YOSEMITE National Park

From the book...

Upper Kerrick Meadow via Barney and Peeler Lakes (Trip 3)

This short, scenic trail leads quickly into breathtaking subalpine terrain, and glittering Peeler Lake, surrounded by frost-shattered and glaciated granite and windswept conifers, mirrors the region's grandeur.

Glacier Point to Yosemite Valley via Four Mile Trail (Trip 66)

This trail provides a very scenic descent to Yosemite Valley—while acquainting you with the Valley's main features. This knee-knocking descent also gives you a feel for the Valley's 3000-foot depth.

Happy Isles to Little Yosemite Valley and Half Dome (Trip 68)

For many camped in Little Yosemite Valley, the ultimate goal is the summit of Half Dome. On a good summer day, hundreds of hikers attempt this summit, but many turn back, either from exhaustion or from fear. If I, as a first-time visitor, were allowed to make only one dayhike in the park, I would unquestionably choose this hike—the one that introduced me to Yosemite and fired my desire to "climb every mountain."

North Wawona to Royal Arch, Buena Vista, and Chilnualna Lakes (Trip 77)

Glaciers originating on the slopes of Buena Vista Peak descended north, south, and west, and then retreated to leave about a dozen small to medium lakes. This hike visits seven of these, plus dashing Chilnualna Fall—one of the park's highest falls outside Yosemite Valley.

YOSEMITE
National Park

A COMPLETE
HIKER'S GUIDE

JEFFREY P. SCHAFFER

 WILDERNESS PRESS · BERKELEY, CA

Yosemite National Park: A Complete Hiker's Guide

1st EDITION 1978
2nd EDITION 1983
3rd EDITION June 1992
4th EDITION June 1999
5th EDITION June 2006

Copyright © 1978, 1983, 1992, 1999, 2006 by Jeffrey P. Schaffer

Front cover photo © 2006 by Sean Arbabi/Arbabi Imagery
Back cover photo © 2006 by Jeffrey P. Schaffer
Interior photos, except where noted, by Jeffrey P. Schaffer
Cover and book design: Larry B. Van Dyke
Book editor: Eva Dienel

ISBN 13: 978-0-89997-383-8
ISBN 10: 0-89997-383-3
UPC: 7-19609-973863-6

Manufactured in the United States of America

Published by: **Wilderness Press**
1200 5th Street
Berkeley, CA 94710
(800) 443-7227; FAX (510) 558-1696
info@wildernesspress.com
www.wildernesspress.com

Visit our website for a complete listing of our books and for ordering information.

Cover photos: A backpacker stands on the south rim, overlooking Yosemite Valley,
from Crocker Point along the Pohono Trail (Trips 61, 65) *(front);*
View of Tenaya Canyon from Half Dome's high point (Trips 42, 68) *(back)*
Frontispiece: Upper Yosemite Fall, from midway traverse north (Trips 28, 59)

SAFETY NOTICE: Although Wilderness Press and the author have made every attempt to ensure that the information in this book is accurate at press time, they are not responsible for any loss, damage, injury, or inconvenience that may occur to anyone while using this book. You are responsible for your own safety and health while in the wilderness. The fact that a trail is described in this book does not mean that it will be safe for you. Be aware that trail conditions can change from day to day. Always check local conditions and know your own limitations.

Dedication

For my wife, Bonnie Myhre, and our daughter, Mary Anne

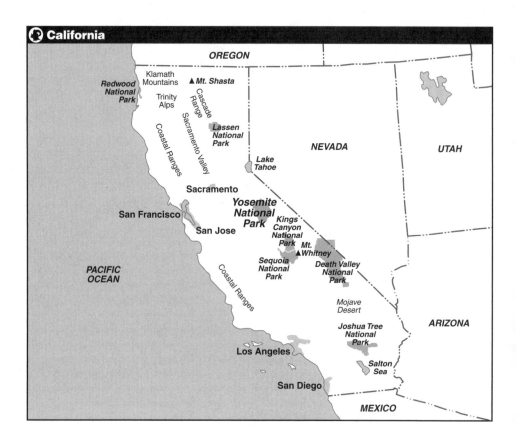

California

OREGON

Redwood
National
Park

Klamath
Mountains

▲ Mt. Shasta

Trinity
Alps

Cascade
Range

Coastal Ranges

Sacramento Valley

Lassen
National
Park

Lake
Tahoe

NEVADA

UTAH

Sacramento

Yosemite
National
Park

Kings
Canyon
National
Park

San Francisco

San Jose

Mt.
▲Whitney

Death Valley
National
Park

Sequoia
National
Park

PACIFIC
OCEAN

Coastal Ranges

Mojave
Desert

ARIZONA

Joshua Tree
National
Park

Los Angeles

Salton
Sea

San Diego

MEXICO

Contents

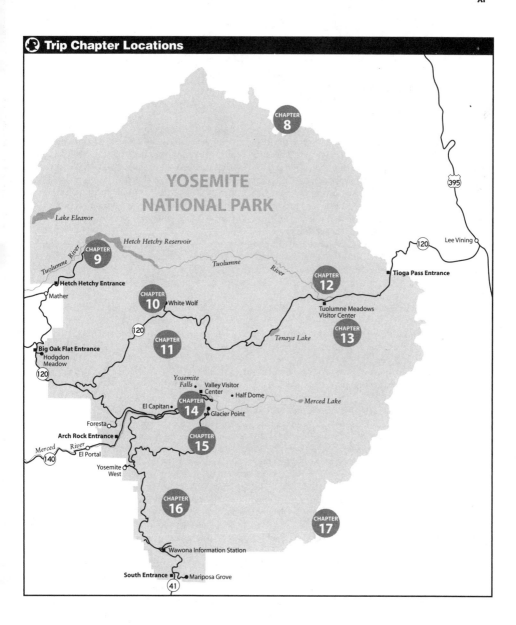

Trip Chapter Locations

YOSEMITE NATIONAL PARK

Lake Eleanor

Hetch Hetchy Reservoir

Tuolumne River

Tuolumne River

Hetch Hetchy Entrance

Mather

White Wolf

Tioga Pass Entrance

Lee Vining

Tuolumne Meadows Visitor Center

Big Oak Flat Entrance

Hodgdon Meadow

Tenaya Lake

Yosemite Falls

Valley Visitor Center

Half Dome

El Capitan

Merced Lake

Glacier Point

Foresta

Arch Rock Entrance

Merced River

El Portal

Yosemite West

Wawona Information Station

South Entrance

Mariposa Grove

LEGEND:

 through refer to general locations of the trips within that chapter.

Acknowledgments

"I'm going to map all the trails of Yosemite and the adjacent area in one summer," I told a park ranger when I was beginning fieldwork on the first edition of this book back in 1976. I had to eat those words. Even if I hadn't had a three-month-long knee ailment, I would have been hard pressed to complete the field mapping in two summers. Fortunately, during the second summer, I had Ben Schifrin, a first-rate mapper and observant naturalist, helping me. Ben, now a medical doctor living in the Sierra's foothills, wrote most of the prose for trips 3, 4, 5, 6, 8, 10, and 12. He made helpful comments for other parts of the original edition and provided photographs for his section and other sections. For later editions, I've revised Ben's sections based largely on prose in his *Emigrant Wilderness and Northwestern Yosemite*, also by Wilderness Press.

Supplying additional original prose was Thomas Winnett, a veteran backpacker and former publisher of Wilderness Press. In the original edition, I borrowed his trail descriptions for about half of the trails in the *Tuolumne Meadows* 15-minute quadrangle, and also for a few sections in the *Mono Craters* 15-minute quadrangle, but I later made changes in his prose to reflect changes in the trails and in the lands they traverse.

In order to understand what really had occurred in the Sierra Nevada, geologically speaking, I reviewed virtually all relevant written research, plus in the 1990s I logged about 150 days in the range while personally examining glacial and uplift evidence. That evidence is considerable, amounting to a book larger than this one, published in 1997 by Wilderness Press: *The Geomorphic Evolution of the Yosemite Valley and Sierra Nevada Landscapes: Solving the Riddles in the Rocks*. The "Acknowledgments" in that book cites persons who have aided me in that fieldwork. Additionally, over the years, I have benefited from geological discussions with Howard Schorn (University of California, Paleontology, retired), and, in the 1990s, with David Jones (US Geological Survey, retired), and with Jeff Middlebrook (a geologically literate Sierran backpacker). The uplift and glacial histories presented in the current geology section of this guidebook differ radically from all previous interpretations, particularly from those of François Matthes, Clyde Wahrhaftig, and N. King Huber, all formerly of the US Geological Survey. In particular, I first wrote (back in 1994) that Sierran uplift was much earlier than previously thought—so early that Sierran rivers had tens of millions of years to cut their deep canyons, which existed long before glaciers flowed through them.

For comments and criticisms on the original biology chapter, I am indebted in part to Dave Graber, a grad student at the University of California during the 1970s while at the same time being Yosemite's bear expert. Also, the late Dr. Carl Sharsmith of the Yosemite Association gave me a solid introduction to alpine wildflowers, and he reviewed an early form of this section. Thanks also go to Dr. Thomas Harvey of San Jose State University, who reviewed the hike into the Mariposa Grove of Big Trees, which deals with giant-sequoia ecology. That hike's description was based largely on work done by Harvey, Richard Hartesveldt, and others. Finally, Len McKenzie, Yosemite's chief park interpreter, read much of the manuscript's natural-history sections.

Giving me encouragement at every step of the way for the first edition was Ron Mackie, Jr., the chief backcountry ranger, who not only shared park philosophy and management problems with me, but also gave me carte blanche to do unrestricted field work in the park. Ron also read all hikes of the manuscript and made numerous valuable comments, particularly with regard to safety. Also, I would like to thank Les Arnberger, a former park superintendent, who contributed the foreword to the original edition.

Finally, I would like to thank my wife, Bonnie, for the moral support I received during the rigorous fieldwork of the 1990s, and my daughter, Mary Anne, who, at age 12 in 1998, typed much of the draft of the fourth edition. During the summers of 2004 and '05, Rudy Goldstein, Ben Schifrin, and my twin, Greg Schaffer, accompanied me on some of the area's rehikes, which I appreciate, given that now that I'm a senior citizen and with accumulated climbing injuries to the neck, back, and knees, I just don't run around the wilderness like I did in the 1960s and '70s.

—Jeffrey P. Schaffer
October 2005

Foreword to the First Edition

Like John Muir more than a century ago, thousands of people have begun to discover in recent years that going to the mountains is going home. Muir spent much of the last 46 years of his life reveling in the "glories" of the High Sierra, basking in its "measureless mountain days," marveling at its breathtaking land forms and intricate subtleties, and breeding a passion for the spectacular yet gentle attributes of this "Range of Light." It was a passion rooted in a boundless sense of wonder and a sense of community with the earth. His zeal and his eloquence nurtured the seeds of an emerging conservation ethic, and his influence was pivotal in molding others' perceptions of wilderness and solidifying the embryonic national park concept.

Today Muir's gift with words is again influencing the ways people perceive and use wilderness, for his written works have enjoyed a resurgence in popularity. The Sierra Nevada is a lodestone that lures a swelling tide of hikers and backpackers each year. They seek the solitude, the excitement, the adventure, the therapeutic qualities, the spirit of freedom—yes, perhaps an element of danger as well—that are inherent in wilderness. For many, a wilderness experience is an escape—from urban pressures, job stress, perhaps the environmental blight spawned by our culture. And, like Muir, they often find—as they should—that going out, they are really going in.

With the spiraling demand for wilderness use have come intensified problems and responsibilities. Wilderness managers have had to exercise the responsibility for its protection by imposing limits on the number of people permitted in the backcountry and some constraints on their activities there. Likewise, it is imperative that individual wilderness users accept those constraints and, as the Indian did, touch the earth softly to help insure that they don't degrade the resources they presumably go to the wilderness to enjoy.

Having logged more than a few miles on Yosemite's trails myself, I have personally discovered Muir's "tonic of wilderness," the balm that soothes the soul and brings spiritual refreshment and rejuvenation. I have also learned that, like a sponge, wilderness has a limited absorption capacity. Its tolerance for human impact is finite; it isn't everything to everyone. To Muir, Yosemite was a temple as sacred as any consecrated by man. Only with constant care and vigilance on the part of all who use the wilderness can the intrinsic qualities and values of this temple remain intact.

This book will provide you a bridge to Yosemite's wilderness. It will not only help you plan a safe and pleasurable backcountry outing, but will sharpen your understanding of Yosemite's physical and biotic character and the processes, both natural and cultural, that have shaped it and govern it today.

Primarily, though, this book is a hiking guide that will heighten your wilderness IQ and bring your experience in Yosemite into sharper focus. Perhaps at least one of these mountain trails will take you "home."

—Leslie P. Arnberger
Superintendent
Yosemite National Park, 1978

Yosemite Valley as viewed from the summit of Half Dome

CHAPTER I

Introduction

Whereas Yellowstone was the first federal land to be set aside as a national park, in 1872, Yosemite was the first federal land to be set aside as a park, in 1864. In that year, President Abraham Lincoln signed a bill that deeded Yosemite Valley and the Mariposa Grove of Big Trees to the state of California, and for good reason. Although the Valley had been discovered only 13 years earlier, its sheer walls and magnificent waterfalls rapidly were attracting national fame, thanks to articles, paintings, photographs, and personal testimonials.

Today, visitors from around the world still come to Yosemite National Park to experience Yosemite Valley firsthand. Who can forget his or her first visit to the Valley, with its enormous granite cliffs, its leaping, dashing waterfalls, and its domes? The Valley's prominent features, if not etched on the mind, are recorded by camera: the monolith of El Capitan; Bridalveil Fall backdropped by the Cathedral Rocks; the Three Brothers opposite the Valley from the Cathedral Spires; the giant tombstone of Sentinel Rock capped by Sentinel Dome; the Lower and Upper Yosemite Falls and adjacent Lost Arrow Spire; the lithic rainbow of Royal Arches and adjacent, vertical Washington Column, both surmounted by North Dome; and the deep, gaping Tenaya Canyon bounded on the north by Basket Dome and Mt. Watkins and on the south and east by Half Dome and Clouds Rest. Finally, there is the curved Glacier Point Apron, sweeping up to a vertical cliff topped by Glacier Point. Its views of Yosemite Valley and of the wilderness lands of the high country beyond it must rank as one of the greatest natural wonders of North America, if not the world.

Most of the visitors of this 1169-square-mile park converge on the few square miles of Yosemite Valley's floor and the square mile of the Mariposa Grove. In contrast, only a few percent of the park's visitors backpack into the wilderness lands of the high country, which comprise the bulk of the park's area. The Sierra Nevada has been called the "gentle wilderness," but if you've backpacked the high country of Sequoia and Kings Canyon national parks, you know that thousands of feet of ascent to a lake basin are anything but gentle. In contrast, Yosemite National Park's high country really is a gentle wilderness, its lakes reached with about half the effort. Part of the reason for this relative ease of backpacking is that the main river canyons, the Merced and the Tuolumne, are only about half as deep as Kings Canyon and none has a major east-side ascent comparable to those out of the Owens Valley up to the Sierran crest. More significantly, most of Yosemite's trailheads are high, ranging

A DAY'S DRIVE THROUGH YOSEMITE

Although this is primarily a hiking guide, if you plan to visit the park for only one day, you'll hardly have time to get out of your vehicle. Given only one day, you can best sample Yosemite's greatness by driving across it.

Starting in Oakhurst or Fish Camp with a full tank of fuel, first drive north up Hwy. 41 to the entrance station, head up to the Mariposa Grove (consider taking a free shuttle from Wawona), and then take a tram tour past the giant sequoias.

Next, continue north from Wawona to the Glacier Point Road, which you take east up to Washburn and Glacier points. Backtrack to the main road and drive down to Yosemite Valley. Park at the Bridalveil Fall lot and walk up the short path toward that waterfall.

Then drive through the Valley and park on either side of Northside Drive west of Yosemite Village but east of shuttle-bus stop 6. From here, take a paved path that parallels Northside Drive 0.2 mile west, to where you will see a nearby building with restrooms. From it, a path heads 0.3 mile north up to a bridge just below Lower Yosemite Fall.

Leave the Valley, drive up to Crane Flat, and then start up the Tioga Road. If the Mariposa Grove was too crowded and you passed it up, head just up the road and branch left into a parking area. Make a 1-mile descent into the Tuolumne Grove of Big Trees, then return.

Drive up into a red fir forest, traverse the Yosemite Creek drainage, and then stop at Olmsted Point, recognized by tourists and tour buses. It is worth it.

Next, descend to nearby Tenaya Lake, seen from the point, and perhaps stop along it to savor its setting as well as to watch climbers ascend various routes on an adjacent domelike ridge. A few minutes beyond the lake, you enter Tuolumne Meadows. If you have a couple hours and considerable energy, make the unforgettable ascent to at least Dog Dome, if not to slightly higher Lembert Dome (both in Trip 38).

Conclude your day by exiting via Tioga Pass, which in late afternoon or evening can have a backdrop of dramatic clouds.

from about 7000 feet to over 9000 feet in elevation, thanks to the Tioga and Glacier Point roads, and since most of the lakes that are visited lie below 10,000 feet in elevation, the effort to reach them is not that great.

From the preceding paragraph, you might conclude that this Yosemite guide is primarily a hiking guide, which is true. Many people return to Yosemite time and time again to experience the appeal of its multifaceted landscape. For these hikers in particular, this book was written. Not being an equestrian, I use the term "hikers," but hopefully equestrians will find my book equally useful. I hope all users will benefit from this book in at least three ways. First, this book describes every single trail in Yosemite that is worth taking, and it also describes many trails just outside the park. With this information, arranged in 83 hiking trips, you can leisurely plan your hike. The table in Chapter 7 (pages 56 to 59) will aid you in planning your hike, for with it, you can see at a glance the basic characteristics of each hike. When you see a hike that matches your desires—say, a two-day hike that is 10 to 15 miles long—turn to that hike and read its description. Often, photos included in the hike will give you a feel for the scenery.

Second, this book is a guide. Yosemite's trails are adequately signed, but if you are caught in a blizzard or are hiking a largely snow-covered trail, then directions may be important. In addition, there are a few places where a trail may not be obvious, and the text identifies these. This book also gives you advice you won't find on signs, such as avalanche dangers, difficult fords, and potentially dangerous sections of trails.

Third, by stressing natural history, this book aims to increase your awareness, understanding, and appreciation of the landscape you traverse. Therefore, natural history is stressed in this book's 83 trips. In addition to trailside nature notes, this book goes into considerable detail about history (Chapter 2), biology (Chapter 3), and geology (Chapter 4).

Fees

There is a fee to enter Yosemite National Park, and the cost depends on which type of pass you purchase (see chart below).

Internet

If you have access to the internet, you might check it for various information on the park, including road conditions, weather conditions, and accommodations both in the park and in surrounding areas. Several websites contain various information, but the only site you may need, since from it you can access others, is: www.nps.gov /yose.

Public Transportation and Yosemite National Park

Especially on the Memorial Day, Fourth of July, and Labor Day weekends, there may be so many people driving to the park that there simply isn't enough parking space for all their vehicles, and then some drivers are turned away at the entrance stations. You can get around this by driving up on other weekends or, better yet, by visiting the park during the week. This is what I prefer, since the popular trails are much less crowded

Type of Pass	Fee	Duration	Access
Standard Pass	$20 per vehicle $10 on foot, motorcycle, bicycle or bus	7 days	Yosemite National Park
Annual Pass	$40	1 year	Yosemite National Park
National Parks Pass	$50	1 year	All national parks
Golden Eagle Pass	$65	1 year	All national parks, monuments, recreation areas, historic sites, & wildlife refuges
Golden Age Passport	$10 (for US citizens or residents 62 or over)	Lifetime	All national parks
Golden Access Pass	Free (for US citizens or residents who are blind or permanently disabled)	Lifetime	All national parks, monuments, recreation areas, historic sites, & wildlife refuges

(especially in Tuolumne Meadows), wilderness-permit quotas are less likely to be full, and you may actually be able to find an available campsite (although this is not likely in Yosemite Valley).

If you've got the time, you can avoid driving hassles by taking public transportation to Merced, a city located along Hwy. 99 west of the park, and catching one of two bus lines that depart daily from Merced and head east up Hwy. 140 to Yosemite Valley: Yosemite Area Regional Transportation System, or YARTS (www.yarts.com), and Gray Line (www.grayline.com). To reach Merced, you can take a bus (Gray Line, www.grayline.com, or Greyhound, www.greyhound.com) or AMTRAK (www.amtrak.com).

Getting Around the Park

There are three free shuttle-bus routes within the park. The first bus route operates year round in the east half of Yosemite Valley, making 21 stops, including at the visitor center, Yosemite Lodge, Curry Village, Ahwahnee Hotel, and the campgrounds. For hiking trips 54 to 56, there is no trailhead parking, so you'll either have to walk to the trailhead or, more conveniently, take one of the shuttles. And although trips 59 and 60, which start nearby, have trailhead parking, it is usually monopolized by the climbers at adjacent Camp 4, so again you ought to plan on a shuttle bus.

The second bus route, in service during the summer season, runs in the south part of the park, from Wawona southeast up to the Mariposa Grove of Giant Sequoias.

The third bus route, also in service during the summer season, runs along Tioga Road, from Olmsted Point northeast to Tenaya Lake, Tuolumne Meadows, and Tioga Pass. Consider taking one of the Tioga Road shuttle buses to the popular trailhead parking areas for Tenaya Lake, Cathedral Lakes, Lembert Dome, and Pothole Dome, which often overflow on weekends.

In addition to these free buses, there are buses operated by the concessionaire: 209-372-1240. During the summer hiking season, this bus leaves daily from Curry Village, stops at Yosemite Lodge, and then heads up the Tioga Road to Tuolumne Meadows, and you can be left off at any roadside trailhead. Additionally, concessionaire buses head up to Glacier Point, and, again, you can be left off at any roadside trailhead. Unfortunately, there are no buses, free or otherwise, from Yosemite Valley south to Wawona or north to Hetch Hetchy.

By using the free and fee buses, you can avoid the need for two cars for point-to-point hiking trips. Those include trips 28, 30, 34, 42, and 44 along the Tioga Road; Trip 60 from Yosemite Valley; and trips 66 and 74 from Glacier Point down to the Valley.

Of course, you can put together custom hikes, starting from one trailhead and ending at another.

Accommodations

Many visitors who stay overnight in the Yosemite area would like to do so in campgrounds, which are shown on this book's topographic map. In addition, every hiking chapter includes information about nearby campgrounds. For a listing of the National Park and National Forest campgrounds, along with private campgrounds and RV parks, outside the park, see Appendix I (page 377). For a listing of the area's hotels, lodges, motels, and resorts, see Appendix II (page 380).

Within the park, reservations are required for sites in Yosemite Valley's North, Upper, and Lower Pines campgrounds. The Valley also has Camp 4 Walk-in Campground, on a first-come, first-served basis. Other park campgrounds requiring reservations are Crane Flat, Wawona (reservations May to September), Hodgdon Meadow (reservations May to September), and half the sites of Tuolumne

Meadows. The park's five other campgrounds, which are smaller and open only in the summer season, are on a first-come, first-served basis, and they fill up fast. These are Bridalveil Creek, along the Glacier Point Road, and, from west to east on or near the Tioga Road, Tamarack Flat, White Wolf, Yosemite Creek, and Porcupine Flat campgrounds.

To make reservations, phone the National Park Reservation System at 800-436-7275 as early as possible within the given time frame. Alternatively, make reservations on the internet at www.reservations.nps.gov. Each time frame begins on the 15th of every month, and you can reserve from as little as one day in advance to as much as five months in advance. For example, if you wanted to camp between June 15th and July 14th, you could reserve as soon as February 15th.

In the park, the hotels, lodges, and camps are operated by the Delaware North Companies Parks & Resorts at Yosemite, Inc (559-253-5635; www.yosemitepark .com). In Yosemite Valley, these are the Ahwahnee Hotel, Yosemite Lodge, and Curry Village. The pricey, world-class Ahwahnee Hotel requires reservations. Yosemite Lodge has comfortable rooms and is moderately priced. Economically priced Curry Village has rooms, cabins, tent cabins, and camping at its nearby, spartan Housekeeping Camp.

The concessionaire also operates the Wawona Hotel, near the park's south border. This historic complex, which is open weekends only from after Christmas until early spring and daily for the rest of the year, is a cut above Yosemite Lodge in both ambiance and price. The company also manages spartan White Wolf and Tuolumne Meadows lodges, both open only typically from mid-June to mid-September. White Wolf Lodge is about a mile off the Tioga Road and halfway between Tuolumne Meadows and Yosemite Valley. Tuolumne Lodge is near the east end of the meadows.

The company also manages the backcountry High Sierra Camps. These are so popular that a lottery is held each December to determine the lucky relative few for the following summer. To obtain a lottery application, contact the concessionaire from early September through late November. In a normal year, these camps open around mid-July and close around mid-September. In years of heavy snowfall, the camps may not open at all! Through Delaware North, you can reserve up to one year and one day in advance.

In addition to accommodations provided by Delaware North, you can also lodge at two other locations. The first is The Redwoods (209-375-6666; www.redwoods-inyosemite.com) in Yosemite, located within a private in-holding in the Wawona area. It has more than 130 units, from one-bedroom cabins up to spacious six-bedroom homes.

The second location is at Yosemite West (www.yosemitewest.com), also on private land but located just outside the park. It is reached from a signed road starting just south of the Glacier Point Road's junction with the Wawona Road. It also has a range of sizes (with matching prices), from studios, condos, cabins, and cottages up to spacious homes, as well as bed and breakfasts. The advantage of Yosemite West is that from it you can reach each of three popular destinations in less than a half hour: Yosemite Valley, Glacier Point, and Wawona.

If you cannot obtain accommodations within the park, you will have to settle for a room in one of the park's satellite towns, and the significant facilities (sans bed and breakfasts, condo rentals, and perhaps a few hotels) are listed in Appendix II. Also, on the internet, check out www.yosemite.com for accommodations and services outside the park.

Along Hwy. 140, heading east toward Yosemite Valley, there are two large, relatively upscale lodges. These are Yosemite View Lodge (888-742-4371), just beyond the park's western border in El Portal, and

Cedar Lodge, about 7 miles to its west. About an hour from the Valley is lodging in the Midpines area and in Mariposa.

Along Hwy. 120, branching from Hwy. 108 a few miles before Sonora, and climbing to the park's Big Oak Flat Entrance Station, there are a few motels, hotels, and bed and breakfasts from Groveland almost to the park's west border. The closest facility of acceptable quality is Yosemite Westgate Lodge (209-962-5281), about 12 miles west of the park. This is fine for visiting the Hetch Hetchy area, but Yosemite Valley will be about an hour's drive.

Along Hwy. 41, heading north to the park's south border and toward the Mariposa Grove of Giant Sequoias and the Wawona environs beyond the grove, Oakhurst has the most accommodations, while Fish Camp, just south of the border, has much less. Alternatively, from between the two settlements, you can branch a few miles east to accommodations at Bass Lake.

This guidebook begins its hiking trips with routes west of Hwy. 395, east of and below the park. There are resorts near the trips' trailheads as well as lodging, from north to south, in the towns of Bridgeport, Lee Vining, and the June Lake-Silver Lake environs. Mammoth Lakes, just southeast of the Yosemite area, is a vacationland unto itself, a bustling Lake Tahoe sans the lake and casinos. You can usually find all kinds of accommodations and services in and about this small city, plus lots of lakes, scenery, and trails nearby. Likewise, lodging along the Sonora-Pinecrest stretch up Hwy. 108, northwest of the Yosemite area, is also a resort land. Whereas one could conceivably drive the one-and-a-half to two hours east to Yosemite Valley from places along this stretch, few do, and so I don't mention Hwy. 108 lodging.

Yosemite Activities Other Than Hiking

Just because this book is mainly a guide to Yosemite's trails doesn't mean that you have to hike to enjoy the park. There are other activities to do here, and the main ones are described here.

Horseback Rides

Weather permitting, from spring through fall, you can ride horses in Yosemite Valley and Wawona, and in summer up in Tuolumne Meadows. In addition, there are pack stations located outside the park, and these offer backpack trips into the park and adjacent wildernesses.

Fishing

Originally, trout were native only to the Merced and Tuolumne rivers below their mid-elevation cascades; the vast majority of Yosemite's streams and virtually all its lakes were barren. Until 1972, about 160 of the park's lakes were regularly stocked with rainbow and brook trout, and, to a lesser extent, with brown, golden, and cutthroat trout. But in the late 1970s, the Park Service greatly reduced the number of lakes it stocked. In 1991, the Park Service completely stopped stocking them, and some of the once-stocked lakes have become barren. As one might expect, lakes close to roads and along popular trails attract the most anglers, so you might do better to select a more remote lake or stream. However, avoid lakes at the higher elevations, such as those above 9000 feet. In Yosemite Valley, you can only do catch-and-release for the native rainbow trout, using only artificial lures or flies with barbless hooks; bait is prohibited. Check the park's latest edition of the *Yosemite Guide*, available at entrance stations, for more information. A California fishing license is required for those 16 or older. Obtain a license in towns en route to the park. For more information, visit the Department of Fish & Game website at www.dfg.ca.gov/fishing.

Swimming, Rafting, and Boating

Many hikers swim in Yosemite's lakes, the warmer of which may approach or even exceed 70°F by midsummer. You can also swim in the Merced River through Yosemite Valley. Although the water temperature is cool, the often hot afternoon air temperatures are great for warming up afterward. There are a number of popular river pools, ranging from lower Tenaya Creek in the east part of the Valley to the Cascades Picnic Area in the west part. During the summer, water temperatures tend to be in the low 60s at the east part and in the mid-60s at the west part. By driving out of the park and down past El Portal, you may spot some of the Merced River's roadside

Tenaya Lake water sports

pools, which can warm up into the 70s. Also check out the South Fork Merced River. There are some rockbound pools located just up from the river's covered bridge, as well as in spots upriver, while some are located beside and downriver from stretched-out Wawona Campground. In addition, Yosemite Lodge and Curry Village each have a large swimming pool open to the public.

If you want to raft, you must wear a life vest. (Ironically, if you swim, which is more dangerous, you don't need one.) During high runoff in late spring and early summer, rafting on the Merced River or South Fork Merced River is prohibited (as is, wisely, swimming). Later on, drifting on an air mattress is relatively safe from Clark Bridge down to El Capitan Bridge. Rafting, however, is limited to a shorter stretch from Stoneman Bridge, just north of Curry Village, west to Sentinel Beach, opposite Leidig Meadow.

In addition to rafting on the Merced River through part of Yosemite Valley, you can use a raft on any lake (such as Tenaya Lake), so long as there is no motor. If you are willing to backpack a raft into any lake—other than Hetch Hetchy Reservoir, a source of drinking water for San Francisco—you can do so. Rental rafts are available in Curry Village.

Non-motorized boats are allowed in Tenaya Lake, whose strong afternoon winds are great for sailing. Kayakers and canoeists will favor the morning. Since the lake lacks a launching ramp, the size of the boat is limited to whatever you and your friends can carry to the lake's shore.

Bicycling

In the central and eastern parts of Yosemite Valley, there are more than 12 miles of paved bike paths. You can rent bikes at both Yosemite Lodge and Curry Village. However, rented bikes are not allowed on the stretch of paved path up to Mirror Lake. California law requires that bicyclists under age 18 must wear a helmet.

Rock Climbing

Yosemite Valley is, in my biased opinion as a former Valley climber, the rock-climbing capital of the world. It offers over a thousand drug-free ways to get high. For the uninitiated or the novice climber, Yosemite Mountaineering School and Guide Service offers safe, affordable introductory lessons. For the more advanced climber, it offers qualified guides. However, for the very difficult climbs (5.10 and above), the rate can be hundreds of dollars per day. During the summer, the climbing service operates out of Tuolumne Meadows; off-season, it operates out of Curry Village in Yosemite Valley. I do not recommend rock climbing from about mid-November through mid-February due to stormy weather, ice-cold rock, and increased rockfall hazard.

On La Escuela, base of El Capitan

Skiing

Both downhill and cross-country skiing are popular at Badger Pass, just off the Glacier Point Road. Lessons and rental equipment are available. The season is brief, at best from about mid-December through late March. Cross-country skiing is also popular in Yosemite Valley, whose floor is typically snow-covered during January and early February. One can rent equipment in the Valley. Other cross-country ski areas with longer-lasting snow are Crane Flat and the Mariposa Grove.

Yosemite Association Field Seminars

The Yosemite Association offers a diverse array of courses from about February through October, but particularly during the summer season. There are courses in astronomy, geology, botany, zoology (especially birding), history, photography, art, writing, dayhiking, and backpacking. Some courses involve little exercise, others a lot, and some are family-oriented. For course information, contact the Yosemite Association: P.O. Box 230, El Portal, CA 95318; 209-379-2646; www.yosemite.org.

Other Activities

Many scheduled activities, such as nature walks and slide shows, are held each week. Consult the *Yosemite Guide*, a seasonal newspaper available at the park entrances, or check at one of the visitor centers or information stations.

CHAPTER 2

Human History

I t was an icy Thursday morning on March 27, 1851, when the 58 members of the Mari-posa Battalion descended north toward the rumored Yosemite Valley. The group, led by Major James D. Savage, was on a mission to find Indian Chief Teneiya and his band of braves, but the battalion was frequently hampered as their horses found themselves chest deep in snow.

Suddenly, they emerged from forest cover on the western brink of the Valley's south wall. Early rumors about the Valley had not prepared the men for the breath-taking view now before them. Later, one of the men, Lafayette Bunnell wrote: "The grandeur of the scene was but softened by the haze that hung over the Valley—light as gossamer—and by the clouds which par-tially dimmed the higher cliffs and moun-tains. This obscurity of vision but increased the awe with which I beheld it, and as I looked, a peculiar exalted sensation seemed to fill my whole being, and I found my eyes in tears with emotion."

He continued: "I have here seen the power and glory of a Supreme being: the majesty of His handy-work is in that 'Testi-mony of the Rocks.'" Then, pointing to El Capitan, he said, "That mute appeal illus-trates it, with more convincing eloquence than can the most powerful arguments of surpliced priests."

Leaving their viewpoint (today's Old Inspiration Point), the battalion descended to the floor of Yosemite Valley and set up camp near the edge of Bridalveil Meadow. That night, at the suggestion of Bunnell, the Valley was christened "Yo-sem-i-ty," which he thought was the name of the tribe of Indians living in it. (They later discovered that the Miwok Indians inhabiting it called it "Ah-wah-nee" and called themselves the "Ah-wah-ne-chee." The name "Yo-sem-i-ty" stuck, but its spelling was changed to "Yosemite" in the first published account of the Valley.)

The Mariposa Battalion was the first group of white men to see and enter the Valley. Joseph Reddeford Walker, crossing the central Sierra Nevada under threatening weather during the autumn of 1833, may have seen the Valley, for his party came to the rim of a deep canyon whose walls appeared to be "more than a mile high." The Valley was certainly viewed and possi-bly entered by William P. Abrams and his companion on October 18, 1849, for his description accurately portrays some of the Valley's landmarks. Nevertheless, it was members of the Mariposa Battalion who first publicized its existence.

Chief Teneiya and the Ahwahnechee

Of course, Yosemite Valley was first discovered by the Indians. Just how many bands of Indians visited or resided in the Valley over thousands of years is unknown; however, the last band to live there was the Ahwahnechee, under the leadership of Chief Teneiya. Growing up with his mother's tribe, the Mono Indians, he spent much of his youth in the Mono Basin. As a young man, he founded his own band, and in the early 1800s he moved west across the Sierra Crest, probably via Mono Pass, to take up residence in Yosemite Valley. Years later, his braves attacked the outpost of James D. Savage, whose site was located along the mouth of the South Fork Merced River. Today, it is passed by motorists driving east along Hwy. 140 toward El Portal.

Savage and his men were not driven away, however. Rather, Savage returned to the area as the Major Savage who entered the Valley with his all-volunteer battalion in spring 1851, and burned the Indian settlements. By June, Chief Teneiya and his band were captured by troops under Captain John Bowling and were escorted to a reservation near Fresno. Life there was unpleasant for the chief, and he made it unpleasant for others, so with some relief, the reservation's officials let him return to the Valley on his own recognizance.

Unfortunately, a group of eight miners who entered the Valley in the spring of 1852 were attacked by the chief's braves, and hostilities were renewed. Realizing that troops would soon be sent, Teneiya and his band fled the Valley and took refuge with his blood relatives, the Mono Indians.

The band apparently returned to the Valley around summer or early autumn in 1853. Soon thereafter, Teneiya's braves returned to the Mono village and stole some horses that the Monos had taken from ranches. Then the braves returned to the Valley. Fired with anger over the way the Ahwahnechee had violated their hospitality, the Monos pursued and killed most of the Ahwahnechee, including Chief Teneiya.

National Park Service

Indians gathering acorns in Yosemite Valley

The Early Tourists

Few Californians believed the first accounts of Yosemite Valley. When Bunnell wrote an article describing the height of the Valley walls as 1500 feet (half their true height), a San Francisco newspaper correspondent suggested he cut his estimates in half. Enraged, Bunnell tore up his manuscript, and Lieutenant Moore thus produced the first published account, in January 1854. However, local Indian trouble instilled fear in potential tourists, so the first ones did not visit the Valley until the 1855 season. Among them were three men who would contribute to the Valley's history: James Hutchings, Thomas Ayres, and Galen Clark.

Word of the beauty and grandeur of Yosemite Valley spread quickly, perhaps due to James Hutchings, who was intent on producing a magazine on California sights. In June 1855, he organized and led the first tourist party to Yosemite Valley, bringing along artist Thomas Ayres to record their discoveries. When he returned to Mariposa, Hutchings wrote up his adventures, which were published in the July 12 issue of the *Mariposa Gazette*. In 1855, California as a state was but five years old and, largely due to the clamor of the Gold Rush, it was an area of interest to many in the eastern states. Hutchings' article was copied in a number of journals and newspapers.

Hutchings was not content to sit idle after his one article, and in July 1856 he began to publish a magazine, *Hutchings' Illustrated California Magazine*, which was devoted to the scenery of California. The first issue contained a lead article on "The Yo-Ham-i-te Valley," illustrated by none other than Thomas Ayres. Later, Hutchings elaborated on this article, producing "The Great Yo-Semite Valley" in a series of four installments, from October 1859 to March 1860. These installments immediately appeared as part of his book, *Scenes of Wonder and Curiosity in California*, which stayed in print well into the 1870s.

During 1856, when Hutchings first began his magazine, Thomas Ayres returned to Yosemite Valley to produce more sketches. These were highly detailed, though not true to form; rather, they exaggerated the angularity of the Valley's walls and the size of the Valley's falls. Nevertheless, Ayres, who also began to write about Yosemite, underestimated the height of the falls, as had most of his predecessors.

Commercialism first came to Yosemite in 1856. In that year, Milton and Houston Mann—two of the 42 tourists to see the Valley in 1855—completed a toll path up the South Fork Merced River and over to the Valley floor. They charged $2 per person—a large sum in those days—but they were later bought out by Mariposa County, and the path became free. Today, you can more or less parallel this historic route by first walking up the South Fork Merced River Trail, ascending the Alder Creek Trail

(Trip 70), and hike from Wawona up to Bridalveil Creek (last half of Trip 71). Next, Trip 62, from Bridalveil Creek to Dewey Point, and Trip 61, from Dewey Point to Yosemite Valley, complete the course.

The Mann brothers needed a way station along their trail, so they convinced Galen Clark, who had just built a cabin in today's Wawona area, to tend to the needs of the tourists. He did this with kindness, and his spirit of devotion to Yosemite profoundly imbued travelers with a similar reverence for this mountain landscape. Meanwhile, a simple structure, later called the Lower Hotel, was being completed as the first tourists rode down the Mann's still-fresh trail into Yosemite Valley. Other trails and hotels quickly followed and tourism increased.

Yosemite Becomes a Park

The Civil War began just months after Hutchings' *Scenes of Wonder and Curiosity in California* appeared, but that didn't deter people from visiting Yosemite. With America locked in Civil War, it is a wonder that anyone visited Yosemite. Still, some people did, and a few of these helped to get park status for Yosemite Valley. A highly influential Unitarian minister, Reverend Thomas Starr King, who had visited the Valley in 1860, saw that homesteading and commercial pursuits in it might be harmful, and he was the first, through his nation-wide audience, to press for a public park. Photographs of the Valley were taken in 1861 by Carleton E. Watkins, and these, together with geographic and geologic data gathered by the Whitney Survey of California, provided legislators with favorable evidence backing King's exhortations.

The call of Yosemite eventually lured Fredrick Law Olmsted, the country's foremost landscape architect, to Yosemite in 1863, and he, too, noted that the Valley and the Mariposa Grove of Big Trees were both being ruined by commercial interests. Though young, he was already very influential, and he convinced California Senator John Conness to introduce a park bill in the Senate. The bill, uncontroversial in the war-torn Congress, easily passed in both houses and was signed by President Abraham Lincoln on June 30, 1864. The bill deeded Yosemite Valley and the Mariposa Grove of Big Trees to the state of California "for public use, resort, and recreation," and these two tracts "shall be inalienable for all time."

It is one thing to create a park on paper; it is another matter to bring it into existence. In September, California's governor proclaimed a board of Yosemite commissioners, which did not form until 1866. The commissioners appointed Galen Clark as the park's first guardian, a position he held on and off through 1896. However, the commissioners at first lacked authority to evict homesteaders, and an 11-year battle ensued.

Josiah D. Whitney, who was the first director of the California State Geological Survey, feared that "Yosemite Valley, instead of being 'a joy forever,' will become, like Niagara Falls, a gigantic institution for fleecing the public." Expressing his concern in his 1870 *Yosemite Guide-Book*, he in part was writing against Hutchings, who, like others, had hoped to gain homesteading rights to 160 of the Valley floor's 2200 acres.

In 1875, the claims of the early settlers were resolved. Hutchings, like three other pre-park landowners, lost his ownership, but he was in part compensated with a state grant of $24,000 for the improvements he made on the Upper Hotel, which he had purchased just months before President Lincoln signed the park bill. Hutchings lost his hotel but still profited from his book, which continued to attract tourists. In 1877, just after his land loss, Hutchings published a second guide, *Hutchings' Tourist Guide to the Yosemite Valley and the Big Tree Groves*, which was very factu-

al and not vindictive toward the park commissioners.

Back on May 10, 1869, the transcontinental railroad had been completed, and during the 1870s a flood of settlers poured into California. These people were potential tourists, but the lengthy horseback ride to Yosemite Valley was a deterrent. However, in the mid-1870s, three stagecoach roads were built to the Valley: the Coulterville Road (June 1874), the Big Oak Flat Road (July 1874), and the Mariposa (Wawona) Road (July 1875). Tourists now came in droves, and this influx resulted in an increase in Yosemite Valley's hotels and services, which were more or less regulated by the commissioners. Still, these men were concerned over the Valley's deteriorating condition, which they wrote up in their 1880 report.

Creating a National Park

While Yosemite Valley suffered from the detrimental effects of tourism, the surrounding countryside fared no better. Its meadows were subjected to overgrazing by sheep (and to a lesser extent by cattle) and its forests faced depletion by loggers. This rape of the landscape was first noted by a young Scotsman, John Muir, who visited Yosemite Valley in 1868 and decided to stay. His exploration of the High Sierra, first while working as a shepherd, convinced him that humans and their animals were destroying the environment. In the mid-1870s, Muir criticized both shepherds and loggers, but to no avail. Lumber was needed to build California's growing communities, and wool export had become big business, with more than 20 million pounds produced annually.

Muir's protestations generally fell on deaf ears until 1889, when he met Robert Underwood Johnson, who was editor of the influential *Century Magazine*. Muir took Johnson on a tour of Yosemite's highlands, including Tuolumne Meadows, and showed him the damage done by "the hooved locusts" as well as by loggers. At a campfire at the meadows' Soda Springs, Muir recapitulated the area's problems, upon which Johnson responded: "Obviously, the thing to do was to make a Yosemite National Park around the Valley on the plan of the Yellowstone [National Park, created in 1872]."

Muir went on to write some articles for *Century Magazine* that conveniently coincided with a park bill introduced in Congress. The Yosemite Act of October 1, 1890, passed without opposition, for communications in those days were still poor—the sheep and lumbermen out West probably knew little, if anything, about the act. This act withdrew lands from "settlement, occupancy, or sale" and protected "all timber, mineral deposits [none in Yosemite], natural curiosities or wonders, and their retention in their natural condition." This included protection against "wanton destruction of the fish and game, and their capture or destruction for purposes of merchandise or profit."

National Park Service

Horse stage on Big Oak Flat Road in 1903

Yosemite Under the Fourth Cavalry

What the Yosemite Act failed to stipulate was how the newly formed Yosemite National Park should be administered. Hence it was, like Yellowstone National Park before it, put under Army jurisdiction. Troops of the Fourth Cavalry, led by Captain Abram Wood, arrived in the new park on May 19, 1891, and set up camp in Wawona, not in Yosemite Valley, for that part of the park still lay under state jurisdiction. Troops were allowed into the Valley, but they had to camp at its west end, in Bridalveil Meadow.

One of several major problems confronting Captain Wood and his men was sheep grazing. Prior to Yosemite's status as a national park, herders led about 100,000 sheep into Yosemite's high meadows each year. But when Yosemite was made a park, this practice became illegal. Wood lacked the legal authority to arrest the trespassing sheepmen, but he devised a technique that discouraged them, which was to escort the herders far away from the herds, which would disperse by the time the herders returned. The herders, however, took their sheep into more remote parts of Yosemite, so the sheep problem did not come under control until the late 1890s. To aid in their pursuit of herders, the troops established a network of trails.

John Muir, who had earlier seen the need to incorporate the Valley into the park, founded the environmental organization the Sierra Club in 1892 and became its first president. With 181 other charter members, Muir pressed for this goal and others, and in 1906, after much lobbying, saw the ceding of Yosemite Valley and the Mariposa Grove to the federal government. However, a price was paid: The area of Yosemite National Park was substantially reduced. (Today, however, more lands are protected than in the 1890 Act, due to the creation of three buffer areas around the

National Park Service

Cavalry F Troop on the Fallen Monarch giant sequoia in 1899

park: the Ansel Adams, Hoover, and Emigrant wildernesses.)

The Hetch Hetchy Reservoir

Though Muir and the Sierra Club could claim partial victory in 1906 with the creation of a unified, if reduced, Yosemite National Park, they had another serious problem to confront. In 1901, the city of San Francisco had applied for permission to dam Hetch Hetchy, a Yosemite-like valley in the northwest part of the park. "Dam Hetch Hetchy!" Muir exclaimed. "As well dam for water-tanks the people's cathedrals and churches, for no holier temple has ever been consecrated by the heart of man." US Department of Interior Secretary Hitchcock concurred with Muir and denied permission. But the city persisted and, despite continued opposition by the Sierra Club and others, it obtained water rights with the passage of the Raker Act in late 1913. The new interior secretary favored dams.

First, a railroad route to the dam site had to be constructed, which took four years to complete. Then, in 1918, construction began, and Hetch Hetchy's granite was dynamited for rocks to make the dam's core, and the canyon floor was cleared of timber. Part of this timber was used in the dam's construction, but more than 6 million board feet of timber logged inside the park was also used. The project was completed in 1923, but in 1938 the dam was increased by 85 feet to its present height. This reservoir could have been located down canyon, just outside Hetch Hetchy, but a lower location would have resulted in reduced hydroelectric power.

Ironically, the reservoir may have preserved more wilderness than it had destroyed. In the early 1900s, the nascent Sierra Club directors, like others, had proposed considerable tourist development in that valley as well as a road system that ascended the Tuolumne River to Tuolumne

Meadows, then south over Tuolumne Pass and down the Merced River to Yosemite Valley.

Exit the Army

With the passage of the Raker Act in 1913, conservationists took a decisive defeat in their battle to save Hetch Hetchy. Muir died shortly afterward, perhaps of heartbreak, though certainly of old age. Just before he died, he expressed hope that "some compensating good must follow [from the Raker Act]." It did—in the form of a new spirit of conservation, of a growing national awareness that Americans must preserve the land, not exploit and destroy it. This mounting consensus played a significant part in the creation of the National Park Act of 1916—though, in addition, Europe was already at war, America was talking war, and the Army probably wanted all of its troops out of the nation's parks.

When the Fourth Cavalry left Yosemite, they left behind an impressive record. They had driven sheep and cattle from the park, had helped to settle property disputes, had laid the foundation for today's trail system, had mapped the park in substantial detail, and had even planted trout in the park's lakes (this, however, would adversely affect the lake's native species).

Many of the cavalry's troops are commemorated today in the names of dozens of the park's backcountry features, such as Rodgers and Foerster peaks, Benson and Smedberg lakes, Fernandez and Isberg passes. For Yosemite, the cavalry had, by and large, "come to the rescue."

Dawn of the Automobile Era

While the intrusion of dammed water into Hetch Hetchy raged as an issue from 1901 to 1913, another intrusion faced the park administrators: automobiles. Thus, when the fledgling National Park Service took over administration in 1916, they were faced with a rapidly growing clientele, and it turned most of their attention to upgrading services. New trails were built, and old ones were brought up to modern standards. In 1916, Tuolumne Meadows Lodge was built, as were camps at Tenaya and Merced lakes, followed in 1924 by precursors of the rest of today's High Sierra Camps. Also in 1916 the Tioga Road was opened to the public. In 1926, the All-Year Highway (Hwy. 140) opened. This highway spelled an end to the Yosemite Valley Railroad, which had started service in 1907. Campgrounds were relocated to forest groves, away from the meadows that had been so important to the previous generations of horseback tourists.

The Yosemite Museum opened in the same year as the All-Year Highway, just four years after the creation of Yosemite's first park naturalist position. The early naturalists relied heavily on work done under Joseph Grinnell and Tracy Storer of the University of California's Museum of Vertebrate Zoology.

During the 1930s Depression years, numerous persons were employed in CCC, CWA, and PWA projects that added refinements to the human imprint on the Yosemite landscape. World War II temporarily put an end to future projects, and, during the war, the park served as an R&R site for almost 90,000 battle-weary troops.

The Postwar Years

After VE and VJ days, America engaged in a pursuit of the good life, and this included traveling in ever-increasing numbers. About three quarters of a million tourists visited Yosemite in 1946, and by 1954, the number had grown to a million. By 1966 (the 50th anniversary of the National Park Service), Yosemite was receiving about 2 million visitors a year.

Hikers and car campers continued to inundate Yosemite in following years. On

the three-day "summer" weekends—
Memorial Day, Fourth of July, and Labor
Day—more than 50,000 visitors, half of
them youths, crammed into Yosemite Valley. By 1970, the Valley scene had become
ugly, with thefts, drugs, rapes, fights, riots,
and even murders.

However, 1970 also marked the start of
a series of projects based on research done
in the Mission 66 program. One was to
remove vehicles from the congested east
end of the Valley and replace them with a
free shuttle-bus system. Tranquility began
to return to the Valley, at least for the priv-
ileged minority who actually could obtain
campsites. Camper frustrations also
occurred above the Valley with the closure
of Tuolumne Meadows' Soda Springs
Campground in 1976, followed by closure
of Porcupine Creek, Smokey Jack, and
Tenaya Lake Walk-in campgrounds.

And what of the backcountry? It, too,
had a population explosion, driven in part
by lightweight backpacking technology
that made carrying food and gear into the
wilderness easier than ever. The backcountry, like Yosemite Valley, developed local
areas of congestion—mostly in Little
Yosemite Valley and at easily reached lakes
off the Tioga Road. The wilderness permit
came to the park in 1972 as an initial step
to monitor use. In succeeding years, rangers

attempted to direct hikers away from popular destinations, and soon initiated a
quota system, which set limits to backcountry sites.

During the 1970s, the number of
Yosemite visitors temporarily stabilized at
about 2 million per year. However, the '80s
saw an upswing, which continued into the
'90s, when annual visitation hovered
around 4 million per year, where it appears
to have peaked. Backpacking also peaked
at about 50,000 people per year in the mid-
1990s, and it has decreased slightly since
then.

The park—particularly Yosemite Valley—can never be returned to the pristine
condition seen by its discovers, the original
Native Americans. However, certain beneficial changes can be made, and are being
made, thanks in particular to the Yosemite
Fund, which in its first 10 years, 1988 to
1997, raised $11.5 million for about 100
projects. What the federal government
could not do, the private sector did. Mother Nature also helped, with "the flood of
the century" in the first few days of January
1997. Expensive damage to structures on
the Valley floor ensured that they would
not be rebuilt. When the second millennium
ended, motor vehicles still had not been
banned from the Valley.

To preserve Yosemite National Park in
the third millennium will require the coop-
eration of all branches of the government
and all aspects of the private sector, including input from communities along the highways to the park. One hopes the park can
be managed in such a way that it will instill
in each new visitor the same awe and reverence that were experienced by those who
first laid eyes on it.

The 1970's "John Muir Freeway," eight
lanes wide, through Tuolumne Meadows

CHAPTER 3

Flora and Fauna

Yosemite's visitors are impressed with enormous granite cliffs of El Capitan and Clouds Rest; the leaping, dashing waterfalls; the domes of Yosemite Valley; Tenaya Canyon; and the peaks soaring above Tuolumne Meadows. But Yosemite is predominantly a landscape of forest green. Driving up highways 41, 120, or 140, you can't help noticing that the natural scene changes with elevation. The most obvious changes are the tree species, but shrubs, wildflowers, grasses, and animals also change with elevation. The distribution of species is controlled by a number of influences, of which climate is probably the foremost. Others include topography, soil, fire, and other species.

Of climatic influences, temperature and precipitation are the most important. Temperature decreases with increasing elevation, and precipitation increases up to mid-elevations, beyond which it decreases slowly to the crest, then rapidly beyond it. Because much of a winter's snow remains through late spring—and some remains throughout summer—most of Yosemite's vegetation has an adequate water supply. In fact, the presence of the subalpine meadows is due to too much water, for conifers aren't able to survive in these seasonally water-saturated soils. In contrast, on alpine rocky slopes, the snow often melts before the start of the growing season. On these dry slopes, then, the wildflowers are often dependent on summer thunderstorms for moisture. During winter, snow on these slopes buries and protects the wildflowers from extreme cold.

The topography indirectly affects the distribution of plants and animals. Irregular topography can create uneven distribution of snow. Well-named Snow Flat is at about the same elevation as Tuolumne Meadows, but because it lies south of Mt. Hoffmann, it receives about twice as much snow as Tuolumne Meadows, which lies just north of the Cathedral Range. This range creates a rain shadow on its north side, so less precipitation falls over the meadows. The Sierra Crest creates an even greater rain shadow, which explains why Mono Lake has such a low precipitation—about 30% of the rate of the mid-elevations. Topography also affects vegetation in other ways. North-facing slopes tend to be heavily forested, while south-facing ones tend to be more open and sometimes brushy. At mid-elevations, red and white firs occur on shady slopes and Jeffrey pines and huckleberry oaks are on sunny ones.

Yosemite's soils are derived primarily from granitic rocks. The decomposition of these rocks creates the soil that High Sierra hikers are so familiar with—gravel-size pieces of feldspar and quartz with a few flecks of mica and hornblende. On mid-elevation slopes, these weathered minerals can accumulate to produce a deep, well-drained soil, which will support a moderately dense forest of pines and firs, such as on slopes along much of the Tioga and the Glacier Point roads. In soils that are extremely porous, a pure stand of Jeffrey pines can develop, as in volcanic soils of the Mono Basin, east of the park. Where a gravelly Sierran soil is also shallow, drought-tolerant shrubs replace pines.

A small fraction of Yosemite's soils are derived from metamorphic rocks, which are found mainly along the park's highest elevations. At these heights, an alpine plant thrives better in the metamorphic soils than in adjacent granitic soils. This is because metamorphic bedrock fractures into smaller pieces than granitic bedrock does, thus creating a greater water-storage capacity for plants. Furthermore, this rock is much richer in dark minerals, so it yields a more nutrient-rich soil. And, being darker in color than their granitic counterparts, metamorphic-derived soils absorb more heat, which is very important to plants at alpine altitudes.

A final point to be made about soils is that in the range, there were a lot of thick soils before glaciers removed them, and this altered the distribution of at least one notable species, the giant sequoia, which, before glaciation, was associated with red firs. John Muir realized this in 1876: Glaciers overran most of the sequoias, eliminating them from their preferred habitat, the red fir belt.

Soils can affect the type and amount of vegetation, but vegetation can also create and change soils. A soil is more than just a combination of loose, moist sand and gravel—it also has an organic component. Each year, the Merced River deposits sterile silt, sand, and gravel at the south end of Washburn Lake. Grasses and sedges take root in these new accumulations and stabilize them. Then, as these plants die over the years, they add an organic component to the sediments, converting them to soil. As the soil develops here, it becomes ripe for invasion by willows, which further modify the new soil. These trap more sediments, and they add detritus to the soil, enriching

it and making it more suitable for other species. Additionally, transpiration by both herbs and shrubs helps to lower the water table: Aspens and lodgepole pines can now invade. In this way, a sterile beach eventually becomes—through activities by a succession of plant species—a rich forest soil.

Animals also influence the development of soils and thus affect the development of vegetation. Most of the Yosemite landscape stands above the range of the lowly earthworm, but at mid-elevations, nature has other soil processors. Foremost among these is the industrious pocket gopher, which works year round, even in the cold of winter when other rodents are either hibernating or living off their stored cache of food. Winter is actually a safer time for the gopher to work, for it can burrow along at the base of a snowpack without danger from its summer predators—hawks, owls, gopher snakes, weasels, badgers, foxes, and coyotes.

In a mountain meadow, a gopher population will churn up tons of soil each year, leading to the development of a richer soil. Bacteria, fungi, and invertebrates attack dead plants and animals, decomposing them into litter and humus. However, because too much litter and humus can prevent seedling germination, fire is an integral part of the park's ecosystem in all but its subalpine and alpine areas.

It has been said that the giant sequoia might not be around today were it not for the roles played by fire, the chickaree (Douglas squirrel), and a cone-boring beetle, all

---

GOPHER ROPES

After the snow melts, the gophers' winter tunneling appears as "gopher ropes." After a gopher digs a tunnel through the snow, he later fills it with soil from his diggings in the ground beneath the snow. When the snow melts, this core of soil is then exposed, looking like a piece of thick rope.

three aiding with the dispersal and germination of seeds. More than 150 species of insects depend in part on the giant sequoia, and it is very dependent on one beetle. Without insects, most wildflowers would disappear for lack of pollination. Then, too, wildflowers receive aid from birds and rodents in the form of seed planting and seed dispersal. Even preying on plants is beneficial; otherwise, plants would undergo a population explosion, cover the earth, and die in their own debris. In short, complex plant-animal interactions help to keep all species' populations relatively stable, neither too low nor too high.

The Role of Fire

The presence or absence of ground fires can really alter the system, for it significantly alters the populations of ground-dwelling plants and animals and everything associated with them. Until 1971, fire suppression was a general Yosemite policy, but it led to the accumulation of thick litter, dense brush, and overmature trees—all prime fuel for a holocaust when a fire inevitably sparked to life. It also led to a change in the distribution of plant and animal species and encouraged root rot (see Trip 58).

Foresters now know that natural fires should not be prevented, but only regulated. These fires, if left unchecked, burn stands of mixed conifers—such as those found in Yosemite Valley—about once every 10 years. At this frequency, only the ground cover is burned over, while the trees remain generally intact. Ultimately, however, stands of trees mature, the trees die, logs accumulate on the ground, and major fires occur.

Some trees are adapted to fire. The giant sequoia, for example, releases its seeds after a fire, as do numbers of conifers, shrubs, and wildflowers. Seeds of the genus *Ceanothus* are quick to germinate in burned-over ground, and some plants of this genus are among the primary foods of deer. With too few burns, shrubs become too woody and unproductive for a deer herd. In like manner, gooseberries and other berry plants sprout after fires and help support a variety of different bird and mammal populations.

Without fires, a plant community evolves toward a climax, an end stage, of plant succession. Red and white firs are the main species in the climax vegetation that is characteristic of the Sierra's mid-elevations. However, a pure stand of any species invites epidemic attacks and therefore can be unstable. At times Yosemite's lodgepole pines have been decimated by lodgepole needleminers—the larval stage of a moth—that turned the living stands into "ghost forests."

Fire is also beneficial in that it unlocks nutrients that are stored up in living matter, litter, topsoil, and even rocks. Vital compounds are released in the form of ash when a fire burns plants and forest litter. Fire also can heat granitic rocks enough to cause them to break up and release their minerals, and it can even cause thin sheets of granite to flake off from boulders. Natural, periodic fires, then, can be very beneficial for a forest ecosystem. After all, for millions of years they have been a common process in most of the Sierra's plant communities.

Biogeography

We have just delved very briefly into the influences regulating the distribution of plants and animals. Of course, not every species is equally affected by these influences. And therefore every plant and animal has its own range, habitat, and niche. The range is the entire area over which an organism may be found. Some species have a very restricted range; others have a very widespread one. The giant sequoia, for example, occurs only in about 75 small groves at mid-elevations in the western Sierra Nevada. An organism's habitat is the kind of place where it lives. The habitat of the sequoia is typically a gently sloping, forested, unglaciated, periodically burned slope that has abundant ground water. An organism's niche is the functional role it plays in its community. For example, the sequoia provides food and shelter for dozens of insects that utilize the tree's needles, branches, bark, and cones, and additional organisms benefit from soil changes created by the sequoia's roots. At the same time, the sequoia receives essential aid from the chickaree, from a long-antennaed beetle, and from fire (see Trip 78). Thus, the niche is a give-and-take relationship.

Some plants and animals have tremendous ranges. For example, the squirreltail is a grass that grows in dry, open habitats from the park's alpine fell-fields down to the park's lowest elevations. Outside the park, it descends to sea level, and its range extends from Mexico north to British Columbia and east to Texas and South Dakota.

In the animal kingdom, the black bear, mule deer, mountain lion, coyote, badger, long-tailed weasel, California ground squirrel, and deer mouse are mammals that range through much of Yosemite. Many birds seen in Yosemite have migrated, if not from the south, then from the lowlands, and they follow the development of a food supply that occurs higher and higher as the winter snowpack retreats. In most of the park, you can expect to see the American robin, dark-eyed junco, Brewer's blackbird, northern flicker, white-crowned sparrow, chipping sparrow, American dipper (water ouzel), red-tailed hawk, and northern harrier (marsh hawk). Reptiles and amphibians, despite their limited mobility and their disadvantageous cold-blooded circulatory system, do include a few well-adapted species that have broad ranges. Seen from the foothills up into the subalpine zone are the western fence lizard, western rattlesnake, and Pacific treefrog. Most of Yosemite's plants and animals have a more restricted distribution, each living in only several of Yosemite's seven plant communities, and some species live in only one community.

We'll now look at some species found in the park's communities.

Plant Communities and Their Animal Associations

In this book, plants and animals are classified according to the dominant plant or plant type of a habitat simply because plants are the most readily observed life forms. Such a group of life forms is called a plant community, even though it includes animals. Because animals move, they can be harder to classify. Birds, for example, typically have a wide—usually seasonal—range, and therefore may be found in many plant communities. In the following list of communities, a species is mentioned in the community in which you, the visitor, are most likely to see it. In addition, only the more prominent and/or diagnostic species are mentioned. Common names, particularly among wildflowers, vary from book to book, so I have attempted to use either the common names appearing in authoritative texts or in popular guidebooks that I feel are the most accurate. To save space, grasses, ferns, lower plants, trout, and invertebrates are excluded. The plant communities listed on the following pages are in approximate order of ascending elevation and decreasing temperature.

Mule deer

Yosemite's Plant Communities

Foothill Woodland

WHERE SEEN: Sunny slopes about and below Hetch Hetchy Reservoir, Arch Rock-El Portal area, lower Alder Creek Trail

TREES: Foothill (gray, Digger) pine, knobcone pine, blue oak, interior live oak, tanbark oak, California buckeye, red willow, arroyo willow, black cottonwood

SHRUBS: Scrub oak, poison oak, Parry manzanita, whiteleaf manzanita, chaparral whitethorn (ceanothus), yerba santa, toyon, western redbud, spice bush, bush poppy, bush monkey flower, mock orange, chaparral currant, bitter gooseberry

WILDFLOWERS: Indian pink, soap plant, California poppy, miner's lettuce, Chinese houses, purple milkweed, star flower, western buttercup

MAMMALS: Gray fox, bobcat, spotted skunk, ringtail, brush rabbit, Merriam's chipmunk, Botta's pocket gopher, dusky-footed wood rat, Heermann's kangaroo rat, brush mouse, pinyon mouse, ornate shrew, small-footed myotis (bat), western pipistrelle (bat)

BIRDS: California thrasher, wrentit, bushtit, plain titmouse, scrub jay, rufous-sided towhee, western bluebird, Nuttall's woodpecker, Hutton's vireo, Bewick's wren, blue-gray gnatcatcher

REPTILES: Common king snake, racer, striped racer, ringneck snake, western whiptail, southern alligator lizard, Gilbert's skink

AMPHIBIANS: Foothill yellow-legged frog, California slender salamander, California newt, arboreal salamander

Ponderosa Pine Forest

WHERE SEEN: Yosemite Valley, Cherry Lake, Mather Ranger Station, Pate Valley, Alder Creek Trail, Wawona, Merced, Tuolumne, and Mariposa groves

TREES: Ponderosa pine, incense-cedar, black oak, sugar pine, white fir, interior live (gold-cup) oak, Douglas fir, giant sequoia (restricted distribution), California laurel (bay tree), big-leaf maple, Scouler's willow, mountain (Pacific) dogwood, white alder, black cottonwood

SHRUBS: Whiteleaf manzanita, mountain misery, western azalea, American (creek) dogwood, buckbrush, deer brush, Sierra gooseberry

WILDFLOWERS: Broad-leaved lupine, harlequin lupine, narrow-leaved lotus, black-eyed Susan, common madia, scarlet monkey flower, blue penstemon, evening primrose, bleeding hearts, wild ginger, false Solomon's seal, mountain dogbane (Indian hemp), umbrella plant (Indian rhubarb), mountain violet, waterfall buttercup

MAMMALS: Black bear, raccoon, striped skunk, gray squirrel, long-eared chipmunk, big brown bat, hairy-winged myotis (bat)

BIRDS: Steller's jay, black-headed grosbeak, western tanager, Townsend's solitaire, acorn woodpecker, white-headed woodpecker, downy woodpecker, band-tailed pigeon, purple finch, solitary vireo, Nashville warbler, black-throated gray warbler, MacGillivray's warbler, winter wren, violet-green swallow, screech owl, spotted owl, golden eagle

REPTILES: California mountain kingsnake, rubber boa, gopher snake, northern alligator lizard

AMPHIBIAN: Ensatina

(continued on page 22)

Yosemite's Plant Communities (continued)

Jeffrey Pine Forest

WHERE SEEN: El Capitan, North Dome-Indian Ridge, old Kibbie Lake Trail, lower West Walker River, slabs above Lake Vernon and Agnew Lake, at most of Yosemite's rocky or dry-gravelly mid-elevation sites, Mono Basin's higher slopes

TREES: Jeffrey pine, red fir, white fir, incense-cedar, sugar pine, western juniper

SHRUBS: Huckleberry oak, greenleaf manzanita, snow bush, tobacco brush, sagebrush, squaw wax currant, curl-leaved mountain mahogany

WILDFLOWERS: Mountain pride (Newberry's penstemon), Bridges' penstemon, showy penstemon, Gray's lupine, single-stemmed senecio, coyote mint (mountain monardella), mule ears, Sierra wallflower, jewel flower (streptanthus), spreading phlox, scarlet gilia, pussy paws, sulfur flower, nude buckwheat, Leichtlin's Mariposa tulip (lily), Sierra sedum

MAMMALS: Sierra Nevada golden-mantled ground squirrel, mountain pocket gopher, bushy-tailed wood rat

BIRDS: Mountain quail, fox sparrow, green-tailed towhee, Townsend's solitaire, olive-sided flycatcher

REPTILES: Western fence lizard, sagebrush lizard, western rattlesnake

Red Fir/Lodgepole Pine Forest

WHERE SEEN: Generally found between 6500 and 9000 feet—the elevation traversed by the bulk of Yosemite's trails; it is the most widespread plant community in the park. Most accessible sites: Tioga Road from Crane Flat to Tuolumne Meadows, White Wolf, Pohono Trail, Badger Pass, Chiquito Pass.

TREES: Red fir, lodgepole pine, western white (silver) pine, white fir, mountain hemlock, aspen, Scouler's willow, MacKenzie's willow

SHRUBS: Bush chinquapin, pinemat manzanita, mountain spiraea, Labrador tea, red heather, Sierra-laurel, Sierra gooseberry, sticky currant, service-berry, bitter cherry, mountain ash, Lemmon's willow, mountain alder

WILDFLOWERS: White-veined wintergreen, pinedrops, snow plant, spotted coralroot, meadow rue, Richardson's geranium, arrow-leaved senecio (butterweed), larkspur, monk's hood, crimson columbine, fringed lungwort (mountain bluebells), alpine (tiger) lily

MAMMALS: Red fox, porcupine, marten, chickaree (Douglas squirrel), lodgepole chipmunk, western jumping mouse, dusky shrew, little brown myotis (bat)

BIRDS: Blue grouse, dark-eyed junco, mountain chickadee, red-breasted nuthatch, golden-crowned kinglet, Williamson's sapsucker, Hammond's flycatcher, Cassin's finch, evening grosbeak, red crossbill, goshawk, great gray owl

Mountain Meadow

WHERE SEEN: Tuolumne Meadows, Dana Meadows, Lyell Canyon, Grace Meadow, Kerrick Meadow, McGurk Meadow, Mono Meadow, Moraine Meadows, Lukens Lake, Cathedral Lakes, Dog Lake, Middle Gaylor Lake, Washburn Lake, Emeric Lake

(continued on page 23)

Yosemite's Plant Communities (continued)

SHRUBS: Arctic (alpine) willow, shining (caudate) willow, Eastwood's willow, Sierra willow, western blueberry, dwarf bilberry, bog kalmia

WILDFLOWERS: Corn lily, Jeffrey's shooting star, cow parsnip, swamp onion, carpet clover, Leichtlin's camas, marsh marigold, Lewis monkey flower, primrose monkey flower, Lemmon's paintbrush, alpine paintbrush, Sierra penstemon, meadow penstemon, slender cinquefoil, sticky cinquefoil, Drummond's cinquefoil, pussytoes, elephant heads

MAMMALS: Belding ground squirrel, white-tailed hare (jack rabbit), montane meadow mouse, water shrew

BIRDS: White-crowned sparrow, Brewer's blackbird, mountain bluebird, spotted sandpiper

REPTILE: Mountain garter snake

AMPHIBIANS: Yosemite toad, Pacific treefrog, mountain yellow-legged frog

Subalpine Forest

WHERE SEEN: Most high lakes and passes, including Dorothy Lake, Peeler Lake, Benson Pass, Virginia Pass, Summit Lake, McCabe Lakes, Gaylor Lakes, Tioga Pass, Mono Pass, Ireland Lake, Vogelsang High Sierra Camp, May Lake, Ten Lakes, Buena Vista Peak, Post Peak Pass, Fernandez Pass, Upper Chain Lake

TREES: Whitebark pine, lodgepole pine, western white pine, mountain hemlock

SHRUBS: Bush cinquefoil, arctic (alpine) willow, Eastwood's willow, Mono willow, Sierra willow, red mountain heather, white heather, Labrador tea, alpine gooseberry, sticky currant

WILDFLOWERS: Sierra wallflower, Davidson's (timberline) penstemon, Coville's lupine, Coville's columbine, mountain sorrel, rock fringe, Lobb's eriogonum, cut-leaved daisy, alpine saxifrage, pink alum root

MAMMALS: Pika, yellow-bellied marmot, white-tailed hare (jack rabbit), alpine chipmunk, ermine (short-tailed weasel), little brown myotis (bat)

BIRDS: Clark's nutcracker, pine grosbeak, mountain chickadee, mountain bluebird, black-backed woodpecker

AMPHIBIANS: Mt. Lyell salamander, Yosemite toad

Alpine Fell-Fields

WHERE SEEN: Most of the Sierra Crest from Matterhorn Peak south, including Mt. Dana, Dana Plateau, Parker Pass, and Donohue Pass; also Mt. Hoffmann and Red Peak Pass

SHRUBS: Snow willow, arctic (alpine) willow, bush cinquefoil, alpine prickly currant

WILDFLOWERS: Sky pilot, alpine gold (hulsea), Brewer's draba, Lemmon's draba, Sierra draba, dense-leaved draba, cushion phlox, Davidson's penstemon, cut-leaved daisy, dwarf alpine daisy, sticky locoweed (oxytrope), Sierra podistera, oval-leaved buckwheat, Muir's ivesia, alpine (pygmy) lewisia

MAMMALS: Pika, yellow-bellied marmot, alpine chipmunk

BIRDS: Rosy finch

The Ahwahnechee

One animal that could be found in all of Yosemite's plant communities was *Homo sapiens*—aboriginal natives of Yosemite Valley. Calling themselves the Ahwahnechee, these people roamed the Yosemite landscape for food gathering, trade, or tribal interactions. Generally, however, they found most of what they needed right in Yosemite Valley.

Annually, the Ahwahnechee burned the vegetation on the Valley's floor, and this was a tradition that had definite benefits. Foremost, it maintained the oak population, and acorns from black oaks alone made up about 60% of their diet. Fire also reduced brush and kept the forests open and parklike, thus reducing the chance of ambush.

Today, Yosemite Valley holds far more humans than its resources could feed. We, however, carry in our own food or buy trucked-in foods. The Indians had to make do with the resources on hand, not only for food, but for all aspects of survival. They made extensive use of the Valley's resources and the resources of other nearby plant communities. The sidebar "Indian Uses of Yosemite Plants" (below), based on work by a former park naturalist, Will Neely, gives an idea of just how extensively they utilized the plants. Animals—both vertebrates and invertebrates—were also extensively utilized.

INDIAN USES OF YOSEMITE PLANTS

FOOD: ACORNS AND LARGE SEEDS black oak, sugar pine, western juniper. When black oak acorns were scarce, the following were used: canyon live oak, interior live oak, foothill pine, buckeye, pinyon pine (east of the Sierra Crest).

SMALLER SEEDS bunchgrass, western buttercup, evening primrose, clarkia (farewell to spring), California coneflower

BULBS, CORMS, ROOTS Mariposa tulip, pretty face (golden brodiaea), common camas, squaw root, Bolander's yampah

GREENS broad-leaved lupine, common monkey flower, nude buckwheat, California thistle, miner's lettuce, sorrel, clover, umbrella plant, crimson columbine, alum root

BERRIES AND FRUITS strawberry, blackberry, raspberry, thimbleberry, wild grape, gooseberry, currant, blue elderberry, western choke cherry, Sierra plum, greenleaf manzanita

DRINKS whiteleaf manzanita, western juniper

MEDICINE: Yerba santa, yarrow, horse mint (giant hyssop), Brewer's angelica, sagebrush, showy milkweed, mountain dogbane, balsamroot, California barberry, fleabane, mint, knotweed, wild rose, meadow goldenrod, mule ears, pearly everlasting, California laurel (bay tree)

SOAP: Soap plant, meadow rue

ROPE AND TWINE: Mountain dogbane (Indian hemp), showy milkweed, wild grape, soap plant

BASKETS: Redbud, American (creek) dogwood, big-leaf maple, buckbrush, deer brush, bracken fern, willows, California hazelnut

BOWS: Incense-cedar, mountain (Pacific) dogwood

SHELTER: Incense-cedar

Western Man in Yosemite

In the late 1850s, tourists, homesteaders, and entrepreneurs began to flock to Yosemite Valley in increasing numbers. By 1864, the Valley was set aside ostensibly for "public use, resort, and recreation," but also to protect it from these people so that future generations could enjoy it. The surrounding high country, however, was not protected, and sheep (and cattle to a lesser extent) were driven up into virtually every High Sierra meadow. Tuolumne Meadows in particular was severely overgrazed by sheep, resulting in deterioration of its soils. Overgrazing was certainly detrimental to the native fauna and flora, but by the mid-1890s, grazing had been virtually eliminated from all parts of the park except Yosemite Valley, where a dairy herd grazed, as did everyone's horses. Fruit orchards displaced native vegetation.

All the introduced animals, together with their masters, inadvertently brought in unwanted alien plants, insects, and associated diseases. Galen Clark, the park's first guardian, noted that in the 30 years that passed after the park was first created, the luxuriant native grasses and flowering plants of Yosemite Valley had decreased to only a quarter of their original number. Part of this was due to grazing, part to other causes, and part to the new plant competition.

Overgrazing on the Valley floor resulted in trampled soil and bare spots, both inviting invasion by ponderosa pines and incense-cedars. Prohibition of fires insured the survival of young conifers, which, as they matured, shaded out the once co-dominant black oaks. Finally, lowering the water table through blasting and ditching hastened this conifer invasion of the meadows. Throughout the 20th century and into the 21st, the Valley's plant community has been largely a dense conifer forest with neatly defined, gardened meadows, not an open conifer-oak woodland.

Thanks to the Yosemite Fund (which you should join), the under-funded Park Service is now able to reverse some of the past damage. It has aided endangered peregrine falcons, great gray owls, and bighorn sheep, and it has restored some meadows to more natural conditions.

But how does one deal with the top predator, man? The millions of annual visitors often has been perceived as the foremost threat to Yosemite's fauna and flora. However, the most pernicious threats usually go unseen and are beyond the control of the Park Service: man-induced global warming, increasing atmospheric pollution, upper-atmosphere ozone depletion, and habitat loss in middle and lower elevations of the Sierra Nevada and elsewhere in the Americas. The latter is of particular concern for Yosemite's birds, which in the fall typically migrate to lower elevations or to lower latitudes, such as to Central America. But everywhere the mounting human population is destroying habitat and the life it once held. For example, each person added to California ultimately causes enough habitat destruction to destroy, on average, up to one ton of animals, plants, and micro-organisms—something to ponder.

Plate 1. **Some Common Yosemite Trees (All Conifers)**

Foothill (gray, Digger) pine

Jeffrey pine

Whitebark pine

Western juniper

Incense-cedar branches

Mountain hemlock

Red fir

Red fir cone (top) and western white pine cone

Western white pine (silver pine)

Plate 2. **Some Common Yosemite Shrubs**

Chinquapin

Tobacco brush

Pinemat manzanita

Mountain ash

Thimbleberry

Mountain spiraea

Red mountain heather

Bog kalmia

Labrador tea

Plate 3. **Some Wildflowers of Foothill Woodlands and Ponderosa Pine Forests**

Indian pink

Mountain dogbane (Indian hemp)

Miner's lettuce

Lemmon's catchfly

Mountain violet

Common madia

Fireweed

Nude buckwheat

California stickseed

Plate 4. **Some Wildflowers of Jeffrey Pine Forests**

Scarlet gilia (desert trumpet)

Pussy paws

Sulfur flower

Mariposa tulip (lily)

Spreading phlox

Mule ears

Mountain pride
(Newberry's penstemon)

Single-stemmed senecio

Wavy-leaved (Applegate's)
paintbrush

Plate 5. **Some Wildflowers of Red Fir/Lodgepole Pine Forests**

Western spring beauty

Bleeding hearts

Branched false Solomon's seal

Spotted coralroot

Pinedrops

Snow plant

White-veined wintergreen

Dwarf lousewort

California Jacob's ladder

Plate 6. **Some Wildflowers of Creeks, Springs, and Bogs**

Wandering daisy

Cow parsnip

Leopard lily

Elephant heads

Common monkey flower

Crimson (red) columbine

Ranger's buttons
(swamp white heads)

Arrow-leaved senecio (butterweed)

Broad-leaved lupine

Plate 7. **Some Wildflowers of Meadows**

Sticky cinquefoil

Corn lily

Monument plant (green gentian)

Hiker's gentian

Shooting star

Marsh marigold

Yarrow

Meadow penstemon

Gray's lovage

Plate 8. **Some Wildflowers of Subalpine Forests and Alpine Fell-Fields**

Alpine gold (hulsea)

Timberline phacelia

Shaggy hawkweed

Flat-seeded rock cress

Newberry's (alpine) gentian

Mountain sorrel

Rock fringe

Sphinx moth and Davidson's penstemon

Alpine saxifrage

Half Dome as viewed from the summit of North Dome

CHAPTER 4

Geology

Evolution of the Yosemite Landscape

Padre Pedro Font, on the second Anza expedition, in April 1776, saw a distant range to the east, as other Spaniards had, but he was the first to give it a name: Sierra Nevada, or Snowy Range. John Muir would see the range almost a century later, in April 1868, but he did not write about it until 1894, in his first book, *The Mountains of California*. In it, he questioned the range's name, saying: "After 10 years spent in the heart of it, rejoicing and wondering... it still seems to me above all others the Range of Light."

But the high country of Yosemite and the rest of the High Sierra would not be very luminous if the overlying rocks intruded by molten "granite" had not been removed, if the volcanic rocks that blanket the northern Sierra had buried the entire range, and if glaciers had not developed on numerous occasions to remove the soil and create vast tracts of barren lands. Foremost, Yosemite National Park was set aside because of its renowned Yosemite Valley, arguably the world's most spectacular, which owes its origin to a unique pattern of major, generally vertical fracture planes in its granitic rock.

How was it produced? The standard answer is that a lowly Sierra was greatly uplifted a few million years ago, and then rivers cut relatively shallow canyons, followed by glaciers that deepened and broadened them. Surprisingly, this answer is not based on any evidence, but rather is based on late 1800s logic proposed by Harvard's William Morris Davis, who fleshed out the views of his Harvard professor, Louis Agas-

siz. Geologists are unaware that Agassiz was a biblical literalist, and his young-earth views might have been abandoned early on were it not for supporting Sierran-uplift "evidence" published in 1865. The evidence does not exist, nor was it ever visited by the Whitney Survey geologists who wrote it up. Nevertheless, geologists embraced this miners' fable, and even embellished it, inventing corroborative, often nonexistent evidence throughout the 1900s and beyond.

In reality, today's Sierran masterpiece was long in the making, the park's lands created mostly over the last 200 million years. In my book, *The Geomorphic Evolution of the Yosemite Valley and Sierra Nevada Landscapes*, I present detailed, verifiable evidence for a long evolutionary history of the Sierran landscape and for minimal glacial erosion. Since volumes of erroneous evidence of uplift and glaciation exist, I felt compelled to document it, covering all of the range's river drainages. This major research manuscript, completed in

2006, is tentatively titled *Seeing the Elephant: How Perceived Evidence in the Sierra Nevada Biased Global Geomorphology.* As the subtitle suggests, not only have the Sierran landscapes been misinterpreted, so have many if not most of the world's landscapes.

Some of the range's relevant uplift and glacial evidence lies in Yosemite National Park, and where each is encountered along some of the hiking routes in this guidebook, I identify and describe it. For example, like the postulated-but-imaginary trans-Sierran river canyon at Deadman Pass, a few miles southeast of the park, there is another equally imaginary river canyon near Rancheria Mountain, and I discuss it in Trip 12.

If magma reaches the surface as eruptions of ash or lava, it becomes volcanic rock. Together, volcanic and plutonic rocks are classified as igneous rocks, which are any that have solidified from a molten mass. There are many kinds of plutonic rocks, but in our area, only four are common. Classified from light-colored to dark-colored (from rich to poor in quartz or from poor to rich in iron and magnesium), these are granite, granodiorite, diorite, and gabbro, of which granodiorite is the commonest. The volcanic equivalents of these four are, respectively, rhyolite, dacite, andesite, and basalt, but none is common within the park.

Igneous Rocks

When continental crust is compressed, the result will be an orogeny, or mountain-building episode. This compression is on a grand scale, resulting in regional metamorphism. Sedimentary rocks are metamorphosed to metasediments, and volcanic rocks to metavolcanics. While the continental crust can't sink, the denser oceanic crust, as well as the dense, upper-mantle rock underlying both crusts, can, and so an oceanic plate will dive under a continental plate—a process called subduction. With increasing pressure and depth, the diving plate will begin to undergo partial melting, and the melt, or magma, ascends through the continental crust. As it ascends through preexisting rock of the upper crust, it alters the existing crustal rocks. This alteration is called contact metamorphism, since, in these rocks, it is greatest near the contact with the magma. In the Sierra, older rocks show signs of being metamorphosed two or more times. Magma that solidifies beneath the surface forms plutonic rock, and a body of this rock is called a pluton. In Sierra Nevada lands, most of this rock is light-gray granitic rock.

OLDEST ROCKS

The oldest rocks in the park's vicinity are about 540 million years old and originated as sandy sediments deposited on the ocean's floor off North America's west coast around the start of the Paleozoic era. These quartz-rich sandstones later were metamorphosed to *quartzites*, which today straddle the park's lightly visited northern-boundary lands. The most accessible remnants occur between Grace Meadow and adjacent Bigelow Peak within the park. Other significant remnants of metamorphic rocks stretch from the Saddlebag Lake environs south to Tioga Pass and into and the northern Ritter Range. These rocks have weathered to earth tones, which locally add color to our area's crest lands. Additionally, the mineral-rich soil they produce results in more plant species and in greater numbers than in adjacent granitic soil.

The Antler, Sonoma, and Nevadan Orogenies

In the vicinity of Yosemite National Park, volcanism began in earnest around 400 million years ago and continued until the Antler orogeny, which occurred from about 365 million to 350 million years ago. In the vicinity of today's range, existing sediments were metamorphosed as a chain of volcanic islands was thrust eastward, compressing, heating, and disrupting them. After the Antler orogeny, which raised the lands through compression, they underwent extension, which caused them to sink and to become buried under accumulating marine sediments.

Eventually, land in our area formed once again with a second round of volcanism, which began about 260 million years ago. This lasted at least until the Sonoma orogeny, which occurred from about 250 million to 240 million years ago, around the time the Paleozoic era gave way to the Mesozoic era. As before, the orogeny was due to a chain of volcanic islands being thrust eastward. During each orogeny, North America proper grew slightly westward as masses of crustal rocks were compressed and metamorphosed and then became accreted terranes, attached because magma rose beneath them, solidifying to form a very stable basement composed of one or more plutons. The earliest surviving plutons in the Sierra Nevada are located in its southern part. They are about 240 million years old and formed as the Sonoma orogeny was waning. The earliest ones in the Yosemite area are about 210 million years old and are found east of the crest, outside the park.

For a third time, the direction of motion of the oceanic plate became increasingly more nearly perpendicular to the North American plate, and another major compressional period began. This was the Nevadan orogeny, named after the Sierra Nevada, where its record is best preserved. Like earlier orogenies, this one metamorphosed the area's previously existing rocks. Compression and uplift may have begun about 180 million years ago, peaked from 160 to 155 million years ago, and then waned for millions of years. During this orogeny, magma mostly intruded an assemblage of older rocks lying west of the park, accreting them as a series of linear terranes. Within the park, plutonism was minimal. During the orogeny's maximum, the Sierra Nevada was a minor length of a major range, a cordillera, which extended along the western edge of both North America and South America.

Extension, Plutonism, and Volcanism

Major changes were needed to create today's largely granitic range, and these were accomplished in part when the compression that brought about the Nevadan orogeny gave way to extension. Faults rifted the upper crust apart, providing space for ascending magma. Extension and plutonism went hand in hand, and from about 115 million to 85 million years ago, Sierran plutonism occurred on an unprecedented scale. Over time, the locus of magma generation migrated episodically eastward across the ancestral Sierra Nevada. Consequently, granitic rocks east of the boundary—say, in the upper part of the Merced Gorge and the west half of Yosemite Valley—are about 105 million to 100 million years old. Those in its east half are about 100 million to 90 million years old, while those farther east, around Tuolumne Meadows, are about 90 million to 85 million years old.

The actual patterns of the spatial distribution and composition of plutons are complex. Some magma intruded older plutons, resulting in younger plutons partly displacing them. And some magma, working upward over millions of years, intruded and displaced outward newly solidified magma. This resulted in a nested, composite pluton called an intrusive suite, whose composition of magma has evolved over time. The largest one in our area, about 450 square miles, is the Tuolumne intrusive suite, which today is exposed over most of the eastern third of the park, but also includes the eastern part of Yosemite Valley, Tenaya Canyon, Little Yosemite Valley, and most of the Illilouette Creek drainage. Its plutonism began about 91 million years ago and continued in surges until about 86 million years ago. The magma's composition evolved toward increasing amounts of lighter-colored minerals (quartz and alkali feldspar).

During the 30-million-year period of abundant plutonism, volcanism locally dominated when extension and plutonism were minimal. Towering stratovolcanoes such as today's Mt. Shasta, Mt. Hood, and Mt. Rainier likely stood at various times above the range's core. During the last

surge of magma in the Tuolumne intrusive suite, one large volcano rose high above what is now Johnson Peak, just south of Tuolumne Meadows. However, a more impressive volcano straddled the park's southeast border about 100 million years ago, centered on the Minarets caldera. A caldera is a large, more or less circular basin at the center of a large volcano. The Minarets caldera was giant—about 18 miles across from near Chiquito Creek northeast to Thousand Island Lake, and 14 miles across from near the San Joaquin River northwest to Washburn Lake. Over its existence, this eruptive center produced an estimated 360 cubic miles of ash and lava.

Magmatism waned in the Sierra Nevada until about 80 million years ago, when the locus of magma generation shifted far east of the range, and it ultimately caused a mountain-building episode in the Rocky Mountains, the Laramide orogeny. The Sierra Nevada now had a core composed of

"Beach ball" landscape near Porphyry Lake

dozens of generally light-gray plutons. These, however, typically lay several miles beneath a largely volcanic landscape—definitely not the Range of Light. More change was in order.

Sierra Nevada Uplift

Until I started doing serious fieldwork in the early 1990s, I, along with the rest of the geoscientist community, believed that glaciers in the Sierra Nevada (and elsewhere around the world) had performed tremendous erosion. However, in glaciated Sierran canyons, I found volcanic remnants, up to 30 million years old on their floors and lower slopes. It was surprising that glaciers from 1000 to 3000-plus feet in thickness had not removed all of the volcanics, but it was even more surprising that they had not eroded the underlying granitic bedrock. Therefore, the range's major canyons, including the Merced River's Yosemite Valley, have been deep for at least 30 million years.

This conclusion posed a problem with regard to uplift. Geoscientists believed that the Sierra Nevada had been tilted westward, mostly in the last few million years, and that this Late Cenozoic uplift raised crest lands in our vicinity by as much as 11,000 feet. But I have found no evidence to support this, and I've found plenty supporting uplift before 30 million (more likely, before 60 million) years ago.

The original view of Sierran uplift began as a miner's tale told California State Geological Survey members in 1862, a year before any of them had set foot in the range. In the following year, when they camped within a few miles of the basis for this theory, they never bothered to check the evidence. Its lava table does exist, but not as they wrote it up as a canyon-bottom lava flow recently uplifted to a ridgetop flow.

Earlier, I said that about 80 million years ago the locus of magma generation shifted far east of the range. In the Sierra

Nevada, extension ensued, and detachment faulting would have developed between the lower and upper crust. In perhaps only a few million years, the upper crust would have been removed from the Sierra Nevada, exposing mainly the upper parts of plutons, but also some lower remnants of metamorphic rocks. With the removal of the upper crust, the lower crust of the Sierran block would have risen—an isostatic rebound upward—although not to its original height.

Origin of a Modern Sierra Nevada

Uplift of the lower crust in response to removal of the upper crust created a range that resembled today's in size and elevations. Uplift also created the Sierra's crest and therefore the valleys east of it. The foremost ones are, from north to south, the Truckee-Lake Tahoe basin (no lake until about 2.25 million years ago), Mono Basin, and Owens Valley. These three (and others) have been considered youthful because faulting and volcanism have occurred in each in the last few million years. However, 1990s mapping and dating of east-side faults demonstrated that some of the faults are extremely old, perhaps almost as ancient as the Nevadan orogeny.

The extensional forces that led to the birth of the modern Sierra Nevada and its east-side basins also fractured the range's recently raised bedrock. It was about then, some 80 million years ago, that the range's modern rivers originated on the newly created surface, cutting into what was once lower crust and having their courses dictated in part by recently formed fractures, or joints. These also dictated the courses of some tributaries, particularly north of the Tuolumne River, where linear canyons are the rule, not the exception.

The composition of bedrock can also influence the development of a landscape. For example, if Yosemite Valley had been carved in diorite instead of granodiorite and granite, it likely wouldn't be part of a national park today (and the Sierra Nevada wouldn't be "the Range of Light"). Diorite does not form massive cliffs and domes.

Joints are more important than the composition of bedrock, as is seen in Yosemite Valley. For example, El Capitan, one of the world's most resistant monoliths, is composed of granite, but just to its west the granitic cliffs are highly fractured, just like the diorite ones west of it, and together these produce a lot of rockfall, creating the Rockslides. When it comes to directing the evolution of the Yosemite landscape, the alignment and spacing of joints are more important than the type of bedrock.

Evolution of Yosemite Valley

At the start of the Cenozoic era 65 million years ago, the dinosaurs had met their demise, and small, primitive mammals, including our ancestors, had inherited the giant-free kingdom. At this time, the granitic Yosemite Valley was continuing to evolve under warm, wet climates. This generated intense chemical weathering, which causes deep, subsurface weathering, such as in the Valley's highly fractured bedrock floor, which was being converted into grus ("decomposed granite"). However, weathering was minimal on essentially joint-free monoliths such as El Capitan and Half Dome, which had already come into existence.

Some 65 million years ago, the main difference from today's lands was that the river canyons were shallower, perhaps half their present depths. In contrast, the topographic features above the canyon ,rims resembled their modern equivalents. Back then, the Valley was developing a generally broad, U-shaped cross profile of steep slopes and a flat floor—one characteristic of today's equatorial and tropical granitic ranges. All of the Valley's major features,

such as El Capitan and Half Dome, should have been recognizable, and their slopes were about as steep as those of today's, governed by similar joint patterns. Also, Ribbon, Upper Yosemite, and Nevada falls may have achieved about two-thirds of their present heights.

Since this time, weathering and erosion have removed only about 100 feet of bedrock from the most resistant summits. Broad, forested uplands may have been perhaps 200 to 500 feet higher than today's lands, so the domes would not have projected as much above their surrounding lands as they do today.

Throughout the first half of the Cenozoic era, Yosemite Valley continued to deepen, but only slowly, since the Merced River was quite ineffective at incising through the massive bedrock west of the Valley. Also during this time, the slopes and cliffs of Yosemite Valley were subject to slow retreat due to mass wasting, which was governed by the spacing and pattern of joint planes.

All of the falls in Yosemite Valley proper most likely achieved their full heights by the time the climate changed profoundly 33 million years ago. Overall, the climate became cooler and drier, and rates of chemical weathering decreased substantially. By this time, Yosemite Valley may have reached 80% of its width and its full depth and then some—the floor is now higher thanks to a few hundred feet of glacial deposits. Virtually all of the Valley's major features existed, including Lower Yosemite and Bridalveil falls. Back then, you could have used today's topographic map of the Valley to navigate along its forested floors, up its forested recesses and side canyons, which would have lacked talus slopes, and across its forested uplands. The same applies to the rest of the Sierra Nevada, from about the northern border of Yosemite National Park southward. North of the park's border, most of the northern Sierran landscape would become buried under various volcanic flows and deposits.

Late-Cenozoic Volcanism

In the northern Sierra, a period of volcanism—one largely of andesitic and basaltic lavas—began about 20 million years ago and climaxed about 10 million to 9 million years ago before waning. Although no major volcano stood within the park, there was at least one just north of it, which produced volcanic deposits in sufficient quantity to bury much of the park's lands north of the Tuolumne River. A small remnant, from an eruption 9.5 million years ago, survives on a lower slope of Hetch Hetchy Valley (see Trip 11 for details). This indicates that in that valley, the deposits originally were at least 4500 feet thick, enough to fill the canyon below Hetch Hetchy to its rim. While most of the deposits are gone, Rancheria Mountain still has considerable deposits because its summit area is quite broad and relatively flat, and therefore was little affected by stream erosion, and because it stood above the glaciers.

Little Devils Postpile

Multiple Glaciations

By around 15 million years ago, the modern Mediterranean climate of California had set in, complete with the cold coastal current and relatively dry summers, although storms, coming north from tropical seas (Central America did not exist back then) caused Great Basin lands to have wetter summers than today's. In these last 15 million years, both chemical and physical weathering have been minimal, and summits such as Yosemite Valley's El Capitan and North Dome have experienced only a few feet of denudation. Unglaciated, granitic Sierran lands 15 million years ago had achieved topography nearly identical to today's. The main difference appears to have been slight canyon deepening by the major rivers, such as the Tuolumne and the San Joaquin, whose glaciated canyons may have deepened by tens of feet, but not much more.

Glacial landscapes developed best near the crest of the Sierra Nevada, but this was due more to mass wasting, particularly earthquake-induced rockfall, than to glacial erosion. The principal role of an alpine, or mountain, glacier in any of the world's glaciated ranges is to transport the products of mass wasting, not to erode by abrading and plucking, which is minimal where the bedrock is resistant, as in most of the Sierra Nevada. Indeed, glaciers failed to remove some pre-glacial volcanic flows and deposits on the floors and/or lower slopes of the South Yuba, North Stanislaus, Tuolumne, South San Joaquin, and Middle Kings river canyons. Nevertheless, glaciers did remove loose rock, soil, and vegetation to expose vast tracts of fresh, generally light-colored bedrock—the final step in transforming the range into John Muir's Range of Light.

The range's earliest glaciation may have occurred as early as 15 million years ago, when the climate cooled, but the glaciers would have been restricted to the heads of canyons below high peaks. In each glacial episode, cold climates would create myriad freeze-and-thaw cycles of ice, which pried rock from steep walls to collect below as talus. As the walls gradually retreated through rockfall, the heads of canyons became broader. The canyon heads are called *cirques,* the small glaciers that occupied them are called *cirque glaciers,* such as below Mt. Lyell. (Be aware that cirques can form in nonglacial, even tropical, lands, and a few in the unglaciated Sierra Nevada may be tens of millions of years old.) About 5.6 million and 5.2 million years ago, *valley glaciers* could have extended many miles down the Sierra Nevada's principal canyons, possibly excavating fractured bedrock to create the range's first lakes.

Glaciation began in earnest by 2 million years ago, and the upper lands may have been glaciated dozens of times; each time, they would have removed lake sediments. Glaciations that occurred before 200,000 years ago collectively are called pre-Tahoe, since they preceded the well-known Tahoe glaciation. On the east side of the range, the Sherwin glaciation, which lasted from about 900,000 to 800,000 years ago, was thought to have produced the largest known glaciers. In contrast, on the west side, there were no large glaciers. How can this be? Actually, most supposed Sherwin deposits are Tahoe deposits; the Sherwin was not larger. Due to the absolutely huge, 150-cubic-mile Long Valley eruption of rhyolite about 760,000 years ago, some Sherwin deposits were buried and preserved.

The Tahoe and Tioga glaciers, which existed, respectively, about 200,000 to 130,000 and 30,000 to 15,000 years ago, were larger in the Merced River drainage than previously supposed, advancing to the lower part of Merced Gorge, about 6 miles beyond the last end moraine (a deposit left by the retreating Tioga glacier) by Bridalveil Meadow. Also, both glaciers were thicker than previously supposed, especially in Little Yosemite Valley, where they were about 2000 feet thick, not 1000. As in all other glaciated canyons studied so far, the Tahoe glacier was slightly larger

A lag deposit (false glacial deposit) atop Turtleback Dome. Glacier Point and other high points along the Valley's rim never were glaciated.

than the Tioga glacier, although in Yosemite Valley the Tioga's ice surface was slightly higher than the Tahoe's simply because some sedimentation had occurred between the two glaciations, giving the Tioga a higher base, and hence a higher ice surface. After the Tioga glacier left the Valley about 15,000 years ago, there was at best a swampy floor, not a lake.

The Holocene Epoch

The last 10,000 years have been classified as the Holocene epoch, which is misleading, for it implies that the glacier-dominated Pleistocene epoch is behind us. Actually, we are only in a short-term interglacial period similar to a preceding, major one that lasted from about 130,000 to 120,000 years ago.

Since 15,000 years ago, when Sierran glaciers had all but disappeared but the lakes had appeared, the park's landscape has changed very little. The massive face of El Capitan has weathered back only a quarter of an inch, if even that, though parts of it have spalled rockfalls.

The largest one identified is the prehistoric fall that dammed Tenaya Creek to create Mirror Lake, estimated to be about 15,000,000 cubic yards. The 1987 Middle Brother rockfall, perhaps the largest historic one, pales in comparison, at about 800,000 cubic yards. Fresh rockfall sites on cliffs are easy to identify, since they expose fresh rock, which, over decades, are covered with medium-gray lichens.

Sierran meadows began to form early on where soils were waterlogged. They are not due to filled-in lake basins, since the sedimentation rate is so slow—about one foot per thousand years—that few, if any, lake basins have been completely filled. Actually, many of the High Sierra meadows, such as Tuolumne Meadows, were forested up to at least the start of the Little Ice Age, when colder conditions developed and the level of ground water rose, drowning the trees. We can therefore be thankful for the Little Ice Age, which became pronounced from about 1550 to 1850 AD, for without it, we wouldn't have the many meadows from which we can view the snow-clad High Sierra landscape. The view-packed Yosemite Valley meadows are also in existence largely due to the presence of a high water table. The meadows once were much more extensive, covering about 745 of the Valley's 1141 acres, but they were greatly reduced by man in part due to the lowering of the water table in order to reduce both flooding and mosquitoes, two problems that plagued early tourism.

The Uniqueness of Yosemite Valley

Yosemite Valley has been hailed as perhaps the premier example of what a glaciated canyon should look like. It certainly was glaciated. Its Tahoe glacier was about 1200 feet thick near El Capitan and about 1600 feet thick near Glacier Point, and it was about 33 miles long. While large, it paled in comparison to the Tahoe glacier in the Grand Canyon of the Tuolumne River, which was about 3500 feet thick near Hetch Hechy's dam, more than 4000 feet thick up-canyon around Pate Valley, and about 58 miles long (it may have flowed 2 to 3 miles past the Tuolumne/Cherry confluence). Despite the enormity of the glaciers, they barely widened and deepened the floor of their canyons.

Most glaciated canyons in the Sierra and elsewhere do not resemble Yosemite Valley. Most do not have broad, flat floors and most do not have steep-to-overhanging cliffs. The Valley's flat floor is easily explained: It is a floodplain atop sediments left by glaciers and by the Merced River between glaciations.

Yosemite Valley, the western Sierra's rockfall capital, is unique because of its different pattern of variations—in size, spacing, and orientation—of its joint planes ("joints" for short). Joints are often linear, usually parallel fractures in bedrock. Most of the Sierra Nevada is granitic and possesses joints, as do other types of rocks, such as massive sandstone, which, in Utah's Zion National Park, is cut by a rectangular grid of streams (and it has glacial features—such as cirques, hanging canyons, and broad floors—despite the *absence* of glaciation). Yosemite Valley has steep-sided walls (with more than 1000 difficult climbing routes up them) because its walls are governed by the presence of vertical joints. Glaciers didn't make the walls vertical— their contribution was minor; the walls were already quite steep long before glaciation.

Chapter 5

Climate

Summer

If you are a typical hiker using this guidebook, you'll probably visit the park during the summer and likely will be taking trails above Yosemite Valley. Unlike most of America's mountain ranges, the Sierra Nevada is summer-dry, receiving only about 1.5 inches of precipitation from the summer solstice, about June 22, until the autumnal equinox, about September 23. The summer solstice, which marks the day with the greatest amount of daylight—about 14 hours and 42 minutes from sunrise to sunset—should be about the time all of us should hike to enjoy a maximum of daylight enjoyment. For Yosemite Valley, the last cold night and/or significant storm usually has just ended, and the days will be in the 80s and the nights down to the 50s (the coolest temperature is not in the middle of the night but actually is a few minutes after sunrise). Temperatures drop with elevation gain, and up at Tuolumne Meadows, which is about 4000 feet higher than the Valley, the summer temperatures are about 15°F (8°C) cooler (see the climate table on page 46 for the Valley's monthly precipitation and temperatures).

At Tuolumne Meadows and other high-elevation areas, early summer temperatures are cool but acceptable. What limits hiker use is lingering snow. Unless the year has had above average snowfall, by the first day of summer, all the park's major roads usually are open, with roads to Tamarack Flat Campground, Yosemite Creek Campground, and the May Lake Trailhead opening by early or mid-July. High trails, however, may be partly to mostly snowbound, so it's best to confine your hiking to below an elevation of about 7500 feet, such as along both rims of Yosemite Valley, up Little Yosemite Valley to Merced Lake, or up from Hetch Hetchy to Laurel Lake and Lake Vernon.

By mid- to late July, most of the area's trails will be snow free or nearly so, and the afternoon temperatures usually are warm and the nights pleasant. However, July, with all the snowmelt and the warm temperatures, is the month of maximum mosquito populations. Should you backpack overnight then, be sure to bring a tent. Furthermore, July seems to get its share of thunderstorms, and the closer you approach the Sierran crest, the more likely you are to experience one. These mostly occur from about mid-afternoon until sunset, and usually they are short lived, drenching a local area for a few minutes before moving on. If ominous clouds are threatening you, be sure to take cover within a forest rather than staying in the open or under an isolated tree. Also by mid- to late July, because snowmelt now is minimal, the volume of Yosemite Falls and other waterfalls is greatly diminished and not very photogenic.

For hikers, the first half of August is best, since chances of a major frontal storm (possibly bringing snow at high elevations) or of an isolated thunderstorm are minimal, and mosquito populations have dwindled to an acceptable level. Also, lakes, which typically reach their maximum temperatures by late July (low to mid-70s for the lower lakes, mid- to high 60s for the higher lakes), are still nearly as warm and are fine for swimming. By the end of August or early September, the lakes definitely are cooling, and the Sierra likely will have had one or two relatively weak frontal storms. After the Labor Day weekend, the park has fewer visitors, mosquitoes are virtually nonexistent, and, for me, this is the most pleasant time to backpack. Should you do so, be sure to check the weather forecast for a possible storm, and certainly bring a tent if you will be out for more than one or two nights. (Weather forecasts usually are accu-rate for two to three days, but not after that, and a storm that was not forecast could hit the Sierra.)

Autumn

The autumnal equinox, about September 23, marks the start of fall, and on this day, the length of daylight has dwindled to 12 hours. Not only is daylight shorter, but the sun at its maximum (1 PM with daylight savings time) rises to only about 52 degrees above the horizon, versus 76 degrees on the summer solstice. Consequently, the days are considerably cooler, as the climate table shows. Yosemite Valley, which has often reached temperatures into the 90s—great for frolicking in the Merced River but not for strenuous hiking or climbing—in the first half of autumn (through early November) is a favorite time for some of us. Whereas the nights may be crisp, the days are ideal, and the colors of turning foliage compensate for the Valley's lack of waterfalls (except for a wispy Bridalveil Fall).

Average Precipitation and Temperatures in Yosemite Valley			
MONTH	PRECIPITATION (inches/cm)	MAXIMUM (F°/C°)	MINIMUM (F°/C°)
January	6.2/15.7	49/9	26/-3
February	6.1/15.5	55/13	28/-2
March	5.2/13.2	59/15	31/-0.5
April	3.0/7.6	65/18	35/2
May	1.3/3.3	73/23	42/5.5
June	0.7/1.8	82/28	48/9
July	0.4/1.0	90/32	54/12
August	0.3/0.8	90/32	53/11.5
September	0.9/2.3	87/30.5	47/8
October	2.1/5.5	74/23	39/4
November	5.5/14	58/14	31/-0.5
December	5.6/14.2	48/9	26/-3

Note: This table is from the park's *Yosemite Guide*.

Backpackers at higher elevations need to be prepared for the season's first major storm, which may strike in early October or not until early November. Although most days are fair weather, I have a rule of thumb that after October 15 I don't backpack more than a few miles from a trailhead, since if a storm does hit and drop a foot or two of snow, I can still plod back to my car in a day's time and hopefully will be able to drive back home (carry chains). The Tioga Road may close briefly in a minor snowstorm, but from about mid-October into November a major one usually hits, and then this road, along with Forest Service roads bordering the park, close for the season.

November through mid-December is a time of solitude. The backcountry is virtually devoid of hikers, save for a few mountaineers who hopefully possess excellent storm-survival skills. Likewise, the Valley is empty, for the days are cool, the nights are nippy, and the ski season has not begun.

Winter

The winter solstice, about December 22, marks the day with the least amount of daylight—about 9 hours and 18 minutes from sunrise to sunset. Furthermore, the sun at noon only rises to about 29 degrees above the horizon, which is not much higher than at the South Pole, where it rises to 23.5 degrees. With the sun staying at low angles, the Valley's floor stays in the shadows, although much of the north wall may be sunlit. With no sunlight on the floor, its temperatures are downright cold. As the climate table shows, both November and December receive a lot of precipitation. At first this is rain, but by around Thanksgiving, most of it will be snow. Snow often covers the Valley's floor from about mid-December to mid-February, after which it may be patchy. By early March, the snow is mostly gone, although one can still get a snowstorm in March and even in April. February, March, and April often have

temperatures that get above freezing during part of the day but then drop below freezing during the night. On the Valley's south walls, ice that melts in the day later refreezes and expands at night, which can dislodge slabs, and so you may be woken up by the sound of rockfall.

Winter is ski season, and most folks driving up to the park head to Badger Pass for downhill or cross-country skiing. Buses still bring in hordes of tourists to the Valley, for, indeed, in the deep of winter, especially after a storm, the Valley is a winter wonderland. Although the four months from November through March produce the most precipitation, about 75% of it, most days are storm free, and when a storm does hit, it usually clears out in a day or two.

Spring

The vernal equinox, on about March 21, is like the autumnal equinox, and, like it, the length of daylight is 12 hours, and the sun at its maximum also rises to about 52 degrees above the horizon. March and April can have quite variable weather, pleasant in some years, wintery in others. You may experience balmy afternoons in the 70s or cold, blustery ones in the 40s or 50s. For plants on the floor of Yosemite Valley, it is still winter. By early May, daylight is about 13.5 hours long, and with daylight savings time in place, the days seem longer. Concurrent with longer daylight, the sun is higher in the sky, providing sufficient insulation to bring spring to the Valley floor. The deciduous trees produce leaves, and the meadows change from matted brown, dead vegetation to a sea of green. The added solar radiation (sunlight) also increases snowmelt, sometimes augmented by the passage of a relatively warm rainstorm, and the Valley's waterfalls reach their zenith from about early May to the first day of summer. The best time to visit these falls is around mid-May, by which time most of the season's storms have abated but the storm of tourists have yet to invade the Valley (which begins around the Memorial Day weekend).

Whereas all of the high country still lies under snow in May, some intermediate elevations are open to hikers. Usually by some date in May you can safely hike from the Valley's floor up to Vernal, Nevada, and Yosemite falls, as well as up the Snow Creek Trail, which goes to the old Big Oak Flat Road. In the Wawona area, south of the Valley, the trail to the top of Chilnualna Falls should be open, while to the northwest, the trail along Hetch Hetchy Reservoir east to Rancheria Creek also should be open. Additionally, all three groves of giant sequoias should be accessible.

In late spring, that is, through most of June, the rims of Yosemite Valley are largely snow free, and so one can hike up the Yosemite Falls Trail, then east along the north rim to North Dome, and then descend the Snow Creek Trail to the Valley's floor. Or, one can start from Glacier Point and either descend the Four Mile Trail or the Pohono Trail to the floor. Finally, usually in June, the Park Service opens the cable route to the summit of Half Dome. While occasional frontal storms sweep through in June, thunderstorms are rare, and so if the morning is nice when you start an ascent of that dome, the afternoon also should be nice.

CHAPTER 6

Traveling the Backcountry

Wilderness Permits

For overnight stays in the backcountry, you need a wilderness permit. There are quotas from May through October, and 60% of each day's trailhead quota is available by reservation; the rest are on first-come, first-served basis. The rest of the year, virtually all of the high country will be under snow, and then very few people will be backpacking, so you won't have to worry about any trailhead having its quota full.

To register in person, see the "Wilderness Permits" section at the start of each hiking chapter. Popular destinations, such as Lyell Canyon, the Cathedral Lakes, the Vogelsang Lake area, and Little Yosemite Valley, can easily reach their quotas, especially for overnight trips beginning on a summer weekend. Therefore, you might want to get a permit well in advance if you are backpacking on a weekend from late June through late September. You can get a permit from 24 weeks to two days in advance of your trip date. You can also get a permit by calling the Valley's Wilderness Center at 209-372-0740, but the reservation phone lines are often busy, and you may not get through. (For general information about wilderness permits and the backcountry, phone the center at 209-372-0745.)

You can also make your request in writing or on the internet at www.nps.gov/yose/wilderness. Written requests are processed simultaneously with phone requests. Write to: Wilderness Permits, PO Box 545, Yosemite, CA 95389. Include the following in your request: name, address, daytime phone, number of people in party, method of travel (e.g., ski, snowshoe, foot, horse), number of stock (if applicable), start and end dates, entry and exit trailheads, and principal destination. Include alternate dates and/or trailheads. A $5 per person non-refundable processing fee is charged for all reservation requests. Payment by check or money order should be made to the Yosemite Association. Credit card payments are accepted with valid card number and expiration date.

Finally, if you begin an overnight trip into a national forest, you'll have to make reservations at an appropriate district office or ranger station. These are mentioned under "Wilderness Permits" in the appropriate chapters.

When to Go

For hikers, the first half of August is best, when the temperatures are good, the mosquito populations have diminished, and the lakes have reached their maximum temperature.

My favorite time of the year for backpacking is October. Although quotas exist in October, not many folks backpack this late in the year, and so quotas likely will not be filled. My advice is to plan a trip in October or the first half of November, verifying the weather before you go and staying only one or two nights in the wilderness (weather reports usually are accurate up to two or three days, but can be fatally wrong beyond that).

Up to mid- or late October, you are probably safe to hike out of Tuolumne Meadows without worrying about a major snow storm closing the Tioga Road and trapping you. After that, I suggest that you only hike out from Happy Isles to Little Yosemite Valley, from the Glacier Point Road, from the Hetch Hetchy Road, from Wawona, or from any of the roads leading up to the trails east of and below the park's Sierran crest, since east-side lands receive less snow. Don't attempt trails out of Cherry Lake or any southern trails, that is, all the ones in Chapter 17.

Wilderness Ethics and Park Regulations

By stressing natural history, this book aims to increase your awareness, understanding, and appreciation of the landscape you traverse. One avid hiker, Keith Schiller, decided to hike every trail in a previous edition, bringing dozens of friends and fellow Yosemite lovers with him to the park. By the time he was nearing completion, he became alarmed at deteriorating conditions in the backcountry, and he resolved to help preserve Yosemite.

In the late 1980s, Keith and his friends founded the East Bay Chapter of the Yosemite Fund, and together they become the initial nucleus for this organization. By 1992, it had raised approximately $200,000 for the restoration of the Happy Isles area in Yosemite Valley. More importantly, in that year, he conceived of and saw established the Yosemite license fund, which raised more than $3 million by the close of the century. For more information on the

Relaxing and fishing at the largest of the Staniford Lakes

Yosemite Fund, contact them at 800-4MY-PARK (469-7275) or at www.yosemitefund.org.

While I don't expect every hiker or equestrian to become as motivated as Schiller, I nevertheless hope that they will gain some appreciation for the park. Too many veteran hikers come to the High Sierra year after year and never extend their natural-history knowledge past the identification of a few prominent tree species. However, the more you know about the environment, the more you will appreciate, protect, and defend it. And you will develop a better feeling for man's role in it.

The following backcountry guidelines should help keep the wild in wilderness.

Camping

- Camp a minimum of 100 feet from any water source.
- Choose a campsite away from trails.
- Never build improvements (fireplaces, rock walls, drainage ditches, etc.).
- Camp on exposed dirt or rock surfaces, not on vegetation.
- Use only downed wood for fires; never cut trees (dead or alive).
- If you must build a fire, use only existing fire rings.
- Never leave a fire unattended.
- Fully extinguish all campfires by thoroughly soaking with water.

Sanitation

- Bury waste 6 inches deep, a minimum of 100 feet from trails, and 500 feet from water sources.
- Pack out toilet paper, or burn it in areas where fires are permissible.
- Cook only the amount of food you can eat to avoid disposing of leftovers.
- Wash and rinse dishes, clothes, and yourself a minimum of 100 feet away from water sources; never wash in lakes or streams.

- Pack out all trash—do not attempt to burn plastic or foil packaging.
- Filter, boil, or purify all drinking water.

On the Trail

- Stay on the trail—don't cut switchbacks.
- Preserve the serenity of the backcountry—avoid making loud noises.
- Yield the right-of-way to equestrians—step off the trail, downhill.
- Avoid traveling in large groups.

Regulations for Yosemite National Park

- Maximum group size for backpackers is 15 people; 8 if you are going cross-country.
- Maximum number of stock in the backcountry is 25.
- Pets are prohibited on trails.
- Bicycles and motorized equipment are prohibited on trails.

Hikers should yield to equestrians

Black bears are adept at climbing trees; use bearproof containers instead of hanging food.

Hetch Hetchy Entrance Station, and the Crane Flat and Wawona stores. They can be returned to any of these locations. Drop bins are available for after-hours returns. Drop bins are also available in the Yosemite Valley's Trailhead Parking area, near Happy Isles. If you've charged your deposit on a credit card, the charge slip will be torn up. If you've used cash, you will have to return the canister during business hours to the site you got it from.

- No hunting: Weapons are prohibited in the park.
- Campfires are prohibited above 9600 feet and at certain lower sites.
- Carry your food in bear canisters, and use bearproof food-storage boxes where they are available (see below).

Bear Canisters

If you backpack in the park, you will need to keep your food in a bear canister, which you can buy at some sporting goods stores or buy or rent one in the park. The only exceptions are for campsites at Little Yosemite Valley and at the High Sierra Camps, which have bear-proof metal food-storage boxes. A park rental canister is $5 for your backpack trip plus a refundable deposit (equal to the cost of the canister) with cash or a credit card.

Canisters are available at the Yosemite Valley and Tuolumne Meadows Wilderness Centers, the Big Oak Flat Information Station, the Wawona Information Station, the

CHAPTER 7

About This Guide

This guide is designed for hikers in search of dayhiking opportunities in and around Yosemite National Park, and for backpackers looking to explore the majesty of the Sierra on short weekend trips up to weeklong trips. Some aspects of the evaluations of the following trails are subjective, but every effort was made to insure that the descriptions are meaningful to the average hiker and backpacker.

The 83 hiking trips in this guide are divided into 10 chapters (arranged more or less from northwest to southeast), each covering an area with a group of related trailheads and their hiking trails. A brief introduction to each area will familiarize you with its features. You'll find information specific to the area, including supplies and services, wilderness permits, and campgrounds. Individual trip descriptions follow the chapter's introductory material.

Selecting Your Trip

If you know where you want to hike, turn to the appropriate geographical section and review its trips. If you need help selecting a trip, start with the Trips Features Chart on page 56 to 59 that offers, at a glance, the basic characteristics of each trip. When you see a trip that matches your desires—say, a two-day trip that is 10 to 15 miles long—turn to that trip and read its description. Often, photos included in the trip will give you a feel for the scenery. You can also look at the enclosed topographic map, which should allow you to envision the park's geography encountered along its trails.

How to Read the Trips

Each trip description begins with a display of symbols denoting the following characteristics.

Trip Difficulty

The ratings are for the minimum distance and do not include any side hikes that are suggested in the hike's description, which are extra. (Of course, you can decrease the difficulty of most hikes by taking longer to do them.)

E = easy

M = moderate

S = strenuous

Type of Trip

⟋ = out and back

⟋ = point to point (shuttle required)

◯ = loop

◯ = semiloop

Duration

This is the length of time that I feel is best for a given hike walked by the average hiker. Elevation, topography, and hiking duration were taken into account in arriving at these recommended times, for a hike will be more exhausting if it is at high altitude, if it involves lots of ascent and descent, or if it is long and therefore requires an initially heavy backpack.

DH = dayhike (single-day outing)

BP = backpack (trip with one or two nights in the wilderness)

BPx = extended backpack (overnight trip with three or more nights in the wilderness)

X = cross-country route (backpack requiring some off-trail travel)

Distance

Distances are given in miles. Mileages for all trips is total mileage.

Elevation

Each trip has two sets of elevations, given in feet (to convert feet to meters, multiply by 0.3). The first set gives the trip's lowest and highest elevations, and since most Sierran trails start low and climb high, these two numbers often (but with many exceptions) represent the elevation at the trailhead and the elevation at the most distant point.

The first two numbers of the second set of numbers represents the total elevation gain and the total elevation loss, which is not the same as the net gain and the net loss. Just as life has its ups and downs, so do trails; you rarely start from a low point and ascend to a high point without some dips along the way. The third number is for the total amount of up and down you will make along your entire trip.

Season

This is the period of the year you should be able to drive to a trailhead and then hike an essentially snow-free trail. On the higher trails, you may experience snow flurries, but your trail will be covered by only a few inches of snow, not a snowpack. Should you choose, you can hike early in the season, when trail use is light or nil, but then be prepared for some route-finding problems due to parts of the trail being under snow. In Yosemite Valley you can hike year round, for it is unlikely you would get lost even with a foot of winter snow on the floor. You may not find the trail, but then, you won't have to, if the snowpack is firm enough for cross-country hiking or skiing.

Use

"Light," "moderate," "heavy," or "packed" is used to describe each trail's popularity. This gives you an idea of how many people to expect. Packed trails are tourist destinations, which may have hundreds of people. On heavy and packed backpack trails, campsites may be in short supply on weekends though probably not on weekdays. Some of this book's hikes have sections that vary significantly in usage.

Lakes

This is fairly obvious. "Yes" means that you will visit one or more lakes. The ones below 9000 feet usually are suitable for swimming, at least from about mid-July through mid-August, while those below 8000 feet may be suitable from early July. Many lakes have trout, but some don't, and with passing time more lakes may become fishless.

Maps

Because this guidebook comes with a topographic map, you don't need any others. Still, some hikers may want a more detailed map, especially if they plan to do some serious cross-country hiking. For them, this entry lists the USGS 7.5-minute quadrangle you need for the lands traversed by each trip. Where more than one quadrangle is required, they are listed in the order you will need them.

Trip Description

This includes an introduction, directions to the trailhead, and a detailed guide to the trail. At the end of the directions to the trailhead is a letter/number combination in boldface type—for example, **H1** for Trip 1—that gives you the location of the trailhead on this guide's topographic map.

In the margins beside the main text you'll find quick-reference icons indicating various features found along the trip route:

⛺ = campsites

≋ = swimming areas

👁 = noteworthy views

✼ = seasonal wildflowers

⚠ = potentially dangerous—
    watch your step

⛰ = geology

◇ = history

Options

Options allow you to extend or vary your trip, and these are side trips, alternate routes, additional cross-country routes, and peaks to climb in the vicinity:

S̲ **SIDE TRIP**

A̲ **ALTERNATE ROUTE**

Trip Features								
TRIP NO.	TYPE OF TRIP	HIKING TIME	DIFFICULTY	HIKING SEASON	HIKER USE	LAKES	LENGTH IN MILES	TOTAL ELEV. GAIN+LOSS

Trips of Yosemite's North Lands

1	↗	1 day	S	Jul–Oct	Light	No	16.4	±6060′
2	↗	6 days	M	Jul–Oct	Mod.	Yes	51.7	±15,190′
3	↗	2 days	M	Jul–Oct	Heavy	Yes	16.4	±6080′
4	↻	6 days	M	Jul–Sep	Mod.	Yes	57.7	±21,600′
5	↗	1–2 days	M	Jul–Oct	Mod.	Yes	9.0	±3600′
6	↗	1–2 days	M	Jul–Oct	Mod.	Yes	11.9	±5270′
7	↻	½ day	E	Jul–Oct	Mod.	Yes	7.6	±1800′

Trips of Yosemite's West Lands

8	↗	4 days	E M	Jul–Sep	Mod.	Yes	21.0	±7440′
9	↗	2 days	M	Jul–Oct	Mod.	Yes	21.2	±9160′
10	↻	4 days	M	Jul–Sep	Light	Yes	44.1	±15,700′
11	↗	1–2 days	M	May–Oct	Mod.	Yes	12.8	±4540′
12	↻	5 days	S	Jul–Sep	Light	Yes	53.7	±24,080′
13	↗	½–2 days	E	Apr–Oct	Light	No	8.6	±1800′
14	↗	2 hours	E	Apr–Oct	Light	No	3.0	±1260′
15	↗	2 days	M	Jun–Oct	Light	No	15.8	±7420′

Trips of Yosemite's West-Central Lands Northwest of the Tioga Road

16	↗	2 hours	M	May–Nov	Mod.	No	3.0	±1140′
17	↗	2 hours	M	May–Nov	Heavy	No	2.4	±980′
18	↗	½ day	E	Jun–Oct	Heavy	Y/N*	5.6	±1140′
19	↗	1–2 days	M	Jun–Oct	Light	Y/N*	19.6	±7600′
20	↻	2 days	S	Jun–Oct	Mod.	Y/N*	20.9	±9400′
21	↗	½ day	E	Jul–Oct	Mod.	Yes	4.6	±940′
22	↗	2 hours	E	Jul–Oct	Mod.	Yes	2.2	±600′
23	↗	2 days	M	Jul–Oct	Heavy	Yes	12.6	±6420′

TRIP NO.	TYPE OF TRIP	HIKING TIME	DIFFICULTY	HIKING SEASON	HIKER USE	LAKES	LENGTH IN MILES	TOTAL ELEV. GAIN+LOSS
			Trip Features					
24	✗	2 hrs.–2 days	**E**	Jul–Oct	Heavy	Yes	2.4	±1120′

Trips of Yosemite's West-Central Lands Between the Tioga Road and Yosemite Valley

TRIP NO.	TYPE OF TRIP	HIKING TIME	DIFFICULTY	HIKING SEASON	HIKER USE	LAKES	LENGTH IN MILES	TOTAL ELEV. GAIN+LOSS
25	✗	½ day	**M**	May–Nov	Light	No	8.2	±3720′
26	✗	2 hours	**E**	Jul–Sep	Light	No	3.0	±1400′
27	✗	1–2 days	**S**	Jul–Sep	Light	No	17.0	±7440′
28	✗	1–2 days	**M**	Jul–Oct	Mod.	No	12.9	±6200′
29	✗	1 day	**M**	Jul–Oct	Light	No	9.2	±3900′
30	✗	1–2 days	**M**	Jul–Oct	Light	Yes	12.6	±5730′

Trips of the Tuolumne Meadows Area North of the Tioga Road

TRIP NO.	TYPE OF TRIP	HIKING TIME	DIFFICULTY	HIKING SEASON	HIKER USE	LAKES	LENGTH IN MILES	TOTAL ELEV. GAIN+LOSS
31	✗	½–2 days	**E**	Jul–Oct	Light	Yes	6.2	±1440′
32	✗	½ day	**E**	Jul–Oct	Mod.	No	6.4	±1180′
33	✗	1–2 days	**M** **E**	Jul–Oct	Heavy	No	18.6	±2660′
34	✗	4 days	**M**	Jul–Oct	Mod.	Yes/No*	31	±11,870′
35	↺	6 days	**M**	Jul–Oct	Heavy	Yes	51.2	±18,180′
36	✗	7 days	**S**	Jul–Oct	Mod.	Yes	76.4	±29,430′
37	♀	2 days	**M**	Jul–Oct	Heavy	Yes	16.4	±6060′
38	✗	½ day	**M**	Jul–Oct	Heavy	Yes	3.0	±2180′
39	✗	½ day	**E**	Jul–Oct	Mod.	Yes	4.0	±2560′

Trips of the Tuolumne Meadows Area South and East of the Tioga Road

TRIP NO.	TYPE OF TRIP	HIKING TIME	DIFFICULTY	HIKING SEASON	HIKER USE	LAKES	LENGTH IN MILES	TOTAL ELEV. GAIN+LOSS
40	✗	½ day	**E**	Jul–Oct	Light	Yes	4.0	±1540′
41	✗	1–2 days	**M**	Jul–Oct	Heavy	Yes	11.6	±5200′
42	✗	1–2 days	**S**	Jul–Oct	Mod.	Yes	21.3	±6380′
43	✗	½–2 days	**M**	Jul–Oct	Mod.	Yes	7.6	±2840′
44	✗	1–2 days	**M**	Jul–Oct	Heavy	Yes	21.7	±9490′

TRIP NO.	TYPE OF TRIP	HIKING TIME	DIFFICULTY	HIKING SEASON	HIKER USE	LAKES	LENGTH IN MILES	TOTAL ELEV. GAIN+LOSS
Trip Features								
45	↗	½–2 days	M	Jul–Oct	Light	Yes	5.4	±3020′
46	↗	½ day	M	Jul–Oct	Heavy	Yes	5.0	±1720′
47	⟳	4 days	M	Jul–Oct	Heavy	Yes	32.8	±11,900′
48	⟳	2 days	M	Jul–Oct	Heavy	Yes	20.3	±5280′
49	↗	3 days	M	Jul–Oct	Heavy	Yes	25.9	±8270′
50	↗	½ day	M	Jul–Oct	Mod.	Yes	8.0	±2800′
51	↗	2 days	M	Jul–Oct	Mod.	Yes	20.0	±9330′
52	↗	½ day	S	Jul–Oct	Heavy	No	5.8	±6600′

Trips in Yosemite Valley and up from its Floor

TRIP NO.	TYPE OF TRIP	HIKING TIME	DIFFICULTY	HIKING SEASON	HIKER USE	LAKES	LENGTH IN MILES	TOTAL ELEV. GAIN+LOSS
53	⟲	½ day	E	Apr–Nov	Mod.	No	6.9	±1100′
54	⟲	½ day	E	Apr–Nov	Mod.	No	6.4	±600′
55	⟲	1 hour	E	Mar–Nov	Packed	No	1.1	±320′
56	⟲	2 hours	E	Mar–Nov	Mod.	No	3.1	±740′
57	⟲	1 hour	E	Apr–Nov	Mod.	No	2.1	±240′
58	⟲	2 hours	E	Apr–Nov	Packed	Yes/No*	3.8	±500′
59	↗	½ day	S	May–Nov	Heavy	No	7.0	±6820′
60	↗	1 day	S	Jul–Oct	Heavy/Mod.	No	17.0	±11,480′
61	↗	1 day	M	Jun–Nov	Light	No	11.0	±7700′

Trips from the Glacier Point Road and Happy Isles

TRIP NO.	TYPE OF TRIP	HIKING TIME	DIFFICULTY	HIKING SEASON	HIKER USE	LAKES	LENGTH IN MILES	TOTAL ELEV. GAIN+LOSS
62	↗	½ day	M	Jun–Oct	Mod.	No	8.2	±2460′
63	↗	2 hours	E	Jun–Oct	Mod.	No	2.6	±840′
64	↗	2 hours	E	Jun–Oct	Heavy	No	2.4	±1060′
65	↗	1–2 days	M	Jul–Oct	Light	No	13.5	±7160′
66	↗	2 hours	E	Jun–Oct	Heavy	No	4.6	±3260′
67	⟳	½ day	S	Jun–Nov	Packed	No	6.5	±4200′
68	⟳	1–2 days	S	Jun–Oct	Packed	No	15.5	±10,800′

TRIP NO.	TYPE OF TRIP	HIKING TIME	DIFFICULTY	HIKING SEASON	HIKER USE	LAKES	LENGTH IN MILES	TOTAL ELEV. GAIN+LOSS
			Trip Features					
69	✦	3 days	M	Jul–Oct	Heavy	Yes	28.4	±8960′

Trips South and East of the Glacier Point Road

TRIP NO.	TYPE OF TRIP	HIKING TIME	DIFFICULTY	HIKING SEASON	HIKER USE	LAKES	LENGTH IN MILES	TOTAL ELEV. GAIN+LOSS
70	✦	½ day	M	Apr–Nov	Light	No	6.4	±3020′
71	☌	3 days	M	Jul–Oct	Light	No	30.2	±11,040′
72	✦	1–2 days	E	Jul–Oct	Heavy	Yes	12.8	±3860′
73	☌	4 days	M	Jul–Oct	Mod.	Yes	30.4	±10,480′
74	✦	1 day	M	Jun–Oct	Heavy	No	9.2	±5230′
75	☌	5 days	S	Jul–Sep	Mod./Light	Yes	51.1	±18,040′
76	✦	½ day	S	May–Nov	Mod.	No	8.2	±4620′
77	☌	4 days	M	Jul–Sep	Mod.	Yes	28.3	±13,140′
78	☌	½ day	M	May–Nov	Packed	No	6.2	±3060′

Trips of Yosemite's Southeastern Lands

TRIP NO.	TYPE OF TRIP	HIKING TIME	DIFFICULTY	HIKING SEASON	HIKER USE	LAKES	LENGTH IN MILES	TOTAL ELEV. GAIN+LOSS
79	✦	2 days	M	Jul–Sep	Light	Yes	19.4	±9260′
80	✦	2 days	M	Jul–Sep	Mod.	Yes	16.4	±5320′
81	☌	1–3 days	E	Jul–Sep	Heavy	Yes	12.3	±5300′
82	☌	6 days	S	Jul–Sep	Mod.	Yes	48.0	±20,500′
83	✦	1–2 days	M	Jul–Sep	Mod.	Yes	18.0	±6620′

* = Harden Lake and Mirror Lake often dry up by late summer

Gilman Lake

CHAPTER 8

Trips of Yosemite's North Lands

Introduction to this Area

There are so many trails leading into Yosemite's north and west backcountry that their descriptions could easily fill a book. Actually, in past years, they have helped to fill four small books: *Pinecrest, Tower Peak, Matterhorn Peak,* and *Hetch Hetchy High Sierra Hiking Guides,* published by Wilderness Press. None of these is in print, though in 1990 *Pinecrest* and *Tower Peak* were replaced by Dr. Ben Schifrin's *Emigrant Wilderness and Northwestern Yosemite.* The *Matterhorn Peak* guide contained only two routes not described in this Yosemite guide. One is through awe-inspiring, although lakeless, Buckeye Creek canyon, which offers a long way in to the backcountry. The other is up a trail south from Mono Village to a use trail that climbs south to a saddle above the head of Spiller Creek canyon. These two routes are shown on this book's map, along with many other undescribed trails outside the park. The trail description in this section includes the shorter and more desirable approaches.

View east down Robinson Creek Canyon

Together with the next chapter, all the trails within Yosemite's north and west backcountry are described. This area's landscape is characterized by many parallel or nearly parallel canyons, which, generally speaking, get progressively deeper toward the east. Many of the canyons lack trails, and the park's management is to be applauded for keeping them that way. In the author's opinion, this Yosemite backcountry and the adjacent Emigrant Wilderness together contain the finest assemblage of cross-country routes to be found in the Sierra Nevada—a last stronghold for the true wilderness experience.

Supplies and Services

Food and limited camper supplies are available in Bridgeport and Lee Vining, both on Hwy. 395. Mono Village, a large resort, has one of the best backpacker-oriented stores to be found in any Sierra mountain resort. Still, by far the greatest selection of gear and food will be found in Mammoth Lakes, with about a dozen sporting goods stores and plenty of food stores. This small city is out of the way unless you are driving north up Hwy. 395 from southern California.

Wilderness Permits

If you want to reserve a permit, rather than get one in person, see page 49. In person, for trips 1 and 2, get your permit at the Summit Ranger Station, located at the Pinecrest Y, or if you are driving along Hwy. 395, get one at the Bridgeport Ranger Station (760-932-7070). For trips 3 to 6, stop at the Bridgeport Ranger Station for permits if you're coming from the north. It is on Hwy. 395 at the east end of Bridgeport, 1 mile east of the town's Twin Lakes Road junction. Should you wish to enter Yosemite National Park via the 20 Lakes Basin (Trip 7), stop at the Lee Vining Ranger Station (760-647-3044), located 1 mile west up Hwy. 120 from its junction with Hwy. 395 at the south end of Lee Vining.

Campgrounds

For Trip 1, if you are driving up from the west, use Baker Campground, located just off Hwy. 108 about 9.2 miles before Sonora Pass. If driving from the east, use Leavitt Meadow Campground, on Hwy. 108, 7.1 miles west of Hwy. 395 and 8 miles east of the pass. Also use this campground for Trip 2. For trips 3 and 4, use any of the five campgrounds along Twin Lakes Road or use the private campground in Mono Village. For Trip 5, use the Green Creek Campground, and for Trip 6, use Turnbull Campground, each near their trip's trailhead. Saddlebag Campground is best for Trip 7, since it is only a minute's walk from the trailhead parking area. Sawmill Walk-in and Junction campgrounds are along the Saddlebag Lake Road, barely west of the road's junction with Hwy. 120. Along this highway, Tioga Lake Campground is just south above the junction, while Ellery Lake Campground is just north below it. Along the lower part of Hwy. 120 (before the start of the steep ascent) are six more campgrounds. Those camping in style with RVs can stay at Twin Lake's Mono Village or at Lee Vining's Mono Vista RV Park.

TRIP 1

Sonora Pass to Kennedy Canyon Crest

S / DH

DISTANCE: 16.4 miles out and back

ELEVATIONS: 9590'/10,880'
+2010'/-1020'/±6060'

SEASON: Mid-July to mid-October

USE: Light

MAPS: *Sonora Pass,*
Pickel Meadow

TRAIL LOG:

2.5   End of climb above the 2-mile-high level

5.5   Start of cross-country ascent to Leavitt Peak

8.2   Closed jeep road

INTRODUCTION: This alpine route, an 8.25-mile segment of the Pacific Crest Trail that was completed in 1977, provides breathtaking panoramas of granitic northern Yosemite National Park and of the volcanic Sonora Pass area. It is presented as a dayhike because there are no acceptable campsites along the route. You can transform it into a backpack trip with camping opportunities by continuing southeast on the trail to Dorothy Lake Pass (the reverse of the last part of Trip 2), which is an extremely scenic way to enter Yosemite National Park.

DIRECTIONS TO THE TRAILHEAD: Drive up Hwy. 108 to Sonora Pass and park at the signed Pacific Crest Trail parking area, whose entrance is about 250 yards west of the pass. Trail begins in map section H1.

DESCRIPTION: From the lower part of the parking area, the Pacific Crest Trail (PCT) traverses about 200 yards southwest over to a highway crossing just 50 yards north of Sonora Pass. We now begin a winding course up the crest of the Sierra Nevada. After only 250 feet of elevation gain, the dominant lodgepole pines are mostly replaced by those harbingers of timberline, whitebark pines. We cross the crest, then dip to cross five closely spaced gullies, which contain our only permanent source of water. Beyond them we circle clockwise, climbing the well-graded trail up a cirque's rubbly headwall back onto the now alpine crest. From it, a panorama explodes into view, ranging from Peak 10641 in the southwest to Stanislaus and Sonora peaks in the north, and down into the West Walker River canyon in the east. Our climb 👁 south stays just a few yards east of the crest, and, on the upper part of this ascent, the narrow trail becomes quite exposed. ⚠ Although this exposure on loose volcanic rock is generally not a problem in mid- or late summer, it can be one before mid-July, when it is apt to be covered by an icy snowfield. Inexperienced mountaineers should not attempt this trail during that season, for then there are also two more hazardous trail sections.

Our 400-foot climb south ends above the 2-mile-high level, leaving one breathless but elated, for all the major climbing is now over, and the trail ahead is generally an easy, contouring route. Its ease is certainly an added plus, for with a full one-third less oxygen than at sea level, the rarefied atmosphere would hinder one's enjoyment if the trail were difficult. Your enjoyment can also be hindered if you haven't dressed for windy weather and if you haven't protected yourself—with hat, dark glasses, and sunscreen—from the more intense ultraviolet radiation that exists up here.

On west slopes within Emigrant Wilderness, we contour south toward Leavitt Peak, the point where three crests unite. Dense, waist-high clumps of whitebark 👁 pines sporadically paint the rusty alpine landscape with patches of green both before and after a crest saddle. At a second saddle, the PCT crosses the crest and then makes a brief, steep switchback and descends gradually—seasonally across a lingering snowfield—to two glacial moraines at the foot of a glacial cirque. These two moraines were left by a glacier during the Little Ice Age. Because the volcanic rock there is so rubbly, it doesn't hold water, so we don't find a lake in the small, deep basin between the two moraines and Peak 11265.

From the moraines, we climb steeply but briefly up to a cleft in a ragged ridge and are almost knocked off our feet by the overpowering view (or perhaps by a gusty wind). You can find higher passes in the Sierra Nevada, but hardly one with a view that surpasses the rugged, alpine view before us. From the cleft, we skirt the base of the ridge, staying high above Latopie Lake, whose barren, rocky shore offers little consolation to the camper. The abundance of large blocks along our traverse testifies to the instability of the volcanic ridge above us, and the possibility of falling rocks is a real concern for early-season hikers. Their final concern will be just ahead, where this short stretch in early season could send an inexperienced hiker quickly down to—and over—the brink of a cliff above Latopie Lake. Luckily, this hazard can be avoided by first climbing southwest up to a level area below Leavitt Peak and then heading southeast on it to a gully.

Beyond the gully, our trail descends gradually across a giant scree slope—the east side of Leavitt Peak. Its instability makes plant growth on it virtually impossible, and thus the landscape is austere. Where the slope curves from southwest to southeast, you can start a cross-country ascent to Leavitt Peak, a loose but safe 800 feet of climbing above you. Otherwise, contour a quarter mile southeast back to the crest of the Sierra Nevada—actually a double crest that has the tendency to become very blustery. Your last 2.25 miles of trail also can be chilly and windy, though most dayhikers will experience pleasant weather. The volcanic slopes here are more stable than the ones we just left, thus you may see alpine gold and other high-altitude wildflowers dotting the landscape. Here, volcanic rocks extend all the way down to the shore of Kennedy Lake, 2800 feet below us. By 7 million years ago, our once granitic landscape had been buried in places to a depth of more than 3000 feet due to the outpouring of dozens of lava flows and other volcanic products. Along your ridge traverse, be sure to stop at the three main crest saddles, all only a few yards away from the trail. The changing views of glaciated Leavitt Creek canyon are well worth the small effort.

Our section of PCT ends at a switchback on a closed jeep road, at 10,580 feet, and from here you retrace your day's course. Alternatively, you can end your hike by first following the jeep road 0.2 mile northeast up to a saddle to start a 2200-foot descent to Hwy. 108. You first take the main jeep road down to the outlet creek of Leavitt Lake, where you can find campsites among small stands of whitebark pines. You may find more protected sites along the drivable road that descends 2.9 miles from the lake to a switchback along Hwy. 108. This junction is 3.7 miles below Sonora Pass. The 1100-plus-foot climb from that junction up to 9556-foot Leavitt Lake makes a relatively easy backpack trip, although many will find the lake's treeline environs too cool, windswept, and shady.

View south from Sonora Pass

TRIP 2

Tower Peak Country via West Walker River

Ⓜ ⟋ X

DISTANCE: 51.7 miles point to point

ELEVATIONS: 7180′/10,880′
+8800′/-6390′/±15,190′

SEASON: Mid-July to early October

USE: Moderate

MAPS: *Pickel Meadow,
Tower Peak,
Piute Mountain,
Tiltill Mountain*

TRAIL LOG:

3.0	Roosevelt Lake
6.2	Red Top Lake Trail
7.2	Fremont Lake Trail
9.2	Lower Piute Meadow
10.1	Long Lakes Trail
10.4	Cascade Creek Trail
11.4	Upper Piute Meadow
15.0	Tower Lake
16.4	Mary Lake
19.8	Reach Tilden Lake
22.0	Outlet of Tilden Lake
23.2	Pacific Crest Trail
31.5	Dorothy Lake Pass
33.9	Cascade Creek Trail
37.0	West Fork Walker River
43.6	Leave jeep road
51.7	Sonora Pass

INTRODUCTION: This route, recommended as a six-day hike, begins along the West Walker River Trail and then climbs into the heart of the Yosemite north country. In these lands, it passes some justifiably popular fishing waters, and then cuts cross-country for 2 miles to reach Tilden Lake, possibly the epitome of the verdant, pas-toral north country. Our exit, via the famous Pacific Crest Trail, provides a rugged, spectacular alpine finale. Rather than do this trip as a point-to-point hike, ending at Sonora Pass, 8 miles from your trailhead, you could do one of two optional semiloop routes back to your trailhead. The first begins north of and below Lake Harriet, and it descends the Cascade Creek Trail to the West Walker River Trail, which you trace back to your trailhead. The second leaves the Pacific Crest Trail just west of the Long Lakes, and it passes these lakes, the Chain of Lakes, and Fremont Lake before dropping to the West Walker River Trail. Compared to the main route, the first option is 6 miles shorter and has 2800 feet less ascent; the second option is 3.6 miles shorter and has 2400 feet less ascent.

DIRECTIONS TO THE TRAILHEAD: Park one vehicle at the trip's end near Sonora Pass. You drive up Hwy. 108 to this pass and park at the signed Pacific Crest Trail parking area, whose entrance is about 250 yards west of the pass. From Sonora Pass, drive a second vehicle 8 miles east down Hwy. 108 to Leavitt Meadow Campground. Park in the trailhead parking area immediately north of the campground. The trail begins in map section H1.

DESCRIPTION: From the trailhead, the West Walker River Trail drops east a few yards to bridge the wide West Walker River under a typical east-slope volcanic-soil forest association: robust, widely spaced Jeffrey pines, squat junipers, streamside Fremont's cottonwoods, and a sagebrush understory. East of the river, our well-trod path climbs briefly east past metamorphic rocks, then traverses briefly south to a west-dropping use trail. From this junction, we climb east momentarily to a low ridge and, 0.3 mile from our trailhead, reach an important junction. From it, the older trail to Roosevelt Lake via Secret Lake continues east before climbing south. This trail is 0.6 mile longer than the newer trail, and its undulating route requires quite a bit more climbing and descending.

We take the newer trail, which swings south and quickly drops to an open, sagebrush-dotted bench on the east side of giant Leavitt Meadow. It stays along this side for 1.4 miles, keeping well above the wide meanders of the West Walker River. Across it, you may hear the shouts of Marine mountain troops practicing rock-climbing techniques on a nearby cliff. Later, we pass the horse trail from Leavitt Pack Station, which is not a recommended route for backpackers due to a deep, dangerous ford of the river. Upon leaving Leavitt Meadow, we begin to climb, and in several minutes reach a junction with another Leavitt Meadow Trail, coming in on our right. In several more minutes, our trail tops out at a diminutive pond. Immediately beyond it, we encounter a long, slender pond, and just past it, a junction with a trail that heads northeast to Secret Lake. Ahead, we traverse about 130 yards to a junction with the last Leavitt Meadow Trail—the route you would take if you were to follow the meadow's westside road.

We continue south, going through a gulch between granitic bluffs. This easy walk leads quickly to the north shore of Roosevelt Lake, which, with its southern twin, Lane Lake, is heavily visited, but it

makes a good lunch stop. Both of these small, shallow lakes—separated by a broad isthmus of sand of possible glacial origin—harbor trout and crayfish, as well as a teeming variety of insect and attendant bird life. In the past, beaver felled lakeside trees, which became covered with plants—a verdure more commonly seen in the volcanic Cascade Range. The two lakes feature an unusual abundance of life, perhaps supported by lake-bottom springs, whose source is nutrient-rich volcanic rocks just above to the east and southeast. Glaciers here were about 1500 feet thick, but despite their enormity, they lacked the erosive ability to remove all of the volcanic rocks that had once buried this ancient, granitic canyon.

The West Walker River Trail passes some adequate camps on the isthmus between Roosevelt and Lane lakes, and then climbs gently above the latter, returning soon to camps at its southern outlet. Here, a newer trail branches from the older one, which can still be followed southwest down to the West Walker River to large, secluded campsites. The newer trail climbs, via switchbacks, southeast up volcanic tuffs to a rising, milelong traverse through open aspen groves and sagebrush flats on a

Roosevelt Lake

bench east of the river. Later, we rejoin the old riverbank route and drop to a lodge-pole-and-aspen grove that borders the river's inner gorge. Here, under a 400-foot bluff of solidified volcanic mud flows, we could share shaded campsites with cattle that range through this canyon. We quickly leave this cooler haven to swing southeast across a side stream, and then steeply attack a stretch that climbs over a chaparral-clothed spur. On it, we have our first up-canyon views of Forsyth Peak. We then descend briefly to the Red Top Lake Trail, branching west.

[S] **SIDE TRIP TO RED TOP AND HIDDEN LAKES:** Although they lie only 10 to 20 minutes from our main trail, Red Top and Hidden lakes are only lightly visited. Red Top Lake is rimmed by sickly lodgepole pines and has poor campsites in the adjacent dense forest. Hidden Lake, just beyond, is smaller, shallower, and less appealing. **END OF SIDE TRIP**

From the trail junction, we resume a pleasant streamside stroll south past good camps under sheltering lodgepoles. After a quarter mile, the West Walker River's course becomes a 15-foot-deep gorge through jointed granodiorite, and we follow it closely on some dynamited tread. Just beyond this gorge, the old trail fords the river, but those on foot will prefer to stay on a newer trail, which continues along the east bank for another half mile to a junction. From it, we head briefly north and cross the river via an easy, sandy ford, and on the far bank we find campsites. Also here is the west bank West Walker River Trail and the Fremont Lake Trail, about 7.25 miles from the trailhead. This lake is a good choice for your first night's camp, but expect company on summer weekends.

[S] **SIDE TRIP TO FREMONT LAKE:** This trail climbs steeply northwest 0.75 mile in deep sand to Fremont Lake, at 8220 feet in elevation. You'll find heavily used camps at the lake's south end. Fishing for brook and rainbow trout is only fair. In this vicinity, ignore lateral trails south from Fremont Lake to Chain of Lakes and Long Lakes. These trails are unpleasantly dusty, and when the latter lakes aren't nearly stagnant, they teem with mosquitoes (but, in all fairness, with trout, too). Fremont Lake lays directly on the route of the pioneers' Sonora Trail route west to the gold fields. In fact, emigrants once had to lower the outlet level of this good-sized lake so that their wagons could pass around its lodgepole-and-juniper-lined western shore! **END OF SIDE TRIP**

If you made the side trip to Fremont Lake, return to the West Walker River. Here, also ignore the longer, less-used west bank trail, as it, too, is sandy, mosquitoey in early summer, and later may reek of cowpies. Regain the east bank trail, southbound, and climb moderately up a wooded gully and over a minor saddle to nearby Long Canyon, up which a trail ascends southeast 4 miles to shallow, subalpine Beartrap Lake. Leap Long Canyon's creek, then continue southward through a forested grove to Lower Piute Meadow. Keeping well back in the dry eastern fringe of lodgepole forest, our way turns south along that sandy grassland, then past it our trail undulates over small ridges to soon reach the Long Lakes Trail, which branches west across a small, often moist meadow. After 0.3 mile of easy walking, we pass the Cascade Creek Trail, part of the first optional route back to your trailhead, and then continue up-canyon in a lodgepole forest.

After a mile of usually easy climbing, we level off at a junction near the north end of large Upper Piute Meadow. From here, the Kirkwood Pass Trail continues ahead along the side of the meadow. Our route branches right, south, and momentarily we cross the West Walker River and reach nearby the Forest Service's Piute Cabin. We now head out into stunningly beautiful Upper Piute Meadow, backdropped by graceful, sweeping Hawksbeak Peak. We head south around the meadow's perimeter, following tread that may be discontinuous. About halfway along this stretch, blazes mark a resumption of good tread, angling slightly uphill into a lodgepole forest. This leads quickly to a small, wetter meadow, then to a nice packer camp on the edge of lovely Rainbow Meadow.

With Tower Lake as an objective, more than 1200 feet above the meadow, we progress south up Tower Canyon, soon crossing its creek, and, in a half mile, recrossing it. You might consider spending your second night along this half-mile stretch, for camping is poorer at Tower and Mary lakes, both near treeline. Our trail crosses a tributary, then parallels the Tower Lake outlet creek midway to the lake. It then crosses this multibranched creek and climbs steeply to very steeply, up to the lake's outlet, at 9523 feet. Taking many breather stops on this ascent, the back-packer can admire the challenging buttress of Tower Peak's north ridge, to the south, or the fine crest of Hawksbeak Peak, to the east. In early fall, this landscape, like Leav-itt Meadow where we started, is painted a brilliant gold as the plants—here willows—change color. Tower Lake and its northern satellite are both tightly rimmed with bedrock, talus, and willows, leaving only tiny spots for camping, the better ones at the satellite. Tower Lake supports a small population of beautiful golden trout. From here onward, the route ahead can be large-ly snowbound before mid-July.

Our route from here is cross-country. From the lake's south shore, we climb south up to a conspicuous saddle. The climb, though steep, is fairly safe for experienced backpackers, the greatest danger perhaps being a careless twist of one's ankle. From the 10,110-foot saddle between Saurian Crest and Tower Peak, we can gaze south-west down Tilden Creek canyon over bar-ren, windswept Mary Lake to long, forest-girded Tilden Lake and its southern guardian dome, Chittenden Peak. Leaving this austere gap, we scramble easily down through a swale of corn lilies and willows to the clustered whitebark pines that afford

the best camps above the inlet of Mary Lake, situated at 9619 feet elevation. Fol-low Mary Lake's rocky northwest shore to reach the outlet, and then descend moder-ately through frost-shattered hummocks and a velvety alpine fell field of reed grass, rice grass, and red heather to about 9420 feet, about a quarter mile below the outlet, where a poor, ducked trail begins to define itself. This use trail leads southwest, always quite near the west bank of raucous, danc-ing Tilden Creek, down through a step-lad-der of delightful meadows and subalpine conifers. Once, at 9120 feet, Tilden Creek makes a small waterfall, and wildflowers explode across the moist slopes, overlooked on the east by mitre-capped Craig and Snow peaks. A long hour below Mary Lake, we traverse the final lumpy meadow to reach the head of lovely Tilden Lake.

A more substantial trail follows the west shore of 2-mile-long, 8900-foot Tilden Lake, which is conspicuously better clothed in lodgepole pines than is the east side, which is slabby and lacking soil. Almost halfway along this narrow gem, we find a sandbar that offers the best swimming beach for miles around. Farther on, our lakeside path bends southwest and enters open subalpine meadows near the base of black-streaked Chittenden Peak. This sum-mit, named for an early Yosemite boundary commissioner, is easily climbed and pro-vides the best overlook of Jack Main Canyon. Rounding south of Chittenden Peak, we find some good camps under a lodgepole canopy, and then reach the end of Tilden Lake's long outlet lagoon. Here, we boulder hop south to find the well-used Tahoe-Yosemite Trail.

⑤ **SIDE TRIP ALONG TILDEN LAKE:** Even if you don't plan to camp at Tilden Lake, you may want to walk 0.75 mile east on this trail for storybook views up-canyon, where Tilden Lake, when the water is calm, mir-rors the cockscombed Saurian Crest. Excel-lent camps are also found here, near emerald shoreline meadows. **END OF SIDE TRIP**

From the outlet of Tilden Lake, the cobbly trail drops moderately west along the slabby, boulder-strewn south banks of frolicking Tilden Creek, where a profusion of shrubs and herbs line our path, including spiraea, shooting star, willow, red heather, corn lily, rosy everlasting, and senecio. Chittenden Peak's south face looms well above us, and we gain views west across the wooded trough of Jack Main Canyon to Schofield and Haystack peaks. Soon, switchbacks appear to ease our way down into thickening forest, always near now cascading, sometimes free-falling Tilden Creek. Below 8400 feet, we turn south through sandy lodgepole forest and trace Jack Main Canyon downstream for a half mile before stepping through a fringe of Labrador tea to the 70-foot-wide, shallow ford of Falls Creek. On the west bank, we find a pleasant camp, and 80 yards later, we reach the Pacific Crest Trail and turn north.

S **SIDE TRIP TO OTTER LAKES:** Should you first want isolated camping, head 0.1 mile south to a creek and ascend its south bank 1 mile west to Otter Lake, located on a subalpine bench with Little Otter Lake and more than a dozen ponds and lakelets. **END OF SIDE TRIP**

The next three days of spectacular hiking will be along the Pacific Crest Trail (PCT). Chittenden Peak and its north satellite serve as impressive reference points as you progress northward, passing two substantial meadows before arriving at the south end of even larger Grace Meadow. Here, the upper canyon opens into plain view, with (east to west) Forsyth Peak, Dorothy Lake Pass, and Bond Pass as the guiding landmarks. Under lodgepole cover along the meadow's edge, you can set up camp.

Leaving Grace Meadow, you soon pass through a small meadow before the ever-increasing gradient becomes noticeable, and people have camped at small sites along this stretch. Our upward climb meets the first of two trails that quickly unite to climb to nearby Bond Pass, on the park's

boundary, the route of the Tahoe-Yosemite Trail. Just beyond these junctions, volcanic sediments and exposures are evident in ever-increasing amounts—a taste of what's to come—before you reach large, exposed Dorothy Lake. Clumps of lodgepoles here provide minimal campsite protection from the winds that often rush up-canyon. Better camping lies ahead. A short climb above the lake's east end takes you up to Dorothy Lake Pass, at about 9500 feet, with the last good view of the lasting snowfields that grace the north slopes of Forsyth Peak.

Leaving Yosemite National Park, we enter Toiyabe National Forest, pass rocky Stella Lake, approach tempting Bonnie Lake, and then switchback east down to campsites along the west shore of 9230-foot Lake Harriet, about 1 mile beyond the pass. Larger, more isolated camps are on the east shore. The PCT crosses Cascade Creek just below the lake, and then it makes short switchbacks down confining terrain, reaching a large campsite in about a half mile. Just 50 yards beyond it, we cross the creek on a footbridge. Ahead, the way is still winding, but it is nearly level, and, after 0.75 mile—just past a pair of ponds—we reach a junction with the Cascade Creek Trail.

A **FIRST ALTERNATE ROUTE TO TRAILHEAD:** This 1.5-mile trail is the first segment of the shorter of two routes back to your trailhead. The Cascade Creek Trail can be divided into three half-mile segments, the first initially traversing northeast and then making a very steep 400-foot descent into the West Walker River canyon. Over the next half mile, the gradient is gentler, giving your knees a rest, and it ends where a short spur trail goes right to a view of pretty Cascade Falls. The last segment begins with switchbacks, and then lower down it crosses a sloping, seasonally boggy meadow before reaching the West Walker River. Look for fallen trees to cross the river, and then trace the first 10.4 miles of your hike back to your trailhead. **END OF ALTERNATE ROUTE**

Onward, we start north, bend west, and pass three ponds before winding down to a creek. Just past it is the Cinko Lake Trail.

[A] **ALTERNATE ROUTE PAST CINKO LAKE:** To the west, the original, more desirable PCT route contorts 1 mile over to Cinko Lake, with adequate campsites. The former PCT route then descends a half mile to the West Fork West Walker River Trail and follows the river, fording it midway along its route, 1.5 miles down to a junction with the newer route. **END OF ALTERNATE ROUTE**

On the official, lackluster segment, we first parallel the creek we've just crossed, and soon pass several gray outcrops of marble, which differ significantly in color and texture from the other metamorphic rocks you've been passing. Beyond them, you curve left into a small bowl and then make a short, steep climb through a granitic notch before dropping west to a seasonal creeklet. After winding briefly northwest from it, the PCT turns northward, taking almost a half mile to descend to the West Fork West Walker River Trail. On it, you descend just a quarter mile down-river to a junction by a pond, choked with sedge.

[A] **SECOND ALTERNATE ROUTE TO TRAIL-HEAD:** The second and longer optional route back to your trailhead takes you past a number of lakes, none of them dramatic. Still, some of them do offer camping, swimming, and fishing opportunities. From the junction's pond, take the Long Lakes Trail 0.2 mile southeast to the northwest end of Upper Long Lake. Linear, 8596-foot Upper Long Lake is at the same elevation as nearby Lower Long Lake. We start north on the Chain of Lakes Trail, looping around the northwest end of Upper Long and, a few minutes beyond it, we arrive at the northwest shore of Lower Long Lake, which has a few large campsites along it. Northward, we walk for another few minutes to the southeast end of a linear, unnamed lakelet. Onward, we have fairly level going in open forest to the southernmost, and largest, of the three Chain of Lakes. You'll find a few adequate camps, the best alongside the largest, southernmost lake. However, on the low, linear ridge east of these lakes, you could establish a camp with sweeping vistas of the West Walker River canyon. From the shallow and grassy northernmost lake, 1.9 miles along the Chain of Lakes Trail, the trail tacks northeast, and over 1.2 miles we follow its undulating course to a junction with the Fremont Lake Trail, mentioned early in this hike. Turning left, you'll quickly reach this popular lake, which is a great last night's stay in the wilderness. Ahead, you'll descend 0.7 mile to the West Walker River Trail, and trace it 7.2 miles back to your trailhead. **END OF ALTERNATE ROUTE**

On the PCT at a junction by a pond, we take a steel bridge across a small gorge that confines the river, and find a large, lodge-pole-shaded campsite immediately past it—the best one this side of Sonora Pass.

A few mountain hemlocks appear as you wind westward a quarter mile in and out of small gullies, and then lodgepoles take over for another quarter mile to the west edge of the southernmost Walker Meadow. Between meadow and granite, the PCT passes through a lodgepole corridor to a crossing of a wide but ephemeral creek, whose water flows mostly underground through the porous volcanic sediments. About a half mile north from this ephemeral creek is another one, which splashes in a two-stage drop into a volcanic alcove—an ideal lunch stop. Your traverse north continues for another half mile, and you can leave the trail at any point to descend to the flat-floored forest just below and make camp.

By the time the trail turns northwest up Kennedy Canyon, granitic bedrock has reappeared, but a half mile up-canyon, not far beyond a potential campsite, it disappears for good. Continuing up this brown-walled, volcanic canyon, you have an easy uphill hike for a mile, cross the canyon's creek, and then labor up an increasingly steeper trail segment to a 9700-foot junction with a jeep road not far north of a broad Sierran crest saddle. We have now left behind all reasonable campsites; none lies between here and Sonora Pass, almost 10 miles away. Ahead, water in frozen form is usually too plentiful, but if snowfall has been scarce, late-season hikers should fill up before climbing to this jeep road, for they may have to hike almost to Sonora Pass to encounter a permanent creek.

Switchbacking northward up the usually closed jeep road, you have ever improving views of Kennedy Canyon and the adjacent volcanic landscape. Whitebark pines, which have been with us since upper Kennedy Canyon, are now wind cropped down to stunted forms. Trees disappear altogether by the time you reach a high crest that presents views westward. Leaving the crest and its expansive views over the northwest Yosemite boundary area, our jeep road climbs quickly up to a junction from where the PCT leaves the jeep road.

[A] **ALTERNATE ROUTE:** Before mid-July, short parts of the remaining stretch to Sonora Pass can be potentially dangerous. If you've been encountering lots of snow, you might consider taking this safety exit route. Continue 0.2 mile up the jeep road to a gate on a saddle, then take the main jeep road 1.5 miles down to the outlet creek of Leavitt Lake. Here you can find campsites among small stands of whitebark pines, although they, too, may be under snow. You may find more protected sites along your road's 2.9 mile descent to Hwy. 108. The alternate route turns left, climbing 2.4 miles northwest to a junction with Road 062, by which you could camp, and then continues 1.3 miles west up to Sonora Pass. **END OF ALTERNATE ROUTE**

Back on trail tread, the PCT begins with a stark, yet stunning, often windy traverse along a 2-mile-high volcanic ridge. Heading northwest, you pass several crest saddles before your trail turns north and finally crosses the Sierra Crest. Should you want to bag Leavitt Peak, 0.75 mile to the northwest, you can start up the crest or else hike

a quarter mile farther along the trail and, in a bowl, start west up a talus slope. About a half mile beyond the bowl, you cross a ridge, which, at 10,880 feet, is the highest point of your trip. Latopie Lake lies well below you and is difficult to reach because of steep slopes. In early season, this short stretch of trail across steep slopes is snowbound and dangerous.

Ahead, beyond a nearby gully, you traverse along the base of an overly steep wall that is avalanche prone in early season. You head through a notch in this wall and bid farewell to the last of your excellent views of the Yosemite hinterlands. The route drops a quarter mile north and then angles northwest, passing two very youthful glacial moraines before climbing to another crest crossing 0.8 mile past the notch. Your route north hovers around tree line, and, with expansive views to the west, you pass dense, isolated clumps of prostrate whitebark pines before you once again cross the crest, 1.2 miles past the former crossing.

Now you tackle a 1200-plus-foot drop to Sonora Pass. In early summer, the first quarter mile of this descent—across steep slopes—is snowbound and potentially lethal if you fall. Near the end of your descent, you cross some closely spaced gullies, with one usually containing water, the first since Kennedy Canyon. Now in open lodgepole forest, you meander slightly up to the Sierra Crest, and then wind down it to cross Hwy. 108.

TRIP **3**

Upper Kerrick Meadow via Barney and Peeler Lakes

Ⓜ **⟋** BP

DISTANCE: 16.4 miles out and back

ELEVATIONS: 7100'/9490'
+2730'/-310'/±6080'

SEASON: Mid-July to early October

USE: Heavy

MAPS: *Buckeye Ridge,*
Matterhorn Peak

TRAIL LOG:

4.6   Barney Lake
7.5   Small saddle
8.2   Peeler Lake

INTRODUCTION: The Robinson Creek Trail is the most popular route through the Hoover Wilderness and into the Yosemite north country, and justifiably so. This short, scenic trail leads quickly into breathtaking subalpine terrain, and glittering Peeler Lake, surrounded by frost-shattered and glaciated granite and windswept conifers, mirrors the region's grandeur. Intimate campsites beside its shore more than compensate for the day's tough climb.

DIRECTIONS TO THE TRAILHEAD: From Hwy. 395 near the west side of Bridgeport, take paved Twin Lakes Road south 13.6 miles to the entrance to Mono Village at the west end of Upper Twin Lake. The trailhead is at road's end in Mono Village. Dayhikers will see a large parking area immediately to their left, alongside the lake. Backpackers need to drive about 0.1 mile farther, to the obvious campground entrance booth. Pay for backpacking here. Mileage is measured from the campground entrance booth, which is about the same distance as from

the backpackers' overnight parking lot. Trail begins in map sections E1-F1.

DESCRIPTION: We begin in Mono Village, a private resort with cabins and a campground, the complex spreading across the alluvial fan of Robinson Creek at the head of Upper Twin Lake. From the campground's entrance booth are two main roads. Take either; both reunite in about 0.2 mile (it's a loop road). From the high end of the loop, by a meadow's edge, your route, a closed road, starts up-canyon. This goes a quarter mile past the meadow, and then 100 yards more to the start of the Robinson Creek Trail. You've done a half mile to here. Just ahead, the road quickly bridges Robinson Creek.

Before starting up the Barney Lake Trail, you might spend a few minutes at the head of Twin Lakes, especially in the fall, when the Kokanee salmon run and hillside aspens turn first amber, then red.

After walking west a couple of minutes, you pass low granitic outcrops that glaciers failed to remove. Just beyond them is a bulletin board with information on the area. The first part of your hike is open forest, dominated by Jeffrey pines on the dry slopes and aspens on wetter soils, particularly near unseen Robinson Creek. On the smooth, white-barked aspens, Basque shepherds carved their names as long ago as the early 1900s, but you're more likely to see much more recent dates carved by hikers. Less common trees include Fremont cottonwood and western juniper, both in more abundance up-canyon.

About 0.6 mile along the Robinson Creek Trail, you reach a persistent stream, chortling down through wild-rose shrubbery from the basin between Victoria and Eagle peaks. Afterward, the trail winds gently up through more open terrain, where bouldery ground moraine and alluvium support sparse conifers, sagebrush, bitterbrush, and barley. Soon, the cobbly, dusty path comes close to Robinson Creek, where its waters veer north around a jutting granitic promontory. From here, about a

THE TIOGA GLACIATION

Twin Lakes lie behind curving recessional moraines, which were left near the end of the last, or Tioga, glaciation. Tioga lateral moraines form obvious bouldery, sagebrush-dotted benches high above both the north and south shores of Twin Lakes, indicating that the last glacier filled the canyon here to a depth of about 1500 feet!

Summits to the north of Twin Lakes, from Eagle Peak to Robinson Peak and Sawmill Ridge, as well as Crater Crest and Monument Ridge to the south, are composed of former volcanic rocks and limestone that originated more than 200 million years ago. Volcanic eruptions ranged in composition from explosive rhyolitic lava to fluid basaltic lava, like those found east of the park today.

During the Nevadan orogeny, all these rocks were metamorphosed, then later were metamorphosed again with the much later intrusion of magma from below, about 85 million years ago, which solidified to form our canyon's walls of Cathedral Peak granodiorite.

mile along the trail, the canyon vistas open up. As our path continues on a westward course, well above lodgepole pines along Robinson Creek, we note the sweeping aprons of avalanche-scoured slope-wash that descend south from ruddy Victoria Peak, contrasting sharply with the spidery cliffs of light-hued granodiorite that form the sharper crests of Hunewill and Kettle peaks, guardians of the upper Robinson Creek basin. Here, the dry surroundings include increasing numbers of mule ears and diminishing numbers of arrow-leaved balsamroots, both of which have large sunflowers. You can tell them apart by the shape of their leaves. At 7600 feet, we pass

through a grove of aspens and then amble through more sagebrush, scattered junipers, and boulders to the Hoover Wilderness boundary, about 2.75 miles from Mono Village. From here, one can head cross-country south to the mouth of Little Slide Canyon, up which can be seen the smooth granitic buttress called the Incredible Hulk, as well as other incredible, but unnamed, rock-climbing goals. Minutes later, we re-enter white fir cover, and can stop for a drink beside tumbling Robinson Creek. This is a good rest spot for the climb ahead.

When you are ready to assault the canyon headwall, gear down to accommodate more than a dozen well-graded switchbacks that lead north through head-high jungles of aspen, bitter cherry, serviceberry, snowberry, and tobacco brush, staying always within earshot of unseen Robinson Creek. Above 8000 feet, we step across a rivulet merrily draining the slopes of Hunewill Peak, a welcome respite that furnishes flowers of American dogwood, Labrador tea, alpine lily, crimson columbine, monk's hood, giant red paintbrush, fireweed, aster, rein orchid, Parish's yampah, Gray's lovage, and other species to delight the eye. Still climbing, we return momentarily to the creekside, where industrious beavers, as above and below, once created dams along Robinson Creek before being decimated, probably in the floods of 1997. Then we climb rockily, bending south, in a gully under aspen shade. Half our ascent to Peeler Lake is behind us when we level out to step across a branch of Robinson Creek that drains the 10,700-foot saddle to our west. From its south side, a use trail up to the saddle and down to South Fork Buckeye Creek formerly climbed west through a tangle of aspens and creek dogwoods up the south side of this creek.

Just ahead, we reach the north end of a large flat that extends to the north shore of Barney Lake, and in times past was littered with campsites. Today, camping on the flat is discouraged, but there are sites east of the creek (sometimes a ford) on a flat behind a granitic mass at the lake's northeast corner. About 4.5 miles from Mono Village, 14-acre Barney Lake, at 8290 feet, is nestled in a narrow, glaciated trough, rimmed on the east by the broken, lichen-mottled north spur of Kettle Peak. The lake's north shore has a sandy beach, good after a swim, and it makes a fine spot for a lunch break.

The western shoreline, which our trail follows, is a dry talus slope mixed with glacial debris. Here, a pair of switchbacks elevate the trail to an easy grade some 100 feet above Barney Lake's inlet. Below, beavers at times have dammed meandering Robinson Creek, drowning the meadow and a grove of lodgepole pines. Farther southwest, cirque-girdled Crown Point dominates the horizon, with Slide Mountain behind its east shoulder, while Kettle Peak flanks to the east, topped by a gendarmed cockscomb.

After a few minutes, we descend several short switchbacks, wind through broken rock and past avalanche-twisted aspens, over two freshets draining Cirque Mountain, then come to a ford of Robinson Creek, about 0.75 mile past the lake and about 2.5 miles before Peeler Lake. This crossing can be a wet ford in early season if industrious beavers have widened the ford by damming the creek in the meadow just downstream. Rainbow and brook trout of handy pan size occur here, as in Barney Lake. From the far bank, we climb easily south in a pleasant forest of lodgepole pine, red fir, western white pine, and a new addition, mountain hemlock, which reflects our higher altitude. The trail soon leads back to the west bank of Robinson Creek, which we cross (using a log, if one is handy). Next, the trail crosses the cascading stream from Peeler Lake, beside which one might rest before ascending a long series of switchbacks just ahead. The first set of gentle, well-engineered swithchbacks traverses a till-covered slope to about 8800 feet, where we level off momentarily for a breather before darting north for a steeper ascent. The vistas east to stunted whitebark pines growing on rough, ice-fractured outcrops of Kettle Peak offer good excuses to stop frequently on this energetic climb. Eventually, we come to a small saddle at 9195 feet, which has a trail bound for Rock Island Pass and Slide Canyon.

Those bound for Peeler Lake now turn northwest, walking moderately up in mixed open forest, to a small, shaded glade beside Peeler Lake creek. We step across this stream twice before switchbacking south moderately up into a narrow gully. The wind can pick up as we ascend it, a sign that we're nearing the ridgetop, and, sure enough, about 8 miles from Mono Village, 9489-foot Peeler Lake's often windswept waters soon come into view, behind car-size granodiorite blocks that dam its outlet. A short descent leads us below this talus-to-dynamited-trail tread on the north shore of Peeler Lake, where its startling blue waters foreground rounded Acker and Wells peaks, in the west. Most of the good campsites, under conifers, are found as we undulate rockily into forest pockets along the north shore—though the east shore has some fine ones too, if a bit out of the way. The lake margin, mostly rock, does have a few stretches of meadowy beach, where one can fly-cast for rainbows and brookies to 14 inches.

Barney Lake and the Sierra Crest

TRIP 4

Kerrick Canyon / Matterhorn Canyon Semiloop

M **Ω** BPx

DISTANCE: 57.7 miles semiloop

ELEVATIONS: 7100'/10,650'
+10,800'/-10,800'/±21,600'

SEASON: Mid-July to late September

USE: Moderate

MAPS: *Buckeye Ridge,*
Matterhorn Peak,
Piute Mountain

TRAIL LOG:

4.6	Barney Lake
7.5	Small saddle
8.2	Peeler Lake
9.5	Junction in Kerrick Meadow
16.5	Pacific Crest Trail
20.9	Seavey Pass
24.0	Benson Lake
28.6	Smedberg Lake
30.5	Benson Pass
35.0	Leave the Pacific Crest Trail
41.2	Burro Pass
46.1	Mule Pass
47.7	Rock Island Pass Trail
48.7	Crown Lake
49.4	Larger Robinson Lake
50.2	Peeler Lake Trail
57.7	Mono Village

INTRODUCTION: Matterhorn Canyon, named for 12,279-foot Matterhorn Peak, which dominates its head, is the most spectacular canyon in the Yosemite north country. Here, former glaciers slightly modified the 13-mile-long trough, giving it a dazzling array of smooth cliffs and aprons, capped with lofty, frost-riven peaks that now support lasting snowfields. Cozy conifer groves make the canyon bottomlands eminently hospitable to campers. After traversing through equally interesting Kerrick Canyon, which has less relief but a marvelous assortment of flanking domes, this hike follows a portion of the Pacific Crest Trail to find Benson and Smedberg lakes, both with good fishing. It then traverses a major part of Matterhorn Canyon, and then passes right under the spiry Sawtooth Ridge at the head of little-visited Slide Canyon.

DIRECTIONS TO THE TRAILHEAD: From Hwy. 395 near the west side of Bridgeport, take paved Twin Lakes Road south 13.6 miles to the entrance to Mono Village at the west end of Upper Twin Lake. The trailhead is at road's end in Mono Village. Dayhikers will see a large parking area immediately to their left, alongside the lake. Backpackers need to drive about 0.1 mile farther, to the obvious campground entrance booth. Pay for backpacking here. Mileage is measured from the campground entrance booth, which is about the same distance as from the backpackers' overnight parking lot. Trail begins in map sections E1-F1.

DESCRIPTION: We begin in Mono Village, a private resort with cabins and a campground, the complex spreading across the alluvial fan of Robinson Creek at the head of Upper Twin Lake. From the campground's entrance booth are two main roads. Take either; both reunite in about 0.2 mile (it's a loop road). From the high end of the loop, by a meadow's edge, your route, a closed road, starts up-canyon. This goes a quarter mile past the meadow, then 100 yards more to the start of the Robinson Creek Trail. You've done a half mile to here. Just ahead, the road quickly bridges Robinson Creek.

After walking west a couple of minutes, you pass low granitic outcrops that glaciers failed to remove. Just beyond them is a bulletin board with information on the area. The first part of your hike is open forest, dominated by Jeffrey pines on the dry slopes and aspens on wetter soils, particularly near unseen Robinson Creek. Less common trees include Fremont cottonwood and western juniper, both in more abundance up-canyon.

About 0.6 mile along the Robinson Creek Trail, you reach a persistent stream, chortling down through wild-rose shrubbery from the basin between Victoria and Eagle peaks. Afterward, the trail winds gently up through more open terrain, where bouldery ground moraine and alluvium support sparse conifers, sagebrush, bitterbrush, and barley. Soon, the cobbly, dusty path comes close to Robinson Creek, where its waters veer north around a jutting granitic promontory. Here, about a mile along the trail, the canyon vistas open up. As our path continues on a westward course, well above lodgepole pines along Robinson Creek, we note the sweeping aprons of avalanche-scoured slope-wash that descend south from ruddy Victoria Peak, contrasting sharply with the spidery cliffs of light-hued granodiorite that form the sharper crests of Hunewill and Kettle peaks, guardians of the upper Robinson Creek basin. Here, the dry surroundings include increasing numbers of mule ears and diminishing numbers of arrow-leaved balsamroots, both having large sunflowers and told apart by the shape of their leaves. At 7600 feet, we pass through a grove of aspens, then amble through more sagebrush, scattered junipers, and boulders to the Hoover Wilderness boundary, about 2.75 miles from Mono Village. Minutes later we re-enter white fir cover, and can stop for a drink beside tumbling Robinson Creek. This is a good rest spot for the climb ahead.

When you are ready to assault the canyon headwall, gear down to accommodate more than a dozen well-graded switchbacks that lead north through head-high jungles of aspen, bitter cherry, serviceberry, snowberry, and tobacco brush, staying always within earshot of unseen Robinson Creek. Above 8000 feet, we step across a rivulet merrily draining the slopes of Hunewill Peak, a welcome respite that furnishes flowers to delight the eye. Still climbing, we return momentarily to the creekside, then we climb rockily, bending south, in a gully under aspen shade. Half our ascent to Peeler Lake is behind us when

View west up Robinson Creek canyon

we level out to step across a branch of Robinson Creek that drains the 10,700-foot saddle to our west.

Just ahead, we reach the north end of a large flat that extends to the north shore of Barney Lake, and in times past was littered with campsites. Today, camping on the flat is discouraged, but there are sites east of the creek (sometimes a ford) on a flat behind a granitic mass at the lake's northeast corner. About 4.5 miles from Mono Village, 14-acre Barney Lake, at 8290 feet, is nestled in a narrow, glaciated trough, rimmed on the east by the broken, lichen-mottled north spur of Kettle Peak. The lake's north shore has a sandy beach, good after a swim, and it makes a fine spot for a lunch break.

The western shoreline, which our trail follows, is a dry talus slope mixed with glacial debris. Here, a pair of switchbacks elevate the trail to an easy grade some 100 feet above Barney Lake's inlet. Below, beavers at times have dammed meandering Robinson Creek, drowning the meadow and a grove of lodgepole pines. Farther southwest, cirque-girdled Crown Point dominates the horizon, with Slide Mountain behind its east shoulder, while Kettle Peak flanks to the east, topped by a gendarmed cockscomb.

After a few minutes, we descend several short switchbacks, wind through broken rock and past avalanche-twisted aspens, travel over two freshets draining Cirque Mountain, and come to a ford of Robinson Creek, about 0.75 mile past the lake and about 2.5 miles before Peeler Lake. This crossing can be wet in early season if industrious beavers have widened the ford by damming the creek in the meadow just downstream. Rainbow and brook trout of handy pan size occur here, as in Barney Lake. From the far bank, we climb easily south in a pleasant forest of lodgepole pine, red fir, western white pine, and a new addition, mountain hemlock, which reflects our higher altitude. The trail soon leads back to the west bank of Robinson Creek, which we cross (using a log, if one is handy). Next, the trail crosses the cascading stream

from Peeler Lake, beside which one might rest before ascending a long series of switchbacks just ahead. The first set of gentle, well-engineered switchbacks traverses a till-covered slope to about 8800 feet, where we level off momentarily for a breather before darting north for a steeper ascent. The vistas east to stunted whitebark pines growing on rough, ice-fractured outcrops of Kettle Peak offer good excuses to stop frequently on this energetic climb. Eventually, we come to a small saddle at 9195 feet, which has a trail bound for Rock Island Pass and Slide Canyon.

Those bound for Peeler Lake now turn northwest, walking moderately up in mixed open forest, to a small, shaded glade beside Peeler Lake creek. We step across this stream twice before switchbacking south moderately up into a narrow gully. The wind can pick up as we ascend it, a sign that we're nearing the ridgetop, and, sure enough, about 8 miles from Mono Village, 9489-foot Peeler Lake's often windswept waters soon come into view, behind car-size granodiorite blocks that dam its outlet. A short descent leads us below this talus to dynamited trail tread on the north shore of Peeler Lake, where its startling blue waters foreground rounded Acker and Wells peaks, in the west. Most of the good campsites, under conifers, are found as we undulate rockily into forest pockets along the north shore—though the east shore has some fine ones too, if a bit out of the way. The lake margin, mostly rock, does have a few stretches of meadowy beach, where one can fly-cast for rainbows and brookies to 14 inches.

You should spend your first night at this lake. On the next day, you leave its northwest end on a path that climbs slightly to a granitic bench dotted with bonsai-stunted lodgepoles, where views back across the outlet show serrated Peak 11581 rising east of Kettle Peak. Now, a short descent leads to the signed Yosemite National Park boundary, beyond which pocket meadows covered with dwarf bilberry and sedge gradually coalesce into the northeastern arm of Kerrick Meadow. Soon, our path ends at a junction in Kerrick Meadow. Here, about 9.5 miles into your trek, you start south through the meadow on the Kerrick Canyon Trail. Kerrick Meadow, covering a vast ground moraine at the head of Rancheria Creek, is a frost-hummocked expanse of sedge, rice-grass, reed-grass, and dwarf bilberry, quite typical of Sierran subalpine meadows. Numerous young lodgepole pines encroach upon the grassland but can die if the soil gets too boggy, as happens in years of abundant snowfall.

Head down-canyon along the path, which can be rutted up to 2 feet deep in the delicate turf, and soon cross the seasonal headwaters of Rancheria Creek. Now you descend easily, ambling along the west margin of Kerrick Meadow, over slabs and dry terraces, typical habitat of sedges. At times, a profusion of birds flit among the open lodgepoles near our route: yellow-rumped warblers, American robins, mountain blue-birds, white-crowned sparrows, northern flickers, dark-eyed juncos, and Brewer's blackbirds. Lemmon's paintbrush and alpine gentian blossom in early summer.

After about 1.5 miles from the previous junction, we come to another one, with the Rock Island Pass Trail, which is an alternate route for our return trip. Still gently descending, we pass through a lodgepole grove, then emerge at the northern end of an even larger meadowed expanse, rimmed on the west by 400-foot bluffs. Long views south down upper Kerrick Canyon are topped by Piute Mountain and other dark, rounded summits near Seavey Pass. After 1.5 miles of rolling, sandy trail, our route crosses a trio of low moraines, then cuts close to an oxbow in 20-foot-wide Rancheria Creek, where the broad canyon pinches off above a low hillock. In this area, you'll find the north-flowing outlet creek of Arndt Lake. This lake, 0.75 mile south, has good campsites. About 13.5 miles from Mono Village, it is a good destination in itself, away from sometimes overly popular Barney and Peeler lakes.

Presently, Rancheria Creek's banks become a broken gorge, and we drop rockily down, only to strike another sandy meadow, this one with a flanking cluster of steep domes. Our path soon leads out of this lupine-flecked flat, down through a bouldery salient of lodgepoles to yet another meadow. Down this we amble south, soon to walk right along the seasonally muddy bank of meandering Rancheria Creek. At the next curve, about 2 miles below Arndt Lake's creek, we cross our creek to a clump of lodgepoles on the east bank, and continue down-canyon. Presently, a master joint in the Cathedral Peak granodiorite bedrock directs Rancheria Creek briefly east, and we follow its splashing course down over broken, porphyritic (large-crystal) bedrock slabs, then back west on another master joint for a half mile on shaded slopes to a junction with the Pacific Crest Trail (PCT)—Trip 36.

Bound for Seavey Pass, 0.7 mile away, our route climbs sometimes steeply, if briefly, up the sandy-cobbly PCT into a dome-girded ravine, at the top of which we glimpse a small pond rimmed with corn lilies and other flowers. The PCT now bends southeast and ascends to the Rancheria Creek/Piute Creek divide, then briefly drops southwest to another gap, the real Seavey Pass, at about 9100 feet.

From this point, our path winds its way down over open benches, soon coming upon a large tarn with vistas over the confusing array of rust-stained cliffs surrounding Piute Creek to Peak 10060 and Volunteer Peak, which form the horizon. From this pond, our route switchbacks west down a shaded draw, then turns steeply southeast, negotiating sometimes brushy slopes first north of, then south of a cascading stream. Glimpsing our second day's goal, Benson Lake, we finally reach the valley bottom, a sometimes swamped tangle of willows and bracken ferns under lodgepoles and firs. At the floodplain's south end, some 2.75 miles from Seavey Pass, is the Benson Lake spur trail. The 0.4-mile spur to 7581-foot Benson Lake ends at a broad, sandy beach—once the lake has dropped a foot or so—and campsites lie just back from the shore. Along the shore, you have vistas over the milelong lake to brushy domes at the outlet. Angling here is for large rainbow and brown trout.

Our third morning finds us retracing our steps to the PCT, where we turn southeast across wide Piute Creek via fallen logs, then climb up into the morning sunlight to a brushy saddle. A short distance later, our route strikes the creek that drains Smedberg Lake, which poses a difficult ford in early summer, usually best solved in the thicket of aspens just upstream. South of that stream, the path climbs rockily up, often at a steep gradient, before crossing the creek twice more, in easier spots, along a more moderate ascent in a tight canyon walled by tremendous bluffs. Once again south of the creek, our route tackles a steep hillside, via moderate switchbacks under increasing numbers of mountain hemlocks. Red heather forms a discontinuous, showy understory here. Almost 700 feet higher, but still under the stony gazes of precipitous Peak 10060 and Volunteer Peak, we find a trail branching southwest to Murdock Lake.

S **SIDE TRIP TO MURDOCK LAKE:** This is a recommended destination for those desiring some isolation, which is usually lacking at Smedberg Lake. The trail southwest is an easy half-mile walk to a level subalpine meadow at 9530 feet, which holds shallow Murdock Lake. Some adequate camps lie in lodgepoles above its west shore and offer interesting views of Volunteer Peak, Matterhorn Peak, and Sawtooth Ridge. **END OF SIDE TRIP**

By climbing east a mere 0.3 mile on the PCT, we reach a meadowy junction with a trail that departs south to Rodgers Lake.

S **SIDE TRIP TO RODGERS LAKE:** This lake has more isolation than Murdock Lake, and it is more appealing, although it requires more effort to reach. The milelong route to it climbs about 330 feet up to a grassy saddle at 9810 feet, where you'll see the stunning sheer profile of nearby Volunteer Peak, which completely dominates a horizon of greater summits throughout the north country—Piute Mountain, Price and Tower peaks, and Crown Point. You then drop 300 feet rather abruptly to subalpine Rodgers Lake, named for the second Yosemite National Park superintendent. This lake is divided into two bodies by a low granitic isthmus; the larger, eastern portion is more open and rockier. There is a handsome grove of lodgepoles and hemlocks on the north shore, and here lie some good camps that afford excellent panoramas over the shallow waters to the ruddy north faces of Regulation and West peaks. **END OF SIDE TRIP**

To reach Smedberg Lake, the PCT over the next mile switchbacks down, then up, to a slabby, polished bench overlooking the lake's south shore. Named for an Army cartographer who, with lieutenants Benson and McClure, mapped the Yosemite backcountry in the early 1900s, 30-acre, 9219-foot Smedberg Lake is dotted with low, grassy islets and rimmed with light granite, strips of sedge-and-bilberry meadow, and pockets of conifers. Pan size rainbow trout are common in its shallow waters, which reflect a sweeping face of streaked granite over the east shore, and the brooding vertical profile of Volunteer Peak on the south. Most camps are found on the west and north shores, and remote camps exist above its northwest and northeast shores in the vicinity of, respectively, Surprise and Sister lakes.

We leave Smedberg Lake by curving south into a hummocky, boulder-and-meadow vale, and soon step across one of its three inlet creeklets to climb northeast toward 10,100-foot Benson Pass, an even 2 miles past the lake. The first rise is moderate, under open mixed conifers; we level out in a small meadow before the last, earnest climb to the pass. Near the top, some of the sandy trail is very steep, but it is soon behind us, and, at the pass, sparingly inhabited by whitebark pines, we stand in coarse granitic sand, catching our breath to views west to Volunteer Peak and northeast over Doghead and Quarry peaks and beyond to Whorl Mountain and Twin and Virginia peaks.

A steep stretch rapidly leads us from Benson Pass down to a gravelly flat; then it becomes a switchbacking descent, under pleasant shade, to the hop-across ford of Wilson Creek in a steep-walled trough. This is a classic glaciated, hanging tributary canyon, widely believed to be hanging because its glacier could not erode downward as fast as the larger glacier in the main canyon. Such is not the case. In resistant bedrock, such as that found in our range, glaciers of all sizes eroded very little; all tributary canyons were hanging before glaciation. Turning down-canyon, the PCT alternately traverses dry openings and lodgepole forests as we cross Wilson Creek twice more. Soon, the gentle-to-moderate descent resolves itself into some two dozen tight, rocky switchbacks as hanging-valley Wilson Creek canyon debauches into deeper Matterhorn Canyon. Bottoming out a few minutes later, we turn up Matterhorn Canyon through dry, sandy, lodgepole-filled flats and pass a large camping complex just before the wide, cobbly ford of Matterhorn Canyon creek. On the east bank, 4.5 miles from Benson Pass and at about 8500 feet elevation, is a trail starting up the canyon.

Leaving the PCT, we start north for a 6.2-mile ascent to Burro Pass, and, if you aren't camping near the ford of Matterhorn Canyon creek, you ought to consider doing so higher up in the canyon. At first, our trail climbs imperceptibly, passing some nearby good camps, and keeping near the large creek past sandy meadow lands. Views within this steep-walled trench are dominated by soaring Peak 10,400-plus, above the canyon's west slopes. In about 1.5 miles, we enter an open, bouldery stretch, then cross Matterhorn Canyon creek via boulders to a small, lush meadow, later recrossing the creek at a horseshoe

bend. About 200 yards later, we see evidence of past winter avalanches, which, descending from high on Quarry Peak, decapitated trees even as they flowed across the canyon and partway up the opposite wall. The massive east face of Quarry Peak, composing part of our canyon's west wall, offers rock climbs up to 10 pitches long in the summer months.

About 0.75 mile upstream, we ford again to the west side, then wind into a boulder-strewn, talus-footed meadow. Willows line the streamside, intermittently making way for rapidly thinning forest patches. Our gently ascending sandy path passes a few very nice, remote camps, your last desirable camping opportunity. Ahead, it's pretty much open going, with Burro Pass clearly in sight, the low point on a light ridge, with Finger Peaks on the west and massive Matterhorn Peak on the east. Standing behind Burro Pass, the jagged Sawtooth Ridge slices into blue skies and billowing afternoon cumulonimbus clouds. Above 9800 feet, under an arc of jagged peaks that stretches from Matterhorn Peak to Whorl Mountain and its unnamed overhanging outlier, the tread becomes steeper, crossing a delicate alpine fell-field sometimes replete with Lemmon's paintbrush, Sierra penstemon, and pussy paws. Soon, the cobbly, riprapped trail becomes steeper still, and resolves into a chaos of eroded, miniature switchbacks through broken granite forming the final slope of Burro Pass, which, at nearly 10,650 feet, is just over 2 miles high.

Up here, where the air pressure is only 80% of the level at sea level, one has a well-deserved rest after the short but arduous ascent to our trip's highest point. From our vantage point with a 360-degree panorama, aptly named Sawtooth Ridge, to the north, throws up a picket line of fractured granite gendarmes, culminating in 12,264-foot Matterhorn Peak. East of us, massive Twin Peaks loom beyond an unnamed peak, dwarfing Whorl Mountain and its 11,920-foot outlier, which together spawn a textbook rock glacier. Vistas back down the trough of Matterhorn Canyon stop at the exfoliating slopes of Quarry Peak, save for a real treat on a clear day, when, over its east flank, you can see Clouds Rest, Quarter Domes, and Half Dome, all near Yosemite Valley. Before our view southwest is blocked by the shoulder of Finger Peaks, we see Doghead Peak, the tip of Volunteer Peak, and distant Central Valley smog. West of Burro Pass, Slide Canyon curves down into pine-clad lower slopes from a pair of beautiful, little-visited alpine lakelets occupying a bench under the gaze of Finger Peaks.

Leaving Burro Pass, our trail drops steeply via rocky switchbacks, often obscured by long-lasting snowfields, to hop across infant Piute Creek in spongy alpine-meadow turf. It then follows that raucous, bubbling stream west on a sometimes steep descent into clustered whitebark pines, which soon become an open forest. Soon, we hop to the south bank of Piute Creek, then wind through a delicate, boggy meadow before recrossing just above an excellent campsite, complete with a small waterfall, in mixed conifers. Leaving this camp, the trail stays farther from the creekside and descends, sometimes via moderate switchbacks, into denser forest. Fair camps are found all the way down to the campsites in willow-understoried forest on the floor of Slide Canyon, our trail's low point along Piute Creek. Truly remote, essentially pristine, trailless camping lies along the creek down this canyon—a worthy layover day.

Now the trail begins to go gently up in sun-dappled forest, and it soon switchbacks moderately near a small branch of Piute Creek. From here, we can look down-canyon to view the feature that gave the names to this canyon and the mountain south of us—the Slide. This feature was first noted by Lieutenant Nathaniel F. McClure, while mapping the Yosemite north country:

> After traveling three and one half miles down the canyon, I came to the most wonderful natural object that I ever beheld. A vast granite cliff, two thousand feet in height, had literally tumbled from the bluff on the right-hand side of the stream with such force that it not only made a mighty dam across the canyon, but many large stones had rolled far up the opposite side.

McClure somewhat overestimated Slide Mountain's 1600-foot wall, but he understated the magnitude of the rockfall. About 2.5 million cubic yards fell, some boulders the size of small houses, and the debris cut a swath across Piute Creek about a quarter mile wide, and rolled almost 200 vertical feet up the far bank!

After a few switchbacks, we find ourselves atop the rim of Slide Canyon, on a sloping subalpine bench. Here, we step across the small stream we've been paralleling, then ascend more steeply west into a rocky gulch. This climb presents ever-improving panoramas east to Burro Pass and the headwaters of Slide Canyon. Our trail climbs north up the gully, then descends gently south into a spongy, boulder-rimmed stepladder meadow. The final rise from this vale to the 10,460-foot saddle, Mule Pass, dividing the Piute and Robinson creek drainages, proceeds on frequently steep, always cobbly tread. Possibly the most interesting view from this windy col, about 4 miles beyond Burro Pass, is to the northeast, over the head of Little Slide Canyon, guarded by the Incredible Hulk and north beyond to the ruddy metamorphic caps of Buckeye and Flatiron ridges.

Leaving behind the Yosemite National Park boundary, our trail leaves the col by first descending a half dozen moderate switchbacks to a stream-braided, marshy terrace fed by an unmapped snowfield in the hollow north of Slide Mountain. At the lower end of this flat lies a small tarn, which we skirt to the south, and then we descend rockily in a maze of head-high whitebark pines and talus blocks along its outlet stream. Soon, the way becomes even steeper, plunging north, losing 500 feet of elevation via excruciatingly rocky switchbacks, to another pocket meadow, where we cross to the stream's west bank. Below, we trace the sharp western lateral-moraine crest, left perhaps by a Little Ice Age glacier from Slide Mountain. It descends to upper Robinson Creek, as do we, where, in a sandy, willowed flat about 1.5 miles from the col, we meet a junction with the Rock Island Pass Trail.

[A] **ALTERNATE TRIP TO SNOW LAKE AND BEYOND:** Here, anglers and hikers who desire a more secluded alpine campsite may turn southwest toward Rock Island Pass. Their route up along the steep southern slopes of Crown Point succumbs to gentle switchbacks and rewards you eventually with a grassy knoll at 10,260 feet, affording a breather and views over the Sierra Crest to the Sawtooth Ridge. Then the trail angles briefly down past snug, sandy camps to sedge-rimmed Snow Lake, containing both rainbow and golden trout. Almost everyone who reaches here, especially photographers, will want to ascend the short, meadowed distance from Snow Lake's inlet to broad Rock Island Pass, 1.5 miles from the previous junction, for lake-reflected vistas of frost-fractured Kettle Peak. Some hikers may decide to descend the moderate trail 2 miles west from the pass down through a quiet subalpine forest to meet the Kerrick Canyon Trail at the lower end of Kerrick Meadow, and then exit Yosemite National park via Peeler Lake, adding an extra half day to their journey. **END OF ALTERNATE TRIP**

Back at the Rock Island Pass Trail junction in the sandy flat, our route turns downstream, through talus boulders and willows. Across the stream, 100 yards east, sits a large, pretty tarn, well worth the side trip for the ecological lessons, views, and secluded alternative camping to sometimes crowded Crown Lake. This lakelet sits on a meadowed bench between granite hillocks. Its outlet stream used to flow northeast, directly down to the head of Crown Lake, but it now starts northwest down into the willow-choked meadow traversed by our trail, then goes around a rocky knob before heading down-canyon. Possibly, rapid

growth of the thick bilberry, sedge, and rush turf surrounding the tarn blocked the original outlet and elevated the lake level until the water found the northwest outlet. Also, frost-heaving of the dense sod during spring months may have closed off the old outlet and further elevated the lake rim. Note that it is markedly higher than the surrounding meadow.

Leaving this interesting lakelet, we return to the Robinson Creek Trail and descend east via gentle switchbacks to the sodden meadow on the west shore of 9460-foot Crown Lake. The path circumvents the meadow to reach Crown Lake's north outlet, from where use trails lead to the only legal campsites, in grouped whitebarks and hemlocks above the lake's rocky east shore. Anglers will be pleased to find a self-sustaining fishery of rainbow trout.

The next leg of our descent leads to the two small Robinson Lakes, on a 9200-foot bench under towering Crown Point. First, we hop Robinson Creek just a minute north of Crown Lake, then descend more and more steeply under open conifer shade. A half mile below our first ford, we jump back to the west bank, just above the larger Robinson Lake, at 9180 feet, where we get nice views north over its shallow, rainbow-breeding waters to Hunewill and Victoria peaks. Meager camps lie on the isthmus between the two Robinson Lakes, although if you camp here, you should look for more ecologically correct ones farther from their shores.

Leaving the isthmus, our trail swings west along the north shore of the swampy, grassy western lakelet, then climbs through a chaos of mammoth talus blocks—the terminal moraine of the Crown Point cirque glacier. One-third mile of dynamited trail through this jumble ends under the quiet shade of a pure mountain hemlock grove that lines a gully containing a seasonal creek. We hop the creek here, turn northeast, and soon climb to a sunny col to meet the Peeler Lake Trail. From here, we retrace our first day's steps downhill all the way to Mono Village at Upper Twin Lake.

TRIP 5

Green Creek Canyon to Green, East, and West Lakes

Ⓜ ╱ DH, BP

DISTANCE: 9 miles out and back

ELEVATIONS: 8000′/9460′
+1630′/-170′/±3600′

SEASON: Mid July to early October

USE: Moderate

MAP: *Dunderberg Peak*

TRAIL LOG:

2.9   Trail junction
3.1   Green Lake
4.4   West Lake
4.5   East Lake

INTRODUCTION: Large, attractive Green Lake is one of the most easily reached backpacker lakes in our area, and the hike up to it is memorable because of the diverse vegetation (especially the wildflowers in July) and of the impressive views down-canyon from the multistep climb. One can continue on to camp at East Lake, set before a dramatic backdrop of Page and Epidote peaks. Or, from Green Lake, one can make a dayhike up to alpine West Lake and even explore cross-country the isolated lakes beyond. For those staying in the Bridgeport area, the relatively short trail up to Green Lake (and even to East Lake) is a great dayhike.

DIRECTIONS TO THE TRAILHEAD: From Bridgeport along Hwy. 395, drive through the town to the Bridgeport Ranger Station, near its south edge. Continue 3.8 miles south on Hwy. 395 to a junction with Green Creek Road 142. If you're traveling north, you'll meet this junction about 8.1 miles north of Hwy. 395's Conway Summit

with its Virginia Lakes Road junction. Take Road 142 about 3.5 miles to a T. (Left, broad, well-graded Dunderberg Meadow Road 020 winds 9 miles south to a junction with Road 021. This has climbed 4.5 miles from Hwy. 395, and, from Road 020, climbs in 1.6 miles past a pack station, resort, and campground to the Virginia Lakes Trailhead. If you are making a one-way hike between the two trailheads, you'll want to take this road rather than descend all the way to Hwy. 395.) To reach the Green Creek Trailhead, branch right at the T and remain on Road 142. Go for about 5 miles to an obvious trailhead parking area, with an outhouse and water spigot, on the right. Just 100 yards past this is Green Creek Campground's Group Unit, on the left, and a quarter mile farther, you enter the campground proper. Trail begins in map section F2.

DESCRIPTION: From the trailhead parking area, take an obvious trail that winds and undulates up-canyon for 0.6 mile to a closed road, which has ascended about a quarter mile from the Green Creek Campground. Start up the road, which continues for about another quarter mile to a creek crossing, from which a trail begins a multistep ascent. After your first 0.1 mile, you end a moderate climb at your first low step, beside a 15-foot-high cliff on your left. You are now beside the top of a small roche moutonnée, which is an asymmetrical hill with a gentle slope up-canyon and a steep one down-canyon.

Whereas we started in a forest dominated by Jeffrey pines, we now ascend through a forest dominated by lodgepole pines and aspens, and then take a dozen short, rocky switchbacks up to another step, which, like others on our route, afford views down-canyon while we catch our breath at these subalpine elevations. In this vicinity and about 1.7 miles into our hike, we enter the Hoover Wilderness and, soon, early-season hikers encounter a stretch of wet trail, which may be a bit of nuisance for some, but the trail cuts up a swath of

ROCHE MOUTONNÉE

Yosemite National Park's most famous roche moutonnée is Lembert Dome, in Tuolumne Meadows, and the asymmetry of these features is almost universally ascribed to glaciers planing down their up-canyon slopes and plucking away at their down-canyon slopes. I say "almost" because, as geologists working in the tropics know, roches moutonnées are common features in tropical canyons that have developed in granitic bedrock. Their shape has nothing to do with glacial erosion. What is unique with our roche moutonnée is a trailside lava strip on the right, about 120 yards past the 15-foot-high cliff. The basalt remnant likely is 5 million to 10 million years old, since basalts in this area have been dated in that age range. Despite some 2 million-plus years of dozens of glacier advances across this roche moutonnée, the pre-glacial lava flow still has not been removed, even though past glaciers were about 1000 feet thick in this vicinity, based on the elevations of lateral-moraine crests, which you can see down-canyon. Consequently, on the up-canyon side of this roche moutonnée, the downward erosion through glacial abrasion is about zero. Massive granitic bedrock is virtually impenetrable to glacial erosion.

luxuriant wildflowers that dazzle the eyes with myriad colors. By mid-season, the display can be gone, but so is the water flowing down the trail.

As lower down, we ascend mostly past lodgepoles and aspens, with isolated junipers adding variety, and then top out on another open step with a restful viewspot. Just ahead, you'll arrive at a trail junction. To the right is a trail that provides access to the northwest shore of Green Lake and to West Lake and its western outliers.

Since no camping is allowed along the northwest shore of Green Lake, and its southwest shore is undesirable (and the trail to it a mere use trail), virtually all users turn left and make a brief jaunt 0.2 mile to a crossing of Green Lake's outlet creek. In early season, this creek can be raging, and you'll need to find a log or two to cross it. Either just before or after this creek, you can head west to the nearby lake and find adequate campsites. At an elevation of 8940 feet, Green Lake can be on the nippy side for swimming, but the relatively large volume and chilly temperatures are ideal for a good-size trout population.

S SIDE TRIP TO WEST LAKE: This windswept lake is deficient in both trees and legal campsites, but it makes a good dayhike, either from the trailhead, or as a part-day excursion from your camp at East Lake. From the trail junction just before East Lake, veer right for a traverse west that is high enough above the north shore of Green Lake to discourage a descent to it (where camping is prohibited). After about a quarter mile, you reach a junction, the trail ahead traversing along the northwest and southwest shores of Green Lake and deteriorating to a use-trail status in the process. From the lake's south end, you could head cross-country up southwest up Glines Canyon to Virginia Pass, which is a grueling 1600-foot ascent, especially with a backpack. But why bother? A far easier entry into Yosemite National Park is on a trail across Summit Pass (next trip). However, if you are looking for relatively isolated excellent campsites, some exist in duff-floored lodgepole-and-hemlock forest above Green Lake's south end.

To reach West Lake, you take an obvious, open ascent via short switchbacks. Wildflowers locally and seasonally may get your attention, but what really gets your attention—and makes this hike worth it—is the ever-improving, expanding panorama across the Green Lake environs. After about a mile, you essentially top out and from a bedrock bench have a phenomenal panorama of the multihued metamorphic and granitic cliffs and peaks above Green Lake. Just ahead lies 9870-foot West Lake with a pittance of whitebark pine clusters and no acceptable, legal campsites. Those who like to explore and have good route-finding and mountaineering skills can tackle the metamorphic slopes above the southwest shore of West Lake for a 600-foot climb to the northernmost of the three Par Value Lakes or parallel West Lake's inlet stream west up a similar elevation gain to rather bleak Bergona Lake. **END OF SIDE TRIP**

From the Green Lake environs, the trail up to East Lake is a moderate ascent through a relatively dense conifer forest. Partway up it, you'll cross the lake's outlet creek, which can be swift in early season; a slip here will send you down its lethal, cascading course. Above, you recross it, and

after about a 500-foot elevation gain, you make a leisurely ascent 0.3 mile up to your last crossing of the creek, just below 9460-foot East Lake. This is a large subalpine lake, fully 0.75 mile long, and the trail parallels its east side for most of its length. From the outlet south to the southeast shore, there are scattered, usually small campsites on granite benches shaded mostly by whitebark pines.

Backpackers won't want to continue onward, since camping possibilities are minimal at the increasingly exposed Nutter, Gilman, and Hoover lakes. The trail past these is described in the reverse direction in the next trip, which begins from the Virginia Lakes Trailhead.

View northeast down Green Creek canyon

TRIP 6

Virginia Lakes Basin to Green Creek

Ⓜ / DH, BP

DISTANCE: 11.9 miles point to point

ELEVATIONS: 8000'/11,120'
+1720'/-3550'/±5270'

SEASON: Mid-July to early October

USE: Moderate

MAP: *Dunderberg Peak*

TRAIL LOG:

0.5	Blue Lake
1.2	Cooney Lake
2.8	Burro Pass
4.3	Junction
5.2	Upper Hoover Lake
6.0	Gilman Lake
6.3	Nutter Lake
6.5	East Lake
7.4	East Lake's outlet
8.8	Green Lake
9.0	Junction
11.9	Green Creek Trailhead

INTRODUCTION: The road up to the Virginia Lakes basin is paved, and for good reason: It attracts a lot of outdoor enthusiasts (hikers, equestrians, anglers) because there is much to offer. For the hiker, there are several general possibilities. First, you can spend a relatively short time exploring one or more of the Virginia Lakes. Second, you can climb above them in rarefied to Burro Pass to enjoy the views. Third, you can either make a long dayhike or a moderate backpack beyond the pass down to the Green Creek Trailhead, passing 10 lakes and several ponds along a mostly descending route. And fourth, you can either dayhike to Summit Lake or backpack

beyond it down into upper Virginia Canyon, which is the easiest-to-reach, classic, glacier-smoothed, subalpine gorge of the Yosemite north country. As well as its own pleasant, sunny lodgepole forests and ever-changing Return Creek, it offers a variety of more rugged alpine options to avoid retracing one's steps on the return trip.

DIRECTIONS TO THE TRAILHEAD: From Bridgeport along Hwy. 395, drive through the town to the Bridgeport Ranger Station, near its south edge. Continue about 12 miles south on Hwy. 395 to Conway Summit and a junction with Virginia Lakes Road 021. From Lee Vining, you reach this summit in about 12.25 miles. On this broad, paved road, you climb 4.5 miles west to a junction with broad, well-graded Dunderberg Meadow Road 020, which winds 9 miles north to a junction with Green Creek Road 142, the road up to the previous trip's trailhead, and the road you would take if you are doing a point-to-point hike. Straight ahead, your Road 021 climbs 1.6 miles to a moderate-size trailhead at road's end, passing along the way the Virginia Lakes Pack Station on the right, the Virginia Lakes Resort (with café) on the left, and then Turnbull Campground on the right. Trail begins in map section F2.

DESCRIPTION: From the parking area at an elevation of about 9830 feet, the Blue Lake Trail traverses briefly west, first rounding above the shore of pretty but sometimes crowded Big Virginia Lake, then entering a stand of aspens. In a minute or two, we turn northeast and ascend briefly to a stand of pines, where we curve left and quickly reach a junction with a horse trail branching right, east, down to Trumbull Lake and the pack station beyond it. Under sparse subalpine shade, our trail quickly passes two tarns just below us and then reaches the Hoover Wilderness boundary. Here, the trail forks: The left branch drops slightly to 9886-foot Blue Lake. Moments later on the higher right trail, Blue Lake comes into view, cupped in steep slopes of ruddy-brown hornfels—a metamorphic rock that lacks foliation. Beside Blue Lake, our two branches briefly merge, and then we veer up from it. As we climb gently to moderately above the north shore of Blue Lake, we cross talus that supports a sparse but lively ground cover of paintbrush, penstemon, buckwheat, and antelope brush. Rickety spires of rusty-weathered Dunderberg Peak loom high to our north, spalling rockfall, resulting in our talus, which is home for yellow-bellied marmots.

At Blue Lake's western headwall, our way climbs steeply, stopping for a moment at a 9950-foot overlook, then rounds an immense talus fan to the verdant banks of Moat Lake's outlet stream, which descends merrily from the north together with its steeply clambering use trail. Now under the prow of a light-colored crag guarding Moat Lake, our trail switchbacks southwest up a forested hillside, presently to find the Gold Start Mine. Just beyond is a switchback, and past it we arrive at the outlet of Cooney Lake, which occupies a low bench in this austere timberline upland. Good camps are found south of the inlet in wind-

tortured knots of whitebark pines, reached by a footpath across the low bench. Also at a bend in the lake is a short path over to several more camps. As we leave the lake, views open to our trip's high point as barren Burro Pass (a local name) saddles the western horizon. Its metamorphosed tuffs look cream-colored against the surrounding, darker, metamorphosed lavas, such as Black Mountain, to the south.

About 1.25 miles into our hike, we leave often windy Cooney Lake and ascend gently west into a rocky-meadowed draw. Here, we easily step across infant Virginia Creek via rocks and logs to find a second, rolling bench, harboring a clutch of small lakelets—the Frog Lakes—named for once numerous mountain yellow-legged frogs, which formerly shared the cold, shallow waters with small eastern brook and rainbow trout. Did the trout eat all of the frogs? Probably not. More likely, we humans brought in unseen pathogens on our clothes. Now we swing south of the meadowy, lowest Frog Lake—a mosquito haven before mid-August—then ascend above some lush alpine turf to the highest

Blue Lake

lake, where good camps are found among scattered whitebark pines.

The next riser on our staircase ascent is steeper than those before and has even less tree cover. Finally, the trail resolves into red-sandy switchbacks, then leaves the last whitebark pines behind for a true alpine ascent along the west wall of a cirque. The relatively warm, mineral-rich, easily weathered, water-holding metavolcanic soil here supports an abundance of alpine wildflowers rarely seen elsewhere along a trail in such numbers: robust, blue-bugled Davidson's penstemon, sour-leaved mountain sorrel, furry-leaved alpine gold, showy skunk-leaved polemonium, and ubiquitous, yellow-headed sulfur flower. Views across the Virginia Lakes basin continue to improve. After a burst of switchbacks, you gain broad and relatively viewless 11,120-foot Burro Pass. By walking north just a minute from the trail's high point, you can also view the Hoover Lakes at the base of Epidote Peak. In the northwest, Summit Lake occupies the saddle under Camiaca Peak's avalanche chutes, backdropped by the dark, brooding temple of distant Virginia Peak.

From the barren, windswept crest, we make an initial descent south, then momentarily switchback northwest toward Summit Lake. Beside the trail, you'll see tight clusters of whitebark pines, the largest cluster offering emergency shelter if you're caught in a blizzard. Our trail switchbacks northwest down through a small, stark side canyon to a sloping subalpine bench, which gives our knees a rest before we hit the third set of switchbacks. After about a 1.5-mile descent from Burro Pass, we arrive at a junction on a small bench, with clusters of whitebark pines, just above 10,000 feet near East Fork Green Creek. Here, you have a choice: Head over to Summit Lake and possibly beyond, or descend a popular route past a half-dozen lakes and several ponds en route to the Green Creek Trailhead. The Summit Lake alternate route will be described first.

A **ALTERNATE TRIP TO GREEN CREEK TRAILHEAD VIA SUMMIT LAKE AND VIRGINIA CANYON:** This route is about 2.5 miles longer than the standard route, a total of about 14.2 to 14.5 miles, depending how much you wind on the cross-country stretches. For strong hikers, this is a possible dayhike, but bring survival gear lest you get stuck in the hinterland. The mileage does not seem much, but you cross two high passes, Burro and Virginia, with a lot of ups and downs along this scenic route.

From the junction on the small bench above Upper Hoover Lake, and with 4.3 miles behind you, you turn southwest and drop momentarily to cross four small freshets in a seasonally verdant meadow where tiny yellow club-moss ivesia plus daisies, Lemmon's paintbrush, and monkey flower all float in a sea of purple-mist grass and alpine timothy. A steep, cobbly ascent ensues, paralleling Summit Lake's outlet stream. Soon, the climb moderates, and we note the avalanche slopes of Camiaca Peak straight on as our ascent over dry sedge flats and benches passes numerous good hemlock-bower campsites. Nearing the outlet of usually windswept Summit Lake, we level off. Campsites are few here, and a tent is advisable, for the scattered whitebark pines offer little wind protection. Sunset views, however, can be quite spectacular. Angling for small brookies is fair.

Our half-mile climb to the lake is replaced with a 0.7-mile traverse, on which we curve west along the north shore past dry flats of Brewer's reed-grass and sagebrush to Summit Pass. On the Yosemite National Park boundary, this barely rises above the 10,195-foot lake.

As we descend into the park, Summit Lake's stunted whitebark pines quickly yield to well-formed lodgepoles and a sagebrush ground cover. After a 1.1-mile descent to about 9350 feet, and 6.6 miles into our trek, we meet a junction with the Virginia Pass Trail, a highly recommended return route that will be described after the description of Virginia Canyon.

GLACIAL TOPOGRAPHY

As recently as 16,000 years ago, a lobe of the massive Virginia Canyon glacier flowed east across this pass and the Summit Lake basin to augment the East Fork branch of the Green Creek glacier. Until the next glaciation, the lake is slowly diminishing in size as winter and spring avalanches carry loose rocks and detritus down into it. Standing at the pass, you can readily identify Virginia Peak, a pointed metamorphic summit that rises above the summits of Stanton Peak and Gray Butte, both south of it. Broad, deep Virginia Canyon, which frames distant Mt. Hoffmann, is a classic example of glacial topography, yet it has been only modestly widened and deepened despite repeated episodes of glaciation over the last 2 million years.

From this junction, the down-canyon trail immediately crosses Return Creek and descends moderately to gently through a lodgepole forest for 4 miles before reaching the Pacific Crest Trail (PCT) at 8540 feet. Most of this canyon, like much of the park's granitic terrain north of the Tuolumne Meadows lands, is composed of Cathedral Peak granodiorite, which solidified in the earth's crust about 85 million to 95 million years ago. Marking our down-canyon progress is an ever-changing view of Shepherd Crest, on our left, whose steep-sided north slopes harbored glacierettes during cold periods of the Little Ice Age. Near the junction of the PCT (Trip 36), you'll find many campsites, popular with backpackers and bears, above both banks of Return Creek. In early season, this creek is dangerous to cross, and you had best camp on the west bank.

Otherwise, backtrack 4 miles up the Virginia Canyon Trail to the junction at 9350 feet, and either retrace your steps to your trailhead or start up the Virginia Pass Trail. This trail initially is on the east bank of Return Creek, but it crosses the stream thrice on its northbound ascent. After 1.2 miles, the trail dies out at 9850 feet, in a thick meadow turf where a stream falls east down from Return Lake, nestled under the red pyramid of Virginia Peak, to our west. One could easily ascend about 400 feet over a long half mile to this lake for nice, secluded camping.

From where the trail dies out, you have a 700-foot elevation gain over about 0.6 mile northeast up steep, open, treeline slopes of sagebrush and whitebark pines to 10,540-foot Virginia Pass. Views here are breathtaking. South down wooded Virginia Canyon, the spiry western Cathedral Range, Half Dome, and Clouds Rest can be seen, bordered on the east by the tips of Mt. Conness and North Peak and the north scarp of Shepherd Crest. More to the west, the upper cirque is guarded by Gray Butte, Stanton Peak, Virginia Peak, and the towering, gendarme-bristled south slope of Twin Peaks. In the northeast, Glines Canyon slopes to forested Green Lake, while the rolling sageland around Bodie marks the horizon. Spend a few minutes examining the metavolcanic schists at often windy Virginia Pass. Note that striations in this hard rock indicate that a lobe of the Virginia Canyon glacier flowed from west to east across this col, as one did at Summit Pass.

Leave this instructional gap at its southeast end, where a use trail—perhaps best treated as cross-country—starts steeply north down into Glines Canyon. After negotiating a slope of moraine and talus, we level off momentarily in a rocky meadow at 10,230 feet. Here, southbound hikers will want to look for the vague route near the first cluster of whitebark pines. Everyone should look for the hexagonal-patterned rock rings that have been heaved up by repeated frost action in this soggy flat. Down-canyon hikers will find a resumption of rudimentary trail along the east side of West Fork Green Creek, which tumbles musically down through Sierra willows, dwarfed pines, red and white heathers, and baby elephant heads. Next, we veer away from the stream for a short while and then drop steeply to a marshy flat, where we rejoin the creek. Here lies a mammoth boulder of marble that is slowly dissolving, and its minerals are precipitating on cobbles lying downstream, causing the stream bed to appear ghostly white.

Across the meadowy flat, we turn momentarily up along Green Creek, then hop north over it just below eye level with another meadow. Our steep descent continues, now under scattered-to-moderate mountain hemlocks that frame vistas of Peak 10880, on the north canyon wall. Soon, a denser hemlock forest on steeper slopes blocks all views, and we come to the ruins of an old stamp mill, in a lush herbaceous jungle. An upward jog a minute later leads to a ruined log cabin in a field of fireweed capping a viewful promontory; yards behind it is a collapsed adit, on the contact between two differing schists. From this site, we switchback north down to cross two streams, the second of which is the outlet from Par Value Lakes, in a patch of swamp onion, yarrow, and dusky horkelia. Just above us lie the ruins of a water-powered, eight-crucible, rocker-arm "Ideal Stamp Mill pat. Oct 8 1899" and a "No. 3 Dodge Rock Brkr" from the Parke and Lacy Co. Old prospect pits dot both hillsides.

Below this amazing testament to strong backs and hopeful, ingenious minds, our use trail sidehills down near scattered lodgepoles, then enters a deeper forest with trail-encroaching hemlocks. The creek stays within easy earshot, and we eventually walk along an old wagon road that supplied the mine. Near the head of Green Lake, our path finally becomes gentle and reaches some excellent campsites, in duff-floored lodgepole and hemlock forest. To reach the northeast end of Green Lake, our trail heads north around the west side of 50-acre lake. Numerous creeks create a boggy path. From Green Lake's north shore, our sometimes overgrown path

climbs up some 50 feet to a dry, mule ears and sagebrush bench, where we meet the descending West Lake Trail. You'll probably be too tired to take this trail, which ascends 900 feet in 1.25 miles. Its best asset is the view you'll get from high up, just before the lake. But you've already gotten great views along your descent from Virginia Pass, so there is little incentive to struggle up to this lake, which has no acceptable, legal campsites. Therefore, make a traverse a quarter mile east to a junction, where you meet those descending the shorter, more popular route. **END OF ALTERNATE TRIP**

Those on the more popular route at the trail junction on the small bench above Upper Hoover Lake begin northeast on the Green Creek Trail, which starts northeast down past a tarn to an excellent overlook down-canyon to the windswept, largely desolate Hoover Lakes. Beyond, light-granitic Kavanaugh Ridge is visible over the massive shoulder of Dunderberg Peak. We drop to step north across East Fork Green Creek, then traverse across talus above the west shore of Upper Hoover Lake before traversing its north shore. At the northeast corner of Upper Hoover Lake, we cross its wide rocky outlet stream, and, in this vicinity, you could hike south briefly upslope to exposed camps on small flats above the lake's east shore. These are best viewed as emergency camps; better ones lie ahead by East Lake and the best ones are beyond at Green Lake. Lower Hoover Lake, just above which our trail traverses via talus, has, in the past, contained rainbow, brook, and brown trout.

Below the lake and 1.1 miles past the trail junction, we drop easily over willowed benches, then circle above less-visited Gilman Lake to cross East Fork and Green Creek in a stand of hemlocks and whitebark pines. Soon afterward, our descent ends and our route rises gently past easily recognized outcrops of conglomerate rocks. Soon, we pass a short spur trail to Gilman Lake, followed closely by small, green

Nutter Lake. Camps lie below our trail in subalpine conifers at Nutter Lake's west end. Off-trail stealth campsites can be found just north of these two lakes. A short northwest climb from Nutter Lake on a mat-manzanita patched slope next presents East Lake, largest of the Green Creek lakes, spread 100 feet below us under the iron-stained talus skirts of crumbly Epidote Peak, Page Peaks, and Gabbro Peak. This is a large subalpine lake, fully 0.75 mile long, and the trail parallels its east side for most of its length. From the outlet south to the southeast shore, there are scattered, usually small campsites on granite benches shaded mostly by whitebark pines. Finally, we reach an extensive camping complex at East Lake's outlet, about 3.1 miles from the last junction. Fishing is good here for rainbow trout.

Your trail makes the first of three outlet creek crossings just below the lake, then you make an easy descent 0.3 mile to where you begin a moderate 500-foot drop in a relatively dense conifer forest to the second crossing. In early season, the creek can be swift, and a slip here will send you down its lethal, cascading course. With more moderate descent, reach your third crossing, and soon the trail levels off, and you can branch left, west, toward Green Lake and its adequate campsites. At an elevation of 8940 feet, the lake can be on the nippy side for swimming, but the relatively large volume and chilly temperatures are ideal for a good-size trout population.

From the lake, you have to cross Green Lake's outlet creek, which can be raging in early season; you'll need to find a log or two to cross it. Once you get back on your trail, you make a brief jaunt 0.2 mile to a junction where those taking the longer Summit Lake route rejoin us for the last 2.9 miles down the Green Creek Trail.

Just down this trail, you have a great view down the Green Creek canyon, one of

Hoover Lakes

several along the descent. Next, the trail soon descends through a swath of luxuriant wildflowers that dazzle the eyes with myriad colors. By mid-season, the display can be gone, but so is the water flowing down the trail. About 1.2 miles beyond the junction, we leave the Hoover Wilderness in a forest dominated by lodgepole pines and aspens and soon descend a dozen short, rocky switchbacks to another view. Below us, the forest is dominated by Jeffrey pines, and you soon come beside the top of a small roche moutonnée, which is an asymmetrical hill with a gentle slope up-canyon and a steep one down-canyon. In this vicinity, about 120 yards before a 15-foot-high cliff, is a remnant of basalt that is a few million years old. Despite past glaciers being about 1000 feet thick in this vicinity, they did not erode below basalt. Roches moutonnées are far more enduring (and pre-glacial) features than geologists have realized.

You complete your descent with a brief drop of 0.1 mile, down to a creek crossing. Next you could make an easier descent a quarter mile down a road from the Green Creek Campground, but, rather, you take a trail branching left, which winds and undulates down-canyon, passing above the campground and, in 0.6 mile, reaching the parking area of the Green Creek Trailhead.

TRIP **7**

Saddlebag Lake Hinterlands

E ♫ DH

DISTANCE: 7.6 miles semiloop

ELEVATIONS: 10,050′/10,360′
+900′/-900′/±1800′

SEASON: Mid-July to early October

USE: Moderate

MAPS: *Tioga Pass,*
Dunderberg Peak

TRAIL LOG:

1.6	Former mining road
1.8	Greenstone Lake
2.5	Wasco Lake
2.7	Former jeep trail
2.8	Steelhead Lake
3.3	Outlet
3.7	Shamrock Lake
4.3	Mill Creek
4.8	Odell Lake
5.2	Lundy Pass
5.4	Hummingbird Lake
5.9	Former mining road
7.6	Trailhead

INTRODUCTION: This splendid semiloop trip travels from Saddlebag Lake to Helen Lake and back, and passes more than one lake per mile, plus a number of ponds. In doing so, it offers you some of the Sierra's finest subalpine scenery along an easy grade. With the high and low elevations only about 400 feet apart, there are no significant ascents and descents. Still, at over 10,000 feet, you will notice the rarefied air if you try to hurry along. This basin's lands are day-use only; camping is not allowed other than at the campground at the trailhead.

Should you wish to backpack, this trip offers an optional mostly cross-country mountaineers' route for a quick way into the McCabe Lakes. Since the crest route above Secret Lake can be dangerous, hikers inexperienced at mountaineering should not attempt to climb it. Be prepared for a sudden summer snowstorm. Chances are you won't be caught in one, but if you are, don't attempt to return to Secret Lake and don't attempt to hike cross-country to Roosevelt Lake. Rather, do as the rangers suggest and take the trail from Lower McCabe Lake west 2.4 miles down to the Pacific Crest Trail, then south 7 miles on it to Glen Aulin High Sierra Camp, and from there continue on the trail out to the Tioga Road in Tuolumne Meadows. During summer, there is a bus service along this road, so you can get a ride to the start of the Saddlebag Lake Road.

DIRECTIONS TO THE TRAILHEAD: Drive 2.1 miles north on Hwy. 120 down from Tioga Pass, then 2.4 miles northwest up to Saddlebag Lake. Trail begins in map section F3.

DESCRIPTION: By Saddlebag Campground is a fairly large trailhead parking area for those hiking north into the Hoover Wilderness. You can get both a wilderness permit and a fishing license at nearby Saddlebag Lake Resort. The resort's store sells fishing supplies and a few groceries, and its café serves breakfast and lunch, but not dinner. The resort also rents small boats, and, on weekdays as well as weekends, Saddlebag Lake often has quite a population of anglers in hot pursuit of the lake's brook, rainbow, and Kamloops trout. If you want to fish here, great, but get off this large lake in a hurry if a thunderstorm approaches— lightning kills. The resort also provides scenic trips on the lake, plus water-taxi service to the lake's far end. The water taxi will pick you up at your own pre-arranged time.

To get to the 10,070-foot lake's far end, you could hike along a closed former mining road that parallels the east shore, but a better, shorter alternative is to hike on a trail that parallels the west shore. From the trailhead parking entrance, you can see a road descending to the base of the lake's dam, then climbing to the dam's west end. Head there, where the trail begins—a blocky tread cutting across open, equally blocky talus slopes.

About a half mile north of the dam, our trail bends northwest, and Mt. Dana, in the southeast, disappears from view. Shepherd Crest, straight ahead, now captivates your attention, in tranquil reflection across the early morning waters of Saddlebag Lake. Among willows and a seasonally fiery field of Pierson's paintbrush, our trail ends by the former mining road at the lake's north end, and we climb west to the east shore of 10,130-foot Greenstone Lake. (Just before reaching the north end of Saddlebag Lake, you could have traversed west across benches to the nearby south shore of Greenstone Lake.) In the early morning, a breathtaking, colorful reflection of North Peak mirrors across the lake's placid waters, beckoning photographers to linger. Following the lake's shore north, we quickly meet the closed mining road that water-taxi riders will be hiking on, and, above this shore, our narrow road enters the Hoover Wilderness. Southwest across Greenstone Lake, a granite wall sweeps up to a crest at Mt. Conness, in whose shade lies the Conness Glacier. Our tread climbs

GRANITIC-ROCK TALUS

This metamorphic-rock talus may be uncomfortable to walk on, but, from an alpine plant's perspective, it is better than granitic-rock talus. Metamorphic bedrock fractures into smaller pieces than granitic bedrock does, thus creating a greater water-storage capacity for plants. Furthermore, it is much richer in dark minerals, so it makes a more nutrient-rich soil. And, because they are darker in color than their granitic counterparts, metamorphic-derived soils absorb more heat, which is very important to plants at these cool altitudes.

northwest, and then at the Z Lake outlet creek, it bends west over to relatively warm Wasco Lake. Beyond the first tarn north of Wasco Lake, our trail enters the drainage of northeast-flowing Mill Creek. Just past the second tarn, we come to a junction with a former jeep trail, the start of interesting side trips.

[S] **SIDE TRIP TO SECRET LAKE AND McCABE LAKES:** To reach Secret Lake, about 1 mile away, this route first descends north to the nearby south shore of Steelhead Lake, bends west, then starts a climb south up a linear gully. Growing in its moist confines are seasonally profuse clusters of Suksdorf's monkey flowers. Typical of many alpine plants, their stems are greatly reduced, thereby making their 1-inch-long yellow flowers seem greatly oversized. You could continue up the gully, then branch southwest to easily reached snowfields below North Peak, but we climb west from the gully to nearby Potter Lake. Its outlet creek immediately cascades noisily into deep Steelhead Lake, and near the cascade are ledges from which brave souls can high-dive into that lake's chilly depths.

The route to the McCabe Lakes is now essentially cross-country, although we'll be following a use trail for most of the way. Just northwest of Potter Lake is a low, broad bedrock ridge that separates Towser Lake from larger Cascade Lake. Start north up this bedrock, and soon you'll be climbing a faint trail up beside a Cascade Lake inlet creeklet. Eventually, this trail crosses the creeklet and then parallels its west bank up to a granite bench that holds icy, barren Secret Lake. Hardly a secret, the 10,860-foot lake sometimes attracts dozens of day-hikers on weekends.

Pausing at Secret Lake to survey your route up the headwall, you see three choices. Adept mountaineers can attack the wall directly, preferably keeping just to the right of the black, lichen-stained vertical streak on the headwall. Hikers who want to put out some extra effort to achieve certainty and lack of steep exposure can arduously pick their way up the scree north of Secret Lake to the lip of what looks like—but isn't—a lake basin. From there, they will traverse slightly upward to their left, under the solid face of the east end of Shepherd Crest, to the low point on the headwall divide.

Probably most people choose a third way, roughly 0.3 mile long. From the south side of Secret Lake, you walk directly up the increasingly steep headwall until, about halfway up, you come to a long ledge that slopes slightly up to the south. Ducks may mark this route, but they are not always easy to see. About 200 yards south up this ledge, you leave it and follow ducks almost directly up to the ridgecrest. Once on it, follow it north to the low point of the divide to find the ducked route descending on the west side of the ridgecrest. From the crest's 11,250-foot saddle—a shallow gap—you can see that an ascent up Shepherd Crest would be tedious but not really dangerous. While you're looking at it, note how icy winds have reduced the whitebark pines on its lower slopes to a knee-high ground cover. To the southeast, pointed Mt. Dana stands high on the horizon above Saddlebag Lake.

The descent from the saddle is easier and safer than the ascent. A ducked route starts among cropped whitebark pines and bush cinquefoils, then descends steeply southwest toward a large, seasonal pond on a flat bench. There can be several primitive, misleading paths down to this pond. The greatest danger—assuming you don't get way off route—is that of knocking loose rock down on your traveling companions. Beyond the pond, you'll come to large, deep, windswept Upper McCabe Lake, at 10,460 feet, and about a half-mile cross-country route from the saddle. Along the lake's north shore are several cramped campsites among stunted whitebark pines—not much protection from wind or storms.

Better campsites lie ahead, so walk about a half mile west along the shore and boulder-hop the lake's wide outlet. Next, climb due west about 0.3 mile up to a shallow gap on a glaciated spur ridge, then descend south about 0.2 mile to a shallow pond behind a low lateral moraine. Beyond the moraine's crest, you drop steeply southwest on a 0.4-mile stretch through an ever-increasing forest that boasts sizable lodgepole pines by the time you reach the north shore of deep Middle McCabe Lake, at 10,230 feet. Since it lacks campsites, follow its outlet creek about 0.6 mile down to shallower Lower McCabe Lake, at 9830 feet and arguably the most photogenic of all three. Traverse 0.4 mile westward to find good campsites beneath lodgepole and whitebark pines, which grow on the moraine atop a buried bedrock ridge that dams this bouldery lake. The added presence of red heather and Labrador tea warns you that mosquitoes will be a pesky problem until late July. By my measurement, these campsites are about 4.2 miles from the start of this mostly cross-country route,

although your mileage will vary. Just south across the lake's outlet creek is a trail that descends about 2.4 miles to the Pacific Crest Trail, Trip 36. **END OF SIDE TRIP**

Along the main loop, you quickly arrive at the south tip of 10,270-foot Steelhead Lake. From it, you follow the former jeep road north alongside deep Steelhead Lake to its outlet. The road continues west above the lake's north shore to the Hess Mine, blocked with boulders. Higher up the road, however, is an unblocked mine that goes 50 yards into the mountainside. Just beyond it, the road ends, and there you have a commanding view of this 20 Lakes Basin, as it is sometimes called. The large, white horizontal dikes on North Peak stand out well, and pointed Mt. Dana pokes its summit just into view on the southeast skyline.

On the west side of Steelhead Lake's outlet—Mill Creek—we go a few yards downstream, then scramble over a low knoll as we follow a faint trail that quickly

North Peak and more distant Mt. Conness (center), from Steelhead Lake

descends to the west shore of tiny Excelsior Lake. At the north end, we go through a notch just west of a low metamorphic-rock knoll that is strewn with granitic glacial erratics. A long, narrow pond quickly comes into view; like many of the lakes, it contains trout. Our trail skirts its west shore, then swings east to the north shore of adjacent, many-armed Shamrock Lake, backdropped by Mt. Conness.

Our ducked route—more cross-country than trail—now continues northeast over a low ridge, then goes past two Mill Creek ponds down to the west shore of Lake Helen. On a trail across talus, we round this lake's north shore to Mill Creek, where our trail dies out just below the lake's outlet—which flows through a tunnel. We go 30 yards up to the tunnel, walk across it, and begin an east-shore traverse south across blocky talus. Don't take the tantalizing trail that follows the lake's outlet creek north; it quickly becomes very dangerous.

Adding warm colors to the dark metamorphic blocks are crimson columbines, white Coville's columbines, and their pink hybrids. Two creeks empty into the lake's southeast end, and we follow the eastern one up a straight, narrow gully that in early season is a snow chute rather than a wildflower garden. After a half mile of southward hiking, mostly up a straight creek, we cross it at the outlet of Odell Lake and parallel the west shore southward while observing the lobes of talus just east of the lake. Like some other metamorphic-rock talus slopes in this glaciated basin, these lobes developed through solifluction—a slow downslope flowage of unstable, water-saturated rock masses.

Near the lake's south end, an old route may still be seen climbing slightly before dying out. In contrast, our route drops to water's edge before climbing from the south shore up to Lundy Pass. At this gap, our path can become vague, but by heading south down toward a pond, we soon reach the outlet of Hummingbird Lake and, here, an obvious trail tread resumes. This tread parallels the east side of the outlet creek a

half mile down to the former mining road. Here, you can descend to the water-taxi dock on Saddlebag Lake and wait for the boat if you made reservations for a return trip, or, if you walk momentarily to the west, you can then retrace your steps on the west-shore trail. Of course, for variety, you can take the closed road back to the lake's south end, a route that is about a half mile longer.

CHAPTER 9

Trips of Yosemite's West Lands

Introduction to this Area

While the previous hiking chapter covers trails heading south into the interior of Yosemite's north country, this chapter covers lower-elevation trails that head north into it from either Cherry Lake or Hetch Hetchy. Taking trips 8, 9, 10, and 12 will get you, in that order, into increasingly remote areas, although Trip 8 to Kibbie Lake does offer an extended hike up-trail and then cross-country to some very desirable, remote lakes. In addition to these lake-blessed routes, this chapter also covers lakeless trails that stay at low to moderate elevations, which have the advantage of a much longer hiking season. The most popular of these is Trip 11, which traverses east above Hetch Hetchy Reservoir to Rancheria Falls Camp, passing Tueeulala and Wapama falls along the way. Many hikers do only the relatively level stretch 2.5 miles to Wapama Falls, which is a worthwhile 5-mile hike before July, when the falls are roaring and possibly dousing you with spray. Trip 13 is the lowest-elevation hike in this guidebook, staying along the lower Tuolumne River between 2400 and 2800 feet. This you can dayhike and backpack enjoyably from April through October, and for even longer in some years. The same season applies to Trip 14,

Hetch Hetchy Reservoir and Wapama Falls

a short hike to rewarding, aptly named Lookout Point. Finally, you can dayhike or backpack Trip 15 up to an even more impressive lookout point, the one atop Smith Peak, which is usually snow free by early June.

Supplies and Services

Absolutely everything you'll need for a Yosemite outdoor experience can be purchased in the western foothills town of Sonora. This includes full backpacking and mountaineering gear, these available at the Sierra Nevada Adventure Company. This town also has several large grocery stores, numerous dining places, and two hospitals.

Groveland, about 24 miles west of the park's Big Oak Flat Entrance Station, is the last town you'll pass on Hwy. 120; however, several resorts, gas stations, and campgrounds are found closer to the park. Gas, meals, and lodging are found at Evergreen Lodge, on Evergreen Road just 0.6 mile before it ends at the Hetch Hetchy Road in Camp Mather (for San Francisco residents).

Wilderness Permits

If you want to reserve a permit, rather than get one in person, see the "Wilderness Permits" section in Chapter 6. In person, those following Trip 8 should get permits at the Groveland Ranger District Office on Hwy. 120 about 8 miles east of Groveland. Also, phone them at 209-962-7825 no more than 24 hours before you start your hike to see if the trailhead quota has been filled. For trips 9 to 12, use either the information station at the park's Big Oak Flat Entrance Station, or use the Hetch Hetchy Entrance Station, by the Mather Ranger Station. The latter is open from about early April through late October. I recommend Trip 15 as a dayhike, but if you backpack it, you will also need a permit. Trip 14 certainly is a short dayhike and is too close to the Hetch Hetchy Road to allow legal camping. Trip 13 is outside the park and not in a wilderness, so you can camp without a permit.

Campgrounds

For Trip 8, use Cherry Valley Campground. From the major intersection near the trailhead parking area, go left a half mile west up Road 1N04, then branch right and go a half mile to the campground's entrance. For all other trips, you could spend the night at Dimond O Campground, about 5.6 miles north on Evergreen Road, which begins from Hwy. 120, just 0.6 mile before the park's boundary below the Big Oak Flat Entrance Station. If you have a wilderness permit, you can stay at the Hetch Hetchy Backpackers Campground, located on the loop road by the O'Shaughnessy Dam Trailhead.

TRIP **8**

Cherry Lake to Boundary Lake and / or Kibbie Lake

E **M** ⟋ BP, BPx, X

DISTANCE: 21 miles out and back

ELEVATIONS: 5880′/7900′
+2870′/-850′/±7440′

SEASON: Early July to late September

USE: Moderate

MAPS: *Cherry Lake North*, *Kibbie Lake*

TRAIL LOG:

1.3	Kibbie Lake Trail
4.0	Kibbie Lake
4.4	Swede's Camp
4.8	Shallow pond
6.6	Sachse Spring
8.9	Large tarn
9.1	Styx Pass
9.4	Many Island Lake
9.9	Boundary Lake Trail
10.5	Boundary Lake

INTRODUCTION: Were it not for the long drive to the trailhead, Kibbie Lake would be a popular dayhike. At 4 miles distance and only about 700 feet between its trail's high and low points, Kibbie Lake is a good choice for beginning backpackers. Serious backpackers will want to visit one or more of about two dozen lakes that appear on the *Kibbie Lake 7.5′* topographic map. Boundary Lake is the only one reached by an official trail, but a use trail continues past it to nearby Little Bear Lake. All of the other lakes are reached by cross-country travel, and you certainly need orienting skills to find most of them.

DIRECTIONS TO THE TRAILHEAD: From Groveland, drive east 13.6 miles on Hwy. 120 to paved Cherry Road 1N07, also known as Forest Route 17, starting just beyond the highway bridge over South Fork Tuolumne River. (A spur road right, immediately before the bridge, leads briefly down to the popular Rainbow Pool day-use area—a refreshing spot to visit after your hike.) Take F. R. 17 5.3 miles to a junction with paved Hetch Hetchy Road (F. R. 12), and branch left. Still on F. R. 17, go 17.6 miles to Cottonwood Road 1N04. The signed Cherry Dam parking area is just yards east down this road.

While you could start your hike from here, most people would prefer to save 4.3 trail miles and a 1200-foot ascent by starting at a newer trailhead. To reach it, drive across Cherry Dam, then continue a half mile beyond it to a T junction with Road 1N45Y. Turn left, north, up this good road, then down, in the next 2 miles passing a succession of signed trailheads and parking lots for, respectively, Lake Eleanor, Kibbie Creek-Flora Lake, and old Kibbie Ridge trails. Onward, the road climbs alongside Kibbie Ridge, just a short distance below the old trail. Three switchbacks eventually lead up to a deadend at 5880 feet. Here are a corral and a sign indicating the way to the Kibbie Ridge Trail.

Be aware that during hunting season, you must park down by the reservoir. This closure is designed by Forest Service biologists to minimize intrusions on the large deer herds that migrate down Kibbie Ridge each fall. To avoid this increased hiking distance, plan to hike this route before late September. Trail begins in map section A3.

DESCRIPTION: From the road's end, we start on a spur trail that leads east-north-east uphill to the nearby Kibbie Ridge Trail. Just about a minute's walk down this main trail is Shingle Spring, with beautiful dog-woods and nearby camps. However, we take the main route north, gaining about 400 feet in elevation as it first climbs to a descending ridge and then curves east into cooler, forested Deadhorse Gulch. Just past its upper end, we reach the main ridge and, in a conifer grove beside a small grass-choked pond, 1.25 miles into our hike, meet the 2.7-mile-long Kibbie Lake Trail. If you are heading to the lakes of the higher country, you'll probably want to skip this lake, although you could visit it on your return trip by making a cross-country route from one of those lakes. If you do hike to Kibbie Lake and back, add 5.4 miles to your total hiking distance. The trip's elevation changes do not include the relatively minor changes to and from Kibbie Lake.

[S] **SIDE TRIP TO KIBBIE LAKE:** Skirting this pond, a lateral trail nears a ridgetop open space freckled by mat lupine, streptanthus, buckwheat, and pretty face (golden brodiaea), the last species eaten by the Miwok Indians. Quickly, it enters Yosemite National Park and drops on rocky tread surrounded by chaparral, lightly forested with Jeffrey pines, into a small canyon. Next, you head north through a sodden bottom land, passing the first lodgepole pines of your trip, which, here, accompanied by white firs, form a dense canopy.

Mountain dogbane (Indian hemp), branched Solomon's seal, bracken fern, Parish's yampah, violet, shooting star, and deadly bleeding hearts thrive in the shadows, enticing the traveler to linger in coolness. In early season, mosquitoes will no doubt urge you on!

The trail leaves the forest, climbing northeast onto granitic slabs mottled by huckleberry oaks to a 6500-foot saddle. The rocky route next descends to cross a tributary of Kibbie Creek under a south-facing dome that offers good rock climbing on its peeling skin. After the step-across ford, we closely parallel smooth, green pools on Kibbie Creek, which is lined by western azaleas, willows, and tall conifers. You pass a good camp on the right, then, just yards later, before a poorer trail climbs up amid huckleberry oak to the right of a granitic outcrop to continue over slabs to the west shore of Kibbie Lake, your route angles down to a 30-foot rock-hop of Kibbie Creek. Across the ford, among lodge-poles, is a very good camp. The trail turns upstream, climbing over blasted granitic ledges, the route indicated by rock ducks.

Granite cliffs provide high-diving opportunities at Kibbie Lake

After passing ice-scoured lagoons presaging 106-acre, 6513-foot Kibbie Lake, you reach its south shore, where camps are found in a lodgepole and Labrador tea fringe. Kibbie Lake is named for pioneer H. G. Kibbie, who traveled throughout the Yosemite north country and constructed small cabins at Frog Creek in the Lake Eleanor vicinity, at Tiltill Meadow, and on Rancheria Mountain. Kibbie Lake is bounded on the west by gently sloping granite, while the east shore is characterized by steep, broken bluffs and polished bosses. The relatively warm lake is mostly shallow, with an algae-coated sandy bottom, where distinctively orange-colored California newts may take your bait if a rainbow trout doesn't. **END OF SIDE TRIP**

From the Kibbie Lake Trail, the Kibbie Ridge Trail starts on its duff tread. After dropping past Sand Canyon, you pass, in quick succession, a marshy flat, a seasonal creek with a good camp (at the Emigrant Wilderness boundary and about 1.25 miles past the trail junction), and a switchback that leads up onto sparsely forested granitic slabs covered with grus (weathered granite). Note how the massive roots of the Jeffrey pines loosen and fracture the peeling rock, hastening the development of soil. Soon re-entering red fir forest, we climb steadily to Lookout Point, with vistas west of the deep cleft of Cherry Creek canyon. Next, we pass Swede's Camp by a corn-lily-filled meadow. Should you camp here, look for a spring-fed creeklet in an adjacent northwest descending shallow gully. In less than a half mile, you make a minor ascent to a large, shallow pond, and again you have an opportunity to camp in the adjacent vicinity. After skirting its sandy north shore, we climb under sparse mixed trees, often at a steep incline, to an open-ridgetop sand flat, where we find the Yosemite National Park boundary. A steep path straight up the sandy ridge, blessed with fine panoramas east-southeast to Mt. Conness, leads to the seasonally muddy, marsh-marigold-dotted vicinity of Sachse Spring,

where there is a good camp. Here you might stop, rest, and consider the ecology of the mule deer that make this area their home in the summer and fall months.

Rested, we continue east from Sachse Spring, on a trail that undulates on morainal material supporting western white pines and red firs. After about a half mile of hiking, you could head north almost 0.2 mile from the trail to reach a large lakelet that offers good campsites along its south shore. Beyond a seasonal creek, our route begins to descend onto open granitic slabs, a harbinger of typical Emigrant Basin terrain to come. Mercur Peak, at 8096 feet elevation, is a domelike summit in the northeast. Like many granitic features in the park, it has exfoliated considerably due to a depressurization caused by the removal of the weight of the last major glacier, which had pressed upon it for thousands of years.

Coming off the slabs into a small lodgepole forest surrounding a murky tarn, we keep right, following blazes and ducks, then continue over sandy slabs on a bearing straight for Mercur Peak. Its summit, reached by an easy scramble up its south slope, provides a fine vantage point for examining the southern Emigrant Basin. In a lodgepole forest south of the peak, our trail reaches a large tarn. You can camp here, although in early season the ground can be quite damp.

⑤ **SIDE TRIP TO MANY ISLAND LAKE:** This tarn marks the start of a cross-country route to aptly named Many Island Lake. Proceed due south through lodgepoles and around early-season ponds to low-angle slabs bounding the north part of the basin that holds this lake. By keeping your feet flat on the sloping rock and pointed downhill, you should have no difficulty descending a total of a half mile to campsites flanking the summer-warm, shallow waters of 7325-foot Many Island Lake, which harbors rainbow trout. **END OF SIDE TRIP**

Just east of the Many Island Lake cross-country route, the Kibbie Ridge Trail passes

MULE DEER

Biologists studying the mule deer herd in this area named it the "Jawbone Herd," after its winter range on Jawbone Ridge and along Jawbone Creek, some 12 miles below Cherry Lake. The mammalogists separated the herd into two distinct groups, the Clavey Unit deer, occupying the rich, brushy, volcanic-earthed Clavey River basin, and the Cherry Unit deer, ranging throughout the Cherry Creek drainage. Mule deer of the Cherry Unit must subsist in poorer conditions than Clavey deer, owing to the prevalence of forage-poor, glacier-polished, granite terrain and food-poor, fire- or logging-caused brushy areas in the Cherry Creek basin. When springtime snows begin to melt, Cherry mule deer begin to drift from their winter range, following budding plants upward, keeping generally 1000 feet below the receding snowline.

By contouring along canyon slopes that are first to sprout new vegetation, most of the deer reach the prime summer range by late June. Once on the summer range, the deer fawn and fatten themselves on forbs and shrubbery. Deer populations are most dense between 6000 and 7500 feet, in forest fringes near meadows and brush. In this habitat, moderate summer deer populations reside below Lookout Point and Kibbie Lake, while deer are rare in higher elevations in the open, soil-deficient granite terrain. On Kibbie Ridge, as elsewhere, deer prefer the open, brush-floored Jeffrey pine community, and they are less common in the shadier red fir community. The most preferred browse species for Jawbone deer in summer months is snow bush, and huckleberry oak is also favored. Aspen and willows are desired foods for pregnant or lactating does, as well as young black oak leaves and mountain misery.

In fall, prompted by the first snowstorms, deer in the Cherry drainage begin a downward migration, the highest deer moving first. They finally reach their winter range by early December. There are two main travel corridors followed by Cherry deer heading south to the winter range. One begins west of Emigrant Lake, heads north of Hyatt Lake to West Fork Cherry Creek, and then goes down Hells Mountain, passing along the ridge west of Cherry Lake. The second migration route begins south of Emigrant Lake and bisects the region visited in this hike by traversing to Lord Meadow, and then going east of Many Island and Kibbie lakes to lower Kibbie Ridge, between Cherry Lake and Lake Eleanor. Other park deer have similar migratory routes.

through a narrow, joint-controlled gully to reach Styx Pass, where it leaves Yosemite National Park some 7.75 miles beyond the Kibbie Lake Trail. We descend to better views of the North and East Fork Cherry Creek drainages, flanked by soaring domes and smooth aprons. Eight tight, rocky switchbacks decorated by clumps of sedge and of red Sierra onion bring us to a long traverse east to the Boundary Lake Trail, 0.75 mile beyond Styx Pass. If not signed, this junction can easily be missed. It is encountered on a steep, broken slope of exfoliating granite right before you make

two small switchbacks and start a traverse northwest down to Lord Meadow.

On the Boundary Lake Trail, we make a switchbacking ascent east-southeast toward a low point on the nearby crest. The ascent presently becomes less steep as it climbs through a jumble of lodgepoles and rocks to a forested tarn. From it, a final rise takes us back into the park, where we immediately confront a pair of seasonal ponds that, in early season, connect with the north shore of 7527-foot Boundary Lake, 0.6 mile beyond the trail junction. Sandy flats with sparse conifers make for good camping on this side of the lake; the east shore has high bluffs. The trail around Boundary Lake's west side winds over granitic outcrops, through patches of huckleberry oak and stands of fir and pine. The undulating path keeps generally away from the irregular rocky shore, but sometimes we head near the shore to find a snug camp near clumps of willows or Labrador tea. You can expect good fishing for rainbow trout.

S **SIDE TRIP TO LITTLE BEAR AND SPOTTED FAWN LAKES:** At Boundary Lake's south end, about 0.75 mile from its northwest shore, you steer through a notched dome, then descend to a step-across ford of the outlet. On the south bank for a moment, you have telescoped views across the lake's slate-gray entirety to Gillett Mountain before you turn south down a joint gully to the marshy north end of 7522-foot Little Bear Lake, situated about 11.5 miles from the trailhead. Heading east of this islet-speckled, 25-acre, rainbow trout fishery, you pass a fine camp on the north shore, then turn south behind a red fir and lodgepole grove entangled in a marshy maze of bracken and manzanita, where the trail peters out. From the south end of Little Bear Lake, you could extend your trip by descending a half mile southeast to granite-cupped, 7327-foot Spotted Fawn Lake, which has adequate camping in its north-shore lodgepole curtain and, like all the lakes of this area, has angling for rainbow trout. Those with considerable mountaineering expertise can continue cross-country a mile southeast to a brink above the Kendrick Creek canyon. Steep slopes and lack of trails make this canyon's half dozen lakes among the least visited in the park. However, an easier, slightly shorter route to these lakes begins from the north shore of Laurel Lake. **END OF SIDE TRIP**

A **ALTERNATE TRIPS TO KIBBIE LAKE:** Rather than retracing your steps, you could start a cross-country route from Many Island Lake, paralleling its outlet, Kibbie Creek, first south and then southwest about 2.5 miles to the northeast shore of Kibbie Lake.

From here, you will likely have to go up cliffs, regardless of which way you go around the lake. To end your hike, retrace your steps to the trailhead.

If you're at Boundary, Many Island, or Spotted Fawn lakes, you'll add a mile or two to your cross-country route to Kibbie Lake. The surest route is to start from a low divide about midway along the west shore of Boundary Lake. From it, descend about 0.3 mile west-southwest to an obvious lakelet, then climb briefly west-northwest to second low divide, from which you traverse, with a 200-foot descent midway along it, about a half mile due west to the northeast shore of Many Island Lake.

Starting from Many Island or Spotted Fawn lakes, you can make additional routes, including one past many lakes, lakelets, and ponds along Bartlett Creek, going as far as Flora Lake before heading more or less across forested terrain to descend to the southeast shore of Kibbie Lake. For any of these additional routes, the *Kibbie Lake 7.5′* topographic map is very useful. Regardless which scale of topographic map you use (including the park's topo map), note that while Sierran lands generally descend southwest, Flora Lake's outlet creek flows in the opposite direction, northeast, down to Bartlett Creek, which continues northeast about 1 mile before curving right and descending southwest through a linear, joint-controlled canyon. Southwest-trending master joints dominate the lands in this northwestern part of the park.

Should you reach Flora Lake, you can either head to Kibbie Lake or take a longer route that goes to Lake Eleanor before reaching your trailhead's road. From Flora Lake, the route west is essentially cross-country. From the west shore, ascend for about a half mile to a horseshoe-shaped lakelet, then ascend northwest for a similar distance to a shallow bowl with a seasonal pond. If you are in luck, you might spot a trail just to its south. It makes a diagonal-trending ascent southwest 0.75 mile up to a sandy divide at a shallow gap with views to the south and southeast. Onward, a hopefully obvious trail descends southwest. After about a mile, it reaches a ridge and follows it about a half mile southwest to a sometimes cryptic junction with a faint, northbound Kibbie Lake Trail. This is located at about 7100 feet elevation in a pleasant, dry, red fir forest. If you continue ahead, you'll drop south off the ridge toward Lake Eleanor. The 1.5-mile-long Kibbie Lake Trail quickly reaches and crosses the crests of three glacial moraines, and then makes rough switchbacks steeply downward. Below 6800 feet, the gradient abates and the trail goes out onto pine-dotted slabs that give vistas southwest down Kibbie Creek. Below this is a moderate descent past pleasant pocket meadows. The gradient becomes gentle about a quarter mile from Kibbie Lake's south shore, where you'll meet the heavily used trail taking you back to the trailhead. **END OF ALTERNATE TRIPS**

A **ALTERNATE TRIP TO TRAILHEAD:** This 6.6-mile route is recommended only for those who want to spend an extra day or two visiting the Lake Eleanor environs. From the sometimes cryptic junction atop the forested ridge, a longer way back to your trailhead is to leave its morainal crest and follow a now better trail tread south, the way becoming very steep, bouldery, and open. As our descent becomes more moderate, once again in forest cover, we approach a seasonal creek, entrenched below us, angle southwest, and then descend often brushy, glaciated terrain for about a mile before we cross the creek. To avoid a smooth whaleback ridge, our trail skirts around its brushy base and then enters another shady forest. We walk southwest down the slopes of a large moraine and then, at its base, angle south and after a 3-mile descent we reach a ford of wide, pot-holed Kibbie Creek—a wet crossing until late summer. Beside the crossing, large-leaved umbrella plant, or Indian rhubarb, whose stalks the Miwoks ate raw, grows along or in the creek. Across the creek you'll discover several small, gravelly campsites.

Beyond the wide ford, we soon reach mile-high elevations, and conifers gradually give way to canyon live oaks as we descend gradually southwest, but they reappear as the dominant plant form after a mile. Over the next half mile, our trail reaches a broad saddle, and, just south, at its lowest point, arrives at a junction with the prominent Lake Eleanor Trail. Those who want to spend one more night in the backcountry can drop east to the west shore of large Lake Eleanor, visible through the pine-and-black-oak cover atop Kibbie Ridge. From here, a good trail leads east moderately down for a quarter mile to a trail junction, from where the left fork continues east down to a shaded peninsula on 27,000-acre-foot Lake Eleanor. This reservoir was created by the city of San Francisco in 1918 to raise, by 35 feet, an existing lake. Travelers may desire to follow the right-hand trail south to the 60-foot-high, 20-caisson concrete dam. At its east end lies the Lake Eleanor NPS Station and a road that follows a part of the south shore of Lake Eleanor, then climbs south and east to Miguel Meadow, where the trail to Laurel Lake begins. From the junction atop the broad saddle west of the reservoir, start northwest down the Lake Eleanor Trail and, in about a quarter mile, strike the trailhead's road. Go but 0.1 mile north on the road to where you'll intersect a lower part of the Kibbie Ridge Trail, which you take 1.75 miles north, gaining about 800 feet to Shingle Spring, just beyond which you drop briefly west on a spur trail to your trailhead. **END OF ALTERNATE TRIP**

TRIP 9

Hetch Hetchy to Laurel Lake and Lake Vernon

Ⓜ ✗ BP

DISTANCE: 21.2 miles out and back

ELEVATIONS: 3810'/6980'
+3860'/1100'/±9160'

SEASON: Early July to mid October

USE: Moderate

MAPS: *Lake Eleanor, Kibbie Lake,
Tiltill Mountain,
Hetch Hetchy Reservoir*

TRAIL LOG:

1.0	Rancheria Falls Trail
2.8	Leave closed road at trail junction
4.6	Linear lakelet
5.3	Southwest-descending trail
7.2	Beehive
8.4	Laurel Lake
8.7	Jack Main Canyon Trail
10.6	Lake Vernon

INTRODUCTION: This relatively low-elevation trip, a good, early-summer conditioner, first visits two relatively large lakes—Laurel and Vernon—both good rainbow trout fisheries. If you hike only to Laurel Lake, your total elevation gain and loss will be about 6680 feet; if you hike only to Lake Vernon, it will be about 8400 feet. These two lakes are popular on summer weekends, and most hikers go no farther. At 6490 feet in elevation, Laurel Lake is the lowest of any large natural lake in the park that is reached by trail, and it provides relatively warm swimming. Being lower, this conifer-ringed lake lacks the inspiring scenery of the park's higher lakes. But in compensation, there are many campsites above its lengthy shore, these allowing for secluded camping even when others are present.

Lake Vernon, at 6564 feet in elevation, is a bit higher; furthermore, you cross a low ridge and then drop 400 feet to the lake. This is a more aesthetic lake, and it has plenty of slabs great for sunbathing, especially for warming up after a swim. If you are looking for variety, you can return to your trailhead from each of these two lakes by using an alternate route. From Laurel Lake, you can descend southwest to Miguel Meadow and then traverse east. From Lake Vernon, you can descend cross-country south along its outlet, Falls Creek, to the brink of Wapama Falls, and then traverse west. Be aware that this somewhat popular cross-country route can be quite dangerous in places if you are not a skilled route finder and mountaineer.

For those with time on their hands and a curiosity for more discovery, these hikes can be extended. From Laurel Lake, you can make a relatively safe, easy cross-country trip north to the Kendrick Creek Lakes. From Lake Vernon, you can climb south and descend east to meadowed Tiltill Valley, an interesting pocket of spring wildflowers and grasses with several isolated creekside campsites. From here, skilled route finders and mountaineers can explore lands along Rancheria Creek east of Tiltill Valley. Be aware that the upper slopes on your descent east into Tiltill Valley can become overgrown with brush. Therefore, first check at the Hetch Hetchy Entrance Station about the trail's condition through the brush.

DIRECTIONS TO THE TRAILHEAD: Just 0.6 mile before the park's boundary below the Big Oak Flat Entrance Station, leave Hwy. 120 and drive north 7.5 miles on Evergreen Road to its junction with the Hetch Hetchy Road. Turn right and go 8.5 miles to a junction left. Backpackers turn here, park in the obvious parking area by the road's start, then walk a half mile on the road to O'Shaughnessy Dam. Dayhikers continue driving 0.7 mile past the junction to the dam, beyond which is parking. Trail begins in map section B3.

DESCRIPTION: For those in great shape, the hike up to Laurel Lake can be done as a long dayhike. Backpackers, starting from their parking area, will add 1 mile to their round-trip distance. Everyone should start early in the morning, since the switchbacking route up from the reservoir is only partly shaded, and summer temperatures can reach into the 90s by noon. Carry sufficient water; in late season it's two or more hours before reaching water.

You begin by starting across the top of O'Shaughnessy Dam (3814 feet) at Hetch Hetchy Reservoir.

On the south wall, the prow of Kolana Rock soars 2000 feet above the reservoir, while to its north, tiered Hetch Hetchy Dome rises about 400 feet higher. In a shaded cleft on the dome's west flank, two-stepped Wapama Falls plunges an aggregate of 1400 feet. In early summer, its

HETCH HETCHY RESERVOIR

Along the curving monolith of O'Shaughnessy Dam, named for the Hetch Hetchy Project's chief engineer, we find bronze plaques posted to commemorate those who made possible this intrusion on a national park, back in 1914, along with similar structures on Lake Eleanor and Cherry Lake. Visitors today can look, but not touch (to protect San Francisco's hygiene, one must assume), so we can only gaze east over the 8-mile-long reservoir. The soaring canyon walls that remain standing above it are good reminders of what Hetch Hetchy Valley once was—a less spectacular sibling of Yosemite Valley. Yosemite Valley, being a popular tourist destination, was saved from dam(nation), but Hetch Hetchy Valley, being quite unknown, was an easy victim.

gossamer companion, Tueeulala Falls, glides down steep slabs farther west.

Across the 600-foot-long dam, we enter a 500-foot-long tunnel that was blasted through solid granite when the original dam was raised 85 feet in 1938. Emerging from this bat haven, the formerly paved road traverses above the rocky west shore of Hetch Hetchy Reservoir in a pleasant grove of Douglas fir, gray pine, big-leaf maple, and bay trees. Sour, blue-blushed California grape, shiny poison oak, and palmlike giant chain ferns grow in the shadier spots. Each of these plants was utilized by the Miwok Indians who visited Hetch Hetchy. One mile into our route, we reach the junction with the Rancheria Falls Trail (Trip 11), just before our route's first switchback.

Keeping to the former road, we ascend moderately steep switchbacks and have better views up the reservoir of LeConte Point and the Grand Canyon of the Tuolumne River.

As we ascend, fairly open, lower slopes give way to oak-shaded slopes, then, near the top, to oak-and-conifer-shaded ones. The last of eight switchbacks swings north into a gully with a trail junction on a small flat, where we leave the closed road. With one third of the distance covered and with half of the elevation gain under your belt, you start up a trail through a partly burned forest of ponderosa pines, sugar pines, and other conifers. In a quarter mile, you reach a mile-high creeklet, which, although diminutive, usually flows through the summer. This is your first reliable water, and people have camped hereabouts. Up the trail about 200 yards past the creeklet and about 3.2 miles from the trailhead, you'll see a shallow gully on your right.

⑤ **SIDE TRIP TO WAPAMA FALLS:** This is the start of a relatively easy 1.5mile cross-country route east to the brink of Wapama Falls. It is the only major year-round waterfall in the park that does not have a trail to its brink. The cross-country route, which I'll leave for you to discern, has been done by so many hikers that a faint use trail exists. Be forewarned that the route is dry, is in rattlesnake habitat, has locally dense brush, and has flower seeds that stick to socks and shoelaces. However, the view from the falls' brink is stupendous, and, after about mid-July, Falls Creek has diminished enough in flow to permit a refreshing swim in a shallow pool just above the brink. If the flow is brisk, do not enter the pool. **END OF SIDE TRIP**

Unlike the closed road you ascended, which maintains a nearly constant grade, your ascending trail varies, being locally steep, moderate, gentle, or even briefly down. You'll eventually climb 1000 feet above the creeklet before the serious climbing ends. About a half mile beyond the creeklet, your trail curves east and levels off, and you may want to rest. Ahead, the trail climbs north, then northwest, and then the serious climbing ends with a curve east

to cross a crest of a lateral moraine. On this ascent, look for linear deposits, which also are lateral moraines. Also look for flat near-trail bedrock exposures into which Indians drilled mortar holes and ground up black oak acorns and sugar pine seeds. Once on top, 4.6 miles into your hike, take a break; you deserve it. While resting, look around.

Your hike ahead is now relatively easy. After rounding the linear lakelet's east end, the trail crosses the broad moraine's crest, drops momentarily, and then ascends 0.4 mile through an open white fir forest to a junction with a southwest-descending trail. Laurel Lake, though only 0.75 mile northwest of us, is at least 2.5 trail miles away by either trail we can take, and one wonders why a trail was not built directly to it. If you've not found water so far, take the trail southwest a quarter mile down to always reliable Frog Creek. Rather than ascend

GEOLOGY LESSONS

The moraine crest you cross is sharp and its rocks are fresh, indicating that it is of Tioga age. Immediately north of it is a shallow, linear lakelet, which holds water well into summer. It appears to be dammed by the moraine, but actually is dammed by bedrock buried under the thin deposits of your moraine. Immediately north of the lakelet is another lateral moraine, judged to be older, of Tahoe age, because it is broad and not sharp-crested, and has fewer boulders. Beyond it, glacial deposits extending up to Laurel Lake are even thinner and more amorphous, and hence judged to be very old, possibly of Sherwin age.

By using these criteria, geologists identified and mapped three episodes of glaciation in Yosemite National Park and other glaciated lands west of the Sierra Crest. The older the deposits are, the more weathered they become, yet if you look at formerly buried boulders exposed by Laurel Lake's outlet creek, you'll see they are fresh, not disintegrated. In 1993, I proposed that the location and shape of glacial deposits are dictated by topography and glacial physics, and that most of the Sierra's thin, amorphous deposits actually are young, that is, of Tioga age—not old, of Sherwin age.

Laurel Lake was an ideal site to test which view was correct. Conventional wisdom called for hundreds of feet of lake sediments and a date of basal sediments some 800,000 years old. My interpretation called for 10 to 20 feet of sediments and a date no more than 16,000 years old. On August 20, 1994, my five-man work party successfully penetrated 14 feet of lake sediments to extract basal sediments, sent them off to be dated, and soon received the results: The sediments are only about 13,000 years old (and the lake, a bit older, would be about 15,000 years old). Glacial deposits throughout most of the Sierra Nevada had been dated under the wrong assumptions.

back to the junction, you might ascend first along the west side of the creek, then along the west side of the lake's outlet creek.

From your junction, 5.3 miles from your trailhead, follow the often shady trail northeast, dip to cross a bracken-bordered creeklet, then soon hike alongside a linear meadow that, in season, is profuse with arrow-leaved senecio and Bigelow's sneezeweed, two kinds of sunflowers. The meadow pinches off at a low gap, beyond which we quickly find ourselves in the southwest corner of a triangular meadow. Staying among white firs and lodgepole pines, we parallel the meadow's edge northeast over to its east corner, called Beehive, where there is a trail junction. About 20 yards before it, just within the meadow, is a usually reliable spring. Just beyond the junction, among trees, is a spacious campsite. Beehive was the site of an 1880s cattlemen's camp, and a log cabin once stood north of the trail junction.

With most of our ascent behind us, we turn left and walk northwest 160 yards on the Laurel Lake Trail to reach another trail junction. Here, a path that loops around Laurel Lake's north shore branches north, while a shorter trail to the lake's outlet strikes west. Following this latter route, we drop easily down into a white-fir-shaded gully and then broad Frog Creek, which could be a wet ford in early season. Along its north bank, we contour west briefly, then ascend steeply to a heavily forested ridge before gently dropping to good camps near Laurel Lake's outlet. A brief stint brings us to a junction with the north-shore loop trail, branching northwest to the best campsites (and more secluded ones beyond). At fairly deep 60-acre Laurel Lake, western azalea grows thickly just back of the locally grassy lakeshore, a fragrant accompaniment to huckleberry and thimbleberry. Fishing is fair for rainbow trout.

By continuing north around Laurel Lake, one will encounter a large packer campsite on the northwest shore. There, the trail turns east through a bracken-over-grown deadfall, negotiates an easy ridge, and drops to a camp beside Frog Creek, here running through cobbles and past tall American dogwood shrubs. Across that stream, the route turns southeast, ascending easily to a junction with the southern Laurel Lake Trail, just north of Beehive.

S **SIDE TRIP TO KENDRICK CREEK LAKES:** Should you want an extended trip with an almost certain guarantee of not meeting other people, consider visiting the Kendrick Creek Lakes, which are among the lowest natural lakes in the park. As such, they are likely the warmest swimming lakes in the park, and afternoon lake temperatures in July and August should be in the mid-70s. From the north shore of Laurel Lake, head north over the low, adjacent ridge, then north down to the west end of an obvious, nearby linear lakelet, then north to the edge of its bench. From it, you could descend 1 mile northwest across open, glacier-smoothed slabs to Eleanor Creek (the merger of Bartlett and Kendrick creeks), where you can find isolated camping, but no lakes. Rather, descend only 0.6 mile north-northwest to an obvious pond on a bench, and, from it, cross the low saddle just to its north and make an undulating traverse up-canyon. On this stretch, try to maintain nearly constant elevation as you encounter many minor ups and downs. After about 2 miles of a winding traverse, you'll come to the east end of a 200-foot cliff that is on the opposite (north) side of Kendrick Creek. Just to its east is the outlet creek from Lake 5683. If you hike up to that lake, you can follow its inlet creek northeast to nearby Lake 5810, then, from its northeast end, bridge a minor divide to adjacent Lake 5774. This empties south to Lake 5728, which is just downstream and is situated along Kendrick Creek. A half-mile walk downstream will get you back to the lower end of Lake 5683's outlet creek. **END OF SIDE TRIP**

A **ALTERNATE TRIP TO TRAILHEAD:** For an alternate return route, leave Laurel Lake near its outlet, heading southwest on the

Frog Creek Trail under a dense canopy of white fir. Within a half mile, this 1.75-mile stretch becomes a gradually steepening descent, down an open nose of fire-damaged conifers. A trail junction is reached midway down the nose, where we must make a choice of return routes. The first contours 1.25 miles east to Frog Creek, then another quarter mile up it to the trail we came in on, leaving you with 5.3 miles of backtracking to Hetch Hetchy. The second—straight ahead—descends to Miguel Meadow.

Should you choose the longer route via Miguel Meadow, head west from the trail junction and drop steeply on sandy tread, with views west over Lake Eleanor and down on conifer-shaded Frog Creek. Beyond an emergency campsite, we easily hop rocks to the south bank and climb a short switchback. Now a traverse leads southwest through dry forest to a nearby ridge saddle clothed in manzanita, from where the Beehive Trail formerly dropped west to Lake Eleanor. We turn south from this saddle, gently descend into the basin of Miguel Creek, and there walk under a pleasant canopy of Jeffrey pines and black oaks, where flickers and white-headed woodpeckers dwell. Below 5400 feet, our path comes out into the open on a bouldery, sunny hillside. Lower down, we pass north of unseen Gravel Pit Lake, then traverse southwest to a road. You could head just 0.3 mile southwest down it to Miguel Meadow, where there is an NPS ranger station and pleasant camping under large black oaks. However, to return to Hetch Hetchy, turn southeast on the road, cross nearby Miguel Creek, wind east for 3.2 miles up a shallow, open-floored canyon, top a mile-high saddle, drop a few hundred yards to the Laurel Lake Trail junction, up which you ascended, and retrace your steps down the switchbacking route to the trailhead. **END OF ALTERNATE TRIP**

If you don't visit Laurel Lake, you'll save about 2.5 miles of hiking and 760 feet of ascent and descent. From the Beehive

junction, we take the eastbound Lake Vernon Trail, which winds easily 1.5 miles up to a moraine-crest junction with the Jack Main Canyon Trail, just below the slightly higher crest of Moraine Ridge. From the junction, we descend to an open granite bench. Now on bedrock, we follow a well-ducked trail down past excellent examples of glacier-smoothed rock—glacier polish—and glacier-transported boulders—glacier erratics. Scattered Jeffrey pines lend occasional shade along a northeast traverse, their roots seeking out cracks in the granite in which they might take hold and help form a soil. On drier, more inhospitable sites grow rugged western junipers, which manage to survive where the Jeffreys don't because their scale-like leaves lose less water to the atmosphere than do the Jeffrey's long needles.

Along this section, we can look across the far wall of Falls Creek canyon until a nearby minor outlier, a half mile southwest of Lake Vernon, obstructs our view, about 1.25 miles from the last junction. Just after this happens, we angle southeast and follow a winding, ducked route up toward the point, but cross a low ridge just north of it. Now below us lies spreading Lake Vernon, flooding part of a broad, flat-floored canyon. During colder times, glaciers occupied this canyon and buried it under as much as 1800 feet of glacier ice. When the last glacier retreated from the canyon by 15,000 years ago, it left minor depressions in the bedrock floor, which quickly filled to become Lake Vernon and its satellite lakes and ponds.

From this inspirational ridge, we descend generally northeast—the trend of this area's master joints—and in 0.3 mile reach a junction with a spur trail. Leaving a small flat with a few nearby aspens among Jeffrey pines, this trail shoots northeast, at first staying close to the base of a similar-trending wall. After a quarter mile of walking, you'll be close to the shore of the unseen lake, and you can head southeast to it. There you'll find a fairly large campsite among lodgepoles. Others lie along this northwest shore of Lake Vernon. The trail continues past a snow-gauge marker and adjacent park cabin, then dies out, about a mile past the lake, by a large camp close to where the creek angles from northeast to north and its gradient increases dramatically.

S SIDE TRIP TO JACK MAIN CANYON TRAIL: From this vicinity, an easy cross-country route follows cascading Falls Creek northeast about 1 mile to a flat. Above it, the route north is steeper, though not dangerously so, if you can discern a proper route up beside the dashing creek. At the top of this milelong ascent, immediately north of the creek's highest cascade, is the Jack Main Canyon Trail. The cross-country route to this point takes no more effort than does the trail route up over Moraine Ridge and down to it. The first offers a cascading creek with a refreshing swimming hole or two, the second, sweeping vistas. **END OF SIDE TRIP**

Rather than take the Lake Vernon Trail, you can take the main trail southeast briefly to a bridge across Falls Creek, then equally briefly northeast around a bedrock slope to Lake Vernon's southwest shore. Additional campsites are found near it. The lake, mostly shallow and lying at about 6564 feet, is one of the warmer park lakes for swimming. Some people choose to camp below the lake, near Falls Creek below the bridge.

A FIRST ALTERNATE TRIP TO TRAILHEAD: A remarkably scenic cross-country route with isolated camping next to several swimming holes goes about 5 miles down Falls Creek to the brink of Wapama Falls, from which a brushy, weedy, viewless route goes about 1.5 miles west to the shallow gully you ascended past on day one. The first part of the cross-country route is past giant potholes the creek carved, probably as a roaring, boulder-choked river beneath a giant glacier. I won't describe the route, but will leave it to you to discover. The route takes a lot more effort than you would imagine,

is locally brushy and bouldery, has one narrow notch and adjacent, steep, potentially dangerous descent to negotiate. Additionally, don't take it in times of high water, such as before mid-July. Below it gets into less scenic, hotter lands, where a rattlesnake encounter is more likely than it is above. This is definitely not a route for the inexperienced or inept. The total distance to the trailhead will be about 9.5 or10 miles, which is a bit shorter than retracing your steps on trail, but the cross-country route is not a stroll in the park, and you'll probably expend as much effort along it as along the trail. **END OF ALTERNATE TRIP**

A SECOND ALTERNATE TRIP TO TRAILHEAD: Most hikers return from Lake Vernon the way they came. Some, along with equestrians, do continue on to Tiltill Valley, which will involve a 2000-foot descent from the following trail's high point. By making this loop, you will hike about 30 miles total. From the lake, you first ascend for about 1000 feet via some three dozen short switchbacks. The view improves with elevation, and the expanding panoramas give us good excuses to take plenty of rests. The views disappear as we enter a minor hanging valley some 700 feet above the lake. Now among firs, we make a short climb up past several lateral moraines until we top the last of them.

With easy hiking ahead, we first dip into a gully, then contour south, passing above two small meadows before crossing another moraine and gently descending to the lower end of a long meadow. The grove of aspens at its upper end may hide a few deer, for aspen leaves are part of their summer diet. Leaving the meadow, we arc southwest up to the crest of a nearby lateral moraine, which, from our vantage point, is only a low ridge, though it stands a full 4000 feet above the inundated floor of the Grand Canyon of the Tuolumne River. The glacier that left this moraine was at least that thick.

Our descent along the brushy hillside provides grand views, but the flanking shrubs at times present thorny problems to hikers in shorts. In addition to snow bush—a favorite food—deer have nearby access to aspen, huckleberry oak, scrubby black oak, gooseberry, and willow. If this stretch of trail is too overgrown, it can become essentially impossible to follow. After an initial brief descent southwest and southeast, the brush abates and the trail traverses east for about a mile, then steepens and, on well-built switchbacks, descends southeast toward seemingly distant Tiltill Valley.

The descent ends where thirst-quenching Tiltill Creek spills out onto flat-floored Tiltill Valley. Where the trail crosses the creek you can walk momentarily along its west bank to a small campsite under incense-cedars and pines, which is enjoyable once the mosquitoes abate, usually after mid-July. A cluster of Miwok Indian mortar holes in bedrock lies nearby, under some large black oaks. Also nearby on both sides of the creek are other campsites.

Beyond Tiltill Creek, the trail stays close to the base of the valley's towering north wall. At times, the trail seems too close to it, for it wanders among large blocks of rockfall-deposited talus; however, a trail built in the meadow would often be waterlogged. After about a half mile, the trail turns south to cross a seasonally boggy meadow, our trail being protected by levees and ditches. Nevertheless, before July, you can expect to get wet feet. By the time the meadow dries out, bunchgrasses can grow to thigh height and harbor abundant rodents as well as their predatory rattlesnakes—be careful here. In the meadow's center, you may find a junction with a rarely used trail that heads northeast to the valley's east end, then switchbacks up a gully, bound for the Pacific Crest Trail.

SIDE TRIP TO RANCHERIA CREEK: Of more interest is the start of a relatively easy cross-country route to Rancheria Creek. From this point, you go about 1 mile east along the floor of an obvious canyon to where you have a choice of routes. Avoid the deep, narrow, inviting canyon on the left and continue east about 0.3 mile to an obvious saddle. Some may find a ducked route that ends just north of this saddle, but it is quite exposed and potentially dangerous. From the saddle, Rancheria Creek lies very close below you, and you can find isolated camping near pools and minor cascades for about 0.75 mile downstream and for about 1.25 miles upstream, to the base of some major cascades. Only serious mountaineers will want to continue farther. Near the base of these cascades is the lower end of Deep Canyon, whose traverse is a disappointment. **END OF SIDE TRIP**

In Tiltill Valley, at about 5600 feet in elevation, the second alternate trip to the trailhead continues by heading south to the base of some steep bluffs that bound the valley on the south. Here, it enters a lush stand of aspens, alders, and willows surrounding a small spring. Both the treelike mountain dogwood and the shrubbier, red-barked American dogwood thrive here, shading lady fern, bracken, thimbleberry, raspberry, and currant. A few Douglas firs hug the hillsides here, sharing the coolness with shrubby mountain maples. Upon reaching the canyon wall, our path starts a short climb, taking some well-engineered switchbacks southwest to a large joint-controlled rift. We follow this gently up southwest, past a small, linear pond decked with yellow pond lilies, then we progress through a forest of white fir and incense-cedar. Seasonally fragrant western azalea is a locally dominant understory shrub, joined in more open spots by uncommon white-bugled Washington's lily. Straight as an arrow, our trail slices through a narrow saddle, at 5780 feet, and then gently descends into another straight-sided canyon, this one also trending southwest. Ahead, we'll face a 1200-foot descent to the vicinity of Rancheria Falls.

After a half mile, we angle west out of this canyon onto open slabs, where we have views south over brushy LeConte Point to somber-cliffed Smith Peak. Now the route begins to descend in earnest, high above the forests below. The trail twists itself into numerous sandy, moderate switchbacks, soon dropping to the 5300-foot level, where the slopes can be too warm in summer, and heat-tolerant vegetation exists, including gray pines and canyon live oaks, which offer meager shade. Here, too, we perceive some slivers of Hetch Hetchy Reservoir, bent around sentinel Kolana Rock to the west. Some 600 feet more of open switchbacking descent follow, depositing us, finally, at a junction with the Rancheria Mountain Trail on a manzanita-cloaked sandy hillside. Here, we turn right, down some easy switchbacks, and after 0.3 mile, bend briefly south to find the cool haven of a large, thick conifer grove, in which a short spur trail heads over to popular, spacious Rancheria Falls Camp, which has adjacent cascades, pools, and rainbow trout. Be warned that this popular camping area is often shared with marauding black bears.

Falls Creek cascade and pool about 1.25 miles below Lake Vernon

To complete your route, hike 6.4 miles west from the camp back to O'Shaughnessy Dam. Briefly, this first traverses 0.3 mile west, descends 0.3 mile to a junction with an old trail down to Hetch Hetchy Reservoir, then descends another 0.3 mile via switchbacks to the oak-and-pine-shaded gorge cut by Tiltill Creek. You can get water just above this bridge by making a cautious traverse over to a pool at the brink of the creek's fall. When the current's not too strong, the pool is great to dip in on a hot day. Here, we cross two bridges, the first one high above the creek.

The 3 miles west to Wapama Falls is on a frequently dynamited trail that undulates along a steep hillside past open chaparral and shaded, fly-infested canyon live oaks. This traverse is not level, for it switchbacks on occasion to circumvent some cliffy spots. Eventually, we reach the first of several bridges below the base of Wapama Falls. During some high-runoff years, even these high, sturdy bridges are inundated by seasonally tumultuous Falls Creek.

The next 1.5-mile stretch begins as we soon make a steep, dynamited ascent through a field of huge talus blocks under a tremendous unnamed precipice. Midway along it, we cross an unnamed, minor stream that descends, until about early summer, hundreds of feet, as Tueeulala Falls. Ahead, the route now is mostly open, and we see the obdurate, warship-like prow of Kolana Rock, which forces a constriction in the 8-mile-long reservoir's tadpole shape. Our traverse along the Rancheria Falls Trail ends at a junction with the road on which we began our hike, and we follow it an easy mile over to O'Shaughnessy Dam and our adjacent trailhead. **END OF ALTERNATE ROUTE**

TRIP 10

Moraine Ridge-Wilma Lake-Tiltill Valley Loop

Ⓜ ◯ BPx

DISTANCE: 44.1 miles loop

ELEVATIONS: 3810′/8630′
+7850′/-7850′/±15,700′

SEASON: Mid July to late September

USE: Light beyond Laurel Lake

MAPS: *Lake Eleanor, Kibbie Lake,*
Tiltill Mountain,
Piute Mountain,
Hetch Hetchy Reservoir

TRAIL LOG:

1.0	Rancheria Falls Trail
2.8	Leave closed road at trail junction
4.6	Linear lakelet
5.3	Southwest-descending trail
7.2	Beehive
8.4	Laurel Lake
9.6	Return to Beehive
11.1	Jack Main Canyon Trail
14.2	Top out
15.1	Falls Creek
18.1	Junction in Jack Main Canyon
21.2	Pacific Crest Trail
21.5	Wilma Lake
23.1	Tilden Canyon Trail
25.6	Junction with the cutoff route
29.0	Tiltill Meadow
34.3	Tiltill Valley
37.7	Rancheria Falls camp
44.1	Trailhead

INTRODUCTION: Following a route used around the turn of the 19th century by both illegal sheepherders and their US Army pursuers, the Jack Main Canyon Trail (named for one of the early sheepmen) visits a succession of small subalpine meadows along the course of delightful, cascading Falls Creek. Wilma Lake, the gem of Jack Main Canyon, marks the northernmost point in that glacier-scoured trough, and offers pastoral camping with the opportunity to visit more than 20 fishing and swimming lakes or climb to more than a dozen viewful summits, each within an easy day's hike!

DIRECTIONS TO THE TRAILHEAD: Just 0.6 mile before the park's boundary below the Big Oak Flat Entrance Station, leave Hwy. 120 and drive north 7.5 miles on Evergreen Road to its junction with the Hetch Hetchy Road. Turn right and go 8.5 miles to a junction left. Backpackers turn here, park in the obvious parking area by the road's start, then walk a half mile on the road to O'Shaughnessy Dam. Dayhikers continue driving 0.7 mile past the junction to the dam, beyond which is parking. Trail begins in map section B3.

DESCRIPTION: On most summer days, you should start early in the morning, since the switchbacking route up from the reservoir is only partly shaded, and summer temperatures can reach into the 90s by noon. Carry sufficient water; in late season it's two or more hours before reaching water. You begin by starting across the top of O'Shaughnessy Dam, then enter a 500-foot-long tunnel blasted through solid granite when the original dam was raised 85 feet in 1938. Emerging from this bat haven, the formerly paved road traverses above the rocky west shore of Hetch Hetchy Reservoir in a pleasant grove of Douglas fir, gray pine, big-leaf maple, and bay trees. One mile into our route, we reach the junction with the Rancheria Falls Trail (Trip 11), just before our route's first switchback.

Keeping to the former road, we ascend moderately steep switchbacks and have better views up the reservoir of LeConte Point and the Grand Canyon of the Tuolumne River.

The last of eight switchbacks swings north into a gully with a trail junction on a small flat, where we leave the closed road. With one third of the distance covered and with half of the elevation gain under your belt, you start up a trail through a partly burned forest of ponderosa pines, sugar pines, and other conifers. In a quarter mile you reach a mile-high creeklet, which, although diminutive, usually flows through the summer. This is your first reliable water, and people have camped hereabouts.

Unlike the closed road you ascended, which maintains a nearly constant grade, your ascending trail varies, being locally steep, moderate, gentle, or even briefly down. You'll eventually climb 1000 feet above the creeklet before the serious climbing ends. About a half mile beyond the creeklet, your trail curves east and levels off, and you may want to rest. Ahead, the trail climbs north, then northwest, and then the serious climbing ends with a curve east to cross a crest of a lateral moraine. On this ascent, look for linear deposits, which also are lateral moraines. Once on top of a

moraine crest, you'll immediately reach a shallow, linear lakelet, which holds water well into summer.

Your hike ahead is now relatively easy. After rounding the linear lakelet's east end, the trail crosses the broad moraine's crest, drops momentarily, and then ascends 0.4 mile through an open white fir forest to a junction with a southwest-descending trail. Laurel Lake, though only 0.75 mile northwest of us, is at least 2.5 trail miles away by either trail we can take, and one wonders why a trail was not built directly to it. If you've not found water so far, take the trail southwest a quarter mile down to always reliable Frog Creek. Rather than ascend back up to the junction, you might ascend first along the west side of the creek, then along the west side of the lake's outlet creek.

From your junction, 5.3 miles from your trailhead, follow the often shady trail northeast, dip to cross a bracken-bordered creeklet, then soon hike alongside a linear

Along Moraine Ridge

meadow that, in season, is profuse with arrow-leaved senecio and Bigelow's sneezeweed, two kinds of sunflowers. The meadow pinches off at a low gap, beyond which we quickly find ourselves in the southwest corner of a triangular meadow. Staying among white firs and lodgepole pines, we parallel the meadow's edge northeast over to its east corner, called the Beehive, where there is a trail junction. About 20 yards before it, just within the meadow, is a usually reliable spring. Just beyond the junction, among trees, is a spacious campsite.

With most of our ascent behind us, we turn left and walk northwest 160 yards on the Laurel Lake Trail to reach another trail junction. Here, a path that loops around Laurel Lake's north shore branches north, while a shorter trail to the lake's outlet strikes west. Following this latter route, we drop easily down into a white-fir-shaded gully and then broad Frog Creek, which could be a wet ford in early season. Along its north bank, we contour west briefly, then ascend steeply to a heavily forested ridge before gently dropping to good camps near the outlet of Laurel Lake, where you spend your first night. A brief stint brings us to a junction with the north-shore loop trail, branching northwest to the best campsites (and more secluded ones beyond). At fairly deep 60-acre Laurel Lake, fishing is fair for rainbow trout.

The next day, return to the Beehive and take the Lake Vernon Trail for a gentle ascent northeast to a forested glade, then moderately above it to a nearby morainal crest, 1.3 miles from the Beehive. Here the more popular Lake Vernon Trail starts a descent northeast to the lake. We, however, veer north on the Jack Main Canyon Trail to begin a long, sandy ascent of Moraine Ridge. In a couple of minutes, we cross a minor saddle, then in a similar time reach a second one, where we reach the actual crest of Moraine Ridge. In 0.3 mile, we make a generally moderate ascent up the crest, then have a nearly level crest traverse for another 0.3 mile. We then resume climbing and, over the first 0.3 mile of this 2-mile ascent,

MORAINE RIDGE

This entire ridge was completely buried under ice by the last glacier, not just by its predecessors, as previously thought. One sees fresh Tioga-age boulders along the entire ascent, and they are especially numerous on the summit area. From just north of it, another "Moraine Ridge" with similar glacial deposits parallels ours southwest. Between the two is a shallow hanging valley that at first appears unglaciated. Not so. The glacial ice down it was thin, and so flowed slowly, taking with it only sparse sediments.

you can obtain water quite easily by descending north about 200 yards to an unnamed creeklet. Drought-tolerant Jeffrey pines dominate the conifers until supplanted above 7500 feet by red firs and western white pines. Along this ascent, there are some views down into the Falls Creek drainage, including glimpses of Lake Vernon, ponds and lakelets beyond it, and the cascading outlet creek of rockbound Branigan Lake. After about 1100 feet of elevation gain, generally at an optimal gradient for backpackers, we top out at about 8120 feet, just below the actual summit of Moraine Ridge.

Around the summit area, we have panoramas to the north and east, stretching from the broken, water-streaked summits of Richardson, Mahan, and Andrews peaks in the foreground to the distant Saurian Crest, Piute Mountain, Sawtooth Ridge, and Mt. Conness. Our trail now begins a 0.3-mile descent, aided with short switchbacks, down to a flat with a dogleg in a sea- sonal creeklet, near which you could camp.

[S] **SIDE TRIP TO OTTER LAKES BASIN:** For remote camping, you could head cross-country about 0.6 mile north gently up through a broad crest gap to the brink of Frog Creek canyon and then visit one or more of its lakes, which include Miwok and Bearup lakes. By following Frog Creek above Bearup Lake, you eventually would reach the Otter Lakes basin, above our trail's destination, Wilma Lake. **END OF SIDE TRIP**

From the flat, our trail toward Wilma is more demanding—steep, tight switchbacks of riprapped and dynamited granite plunge down along a joint-controlled ravine to a hop across our seasonal creeklet. Immediately beyond it is Falls Creek, which begins a seriously cascading descent toward Lake Vernon. If you took a trail northeast from that lake and then a cross-country route north up the cascades, you would join the trail here. We now begin our ascent of Jack Main Canyon, and the first mile of walking along Falls Creek sets the tone for the rest of our journey: The trail undulates moderately, alternately visiting benches of sunny, glaciated granite dotted with huckleberry-oak thickets and precariously rooted western junipers, and pocket stands of lodgepoles and stately red firs, their canopy shading twinberry, mountain ash, and red elderberry. We pass above a triad of sand-banked pools, then descend slightly to a horseshoe bend in Falls Creek that has a grove of red firs with good camping nearby. East of this bend our still-undulating trail winds among open slabs and up to a piney bench.

⑤ **SIDE TRIP TO ANDREWS AND BRANIGAN LAKES:** Here, one may choose to leave the trail and strike south across Falls Creek and up through a gap west of striated Andrews Peak to Andrews and Branigan lakes. **END OF SIDE TRIP**

Our path turns north, dropping to the largest and most beautiful of a number of unnamed lakelets in lower Jack Main Canyon. Shaped somewhat like a horseshoe, this shallow lakelet reflects the broken south face of Mahan Peak while supporting a shoreline garden of Parish's yampah and Bigelow's sneezeweed.

Our route skirts its north shore, then veers south around another pond, following T blazes back to the north bank of Falls Creek. Here, we turn east, on a 30-foot-wide isthmus between the stream and an aspen-bordered pond that lies just north of the trail, fed only by ground water. From the head of this pond, we climb north to a gap, then drop easily to a large meadow known as Paradise Valley. Here, our path keeps near the screen of infringing lodgepole pines, leaps the outlet stream of Mahan Lake, and comes to a large complex of streamside campsites surrounding a junction, 3.3 miles up Jack Main Canyon, with a cutoff east to Tilden Canyon.

⑤ **SIDE TRIP TO BRANIGAN LAKES:** This hot, unworthy route is recommended only for those headed for the Branigan Lakes. To take it, wade across sandy Falls Creek just below a wide pool and find the vague trail as it swings east around the south side of a grassy mosquito pond. The little-used route then climbs tortuously southeast through pockets of mat manzanita and open lodgepole pines to a viewful knoll. Next, this route drops momentarily east, then turns southwest up a narrow rock corridor. Near the head of this herbaceously floored ravine, where further progress seems blocked by a talus slide, the path turns abruptly and steeply up to the east. By heading cross-country southwest in a linear, joint-controlled canyon, you would reach Upper Branigan Lake in a half mile. Ahead, the cutoff trail bends back to the northeast and climbs easily to a tarn-dotted flat. From here, you switchback steeply east over gneissic-banded intrusive rocks into a forested canyon. Lodgepoles and hemlocks shade the way as the drainage heads northeast, then south, to 8575 feet, where the route tops out in a narrow gap. From this pass, this lateral trail drops southeast to the nearby Tilden Canyon Trail. **END OF SIDE TRIP**

To finish our hike up Jack Main Canyon to Wilma Lake, 3.3 miles away, we slog through sand beyond the Tilden

Canyon cutoff, quickly reaching the lodge-pole-shaded shores of a lake that is back-dropped by a lichen-covered cliff. Beyond it, we're led back through a gap to Falls Creek, now a wide lagoon, and we walk north near its meanders, which are hidden by tall willows. Above us, the ancient Falls Creek glacier enhanced the resistant rock of Peak 8273 with some fantastic fins, which, today, provide excellent multipitch rock climbs. Later, Sybol Lake, a seasonal lily pond in an encroaching meadow, is passed with only a glimpse of it through lodge-poles and aspens.

North of Sybol Lake, Falls Creek, true to its name, tumbles through a narrow gorge of mafic rock and slides over some smooth slabs that are ideal for bathers, and our path takes some rocky, dynamited switchbacks up along it. Above the gorge, our streamside way is more gentle as it winds northeast over slabs dotted with erratic boulders, mat manzanita, and hummocks bearing dense stands of lodgepoles. Note that many of the lodgepoles here-abouts have prominent "witches' brooms"—bizarrely twisted branches of too-dense needles—that are caused by a virus that disrupts their growth pattern. Presently, we spy turf-bounded Wilma Lake lying across the stream, in a pleasant mixed-conifer forest. Now our route ascends a final shoulder and drops to a large, dry flat where the Pacific Crest Trail leads up Jack Main Canyon (Trip 36). You'll see a seasonal rangers' cabin nearby.

On the PCT, we turn east to wade broad Falls Creek near some heavily used camps, then striking southeast, we soon reach Wilma Lake, which has rainbow trout. The PCT skirts close along the lake's south shore, past lodgepoles and hemlocks. We then wind moderately up a canyon past two pleasant tarns to a junction with the Tilden Lake Trail, which ascends north to its namesake.

At this junction, we turn south down the PCT for 110 yards to the Tilden Canyon Trail, and take it southwest down along Tilden Canyon Creek under an often

mosquitoey lodgepole canopy. This shady walk soon reaches a pear-shaped, grassy tarn rimmed with Labrador tea and bilberry. From its west end, we bend south, following blazes and ducks in open lodgepole stands interspersed with erratics and glaciated slabs. In about a mile, we again come close to Tilden Canyon Creek—here, a wide lagoon cut deep through meadow turf—where one might disturb a family of mallard ducks. Pressing on, we negotiate a small rise, then ascend once more, this time via steep, eroded, rocky switchbacks, past a junction with the cutoff route west to lower Jack Main Canyon. The grind abates minutes later, when we level off at about 8630 feet just below a low summit on a glacier-smoothed ridge. It is well worth a minute taken to reach it, for it presents sweeping panoramas of northern Yosemite. You can look all the way up Jack Main Canyon to Bond Pass; then, swinging your gaze east, spot Tower Peak, Matterhorn Peak, Piute Mountain, and the Cathedral Range from Fairview Dome to Mt. Lyell.

Resuming our trek, we walk south along a low, broad ridge, then drop on a switchback to an easy traverse that is shaded by red firs, mountain hemlocks, and western white pines. Uncommon bleeding hearts and common dwarf lousewort grow in the shade here.

⑤ **SIDE TRIP TO LAKE 8576 AND LAKE 8531:** After about a quarter mile, you can leave the trail and head west about 200 yards to a small lake with isolated camping. For even more remote camping, follow its outlet creeklet just over a half mile south to a larger lake by the east base of Tiltill Mountain. **END OF SIDE TRIP**

Presently, we ascend to a broad, forested saddle, which ties with the previously mentioned elevation of 8630 feet for our route's high point, then we descend to a diminishing lakelet, our last permanent water source for about 8 miles, in Tiltill Valley. Below the lakelet, we walk for a while beside its meadowed outlet creek, then veer away on a rocky descent around a steep bluff before resuming a creekside route under moderate forest cover. We walk easily for a mile down through an understory of yarrow, meadow rue, aster, senecio, and corn lily to small Tiltill Meadow, in which once stood a cabin built by H. G. Kibbie.

South of Tiltill Meadow, we continue in the same easy manner for a half mile, then turn southwest down a dry morainal slope to a red fir grove beside a small meadow drained by a step-across branch of Rancheria Creek. Now begins a 2300-foot descent to Tiltill Valley. Chaparral areas allow views south and east over the bluffs of Smith Peak and Rancheria Mountain. Moderate switchbacks ease our descent to 7300 feet, and then we drop more gently southwest down a sandy canyon and look west to a brush-covered Mt. Gibson. Next, we work south along a bouldery, brushy bench, and then begin the final 1300-foot plunge. At first we stay on the north side of a ridge, descending steeply on sand in the relative shade of tall huckleberry-oak brush and scattered Jeffrey pines. But below 6600 feet, we swing onto the ridge's south face, which allows our first views of lush Tiltill Valley and, beyond it, Hetch Hetchy Reservoir. But the south face also subjects us to the full heat of the midday sun.

Eventually, at 6320 feet, we reach a gap on the ridge, which affords some shade and a good spot to appreciate the size of the Rancheria Creek and Tuolumne River glaciers. At this elevation, during the height of the last glaciation, we would have been buried under about 1700 feet of ice, since, in our vicinity, the sea of ice of the Yosemite north country had a surface elevation of about 8000 feet, if not more. Below this instructional rest stop are more steep, rocky, exposed switchbacks, this time leading east through canyon live oak scrub. Eventually, the trail bends south and lowers us to the long-awaited shade of a grove of incense-cedars, black oaks, and Jeffrey pines at the eastern edge of Tiltill Valley, at 5600 feet elevation.

In Tiltill Valley, find a trail that heads south to the base of some steep bluffs that bound the valley on the south. Here, it enters a lush stand of aspens, alders, and willows surrounding a small spring. Upon reaching the canyon wall, our path starts a short climb, taking some well-engineered switchbacks southwest to a large joint-controlled rift. This we follow gently up southwest, past a small, linear pond decked with yellow pond lilies, then we progress through a forest of white fir and incense-cedar. Seasonally fragrant western azalea is a locally dominant understory shrub, joined in more open spots by uncommon white-bugled Washington's lily. Straight as an arrow, our trail slices through a narrow saddle, at 5780 feet, and then gently descends into another straight-sided canyon, this one also trending southwest. Ahead, we'll face a 1200-foot descent to the vicinity of Rancheria Falls.

After a half mile, we angle west out of this canyon onto open slabs, where we have views south over brushy LeConte Point to somber-cliffed Smith Peak. Now the route begins to descend in earnest, high above the forests below. The trail twists itself into numerous sandy, moderate switchbacks, soon dropping to the 5300-foot level, where the slopes can be too warm in summer, and heat-tolerant vegetation grows, including gray pines and canyon live oaks, which offer meager shade. Here, too, we perceive some slivers of Hetch Hetchy Reservoir, bent around sentinel Kolana Rock to the west. Some 600 feet more of occasionally open switchbacking descent follow, depositing us, finally, at a junction with the Rancheria Mountain Trail on a manzanita-cloaked sandy hillside. Here, we turn right, down some easy switchbacks, and after 0.3 mile bend briefly south to find the cool haven of a large, thick conifer grove, in which a short spur trail heads over to popular, spacious Rancheria Falls Camp, which has adjacent cascades, pools, and rainbow trout. Be warned that this popular camping area is often shared with marauding black bears.

To complete your route, hike 6.4 miles west from the camp back to O'Shaughnessy Dam. Briefly, this first traverses 0.3 mile west, descends 0.3 mile to a junction with an old trail down to Hetch Hetchy Reservoir, then descends another 0.3 mile via switchbacks to the oak-and-pine-shaded gorge cut by Tiltill Creek. You can get water just above this bridge by making a cautious traverse over to a pool at the brink of the creek's fall. When the current's not too strong, the pool is great to dip in on a hot day. Here, we cross two bridges, the first one high above the creek.

The 3 miles west to Wapama Falls is on a frequently dynamited trail that undulates along a steep hillside past open chaparral and shaded, fly-infested canyon live oaks. This traverse is not level, for it switchbacks on occasion to circumvent some cliffy spots. Eventually, we reach the first of several bridges below the base of Wapama Falls. During some high-runoff years, even these high, sturdy bridges are inundated by seasonally tumultuous Falls Creek.

The next 1.5-mile stretch begins as we soon make a steep, dynamited ascent through a field of huge talus blocks under a tremendous unnamed precipice. Midway along it, we cross an unnamed, minor stream that descends, until about early summer, hundreds of feet, as Tueeulala Falls. Ahead, the route now is mostly open, and we see the obdurate, warship-like prow of Kolana Rock, which forces a constriction in the 8-mile-long reservoir's tadpole shape. Our traverse along the Rancheria Falls Trail ends at a junction with the road on which we began our hike, and we follow it an easy mile over to O'Shaughnessy Dam and our adjacent trailhead.

TRIP 11

Hetch Hetchy to Rancheria Falls Camp

Ⓜ ↗ DH, BP

DISTANCE: 12.8 miles out and back

ELEVATIONS: 3810'/4520'
+1490'/-780'/±4540'

SEASON: May to October

USE: Moderate

MAPS: *Lake Eleanor,
Hetch Hetchy Reservoir*

TRAIL LOG:

1.0	Rancheria Falls Trail
2.5	Wapama Falls
5.5	Tiltill Creek
6.4	Rancheria Falls camp

INTRODUCTION: A stately grove of pines and incense-cedars harboring a spacious camping area near Rancheria Falls marks the terminus of this hike. Its cascades and pools are the goals for some, but also rewarding are inspirational vistas of the awesome cliffs and early-summer waterfalls seen along the undulating path on the north wall of Hetch Hetchy Reservoir. Since you are traversing above a reservoir, you might think that this is an easy hike. Well, it basically is easy to Wapama Falls, but then you face gains and losses of hundreds of feet. Also, the route, being quite open and at a relatively low elevation, can be quite sunny and hot, and so on a summer's day, it is best begun in early morning.

DIRECTIONS TO THE TRAILHEAD: Just 0.6 mile before the park's boundary below the Big Oak Flat Entrance Station, leave Hwy. 120 and drive north 7.5 miles on Evergreen Road to its junction with the Hetch Hetchy Road. Turn right and go 8.5 miles to a junction left. Backpackers turn here, park in the obvious parking area by the road's start, then walk a half mile on the road to O'Shaughnessy Dam. Dayhikers continue driving 0.7 mile past the junction to the dam, beyond which is parking. Trail begins in map section B3.

DESCRIPTION: Our trail starts across the top of O'Shaughnessy Dam and, after 1 mile along a road just above Hetch Hetchy Reservoir, it reaches the junction with the Rancheria Falls Trail. On it, we descend gently first south and then east across an exfoliating granitic nose, and then switchback once down to a broad, sloping ledge, sparingly shaded by grayish-green foliage of gray pines and scrubby mountain mahogany. From April through June, you may see an assortment of wildflowers in bloom, along with patches of mosslike selaginella, a relative of ferns. We follow this ledge a half mile to an unnamed, minor stream that descends, until about early summer, hundreds of feet as Tueeulala Falls. Beyond it, we wind down along the north shore of Hetch Hetchy Reservoir to a bridge over a steep ravine, where our views east to the lake's head expand impressively. On the north wall stands multifaceted Hetch Hetchy Dome, guarding split-level Wapama Falls. Opposite this monolith towers the obdurate, warship-like prow of Kolana Rock, which forces a constriction in the 8-mile-long reservoir's tadpole shape.

A few minutes of easy traverse east from here end at a steep, dynamited descent through a field of huge talus blocks under a tremendous unnamed precipice. Soon, if we're passing this way in early summer, flecks of spray dampen our cobbly path, as we come to the first of several bridges below the base of Wapama Falls. During some high-runoff years, even these high, sturdy bridges are inundated by seasonally tumultuous Falls Creek.

East of Wapama Falls, our rocky path leads up around the base of a steep bulge of glacier-polished and striated granite under a fly-infested canopy of canyon live oak,

Tueeulala Falls

bay tree, poison oak, and wild-grape vines. Huge flakes of shattered granite also dot this bench, spalled from the walls above. After our terrace tapers off, the frequently dynamited trail undulates along a steep hillside in open chaparral of yerba santa and mountain mahogany, switchbacking on occasion to circumvent some cliffy spots. Eventually, our path descends to the oak-and-pine-shaded gorge cut by Tiltill Creek, and we cross two bridges, the second one high above the creek. You can get water just above this bridge by making a cautious traverse over to a pool at the brink of the creek's fall. When the current's not too strong, the pool is great to dip in on a hot day.

Beyond the creek, our route climbs the gorge's east slope via a set of tight switchbacks to emerge 250 feet higher on a gentle hillside of sunny, gray-lichened slabs, gray pines, and whiteleaf manzanitas. Where this ascent eases off, you may see, on your right, the start of an old, abandoned trail, which nevertheless is in very good condition. It follows a descending ridge just south of Tiltill Creek, ending just above Hetch Hetchy Reservoir. Signs down there advise you that no camping is allowed within 200 feet of the shoreline. Camping in this vicinity avoids the crowds that are sometimes found at the Rancheria Falls Camp.

Soon, our way levels off, and we spy Rancheria Creek. By walking a few paces right, we have an excellent view of it. The creek here slides invitingly over broad rock slabs, its pools superb for skinny-dipping. Every step of your way has been on granite, but just 0.2 mile past your vantage point you may note a different substrate: a small deposit, essentially granitic, which is a tiny remnant of a much larger deposit that was transported to this spot in a south-directed eruption of latite tuff about 9.5 million years ago. More important, the deposit shows that no erosion of the bedrock here has occurred, despite repeated passage by glaciers up to 4000 feet thick. If you could have hiked here 9.5 million years ago, you would have seen that the Hetch Hetchy canyonland would have been almost as deep and wide back then as it is today. Conventional wisdom, based on ignorance of canyon-bottomland deposits, posits that today's deep canyon was shallow (and the Sierra low) back then.

Just 0.1 mile past the volcanic remnants, we reach a junction with a short trail to the spacious Rancheria Falls Camp. Rancheria Creek is a moment's walk away, and you can head up and down it in pursuit of cascades and pools. One nearby cascade is a small fall, about 25 feet high, which, in high volume, shoots over a ledge of resistant dark intrusive rock. Fishing below the falls might yield pan-size rainbow trout. Be warned that this popular camping area is often shared with marauding black bears.

TRIP 12

Rancheria Mountain-Pleasant Valley-Bear Valley-Tiltill Valley Semiloop

S **♫** **BPx**

DISTANCE: 53.7 miles semiloop

ELEVATIONS: 3810′/9490′
+12,040′/-12,040′/±24,080′

SEASON: Mid-July to late September

USE: Light

MAPS: *Lake Eleanor,
Hetch Hetchy Reservoir,
Ten Lakes, Piute Mountain,
Tiltill Mountain*

TRAIL LOG:

1.0	Rancheria Falls Trail
2.5	Wapama Falls
5.5	Tiltill Creek
6.4	Rancheria Falls camp
11.7	Reliable stream
16.2	Pleasant Valley Trail
20.7	Bear Valley
21.8	Bear Valley Lake
23.8	Pacific Crest Trail
26.3	Stubblefield Canyon creek
29.7	Tilden Lake Trail
31.2	Wilma Lake
32.7	Tilden Canyon Trail
43.9	Tiltill Valley
47.3	Rancheria Falls camp
53.7	Trailhead

INTRODUCTION: The broad, conifer-robed massif of Rancheria Mountain affords a generally snow-free, early-summer route into the Yosemite north country. Hikers who don't demand a spectacular, high-level trail will find that the floral gardens and the serene forests on this north rim of the Grand Canyon of the Tuolumne, coupled with secluded hemlock-bower camping beside Bear Valley Lake, compensate for the prolonged climb in.

This trip also includes an alternate route, which is this book's longest trip in the Yosemite north country, with a distance of 69.8 miles and an elevation gain and loss of 38,920 feet. This route also visits the greatest variety of subalpine settings to be found anywhere in the park. This lightly traveled path through Pleasant Valley to subalpine Rodgers Meadow is a more isolated alternative to using the Pacific Crest Trail to reach the Benson Lake region.

DIRECTIONS TO THE TRAILHEAD: Just 0.6 mile before the park's boundary below the Big Oak Flat Entrance Station, leave Hwy. 120 and drive north 7.5 miles on Evergreen Road to its junction with the Hetch Hetchy Road. Turn right and go 8.5 miles to a junction left. Backpackers turn here, park in the obvious parking area by the road's start, then walk a half mile on the road to O'Shaughnessy Dam. Dayhikers continue driving 0.7 mile past the junction to the dam, beyond which is parking. Trail begins in map section B3.

DESCRIPTION: Our trail starts across the top of O'Shaughnessy Dam and, after 1 mile along a road just above Hetch Hetchy Reservoir, it reaches the junction with the Rancheria Falls Trail. On it, we descend gently first south and then east across an exfoliating granitic nose, then switchback once down to a broad, sloping ledge, sparingly shaded by grayish-green foliage of gray pines and scrubby mountain mahogany, with an assortment of wildflowers in bloom from April through June. We follow this ledge a half mile to a minor stream below seasonal Tueeulala Falls. Beyond it, we wind down along the north shore of Hetch Hetchy Reservoir to a bridge over a steep ravine, where our views east to the lake's head expand impressively. On the north wall stands multifaceted Hetch Hetchy Dome, guarding split-level Wapama Falls. Opposite this monolith towers the obdurate, warship-like prow of Kolana Rock, which forces a constriction in the 8-mile-long reservoir's tadpole shape.

A few minutes of easy traverse east from here end at a steep, dynamited descent through a field of huge talus blocks under a tremendous unnamed precipice. Soon, if we're passing this way in early summer, flecks of spray dampen our cobbly path, as we come to the first of several bridges below the base of Wapama Falls. During some high-runoff years, even these high, sturdy bridges are inundated by seasonally tumultuous Falls Creek.

East of Wapama Falls, our rocky path leads up around the base of a steep bulge of glacier-polished and striated granite under a fly-infested canopy of canyon live oak, bay tree, poison oak, and wild-grape vines. Huge flakes of shattered granite also dot this bench, spalled from the walls above. After our terrace tapers off, the frequently dynamited trail undulates along a steep hillside in open chaparral of yerba santa and mountain mahogany, switchbacking on occasion to circumvent some cliffy spots. Eventually, our path descends to the oak-and-pine-shaded gorge cut by Tiltill Creek, and we cross two bridges, the second one high above the creek. You can get water just above this bridge by making a cautious traverse over to a pool at the brink of the creek's fall. When the current's not too strong, the pool is great to dip in on a hot day.

Beyond the creek, our route climbs the gorge's east slope via a set of tight switchbacks to emerge 250 feet higher on a gentle hillside of sunny, gray-lichened slabs, gray pines, and whiteleaf manzanitas. Where this ascent eases off, you may see, on your right, the start of an old, abandoned trail, which nevertheless is in very good condition. It follows a descending ridge just south of Tiltill Creek, ending just above Hetch Hetchy Reservoir. Signs down there advise you that no camping is allowed within 200 feet of the shoreline. Camping in this vicinity avoids the crowds that are sometimes found at the Rancheria Falls Camp.

Hetch Hetchy Reservoir, from high on closed road

Soon, our way levels off, and we spy Rancheria Creek. By walking a few paces right, we have an excellent view of it. The creek here slides invitingly over broad rock slabs, its pools superb for skinny-dipping. Just 0.3 mile past the vantage point, we reach a junction with a short trail to the spacious Rancheria Falls Camp, and here we spend our first night. Rancheria Creek is a moment's walk away, and you can head up and down it in pursuit of cascades and pools. One nearby cascade is a small fall, about 25 feet high, which, in high volume, shoots over a ledge of resistant dark intrusive rock. Fishing below the falls might yield pan-size rainbow trout. Be warned that this popular camping area is often shared with marauding black bears.

The next morning, ascend 0.3 mile moderately up to a junction with the Tiltill Valley Trail, which we will descend, then 300 yards beyond to a bridge over Rancheria Creek. This stream bumps and slides frothily below through a series of well-worn potholes and slabs, inviting divers, swimmers, and sunbathers. Tank up on water at this creek, for your next source will be after an often hot 3200-foot ascent

and 5 miles farther, on the west slope of Rancheria Mountain. Our trail now ascends briefly south past brush and scattered gray pines, then commences a 1300-foot switchbacking ascent. The slopes are fairly open, though you can stop and rest in the shade of black oaks, which are the dominant tree along this stretch. As we progress higher, vistas west over the reservoir and Kolana Rock improve. About 2 miles past Rancheria Creek, we finally top a 6200-foot nose, littered with gravel and boulder glacial deposits.

[S] **SIDE TRIP TO LECONTE POINT:** This lies just east of an obvious saddle, from which many hikers climb a crest to its summit, LeConte Point, at 6388 feet. Should you wish to visit this spectacular viewpoint—a sometimes pilgrimage destination for Sierra Club hikers—leave the trail before the nose, at any point where you feel comfortable heading to the saddle. **END OF SIDE TRIP**

Onward, our trail traverses a half mile east along sandy chaparral slopes to the head of a minor hanging canyon, in which we encounter the first white firs of our journey. The ascent resumes on dusty switchbacks up past some fire-cleared forest openings that now support a thriving population of deer. At 6750 feet, we swing onto a south-facing chaparral slope and can look south across the Grand Canyon of the Tuolumne River to the rolling upland region across it. This harbors hidden White Wolf Resort and Campground, a mere 5 air miles away, but some four times that by extremely strenuous trails. From a minor bench, our path enters a burned area and first ascends on a comfortable gradient then begins to switchback after a half mile. We tediously zigzag up them, climbing 300 feet in elevation, then enter forest slopes, mantled with volcanic deposits, as we approach a reliable stream. This we parallel east for 0.3 mile before crossing it at about 7700 feet elevation. Above its opposite bank is a mostly open, gentle, gravelly slope adequate for camping.

Onward, our trail soon ascends under lodgepoles and red firs to another creek, a half mile farther. In a pleasant glade on its north bank is the site of a former log cabin, constructed, like the one in Tiltill Meadow, by pioneer fish-propagator H.G. Kibbie. Beyond this site, we briefly parallel the creek, then angle northeast away from it, ascending up over a moraine divide back to the first creek that we met, 1.75 miles beyond where we first crossed it, and now up at an elevation of about 8250 feet. Standing almost head high in the height of flowering season are stalks of blue-bonnet larkspur, slender lupine, umbrella-leaved cow parsnip, red elderberry, and four-petalled monument plant. Reaching to between knee height and waist height are lacy meadow rue, purple aster, white yarrow, yellow senecio, aromatic mint, and leather-leaved mule ears. Under all these, at times, can be a mat of Jacob's ladder, which can grow in large numbers. The abundance of these wildflowers is due in part to the streamside environment, but also to volcanic soils, which are more nutrient rich than are granitic soils. The 7-plus-mile route from the Rancheria Falls camp leaves many hikers exhausted, since they'll have ascended some 4000 feet with a heavy pack. You may find yourself camping in this vicinity, too weary to continue.

From this flower garden, our path turns east-northeast up a broad, shallow swale and soon leaves lush surroundings behind as it climbs easily along dry volcanic slopes of a broad, low, west-heading ridge from the northeast summit of Rancheria Mountain.

This volcanic-mudflow material and the overlying darker layer of harder andesite, which caps three summits, settled here some 9.5 million years ago, having come from the Little Walker caldera, about 28 miles to the north. Enough material was transported to not only deeply bury the park's northern uplands, but also to fill the already deep Tuolumne River canyon sufficiently to spill over its two rims below Hetch Hetchy Valley. Most of the easily erodible material in the park was removed by thick glaciers, but since our summit was blanketed with only thin, barely flowing ice, much of it still persists.

After a mile past the creek, our way becomes a ridgetop amble, bringing us, in a half mile, to our high point on Rancheria Mountain, at 8670 feet. Ahead, we have a 1.2-mile-long, two-stage descent of about 600 feet, first to cross one minor saddle, then to reach a second, larger one. Five switchbacks spare our knees on the descent, and, where the trees disperse momentarily, we look northeast to Sawtooth Ridge and closer Volunteer Peak. A short distance later, atop an 8060-foot saddle some 16.25 miles from our trailhead, we reach a junction with the Pleasant Valley Trail.

A ALTERNATE TRIP TO PLEASANT VALLEY AND BEYOND: Whereas the main route takes 15 miles to reach Wilma Lake, those wanting an extended wilderness experience can take 32 miles to reach it by starting on the Pleasant Valley Trail. On it, you branch southeast, then head more eastward down a shallow draw to the rim of Piute Creek canyon's 1200-foot western scarp. Emerging from a thick stand of aspens, you are treated with superb vistas northeast over sparsely forested Pleasant Valley to a rolling landscape of dark exfoliating domes and slopes above Piute Creek, terminating this side of spiry Sawtooth Ridge. A part of little-visited Irwin Bright Lake, one of several shallow, granite-rimmed lakes arcing around Pleasant Valley, can be seen on a forested bench below. We switchback moderately to steeply downward across slopes of volcanic deposits, which, viewed from the opposite side of Piute Creek canyon, appear as a broad V.

Around the start of the 20th century, Henry W. Turner saw it and inferred that an ancient Tuolumne River once flowed west through a canyon now buried by the volcanic deposits. Actually, these V-shaped deposits are merely uneroded remnants filling V-shaped side gullies of canyons. Nevertheless, this ancient idea of a buried river, like other Sierran geomyths, refuses to die.

Below 7500 feet, the trail swings northeast past huckleberry oaks, scattered conifers, and black oaks. Soon, we reach a hanging-valley aspen grove and walk in the seasonal creek bed that drains it, then descend along the stream in a narrow chute. A few short switchbacks lead us north from this ravine down to the floor of Pleasant Valley, at 6860 feet, and 1.9 miles beyond the trail junction. Here we find a mixed forest of dominant lodgepole pines plus red and white firs, Jeffrey pines, junipers, and incense-cedars. Not seen are singleleaf pinyon pines, which are rare in the park; the closest grove is about a mile south and 400 feet below us, on dry slopes west above Piute Creek.

A few minutes' amble through the forest brings us to a trail branching northeast 0.2 mile to large packer camps beside a pool on Piute Creek. From this spur trail, our main path veers south to momentarily reach shaded Piute Creek, incised deeply in cobbly alluvium. This ford could be a 50-foot-long wade in early summer. On the east bank, another spur trail heads upstream to more camps, but we turn

downstream to soon begin a moderate, if short, ascent up dark slopes of diorite. From the south shoulder of a low ridge, the trail then dips easily to a crossing of Table Lake's outlet stream, 0.9 mile past our arrival at Pleasant Valley. The best campsites by Table Lake are reached by ascending north along an open bench just before crossing this stream. Between the main lake, which is ringed with low, broken bluffs and shrubs, and its southern arm, which is shallow and dotted with pond lilies, is a dry peninsula, with sparse Jeffrey pines and the best campsites. Fishing for rainbow trout in Table, Irwin Bright, and Saddle Horse lakes is good due to a scarcity of anglers.

Eastward from the Table Lake environs, the main trail passes through an aspen grove, in which an old trail once headed north for Irwin Bright Lake. Near this old junction, we hop a stream, and then ascend rapidly onto brushy slopes. Soon, we pant up the inevitable rocky switchbacks and are partly consoled by an improving picture of Pleasant Valley. Our zigzag course persists until 7600 feet, where we top a bench to find, in another aspen grove, the stream we crossed lower down. Now our climb moderates, proceeding southeast through alternately well-watered and dry-rocky plant associations, to a ridgetop just under 8000 feet. This open spot lets us look south down Piute Creek's gorge and beyond to 9782-foot Double Rock, and it also marks the start of an undulating traverse south. On it, we cross numerous small, steep gullies, usually under shade, above Piute Creek's gaping canyon, and, in a mile, reach a sloping aspen glade, which has a junction with the southwest-descending Pate Valley Trail, 2.4 miles past the outlet stream.

SIDE TRIP TO PATE VALLEY: Probably no one would want to make this dry 3500-foot drop over 4.7 miles to Pate Valley. Furthermore, when this steep trail is not maintained, it can become seriously overgrown with brush. However, if you are trying to follow the Tuolumne River canyon from Hetch Hetchy up to Tuolumne Meadows, you would need to descend this trail to the valley before hiking 20.5 miles up-canyon to the meadows (parts of trips 34 and 33, hiked in reverse). **END OF SIDE TRIP**

From this junction, you have a 4.2-mile stretch to Rodgers Meadow. The route starts initially southeast and quickly climbs south across an open volcanic slope, where a small spring trickles across the path. Excellent views and myriad wildflowers recommend this spot for a break. Then we gear down for a short but initially steep ascent east to the crest of a bouldery, conifer-robed moraine. From it, we descend east across volcanic slopes and, in about a mile, reach our low point along the north rim of the Grand Canyon of the Tuolumne River. Here, in a field of glacial erratics, we are face to face with cliff-girded Colby Mountain, named for an early president of the Sierra Club who was on its board of directors for 49 years.

Just a few minutes later, we enter Rodgers Canyon, then abruptly turn uphill. The trail ascends a series of well-forested glacial steps to come alongside seasonally large Rodgers Canyon creek just under 8000 feet. For the next 1.5 miles, our gently to moderately climbing trail keeps west of the creek, passing through typical subalpine pockets of lodgepoles that cluster near the cascading stream. After one cobbly pitch, we soon emerge on the south edge of lengthy Rodgers Meadow. Here, Rodgers Canyon creek cuts a broad, lazy snake through the sedge turf, overshadowed by a small dome near Neall Lake, above the meadow's north end. Over our next stretch of 0.8 mile, we at first stay near the forest that demarcates the west side of Rodgers Meadow as we amble north to find a very good campsite among lodgepoles. A few yards north of this camp, we leave the meadow and cross to the east bank of Rodgers Canyon creek, only to cross back moments later. Now we come abruptly to a

trail junction at 8800 feet. By continuing north, you can take a shorter route to the PCT, via Murdock Lake.

SIDE TRIP PAST MURDOCK LAKE: If you don't take the scenic longer route, take this trail northward moderately up along slopes, quickly leaving behind the canyon-floor forest. Soon, you tackle a set of very steep, sandy switchbacks, then angle northeast, passing below a small spring. The remainder of this ascent ends abruptly on a level subalpine meadow at 9530 feet, about a mile beyond the junction. Shallow Murdock Lake is cupped in a depression in this rolling grassland. Some adequate camps lie in lodgepoles above its west shore and offer interesting views of Volunteer Peak, Matterhorn Peak, and Sawtooth Ridge. Leaving the ridgetop meadowland, the trail descends a half mile back into mixed conifers and soon reaches the PCT. **END OF SIDE TRIP**

Most hikers will branch right on the 1.75-mile-longer, far more scenic trail to Neall and Rodgers lakes. This route heads east to Neall Lake's outlet creek, then climbs pleasantly east along its north bank. Less than a mile past the trail junction, we find a short spur trail going south to Neall Lake, which has fine campsites nestled by its outlet. Cupped by a terminal-moraine arc under the sharp crest of West Peak, small Neall Lake, at 9175 feet, reflects surrounding cliffs, blue sky, fringing conifers, and willowy fell-fields. Secluded campsites lie everywhere but on the talus of the south shore. Fishing for rainbow trout is excellent.

Heading toward Rodgers Lake, about a half mile away, the main trail steeply ascends a cobbly ridge under a western outlier of Regulation Peak. Soon, we swing north, wind over terraced sedge flats, and come to the south shore of long, subalpine, 9507-foot Rodgers Lake, named for the second Yosemite National Park superintendent. This lake is divided into two bodies by a low granitic isthmus. The larger, eastern portion is more open and rockier. Our way rounds the lake to a handsome grove of lodgepoles and hemlocks on the north shore. Here lie some good camps that afford excellent panoramas over the shallow waters to the ruddy north faces of Regulation and West peaks. Farther east, we pass another group of camps, then begin to switchback north over metasediments that have been intruded by a netlike swarm of quartz veins.

Presently, we arrive atop a grassy saddle at 9810 feet, where, on the highest point of our trip, we see the stunning sheer profile of nearby Volunteer Peak, which completely dominates a horizon of greater summits throughout the north country—Piute Mountain, Price and Tower peaks, and Crown Point. Descending north from this gap via short switchbacks, we soon re-enter forest and wind past huge talus blocks, seasonal willow-fringed tarns, and hummocky meadows to a junction with the Pacific Crest Trail. Here, under the brooding face of Volunteer Peak, which has been frost-riven into myriad vertically oriented flakes, go but 0.3 mile on the PCT to the Murdock Lake Trail, the shortcut from upper Rodgers Canyon. From this junction, you have about 11 miles of descents and ascents on the PCT to the Bear Valley Trail junction, where you join the shorter, main route.

The 2.9-mile descent to the Benson Lake spur trail begins with two dozen short switchbacks down to a ford of Smedberg Lake's outlet creek. Now on the creek's north bank, you pass a small pond before commencing a steady, moderate creekside descent to a second ford—a slight problem in early season. Back on the south bank, you make a winding, switchbacking descent over metamorphic rock down to the last, sometimes tricky ford of the creek. The next 0.3 mile of trail climbs up to a brushy saddle just east of a conspicuous knoll, then descends into a shady forest of giant firs before crossing wide Piute Creek. To keep your feet dry, look for one or more large, fallen logs.

SIDE TRIP TO BENSON LAKE: Virtually no one makes this long descent from Benson Pass without visiting giant Benson Lake. Down at 7590 feet, about 2500 feet below Benson Pass, the Benson Lake spur trail winds southwest along the shady, often damp forest floor a short half mile to a section of beach near Piute Creek's inlet. Remember this spot, for, otherwise, the route back can be hard to locate. Many campsites at 7580-foot Benson Lake lie just within the forest's edge, and they testify to the popularity of this broad, sandy beach. If you've brought in a portable folding boat or raft, you'll probably have the whole lake to yourself. Swimming in this large, deep lake is brisk at best, but sunning on the beach can be superb—in late summer, after the water line drops. However, strong, up-canyon afternoon winds can quell both activities. Anglers can anticipate a meal of rainbow or brook trout. **END OF SIDE TRIP**

From the Benson Lake spur trail, prepare for a grueling 1500-foot climb north 2.7 miles to Seavey Pass. Thankfully, the descent from it will be minor—about a 400-foot drop. At first brushy, the ascent northwest provides views of pointed Volunteer Peak and closer, two-crowned Peak 10060. You cross a creek, continue switchbacking northwest along the base of spectacular Peak 10368, then climb north briefly, only to be confronted with a steep 400-foot climb east. On it, you are eventually funneled through a narrow, steep-walled, minor gap, which rewards your climbing efforts with the sight of a relatively wind-free, sparkling pond. Just past its outlet, you'll find a trailside rock from which you can dive into its reasonably warm waters. The PCT parallels the pond's shore, curves east around a minuscule pond, then climbs northeast through wet meadows before switchbacking up to a second gap. At its north base lies a shallow, rockbound pond, immediately beyond which is a third gap, Seavey Pass.

A small meadow separates it from a fourth gap, beyond which you reach a more noteworthy—and the highest—gap. Now you bend northwest, travel past the head of a linear lake to a sixth gap, and switchback quickly down into a southwest-trending trough, spying a shallow pond 200 yards off in that direction. Turn right and immediately top your last gap, from which you descend northeast a quarter mile to a junction in Kerrick Canyon, 0.7 mile beyond Seavey Pass. The south-descending the Kerrick Canyon Trail, which Trip 4 follows, ends here. A cursory glance at the map suggests that it is an easy, 3-mile, down-canyon walk to the Bear Valley Trail junction, but closer scrutiny reveals a 3.7 mile, winding, too often ascending route. A short northward jog of your Kerrick Canyon Trail segment ends at the Bear Valley Trail junction, where you join those on the shorter main route. **END OF ALTERNATE ROUTE**

Back atop an 8060-foot saddle at the junction with the Pleasant Valley Trail, we begin the Bear Valley Trail. In the first mile, the Bear Valley Trail crosses the timbered saddle, then climbs north up a steep, shaded pitch to a small, grassy pond. This knee-deep lakelet does have a fair campsite just behind the fringe of Labrador tea. We climb gently north from this pond along a sandy ridge to the willowy east bank of an unnamed creek in a half mile. Then, after another half mile, we cross it so that we can climb northwest through a grassy meadow to top a lateral moraine and, after a third half mile, find yet another unnamed creek. After jumping to its west bank, we ascend for 1.25 miles, starting gently north on a sparsely timbered slope. Soon, our lightly traveled trail fades to a faint depression in meadow turf. Small cairns and ducks may guide you, but you cannot miss your goal, our trip's high point at 9490 feet, a saddle flanked by huddled whitebark pines. Beyond, 700 feet below, is pastoral Bear Valley, overshadowed by knife-edged Bear Valley Peak. Farther north, the Yosemite north country rears its shining ivory sum-

mits, and red-volcanic Relief Peak, near Sonora Pass, touches the horizon.

Raucous Clark's nutcrackers may oversee our knee-jarring plummet north down the cirque wall of Bear Valley. At first, our path is contorted into short, tight, rocky switchbacks, but later, the legs lengthen as we descend a seasonally wet route through a lush thicket of willows, mountain maple, meadow rue, and seasonal forbs. After rapidly losing 500 feet of altitude, the descent becomes gentler and turns northwest down to the south side of meadowed Bear Valley, where the path can be lost for some 150 yards north across the hummocky, frequently soggy grassland.

We then climb easily over a forested moraine and drop to the east end of a small, hospitable lakelet circled by lodgepoles and western white pines. Just a minute north of it, we hop across Breeze Creek, then ascend northeast along it over open, slabby terrain. After about 300 feet of elevation gain, the trail levels off through a delightful open stand of pines and hemlocks and we quickly arrive at the outlet of long-awaited Bear Valley Lake. This shallow gem, at 9154 feet, sits in a washboard-bottomed glacial trough, and numerous outcrops of polished granite break the lake's surface. These picturesque islets, combined with a shoreline of short grasses, red heather, and dwarf bilberry, provide a stunning foreground for soaring, photogenic Bear Valley Peak. Excellent camps lie among conifers back from the north shore.

The next morning, we walk a short distance northwest from the lake's outlet to a small gap between two low domes and gird ourselves for a 1200-foot descent north into Kerrick Canyon, involving the better part of 100 moderate-to-steep switchbacks. For the first 400 feet of this direct descent, our way is shaded by hemlocks and western white pines, and we can survey north over intervening ridges to Snow Peak and ragged Tower Peak. Lower down, however, the views are hidden by a rising horizon and a thick growth of hemlocks and lodgepoles. Finally reaching morainal till rearranged by sometimes raging Rancheria Creek, our descent abates and we turn east through dry lodgepole flats to arrive at a junction with the Pacific Crest Trail, where it bends north to cross Rancheria Creek.

Immediately beyond the trail junction, we cross voluminous Kerrick Canyon's bouldery Rancheria Creek. Major joints cut across this area's canyons, and this creek has eroded along some of them, so that now it has an angular, joint-controlled course. After crossing this creek, which can be a rough ford through mid-July, locate a north-bank spur trail striking east up to popular campsites.

The PCT climbs west, affording dramatic cross-canyon views of Bear Valley Peak and Piute Mountain. The trail eventually climbs north, gaining 700 feet in elevation up to a shallow gap, and, just east of it, you'll find a campsite near the west end of a small lakelet. Proceeding north from the gap, we have the usual knee-shocking descent on a multitude of short, steep switchbacks down almost 1000 feet to the mouth of Thompson Canyon. Here, we make a shady, short descent west to a large camp beside Stubblefield Canyon creek. The main trail meets the creek just below the camp, and across from it, a spur trail up the opposite bank quickly meets the main trail. Cross where you will, locate the main trail near the opposite bank, and start down-canyon. In a quarter mile, you leave the shady floor for slabs and slopes, in an hour arriving at a false pass. A short, steep descent west leads to a corn-lily meadow, from which you wind a quarter mile northwest up to the true Macomb Ridge pass, about 1100 feet above Stubblefield Canyon creek. With the deep canyons at last behind, the 550-foot descent northwest into Tilden Canyon seems like child's play. Just beyond the west bank of Tilden Canyon Creek, you meet the Tilden Canyon Trail, which we will take back to our trailhead. From this junction, we hike up-canyon north on the Tilden Lake Trail just 110 yards to a second junction.

S SIDE TRIP TO TILDEN LAKE: Rather than spend the night at Wilma Lake, you could spend it at huge, linear Tilden Lake, which has many near-shore campsites and a healthy population of rainbow trout. Its backdrop is more dramatic than at Wilma, but, at about 8900 feet, the lake is about 1000 feet higher than Wilma, and so the temperatures will be several degrees cooler. Also, the relatively easy hike to it is 3.25 miles long versus 1.5 miles to Wilma. END OF SIDE TRIP

Our main route adheres to the PCT, which goes left at this junction and winds northwest past several ponds, nestled on a broad gap, before descending west and dropping about 500 feet to reach relatively large, shallow 7946-foot Wilma Lake. Like so many of Yosemite's High Sierra lakes, it contains rainbow trout. Good campsites are found just beyond it, along broad, tantalizing Falls Creek. Alternatively, you could make a few minutes' walk northwest up-canyon to a shallow, broad ford of the creek to spacious campsites just before a junction with the Jack Main Canyon Trail.

The following day, retrace your steps 1.5 miles to the Tilden Canyon Trail, and take it southwest down along Tilden Canyon Creek under an often mosquitoey lodgepole canopy. This shady walk soon reaches a pear-shaped, grassy tarn rimmed with Labrador tea and bilberry. From its west end, we bend south, following blazes and ducks in open lodgepole stands interspersed with erratics and glaciated slabs. In about a mile, we again come close to Tilden Canyon Creek—here a wide lagoon cut deep through meadow turf—where one might disturb a family of mallard ducks. Pressing on, we negotiate a small rise, then ascend once more, this time via steep, eroded, rocky switchbacks, past a junction with the cutoff route west to lower Jack Main Canyon. The grind abates minutes later, when we level off at about 8630 feet just below a low summit on a glacier-smoothed ridge. It is well worth a minute taken to reach it, for it presents sweeping panoramas of northern Yosemite. You can look all the way up Jack Main Canyon to Bond Pass; then, swinging your gaze east, spot Tower Peak, Matterhorn Peak, Piute Mountain, and the Cathedral Range from Fairview Dome to Mt. Lyell.

Resuming our trek, we walk south along a low, broad ridge, then drop on a switchback to an easy traverse that is shaded by red firs, mountain hemlocks, and western white pines. Uncommon bleeding hearts and common dwarf lousewort grow in the shade here.

Presently, we ascend to a broad, forested saddle, which ties with the previously mentioned elevation of 8630 feet for our route's high point, then we descend to a diminishing lakelet, our last permanent water source for about 8 miles, in Tiltill Valley. Below the lakelet, we walk for a while beside its meadowed outlet creek, then veer away on a rocky descent around a steep bluff before resuming a creekside route under moderate forest cover. We walk easily for a mile down through an understory of yarrow, meadow rue, aster, senecio, and corn lily to small Tiltill Meadow, in which once stood a cabin built by H. G. Kibbie.

South of Tiltill Meadow, we continue in the same easy manner for a half mile, then turn southwest down a dry morainal slope to a red-fir grove beside a small meadow drained by a step-across branch of Rancheria Creek. Now begins a 2300-foot descent to Tiltill Valley. Chaparral areas allow views south and east over the bluffs of Smith Peak and Rancheria Mountain. Moderate switchbacks ease our descent to 7300 feet, and then we drop more gently southwest down a sandy canyon and look west to a brush-covered Mt. Gibson. Next, we work south along a bouldery, brushy bench, and then begin the final 1300-foot plunge. At first, we stay on the north side of a ridge, descending steeply on sand in the relative shade of tall huckleberry-oak brush and scattered Jeffrey pines. But below 6600 feet, we swing onto the ridge's south face, which allows our first views of lush Tiltill

Valley and, beyond it, Hetch Hetchy Reservoir. But the south face also subjects us to the full heat of the midday sun. Eventually, at 6320 feet, we reach a gap on the ridge, which affords some shade. Below this rest stop are more steep, rocky, exposed switchbacks, this time leading east through canyon live oak scrub. Eventually, the trail bends south and lowers us to the long-awaited shade of a grove of incense-cedars, black oaks, and Jeffrey pines at the eastern edge of Tiltill Valley, at 5600 feet elevation.

In Tiltill Valley, find a trail that heads south to the base of some steep bluffs that bound the valley on the south. Here it enters a lush stand of aspens, alders, and willows surrounding a small spring. Upon reaching the canyon wall, our path starts a short climb, taking some well-engineered switchbacks southwest to a large, joint-controlled rift. This we follow gently up southwest, past a small, linear pond decked with yellow pond lilies, then we progress through a forest of white fir and incense-cedar. Seasonally fragrant western azalea is a locally dominant understory shrub, joined in more open spots by uncommon white-bugled Washington's lily. Straight as an arrow, our trail slices through a narrow saddle, at 5780 feet, and then gently descends into another straight-sided canyon, this one also trending southwest. Ahead, we'll face a 1200-foot descent to the vicinity of Rancheria Falls.

After a half mile, we angle west out of this canyon onto open slabs, where we have views south over brushy LeConte Point to somber-cliffed Smith Peak. Now the route begins to descend in earnest, high above the forests below. The trail twists itself into numerous sandy, moderate switchbacks, soon dropping to the 5300-foot level, where the slopes can be too warm in summer, and heat-tolerant vegetation grows, including gray pines and canyon live oaks, which offer meager shade. Here, too, we perceive some slivers of Hetch Hetchy Reservoir, bent around sentinel Kolana Rock to the west. Some 600 feet more of occasionally open switchbacking descent follow, depositing us, finally, at a junction with the Rancheria Mountain Trail on a manzanita-cloaked sandy hillside. Here, we turn right, down some easy switchbacks, and, after 0.3 mile, bend briefly south to find the cool haven of a large, thick conifer grove, in which a short spur trail heads over to popular, spacious Rancheria Falls Camp, which has adjacent cascades, pools, and rainbow trout. Be warned that this popular camping area is often shared with marauding black bears.

To complete your route, hike 6.4 miles west from the camp back to O'Shaughnessy Dam. Briefly, this first traverses 0.3 mile west, descends 0.3 mile to a junction with an old trail down to Hetch Hetchy Reservoir, then descends another 0.3 mile via switchbacks to the oak-and-pine-shaded gorge cut by Tiltill Creek. You can get water just above this bridge by making a cautious traverse over to a pool at the brink of the creek's fall. When the current's not too strong, the pool is great to dip in on a hot day. Here, we cross two bridges, the first one high above the creek.

The 3 miles west to Wapama Falls follows a frequently dynamited trail that undulates along a steep hillside past open chaparral and shaded, fly-infested canyon live oaks. This traverse is not level, for it switchbacks on occasion to circumvent some cliffy spots. Eventually, we reach the first of several bridges below the base of Wapama Falls. During some high-runoff years, even these high, sturdy bridges are inundated by seasonally tumultuous Falls Creek.

The next 1.5-mile stretch begins as we soon make a steep, dynamited ascent through a field of huge talus blocks under a tremendous unnamed precipice. Midway along it, we cross an unnamed, minor stream that descends, until about early summer, hundreds of feet as Tueeulala Falls. Ahead, the route now is mostly open, and we see the obdurate, warshiplike prow of Kolana Rock, which forces a constriction in the 8-mile-long reservoir's tadpole shape. Our traverse along the Rancheria

Falls Trail ends at a junction with the road on which we began our hike, and we follow it an easy mile over to O'Shaughnessy Dam and our adjacent trailhead.

TRIP 13

Preston Flat Trail

E ⬈ DH, BP

DISTANCE: 8.6 miles out and back

ELEVATIONS: 2410′/2810′
+640′/-260′/±1800′

SEASON: Early April to late October

USE: Light

MAP: *Cherry Lake South*

TRAIL LOG:

4.3   Preston Falls

INTRODUCTION: In previous editions, I described the Poopenaut Valley Trail, which has a trailhead 3.9 miles past the Mather Ranger Station, at a clockwise turn in the road to Hetch Hetchy. This old trail is the steepest trail I know: If it was only slightly steeper, many hikers would take spills. The only reason I justified this trail was to take a dip in the Tuolumne River after a long backpack trip, but since the ascent back to the trailhead is so exhausting, you'll be dripping sweat and will need to descend for another dip! In the past, one could camp down there, say in early or late season, when Hetch Hetchy's high country lay under snow, but because Poopenaut Valley is within a mile of a park road, camping now is prohibited.

A more recent, 1980s vintage alternative, located west of the park, is the Preston Flat Trail, which parallels the Tuolumne River up-canyon. Most of it is easy, although there are steep, but short, sections to surmount minor ridges. The discharge of the Tuolumne River is controlled by how much water is released from O'Shaughnessy Dam, about 8 miles upstream, so don't swim in the river if the current is fast. The Preston Flat Trail has a spectacular

ending, a view of the Tuolumne River plunging over a low escarpment. Be forewarned that poison oak grows along both trails, especially along the latter, and you are in prime rattlesnake country, so watch your step.

DIRECTIONS TO THE TRAILHEAD: Just 0.6 mile before the park's boundary below the Big Oak Flat Entrance Station, leave Hwy. 120 and drive north 7.5 miles on Evergreen Road to its junction with the Hetch Hetchy Road. Turn left and go 7.7 miles west on Road 12 to a junction with Road 17, bound for Cherry Lake (this junction is 5.3 miles from the Hwy. 120/Road 17 junction). Descend Road 17 for 3.1 miles to a bridge across the Tuolumne River, turn right, and ascend a road 0.8 mile to a trailhead parking area at its end. Trail begins in map section A3.

DESCRIPTION: The Preston Flat Trail, being relatively new, is not shown on the park map. However, since it follows the Tuolumne River upstream, you can't get lost. It starts as an old road that goes a quarter mile to a stream-gauging station. Ahead is a generally very good trail, usually shaded with ponderosa pine, incense-cedar, Douglas fir, and black and live oaks. In spring, buckeye trees have very showy flowers on stalks, but with summer's heat, they soon drop both flowers and leaves. The heat brings out the aroma of a lowly shrub, mountain misery, with sticky, finely divided foliage. About 0.3 mile from the trailhead, you reach a small campsite on a bouldery flat beside the river. The trail ahead rises and falls from the riverbank several times, and each time you reach the river, you can usually find adjacent camping. If you build a fire here or elsewhere, you'll need to get a permit first from the Forest Service office in Groveland.

After about 1.75 miles, the trail may appear to end at the base of a sloping, granitic slab. Here, beside the lower end of a short, inner gorge, is a good campsite, as well as mortar holes drilled in the granite by former Native Americans. The route up the slab stays close to the brink of the inner gorge, before climbing just above it. Along a short traverse are small patches of smooth rock, and, if the lighting is right, you may see faint striations cut by glacier-transported rocks.

Although this canyon was repeatedly occupied by giant glaciers, it is a classic V-shaped canyon, not a U-shaped one. The last two glaciers flowing through here were about 2000-plus-feet thick, which was enough to spill ice across the canyon's south rim. In contrast, the last two glaciers flowing through Yosemite Valley averaged only about 1400 feet in thickness. In both areas, glaciers performed very little erosion; before glaciation, the Tuolumne River canyon and Yosemite Valley looked very much as they do today. In the former, the last two glaciers ended at about 2000 feet elevation at an estimated 2 to 3 miles beyond the Tuolumne River's confluence with Cherry Creek, west of our trailhead.

The trail soon descends to the river and continues its generally shady traverse, but around 3.5 miles into the route, you reach a meadow, which, in spring, can have a conspicuous waterfall plunging toward it. Then, the meadow can be a boggy traverse. About 0.75 mile beyond the meadow, the trail ends at a campsite beside a low, granitic slab. From the slab, you have a view across a 100-yard-diameter pool of Preston Falls, a 15-foot thunderous drop in the Tuolumne River at the lower end of an inner gorge.

TRIP 14

Lookout Point

E ⟋ DH

DISTANCE: 3 miles out and back

ELEVATIONS: 4740'/5310'
+600'/-30'/±1260'

SEASON: Early April to late October

USE: Light

MAP: *Lake Eleanor*

TRAIL LOG:

1.5   Lookout Point

INTRODUCTION: For good views of the lower Tuolumne River canyon, the hike to Lookout Point is an excellent choice. It is particularly enjoyable in springtime, when temperatures are mild, water is present, and wildflowers abound.

DIRECTIONS TO THE TRAILHEAD: Just 0.6 mile before the park's boundary below the Big Oak Flat Entrance Station, drive north 7.5 miles on Evergreen Road to its junction with Hetch Hetchy Road 12. Here in Camp Mather, turn right and drive 1.25 miles north east to the Hetch Hetchy Entrance Station (Mather Ranger Station). Since parking is limited, ask a ranger where to park. Trail begins in map section B3.

DESCRIPTION: This hike is best done in the morning, when temperatures are still fairly cool and shadows are good for photography. Our starting point, Mather Ranger Station, sits on a broad, glaciated granitic bench that has a shady, fairly dense cover of ponderosa pines, incense-cedars, and black oaks. From the station's east side, we follow a trail briefly south to a junction with a trail heading right to nearby Camp Mather. We turn left and parallel Hetch Hetchy Road east, quickly entering lands burned by an extensive 1996 fire. Our trail roller-coasters across rocky slopes rich in spring-time flowers, then climbs briefly up a gully, which, in springtime, usually has a flowing creeklet and lush displays of water-loving flowers. Above the gully, we level off and parallel its seasonal creeklet northeast to a quick junction, 1.2 miles from our trail-head, with the Lookout Point spur trail.

Branching left on it, we walk north for a minute, skirt around a seasonal pond, then circle counterclockwise up the north-east side of a largely barren, glacier-smoothed knoll. The trail tread dies. Before climbing up bedrock slopes to the nearby obvious summit, check this spot, since it easily can be missed on your descent. Around the summit grow a few dwarfed Jeffrey pines and clumps of lowly penstemons known as mountain pride, both species sending their roots along cracks, helping to oh-so-slowly disintegrate this summit. Give them a few tens of millions of years to complete the job.

The knoll stands despite repeated glaciation; the last two major glaciers were about 700 feet thick at your summit and about 2500 feet thick at the unseen floor of the Tuolumne River canyon about 1 mile northwest of you. The last glacier retreated by or before 15,000 years ago. Smoothed rock, faint striations, and chatter (gouge) marks comprise the evidence here. Additional evidence is found on the barren knolls southwest and northwest of us, which have large, glacier-transported boulders strewn over their surfaces. Erosion by the last glacier here was so minimal that the very shallow solution potholes, which existed before that glacier existed, remain virtually unchanged.

Atop Lookout Point you have a 360-degree panorama, although the most interesting scenery is clockwise from west to northeast—that is, down the Tuolumne River canyon and then up to Hetch Hetchy Reservoir. Above the reservoir, Tueeulala Falls adds accent to the springtime land-scape, while, to the right, voluminous Wapama Falls, fed by Falls Creek, which originates at the Sierra Crest, flows year round.

A lone Jeffrey pine and glacial chatter (gouge) marks atop Lookout Point

TRIP 15

Mather Ranger Station to Smith Peak

Ⓜ ↗ BP

DISTANCE: 15.8 miles out and back

ELEVATIONS: 4740′/7750′
+3360′/-350′/±7420′

SEASON: Early June to late October

USE: Light

MAPS: *Lake Eleanor,*
Hetch Hetchy Reservoir

TRAIL LOG:

2.7 Aspen Valley Trail junction
6.4 Westbound trail from White Wolf
7.9 Smith Peak

INTRODUCTION: Smith Peak, with its all-encompassing view of the northwest half of Yosemite National Park, can be reached from White Wolf or from the Hetch Hetchy Road. This trip and Trip 19, from White Wolf, are similar both in length and in amount of elevation gain and loss. So, which should you choose? The seasons determine the answer. If you are hiking in May, June, or October, then take this hike to avoid snow problems. If you are hiking in July, August, or September, take Trip 19 to avoid the summer's heat found on the lower part of Trip 15.

DIRECTIONS TO THE TRAILHEAD: Just 0.6 mile before the park's boundary below the Big Oak Flat Entrance Station, drive north 7.5 miles on Evergreen Road to its junction with Hetch Hetchy Road 12. Here in Camp Mather, turn right and drive 1.25 miles northeast to the Hetch Hetchy Entrance Station (Mather Ranger Station). Since parking is limited, ask a ranger where to park. Trail begins in map section B3.

DESCRIPTION: The preferred route described here is the one requiring the least effort. From our starting point, Mather Ranger Station's east side, we follow a trail briefly south to a junction with a trail heading right to nearby Camp Mather. We turn left and parallel Hetch Hetchy Road east, quickly entering lands burned by an extensive 1996 fire. Our trail rollercoasters across rocky slopes rich in springtime flowers, then climbs briefly up a gully, which in springtime usually has a flowing creeklet and lush displays of water-loving flowers. Above the gully, we level off and parallel its seasonal creeklet northeast to a quick junction, 1.2 miles from our trailhead, with the Lookout Point spur trail. If you hike up to and back from the point—a worthwhile objective while you're fresh—add 0.6 mile to your total distance.

[S] **SIDE TRIP TO SMITH MEADOW:** You could also begin on another equally long trail starting from the Hetch Hetchy Road beside a prominent gully about 6 miles beyond the Mather Ranger Station. This climbs about 1.5 miles to a junction with a little-used trail to the ranger station, then about 4 miles more up to Smith Meadow. Its disadvantage is that, because it starts lower, you have an additional 500 feet of climbing. On the other hand, Cottonwood and Smith meadows can be quite soggy through spring, and this alternate route avoids both. **END OF SIDE TRIP**

From the junction, continue ahead just 0.2 mile to another, and if you would continue straight ahead for a similar distance, you would reach a linear lakelet. This lakelet is along the aforementioned little-used trail, which rambles for a total of 3.5 miles to the alternate trail.

At our second junction, we turn right to begin a well-graded, winding ascent a half mile to a broad saddle, where a trail formerly descended west to Camp Mather. We traverse east just over a half mile to a junction with the Base Line Camp road, which climbs initially southwest before eventually dropping on a circuitous route to Camp

Mather. The elevation here, about 5500 feet, is high enough for sugar pines, with their long cones hanging at the ends of branches. East, we traverse a similar distance to another junction, this one with a winding trail 6.5 miles south to Aspen Valley.

Before the new Big Oak Flat Road opened in 1940, the old Hwy. 120 was routed along part of Evergreen Road, then east up the old Tioga Road to Aspen Valley, where you entered the park. Before then, traffic was so light that motorists were requested to sound the horn to get the attention of the attendant, who would often be off doing other chores. These days, at the Big Oak Flat Entrance Station, you may hear weekend motorists sounding their horns to protest the long wait to get in, due to sheer numbers of visitors.

From the Aspen Valley Trail junction, the Base Line Camp road quickly ends, and, from it, a trail climbs to a reliable creek with a water tank, the source of water for the Mather area. Again, we tick off another half mile east, this time a moderate climb to the crest of a broad ridge.

This is a lateral moraine, 2500 feet above Poopenaut Valley, and it represents the minimum thickness of the last glacier that flowed down the Tuolumne River canyon, retreating from this site perhaps 16,000 years ago. At its maximum, this glacier may have been thick enough to spread laterally eastward across the Cottonwood Creek drainage. In preglacial time, Cottonwood Creek may have drained west down to the Tuolumne River in western Poopenaut Valley, but today the moraine forces the creek to drain southwest down to the much smaller Middle Tuolumne River.

Jeffrey pines began to replace ponderosa pines on our ascent, and now, in the Cottonwood Creek drainage, we find white firs quite common and lodgepole pines bordering nearby lower Cottonwood Meadow. Also bordering it are aspens, which are related to cottonwoods, which, if present, are not conspicuous. Once we leave this meadow, the lodgepoles disappear, for conditions are now drier, and, about a half mile beyond it, you will notice a trailside slab on your left with more than three dozen mortar holes.

Sugar pines, known as *hi 'ymachi* by the local Native Americans, grow in this vicinity, and the Native Americans ate the seeds probably after grinding them here. They also made use of the tree's whitish sugar, which they considered a delicacy. About a mile northwest of this mortar site are black oaks, whose acorns were a major part of their diet, in ground form providing them with bread, mush, and even soup.

A mile farther, we enter upper Cottonwood Meadow, and, in it, we cross Cottonwood Creek, which is generally a wet ford before July. Continuing northeast, we soon climb moderately up to a broad ridge and descend briefly to its opposite side, beside which flows Cottonwood Creek along the southwest edge of Smith Meadow. If the

Solution pockets on Smith Peak's summit

creek is too broad to jump across, look for one or more nearby logs across it. Like the nearby peak, the meadow is named for a sheep rancher who claimed that this part of Yosemite belonged to him. Ignoring the land's park status, he grazed his sheep in its meadows well into the 1920s. We continue northeast up this sloping meadow on a trail that can be boggy and obscure before July. Immediately above its northeast corner, just within forest cover, we reach an intersection with the westbound trail from White Wolf (Trip 19). Had you taken the alternate trip up to Smith Meadow, you would have ended here.

If you are backpacking, you won't want to carry a heavy pack 1370 feet up to the 7751-foot summit of Smith Peak. Look for adequate campsites on gentle, forested slopes about 100 to 200 yards west of the trail intersection. The trail to the summit is direct and steep, so, before you start, you might want to get some water at a trickling creeklet only a few yards from the intersection. If conditions are dry, you'll have to get water at Cottonwood Creek, which you crossed about a quarter mile back.

We start our climb in a forest of white firs, sugar pines, and incense-cedars, and by the time we reach the first of three seasonally wet meadows—all of them rich in summer wildflowers—we have left the incense-cedars behind. If you're hiking this trail before July, you're likely to run into snow patches from here on. Although you may lose the trail beneath them, you won't lose your way, as long as you keep heading northeast upslope. A second wet meadow, marking the halfway point, is quickly passed; we pass a third one midway between it and the Tuolumne River canyon crest. By the time we reach the crest, red firs have become the dominant forest tree, with Jeffrey pines occupying the drier, sunnier spots, and white firs in between. If you came up on horses, leave them at the canyon-crest saddle, for the footpaths ahead are steep and narrow.

The final 250-foot elevation gain can be made by any of several brush-lined paths.

GEOLOGY OF GRAND CANYON OF THE TUOLUMNE RIVER

During the last two major glaciations, glaciers filled the canyon below us to a depth of 3500 feet or more, coming to within 500 or 600 feet of our summit. Being so thick, these glaciers exerted a force of about 100 tons per square foot on the canyon's bottom.

Nevertheless, the shape and depth of the canyon haven't changed all that much, despite repeated glaciation over at least the last 2 million years. Indeed, it hasn't deepened much in the last 10 million years, if not considerably longer. As you can see, the canyon is distinctly V-shaped in cross profile, as it is below the reservoir. From its dam site, the two glaciers advanced about 20 or so miles farther down-canyon.

You can also see that much of the Yosemite landscape north, south, and west of the river's canyon is a gentle, rolling uplands topography, which has evolved only very slowly over the last 80 million years.

Perhaps the safest and most frequently used path is the one that climbs the west slope, then traverses along the south slope. To reach the best viewpoint, atop pitted granitic rocks, you'll have to plow through a dense, brushy cover of huckleberry oaks. The solution pockets—some of them filling with water after recent rains—result from extremely slow weathering locally found on gentle-sloped surfaces of granitic rock. Solution pockets rarely form on metamorphic or volcanic rock.

From the pocketed rocks, you can gaze down into the deep Grand Canyon of the Tuolumne River and see the Hetch Hetchy Reservoir, about 4000 feet below you.

Scanning the northeast skyline, keen map users should be able to identify, from east to northeast, Mt. Hoffmann, plus the prominent crest summits of Mt. Conness, Matterhorn Peak, and Tower Peak. Across the main canyon, Tiltill Creek canyon descends toward us, its floor and slopes stripped bare of soil by glaciers, exposing naked granite. In contrast, Rancheria Mountain, above its east slopes, is quite forested. Volcanic deposits are rare within the park, and the bulk of them are on or near this flat-topped mountain, which stood above glaciers.

Unless a storm is approaching, don't be in a hurry to leave this view-packed summit. Scarcity of water prevents tall conifers from overpowering it and blocking our views.

The shallow, dry soils, however, are the perfect medium for the densely packed, shrubby huckleberry oaks, whose small, evergreen leaves keep the plant's water loss at a minimum. On the more snowbound slopes of Smith Peak grows the bush chinquapin, a distant cousin of the huckleberry oak. Also found here are a few black oaks, which stand hardly more than knee high, though in Yosemite Valley, they grow up to 80 feet tall. This oak prefers sunny slopes, and, in the absence of conifers, it has managed to survive. At about 7750 feet in elevation, this patch of black oaks may be the highest one in Yosemite; only in a few other parts of the park are they seen at the 7500- to 7600-foot level. This oak, together with whitebark pine, are the only two Yosemite trees that reduce to shrub height as they approach the upper limit of their ranges. A final bush worth noting is the snow bush, a spiny *Ceanothus* that prefers dry, gravelly granitic soils. We've seen it along drier sections of the Cottonwood Creek drainage.

After your stay on the summit, descend to Smith Meadow, then retrace your steps to the trailhead.

CHAPTER 10

Trips of Yosemite's West-Central Lands Northwest of the Tioga Road

Introduction to this Area

This chapter and the next one cover lands situated between the park's low western lands and its high eastern lands. The chapter's title is slightly misleading in that Trip 16, the Merced Grove of Big Trees, does not lie along the Tioga Road, but rather along the Big Oak Flat Road about 3.75 miles west of the Tioga Road junction in Crane Flat. And then, it lies on the south side of that road, not the north. However, I could not have a one-trip chapter, so I put it in this one, since the first trip along the Tioga Road, Trip 17, is very similar, a hike to the Tuolumne Grove of Big Trees. Elevations range from about a mile high, down in the Merced Grove, to 2 miles high atop the summit of Mt. Hoffmann, Trip 24. Standing near the park's center, it provides commanding views over most of the park's landscape. Between these antipodes lie trails with one or more lakes, save for Trip 20 down

The Tunnel Tree, Tuolumne Grove

to Pate Valley, and that is if you take the short way out. This is the only strenuous hike, since you descend almost 4000 feet and then have to climb back up. Still, the spacious lands extending from Pate Valley proper do offer a feeling of wilderness and isolation not found at most of the High Sierra's trailside—and, therefore, popular—lakes. Short, easy hikes take you to Harden, Lukens, and May lakes. The first is fishless and, in late season, too shallow for swimming; the second is great for fishing and swimming; and the third is good for fishing but on the cool side for swimming. In my opinion, the best cluster of lakes in the park is along Trip 23 to the Ten Lakes Basin. Too many folks visit only the three easily reached lakes, leaving the other four with only moderate to light use. As you proceed from Trip 16 to Trip 24, the length of the hiking season lessens, from about seven months to about four months.

Supplies and Services

Absolutely everything you'll need for a Yosemite outdoor experience can be purchased in the western foothills town of Sonora. This includes full backpacking and mountaineering gear, these available at the Sierra Nevada Adventure Company. This town also has several large grocery stores, numerous dining places, and two hospitals.

Groveland, about 24 miles west of the park's Big Oak Flat Entrance Station, is the last town you'll pass on Hwy. 120; however, several resorts, gas stations, and campgrounds are found closer to the park. Gas, meals, and lodging are found at Evergreen Lodge, on Evergreen Road just 0.6 mile before it ends at the Hetch Hetchy Road in Camp Mather (for San Francisco residents).

Once inside the park, you can find virtually anything you'll need—other than fuel—down in Yosemite Valley, but this is crowded and is out of your way. Should you need last-minute food or fuel, you can get them at Crane Flat. Fewer supplies are at White Wolf Lodge, the center for trips 18 to 21, though it offers breakfast and dinner.

Wilderness Permits

If you want to reserve a permit, rather than get one in person, see the "Wilderness Permits" section in Chapter 6. In person, if you are driving east up Hwy. 120, get a permit at the Big Oak Flat Information Station, which is immediately past the park's entrance station. Note that from about early April through late October, you can get a permit at the Hetch Hetchy Entrance Station (by the Mather Ranger Station). You cannot get a permit in the White Wolf area. If you are driving up Hwy. 140 or Hwy. 41, get your permit at the Visitor Center in Yosemite Valley, and if you are driving west down Hwy. 120, stop in Tuolumne Meadows.

Campgrounds

Within the park, you can stay at Hodgdon Meadow Campground, reached by turning left immediately after passing through the Big Oak Flat Entrance Station. This is good for trips 16 and 17. Driving east on Hwy. 120, you'll reach another possibility, Crane Flat Campground, just a quarter mile before Crane Flat, which is ideal for trips 16 and 17. Both these campgrounds are on a reservation system; see Chapter 1 for details. After turning left at the flat's junction, you then drive 14.5 miles up the Tioga Road (Hwy. 120) to the White Wolf Road. Opposite this road's White Wolf Lodge is the entrance to the White Wolf Campground, ideal for trips 18 to 21. Those taking trips 22 to 24 can also stay here or at Porcupine Flat Campground, on the Tioga Road, 9.2 miles past the White Wolf Road junction. During the summer season, all these campsites can be full, so plan to find a campsite early in the day.

TRIP 16

Merced Grove of Big Trees

M ↗ DH

DISTANCE: 3 miles out and back

ELEVATIONS: 5380´/5900´
+40´/-530´/±1140´

SEASON: Early May to
mid-November

USE: Moderate

MAPS: *Ackerson Mountain,
El Portal*

TRAIL LOG:

1.5   Merced Grove

INTRODUCTION: Having only a few parking spaces, the trailhead parking area limits the number of visitors to this smallest of the park's three groves. So, if you want to see giant sequoias *and* avoid crowds, this hike is for you. Both the Merced Grove and the nearby Tuolumne Grove (next hike) have more than a dozen trees at least 10 feet in diameter near the base, which pale in comparison with the much larger Mariposa Grove's (Trip 78) approximately 200 trees of similar or larger size. In each of the two small groves, a few trees reach about 15 feet in diameter, the largest being about 10 feet short of the diameter of the Mariposa Grove's Grizzly Giant. Although you are likely to see a few more of the larger specimens in the Tuolumne Grove than in the Merced Grove, you will almost certainly see more tourists, since its trailhead parking area is quite large and is often quite full.

DIRECTIONS TO THE TRAILHEAD: This is located along the Big Oak Flat Road where it crosses a divide about 4.25 miles east of the Big Oak Flat Entrance Station and about 3.75 miles west of the Tioga Road

junction in Crane Flat. Trail begins in map section B4.

DESCRIPTION: In the area covered by this book's map, there are three sequoia groves: Merced, Tuolumne, and Mariposa. However, about 5 miles due south of the Mariposa Grove (just off the map) lies the Nelder Grove. Perhaps before 15 million years ago, when the summers were wetter, the Merced and Tuolumne groves probably were one large grove, as probably were the Mariposa and Nelder groves. What all four have in common today are similar elevations, between 5000 and 6000 feet, and, perhaps more importantly, some underlying metamorphic bedrock. Indeed, the Merced and Tuolumne groves grow entirely on metamorphic bedrock. There are many suitable alcoves at the proper altitude in our area, but almost all lie in granitic bedrock. Metamorphic bedrock weathers to produce soils with more nutrients and more groundwater capacity than soils derived from granitic bedrock, and, in times of warmer, drier climates, such as a few thousand years ago, metamorphic soils may have enabled our sequoias to survive.

Unlike on the next hike, mountain bikes are allowed along this one. The first half of our hike is along a nearly level, gated, limited-access road, shaded by white firs and, to a lesser extent, incense-cedars and ponderosa pines. A fire almost razed the grove, but, fortunately, it stopped just above part of the road, and shrubs have taken over in the burned area. After about 0.7 mile, we reach a junction with a closed road and branch left on it. This makes a counterclockwise, moderate descent through a gully shaded by Douglas firs, white firs, and sugar pines—typical sequoia associates at this latitude. In late spring and early summer, you're also likely to see mountain dogwood in bloom, the tree's large, white bracts making up "petals" around the cluster of small, green, actual flowers in the center of the bracts.

The road next makes a clockwise, moderate descent out of the gully, briefly paralleling audible Moss Creek before curving into a dry gully, about 1.4 miles from the trailhead. Here grow a half dozen sequoias, ranging, at breast height (the standard, if arbitrary height for measurement), between 5 and 8 feet in diameter. As a generality, for the first 800 years, the sequoia adds a foot in diameter per century, making these about 500 to 800 years old. To reach 12 feet takes about 1500 years, and 15 feet takes about 2000 years. Although the sequoias in this gully are relatively young, they nevertheless are close to a maximum average height of about 250 feet. Water should flow down this gully during the wet season, but there is no sign of a creek bed. Sequoias are thirsty individuals, like their cousins, the coast redwoods, and they soak up a lot of ground water.

We pass several more giants midway to several more that are opposite a cabin in the heart of Merced Grove, some 1.5 miles from the trailhead. Above the cabin are two outhouses, should you need one. In this vicinity, you'll see a number of sequoias, from about 14 feet in diameter and up to 270 feet high, down to saplings. Large trees are few in number, and the last large one you'll see is about 200 yards down the road. Superficially, one gets the impression that the trees are not regenerating. However, small trees are easily missed and also they may be confused with incense-cedars, which have similar bark, but different leaves and cones. As many as 200 saplings grow within the grove, the great bulk of them in the lower part of the grove.

Giant sequoias

TRIP **17**

Tuolumne Grove of Big Trees

Ⓜ ↗ DH

DISTANCE:　2.4 miles out and back

ELEVATIONS: 5700´/6190´
　　　　　　　+0´/-490´/±980´

SEASON:　　Early May to
　　　　　　　mid-November

USE:　　　　Heavy

MAP:　　　*Ackerson Mountain*

TRAIL LOG:

　1.2　Tuolumne Grove

INTRODUCTION: Having only a few parking spaces, the trailhead parking area limits the number of visitors to this smallest of the park's three groves. So, if you want to see giant sequoias *and* avoid crowds, this hike is for you. Both the Merced Grove and the nearby Tuolumne Grove have more than a dozen trees at least 10 feet in diameter near the base, which pale in comparison with the much larger Mariposa Grove's (Trip 78) approximately 200 trees of similar or larger size. In each of the two small groves, a few trees reach about 15 feet in diameter, the largest being about 10 feet short of the diameter of the Mariposa Grove's Grizzly Giant. (For details about the elevations and soils the giant sequoias inhabit, see the beginning of Trip 16's hike description on page 141.) Although you are likely to see a few more of the larger specimens in the Tuolumne Grove than in the Merced Grove, you will almost certainly see more tourists, since its trailhead parking area is quite large and is often quite full.

DIRECTIONS TO THE TRAILHEAD: Drive to the junction of the Big Oak Flat Road with the Tioga Road, at Crane Flat, then drive a half mile up the Tioga Road to a large parking area on your left. Trail begins in map section B4.

DESCRIPTION: The route is obvious, an old closed road for hikers only. It first curves a quarter mile over to a gully below the back side of the Yosemite Institute, which provides weeklong outdoor education to groups of students and to other groups. The road then takes on a steep gradient as it first descends to a switchback west, then to one north. Just past it, about 0.9 mile into your hike, you enter the Tuolumne Grove, and, about 0.2 mile farther down the road, you come to a junction beside an impressive sequoia about 15 feet in diameter. You could continue down the main road, but the alternate road is more desirable. About 130 yards along it, you pass through the Tunnel Tree, a dead, charred hulk with a base diameter of 29.5 feet. In its glory, it must have been one of Yosemite's tallest specimens. A tunnel was carved in it back in 1878, before two were carved in the Mariposa Grove. From the Tunnel Tree, the alternate road goes 160 yards down to a reunion with the main road. Here, in the heart of the Tuolumne Grove, is a picnic area plus two ends of a self-guiding nature trail that winds through a group of sequoias. Taking this informative trail adds about a half mile to the total length of your hike.

Most folks turn around at the picnic area, if not sooner, but you can descend the main road a quarter mile beyond it to the lower, northern edge of the grove. If you look to your left, you'll see a lone giant sequoia at the far edge of a gently sloping flat, among mature sugar pines and white firs. What sets it apart, besides its isolation, is that it is growing along the brink of North Crane Creek's gully. Should this tree live long enough, it may be undercut by erosion. Beyond the grove's northern edge, the road descends about 4.5 miles to Hodgdon Meadow Campground, which lies just east of the Big Oak Flat Entrance Station.

TRIP 18

White Wolf to Harden Lake

E ⬈ DH

DISTANCE: 5.6 miles out and back

ELEVATIONS: 7480′/7870′
+90′/-480′/±1140′

SEASON: Mid-June to mid-October

USE: Heavy

MAPS: *Tamarack Flat,*
Hetch Hetchy Reservoir

TRAIL LOG:

1.8   Trail junction
2.5   Harden Lake Road
2.8   Harden Lake

INTRODUCTION: Only about an hour's hike from White Wolf Campground, this lake attracts quite a number of summer visitors. From early July through early August, this shallow lake can be fine for swimming, but the lake lies in a leaky basin, and by mid-August it usually has dwindled to an oversized wading pool. Don't expect to catch any fish since the lake becomes far too shallow by late summer to support any.

DIRECTIONS TO THE TRAILHEAD: From Crane Flat, drive northeast 14.5 miles up Hwy. 120 to the White Wolf turnoff and follow that road down to where it is closed to motor vehicles, just past the entrance to White Wolf Campground. Trail begins in map section C4.

DESCRIPTION: Our route, a closed fire road (part of the old Tioga Road), bridges the infant Middle Tuolumne River in less than a half mile, then parallels its sometimes splashing course down unglaciated granitic terrain that sustains a healthy stand of lodgepole pines. After 1.2 miles of easy descent along our road, we come to a closed spur road that goes to a sewage-treatment pond, constructed in the mid-1970s as part of a parkwide program to upgrade treatment plants to tougher environmental standards. Over the next 0.6 mile, our road first climbs over a low ridge of glacial deposits before dipping into a shady alcove of lodgepole pines and red firs. In days past, the park had far more camping than it unfortunately has at present, and a primitive campground once lay here, done in by tougher environmental standards. Today, only a trail junction exists.

We take the trail, which traverses the slope of a large glacial moraine. The well-drained sediments of this moraine support a different plant community than our generally rocky-road descent. On this moraine, a forest of Jeffrey pines grows together with some firs and aspens. Thousands of bracken ferns seek the forest shade together with chinquapins, the bushes with spiny, seed-bearing spheres. Seeking the sun are snow bushes, which have spine-tipped branches. In 0.75 mile, our trail ends at the Harden Lake Road. This formerly maintained road leaves the main road about a half mile west of our trail junction. The main road parallels the Middle Tuolumne River almost the whole distance of 8 miles to Aspen Valley, which is a private in-holding that once was the west entrance to Yosemite National Park. Today, that gently graded road is a pleasant stroll for those looking for a lightly used creekside excursion. Meanwhile, those on the last part of the Harden Lake

HARDEN LAKE

Seasonal Harden Lake has a rather uncommon origin, for it occupies a small depression that formed between two lateral moraines. Most Sierran lakes have existed for only 13,000 to 16,000 years, but Harden could have originated earlier. This shallow, 9-acre lake has no surface inlet or outlet, and not long after adjacent snow patches melt, the lake's level begins to drop. In the drought year of 1977, this lake dwindled to barely a pond by summer's end, and its stocked rainbow trout died, and were not replanted. The lake's diminishing size not only reduced food and oxygen available to these trout, but it also raised the water temperature into the mid-70s—great for swimming but fatal for trout. Except when the lake is at its highest level, it is usually shallow enough to wade across. Bathers, if they are careless, could scrape their feet on the lake's many submerged glacier-transported boulders.

Road walk across relatively flat glacial sediments, passing a seasonally delightful meadow midway along this short traverse to a gravelly junction with a trail to Pate Valley. We branch right, northeast, on the trail and in a minute's time arrive near the southwest corner of Harden Lake.

Boulder-dotted Harden Lake, from east shore

TRIP 19

White Wolf to Smith Peak

Ⓜ 🡕 DH, BP

DISTANCE: 19.6 miles out and back

ELEVATIONS: 7480'/7750'
+1840'/-1960'/±7600'

SEASON: Late June to mid-October

USE: Light beyond Harden Lake

MAPS: *Tamarack Flat,*
Hetchy Reservoir,
Lake Eleanor

TRAIL LOG:

1.8   Trail junction
2.5   Harden Lake Road
2.8   Harden Lake
8.3   Smith Meadow
9.8   Smith Peak

INTRODUCTION: Looking for a nice weekend hike without the summer crowds? Take this one. Its elevation range is perfect for summer hiking—not too cold, hot, windy, or exposed. Near the end of your hike, you can enjoy a refreshing swim at Harden Lake—that is, before it drops substantially in late summer.

DIRECTIONS TO THE TRAILHEAD: From Crane Flat, drive northeast 14.5 miles up Hwy. 120 to the White Wolf turnoff and follow that road down to where it is closed to motor vehicles, just past the entrance to White Wolf Campground. Trail begins in map section C4.

DESCRIPTION: Ironically, our trailhead is about 120 feet *higher* than the summit views we'll attain. Our route, a closed fire road, bridges the infant Middle Tuolumne River in less than a half mile, then parallels its sometimes splashing course down unglaciated granitic terrain that sustains a

healthy stand of lodgepole pines. After 1.2 miles of easy descent along our road, we come to a closed spur road that goes to a sewage-treatment pond, constructed in the mid-1970s as part of a parkwide program to upgrade treatment plants to tougher environmental standards. Over the next 0.6 mile, our road climbs over a low ridge of glacial deposits before dipping into a shady alcove of lodgepole pines and red firs. In days past, the park had far more camping than it unfortunately has at present, and a primitive campground once lay here, done in by tougher environmental standards. Today, only a trail junction exists.

We take the trail, which traverses the slope of a large glacial moraine. The well-drained sediments of this moraine support a different plant community than our generally rocky-road descent. On this moraine, a forest of Jeffrey pines grows together with some firs and aspens. Thousands of bracken ferns seek the forest shade together with chinquapins, the bushes with spiny, seed-bearing spheres. Seeking the sun are snow bushes, which have spine-tipped branches. In 0.75 mile, our trail ends at the Harden Lake Road. This formerly maintained road leaves the main road about a half mile west of our trail junction. On the last part of the Harden Lake Road, we walk across relatively flat glacial sediments, passing a seasonally delightful meadow midway along this short traverse to a gravelly junction with a trail to Pate Valley. Although we're bound for Smith Peak, Harden Lake is so close that you ought to take a minute to walk to its southwest corner.

From the junction by the lake, we now take a trail that starts northwest, hemmed in by a meadow on the left and a bouldery moraine on the right. Soon, we cross the crest of the moraine, which sits almost 4000 feet above the unseen east end of Hetch Hetchy Reservoir. The glacier that left it was at least this thick. On slopes, we now traverse west through a red fir forest, crossing two small meadows before briefly descending to a larger one atop a broad saddle. Meadows, being often wet, support all too many mosquitoes, but usually by late July most of them have died, as the meadow's soils have dried out, and then this meadow is particularly enjoyable for botanizing. Here you may find a rainbow of colors in the flower blossoms: white-flowered cow parsnip and Richardson's geranium, creamy corn lily and bistort, yellow senecio and monkey flow, orange alpine lily, red columbine, maroon shooting star, blue-violet lupine, and blue Leichtlin's camas. On the nearby drab forest floor, bits of color may be seen in the whitish-yellow-stemmed coralroot and the all-red snow plant. Both plants are saprophytes—they derive their food from soil fungi rather than by photosynthesizing scarce sunlight.

From the broad saddle's meadow, we climb a quarter mile north to a forested saddle. Here, about 1.5 miles along this trail, we are at an elevation of about 7700 feet, which is almost the elevation of Smith Peak. Unfortunately, the terrain between our saddle and the peak is not flat, and we'll drop about 1300 feet, only to make it up. Red firs yield to white firs and Jeffrey pines as we begin a diagonal descent across south-facing slopes. Bracken ferns and snow bushes also thrive on the forest

slopes, and scrubby black oaks make a showing just before we reach the crest of a glacial moraine. As we traverse a quarter mile west down this crest, we can see Smith Peak, to the northwest, through the trees. North from the crest, we descend shady slopes and exchange the company of Jeffrey pines for that of red firs, then white firs, and by the time we reach a creeklet, incense-cedars join us. Soon we cross the creeklet, which is lined with alders, azaleas, thimbleberries, bracken ferns, and water-loving wildflowers, and we follow it down to a seasonally wet meadow. Just beyond the meadow, you'll cross Cottonwood Creek and arrive at eastern Smith Meadow. At times, your trail through it can be hard to follow, but it generally goes northwest, re-entering forest cover near the meadow's north edge. Then, to avoid damp soil, the trail stays close to the base of Smith Peak as it traverses northwest to western Smith Meadow, by which you'll find a junction with the Smith Peak Trail (Trip 15). If you are backpacking, you won't want to carry a heavy pack 1370 feet up to the 7751-foot summit of Smith Peak. Look for adequate campsites on gentle, forested slopes about

Shallow pools in Middle Tuolumne River below White Wolf

100 to 200 yards west of the trail intersection.

The trail to the summit is direct and steep, so before you start, you might want to get some water at a trickling creeklet only a few yards from the intersection. If conditions are dry, you'll have to get water at Cottonwood Creek, which you crossed about a quarter mile back.

We start our climb in a forest of white firs, sugar pines, and incense-cedars, and by the time we reach the first of three seasonally wet meadows—all of them rich in summer wildflowers—we have left the incense-cedars behind. If you're hiking this trail before July, you're likely to run into snow patches from here on. Although you may lose the trail beneath them, you won't lose your way, as long as you keep heading northeast upslope. A second wet meadow, marking the halfway point, is quickly passed; we pass a third one midway between it and the Tuolumne River canyon crest. By the time we reach the crest, red firs have become the dominant forest tree, with Jeffrey pines occupying the drier, sunnier spots and white firs in between. If you came up on horses, leave them at the canyon-crest saddle, for the footpaths ahead are steep and narrow.

The final 250-foot elevation gain can be made by any of several brush-lined paths. Perhaps the safest and most frequently used path is the one that climbs the west slope, then traverses along the south slope. To reach the best viewpoint, atop pitted granitic rocks, you'll have to plow through a dense, brushy cover of huckleberry oaks.

From the pocketed rocks, you can gaze down into the deep Grand Canyon of the Tuolumne River and see the Hetch Hetchy Reservoir, about 4000 feet below you.

After your stay on the summit, descend to Smith Meadow, then retrace your steps to the trailhead. Alternatively, if someone is willing to drive to Mather Ranger Station, you can follow Trip 15 for 8.3 miles down to it, which is easier than climbing back up to White Wolf.

GLACIATION AND VIEWS AT GRAND CANYON OF THE TUOLUMNE

During the last two major glaciations, glaciers filled the canyon below us to a depth of 3500 feet or more, coming to within 500 or 600 feet of our summit. Being so thick, these glaciers exerted a force of about 100 tons per square foot on the canyon's bottom; nevertheless, the shape and depth of the canyon haven't changed all that much despite repeated glaciation over at least the last 2 million years. Indeed, it hasn't deepened much in the last 10 million years, if not considerably longer. As you can see, the canyon is distinctly V-shaped in cross profile, as it is below the reservoir. From its dam site, the two glaciers advanced about 20 or so miles farther down-canyon.

You can also see that much of the Yosemite landscape north, south, and west of the river's canyon is a gentle, rolling uplands topography, which has evolved only very slowly over the last 80 million years.

Scanning the northeast skyline, keen map users should be able to identify, from east to northeast, Mt. Hoffmann, plus the prominent crest summits of Mt. Conness, Matterhorn Peak, and Tower Peak. Across the main canyon, Tiltill Creek canyon descends toward us, its floor and slopes stripped bare of soil by glaciers, exposing naked granite. In contrast, Rancheria Mountain, above its east slopes, is quite forested. Volcanic deposits are rare within the park, and the bulk of them are on or near this flat-topped mountain, which stood above glaciers.

TRIP **20**

White Wolf to Pate Valley

S 🔍 BP

DISTANCE: 20.9 miles semiloop

ELEVATIONS: 4230'/7980'
+600'/-4100'/±9400'

SEASON: Late June to mid-October

USE: Moderate

MAPS: *Tamarack Flat,*
Hetch Hetchy Reservoir,
Ten Lakes

TRAIL LOG:

4.2	Pate Valley Trail
6.4	Morrison Creek
10.4	Pate Valley
16.6	White Wolf Trail
18.1	Harden Lake
20.9	White Wolf

INTRODUCTION: Pate Valley is sort of a miniature Yosemite Valley without the automobiles and tourists. It therefore attracts quite a number of backpackers, who, in turn, attract a few bears. Nevertheless, if you want to have a warm, spacious camp along the Tuolumne River, Pate Valley proper or its outlying areas may just be for you. Be forewarned that the switchbacking trail down to the floor west of Pate Valley involves a mostly unrelenting 3700-foot descent, which can be hard on the knees. And then, of course, you'll later have to make the climb back up. However, by doing this descent and ascent, you a gain an appreciation of the great depth of the Grand Canyon of the Tuolumne River. Amazingly, past glaciers flowing through this canyon were so thick that they overflowed its rims and spilled laterally onto adjacent bench lands.

DIRECTIONS TO THE TRAILHEAD: From Crane Flat, drive northeast 14.5 miles up Hwy. 120 to the White Wolf turnoff and follow that road down to where it is closed to motor vehicles, just past the entrance to White Wolf Campground. Trail begins in map section C4.

DESCRIPTION: This hike is described as a semiloop, since I feel that both trails leading to the Pate Valley Trail are worth taking. However, if mosquitoes in the White Wolf area are intolerable, often until mid-July, you should first hike down to Harden Lake, following the last 2.8 miles of this trip's description in reverse. Also before mid-July, you may find significant patches of snow on the route starting east. Regardless which way you take, be aware that by late summer, the route *may* be dry, so bring sufficient water to last for a half-day hike.

For the described route, walk a short distance from your trailhead parking area to a trail starting east from trailhead opposite White Wolf Lodge. The trail first skirts the south edge of White Wolf Campground and then traverses east about 0.8 mile through a shady lodgepole pine forest to a crossing of the Middle Tuolumne River—maybe a ford in early season—about a quarter mile before reaching a junction with a trail right to Lukens Lake (Trip 21). We go left, northwest, and continue a traverse across the flat, forested floor. A short climb soon follows, which ends on a broad, shallow gap, which, at 7980 feet, is our route's highest point.

Leaving the crest, we descend northwest down a gully to the east edge of a meadow, beyond which we enter level terrain strewn with glacial sediments. Only one significant creek drains this terrain, seasonally rich in ground water, and, by late summer, it can be dry. Just beyond the creek, we climb to the crest of a lateral moraine. Amid red firs, we now start the long descent to Pate Valley, hiking over or past the crests of four more moraines, these left by a Tioga-age glacier that retreated from this area by 15,000 years ago. By the time our 1.3-mile descent and its dozen-plus switchbacks end, more than 600 feet lower at a junction with the Pate Valley Trail, the forest cover has changed from red firs and western white pines to white firs, Jeffrey pines, and incense-cedars. Bushy black oaks are also found near the junction.

Our return route goes west to Harden Lake, but we strike east on a sympathetic trail that drops only very gently, thus giving our knees a chance to recover from our first switchbacking descent. In a half mile, you'll cross a spring-fed creeklet whose banks are hidden among a luxuriant growth of water-loving vegetation—alders, aspen, American dogwoods, bracken ferns, thinbleberries, and currants. In late summer, this is your last *usually* reliable source of water until you reach the floor of the Grand Canyon of the Tuolumne River. In a few minutes, we cut through a flat-floored notch high on this canyon's south wall, then, after a few more minutes of gentle descent, we reach seasonal Morrison Creek, about a quarter mile beyond the spring-fed creeklet. Here you are at about 6750 feet elevation, and have performed the first third of your descent into the canyon. After paralleling it for a quarter mile, we come to a low, rocky knoll, on our left. Here you may be scolded by Steller's jays—avian indicators of a warmer plant community. This is a good spot for a rest, and you might do it from the knoll, which offers quite a view west-north-west down the trough holding Hetch Hetchy Reservoir to Wapama Falls, dashing into the reservoir's far end.

Onward, we start our second set of short switchbacks—about four dozen of them—that lead us on a descent to a crossing of Morrison Creek. Along this descent through a white fir forest, note that sugar pines appear, incense-cedars grow in numbers, and black oaks now have tree stature. On the dry, rocky ridge paralleling our descent grow scraggly western junipers and pervasive huckleberry oaks. Finally, we come to a crossing of Morrison Creek, at about 5600 feet, and you've completed almost two-thirds of your descent. In late summer, the creek can be bone dry, and then flies can be a special nuisance. During this season, they can become almost unbearable on the canyon floor, way below you, if you are covered with sweat, but they aren't bad once you've bathed in the river and have gotten into fresh clothes.

Our last set of switchbacks—about 55 of them down to the river—begins just past Morrison Creek. Along this descent, you'll get numerous views of the Grand Canyon of the Tuolumne River, whose distant floor gradually draws nearer. Black oaks tend to be the dominant shade tree at first, but halfway down, after we cross a dramatic water-polished gully that descends the canyon's south wall, the vegetation soon changes. Canyon live oaks and bay trees slowly put in an appearance. Summer afternoon temperatures can be hot, even under the trees, by the time we cross a granite gap, about 250 feet above the canyon's floor. Greenleaf manzanitas, seen higher up, are now replaced by whiteleaf manzanitas.

Beyond the gap is a grassy pond, which can dry up in late season; however, before then, it makes a warm swimming hole. At the pond's east end, we cross the crest of a low moraine, then negotiate the few remaining switchbacks down to the flat floor of this great river canyon. Here, the forest composition is nearly identical to that of Yosemite Valley, dominated by ponderosa pines, black oaks, and incense-cedars. Over the next 2 miles of fairly level hiking, you'll pass several near-river campsites, and isolated camps could be set up in a number of places. Only several hundred yards before two crossings of the Tuolumne River, you'll enter Pate Valley proper and pass through a very large riverside camping area popular with equestrians.

Backpackers can find more isolated sites by crossing the two bridges over the often chilly Tuolumne River, then climbing through a narrow bedrock notch and arriving at the north bank of the river's main branch. About a minute's walk beyond the north-bank camps you'll come to a trail junction.

[S] **SIDE TRIP TO PLEASANT VALLEY:** For most, the dry, 4.7-mile climb to the Pleasant Valley Trail—3500 feet higher—is not worth the toil and sweat. Furthermore, when this steep trail is not maintained, it can become seriously overgrown with brush. However, some may want to do the first 0.75 mile, with about 500 feet of ascent, to where the trail levels off, then, in the next half mile, before serious climbing starts, leave it for good-to-excellent camping near either bank of Piute Creek.

For those who want to reach Pleasant Valley, after the 4.7-mile climb, you traverse about 1 mile north before dropping about 850 feet, mostly on short switchbacks, 1.2 miles northwest down to the outlet creek of a lakelet. The lakelet is just off the trail, and Table Lake is just north of it. You should see both of these along your descent, as well as Irwin Bright Lake north of Table Lake, separated by a low, broad divide. If these aren't remote enough for you, then head to Saddle Horse Lake, reached by going around either side of a conspicuous dome-like hill west of Irwin Bright Lake. **END OF SIDE TRIP.**

To return to your trailhead, retrace your steps 6.2 miles southwest back up to the junction with the White Wolf Trail, 0.75 mile west of Morrison Creek. On this ascent, start early, while it is still cool, take it easy, resting often, and carry *at least* one quart of water. When you reach the mentioned junction, head for Harden Lake on a trail whose first mile is a comfortable contour. Many aspens are passed along the second half of this contour. These aspens fill their thirsty appetites by tapping the large "reservoir" of water stored within the morainal sediments we traverse across. One source of this "reservoir" is our immediate goal, Harden Lake, which has no surface outlet, but rather loses some of its water via percolation through the morainal sediments. To reach Harden Lake, we climb moderately to steeply up about 20 switch-

backs, entering a forest of lodgepole pines, then of red firs and western white pines.

When you arrive at Harden Lake, you'll need a rest and probably a refreshing swim—if this seasonal lake hasn't already leaked so much that it is barely a mud hole. From the lake, your trail quickly ends at a road, which you follow southeast for a quarter mile, then take a left-branching trail 0.75 mile over to the old Tioga Road, which heads 1.8 miles up along the infant Middle Tuolumne River to White Wolf. If Harden Lake was dry, you can get water from the river. It's not deep enough to swim in, but there are several small pools deep enough to lie in, should you be filthy dirty and want to get clean before reaching your vehicle.

TRIP 21

White Wolf to Lukens Lake

E ↗ DH

DISTANCE: 4.6 miles out and back

ELEVATIONS: 7870´/8240´
+420´/-50´/±940´

SEASON: Early July to mid-October

USE: Moderate

MAPS: *Tamarack Flat,*
Yosemite Falls

TRAIL LOG:

0.9 First junction
1.8 Second junction
2.3 Lukens Lake

INTRODUCTION: This is the longer, yet more popular route to Lukens Lake. The second route, Trip 22, would be more popular if its trailhead were better signed. Since Lukens Lake is already heavily visited, however, it is perhaps best that the shorter route's trailhead is not that conspicuous. Lukens Lake is very similar to seasonal Harden Lake (Trip 18), except that Lukens never dries up! If you enjoy one, you'll enjoy the other. Before mid-July, you can expect patches of snow along the White Wolf-Lukens Lake route.

DIRECTIONS TO THE TRAILHEAD: From Crane Flat, drive northeast 14.5 miles up Hwy. 120 to the White Wolf turnoff and follow that road down to where it is closed to motor vehicles, just past the entrance to White Wolf Campground. Trail begins in map section C4.

DESCRIPTION: Our trail to Lukens Lake skirts the south edge of White Wolf Campground and traverses east about 0.75 mile through a shady lodgepole pine forest to a crossing of the Middle Tuolumne River—

maybe a ford in early season—about a quarter mile before reaching a junction with a trail north to Pate Valley (Trip 20). Until mid-July, the mosquitoes can be particularly abundant along this level stretch, for the ground is nearly saturated with water. From the junction, we hike east upstream for a nearly level, shady, short mile and come to a second junction. The trail east toward Ten Lakes first climbs and then descends, for a total of 3.8 miles, to the shorter, more popular Ten Lakes Trail (Trip 23).

Leaving the junction, we head south a few steps, jump across the infant Middle Tuolumne River, then begin a continuous, generally moderate, half-mile ascent to Lukens Lake. Climbing this trail segment, we cross at least four glacial moraines, the final one forming a rim along the north shore of Lukens Lake.

Along Lukens Lake's north shore, we now find a well-mixed conifer forest, with red firs, western white pines, and mountain

WILDLIFE AT WHITE WOLF

If you stay at White Wolf Campground and rise early in the morning, you just might be fortunate enough to see a great gray owl perched on the trailhead sign or on a small lodgepole that has invaded White Wolf meadow. With keen, alert senses, this largest species of the North American owls waits for one of the meadow's many rodents to make a move. In this mid-elevation meadow, the likely prey would be a shrew, deer mouse, meadow mouse, western jumping mouse, Belding ground squirrel, or perhaps even a pocket gopher. Also preying on these rodents is the more abundant coyote, a predator that is found in all of Yosemite's plant communities except the alpine one. Coyotes and great gray owls may also be seen in another similar habitat, Crane Flat meadow.

hemlocks, joining the lodgepole pines, which have dominated so much of our route. Like Harden Lake, Lukens Lake is a 9-acre, shallow, warm lake, and it lacks views of stunning peaks. Be aware that because this lake is less than 1 mile from the Tioga Road (via the next trip), overnight camping is prohibited.

GEOLOGY OF LUKENS LAKE

The lateral moraine along the north shore of Lukens Lake, like the other glacial moraines, was created late in the Tioga glaciation as the huge Tuolumne glacier system was waning about 16,000 years ago. Before then, at the height of the glaciation some 20,000 years ago, the glacier was thicker and had filled the Lukens Lake basin with thin, stagnant ice. During the preceding Tahoe glaciation, the same thing happened, but Tahoe deposits were obliterated by the following Tioga glaciation. The ice surface of each glacier was not quite thick enough to spill south through the saddle crossed in the next trip.

Also, like Harden, Lukens is one of the Sierra's rare moraine-dammed lakes. Unlike Harden, Lukens has trout—rainbow, brook, and brown— and it tends to have a grassy bottom, not a bouldery one, because the glacial ice here was so thin it hardly flowed, and so precious little deposits were left. Also unlike Harden, the moraine dam here is sufficiently thick to prevent serious leakage, so Lukens' water level does not drop dramatically, as does the water level at Harden. This makes Lukens Lake a good swimming lake, especially with its grassy bottom. No toe-stubbing here.

Lukens Lake, view southeast

TRIP 22

Tioga Road to Lukens Lake

E ↗ DH

DISTANCE: 2.2 miles out and back

ELEVATIONS: 8190'/8340'
+170'/-130'/±600'

SEASON: Early July to mid-October

USE: Moderate

MAP: *Yosemite Falls*

TRAIL LOG:

0.4 Saddle
1.1 Lukens Lake

INTRODUCTION: This is the shorter approach to Lukens Lake, about half the length as along the trail east from White Wolf (Trip 21). No overnight camping is allowed.

DIRECTIONS TO THE TRAILHEAD: From Crane Flat, drive northeast 14.5 miles up Hwy. 120 to the White Wolf turnoff, then continue an additional 1.9 miles to a paved turnout on the highway's south side. Trail begins in map section D4.

DESCRIPTION: From the Hwy. 120 turnout, located in a shady gully near a curve in the highway, look for a signed trailhead on the north side of the road. Among red firs and western white pines, make an easy climb north to a viewless saddle, which the mighty Tuolumne River glaciers failed to top (see Trip 21 for more details). On the fairly open bedrock slope ascending west from the saddle are scattered rocks that may look like glacial deposits—but they are not. These collectively are a lag deposit, a rare feature in our area. If you walk a hundred yards or so up this slope, you can see where the bedrock is exfoliating, producing the scattered rocks that form this local deposit.

Leaving the saddle, you make an equally easy descent to the southeast end of a sedge-dominated meadow that also contains conspicuous corn lilies and, as usual, willows. From this meadow's corner, the main trail strikes 0.2 mile northwest toward the north shore of Lukens Lake, 〰 while a lesser trail—one of use—strikes west toward its south shore. For more information about this lake, see the sidebar "Geology of Lukens Lake," on page 152.

Lag deposit on bedrock slope ascending west from saddle

TRIP 23

Ten Lakes Basin via Yosemite Creek

Ⓜ ↗ DH, BP, X

DISTANCE: 12.6 miles
out and back to Lake 2

ELEVATIONS: 7500'/9670'
+2330'/-880'/±6420'

SEASON: Mid-July to mid-October

USE: Heavy

MAPS: *Yosemite Falls, Ten Lakes*

TRAIL LOG:

2.3	Junction with trail to White Wolf
4.3	Half Moon Meadow
5.2	Junction with trail to Grant Lakes
5.4	Ten Lakes Pass
6.3	Lake 2
6.3	Lake 3
6.5	Lower Grant Lake
6.8	Lake 1
6.8	Lake 4
7.3	Lake 5
7.7	Lake 6
8.0	Lake 7

INTRODUCTION: The Ten Lakes Basin is extremely popular with weekend backpackers. With only a few hours' hiking effort, you can attain any of its seven major lakes. The three most accessible receive moderate-to-heavy use, but the other four, off the beaten track, are worth the effort for those who want relatively secluded camping. These lakes, plus the two Grant Lakes, are situated at about 8950 to 9400 feet, making them subalpine. Still, at least the three lowest of the Ten Lakes Basin warm sufficiently for enjoyable midsummer swimming.

At the end of the description is a longer, lightly used alternate route into Ten Lakes Basin, which takes 14.6 miles, versus 7.7 miles, to reach Lake 6, a large, eastern trailside lake. Besides being longer, this alternate route involves about an extra 4000 feet of elevation gain and loss. However, it does have some great views, which the standard trail lacks. Also, you might consider hiking in one trail to the Ten Lakes Basin and taking the other one out, a total distance of 22.3 miles. To reach the May Lake Trailhead from Crane Flat, drive northeast 27 miles up Hwy. 120 to the old Tioga Road. This junction is 3.7 miles west of the trailhead parking area by the southwest shore of Tenaya Lake. Take the old Tioga Road, signed for May Lake, 1.75 miles northeast up to an obvious trailhead parking area.

DIRECTIONS TO THE TRAILHEAD: From Crane Flat, drive northeast 19.6 miles up Hwy. 120 to the trailhead parking area, on *both* sides of the highway, immediately before the highway bridges signed Yosemite Creek. Trail begins in map section D4.

DESCRIPTION: From the west end of the highway's north parking lot, a spur trail goes 90 yards northwest to the main trail, the Ten Lakes Trail. On it, we hike up-canyon, first through a lodgepole pine flat, and soon we climb away from unseen Yosemite Creek and encounter Jeffrey pines and huckleberry oaks. Next, we meet shaggy-barked western junipers as we climb moderately but relatively briefly up to drier granitic slopes. This ascent, which may seem unnecessary, takes us above most of the lodgepoles, which tend to harbor mosquitoes. Also, the climb gives us views of Yosemite Creek canyon, Mt. Hoffmann, and the county-line crest north of it. Soon after we get these views, the trail levels, enters a forest of red firs and lodgepoles, and then, about 2.25 miles into our hike, reaches a creekside junction with a trail leading 5.6 miles to White Wolf, its road, lodge, and campground.

From the junction, we boulder hop the creek and leave a nearby campsite to begin a moderate climb up a well-forested moraine left after the retreat of a large glacier 15,000 years ago. Our climbing in a forest of red fir and western white pine ends at the top of a moraine. Behind it lies crescent-shaped, seasonally wet Half Moon Meadow, which probably exists because the moraine impedes the meadow's drainage. The trail cuts across the meadow's relatively dry north edge, which nevertheless contains enough water to support a healthy crop of corn lilies. By its northeast corner, about 4.5 miles from the trailhead, is a campsite, nestled under lodgepoles and close to a creek. The next stretch of ascent is steep and dry, so rest here and perhaps get a drink.

Roughly three dozen short, steep switchbacks guide us about 0.75 mile up, almost to the Tuolumne/Mariposa county-line crest, from which we veer away to a junction with a trail to Grant Lakes. From it, a poorly designed trail drops about 400 feet in its 1.2-mile length to Lower Grant Lake. A far better route, at least for cross-country hikers, is to start from the south corner of Half Moon Meadow and climb southeast cross-country up about 400 feet of slopes to this lake. There is no maintained trail to Upper Grant Lake, but rather just a faint, discontinuous use trail. The more popular lower lake has better campsites than the upper lake, though fishing for rainbow trout may be better at the less visited upper lake.

Leaving the Grant Lakes Trail junction, the Ten Lakes Trail climbs gently across a gravelly slope that can be covered in midsummer with large, deliciously scented lupines. These taper off just before we cross the county-line crest, Ten Lakes Pass, which here is a broad, level, unglaciated surface that has weathered very little over many millions of years. Leaving Merced River drainage, we enter Tuolumne River drainage as we descend briefly north to a shallow saddle. Just beyond it is a small summit and, to the left of it, is flat-topped

Colby Mountain, which crowns the west rim of the Ten Lakes Basin. This undistinguished summit is named for a very distinguished man, William Colby, the third president of the Sierra Club—just after John Muir and Professor Joseph LeConte. Colby served the club for nearly half a century and was truly one of the greatest conservationists in the early days of Yosemite National Park.

As we start a descent from the shallow saddle, a panorama of steep-sided, glaciated Ten Lakes Basin opens all around us, and three of the western lakes are clearly evident. On our descent of short-switchbacks into Ten Lakes Basin, the trail veers north far enough three times to get partial views down into the upper part of the Grand Canyon of the Tuolumne River, which is so deep that you can't see the canyon bottom. Beyond the canyon, you see northern park lands extending to the park's Sierran-crest boundary.

The descent, which started close to some windblown whitebark pines growing on the county-line crest, ends at a creek that flows from Lake 3 to Lake 2, in a forest of mountain hemlocks and lodgepole and western white pines. The presence of hemlock and lodgepole, together with lakeside red heather and Labrador tea, indicates prime mosquito country—at least before August. Until then, use a tent to escape their bloodthirsty attacks. However, camping is quite enjoyable by early August, when the lakes are at their warmest temperatures, and also during September, after most hikers have left. It is then that a common, easily missed plant, the dwarf bilberry, makes its thumb-size presence known by turning to a blazing crimson color.

Ten Lakes Basin has seven prominent lakes that appear on the park's topographic map, and for the sake of easy reference, I refer to them by number, starting with the northwesternmost, Lake 1, situated just west of and below Grand Mountain, a misnamed ridge. To its south is Lake 2, the most popular because it is the first lake one reaches and the largest of the western lakes (just north of and below the trail). (The elevation changes mentioned at the start of this trip are to Lake 2; all other lakes involve additional elevation changes.) Not far south of and above the trail is Lake 3, followed by Lake 4. Continuing counterclockwise, we head east up to Lake 5, then northeast down to large, eastern Lake 6, also popular because it is along the trail. North of the trail and considerably below it is Lake 7. The popular lakes 2 and 6 are also the largest, at 21 and 24 acres, respectively. Lake 3 receives moderate use, Lake 1, lighter use, and lakes 4, 5, and 7, very little use. All lakes have adjacent barren slopes or cliffs, making all photogenic.

From a boulder hop or log cross of the creek, you go just 80 yards east on main trail to a use trail branching south to lakes 3 and 4. This trail will be described later. First, you are about 100 yards above Lake 2, which you can expect to have as many campers as are at the other six lakes combined. To reach Lake 2, just head downslope to the lake. Several ample campsites exist on the broad, low ridge above the lake's west shore; more can be found along its west shore. East along its south shore are obvious diving rocks. From mid-July to

Lake 3 with a dramatic cliff for a backdrop

mid-August, expect afternoon water temperatures to reach the mid- to high 60s. The northwest corner of the lake is almost cut off from the main part. Here you'll find bedrock benches and small rock islands, as well as the warmest swimming, although it's mostly fine for wading. This is a great lake for basking on rocks but a poor one for fishing, given its popularity.

Just east of the outlet at the lake's north tip, you may see a primitive trail climbing north to northeast toward Lake 1. This dies out among bedrock, along which you may find more than one ducked route. To reach Lake 1, just maintain a north-northeast bearing up to a minor gap in the crest, about 100 feet above Lake 2. (If you're heading north *downward*, you're on your way to a very steep drop into the Grand Canyon of the Tuolumne River.) From the crest, Lake 1 is in plain view, and you drop about 70 feet in elevation to reach it in a couple of minutes. Lake 1 has a beautiful backdrop by the east cliff above it (the west side of Grand Mountain). Small camps exist on a bench beside the north shore, and from its edge you have tree-filtered views across the Grand Canyon. Lake 1 competes with Lake 7 as the warmest lake. Afternoon water temperatures can reach 70 degrees or more. You can dive into the lake from its northeast shore or from a linear island along the east shore, near good basking rocks. From here, you can reach Lake 7, about 0.6 mile to the east as the nutcracker flies, but you'll take about 1 mile. From the lake's southeast corner, head south up to the top of a minor ridge, then east up steep but safe, forested slopes to a broad crest, then descend more or less due east a half mile to the west shore of Lake 7. An easier way to reach it is from the main trail between lakes 2 and 6. From the junction between lakes 2 and 3, this trail climbs about 500 feet to a divide south of Grand Mountain, then drops southeast en route to Lake 6. Where the trail levels out just before Lake 6, just head downslope. Don't try to follow the outlet creek of Lake 6, since the slopes get steep along one stretch.

Keep to its west side, and where the gradient nearly flattens to zero, head east-north-east about a quarter mile to Lake 7. This may be the least visited lake. It is grass lined and may be the most mosquito prone. It is shallow and warm, good for swimming from basking slabs by its northeast shore. This lake rivals Lake 2 for camping area: There is about an acre of nearly flat land beyond the north shore east of the outlet creek.

From the junction just above popular Lake 2, a fair number of hikers make the mile-long hike up and then down and then up to Lake 6. Its northwest shore has quite a lot of flat land along it, a large camping area that can hold a couple dozen campers. It tends to be a bit cooler than Lake 2, but probably has better fishing, due to cooler water and fewer anglers. From the west shore of this lake, you have an easy cross-country hike southwest a half mile to chilly Lake 5. (See directions in reverse that follow.)

Back at the junction just above Lake 2, about 80 yards beyond the creek crossing, go just 0.1 mile south up a use trail to reach the north end of Lake 3. Lakes 3, 4, and 5 are best for fishing, since they are coldest. Lake 3 may have the most dramatic backdrop, since an impressive crest looms high above it. It also has good camping above its north shore, as well as small sites along its east shore. The use trail continues south along lake's east shore, then more or less follows the creek connecting lakes 3 and 4. This trail receives less use than below, and it becomes somewhat obscure about the last 200 yards before reaching Lake 4. Also dramatic, this lake is nestled in a very confining cirque. This lake probably is not popular because it is about a half mile off the main trail, and this seems to be for the better, given the minimal camping possibilities. To reach Lake 5, you go cross-country. I prefer heading more or less east directly upslope rather than following the winding creek, which saves about a quarter mile of walking. Like Lake 4, Lake 5 is chilly and hemmed-in. And like Lake 7, it is

virtually unused, and so it may have great fishing. Look for small campsites on gentler slopes high above the northeast shore. From this lake, you make a relatively easy cross-country jaunt over to Lake 6. From the outlet, you head north about a quarter mile up to a lakelet, then about 250 yards northeast to a minor gap in the lower part of a northwest-trending ridge, then descend a quarter mile northeast to the northwest shore of Lake 6, a large, eastern trailside lake.

After visiting one or more of the basin's sparkling gems, hike back out the way you came—or, from the large eastern trailside lake, follow the long trail out to May Lake (the reverse of the following route to it). Alternatively, you can hike in to the Ten Lakes Basin from the May Lake Trailhead.

[A] **ALTERNATE ROUTE TO TEN LAKES BASIN:** The 1.2-mile trail to May Lake begins by the southwest side of a small pond on Snow Flat. Our sandy trail ascends gently through forest cover, where we recognize the western white pine by its long, narrow cones and checkerboard bark pattern, and we notice how the red fir cones, near the tops of these trees, stand upright on the branches, unlike the hanging cones of pines and hemlocks. The initial ascent leads up open granite slabs dotted with lodgepoles. Then, as we switchback west up a short, steep slope, we have fine views of Cathedral Peak in the east, Mt. Clark in the southeast, and Clouds Rest and Half Dome in the south. Near the top of the slope, the forest cover thickens and the western white pines become larger and more handsome. Just beyond the crest, we find ourselves in a flat beneath a half dozen superb, large hemlocks by deep, often chilly May Lake.

Continue along its east shore to its north shore, then leave the lake on the High Sierra Camps Loop Trail, climbing to a quickly reached shallow pass. The trail soon begins a switchbacking descent that provides views of Cathedral Peak, standing high above Polly Dome. After about a dozen switchbacks, our descending trail's gradient eases, and, in forest shade, we wind southeast, crossing four seasonal creeklets before sighting Raisin Lake, located just off the trail and 3 miles from our trailhead. Because it is shallow and has no icy creeks to feed it, this can be one of the warmest swimming holes in the park.

Beyond the lake, our trail goes briefly east toward a low knoll, then heads north beside it up to a nearby, second shallow pass. At it, a panorama of the High Sierra unfolds, with Mt. Conness dominating the Sierra Crest. Note that Polly Dome is very *un*-domelike and rather is basically rectangular. Leaving the pass and its southward view of Clouds Rest, we descend some rocky switchbacks, then traverse north for 0.75 mile, staying high on the slopes above Murphy Creek and its largely hidden trail (Trip 31). At the end of the traverse, we cross our third shallow pass in a stand of lodgepoles that obstruct a backward view of Tenaya Lake. As our trail descends north-facing slopes for a quarter mile to a junction, the forest cover becomes increasingly dominated by mountain hemlocks, which do well in areas of long-lasting snow cover.

At the trail junction, 4.7 miles from our trailhead, we leave the popular High Sierra Camps Loop Trail (Trip 35), and start southwest on the lightly used eastern part of the Ten Lakes Trail. After a quarter mile, the trail veers north, and, as we hike in that direction, lodgepole pines, red firs, and western white pines increase in numbers. They soon diminish as we gain altitude, giving us fair views east toward the Cathedral Range. Moderately graded switchbacks take us up to a crest saddle—a good breather stop—and then we continue almost a half mile farther, first up to a crest—this route's highest point at 9870 feet—and then briefly down to a nearby pond. This is a good rest spot, although, at 7.7 miles from the trailhead, one might look for isolated campsites in this vicinity, first obtaining drinking water from the pond. From sites about here, one can experience beautiful sunrises. Also from here,

one can head about a half mile southwest up a ridge to steeper slopes of Tuolumne Peak proper, which can be scrambled up—cautiously—without a rope.

From the pond, our trail climbs, drops, and winds westward to a good overlook point high above the South Fork Cathedral Creek canyon. Short, rocky switchbacks carry you down toward the canyon floor, and then you veer south on a long contour just below a low-angle cliff, only to resume more switchbacks. You reach the South Fork in minutes, and, when hiking down along it, you can find suitable campsites on either side of this creek. After 2 miles of winding trail, you cross the South Fork, 12.3 miles from the trailhead. This is a ford in early season, and from it you go briefly downstream, then prepare for a two-dozen-switchback climb of a generally open, juniper-dotted slope. Your last chance for secluded camping is in this vicinity, below the crossing.

As you labor up the switchbacks, stop and rest and take in the ever-expanding views of northern Yosemite, from Mt. Gibbs westward, with the north wall of the mighty gorge of the Tuolumne River dominating the foreground. As the switchbacks abate, the trail enters forest shade and then climbs a mile to a seasonal pond. Beyond it, about 150 feet below, is the large, eastern lake (Lake 6) of the Ten Lakes Basin, 14.6 miles from the trailhead. **END OF ALTERNATE ROUTE.**

TRIP **24**

Old Tioga Road to May Lake and Mt. Hoffmann

Ⓔ ↗ DH, BP

DISTANCE: 2.4 miles out and back

ELEVATIONS: 8840'/9350'
+530'/-30'/±1120'

SEASON: Mid-July to mid-October

USE: Heavy

MAP: *Tenaya Lake*

TRAIL LOG:

1.2 May Lake

INTRODUCTION: May Lake is a very popular destination because it is such a short hike. Dayhikers can reach it in less than a half hour, and all but the slowest backpackers in less than an hour. At 1.2 miles from the trailhead, May Lake has the most easily accessible campsites in the park, and so may be ideal for novice backpackers or for those with young children. Additionally, these are good basecamp sites for an ascent of Mt. Hoffmann, although strong hikers can reach that summit in about an hour. Mt. Hoffmann, centrally located in Yosemite National Park, provides the best all-around views of this park's varied landscapes. The 3-mile hike up to it is offered as a side trip, and if you do it, you will have a total ascent and descent of about 4200 feet.

DIRECTIONS TO THE TRAILHEAD: From Crane Flat, drive northeast 27 miles up Hwy. 120 to the old Tioga Road; this junction is 3.7 miles west of the trailhead parking area by the southwest shore of Tenaya Lake. Take the old Tioga Road, signed for May Lake, 1.75 miles northeast up to an obvious trailhead parking area. Trail begins in map section E4.

DESCRIPTION: Although this walk is treated here as a dayhike, there is no reason that one should not stay overnight at the May Lake High Sierra Camp. Its cabins, however, usually are reserved months in advance, leaving the majority of overnighters to stay in a hikers' camp just above the lake's south shore. Like at other High Sierra Camps you'll find bearproof food-storage boxes.

The trail begins by the southwest side of a small pond on Snow Flat in a moderately dense stand of hemlock, red fir, and western white and lodgepole pines. To the northwest is Mt. Hoffmann, which is at the geographic center of the park. In a little vale to the east of the trail, water lies late in the season, permitting corn lilies to bloom into August. Our sandy trail ascends gently through forest cover, where we recognize the western white pine by its long, narrow cones and checkerboard bark pattern, and we notice how the red fir cones, near the tops of these trees, stand upright on the branches, unlike the hanging cones of pines and hemlocks.

The initial ascent leads up open granite slabs dotted with lodgepoles. Then, as we switchback west up a short, steep slope, we have fine views of Cathedral Peak in the east, Mt. Clark in the southeast, and Clouds Rest and Half Dome in the south. Near the top of the slope, the forest cover thickens and the western white pines become larger and more handsome. Just beyond the crest, we find ourselves in a flat beneath a half dozen superb, large hemlocks by deep, chilly May Lake. Swimming is not allowed, but you may try your luck at catching the lake's brook or rainbow trout while contemplating the lake's beautiful backdrop of the east slopes of massive Mt. Hoffmann.

Ⓢ **SIDE TRIP TO MT. HOFFMANN:** Perhaps more hikers ascend Mt. Hoffmann than any other 10,000-plus-foot peak in the park, with only Mt. Dana (Hike 52) challenging its popularity. As with any high peak ascent, wear dark glasses and lots of sunscreen, for there's about 30% less air on

A summit view east: May Lake, Tenaya Lake, and the Sierra Crest from Tioga Pass to Mt. Lyell complex

the summit, and the ultraviolet rays come on strong. Also, avoid altitude sickness, which is brought on by overexerting yourself, particularly after a large meal. If you are not in shape, camp overnight at May Lake to get partly acclimatized, then climb the peak the next day. Take it easy, for the route is short. However, abandon your attempt if a thunderstorm is approaching.

From May Lake's southeast corner, you'll see a trail striking west. On it, you pass a backpackers' camp that extends westward, and then you traverse across metasedimentary rocks cropping out above the lake's southwest shore. You now follow it south, first through a small gap, then through a boulder-strewn wildflower garden. You might lose the trail here, but the route south—up a shallow gully to a small, linear meadow—is quite obvious. From the meadow's south end, near a saddle, the trail goes 100 yards southwest and then climbs northwest up to the lower end of the broad, sloping, lupine-decked summit area. Numerous summits exist, but the western

summit is the highest, at 10,850 feet, and you have an easy, safe scramble to its top.

Using this guidebook's topo map of the park, you can identify almost every major peak in it, since most are visible from here. Note how Mt. Hoffmann's nearly flat summit plateau contrasts with the mountain's steep sides. Mass wasting, accelerated by the presence of past glacial climates, has caused retreat through rockfall on all sides of this mountain, diminishing the size of the plateau. The same has occurred on summit areas of Mt. Conness, Dana Plateau, Dore Pass, and a few other spots that once were part of an extensive, rolling landscape back in the late days of the dinosaurs some 80 million to 65 million years ago. When you return, don't be tempted to take any shortcuts, since other routes are steeper, have loose rock, and are potentially dangerous. **END OF SIDE TRIP.**

CHAPTER 11

Trips of Yosemite's West-Central Lands Between the Tioga Road and Yosemite Valley

Introduction to this Area

O f all this guide's sections, this is the only one that lacks a prominent, nearby peak. It is chiefly a heavily forested uplands landscape of rolling, gentle topography. However, along this land's southern perimeter, the slopes end in steep-walled cliffs that make up the north wall of Yosemite Valley. Lacking alpine scenery, the trails in this section get only light-to-moderate use except for the stretch of trail that descends from the brink of Upper Yosemite Fall to the Valley floor. Compensating for the alpine deficiencies are five spectacular viewpoints along the Valley's north rim: El Capitan, Eagle Peak, the Upper Yosemite Fall brink, Yosemite Point, and North Dome. There are also great views from the Devils Dance Floor, reached by a short cross-country route described as Trip 26. Finally, you can

Half Dome from Indian Rock

study the ever-changing perspective of Half Dome along your descent along Trip 30 into Tenaya Canyon.

Supplies and Services

Absolutely everything you'll need for a Yosemite outdoor experience can be purchased in the western foothills town of Sonora. This includes full backpacking and mountaineering gear, these available at the Sierra Nevada Adventure Company. This town also has several large grocery stores, numerous dining places, and two hospitals.

Groveland, about 24 miles west of the park's Big Oak Flat Entrance Station, is the last town you'll pass on Hwy. 120; however, several resorts, gas stations, and campgrounds are found closer to the park. Gas, meals, and lodging are found at Evergreen Lodge, on Evergreen Road just 0.6 mile before it ends at the Hetch Hetchy Road in Camp Mather (for San Francisco residents).

Wilderness Permits

If you want to reserve a permit, rather than get one in person, see the "Wilderness Permits" section in Chapter 6. To get permits in person, go to the Groveland Ranger District Office on Hwy. 120 about 8 miles east of Groveland. Also, phone them at 209-962-7825 no more than 24 hours before you start your hike to see if the trailhead quota has been filled. You can also use either the information station at the park's Big Oak Flat Entrance Station, or use the Hetch Hetchy Entrance Station, by the Mather Ranger Station. The latter is open from about early April through late October.

Campgrounds

All the campgrounds mentioned in the "Campgrounds" section of Chapter 9 can be used, plus the two described here. After driving east 3.75 miles up the Tioga Road from Crane Flat, branch right immediately before Gin Flat and follow the old Big Oak Flat Road 3 winding miles to Tamarack Flat Campground. This camp is best for trips 26 and 27. The second campground is also off the highway. Just 0.3 mile past the White Wolf Road junction is a junction with the old Tioga Road, on your right. Follow it 4.75 miles to the Yosemite Creek Campground, best for Trip 28, although for it and trips 29 and 30, you could also stay at Porcupine Flat Campground, on the Tioga Road, 9.2 miles past the White Wolf Road junction. Only the Hodgdon Meadow and Crane Flat campgrounds are on the reservation system; all others are on a first-come, first-served basis, and if you hope to stay at any of them, try to look for a site in midmorning, when most campers leave.

TRIP 25

New Big Oak Flat Road to Cascade Creek

M / DH

DISTANCE: 8.2 miles out and back

ELEVATIONS: 4840'/6040'
+1510'/-350'/±3720'

SEASON: Early May to mid-November

USE: Light

MAP: El Capitan

TRAIL LOG:

1.6   Wildcat Creek
2.7   Tamarack Creek
4.0   Old Big Oak Flat Road
4.1   Cascade Creek bridge

INTRODUCTION: During late spring, when most of Yosemite's trails are under snow, this trail is at its best. Views are few and lakes are nonexistent, so it will appeal only to those who want an invigorating yet not exhausting walk and to those who appreciate the finer details of mid-Sierran ecology.

DIRECTIONS TO THE TRAILHEAD: From Crane Flat, drive east 5.8 miles toward Yosemite Valley down the new Big Oak Flat Road to a small but signed trailhead parking area, on the south, which is a quarter mile before the Foresta Road junction. Trail begins in map section C5.

DESCRIPTION: The first 1.25 miles of our route was burned in an August 1990 lightning-caused fire that raged for two weeks and burned more than 24,000 acres of mostly forested land as well as some homes in the private in-holding of Foresta, below the trailhead. This extensive fire left charred snags, but it also allowed much

more light to reach the ground—hence the profusion of shrubs and wildflowers. Over time, the snags have fallen down and oaks are reasserting themselves, growing taller than the whiteleaf manzanitas. Eventually, in the absence of another fire, they will shade out both the manzanitas and most of the wildflowers.

We begin opposite the trailhead parking area, and the trail initially makes a switchbacking, moderate ascent northeast, gaining 400 feet in elevation as it climbs a half mile to a ridge. Rounding it, we have our first views of the top of El Capitan and of Half Dome, and Yosemite Valley views continue for about the next half mile as the trail first ascends moderately, then levels off, passing a moist area with a seasonal spring. The trail soon begins a gentle descent, and, about 1.3 miles into our hike, we enter unburned forest. Over the next quarter mile, we descend to usually flowing Wildcat Creek. Soon, we begin to climb again, and do so for almost a mile until we start a short, steep descent along a ridge, which offers a view, across the Merced River canyon, of the Wawona Road traversing the flanks of Turtleback Dome. The steep descent continues down to nearby Tamarack Creek, which, in summer, flourishes with giant-leaved umbrella plants growing from its stream bed. At times this creek is a wet ford.

Again, we make a mile-long climb, then make a momentary drop to a Cascade Creek tributary, which we boulder hop only yards before reaching the old Big Oak Flat Road. At this creek crossing, serviceberries hug the bank of a small pool fed by a photogenic cascade. Once on the road, we have a brief walk down to the Cascade Creek bridge—a good spot for a lunch break (camping prohibited). In late summer, the flow of Cascade Creek is slow and warm enough for safe and enjoyable splashing around in the small pools immediately downstream. During summer, when the road to Tamarack Flat Campground is open, you'll want to take the much shorter first part of Trip 27 down to Cascade

Creek, as well as to El Capitan. When the road down to the campground is closed, you can expect much of the El Capitan Trail to be under snow.

TRIP **26**

Tamarack Flat Campground to Devils Dance Floor

Ⓔ ↗ DH, X

DISTANCE: 3 miles out and back

ELEVATIONS: 6340'/6836'
+600'/-100'/±1400'

SEASON: Mid-July to early September

USE: Light

MAPS: *Tamarack Flat, El Capitan*

TRAIL LOG:

1.5 Devils Dance Floor

INTRODUCTION: This trip and the next one usually are mostly snow free by early July, if not sooner, and they stay that way usually until mid- or late October. The reason both trips have a relatively short hiking season is because the road down to Tamarack Flat Campground is open only from about mid-July to early September.

Around midmorning, Tamarack Flat Campground becomes temporarily abandoned, only to receive another flood of motorized campers in late afternoon. Take the time to enjoy the campground during the tranquil part of day, and, while you're in the vicinity, you might make this cross-country hike with great views and an incredibly interesting (geologically speaking) "dance floor."

Generally, I wouldn't include a route that is entirely cross-country, but back in the 1990s, a certain seasonal naturalist raved about the Devils Dance Floor and was leading tourists to it. Well, if it's good enough for the Park Service, then it's good enough to be included in this guidebook.

DIRECTIONS TO THE TRAILHEAD: From Crane Flat, drive northeast 3.75 miles up the Tioga Road to the Tamarack Flat Campground turnoff, immediately before the Gin Flat scenic turnout. Drive southeast down the old Big Oak Flat Road to the east end of Tamarack Flat Campground, 3.25 miles from the Tioga Road. Trail begins in map section C4.

DESCRIPTION: There is no correct way to start and distances will vary a bit depending on your route. I prefer walking southwest through Tamarack Flat Campground to where the campsites end. There are relatively steep slopes just to the south, and you can tackle them head-on or else veer to the east or to the west (my preference) to find more moderate slopes. After about 100 feet of elevation gain, you'll reach gentler slopes, and then you take the path of least resistance up to the Devils Dance Floor's northern satellite summit.

To reach the Devils Dance Floor you can head south, downslope, directly to it, but there is a short drop-off that might trouble nonclimbers. So, more prudently, you might look for gentler slopes on the east side of the satellite summit and take them southeast down to a gully. Rather than following it southwest up to its head, from which you'd have to climb some relatively steep slopes to the summit, you'll find it safer to traverse south out of the gully on to the gentler, safer eastern slopes of the Devils Dance Floor and take a path of least resistance to its top, hopefully passing an enormous, grotesquely weathering boulder. From the actual summit, descend slightly south to the brink of Devils Dance Floor for your rewarding views. Don't get too close to the brink, for a slip off it could be fatal.

From the brink's slowly forming solution holes, you see below to the south an ancient granitic bench containing Big Meadow and the private in-holding of Foresta, which was largely burned down in a 1990 lightning-caused fire that quickly got out of control.

François Matthes described glacial evidence down there, but none exists. His "moraine" is bedrock and his "erratics" are either protruding bedrock knobs or detached bedrock. To your southeast is Turtleback Dome, above the Merced River's gorge. It, too, was unglaciated, although, to uncritical geologists, the large boulders and the deposit atop it do look like, respectively, glacial erratics and a moraine. In actuality, both the boulders and lag deposit are locally derived. To the east is a dramatic view of the western part of Yosemite Valley, perhaps the world's most misinterpreted landscape.

HOW DEVILS DANCE FLOOR GOT ITS GROOVES

How does one explain how the Devils Dance Floor's gently westward sloping summit got its "standing waves," up to 3 feet high, frozen in the rock, like giant ripple bars left by a giant flood?

Between the crests of these "waves" are water troughs similar to ones you might find on bedrock that once lay beneath a giant glacier. Furthermore, several giant boulders lie on the summit, and they can easily be interpreted as erratics, but they are locally derived. There is no evidence of a mega-flood or a mega-glacier. As in some other Sierran localities, this is a very ancient landform, one that originated during warmer, wetter weather.

I suspect that this unique landform had a very unassuming beginning in which several parallel, barely noticeable grooves on the sloping surface slowly widened and deepened through weathering over 80 million or so years to evolve into today's deep troughs separating the "standing waves."

Finally, to the northeast is a relatively gentle upland landscape that contains dozens of bald summits, ridges, and slopes much like your bald summit. Because it is in the altitudinal zone of maximum precipitation, this landscape should be completely forested, but, like many well-watered granitic landscapes around the world, it defies common reason. The Sierra Nevada has many areas with clusters of "balds," but this one, about 25 square miles in area, is one of the most accessible. Still, perhaps not one in a million park visitors ever sets foot into it. If you are a competent cross-country hiker (orientation is a must!), you've got this whole "baldland" to yourself.

TRIP **27**

Tamarack Flat Campground to El Capitan

S ↗ DH, BP

DISTANCE:	17 miles out and back
ELEVATIONS:	5800′/7730′ +2470′/-1250′/±7440′
SEASON:	Mid-July to early September
USE:	Light
MAPS:	*Tamarack Flat, El Capitan*

TRAIL LOG:

2.4	Cascade Creek bridge
2.9	North Rim Trail
6.2	Ribbon Meadow
7.2	Ribbon Creek
8.3	El Capitan spur trail
8.5	El Capitan's summit

INTRODUCTION: The vertical walls of 3000-foot El Capitan attract rock climbers from all over the world, and more than five dozen extremely difficult routes ascend it. For nonclimbers, this hike provides a much easier, safer way to attain El Capitan's summit, which stands only 15 feet above the north-side approach. This trip is mostly snow free by early July and stays that way usually until mid- or late October. The reason it has a relatively short hiking season is because the road down to Tamarack Flat Campground is open only from about mid-July to early September. When the road down to the campground is closed, you'll have to take Trip 25 to the Cascade Creek bridge, which adds 1.7 miles, each way, to your hike, making it a hefty 20.4-mile excursion.

DIRECTIONS TO THE TRAILHEAD: From Crane Flat, drive northeast 3.75 miles up the Tioga Road to the Tamarack Flat Campground turnoff, immediately before the Gin Flat scenic turnout. Drive southeast down the old Big Oak Flat Road to the east end of Tamarack Flat Campground, 3.25 miles from the Tioga Road. Trail begins in map section C4.

DESCRIPTION: Tamarack Flat derives its name from its extreme predominance of tamaracks, known today as lodgepole pines. The road through this flat and down to Yosemite Valley opened in 1874, and early visitors on crowded, uncomfortable stagecoaches had already traveled about 100 miles or more just to reach it and still had a few more anxious miles to go. Until the mid-1970s, you could drive from Tamarack Flat Campground down to Cascade Creek, but now that the road is closed to motor vehicles.

From Tamarack Flat Campground, you immediately cross Tamarack Creek and then ascend slopes on the old (original) Big Oak Flat Road for a 100-foot elevation gain. Here, white firs become dominant, and, along both sides of the road, you'll see large, partly buried granitic boulders.

These were not carried here by glaciers, as John Muir once supposed, for this local terrain was never glaciated. Instead, they developed right where you see them, being resistant enough to subsurface weathering that they finally emerged at the surface quite intact, while the adjacent, less resistant, more fractured bedrock was chemically broken down and slowly stripped away by erosion. Thus these boulders did not "grow" out of the ground, but rather, the ground around them was slowly removed—a process that took millions of years.

Just before you reach a prominent cluster of rocks—ideal for rock-climbing practice— your road begins a steady descent to Cascade Creek. At a road switchback just 240 yards before the bridge across this creek, you'll see a junction with a trail to the new Big Oak Flat Road, Trip 25. Down at this lower, warmer, drier elevation, you'll

find Jeffrey and sugar pines intermingled with the firs. Along the first 200 yards below its bridge, Cascade Creek splashes down low cascades into small pools, and, in late season, these make nice "swimming holes." Before then, the creek is likely to be too swift for safe frolicking, particularly since the water-polished rock can be quite slippery. Rooted in this creek are large-leaved umbrella plants, and growing just beside the water's edge are creek dogwoods, willows, western azaleas and serviceberries. Huckleberry oaks crowd the dry rocks above the banks.

Some folks go no farther than here, perhaps having a creekside picnic, under shady, spacious conifers, before returning to the campground. Those bound for El Capitan continue a half mile down the old Big Oak Flat Road—now more like a trail—to a junction with Yosemite Valley's North Rim Trail. Or, continue *only* 200 yards below Cascade Creek to a well-graded, abandoned road, on the left, and follow it a quarter mile up to the El Capitan Trail. Since the Big Oak Flat Road down to the Valley floor is quite abandoned, the Park Service ought to also abandon the current

Cascade Creek's northwest tributary

trail junction and place it at the junction with the abandoned road. This change would save hikers almost a half mile. From either junction, a major climb of almost 2000 feet confronts us. Along the lands between here and El Capitan, USGS geologist François Matthes mapped seven glacial moraines, extensive, scattered glacial deposits, and 20 glacial erratics. None of the moraines or deposits exist, and all of the erratics are merely locally derived boulders. None of your route ahead was ever glaciated.

Starting in a summer-warm forest of incense-cedar, ponderosa and sugar pines, and white fir, we climb hundreds of feet—steeply at times—up to drier slopes with clusters of greenleaf manzanita and huckleberry oak. Also growing in the gravelly soils are some common drought-tolerant wildflowers—streptanthus, pussy paws, spreading phlox, and mat lupine. When we do re-enter forest, it is one of white firs and Jeffrey pines. Occasionally, we see black oaks, but these diminish to shrub height as we climb higher, disappearing altogether by the time we reach a small drop on a ridge. In this vicinity, chinquapins compete with huckleberry oaks, and they herald the imminent encounter with red firs, which we find growing near the top of the crest.

Three miles from the old road, lodgepoles join in the ranks as we make a short descent from it down to a sedge-filled damp meadow, the western outskirts of Ribbon Meadow, which sprouts short-blooming shooting stars, marsh marigolds and other water-loving wildflowers. (To the north lies an incredible, fairly gentle terrain I call the "baldland," which virtually no one has explored; see more on page 166.) The meadow guides us to a crossing of a Ribbon Creek tributary—a wide bog in early summer—and then we parallel it east 1 mile down to Ribbon Creek. Ribbon Meadow, which we traverse on the first part of this descent, is more forest than meadow, and, on the bark of lodgepoles, you'll see blazes to guide you where the route becomes a little vague. Along the

banks of Ribbon Creek are the trail's only acceptable campsites—but they are waterless when the creek dries up about midsummer.

Now only 1.25 miles from our goal, we make a brief climb, an equally brief descent, and then an ascending traverse east to the top of El Capitan Gully. One Yosemite Valley's mountaineering tragedies occurred in the upper part of this gully on June 5, 1905, when Charles Bailey fell to his death. His partner, J.L. Staats, became the first known person to ascend the gully successfully. Every year, a few climbers are killed on the walls of Yosemite Valley. This shouldn't happen, for rock climbing has the potential to be a very safe sport. All too often, however, it attracts reckless individuals who spurn safety precautions.

Your first views of El Capitan and the south wall of Yosemite Valley appear on this traverse to El Capitan Gully, and views continue through the sparse stand of Jeffrey pines as you climb south from the gully past dense shrubbery to a junction with the El Capitan spur trail. If you are hiking this trail in late summer, after Ribbon Creek has dried up, you may want to continue on the main trail a half mile northeast to two trickling springs. The trail beyond them is not all that interesting, but it does get you to Eagle Peak (see trips 28 and 59).

Along the short spur trail south to El Capitan's broad, rounded summit, you can gaze up-canyon and identify unmistakable Half Dome, at the Valley's end, barely protruding Sentinel Dome, above the Valley's south wall, and fin-shaped Mt. Clark, on the skyline above the dome. Take your time exploring El Capitan's large, domed summit area, but don't stray too far from it. The first 200 yards below it are safe, but then the summit's slopes gradually get steeper and you could slip on loose, weathered crystals, giving you a one-way trip to the bottom. Remember that many climbing deaths occur after the triumphant party has reached the summit.

TRIP 28

Tioga Road to Yosemite Valley via Yosemite Creek

(M) / DH, BP

DISTANCE: 12.9 miles point to point

ELEVATIONS: 3980′/7500′
+1340′/-4860′/±6200′

SEASON: Early July to mid-October

USE: Moderate

MAPS: *Yosemite Falls, Half Dome*

TRAIL LOG:

2.7	Yosemite Creek Campground Trailhead
4.6	Lightly used trail
8.5	Eagle Peak Trail
9.1	Trail east
9.4	Upper Yosemite Fall
9.7	Back to the main trail
12.9	Floor of Yosemite Valley

INTRODUCTION: This is perhaps the best hike along which to observe the differences between two distinct landforms: steep-walled Yosemite Valley and the rolling uplands of Yosemite Creek. This route also takes you to the dramatic viewpoint at the brink of Upper Yosemite Fall with only a third the climbing effort of Trip 59, which starts from the floor of the Valley. Unfortunately, when the waterfall is at its best—before late June—snow patches and mosquitoes are prevalent along the Yosemite Creek Trail. By late July, Upper Yosemite Fall will be seriously waning, and by late August it could be little more than a gossamer mist. Surprisingly, folks still hike in September and October, when the fall can cease to exist, because the view of Yosemite Valley from near the brink of the fall makes the effort worth it.

DIRECTIONS TO THE TRAILHEAD: From Crane Flat, drive northeast 19.6 miles up Hwy. 120 to the trailhead parking area, on *both* sides of the highway, immediately before the highway bridges signed Yosemite Creek. Trail begins in map section D4.

DESCRIPTION: You begin by walking on the Tioga Road 120 yards west from the parking area to the signed trailhead. Except perhaps for snow patches, your route ahead is quite clear. Being a mid-elevation, near-creek hike, the route is dominated by lodge-poles, though red firs and western white pines thrive on shady slopes, and junipers and Jeffrey pines grow on dry, rocky ones. After a mile of rambling trail, we reach and boulder hop wide Yosemite Creek. An additional mile of walking, this one close to the creek's east bank, gets us to the north end of Yosemite Creek Campground.

Along the campground's east sites, we follow a dirt road south several minutes to a junction with the old Tioga Road, and then tread its rutted surface southwest down-canyon 0.4 mile to a bridge across Yosemite Creek. Unfortunately, the bridge was damaged in a storm, and so all of the east sites were off limits to campers. Such damage occasionally happens, but damaged structures usually are replaced. Unless a replacement bridge is destroyed, the east-side campsites will be open. Beyond the bridge, we soon enter the campground proper, with a telephone booth, then cross an often-sluggish tributary, and, in 25 yards, come to a resumption of the trail. You could drive to this point and start here, saving 2.7 miles of walking. However, the road to the campground usually is only open from about mid-July to early September. To get to it in a vehicle, start from Crane Flat and drive northeast 14.5 miles up the Tioga Road to the White Wolf turnoff, then an additional 0.3 mile on the highway to a junction with the old Tioga Road. Turn right and follow its rambling course 5 miles to this Yosemite Creek Campground Trailhead.

From the campground, we hike south through a fairly open forest on a trail that stays a short distance from the creek. After 1.5 miles, you'll climb up a ridge away from the creek. Glaciers advancing from Mt. Hoffman scoured this countryside, but our route up across the barren bedrock is adequately marked. Large boulders resting atop polished slabs constitute evidence of glaciation. From the ridge, we can look across the canyon and see a low dome that is exfoliating—shedding slabs of granite as a giant onion might peel its layers.

Short switchbacks guide us down from the ridge, and then the trail shoots west over to three closely spaced creeks of a tributary canyon. Between the first and second is a junction with a northbound lightly used trail, which heads about 2.7 miles up the canyon to the old Tioga Road, then 0.8 mile past it to the new Tioga Road. On the opposite side of this road is the start of the short trail to Lukens Lake (Trip 22). About a half mile southeast from this junction, we join the west bank of Yosemite Creek at a spot where the creek's course has migrated laterally west to abut against granitic bedrock. Small pools soon appear in the creek bed as we descend south; then, farther downstream, the pools are interspersed with water-polished slabs. None of the pools is large enough for a swim, though many are suitable for a refreshing dip. Along this section of creek, you may see a small campsite; then, just past it, the trail makes a short, winding drop down a low ridge, touches the creek, ducks into a small cluster of aspens, and, in a quarter mile, becomes almost level. The trail now hugs the creek for 0.6 mile before temporarily veering away from it to skirt around a large gravel bar. Beyond it, the trail winds southeast for a half mile, then comes to seasonal Eagle Peak Creek. A moderate-sized campsite lies between it and Yosemite Creek—worth considering since camping is illegal within a half mile of the Valley's brink.

Climbing from the shady campsite, we hike a quarter mile south up a gully to a divide; on it, we meet the Eagle Peak Trail, mentioned in the last part of Trip 59, striking west. If you've got the time, you might make the 7-mile round trip to Eagle Peak and back. It involves only about 1000 feet of climbing, and the peak's panoramic views are certainly worth the effort. Beyond this trail junction, we descend into a second gully, climb out of a third and descend to a fourth. All four lie in a straight line, which probably represents a major fracture in the bedrock.

In this fourth gully is a junction with a trail east, and, up it, we make a brief climb to an adjacent broad crest and a trail south to Upper Yosemite Fall. If you are backpacking to this vicinity, continue east just a bit farther to a conspicuous use trail that goes 200-plus yards north to a large camping area near the west bank of Yosemite Creek. You can find relatively isolated campsites by going either west or north of this area. If you just need water, continue on the eastbound trail briefly down to a bridge over Yosemite Creek and obtain water. However, be careful! Occasionally, people, wading in the creek's icy water, slip on the glass-smooth creek bottom and are swiftly carried over the fall's brink. From the creek's bridge, you could continue eastward 0.75 mile up a trail to Yosemite Point, a highly scenic goal (passed along Trip 60).

Those bound for the fall keep to the crest, following the southbound trail almost to the Valley's rim; then, at a juniper, you veer east and descend more steps to a fenced-in viewpoint. If you're acrophobic, you should not attempt the last part of this descent, even though it has a hand railing, for it is possible, though unlikely, that you could slip on loose gravel or smooth bedrock and tumble over the brink. Standing just above the lip of Upper Yosemite Fall, you see and hear it plunge all the way down its 1430-foot drop to the rocks below. Just beyond the fall is a large roof—one that indicates the size of a slab that broke loose from this cliff in the not too distant past. On the skyline beyond the roof stands the pride of the Clark Range, finlike Mt. Clark.

About 20,000 years ago, at the height of the last glaciation, a glacier advancing down the Yosemite Creek drainage was about 600 feet thick where you are standing, and it calved massive icefalls over the cliff onto the Valley's trunk glacier, more than 1000 feet below.

From the brink of Upper Yosemite Fall, retrace your steps back to the main trail and prepare for the first leg of the 3.2 miles of descent along the Yosemite Falls Trail. There are about 135 switchbacks along this trail, and some of them are overly steep and too often gravelly, so watch your step, especially if you are wearing a backpack. For most of the first leg, you are switchbacking through brush, but as you get near its end, oaks, bay trees, and Douglas firs appear, the latter possible due to gusts of wind-blown moisture from Upper Yosemite Fall's spray. Also lower down, views of the fall appear. After about 65 switchbacks and 1600 feet of descent, you begin a second leg, which is a traverse south, then southwest. Along the traverse south, you have views of Upper Yosemite Fall, then you reach a gate and immediately switchback briefly up to the bend southwest. Here, at a minor low spot in the trail, is a cryptic junction.

[S] SIDE TRIP TO OH MY GOSH ROCK: On your right is the start of a 50-yard trail that descends to a railing, from which you look almost directly down on Lower Yosemite Fall and can trace Yosemite Creek up past its cascades to Upper Yosemite Fall. Be forewarned, however, that the trail is somewhat exposed, and a careless step could result in a fatal slip over the brink of a cliff. END OF SIDE TRIP.

With 1.6 miles to go to trail's end, we make a mostly shady traverse 0.4 mile to Columbia Rock, which is reached at the end of a short, steep, switchbacking descent down an unstable, gravelly slope. From the railing at Columbia Rock, which, at 5031

feet elevation, is just over 1000 feet above the Valley floor, we have a panoramic view of most of Yosemite Valley, from Half Dome and the Quarter Domes in the east to the Cathedral Spires in the west.

Now we start our last leg, which is a mostly viewless descent of more than 60 short switchbacks under the shade of canyon live oaks, and mostly across talus, which is derived from past rockfalls. The switchbacking ends at the intersection of the Valley's north-side trail (Trip 54), and, on it, we walk east about 25 yards to a south-descending trail that separates Camp 4 Walk-In Campground from its adjacent parking lot. On it ,we go about 200 yards to trail's end by Northside Drive, on the floor of Yosemite Valley.

Lower Yosemite Fall from Oh My Gosh Rock

TRIP 29

Tioga Road to North Dome

Ⓜ ↗ **DH**

DISTANCE: 9.2 miles out and back

ELEVATIONS: 7610′/8130′
+680′/-1270′/±3900′

SEASON: Mid-July to mid-October

USE: Light

MAP: Yosemite Falls

TRAIL LOG:

0.7   Porcupine Creek
1.8   Junction
2.9   Second junction
4.1   Junction with Trip 60
4.6   Summit of North Dome

INTRODUCTION: North Dome, which looks so inaccessible from the Yosemite Valley floor, can be reached in a couple of hours by this route. From the dome, you get perhaps the best views of the expansive faces of Half Dome and Clouds Rest, as well as excellent views of Yosemite Valley. Along this hike, you can also visit one of Yosemite's few known natural arches. Another one is, surprisingly, underwater, near Tuolumne Meadows Lodge (Trip 55). Additionally, you can visit Indian Rock, which provides a 360-degree panorama of the Valley's eastern uplands.

DIRECTIONS TO THE TRAILHEAD: From Crane Flat, drive northeast 23.7 miles up the Tioga Road to the Porcupine Flat Campground, then an additional 1.1 miles to a closed road, on your right. If you're westbound, the trailhead is 2.1 miles west of the May Lake turnoff. Trail begins in map section D4.

DESCRIPTION: Through 1976, you could drive to primitive Porcupine Creek Camp-

ground, its road beginning at the west end of the trailhead parking strip. You could start there, where it is blocked off, or, preferably, start from a trailhead sign near the outhouse. From there, a trail descends shortly to the nearby closed road. On it, you descend 0.6 mile to Porcupine Creek.

The Porcupine Creek Campground is alongside Porcupine Creek, which, in early season, can be a wet ford if you don't find a log to cross it. From its west bank, our trail makes a rolling traverse for a little over a mile to a junction atop a shady saddle dominated by red firs.

Ⓐ ALTERNATE TRIP TO MIRROR LAKE: This shady trail, 2.8 miles long, descends east to cascades along Porcupine Creek and then, in the realm of white firs, descends south to a junction near a bridge across Snow Creek. The acres of lands just east of the creek are nearly level, and there is abundant space for camping.

PORCUPINES

Porcupine Creek and Porcupine Flat above it by the Tioga Road are well named, for they are located in a nearly pure stand of lodgepole pines—the favorite food of the park's porcupines. They seem to prefer lodgepoles among all conifers because of this tree's thin bark, and they usually attack the tree's upper section, where the bark is especially thin. They relish the tree's soft-growing tissues immediately beneath the bark. The porcupine's chief enemy is the fisher, a minklike carnivore only one quarter the size of the porcupine that can swiftly attack its vulnerable, unprotected belly. Coyotes, mountain lions, and bobcats are less adept at killing porcupines, and they often receive a good share of quills in their attempts. The porcupine population also may be controlled by diseases and internal parasites.

SIDE TRIP TO SNOW CREEK POINT: The 2.6-mile trail ahead to the floor of Tenaya Canyon has the greatest gradient of any trail into (and out of) Yosemite Valley—just over 20%—and, when wet, it can be treacherous. Before commencing this descent, you first might want to make brief a diversion 0.2 mile southeast over to what I call Snow Creek Point for a good rest. Leave your trail about 250 yards from the junction near the bridge. You cross a broad area out to a minor but obvious high point of 6700 feet. From it, you have a view directly across to Half Dome as well as up-canyon to Clouds Rest, partly blocked by the dome-like mass of Mt. Watkins. **END OF SIDE TRIP.**

Along the alternate trip to Mirror Lake, you make a spectacular descent to the floor of Tenaya Canyon, then walk southwest 1.1 miles to Mirror Lake. Since you're bound to be tired, end your hike by taking the shortest route—the 1.2-mile paved bike path—down to the shuttle-bus stop just east of Clarks Bridge. **END OF ALTERNATE TRIP.**

Just 20 yards beyond the crest of our saddle, the trail to North Dome reaches a second junction, and here a trail forking right descends 1.6 miles down along Lehamite Creek to Yosemite Valley's north rim trail (Trip 60). We fork left and traverse 0.3 mile to a spur ridge with a large boulder on it, from whose top you can see Sentinel Dome. The view of Yosemite Valley improves as you walk beyond the boulder, although much better ones lie ahead. The vicinity here is flat, and hikers occasionally dry-camp on it. Past the spur ridge, we contour 0.3 mile, then drop to a gully before climbing steeply to a second junction located only yards short of a second red fir saddle.

S SIDE TRIP TO INDIAN ROCK: Veering left is a trail signed for Indian Rock. The trail actually climbs very steeply a quarter mile up brushy slopes to a delicate arch (see

Broad dike on lower (south) part of Indian Ridge

page 289), not a rock. About 1.5 feet thick at the thinnest part of its span, this 20-foot arch came into existence when the highly fractured rock beneath it broke away. After investigating this curious feature, which is quite easily reached from the northwest, you can return to the main route or continue north a half mile up Indian Ridge to its north end, Indian Rock. This summit was one of the key points on the 1864 Yosemite Valley boundary. From the arch, a use trail is fairly obvious until the ridge gives way to a headwall. You can go either right or left around it; I prefer the right (east) side, despite a short bit of brush. (On the left side, you first drop from and then climb considerably back to the ridge.) Once back on the ridge, you quickly reach the summit area, which, contrary to the topographic map, is not a small dome but rather are two small (and I do mean small!) summits of nearly equal elevation. Each can be reached by more than one route, all of them requiring a short but fairly steep scramble. If you are uncomfortable with climbing, don't attempt either. Their views are almost identical from those you obtain from the immediate vicinity, which entails no risk. **END OF SIDE TRIP.**

From the saddle, which, at 8130 feet, is at the same elevation as our trailhead, the main trail descends briefly south, then follows Indian Ridge proper south, traversing across two low, broad ridge knolls before veering east off the now-descending ridge. While most folks take the trail, some merely walk down the view-blessed ridge. After about a 250-foot elevation loss, the trail heads southwest across ridge, from where the ridge-descenders join us. Just before your trail comes to a pine-shaded junction, you'll note a large dike (which you may have noticed above), composed of resistant aplite, standing several feet above its adjacent bedrock.

At this junction with Trip 60, coming from the west, we turn left and take the half-mile spur trail out to the bald, rounded summit of North Dome. Be careful on the first part of this trail, for a slip on loose gravel could send you sliding down a dangerously steep slope. Your brief descent ends on a forested saddle, and one might think, by studying the map, that a half-mile traverse northeast to Basket Dome would be an easy jaunt. While its summit area is an easy scramble, beneath the forest between the saddle and the summit is a lot of dense brush. The same is true of slopes northeast of the dome. It is most unfortunate that the Park Service never cleared a trail through the brush to the saddle north of Basket Dome and then northeast down to Snow Creek. Doing so would have added one more great summit view to Yosemite Valley's north rim traverse, but, more importantly, this new route would have been about 4 miles shorter than the current Yosemite Falls-Snow Creek route.

From the North Dome summit area, you can probably see more of Yosemite Valley and its adjacent uplands than can be seen from any other summit except Half Dome. (The views from about 200 yards south of and below the summit area are even better.) Note that severely glaciated Tenaya Canyon, to the east, is distinctly V-shaped in cross section, not U-shaped as glaciated canyons are said to be. The enormous 4000-foot face of Clouds Rest dominates the canyon's east side, and, to the south and west of it, stands mighty Half Dome, perhaps Yosemite's best-remembered feature. Continuing our clockwise scan, we next recognize Mt. Starr King, a steep-sided dome above Little Yosemite Valley. West of this unseen valley is joint-controlled Panorama Cliff, which bears the scar of a large rockfall near Panorama Point, close to Illilouette Fall. Extremely popular Glacier Point stands west of the fall's gorge, and, above and right of the point, Sentinel Dome bulges up into the sky. Looking down Yosemite Valley, we see Sentinel Rock, with its near-vertical north face, which is due to the unloading of slabs along the rock's near-vertical joint planes. Opposite the rock stand the Three Brothers, also shaped by joint planes, and beyond them protrudes the brow of El Capitan, opposite the Cathedral Rocks. Note the broad, gentle surface north of El Capitan, a surface that has changed but little in at least the last 30 million years. But neither has Yosemite Valley changed that much; it was about as deep back then as it is today. However, it has widened by hundreds of feet. Before leaving North Dome, investigate some of its exfoliating slabs—features common to all of Yosemite's domes.

TRIP **30**

Tenaya Lake to Yosemite Valley via Snow Creek

Ⓜ **↗** DH, BP

DISTANCE: 12.6 miles point to point

ELEVATIONS: 3990′/8490′
+780′/-4950′/±5730′

SEASON: Mid-July to mid-October

USE: Light

MAPS: *Tenaya Lake,
Yosemite Falls, Half Dome*

TRAIL LOG:

1.7	Gap below Olmsted Point
6.0	Trail from Tioga Road
7.7	Porcupine Creek- North Dome Trail
10.3	Tenaya Canyon Trail
11.4	Mirror Lake
12.6	Clarks Bridge

INTRODUCTION: When linked with a trail that parallels the Tioga Road from Tuolumne Meadows' Cathedral Lakes Trailhead, this hike provides the shortest route from the meadows to Yosemite Valley, only 21 miles. Though not nearly as scenic as other routes from the meadows to the Valley, Trip 30 is shorter and considerably easier, making it best for an unacclimated hiker.

Note that this trip is just one of three trails that converge in Snow Creek canyon before uniting to descend to Mirror Lake. Of the two others, one comes from Porcupine Creek and North Dome (Trip 29), and another, which is mentioned in the following text, from the Tioga Road. This is the shortest.

DIRECTIONS TO THE TRAILHEAD: On the Tioga Road at the Tenaya Lake Trailhead parking area, at a highway bend near the lake's southwest shore, located 30.5 miles northeast of Crane Flat and 8.5 miles southwest of the Tuolumne Meadows Campground. Trail begins in map section E4.

DESCRIPTION: The first part of this trail approximates the route taken (in the opposite direction) by Captain Bowling and his 35 men in search of Chief Teneiya's band. In early June 1852, they surprised this band at Py-wi-ack—"Lake of the Glistening (glacier-polished) Rocks." This lake was named by Lafayette Bunnell in memory of the old chief, and, before departing for an Indian reservation, both Indians and troops spent the night in what is now the west side of today's trailhead parking area.

From the Tenaya Lake Trailhead parking area at 8160 feet, you may spy a spur trail that heads south through lodgepoles to the edge of a nearby meadow. Along its edge is the main trail, which goes east to the Sunrise Lakes and Sunrise High Sierra Camp, and connects with other trails to Clouds Rest, Happy Isles, Tuolumne Meadows, and other destinations. On this main trail, we make a traverse southwest across the sometimes boggy meadow for a half mile before reaching a junction with a little-used spur trail that goes a quarter mile north to the Tioga Road. Along this meadow traverse, we get backward glances at Polly Dome, rising above the dense lodgepoles that ring our meadow. Few wildflowers are seen in this typical Sierran meadow; rather, it is dominated by sedges and dwarf bilberries. The latter aren't obvious until late August, when they turn a blazing crimson color.

From the spur-trail junction, we walk south a quarter mile along the west edge of a meadow; then, after another quarter mile past lodgepoles, we cross a head-high glacial moraine and momentarily spy a knee-deep pond, lying just 60 yards east. Beyond it, our trail begins to climb, and, in a small clearing, we can look back and see distant Mt. Conness between Polly Dome and Medlicott Dome—each a ridge, not a dome.

Beyond this clearing, we enter forest, now containing numerous mountain hemlocks, and climb, ultimately by short switchbacks, up to a gap that lies immediately below perhaps the most popular scenic turnout along the Tioga Road. The turnout, Olmsted Point, is 130 yards north of us, and it provides a view northeast toward stirring Tenaya Lake, and a view south toward Clouds Rest and Half Dome. The actual point is atop the low knoll 170 yards south of the gap, and it provides stunning views down Tenaya Canyon and across to Clouds Rest. Atop this low knoll, partly clothed with scattered lodgepole, western white and Jeffrey pines, are erratic boulders left behind as a glacier retreated up-canyon by 15,000 years ago.

The next half mile of trail west from the gap is an incredibly winding one, for the trail avoids many bedrock protuberances and one overhanging cliff. Beyond these, our erratic-strewn course tops a low crest, which, at 8490 feet, is our high point. We then begin to veer away from the nearby Tioga Road, coming within 0.3 mile of unseen Hidden Lake, where it begins to switchback down into a forested, damp-floored canyon with plenty of moisture-loving wildflowers.

S SIDE TRIP TO HIDDEN LAKE: From the top of the switchbacks, you can contour 0.3 mile south to the lake, but because the slopes are somewhat steep, it's safer to reach the lake by starting a quarter mile sooner, where your trail is briefly beside the Tioga Road. Start south up an easy ridge, and before reaching its top, veer right to attain its subordinate west-trending ridge. From it, the descent southwest to the lake is obvious. From early July through mid-August, this is a good swimming lake. Because the lake is so close to the road, camping is forbidden. From the lake's south end, you can walk briefly south to a brink with a great view into Tenaya Canyon,

Tenaya Lake from Olmsted Point

although a similar view is attained with less effort back at Olmsted Point. **END OF SIDE TRIP.**

Our westbound trail crosses two ephemeral creeks, then angles southwest and descends this glaciated canyon—rich in mosquitoes before August—for a mile before climbing 300 feet up to a crest. Erratic boulders atop it testify to the presence of a past glacier, and the huge, ice-smoothed southeast wall of Tenaya Canyon, opposite us, adds further evidence.

S **SIDE TRIP TO MT. WATKINS:** From here, you can make an easy cross-country walk south along a ridge and then southwest up it to the gentle summit of 8500-foot Mt. Watkins, a low dome located just 0.9 mile from your trail and only 250 feet above it. Alternatively, you can make an even easier cross-country walk to its slightly lower eastern satellite. After walking about 0.3 mile south, to where the ridge turns southwest and begins to climb, veer left onto a nearly level ridge and follow it south 0.4 mile to its low summit. The satellite has a precipitous east face, so don't get too far from the summit. Both summits provide extraordinary views down into Tenaya Canyon as well as of Clouds Rest, directly across from the your summits. **END OF SIDE TRIP.**

Next, we switchback down into a forested side canyon, traversing below two smooth-sloped domes before arriving at a junction with a trail from Tioga Road.

A **ALTERNATE TRIP TO SNOW CREEK CANYON:** This is under the short trip to Mirror Lake that was mentioned in the introduction. Should you take it, you'll find the trailhead at a Tioga Road parking area immediately east of a road cut through a signed glacial moraine, 0.6 mile east of the May Lake turnoff and 3.1 miles west of the Tenaya Lake Trailhead parking area. You can't ask for a better glacial moraine to examine than the one beside our trailhead, where the Tioga Road cuts through the crest of a lateral moraine. Note its characteristic composition, a gravelly, unsorted matrix containing boulders of all sizes. Note that all the boulders are fresh, a characteristic of the most recent, or Tioga, glaciation.

This 2.8-mile alternate trail, a continuation of one from May Lake, starts from the Tioga Road just by the west side of a nearby closed road that goes 250 yards south to a heliport. From this dirt road, the trail climbs west to the crest of the lateral moraine, turns south on it, and, after about a half mile, the crest traverse comes to a giant trailside boulder—an erratic—that was dropped here by a glacier. The glacier, descending the canyon immediately east of us, must have been at least 700 feet thick, and we can appreciate its power by marveling at the size of this particular erratic, which weighs at least 100 tons. (Elsewhere in the range, I've seen an erratic, left by a similar-size glacier, which I estimated at 1100 tons!) Before leaving the boulder, you might note unmistakable Cathedral Peak, to the east, and the Echo Peaks, just south of it. After hiking a couple of minutes past the boulder, our route begins a wandering, 2-mile, 1000-foot drop to a junction with the trail from Tenaya Lake. **END OF ALTERNATE TRIP.**

Around this junction with the trail from Tioga Road, white firs begin to compete with red firs for space, and Jeffrey pines, with us for some time now, become more numerous.

Switchbacks drop us well into Snow Creek canyon, and then we head south for a mile, dropping 500 feet to campsites under white firs along the banks of Snow Creek. While chickarees (Douglas squirrels) live in red firs higher up, down here, western gray squirrels are more common, living in white firs. About 1987, a fire raged through part of the creek's drainage basin, but you won't see any fire damage along the trail down by the creek. The acres of lands just east of the creek are nearly level, and there is abundant space for camping. In this vicinity, the trail bridges the reliable creek and starts down beside Snow Creek, arriving in 140 yards at a junction with the Porcupine Creek-North Dome Trail (Trip 29). From the junction, our southbound trail traverses for 0.3 mile through a forest of white firs, Jeffrey pines, and—surprisingly—ponderosa pines before emerging on more open slopes to begin a 108-switchback descent to the floor of Tenaya Canyon, 2500 feet below us.

[S] **SIDE TRIP TO SNOW CREEK POINT:** The trail ahead has the greatest gradient of any trail into (and out of) Yosemite Valley, just over 20%, and, when wet, it can be treacherous. Before commencing this descent, you first might want to make brief diversion 0.2 mile southeast over to what I call Snow Creek Point for a good rest. Leave your trail about 250 yards from the junction, that is, about halfway along the 0.3-mile traverse. You cross a broad area out to a minor but obvious high point, 6700 feet elevation on the Valley's topo map, and, about halfway to it, you may see a campsite along the east side, near Snow Creek. From the point, you have a view directly across to Half Dome, as well as up-canyon to Clouds Rest, partly blocked by the dome-like mass of Mt. Watkins. Besides a relaxing and scenic rest spot, this is one of glacial interest. According to the glacial map in François Matthes' US Geological Survey "Professional Paper 160," an ancient glacier covered this broad area with at least 1500 feet of ice. When that glacier melted and diminished in thickness, it would have left dozens of glacial erratics on it, but there are none. As elsewhere, Matthes' Yosemite rim glacial evidence existed only in his mind, not on the ground. **END OF SIDE TRIP.**

As you start your switchbacking descent, your first views include the massive northwest face of Half Dome plus short-lived views of Watkins Pinnacles, to the east, and the top of Mt. Clark, behind Half Dome. About a dozen switchbacks down, you enter a gully and encounter a small community of trees that include—

surprisingly again—Douglas firs, which usually aren't found up at this elevation (6300 feet). The trail continues down this gully for another 40 switchbacks, many of them obliterated in an April 1987 rockslide, and then rebuilt. Along the upper part of this descent, you'll have views just to the west of a large half-arch, descending away from you. On the lower part of it are views of another half-arch, smaller, but much more dramatic, for it is greatly overhanging, even more so than the famous, larger Royal Arches, and it looks like it could break away at any moment.

After about 50 short switchbacks, you are about halfway down, and now you diagonal east down across open slopes that provide ground for whiteleaf manzanitas and seasonally blooming wildflowers such as the brilliantly colored wavy-leaved paintbrush and the equally colorful showy penstemon. Among rocks here is bird's foot fern, specially adapted—unlike most ferns—to this hot, dry environment.

Another 50-plus short switchbacks await us, and Clouds Rest and Half Dome continue to dominate the views as we switchback down even lower, and we also take note of Tenaya Creek plunging over a long vertical wall before it dries up, usually in late summer. About 10 switchbacks from the canyon floor, the trail enters a forest dominated by canyon live oaks. Also in it are bay trees, easily identified by the aroma given off from the crushed leaves. On the floor of Tenaya Canyon, near the wide, bouldery bed of Tenaya Creek, our trail meets the Tenaya Canyon Trail (Trip 58's side trip up lower Tenaya Canyon), and, on it, we walk a fairly level 1.1 miles west to our trail's end, beside a former parking area of a now closed road, just above the west edge of Mirror Lake, which, these days, is little more than a wide part of Tenaya Creek. Now you take the shortest route—the 1.2-mile paved bike path—down to the shuttle-bus stop just east of Clarks Bridge. Taking the path down only to the first shuttle-bus stop, east of the stop by Clarks Bridge, cuts your distance by 0.3 mile.

CHAPTER 12

Trips of the Tuolumne Meadows Area North of the Tioga Road

Introduction to this Area

Although this section generally describes trails lying north and west of Tuolumne Meadows, it also describes two that extend beyond this regional area. Trip 35, the High Sierra Camps Loop Trail, wanders more than half of its length in the country south of the Tioga Road, and Trip 36, the northbound Pacific Crest Trail, goes through the park and then winds over to Sonora Pass. Trip 36, at 76 miles, is the longest one described in this guide; Trip 32, at about a half mile if you go *only* to the top of Pothole Dome, is the shortest. Between these two extremes, you'll find a hiking length ideal for you as you explore this subalpine wonderland. This section's highlights are too numerous to mention. Of all its hikes, only Trip 31 would not receive a spectacular rating. Ragged peaks, crystal-clear lakes, glaciated domes, long canyons, and roaring cascades await the High Sierra hiker here.

Rudy Goldstein

Waterwheel Falls

The first trail begins beside Tenaya Lake, and, if you plan to swim in this chilly lake, do so at the bouldery southwest shore. The sandy beach of the northeast shore is lacking here, but so, too, are the strong up-canyon winds that were needed to form it. Besides, here you'll find a few small boulder islands worth swimming or wading to—something lacking near the northeast shore. From various points along the lake's shore, you may see some protruding tree stumps. There is a myth that during a lengthy former drought, this lake dried up and a forest grew on its floor, and then, centuries later, when the rains returned, the forest was submerged beneath the lake's water. Actually, rockfalls carry trees into this 180-foot-deep lake, and their heavier ends can become lodged in the lake's sediments. You don't see stumps at other lakes because they lack one or more of the three necessary ingredients: steep cliffs, forested slopes, and deep water.

Supplies and Services

Information, guidebooks, natural-history books, and topographic maps are available at the Tuolumne Meadows Visitor Center, which is 7.5 miles northeast up the Tioga Road from the Tenaya Lake Trailhead parking area and an even 8 miles southwest down the road from Tioga Pass. Just under 1 mile east of the center are useful facilities, which, west to east, are: a dump station for RVs, a service station, a mountaineering school and sports shop, a store, cafe, and post office. Just beyond the last of these is the Tuolumne Meadows Campground entrance, and just beyond it is a bridge across the Tuolumne River. Immediately past it is a road branching left (west) to the Tuolumne Meadows Stable, which offers horseback rides ranging from several hours to several days.

Those wanting to stay in the Tuolumne Meadows area in a rustic style should stay at Tuolumne Meadows Lodge. To reach it, drive 0.6 mile northeast on the Tioga Road from the campground entrance, then turn right on the lodge's spur road and follow it to its end. Accommodations at the lodge consist of canvas tents on wooden platforms. Breakfast and dinner are served here, and you can get them without being a guest. On weekends, however, reserve your spot at the dinner table early in the day. Showers are also available; inquire at the office.

Just 2 miles outside the park, you'll find the Tioga Pass Resort, with some supplies, meals, and lodging—an alternative to the crowded Tuolumne Meadows area. This resort is usually open to travelers from late May until mid-October. Most of the Tuolumne Meadows facilities are open for a shorter duration, usually from mid-June until mid-September. The Tuolumne Meadows Campground and the visitor center stay open a few weeks longer. All-year services are available in Lee Vining, just north of the Tioga Road's (Hwy. 120's) junction with Hwy. 395. This town is about 19.5 miles from the Tuolumne Meadows Campground.

Wilderness Permits

If you want to reserve a permit in advance, rather than get one in person, see the "Wilderness Permits" section in Chapter 6. In person, get your permit at a booth in the parking lot a short way down the Tuolumne Meadows Lodge spur road. From late June through the Labor Day weekend, this booth is open on Friday nights, and it opens as early as 6 AM on Saturdays. After the Labor Day weekend, get your permits at the Information Center.

Campgrounds

For Trip 31, camp at Porcupine Flat Campground on the Tioga Road, 9.2 miles east past the White Wolf Road junction and 6.9 miles west from the Tenaya Lake Trailhead parking area, at a highway bend near the lake's southwest shore. This campground is also ideal for Chapter 13's trips 40 to 42. For the remaining hikes, camp at large

Tuolumne Meadows Campground, whose entrance is just southwest of the Tuolumne River bridge. You may also want to try equally full Tioga Lake and Junction campgrounds, just outside the park below Tioga Pass.

TRIP **31**

Polly Dome Lakes via Murphy Creek

E ⟋ DH, BP, X

DISTANCE:	6.2 miles out and back
ELEVATIONS:	8160′/8720′
	+640′/-80′/±1440′
SEASON:	Mid-July to mid-October
USE:	Light
MAP:	*Tenaya Lake*

TRAIL LOG:

2.6   Trailside pond
3.1   Largest Polly Dome Lake

INTRODUCTION: This hike is for those who want to visit a readily accessible lake that isn't being visited by everyone else. A small amount of cross-country hiking is required, but you don't have to be an expert to do it. As long as you don't cross over any divide, you really can't get lost, for if you can't find the Polly Dome Lakes, you can always head back down-canyon—toward Tenaya Lake —and find your trail again.

DIRECTIONS TO THE TRAILHEAD: Across from a picnic area midway along Tenaya Lake. Trail begins in map section E4.

DESCRIPTION: Our trail, along seasonally flowing Murphy Creek, climbs 3 miles north to a junction with the High Sierra Camps Loop Trail (Trip 35). We begin our uneventful trail by passing a trail branching west across adjacent Murphy Creek, 0.3 mile into our hike. This trail descends south to a main trailhead parking area near the southwest corner of Tenaya Lake.

Midway along your hike is ample evidence of glacier action: glacier-transported boulders and glacier-polished bedrock slabs. Across these slabs, the trail can disappear, so watch for ducks (manmade stone piles). Near the divide at the head of Murphy Creek and 0.3 mile before the High Sierra Camps Loop Trail, you'll reach a trailside pond, on your right. Leave the trail here and progress cross-country a half mile southeast to the north shore of the largest Polly Dome Lake. Any cross-country route you might take will tend to get a little damp and/or brushy, but the distance is short and the lake is almost impossible to miss, particularly since it lies at the base of Polly Dome. The best campsites are along the west shore of this warm, shallow, boulder-dotted lake. The small lakes northeast of it aren't worth your effort unless you are a serious botanist.

TRIP **32**

Pothole Dome, the Tuolumne River, and Little Devils Postpile

E ↗ DH, BP, X

DISTANCE: 6.4 miles out and back

ELEVATIONS: 8340'/8610'
+160'/-430'/±1180'

SEASON: Early July to mid-October

USE: Moderate

MAP: *Falls Ridge*

TRAIL LOG:

1.2	Tuolumne River's pools
3.0	Little Devils Postpile
3.2	Pacific Crest Trail

INTRODUCTION: Because Pothole Dome is Yosemite's most accessible dome, more people climb it than any other in the park, except perhaps Lembert Dome (Trip 38), Sentinel Dome (Trip 64), or Half Dome (Trip 68). Its upper slopes and summit provide outstanding views of Tuolumne Meadows and the surrounding peaks and domes. Not all visitors climb the dome; many instead take a use trail to granite slabs along a very scenic stretch of the Tuolumne River, and a few geologically inclined visit Little Devils Postpile, named for its larger and more famous analog, Devils Postpile, about 12 miles beyond the park's southeast boundary. Also, a few find this use trail a more scenic and mile-shorter route to Glen Aulin and Waterwheel Falls (Trip 33). However, it is not recommended for backpackers since you encounter several brief stretches across sloping (and sometimes polished) bedrock where you could slip and possibly slide into the river should your pack throw you off balance.

DIRECTIONS TO THE TRAILHEAD: Park opposite Pothole Dome at a turnout at the westernmost edge of Tuolumne Meadows, 1.5 miles west from the Tuolumne Meadows Visitor Center. Trail begins in map section E3.

DESCRIPTION: From the trailhead, take a trail that starts northwest along an often boggy meadow, then, from its tip, heads east along the base of the dome, and you can climb initially steep slopes to its summit wherever you feel it is safe. The safest routes are to begin your ascent after 0.3 mile from the start, where your trail curves from east to northeast. (Once the boggy meadow becomes less waterlogged, you can reach this point by starting from a parking area about 200 yards of the official one and taking a use trail directly north to it. Do not make your own path across this fragile meadow.)

S SIDE TRIP TO TOP OF POTHOLE DOME: From this spot or any spot north of it, your ascent is only a walk up, with an average gradient of about 20%. This is the gradient you'd find on a very steep trail, and because you are above 8500 feet in elevation, the air is thin and the ascent is an effort. A beeline to the summit would be a quarter mile long, but the ascent is easier if you switchback up the open bedrock. You need not go all the way to the summit, for, after about 200 yards of ascent, you are above the tops of the lodgepoles along the dome's base and have an unobstructed view across Tuolumne Meadows and north, east, and south toward the high peaks beyond the meadows. From the actual summit, you have a 360-degree panorama that includes most of the park's north country. With your book's map in hand, you should be able to identify many prominent peaks and domes. On some days, you may see beginning climbers practicing on the dome's steep west-side drop off.

Like other glaciated Yosemite domes, Pothole Dome has gentle up-canyon slopes and steep down-canyon slopes, as do most unglaciated domes of the Sierra Nevada.

Glaciers did not transform any of them from symmetrical to asymmetrical. Glacial evidence includes slopes of highly polished bedrock plus anomalous boulders—erratics—resting on them, which could have reached their present locations only by glacier transport. Pothole Dome differs from other domes because it has several large potholes, particularly on its south slopes. Potholes are usually found in streams, where boulders swirl around in a bedrock depression and gradually drill out a hole. Obviously, streams did not flow up over Pothole Dome, but glaciers did. The potholes were formed by flowing watercourses trapped beneath a glacier, and these courses did flow uphill over the dome. Another interesting geologic feature is the presence of large, blocky crystals of potassium feldspar that are so characteristic of this hiking section's landscape. These crystals and their surrounding matrix solidified around 85 million years ago, and the resulting large-scale granite body that formed is known as the Cathedral Peak pluton, which covers much of the Yosemite high country from Tower Peak (Trip 2) south almost to Merced Lake (Trip 47). **END OF SIDE TRIP.**

To reach the Tuolumne River, stay on the trail beyond its curve from east to north, traversing along the dome's base. You are likely to see two parallel trails, one

Fairview Dome and Mariuolumne Dome, from Pothole Dome

just above the base of the dome, and the other along the west edge of the meadow. In 0.4 mile, the slightly higher trail heads northwest, and, in a quarter mile, crosses a very minor divide. This is the route to take when the Tuolumne River is flowing swiftly, usually until mid-July, since the route straight ahead in spots traverses just above the river. Ahead, your use trail may be ill-defined, so if you can't follow it, curve north over to the often audible river. This stretch has pools and rapids, and when the water is low, the pools may be safe for swimming, but not when the flow is swift. The water is never warm, but summer days often are, and on those days, you can warm up on glacier-smoothed slabs after a brisk swim. The more scenic, slightly lower trail reaches the pools and rapids by continuing north along the meadow's edge to the Tuolumne River, and then traverses for about 200 yards downstream along the lower slopes of an obvious knoll. Because these slopes are water polished in spots, and therefore slippery, don't take it in times of high water, when a slip into the raging river could be fatal.

Most folks don't go beyond the initial stretch of pools and rapids, and, ahead, you generally have the terrain all to yourself. Basically, you parallel the river's edge past more pools and rapids for about a half mile to where you reach the edge of large meadow, and the river veers from west to north. The meadow becomes increasingly boggy toward its west side, so before early or mid-August, don't strike directly across it. Stay near its southern edge as you traverse west for about 0.3 mile to the edge of a lodge-pole forest. Within it, you stay near the base of some slopes as you traverse north-west for a similar distance to a low, narrow, obvious ridge, another feature (of countless thousands) that Sierran glaciers failed to eradicate, despite multiple glaciations and ice here about 2000 feet thick. From the ridge, you traverse about a quarter mile northwest back to the river's edge and again briefly traverse glacier-and-water-polished slopes at the base of descending

ridge. Just beyond it, you see Little Devils Postpile, reached in an equally short traverse.

This looks like any other Sierran lava flow, but on the USGS *Tuolumne Meadows* geologic quadrangle map, this basaltic lava is identified as a plug, not as surface lava. But it is named for Devils Postpile, and one has denied that this is a remnant of a lava flow, so why should a smaller version be any different? Simply, geoscientists believe that glaciers greatly deepen canyons through erosion, and so past Tuolumne glaciers must have cut down through granite to expose the basalt. The evidence against this is twofold. First, most Sierran canyon floors have remnants of intact lava or tuff (from 4 million to 30 million years old), and, despite massive glaciers repeatedly advancing down-canyon over the last 2-plus million years, they have not been able remove these remnants and erode the bedrock below them. Second, the minerals and columns of plugs and other shallow intrusions are much larger than those of Little Devils Postpile. This has nearly microscopic crystals and columns a half foot to 1 foot in diameter. In contrast, Wyoming's Devils Tower has crystals one-eighth to one-quarter inch across, and hexagonal columns about 6 to 12 feet in diameter.

Those bound for Glen Aulin and beyond traverse across Little Devils Postpile, which is about 100 yards in diameter, and immediately confront a brief traverse along a use path across a 30-degree slope. You don't want to slip and fall into the river below, especially if it is raging. If the traverse bothers you, either don't do it or head up the slope to safer ground and then traverse. Beyond it, you walk on a flat for about 100 yards, passing a campsite on your left about midway to the Pacific Crest Trail (Trip 33) where it bridges the Tuolumne River.

TRIP 33

Tuolumne Meadows to Glen Aulin and Waterwheel Falls

Ⓜ Ⓔ / DH, BP

DISTANCE: 12 or 18.6 miles
out and back

ELEVATIONS: 7870'/8650'
+310'/-1020'/±2660'

SEASON: Early July to mid-October

USE: Heavy

MAPS: *Tioga Pass, Falls Ridge*

TRAIL LOG:
0.8   Soda Springs
2.0   Young Lakes Trail
4.7   Tuolumne River bridge
5.8   Trail to May Lake
6.0   Glen Aulin High Sierra Camp
9.3   Waterwheel Falls

INTRODUCTION: This trail comprises the easiest section of the High Sierra Camps Loop Trail (Trip 35). It is also a section of the Pacific Crest and Tahoe-Yosemite trails. This popular hike to Glen Aulin is noted for the scenic pools, rapids, cascades, and falls it passes. Because the hike is virtually all downhill, it is ideal for hikers unaccustomed to high elevations. Spending a night at Glen Aulin gets you partly acclimated, preparing you for the hike back up to your trailhead.

If you are hiking while the river is still swift, which usually is before mid-July, it is worth your while to descend an additional 3.3 miles to Waterwheel Falls, which are most dramatic during maximum runoff. Strong hikers can make the trip to Waterwheel Falls (Trip 41) in six to eight hours or less, particularly if they take the preceding

trip to Glen Aulin, which results in about a 16-mile round trip instead of about an 18-mile one via the official trail. Descending from Glen Aulin to Waterwheel Falls and ascending back to it has an overall elevation gain and loss of about 2550 feet, which effectively doubles the elevation gain and loss along the trip to and from Glen Aulin.

DIRECTIONS TO THE TRAILHEAD: Drive along the Tioga Road to a dirt road starting west from the base of Lembert Dome, this spot located at the east end of Tuolumne Meadows and immediately north of the Tuolumne River. Alternatively, from the trailhead parking area at this spot, you can drive 0.3 mile west on the dirt road to a gate, from which point the main road turns north, bound for the nearby stables, which will save you 0.3 mile each way. The mileage is measured from the trailhead parking area. Trail begins in map section F3.

DESCRIPTION: From the Lembert Dome parking area west of the Tioga Road, we first walk west 0.3 mile along a dirt road to its bend, and then continue west on a gated service road that contours the lodgepole-dotted flank of Tuolumne Meadows. On it, we are treated to fine views south across them toward Unicorn Peak, Cathedral Peak, and some of the knobby Echo Peaks. You may also see an occasional marmot foraging for food, or Belding ground squirrels standing upright by their rodent holes. After about a quarter mile, we meet a trail heading northeast to the horse stables, and, about 200 yards past this junction, we face a split. The left branch heads over to a nearby bridge across the Tuolumne River, which proffers inspiring views. Our road veers right, slightly uphill, and quickly encounters a trail that leads to the still-bubbling natural Soda Springs. You can take this trail west across this vicinity to our road, or take the road, which arcs counterclockwise across the former site of the old Soda Springs Campground.

From the effervescent Soda Springs, our westbound trail undulates through a forest of sparse, small lodgepole pines, and, in just under a mile, descends to Delaney Creek, reached about 100 yards after a stock trail from the stables back in the meadows comes in on the right. In early season, look for a log to cross it; later on, boulder hopping will do. After 0.3 mile, you reach the Young Lakes Trail, on which those taking Trip 37 branch right, north.

Leaving this trail, we continue westward on our rambling traverse, and, after more winding through scattered lodgepoles, we descend some bare granite slabs and enter a flat-floored forest. A mile's pleasant walking since the last junction brings us to the bank of the Tuolumne River, just before three branches of Dingley Creek, near the west end of the huge meadows. From here, the nearly level trail often runs along the river, and, in these stretches by the stream, there are numerous glacier-smoothed granite slabs on which to take a break—or dip, if the river's current is slow.

After a mile-long, winding traverse, the trail leaves the last slabs to climb briefly up a granite outcrop to get around the river's gorge. You can leave the trail and walk toward a brink, from which you'll see, on the south side of the gorge below you, Little Devils Postpile.

Back on the trail, you wind down, eventually toward a sturdy Tuolumne River bridge, and, from the far bank, you can hike upriver cautiously to Little Devils Postpile. Immediately beyond the bridge, you can look north up long Cold Canyon to Matterhorn Peak and Whorl Mountain, and, to their right, Mt. Conness. As the river soon approaches nearby Tuolumne Falls, it flows down a series of sparkling rapids separated by large pools and wide sheets of water spread out across slightly inclined granite slopes. Beyond this beautiful stretch of river, the trail descends, steeply at times, past Tuolumne Falls and White Cascade to a junction with the trail to May Lake (Trip 35). From here, it is only a few minutes' walk to Glen Aulin High Sierra Camp, reached by crossing the river on a bridge below roaring White Cascade. During high runoff, you may have to wade just to reach this bridge! From the camp is a short trail to sites in the heavily used Glen Aulin backpackers' camp, complete with bearproof food-storage boxes, which are found at all the High Sierra Camps. Only 15 yards beyond the spur trail across Conness Creek to Glen Aulin High Sierra Camp is the Tuolumne Canyon Trail, going left.

Tuolumne Falls

LITTLE DEVILS POSTPILE

This is a 9.4-million-year-old lava remnant that has been interpreted by the US Geological Survey as a conduit of a former volcano. Not so. Conduits have nearly vertical columnar lava, but, as you can see, the columns beside the river are nearly horizontal, indicating that they formed on the surface in contact with adjacent granitic bedrock. Additionally, had the lava been a conduit, the columns would have been several feet in diameter, not a half foot to 1 foot in diameter. Despite repeated attacks by likely dozens of glaciers, this basalt flow remains, standing as mute testimony to the impotence of glaciers' ability to erode.

S **SIDE TRIP TO WATERWHEEL FALLS:** The Tuolumne Canyon Trail leaves the northbound Cold Canyon Trail (Trip 36) and climbs over a low knoll that sports rust-stained metamorphic rocks. From it is an excellent view west down the flat-floored, steep-walled canyon. It looks like a glaciated canyon should look: U-shaped in cross section. However, the flat, broad Tuolumne Meadows vicinity upstream and the V-shaped Grand Canyon of the Tuolumne River downstream were also glaciated and are certainly not U-shaped. In Yosemite, it is the joint (fracture) pattern of the resistant granitic bedrock that determines a canyon's shape, not the process of glaciation.

Leaving the low knoll, you switchback quickly down into Glen Aulin proper, and, paralleling the Tuolumne River through a lodgepole pine forest, you soon reach a backpackers' camp. Between here and Waterwheel Falls are several dwarfish, generally cryptic near-trail camps, and, at any along this trail, you can expect a nighttime visit by a local bear. Also, between here and Pate Valley is abundant evidence of a former, major fire. We tread the gravelly flat floor of the glen for more than a mile, and then, on bedrock, quickly arrive at the brink of cascading California Falls, perched at the base of a towering cliff. Be cautious around these falls and other falls downstream, for the bedrock often is polished and slippery, even when dry.

Switchbacking down beside the cascade, you leave behind the glen's thick forest of predominantly lodgepole pines with associated red firs and descend past scattered Jeffrey pines and junipers and through lots of brush. At the base of the cascade, lodgepoles, western white pines, and red firs return once more as you make a gentle descent north. Near the end of this short stretch, you parallel a long pool, which is a good spot to break for lunch or perhaps take a swim. However, stay away from the pool's outlet, where the Tuolumne River plunges over a brink.

The trail parallels this second cascade as it generally descends through brush and open forest. On this descent, notice that red firs have yielded to white firs. Sugar pines also put in their first appearance as you reach the brink of broad LeConte Falls, which cascades down fairly open granite slabs. On a flat-floored section of canyon, incense-cedar joins the ranks of white fir, Jeffrey pine, and sugar pine, with few, if any, lodgepoles to be found. In this forest, we reach our fifth and final cascade, extensive Waterwheel Falls. This cascade gets its name from the curving sprays of water tossed into the air, which occur when the river is flowing with sufficient force. It is worth the trip in early season to see the white water turning to rainbow as it sprays the canyon full of light and color. The cascade's classic views are from midway between its brink and its base. You'll probably spot a use trail out to this vicinity. On the slabs, the falls descend; use extreme caution even where the rock is dry. **END OF SIDE TRIP.**

TRIP 34

Tuolumne Meadows to White Wolf via Pate Valley

Ⓜ ↗ BPx

DISTANCE: 31 miles point to point

ELEVATIONS: 4230′/8650′
+5580′/-6290′/±11,870′

SEASON: Early July to mid-October

USE: Moderate

MAPS: *Tioga Pass, Falls Ridge, Ten Lakes, Hetch Hetchy Reservoir, Tamarack Flat*

TRAIL LOG:

0.8	Soda Springs
2.0	Young Lakes Trail
4.7	Tuolumne River bridge
5.8	Trail to May Lake
6.0	Glen Aulin High Sierra Camp
9.3	Waterwheel Falls
16.0	Register Creek
20.5	Pate Valley
24.5	Morrison Creek
26.7	White Wolf Trail
28.2	Harden Lake
31.0	White Wolf

INTRODUCTION: Rather than take Trip 22 to Pate Valley, you can take this route, which is longer but more spectacular. On it, a lot of hikers go no farther than Waterwheel Falls, which, at 3.3 trail miles from Glen Aulin, is the westernmost of the Tuolumne River's five major cascades. Go before mid-July to see the "waterwheels" at their best. Horseback riders should check with rangers if they intend to travel beyond Waterwheel Falls; there may be an early-season, high-water problem.

This trip is rated moderate in difficulty, but that is an average. The bulk of the hike is a mostly easy downhill route, but then you end with a strenuous ascent of about 4000 feet to climb out of the Grand Canyon of the Tuolumne River. While exhausting, this ascent does give you an appreciation of the magnitude of this major Sierran canyon. Alternatively, you can avoid this climb and return the way you came, for a total of about 40.5 miles. Although 10 miles longer, this less strenuous variation gives you a second chance to visit all the falls and cascades.

DIRECTIONS TO THE TRAILHEAD: Drive along the Tioga Road to a dirt road starting west from the base of Lembert Dome; this spot is located at the east end of Tuolumne Meadows and immediately north of the Tuolumne River. Alternatively, from the trailhead parking area at this spot, you can drive 0.3 mile west on the dirt road to a gate, from which the main road turns north, bound for the nearby stables, which will save you 0.3 mile each way. The mileage is measured from the trailhead parking area. Trail begins in map section F3.

DESCRIPTION: From the Lembert Dome parking area west of the Tioga Road, we first walk west 0.3 mile along a dirt road to its bend, and then continue west on a gated service road that contours the lodgepole-dotted flank of Tuolumne Meadows. On it, we are treated to fine views south across them toward Unicorn Peak, Cathedral Peak, and some of the knobby Echo Peaks. After about a quarter mile, we meet a trail heading northeast to the horse stables, and, about 200 yards past this junction, we face a split. The left branch heads over to a nearby bridge across the Tuolumne River, but our road veers right, slightly uphill, and quickly encounters a trail that leads to the still-bubbling natural Soda Springs. You can take this trail west across this vicinity to our road, or take the road, which arcs counterclockwise across the former site of the old Soda Springs Campground.

Westward, our trail undulates through a forest of sparse, small lodgepole pines, and, in just under 1 mile, it descends to Delaney Creek, reached about 100 yards after a stock trail from the stables back in the meadows comes in on the right. In early season, look for a log to cross it; later on, boulder hopping will do. After 0.3 mile, you reach the Young Lakes Trail, on which those taking Trip 37 branch right, north.

Leaving this trail, we continue westward on our rambling traverse, and, after more winding through scattered lodgepoles, we descend some bare granite slabs and enter a flat-floored forest. A mile's pleasant walking since the last junction brings us to the bank of the Tuolumne River, just before three branches of Dingley Creek, near the west end of the huge meadows. From here, the nearly level trail often runs along the river, and, in these stretches by the stream, there are numerous glacier-smoothed granite slabs on which to take a break—or dip, if the river's current is slow.

After a mile-long winding traverse, the trail leaves the last slabs to climb briefly up a granite outcrop to get around the river's gorge. You can leave the trail and walk toward a brink, from which you'll see, on the south side of the gorge below you, Little Devils Postpile, a 9.4-million-year-old remnant of a lava flow. Despite repeated attacks by likely dozens of glaciers, this basalt flow remains, standing as mute testimony to the impotence of glaciers' ability to erode.

 Back on the trail, you wind down eventually toward a sturdy Tuolumne River bridge, and from the far bank, one can hike upriver cautiously to Little Devils Postpile. Immediately beyond the bridge, you can look north up long Cold Canyon to Matterhorn Peak and Whorl Mountain, and, to their right, Mt. Conness. As the river soon approaches nearby Tuolumne Falls, it flows down a series of sparkling rapids separated by large pools and wide sheets of water spread out across slightly inclined granite slopes. Beyond this beautiful stretch of river, the trail descends, steeply at times,

past Tuolumne Falls and White Cascade to a junction with the trail to May Lake (Trip 35). From here, it is only a few minutes' walk to Glen Aulin High Sierra Camp, reached by crossing the river on a bridge below roaring White Cascade. During high runoff, you may have to wade just to reach this bridge! From the camp is a short trail to sites in the heavily used Glen Aulin backpackers' camp, complete with bearproof food-storage boxes, which are found at all the High Sierra Camps.

Only 15 yards beyond the spur trail across Conness Creek to Glen Aulin High Sierra Camp is the Tuolumne Canyon Trail, going left. On it, we leave the northbound Cold Canyon Trail (Trip 36) and climb over a low knoll that sports rust-stained metamorphic rocks. From it is an excellent view west down the flat-floored, steep-walled canyon. Now you switchback quickly down into Glen Aulin proper, and, paralleling the Tuolumne River through a lodgepole pine forest, soon reach a backpackers' camp. Between here and Waterwheel Falls are several dwarfish, generally cryptic near-trail camps. At any camps along this trail, you can expect a nighttime visit by a local bear. Also, between here and Pate Valley is abundant evidence of a former, major fire. We tread the gravelly flat floor of the glen for more than a mile, and then, on bedrock, quickly arrive at the brink of cascading California Falls, perched at the base of a towering cliff. Be cautious around these falls and other falls downstream, for the bedrock often is polished and slippery, even when dry.

Switchbacking down beside the cascade, you leave behind the glen's thick forest of predominantly lodgepole pines with associated red firs and descend past scattered Jeffrey pines and junipers and through lots of brush. At the base of the cascade, lodgepoles, western white pines, and red firs return once more as you make a gentle descent north. Near the end of this short stretch you parallel a long pool, which is a good spot to break for lunch or perhaps take a swim. However, stay away

California Falls

from the pool's outlet, where the Tuolumne River plunges over a brink.

The trail parallels this second cascade as it generally descends through brush and open forest. On this descent, notice that red firs have yielded to white firs. Sugar pines also put in their first appearance as you reach the brink of broad LeConte Falls, which cascades down fairly open granite slabs. On a flat-floored section of canyon, incense-cedar joins the ranks of white fir, Jeffrey pine, and sugar pine, with few, if any, lodgepoles to be found. In this forest, we reach our fifth and final cascade, extensive Waterwheel Falls. This cascade gets its name from the curving sprays of water tossed into the air, which occur when the river is flowing with sufficient force. It is worth the trip in early season to see the white water turning to rainbow as it sprays the canyon full of light and color. The cascade's classic views are from midway between its brink and its base. You'll probably spot a use trail out to this vicinity. On the slabs the falls descend, use extreme caution even where the rock is dry.

Starting on a trail segment recommended by John Muir and completed in 1925, you follow switchbacks down to the cascade's base, then continue to descend past a smaller set of cascades, beyond which you reach a small campsite beside a Tuolumne River pool. About 200 yards past it, a larger campsite is reached, this one located by the east bank of Return Creek. On the map, Return Creek up Virginia Canyon looks like a good cross-country tour, but, in reality, it is overgrown with huckleberry oak and other shrubs, making an ascent up it a sweaty, dusty experience.

Just past Return Creek, you'll note a swimming hole between two low cascades—one of many possible swimming holes you'll see before reaching Pate Valley. Unfortunately, these pools are best in August, but, if you go then, the river's flow has diminished sufficiently to make Waterwheel Falls just an ordinary cascade. Upon descending to lower elevations—now characterized largely by incense-cedars, black oaks, and canyon live oaks—hikers may face pesky hordes of flies. Continuing down-canyon, you pass a massive south-wall cliff before coming to a fair campsite, and then, in a half mile, cross a low ridge. During most of the summer, the afternoon temperatures at our now-lower elevations are distinctly warm, if not hot, but most of the route is shaded, and the Tuolumne River is usually close by for dipping. At these elevations, ground squirrels and other rodents abound, so rattlesnakes are likely, too. At first, the route is along a shady, flat-floored valley, into which only a minimal amount of talus has fallen in about the last 15,000 years, the time when the last glacier—about 4000 feet thick at its maximum—retreated up this canyon. After a mile, you begin a curve north around the base of a half-mile-high buttress of Colby Mountain, standing on the west rim of the Ten Lakes Basin.

Beyond this buttress, the Tuolumne River Trail begins a climb up and around the Muir Gorge. Under shade, it climbs 400 feet to a viewless subsidiary ridge, arcs counterclockwise across fairly open slabs to a larger ridge, and then encounters a low, joint-controlled trough, which obstructs views, although immediately east, west, and south of it are excellent ones. You can now look south straight up the glaciated, plunging Ten Lakes canyon. Your struggle down-canyon is not yet over, for after you descend two dozen switchbacks—a 500-foot drop—you climb again. This, however, is short-lived, and you very quickly pass through a notch, which has been cleft straight as an arrow. It, like so many other geomorphic features, lies along a straight fracture in the granitic bedrock. Now you switchback down to a bridge over Register Creek, near its 60-foot plunge into a walled-in pool, and immediately bridge smaller Rodgers Canyon creek. Both creeks may be dry after Labor Day. Just beyond them, you can peer through the canyon live oaks and black oaks and look straight "down the throat" of linear Muir Gorge— a product of the Tuolumne River's cutting down along a major fracture. John Muir was probably the first white man to descend the gorge, and, in 1931, two Sierra Club parties became the first successful groups to duplicate this feat. Even in times of low water, this hike/swim feat can be dangerous.

After a few descending switchbacks, the trail leaves the mouth of the Muir Gorge behind and traverses a very level mile before presenting views of an incredible section of the canyon's north wall. Above you towers a giant wall, with fresh polish and striations, which are dark gray and pale orange. The wall presents an opportunity for good early-morning color photography. The gray color is not the color of the bedrock, but rather of the lichens growing on it.

Continuing your descent west down the Grand Canyon of the Tuolumne River, you might see wild grapes growing along the trail. The river is forced south by a "mountain"—a large, glacier-defying bedrock mass within the canyon—and, across its lower slopes, your trail parallels the river to shadier, easier terrain. The last mile of trail to the Pate Valley junction is nearly flat, and along it you may see burned snags and flood-strewn logs. From the Pate Valley junction, head for riverside campsites, about 100 to 200 yards west, or continue several hundred yards beyond the two Tuolumne River bridges to even more campsites, in Pate Valley proper. Here, the forest composition is nearly identical to that of Yosemite Valley, dominated by ponderosa pines, black oaks, and incense-cedars.

To reach White Wolf, it is best to start early, while it is still cool, and to take it easy, resting often. Carry at least one quart of water. You begin with fairly level hiking down-canyon, and you'll pass several near-river campsites, and isolated camps could be set up in a number of places. After about 2 miles from Pate Valley proper, you begin your climb, and, with sufficient water, you ascend a few switchbacks to a seasonal, grassy pond, then cross a granite gap, about 250 feet above the canyon's floor.

Onward, we start our first of two major sets of short switchbacks, and we ascend about four dozen of them over 2 miles to a crossing of Morrison Creek. Along this ascent, black oaks and incense-cedars and scraggly western junipers and pervasive huckleberry oaks give way to sugar pines, and then to a forest of white firs. You may want to rest often, and numerous views of the Grand Canyon of the Tuolumne River provide an excuse for doing so. Finally, you come to a crossing of seasonal Morrison Creek, at about 5600 feet elevation. You've completed just over one-third of your ascent.

The second major set of short switchbacks is up alongside Morrison Creek, and these end beside a low, rocky knoll, on our right. This is a good spot for a rest, and you might do it from the knoll, which offers quite a view west-northwest down the trough holding Hetch Hetchy Reservoir to Wapama Falls, dashing into the reservoir's far end. On an easier grade, we now parallel Morrison Creek for a quarter mile, where we finally leave it at about 6750 feet elevation. If the creek has been dry, you may find water just a quarter mile ahead at a spring-fed creeklet. About 0.8 mile after leaving Morrison Creek, we reach the White Wolf Trail.

Rather than make a steep, switchbacking climb south up to White Wolf, continue west on a trail bound for Harden Lake, whose first mile is a comfortable contour. Many aspens are passed along the second half of this contour, and they fill their thirsty appetites by tapping the large "reservoir" of water stored within the morainal sediments we traverse across. One source of this "reservoir" is our immediate goal, Harden Lake, which has no surface outlet but, rather, loses some of its water via percolation through the morainal sediments. To reach Harden Lake, we climb moderately to steeply up about 20 switchbacks, entering a forest of lodgepole pines, then of red firs and western white pines.

When you arrive at Harden Lake, you'll need a rest and probably a refreshing swim—if this seasonal lake hasn't already leaked so much that it is barely a mud hole. From the lake, your trail quickly ends at a road that you follow southeast for a quarter mile, then take a left-branching trail 0.75 mile over to the old Tioga Road, which heads 1.8 miles up along the infant Middle Tuolumne River to White Wolf. If Harden Lake was dry, you can get water from the river. It's not deep enough to swim in, but there are several small pools deep enough to lie in, should you be filthy dirty and want to get clean before reaching your vehicle.

TRIP **35**

High Sierra Camps Loop

M Q BPx

DISTANCE: 51.2 miles loop

ELEVATIONS: 7220´/10,670´
+9090´/-9090´/±18,180´

SEASON: Mid-July to early October

USE: Heavy

MAPS: *Tioga Pass, Falls Ridge, Tenaya Lake, Merced Peak, Vogelsang Peak*

TRAIL LOG:

6.0	Glen Aulin High Sierra Camp
10.3	Murphy Creek Trail
10.9	Ten Lakes Trail
12.6	Raisin Lake
14.4	May Lake High Sierra Camp
15.6	May Lake Trailhead
17.5	Tenaya Lake
23.3	Sunrise High Sierra Camp
33.6	Merced Lake High Sierra Camp
42.6	Vogelsang High Sierra Camp
51.2	Trailhead

INTRODUCTION: Along this loop are six High Sierra Camps, each spaced a convenient day's hike from the next. Many visitors make this loop on horseback. Others hike the trail carrying little more than a daypack, since the camps provide meals and bedding. Unfortunately, the camps are so popular that a lottery is held each December to determine the lucky relative few for the following summer. To obtain a lottery application, phone the camp-management company at 559-253-5674 between October 15 and November 30.

The High Sierra Camps Loop hike became very popular years ago, and a quota to limit the number of hikers using it is often filled. Therefore, if you plan to hike it without having camp reservations, you might plan to do it before the camps open around mid-July or after they close around mid-September. However, if you are hiking it then, do plan for the possibility of sudden snow storms and know what to do if you're caught in one. You could hike this loop trail either clockwise or counterclockwise from either the Tuolumne Meadows or the Tenaya Lake environs. I prefer counterclockwise from the former, since this way, on your first day, when your pack is heaviest and you perhaps are not in the best of shape, your route is mostly level and downhill.

During the summer season, buses run along the Tioga Road, and this conveniently allows you to do just part of the loop if you don't have time for its entirety. You can hike either from Tuolumne Meadows to the Glen Aulin and May Lake high sierra camps, and then to the Tioga Road at Tenaya Lake and take a bus back to your trailhead; or you can take the bus to Tenaya Lake and then hike to Sunrise, Merced Lake, and Vogelsang high sierra camps, and then hike back out to your trailhead in Tuolumne Meadows.

On all the other long, multiday backpack trips in this guidebook, you can camp at many locations, hiking as far as you choose for each day. In contrast, Trip 35 is unique in that you ideally hike a specific distance each day and then camp only by each High Sierra Camp. Because the distances and elevation gains and losses are fixed, I'm presenting them here in tabular form, so that you can immediately grasp the severity of each day's hike.

DIRECTIONS TO THE TRAILHEAD: Of the several possibilities, I recommend the parking area at the base of Lembert Dome, which is located immediately off the Tioga Road and immediately north of a bridge across the Tuolumne River. Mileages are measured from here. You could also drive to the large parking lot just beyond the start of the Tuolumne Meadows Lodge spur road. This road is reached by driving 0.6 mile northeast from the Tuolumne Meadows Campground entrance. During most of the summer, this large lot, immediately west of the spur road, has a small booth that dispenses wilderness permits. Trail begins in map section F3.

DESCRIPTION: From your parking lot, follow a trail west down the Tuolumne River to the backpackers' camp at Glen Aulin High Sierra Camp, the place most hikers spend their first night. This trail begins from the Lembert Dome parking area west of the Tioga Road. We first walk west 0.3 mile along a dirt road to its bend, and then continue west on a gated service road that contours the lodgepole-dotted flank of Tuolumne Meadows. On it, we are treated to fine views south across them toward Unicorn Peak, Cathedral Peak, and some of the knobby Echo Peaks. After about a quarter mile, we meet a trail heading northeast to the horse stables, and, about 200 yards past this junction, we face a split. The left branch heads over to a nearby bridge across the Tuolumne River, but our road veers right, slightly uphill, and quickly encounters a trail that leads to the still-bubbling natural Soda Springs. Take this trail west across this vicinity to our road, or take the road, which arcs counterclockwise

DISTANCE AND ELEVATION FOR TRIP 35				
Day 1	Trailhead to Glen Aulin	6.0 miles	310′ gain	1020′ loss
Day 2	Glen Aulin to May Lake	8.4 miles	2220′ gain	740′ loss
Day 3	May Lake to Sunrise	8.9 miles	1980′ gain	1990′ loss
Day 4	Sunrise to Merced	10.3 miles	610′ gain	2730′ loss
Day 5	Merced to Vogelsang	9.0 miles	3740′ gain	840′ loss
Day 6	Vogelsang to Trailhead	8.6 miles	230′ gain	1770′ loss

across the former site of the old Soda Springs Campground.

Westward, our trail undulates through a forest of sparse, small lodgepole pines, and, in just under 1 mile, descends to Delaney Creek, reached about 100 yards after a stock trail from the stables back in the meadows comes in on the right. In early season, look for a log to cross it; later on, boulder hopping will do. After 0.3 mile, you reach the Young Lakes Trail, branching right, north.

Leaving this trail, we continue westward on our rambling traverse, and after more winding through scattered lodgepoles, it descends some bare granite slabs and enters a flat-floored forest. A mile's pleasant walking since the last junction brings one to the bank of the Tuolumne River, just before three branches of Dingley Creek, near the west end of the huge meadows. From here, the nearly level trail often runs along the river, and, in these stretches by the stream, there are numerous glacier-smoothed granite slabs on which to take a break—or dip, if the river's current is slow.

After a mile-long winding traverse, the trail leaves the last slabs to climb briefly up a granite outcrop to get around the river's gorge. You can leave the trail and walk toward a brink, from which you'll see, on the south side of the gorge below you, Little Devils Postpile, a 9.4-million-year-old remnant of a lava flow.

Onward, you wind down, eventually, toward a sturdy Tuolumne River bridge, and, immediately beyond it, you can look north up long Cold Canyon to Matterhorn Peak and Whorl Mountain, and, to their right, Mt. Conness. As the river soon approaches nearby Tuolumne Falls, it flows down a series of sparkling rapids separated by large pools and wide sheets of water spread out across slightly inclined granite slopes. Beyond this beautiful stretch of river, the trail descends, steeply at times, past Tuolumne Falls and White Cascade to a junction with the trail to May Lake. From here, it is only a few minutes' walk to Glen Aulin High Sierra Camp, reached by crossing the river on a bridge below roaring White Cascade. During high runoff, you may have to wade just to reach this bridge! From the camp is a short trail to sites in the heavily used Glen Aulin backpackers' camp, complete with bearproof food-storage boxes, which are found at all the High Sierra Camps.

Bridge immediately above Tuolumne Falls

The second day's hike is from the Glen Aulin to the May Lake High Sierra Camp. From the junction immediately south of and above Glen Aulin's bridge across the Tuolumne River, you briefly curve northwest through a notch, and then your duff trail ascends gently southwest, soon crossing and recrossing McGee Lake's northeast-flowing outlet, which dries up by late summer. Where the trail levels off, McGee Lake, long and narrow and bordered on the southwest by a granite cliff, comes into view through the lodgepole trees. The dead snags along the shallow margin, and the fallen limbs and downed trees make fishing difficult, and, in late summer, the lake may dwindle to a stale pond. Adept campers can find isolated, level spots, some with views, on slopes north of the lake, beneath the east end of Falls Ridge.

Beyond the lake, your trail descends along its southwest-flowing outlet for 0.75 mile, and then you cross it. Soon, you have a view northwest through the shallow Cathedral Creek canyon to hulking Falls Ridge, which Cathedral Creek has to detour around in order to join the Tuolumne River. After several minutes, we reach 20-foot-wide Cathedral Creek, which can be a ford in early season, a boulder hop later on. Starting a moderate ascent beyond the creek, we soon reach a stand of tall, healthy red firs, and the contrast with the small, overcrowded lodgepole pines earlier on the trail is inescapable.

Higher on the trail, there are good views, and, after 3 miles of walking through moderate and dense forest, the panorama seems especially welcome. In the distant northeast stand Sheep Peak, North Peak, and Mt. Conness, encircling the basin of Roosevelt Lake. In the near north, Falls Ridge is a mountain of pinkish granite that contrasts with the white and gray granite of the other peaks. When we look back toward McGee Lake, the route appears to be entirely carpeted with lodgepole pines.

The trail continues up a moderate slope on gravel and granite shelves, through a forest cover of hemlock, red fir, and lodge-pole. After arriving at a branch of Cathedral Creek, you cross it, then continue for a half mile to a junction shaded under some tall hemlocks. The Murphy Creek Trail departs from this junction to go down to Tenaya Lake (Trip 30). Down this trail, a short half mile before the lake, a lateral trail departs southwest, parallels the Tioga Road, and ends at a bend in the highway by a trailhead parking area. We'll reach this spot by a longer route.

A half mile from the hemlock-shaded junction, you reach a junction with the Ten Lakes Trail (Trip 23), which climbs slopes beneath the very steep east face of Tuolumne Peak. Here, you branch left and ascend briefly to a long, narrow, shallow, forested saddle beyond which large Tenaya Lake is visible in the south. After traversing somewhat open slopes of sagebrush, huckleberry oak, and lupine, you reach a spring, and then momentarily come to a series of switchbacks. Progress up the long, gentle gradient of these zigzags is distinguished by the striking views of Mt. Conness, Mt. Dana, and the other giants on the Sierra Crest/Yosemite border. The trail then passes through a little saddle just north of a glacier-smoothed peak, and, ahead, suddenly, is another Yosemite landmark, Clouds Rest, rising grandly in the south: You see a part of this largest expanse of bare granite in the park.

Now the trail descends gradually over fairly open granite to a forested flat and bends west above the north shore of Raisin Lake, which is one of the warmest "swimming holes" in this section. It also has campsites, including waterless, isolated ones with views, located about a quarter mile south of the lake. From the lake's vicinity, the trail continues beside a flower-lined runoff stream bed under a sparse forest cover of mountain hemlock and western white and lodgepole pines, and then it swings west to cross three unnamed, seasonal streams.

Finally the trail makes a steep, half-mile ascent up to May Lake, across a slope sparsely dotted with red firs, western white pines, and other conifers. Views improve constantly, and, presently, you have a panorama of the peaks on the Sierra Crest from North Peak south to Mt. Gibbs. The Tioga Pass notch is clearly visible. At the top of this climb is a gentle upland where several small meadows are strung along the trail, with corn lilies growing at an almost perceptible rate in early season, while aromatic lupine commands your attention later on. In the west, Mt. Hoffman dominates. Now you swing south at the northeast corner of the lake and parallel its east shore to the May Lake High Sierra Camp. From May Lake's southeast corner, you'll see a trail striking west and it has a backpackers' camp that extends westward.

You begin the third day's hike by taking the lake's short trail 1.2 miles down to the May Lake Trailhead on Snow Flat, along the old Tioga Road. From here, you follow the road northeast for two minutes to where it is blocked off, then descend the closed stretch of road southeast to the Tioga Road, cross it, and parallel it northeast about 0.6 mile to a fairly large trailhead parking area near the southwest corner of Tenaya Lake. During the summer season, shuttle buses ply the road between here and Tuolumne Meadows, offering you a free ride back to your trailhead, should you want or need to cut your trip short.

From the trailhead parking area, take a trail that heads east, and you soon cross the usually flowing outlet of Tenaya Lake. Just beyond this crossing, you reach a trail junction. The trail left goes northeast to start a loop around the lake, and then it continues another 7 miles to the Cathedral Lakes Trail in Tuolumne Meadows. You veer right on a trail that heads south for a quarter mile along Tenaya Creek. Over the next half mile, our trail ascends southeast in sparse forest over a little rise and drops to a ford of Mildred Lake's outlet, which, like the other streams between Tenaya Lake and the Sunrise Trail junction, can dry up in late season. Beyond the Mildred Lake stream, the trail undulates and winds generally south, passing several pocket meadows

browsed by mule deer. The trail then begins to climb in earnest, through a thinning cover of lodgepole pine and occasional red fir, western white pine, and mountain hemlock. As your trail rises above Tenaya Canyon, you pass several vantage points from which you can look back upon its polished granite walls, though you never see Tenaya Lake. To the east, the canyon is bounded by Tenaya Peak; in the northwest are the cliffs of Mt. Hoffman and Tuolumne Peak.

Now on switchbacks, one sees the Tioga Road across the canyon and can even hear vehicles, but these annoyances are infinitesimal compared to the pleasures of polished granite expanses all around. These switchbacks are mercifully shaded, and where they become steepest, requiring a great output of energy, they give back the beauty of the finest flower displays on this trail, including lupine, penstemon, paintbrush, larkspur, buttercup, and sunflowers such as aster and senecio. Finally, the switchbacks end and the trail levels as it arrives at a junction on a shallow, forested saddle, 2.9 miles beyond the trailhead.

The trail ahead goes to Clouds Rest and beyond, but we turn left, and, over a half mile, we first contour east, cross a low gap, and descend north to lower Sunrise Lake. Climbing from this lake and its small campsites, we reach a crest in several minutes; from it, you could descend cross-country an equally short distance north to more isolated, island-dotted middle Sunrise Lake. Our loop trail, however, veers east and gains a very noticeable 150 feet in elevation as it climbs to upper Sunrise Lake, the largest and most popular lake of the trio. Campsites are plentiful along its north shore, away from the trail.

With 1.7 miles remaining to our day's goal, we leave this lake and climb south up a gully, cross it, and then soon climb up a second gully to the east side of a broad gap, from which you see the Clark Range head-on, piercing the southern sky. From the gap, which is sparsely clothed with mountain hemlocks, whitebark pines, and western white pines, you descend south into denser cover, veer east, and then veer north to make a steep descent to a backpackers' camp. By walking briefly north from it, you'll reach Sunrise High Sierra Camp. An overnight stay at either camp gives you an inspiring sunrise over Matthes Crest and the Cathedral Range.

You begin the fourth day's hike by treading the John Muir Trail 0.8 mile, first east and then north to the Echo Creek Trail, on which you will immediately ford Long Meadow's creek on boulders. This trail, which takes us 7.2 miles to the Merced Lake Trail, quickly switchbacks up to the top of a forested ridge, about 200 feet above the meadow. It then descends through dense hemlock-and-lodgepole forest to a tributary of Echo Creek. Cross this, descend along it for 0.3 mile, recross it, and then momentarily reach the west bank of Echo Creek's Cathedral Fork, about 1.5 miles beyond Long Meadow.

From our trail beside the Cathedral Fork, we have fine views of the creek's water gliding down a series of granite slabs, and then the trail veers away from the creek and descends gently above it for more than a mile. Even in late season, these shaded slopes are watered by numerous rills that are bordered by still-blooming flowers. On this downgrade, the trail crosses the Long Meadow creek, which has found an escape from that meadow through a gap between two small domes high above our trail. The route then levels out in a mile-long flat section of this valley, where the wet ground yields wildflowers all summer but also many mosquitoes in the early season. Beyond this flat "park," the trail descends more open slopes, and, eventually, you can see across the valley the steep course of Echo Creek plunging down to its rendezvous with its western Cathedral Fork. By the Cathedral Fork, your trail levels off and passes good campsites immediately before you take a bridge over Echo Creek.

Beyond the bridge, your trail leads down the forested valley and easily fords a tributary stream, staying well above the main creek. This pleasant, shaded descent soon becomes more open and steep, and it encounters fibrous-barked juniper trees and butterscotch-scented Jeffrey pines as it drops to another bridge 1.3 miles from the first one. Beyond it, the trail rises slightly and the creek drops precipitously, so that you are soon far above it. Then the sandy tread swings west and diagonals down a brushy slope. Across it, the views are excellent of Echo Valley, which is a wide place in the great Merced River canyon below. On this slope, you arrive at a junction with the High Trail, which goes 3 miles west to a junction with the John Muir Trail. Leaving the dense growth of huckleberry oak, chinquapin, greenleaf manzanita, and snow bush behind, start southeast and make a drop 450 feet over 0.7 mile to the Merced Lake Trail junction in Echo Valley.

There is adequate camping here, but our goal is only 2.3 miles ahead. We go east, immediately bridging Echo Creek, pass through a burned but boggy area, then climb east past the Merced River's largely unseen, but enjoyable, pools to Merced Lake's west shore. Don't camp here, but rather continue past the north shore to Merced Lake High Sierra Camp and the adjacent campground, which you reach just before the camp.

While day five isn't the longest, it easily has the most elevation to gain, about 3740 feet. Fortunately, by now you should be well acclimatized, should be somewhat in shape, and should have a lighter pack. You begin day five with an easy warm-up by hiking a level mile east to the Merced Lake Ranger Station and an adjacent trail junction. From it, you struggle 1.5 miles in a 1000-foot climb northeast up the Lewis Creek Trail to another trail junction. Here, you branch left on the Fletcher Creek Trail and descend on short switchbacks to a bridge over Lewis Creek. Just 50 yards past it is a good campsite, and then the trail enters more open slopes as it climbs moderately on a cobbled path bordered with proliferating bushes of snow bush and huckleberry oak. Just past a tributary a half mile from Lewis Creek, you have fine views of Fletcher Creek cascading down from the notch at the base of the granite dome before it leaps off a ledge in free fall. The few solitary pine trees on this otherwise blank dome testify to nature's extraordinary persistence. At the notch, your trail levels off and reaches the Babcock Lake Trail, which won't be worth the 3-mile round trip effort.

Onward, the sandy Fletcher Creek Trail ascends steadily through a moderate forest cover, staying just east of Fletcher Creek. After 0.75 mile, this route breaks out into the open and begins to rise more steeply via rocky switchbacks. From these, one can see nearby in the north the outlet stream of Emeric Lake—though not the lake itself, which is behind a dome just to the right of the outlet's notch. Continue up the trail into a long meadow guarded in the west by a highly polished knoll and presided over in the east by huge Vogelsang Peak. When you come to the scissors junction near Emeric Lake, branch right and hike 2.3 miles northeast up to the Vogelsang High Sierra Camp.

Your last day is the easiest; it is one of the shortest legs, and almost all of it is downhill or level. You begin by dropping slightly as you traverse 0.8 mile north across slopes to Tuolumne Pass. From it is a large, linear meadow, and descending about 1.5 miles north through it, you have views north to the Sierra Crest between Tioga Pass and Mt. Conness and views behind to cliff-bound, dark-banded Fletcher Peak and Vogelsang Peak to the right of it. Where you leave the meadow, you have a 3.7-mile descent on the Rafferty Creek Trail. You go a viewless half mile down to a meadow, which is about a half mile long, but the trail stays just within the confines of a lodgepole pine forest. Beyond the meadow, the trail descends its namesake creek for about 2.3 viewless miles to a junction with the John Muir Trail.

Ahead, the route is almost flat. You traverse 0.6 mile west to a junction, leave the westbound trail ahead to Tuolumne Camp-

ground, and branch north on the route of the John Muir Trail. In about 70 yards, you reach two bridges across branches of the Lyell Fork of the Tuolumne River. The meadows above these bridges are among the most delightful in all the Sierra, and anytime you happen to be staying all night at the lodge or nearby, the bridges are a wonderful place to spend the last hour before dinner, something you might consider for your hike out to your trailhead. Mt. Dana and Mt. Gibbs glow on the eastern horizon, catching the late sun, while trout dart along the wide Lyell Fork.

Past the second bridge, the John Muir Trail leads over a slight rise and descends to a trail junction by the Dana Fork. Here, a trail begins an ascent to the Gaylor Lakes. After a brief walk downstream, we bridge the Dana Fork and find a spur trail that goes shortly over to the west end of the parking lot of the Tuolumne Meadows Lodge. Rather, we continue downstream 0.3 mile to the large parking lot just beyond the start of the Tuolumne Meadows Lodge spur road. If you parked here, your trip is over, but if you parked at the base of Lembert Dome, from where the High Sierra Camps Loop description began, you continue a half mile farther.

TRIP 36

Tuolumne Meadows to Sonora Pass via Pacific Crest Trail

S ⬈ BPx

DISTANCE: 76.4 miles point to point

ELEVATIONS: 7580'/10,100'
+15,220'/-14,210'/±29,430'

SEASON: Mid-July to late September

USE: Moderate

MAPS: *Tioga Pass, Falls Ridge, Matterhorn Peak, Dunderberg Peak, Piute Mountain, Tiltill Mountain, Tower Peak, Pickel Meadow, Sonora Pass*

TRAIL LOG:

INTRODUCTION: Deep, spectacular glaciated canyons, crossed one after another, characterize this hike. As a backpacker here, you may feel as if you are doing more vertical climbing than horizontal walking. Nearing the north end of this hike, you leave the expansive granitic domain behind and enter Vulcan's realm—thick floods of volcanic flows and sediments that buried most of the northern Sierra Nevada. By hiking these 76 miles, you will have completed almost 3% of the entire Pacific Crest Trail, which extends from the Mexican border north. Although you might think that in Yosemite's hinterlands traversed by the Pacific Crest Trail there would be no bears, such is not the case. As on other Yosemite trails, bears, deer, and mountain lions all use the trail.

DIRECTIONS TO THE TRAILHEADS: Drive along the Tioga Road to a dirt road starting west from the base of Lembert Dome. This spot is located at the east end of Tuolumne Meadows and immediately north of the Tuolumne River. Alternatively, from the trailhead parking area at this spot, you can drive 0.3 mile west on the dirt road to a gate, from which the main road turns north, bound for the nearby stables, which will save you 0.3 mile each way. The mileage is measured from the trailhead parking area. This trail begins in map section F3. To reach the trailhead at the trip's end, drive up Hwy. 108 to Sonora Pass and park at the signed Pacific Crest Trail parking area, whose entrance is about 250 yards west of the pass. This trail head is in map section H1.

DESCRIPTION: From your parking lot, follow a trail west down the Tuolumne River to the backpackers' camp at Glen Aulin High Sierra Camp, the place most hikers spend their first night. This trail begins from the Lembert Dome parking area west of the Tioga Road. We first walk west 0.3 mile along a dirt road to its bend, and then continue west on a gated service road that contours the lodgepole-dotted flank of Tuolumne Meadows. On it, we are treated to fine views south across them toward Unicorn Peak, Cathedral Peak, and some of the knobby Echo Peaks. After about a quarter mile, we meet a trail heading northeast to the horse stables, and, about 200 yards past this junction, we face a split. The left branch heads over to a nearby bridge across the Tuolumne River, but our road veers right, slightly uphill, and quickly encounters a trail that leads to the still-bubbling natural Soda Springs. You can take this trail west across this vicinity to our road, or take the road, which arcs counterclockwise across the former site of the old Soda Springs Campground.

Westward, our trail undulates through a forest of sparse, small lodgepole pines, and, in just under 1 mile, descends to Delaney Creek, reached about 100 yards after a stock trail from the stables back in the meadows comes in on the right. In early season, look for a log to cross it; later on,

boulder hopping will do. After 0.3 mile, you reach the Young Lakes Trail, 2 miles into our route and branching right, north.

Leaving this trail, we continue westward on our rambling traverse, and, after more winding through scattered lodgepoles, it descends some bare granite slabs and enters a flat-floored forest. A mile's pleasant walking since the last junction brings you to the bank of the Tuolumne River, just before three branches of Dingley Creek, near the west end of the huge meadows. From here, the nearly level trail often runs along the river, and, in these stretches by the stream, there are numerous glacier-smoothed granite slabs on which to take a break—or a dip, if the river's current is slow.

After a winding, mile-long traverse, the trail leaves the last slabs to climb briefly up a granite outcrop to get around the river's gorge. You can leave the trail and walk toward a brink, from which you'll see, on the south side of the gorge below you, Little Devils Postpile, a 9.4-million-year-old remnant of a lava flow.

Onward, you wind down, eventually toward a sturdy Tuolumne River bridge, 4.7 miles into our route. Immediately

Tuolumne River, Unicorn Peak, and Cathedral Peak, from near Soda Springs

beyond it, you can look north up long Cold Canyon to Matterhorn Peak and Whorl Mountain, and, to their right, Mt. Conness. As the river soon approaches nearby Tuolumne Falls, it flows down a series of sparkling rapids separated by large pools and wide sheets of water spread out across slightly inclined granite slopes. Beyond this beautiful stretch of river, the trail descends, steeply at times, past Tuolumne Falls and White Cascade to a junction with the trail to May Lake. From here, it is only a few minutes' walk to Glen Aulin High Sierra Camp, reached by crossing the river on a bridge below roaring White Cascade. During high runoff, you may have to wade just to reach this bridge! From the camp is a short trail to sites in the heavily used Glen Aulin backpackers' camp, complete with bearproof food-storage boxes, which are found at all the High Sierra Camps. This is a good place to spend the night if you're taking seven or more days to do this hike.

Leaving Glen Aulin, your trail—the Pacific Crest Trail, or PCT—climbs north, sometimes along Cold Canyon creek, 3 miles to a forested gap. It then descends a half mile to the south edge of a large, usually soggy meadow. Midway across it, you'll notice a huge boulder, just west. Its overhanging sides have been used as an emergency shelter, but in a lightning storm, it is a prime-strike target. Beyond it, your route continues north, first for a mile through meadow, then on a gradual ascent through forest to a crest junction with the McCabe Lakes Trail.

[S] **SIDE TRIP TO LOWER MCCABE LAKE:** A long, half-mile walk northeast up this trail would get you to a small campsite just above McCabe Creek; an hour's walk up it would get you to larger, better campsites at scenic Lower McCabe Lake. If you took Trip 7's mountaineering route to the McCabe Lakes and you are caught in a snow storm, exit via this route, *not* by the route you came in on, for the Secret Lake pass is far too treacherous when snowbound. **END OF SIDE TRIP.**

If you're trying to do Trip 36 in six days, your first night's goal should be campsites along Return Creek or lower McCabe Creek, both down in Virginia Canyon—a *long* 14 miles from the trailhead if you're carrying a heavy pack. (But then, tri-state PCT trekkers typically average about 20 miles per day!) You switchback down to this canyon's floor, cross McCabe Creek—a wet ford before July— and look for nearby campsites or advance briefly to a junction with a spur trail heading briefly up-canyon past additional campsites.

The next morning, ford seasonally powerful Return Creek, which usually is a wet ford and, in early season, can be a dangerous one, especially in the afternoon, when snow is melting rapidly. At times of high water, look as much as a half mile up-canyon for slower-flowing water rather than attempting to cross here. Don't rope up, since hikers have been known to drown before they could untie their rope after they slipped. On the west bank, you walk but a few steps southwest before your trail veers right and meets the Virginia Canyon Trail (mentioned in Trip 6's alternate route). On the PCT, you start down-canyon, climb west up into Spiller Creek canyon, and then, halfway to a pass, cross the canyon's high-volume creek. A favorite route among mountaineers is to hike from Twin Lakes up Horse Creek canyon to the park's boundary—a de facto trail most of the way—and then to descend Spiller Creek canyon to this PCT crossing.

Beyond Spiller Creek, we soon start up two dozen switchbacks that transport us 2 miles up to a forested pass, 800 feet above the creek, and, up here, there are fair camps when there is enough snow to provide water. Most hikers continue 1.5 miles southwest along an undulating route that goes slightly down to shallow Miller Lake, at 9446 feet and with good campsites along its forested west shore. From the lake, you parallel a meadow north up to a low gap, and then execute more than two dozen often steep switchbacks down about 1200 feet to a canyon floor and a junction with the northbound Matterhorn Canyon Trail. Trip 4 goes north up-canyon, but the PCT descends southwest, reaching this majestic canyon's broad creek in 80 yards. Immediately beyond the often wet ford lies a large, lodgepole-shaded campsite with ample space to stretch out and dry your feet.

Heading down-canyon for a mile, you pass less obvious and more secluded campsites, then soon leave the glaciated canyon to begin the usual two dozen, short, steep switchbacks—this time west up into Wilson Creek canyon. This is a typical glaciated side canyon that hangs above the main canyon, but not—as is widely believed—because its smaller glacier couldn't erode the landscape as rapidly as the trunk-canyon glacier could. River drainages in the Sierra Nevada have numerous *unglaciated,* hanging, tributary canyons.

We twice ford Wilson Creek, and then ford it a last time and start a switchbacking climb up to windy, gravelly Benson Pass, registering a breathtaking height of 10,100 feet. As the passes have become deeper, so, too, have the canyons, and our multistage descent to and then ascent up from Benson Lake is exhausting. In about 6 miles, we'll go from the route's highest elevation down to its lowest, at the Benson Lake spur trail. We begin uneventfully, with an easy descent to a large meadow, reaching its peaceful creeklet just before a dropoff. Veering away from the creeklet, we soon begin a switchbacking descent that, in 2 miles, ends at a south-shore peninsula on 9219-foot Smedberg Lake. Most of the campsites, however, lie along the lake's west and north shores.

From the lake's south-shore peninsula—below the steep-walled sentinel, Volunteer Peak—you continue west, passing a spur trail to the west-shore campsites before winding southwest up a slab-rock trail to a nearby gap. From it, the trail switchbacks down joint-controlled granite slabs, only to climb south high up to a meadowy junction with the Rodgers Lake Trail.

S **SIDE TRIP TO RODGERS LAKE:** This lake has more isolation than Murdock Lake, just ahead, and it is more appealing, although it requires more effort to reach. The mile-long route to it climbs about 330 feet up to a grassy saddle at 9810 feet, where you'll see the stunning sheer profile of nearby Volunteer Peak, which completely dominates a horizon of greater summits throughout the north country—Piute Mountain, Price and Tower peaks, and Crown Point. You then drop 300 feet rather abruptly to subalpine Rodgers Lake, named for the second Yosemite National Park superintendent. This lake is divided into two bodies by a low granitic isthmus, the larger, eastern portion being more open and rockier. There is a handsome grove of lodgepoles and hemlocks on the north shore, and here lie some good camps that afford excellent panoramas over the shallow waters to the ruddy north faces of Regulation and West peaks. **END OF SIDE TRIP.**

By descending west a mere 0.3 mile on the PCT, we reach a meadowy junction with a trail that departs south to Murdock Lake.

S **SIDE TRIP TO MURDOCK LAKE:** This is a recommended destination for those desiring some isolation, which is usually lacking at Smedberg Lake. The trail southwest is an easy half-mile walk to a level subalpine meadow at 9530 feet that holds shallow Murdock Lake. Some adequate camps lie in lodgepoles above its west shore and offer interesting views of Volunteer Peak, Matterhorn Peak, and Sawtooth Ridge. **END OF SIDE TRIP.**

The next step down to Benson Lake is a typical descent down two dozen short switchbacks to a ford of Smedberg Lake's outlet creek. The PCT from that lake to here will be virtually impossible to follow in the snowbound early season. During those times, hikers will want to make a steep cross-country descent west down to this spot on an almost level canyon floor.

Now on the creek's north bank, you pass a small pond before commencing a steady, moderate, creekside descent to a second ford—a slight problem in early season. Back on the south bank, you make a winding, switchbacking descent over metamorphic rock down to the last, sometimes tricky ford of the creek. The next 0.3 mile of trail climbs up to a brushy saddle just east of a conspicuous knoll, then descends into a shady forest of giant firs before crossing wide Piute Creek. To keep your feet dry, look for one or more large, fallen logs.

S SIDE TRIP TO BENSON LAKE: Virtually no one makes this long descent from Benson Pass without visiting giant Benson Lake. Down at 7590 feet, about 2500 feet below Benson Pass, the Benson Lake spur trail winds southwest along the shady, often damp forest floor a short half mile to a section of beach near Piute Creek's inlet. Remember this spot, for, otherwise, this route back can be hard to locate. Many campsites at 7580-foot Benson Lake lie just within the forest's edge, and they testify to the popularity of this broad, sandy beach. If you've brought in a portable folding boat or raft, you'll probably have the whole lake to yourself. Swimming in this large, deep lake is brisk at best, but sunning on the beach can be superb in late summer, after the water line drops. However, strong, up-canyon afternoon winds can quell both activities. Anglers can anticipate a meal of rainbow or brook trout. **END OF SIDE TRIP.**

From the Benson Lake spur trail, prepare for a grueling 1500-foot climb north to Seavey Pass. Thankfully, the descent from it will be minor—about a 400-foot drop. At first brushy, the ascent northwest provides views of pointed Volunteer Peak and closer, two-crowned Peak 10060. You cross a creek, continue switchbacking northwest along the base of spectacular Peak 10368, and then climb north briefly, only to be confronted with a steep 400-foot climb east. On it, you are eventually funneled through a narrow, steep-walled, minor gap that rewards your climbing efforts with the sight of a relatively wind-free, sparkling pond. Just past its outlet, you'll find a trailside rock from which you can dive into its reasonably warm waters. The PCT parallels the pond's shore, curves east around a minuscule pond, and then climbs northeast through wet meadows before switchbacking up to a second gap. At its north base lies a shallow, rockbound pond, immediately beyond which is a third gap, Seavey Pass. A small meadow separates it from a fourth gap, beyond which you reach a more noteworthy—and the highest—gap. Now you bend northwest, travel past the head of a linear lake to a sixth gap, and switchback quickly down into a southwest-trending trough, spying a shallow pond 200 yards off in that direction. Turn right and immediately top your last gap, from which you descend northeast a quarter mile to a junction in Kerrick Canyon. Trip 4, which descends the Kerrick Canyon Trail south to this junction, follows the PCT east to Matterhorn Canyon before turning to climb back north.

A cursory glance at the map suggests that it is an easy 3-mile, down-canyon walk to the Bear Valley Trail junction. But closer scrutiny reveals a longer, winding, too often ascending route. A short northward jog of your Kerrick Canyon Trail segment ends at the Bear Valley Trail junction. Although Bear Valley Lake is less than a straight mile south of us, the lengthy, switchbacking climb up 1200 feet to the valley is not worth the effort for most backpackers. Immediately beyond the trail junction, we cross voluminous Kerrick Canyon's bouldery Rancheria Creek. Major joints cut across this area's canyons, and this creek has eroded along some of them, so that now it has an angular, joint-controlled course. After crossing this creek, which can be a rough ford through mid-July, locate a north-bank spur trail striking east up to popular campsites.

The PCT climbs west, affording dramatic cross-canyon views of Bear Valley peak and Piute Mountain. The trail eventually climbs north, gaining 700 feet in elevation up to a shallow gap, and, just east of it, you'll find a campsite near the west end of a small lakelet. Proceeding north from the gap, we have the usual knee-shocking descent on a multitude of short, steep switchbacks down almost 1000 feet to the mouth of Thompson Canyon. Here, we make a shady, short descent west to a large camp beside Stubblefield Canyon creek. The main trail meets the creek just below the camp, and, across from it, a spur trail up the opposite bank quickly meets the main trail. (If you hike this route in reverse, you probably won't see this large creekside camp. From it you can rock hop—in late season only—to the north end of our large camp.) Cross where you will, locate the main trail near the opposite bank, and start down-canyon. In a quarter mile, you leave the shady floor for slabs and slopes, and arrive at a false pass in an hour. A short, steep descent west leads to a corn-lily meadow, from which you wind a quarter mile northwest up to the true Macomb Ridge pass, about 1100 feet above Stubblefield Canyon creek.

With the deep canyons at last behind, the 550-foot descent northwest into Tilden Canyon seems like child's play. Just beyond the west bank of Tilden Canyon Creek, you meet the Tilden Canyon Trail, on which Trip 10, from Wilma Lake, heads south. From this junction, we hike up-canyon north on the Tilden Lake Trail just 110 yards to a second junction. From here, the PCT heads west to Wilma Lake and then goes up Jack Main Canyon.

[A] **ALTERNATE ROUTE PAST TILDEN LAKE:** A slightly longer alternate route continues north, gently up to huge, linear Tilden Lake, at about 8900 feet. This lake has many near-shore campsites and a healthy population of rainbow trout. From the lake's outlet, this route then descends west to Falls Creek and the adjacent PCT. **END OF ALTERNATE ROUTE.**

Our main route adheres to the PCT, which goes left at this junction and winds northwest past several ponds, nestled on a broad gap, before descending west and dropping about 500 feet to reach relatively large, shallow 7946-foot Wilma Lake. Like so many of Yosemite's High Sierra lakes, it contains rainbow trout. Good campsites are found just beyond it, along broad, tantalizing Falls Creek. A few minutes' walk northwest up-canyon takes you to a shallow, broad ford of the creek, and then past spacious campsites to a junction with the Jack Main Canyon Trail, which Trip 10 has ascended north.

From our junction, which is near a seasonal ranger's cabin, the PCT first winds northward up-canyon, touching the east bank of Falls Creek only several times before reaching a junction with a trail east to Tilden Lake. Chittenden Peak and its north satellite serve as impressive reference points as you progress northward, passing two substantial meadows before arriving at the south end of even larger Grace Meadow. Here, the upper canyon opens into plain view. The guiding landmarks are, from east to west, Forsyth Peak, Dorothy Lake Pass, and Bond Pass. Under lodgepole cover along the meadow's edge, you can set up camp.

Leaving Grace Meadow, you soon pass through a small meadow before the ever-increasing gradient becomes noticeable. People have camped at small sites along this stretch. Our upward climb meets the first of two trails that quickly unite to climb to nearby Bond Pass, on the park's boundary, the route of the Tahoe-Yosemite Trail. Just beyond these junctions, volcanic sediments and exposures are evident in ever-increasing amounts—a taste of what's to come—before you reach large, exposed Dorothy Lake. Clumps of lodgepoles here provide minimal campsite protection from the winds that often rush up-canyon. Better camping lies ahead. A short climb above the lake's east end takes you up to Dorothy Lake Pass, at about 9500 feet, with the final good view of the lasting snowfields that grace the north slopes of Forsyth Peak.

Leaving Yosemite National Park, we enter Toiyabe National Forest, pass rocky Stella Lake, approach tempting Bonnie Lake, and then switchback east down to campsites along the west shore of 9230-foot Lake Harriet, about 1 mile beyond the pass. Larger, more-isolated camps are on the east shore. The PCT crosses Cascade Creek just below the lake, and then it makes short switchbacks down confining terrain, reaching a large campsite in about a half mile. Just 50 yards beyond it, we cross the creek on a footbridge. Ahead, the way is still winding, but it is nearly level, and, after 0.75 mile, just past a pair of ponds, we reach a junction with a connecting trail that descends 1.5 miles northeast to the West Walker River Trail. Onward, we start north, then bend west and pass three ponds before winding down to a creek. Just past it is the Cinko Lake Trail.

A **ALTERNATE ROUTE PAST CINKO LAKE:** West, the original, more desirable PCT route contorts 1 mile over to Cinko Lake, with adequate campsites. The former PCT route then descends 0.5 mile to the West Fork West Walker River Trail and follows the river, fording it midway along its route 1.5 miles down to a junction with the newer route. **END OF ALTERNATE ROUTE.**

On the official, lackluster segment, we first parallel the creek we've just crossed, and soon pass several gray outcrops of marble, which differ significantly in color and texture from the other metamorphic rocks we've been passing. Beyond them, you curve left into a small bowl, and then make a short, steep climb through a granitic notch before dropping west to a seasonal creeklet. After winding briefly northwest from it, the PCT turns northward, taking almost a half mile to descend to the West Fork West Walker River Trail. On it, you descend just a quarter mile downriver to a junction by a pond, choked with sedge and lying just northwest of Upper Long Lake. Linear, 8596-foot Upper Long Lake, which is at the same elevation as Lower Long Lake just north of it, has a few large campsites along it. From the junction, we take a steel bridge across a small gorge that confines the river, and find a large, lodgepole-shaded campsite immediately past it—the best one this side of Sonora Pass.

A few mountain hemlocks are visible as you wind westward a quarter mile in and out of small gullies, and then lodgepoles take over for another quarter mile to the west edge of the southernmost Walker Meadow. Between meadow and granite, the PCT passes through a lodgepole corridor to a crossing of a wide but ephemeral creek, whose water flows mostly underground through the porous volcanic sediments. About a half mile north from this ephemeral creek is another one that splashes, in a two-stage drop, into a volcanic alcove—an ideal lunch stop. Your traverse north continues for another half mile, and you can leave the trail at any point to descend to the flat-floored forest just below and make camp.

By the time the trail turns northwest up Kennedy Canyon, granitic bedrock has reappeared, but a half mile up-canyon, not far beyond a potential campsite, it disappears for good. Continuing up this brown-walled, volcanic canyon, you have an easy uphill hike for a mile, cross the canyon's creek, and then labor up an increasingly steeper trail segment to a 9700-foot junction with a jeep road not far north of a broad Sierran crest saddle. We have now left behind all reasonable campsites; none lies between here and Sonora Pass, almost 10 miles away. Ahead, water in frozen form is usually too plentiful, but if snowfall has been scarce, late-season hikers should fill up before climbing to this jeep road, for they may have to hike almost to Sonora Pass to encounter a permanent creek.

Switchbacking northward up the usually closed jeep road, you have ever-improving views of Kennedy Canyon and the adjacent volcanic landscape. Whitebark pines, which have been with us since upper Kennedy Canyon, are now wind cropped down to stunted forms. Trees disappear altogether by the time you reach a high crest that presents views westward. Leaving the crest and its expansive views over the northwest Yosemite boundary area, our jeep road climbs quickly up to a tight switchback, and here we leave the jeep road.

A **ALTERNATE ROUTE:** Before mid-July, short parts of the remaining stretch to Sonora Pass can be dangerous. If you've been encountering lots of snow, you might consider taking this safety exit route. Continue 0.2 mile up the jeep road to a gate on a saddle, and then take the main jeep road 1.5 miles down to the outlet creek of Leavitt Lake. Here you can find campsites among small stands of whitebark pines, although they, too, may be under snow. You may find better-protected sites along your road's 2.9 mile descent to Hwy. 108. The alternate route turns left, climbing 2.4 miles northwest to a junction with Road 062, by which you could camp, and then continues 1.3 miles west up to Sonora Pass. **END OF ALTERNATE ROUTE.**

Back on trail tread, the PCT begins with a stark, yet stunning, often windy traverse along a 2-mile-high volcanic ridge. Heading northwest, you pass several crest saddles before your trail turns north and finally crosses the Sierra Crest. Should you want to "bag" Leavitt Peak, 0.75 mile to the northwest, you can either start up the crest or hike a quarter mile farther along the trail and, in a bowl, start west up a talus slope. About a half mile beyond the bowl, you cross a ridge, which, at 10,880 feet, is the highest point of your trip. Latopie Lake lies well below you and is difficult to reach because of steep slopes. In early season, this short stretch of trail across steep slopes is snowbound and dangerous.

Ahead, beyond a nearby gully, you traverse along the base of an overly steep wall that is avalanche prone in early season. You head through a notch in this wall and bid farewell to the last of your excellent views of the Yosemite hinterlands. The route drops a quarter mile north, then angles northwest, passing two very youthful glacial moraines before climbing to another crest crossing 0.8 mile past the notch. Your route north hovers around treeline, and, with expansive views to the west, you pass dense, isolated clumps of prostrate whitebark pines before you once again cross the crest 1.2 miles past the former crossing.

Now you tackle a 1200-plus-foot drop to Sonora Pass. In early summer, the first quarter mile of this descent—across steep slopes—is snowbound and potentially lethal if you fall. Near the end of your descent, you cross some closely spaced gullies, one of which usually contains water— the first since Kennedy Canyon. Now in open lodgepole forest, you meander slightly up to the Sierra Crest, and then wind down it to cross Sonora Pass on Hwy. 108.

TRIP 37

Tuolumne Meadows to Young Lakes

Ⓜ ♫ BP

DISTANCE: 16.4 miles semiloop

ELEVATIONS: 8580´/10,220´
+3030´/-3030´/±6060´

SEASON: Mid-July to early October

USE: Heavy

MAPS: *Tioga Pass, Falls Ridge*

TRAIL LOG:

0.8	Soda Springs
2.0	Young Lakes Trail
5.7	Dog Lake Trail
7.6	Lower Young Lake
8.0	Middle Young Lake
8.6	Upper Young Lake
11.5	Dog Lake Trail
14.3	Delaney Creek
15.1	Lateral to Dog Lake
16.4	Lembert Dome parking area

INTRODUCTION: The Young Lakes are the only reasonably accessible lakes north of Tuolumne Meadows at which camping is allowed. This isolated cluster of lakes, backdropped by the scenic Ragged Peak crest, is quite popular, though not over-crowded like the Cathedral Lakes and the lakes near Vogelsang High Sierra Camp. Whereas most visitors will backpack to the Young Lakes, those in good shape can day-hike to and from them. This is a relatively long dayhike, but the lakes are only about 1500 feet above the trailhead, and, for most of the ascent, the trail gradient is relatively easy. The advantages of dayhiking are that you don't need a wilderness permit (and the lakes on busy weekends can reach their backpacking quotas), and that you

don't have to carry a heavy pack. If you visit only the lowest lake, you can shave 2 miles off the total distance.

DIRECTIONS TO THE TRAILHEAD: Drive along the Tioga Road to a dirt road starting west from the base of Lembert Dome. This spot is located at the east end of Tuolumne Meadows and immediately north of the Tuolumne River. Alternatively, from the trailhead parking area at this spot, you can drive 0.3 mile west on the dirt road to a gate, from which the main road turns north, bound for the nearby stables, which will save you 0.3 mile each way. The mileage is measured from the trailhead parking area. Trail begins in map section F3.

DESCRIPTION: From the Lembert Dome parking area west of the Tioga Road, we first walk west 0.3 mile along a dirt road to its bend, and then continue west on a gated service road that contours the lodgepole-dotted flank of Tuolumne Meadows. On it, we are treated to fine views south across them toward Unicorn Peak, Cathedral Peak, and some of the knobby Echo Peaks. After about a quarter mile, we meet a trail heading northeast to the horse stables, and, about 200 yards past this junction, we face a split. The left branch heads over to a nearby bridge across the Tuolumne River, but our road veers right, slightly uphill, and quickly encounters a trail that leads to the still-bubbling natural Soda Springs. You can take this trail west across this vicinity to our road, or take the road, which arcs counterclockwise across the former site of the old Soda Springs Campground.

Westward, our trail undulates through a forest of sparse, small lodgepole pines, and, in just under 1 mile, descends to Delaney Creek, reached about 100 yards after a stock trail from the stables back in the meadows comes in on the right. In early season, look for a log to cross it; later on, boulder hopping will do. After 0.3 mile, you reach the Young Lakes Trail, on which we branch right, north.

Turning right, you ascend slightly and cross a broad expanse of boulder-strewn, grass-pocketed glaciated sheet granite. An open spot affords a look south across broad Tuolumne Meadows to the line of peaks from Fairview Dome to the steeple-like spires of the Cathedral Range. After ascending the open, glacier-polished granite, following a line of boulders that mark the trailless route, the trail tread resumes and climbs northward up a tree-clothed slope—the first 2 miles moderately, the next mile gently—to a ridge. On the other side of the ridge, a new panoply of peaks appears in the north—majestic Tower Peak, Doghead and Quarry peaks, the Finger Peaks, Matterhorn Peak, Sheep Peak, Mt. Conness, and the Shepherd Crest. From this high viewpoint, a moderate descent leads 0.3 mile to a ford of a usually flowing tributary of Conness Creek. Just 60 yards up from this tributary is a junction with the southeast-climbing Dog Lake Trail, our return route.

Now we start a rollercoaster traverse northeast through a forest of mountain hemlocks and lodgepole and western white pines. On a level stretch of trail, we cross a diminutive branch of Conness Creek, and then switchback a quarter mile up to a plateau, from which the view is fine of the steep northwest face of Ragged Peak. After rounding the edge of a meadow, we descend to Lower Young Lake, whose north shore easily has the most campsites of the three lakes, and some hikers go no farther. At about 9900 feet, it lies in the subalpine realm, but it still has sufficient trees for shade and to diminish the sometimes strong late afternoon winds. From the lake's northeast corner, you can hop its outlet creek—possibly a wet ford in early season, if logs aren't available—and take a trail east that parallels the creek about a quarter mile east moderately up to relatively small Middle Young Lake. As at the lower lake, you can camp on a rocky ridge above its north shore. If you camp at either

Lower Young Lake and Ragged Peak

lake, bring a tent, since at both lakes there can be hordes of mosquitoes in the morning and evening until late July or early August. Furthermore, afternoon-to-evening thunderstorms can occur near the Sierran crest, and you are only a couple of miles from it.

You may see a use trail following a creek to the upper lake, but avoid it. A better, if sometimes cryptic, use trail stays farther to the north, meandering eastward up to bench lands north of the upper lake. From these lands, serious backpackers or mountaineers can start cross-country to Roosevelt Lake or Mt. Conness. Most likely, however, you'll want to make an easy, nearly level, open, scenic traverse southeast to Upper Young Lake. At about 10,220 feet, it lies in the lower alpine realm, and small clusters of whitebark pines offer little protection from the elements. You could camp above its north shore, but the small sites are marginal, and most of the alpine turf is fragile.

After exploring the Young Lakes area, retrace your steps to the Dog Lake Trail junction. Turn left and make a steep ascent up a boulder-dotted slope under a forest cover of lodgepoles and hemlocks. As the trail ascends, the trees diminish in density and change in species, to a predominance of whitebark pine, the highest dwelling of Yosemite's trees. From the southwest shoulder of Ragged Peak the trail quickly enters and then descends through a very large, gently sloping meadow. This broad, well-watered expanse is a wildflower garden in season, laced with meandering brooks. Species of wildflowers in the foreground set off the marvelous views of the entire Cathedral Range, strung along the southern horizon.

Near the lower edge of the meadow, you cross the headwaters of Dingley Creek and then descend, steeply at times, some 300 feet past exfoliating Peak 10410, through a moderately dense forest of lodgepoles and a few hemlocks, to a seasonal creek. Another seasonal creek is crossed in 0.3 mile, and then we make a short but noticeable climb up to the crest of a large, bouldery ridge. Down its gravelly slopes, we descend to a very large, level meadow, above which the reddish peaks of Mt. Dana and Mt. Gibbs loom in the east. Here, Delaney Creek meanders lazily through the sedges and grasses, and Belding ground squirrels pipe away. Delaney Creek is a wet, deep crossing in early season, but shallower fords may be found up- or downstream from the trail. Particularly downstream, you may find a narrow spot you can jump across.

After climbing briefly over the crest of a second bouldery ridge, your route drops once more toward Tuolumne Meadows. Lembert Dome, the "first ascent" of so many visitors to Tuolumne Meadows, can be glimpsed through the trees along this stretch of trail. After 0.4 mile of easy descent east, your trail levels off in a small, linear meadow and turns south to parallel it. Should you wish to visit Dog Lake, which definitely is worthwhile, the quickest way to it is to leave the trail at this bend and continue east to reach it in less than 200 yards. By adhering to the trail, you'll parallel the linear meadow for about 250 yards south to a junction with the ascending, quarter-mile lateral to Dog Lake (Trip 38). Be aware that no camping is allowed in this vicinity since the lake is within 1 mile of the Tioga Road.

About 230 yards below the junction, your route passes another junction, this time with a trail that leads east along the north side of Dog Dome, the lower adjunct of Lembert Dome. We keep southwest, parallel a creek from Dog Lake, and begin a 450-foot switchbacking descent that is terribly dusty due to the braking efforts of descending hikers on this overly steep section. At the bottom of the deep dust, the trail splits into two paths. The right one leads west to the stables, and the left one heads south to the west side of the Lembert Dome parking area. Just before it is a second lateral to this stables, first branching west and quickly turning northwest.

TRIP 38

Lembert Dome and Dog Lake

Ⓜ ↗ DH

DISTANCE: 3 miles out and back

ELEVATIONS: 8650'/9450'
                (Lembert Dome)
                +1090'/-1090'/±2180'

SEASON: Early July to mid-October

USE: Heavy

MAP: *Tioga Pass*

TRAIL LOG:

    1.1   Lembert Dome
    1.5   Dog Lake

INTRODUCTION: This is perhaps the finest dayhike you can take in the Tuolumne Meadows area. If you have only a few hours to spare, hike simply to the top of Lembert Dome. However, don't overexert yourself, for, at this area's elevation, you can easily get altitude sickness. If you hike only to the top of the dome, the round-trip distance is 2.2 miles; if you go to the lake, the round-trip distance is 3 miles.

DIRECTIONS TO THE TRAILHEAD: Large parking lot for hikers and backpackers 0.3 mile west of the Tuolumne Meadows Lodge parking lot. To reach this lot from Tuolumne Meadows Campground, drive 0.6 mile northeast on the Tioga Road, turn right on the Tuolumne Lodge spur road, and follow it 0.4 mile to the lot, on your left. Trail begins in map section F3.

DESCRIPTION: From the north end of the parking lot, you make a brief, moderate climb up an obvious trail to a crossing of the Tioga Road. Onward, you switchback at a generally moderate grade up to a junction, about 0.6 mile into your route and just 80 yards shy of a broad, lodgepole-

forested saddle. To climb Lembert Dome, branch left and ascend westward on a trail that at first stays just below the crest. In about 0.3 mile, it reaches a minor gap, from which you can make a brief, safe ascent north to the adjacent summit of Dog Dome, with its precipitous north face.

To reach the summit of Lembert Dome from the minor gap, you head about 0.2 mile up the bedrock slopes to its summit. While one can tackle it head on up a steep slope, most hikers first veer to the left and then arc right up to it. Both routes are somewhat intimidating, so if you feel unsure, don't do it! Your view from 150-foot-higher Lembert Dome is nearly identical to the one from Dog Dome. After exploring the Lembert Dome summit, first return to the trail at the minor gap. This descends first briefly west and then too steeply southwest—not a desirable route for those descending to the Tioga Road. Rather, retrace your steps.

To reach Dog Lake from the minor gap, retrace your steps to a junction, and then turn sharply left. In 80 yards, you'll reach the aforementioned broad, lodgepole-forested saddle. Beyond it, you drop briefly west-northwest, and then traverse in the same direction, having a view of the north cliffs of Dog Dome and skirting past a pond that seasonally has wild onions growing in wet ground near its shore. Just 100 yards beyond it, you cross the outlet creek of an unseen, sedge-filled pond. In 150 more yards, reach a trail junction. An alternate, less desirable, longer return route to your trailhead would be to descend this overly steep trail southwest to a parking lot at the foot of Lembert Dome, and then cross the Tioga Road and follow a trail—mostly an abandoned road—back to your starting point.

To reach Dog Lake, first head about 230 yards northwest up this trail to a junction from which a trail continues about 5 miles to the first of three Young Lakes (Trip 37). Veer right and make an easy ascent a quarter mile to the outlet of Dog Lake, at its western end. The official trail ends here,

THE SHAPE OF A DOME

Like all domes in the Tuolumne Meadows area, Dog Dome is domelike in appearance only from a certain angle, and it is generally un-domelike from most other angles. This is because it is gentle-sloped on its up-canyon side and steep-sloped on the opposite side. The asymmetrical shapes of such "domes" have nothing to do with glacial erosion, for they are locally common in parts of the unglaciated southern Sierra as well as in granitic lands of the tropics.

On Dog Dome, you'll see several large boulders left behind by a former glacier. Like the bedrock of Dog Dome, they are granitic, but unlike it, they lack the large, blocky feldspar crystals, and they came from an eastern source. Also interesting on Dog Dome is its precarious north slopes. Whereas glaciers supposedly pluck away at a dome's down-canyon slopes, transforming them into steep cliffs, such as Lembert Dome's west slopes, Dog Dome's west slopes are minor compared to its north slopes. The logical reason for this is that the cliffs of each dome developed along nearly vertical sets of joints long before any glaciation occurred. Indeed, the unglaciated Dome Land Wilderness of the southern Sierra Nevada has far more domes than the park does, and many, if not most, are asymmetrical.

Glaciers also left other evidence of their presence. In some places, the bedrock has been polished by the fine layer of transported basal sediment. These striations mark the direction the glacier traveled—generally westward. Another feature you might note is the presence of chatter marks. These may be due to erratic gouges made by large boulders, or they may be due solely to the enormous force of thick, moving glaciers acting against irregularities in the bedrock. Whereas a glacier smooths and polishes the stoss, or up-canyon, side of a dome, it may quarry the lee, or down-canyon, side.

In the Sierra Nevada, both quarrying and abrasion have been minimal. Lembert Dome is not really a dome; rather, it is, like most of Yosemite's domes, a giant roche moutonnée. Other prominent examples of roches moutonnées are Fairview Dome and Pywiack Dome, both seen along the Tioga Road. In Yosemite Valley, Liberty Cap and Mt. Broderick are examples. However, Sentinel Dome and Mt. Starr King, both unglaciated, are true domes.

Lembert Dome, from Dog Dome

but you could go either right, along the lake's south shore, or left, along its north shore. Encircling the lake is difficult, due to boggy ground by its eastern end. Be aware that no camping is allowed in this vicinity since the lake is within 1 mile of the Tioga Road.

From the lake's west shore just north of the outlet creek, you may obtain reflected views of Mt. Dana, Mt. Gibbs, and Mt. Lewis. A long peninsula extends east into the lake from your shoreline, and on it you can walk—usually in knee-deep water— well out into the middle of this large but shallow lake. Because it is shallow, it is one of the high country's warmest lakes, suit-able for swimming and for just plain relaxing. Camping, however, is prohibited. Like many High Sierra lakes, this one is visited in the summer by spotted sandpipers, which usually nest close to the lake's shore. Among the shore boulders, you may find metamorphic ones—rocks that could have gotten here via glacier transport from their source area, the Gaylor Peak/Tioga Hill area. Leaving Dog Lake, retrace your steps back to your trailhead.

TRIP **39**

Tioga Pass to Gaylor Lakes, Great Sierra Mine, and Granite Lakes

E   ↗   DH

DISTANCE:	4 miles out and back
ELEVATIONS:	9940′/10,780′ +1280′/-1280′/±2560′
SEASON:	Mid-July to mid-October
USE:	Moderate
MAP:	*Tioga Pass*

TRAIL LOG:

0.8	Middle Gaylor Lake
1.4	Upper Gaylor Lake
2.0	Great Sierra Mine

INTRODUCTION: Five subalpine lakes await those who take this hike, although most visitors probably visit only Middle and Upper Gaylor Lake and perhaps the mining cabins above them. To reach the Granite Lakes you take a cross-country hike. You can also reach the Gaylor Lakes Basin from Tuolumne Meadows Lodge by first taking a trail 2 miles east from it up the Dana Fork to the Tioga Road, crossing it, and going 2.5 miles up to Lower Gaylor Lake (see start of Trip 47). However, the route description that follows is about 8 miles shorter, round trip. Camping is *not* allowed in the Gaylor Lakes area, which includes the Granite Lakes.

DIRECTIONS TO THE TRAILHEAD: Beside the Tioga Pass Entrance Station. Trail begins in map section F3.

DESCRIPTION: From the restrooms by the Tioga Pass Entrance Station, your rocky trail ascends steeply through a forest of lodgepole, and in season you pass a profusion of wildflowers, including single-stemmed senecio, Sierra penstemon, Gray's lovage, daisy, pussytoes, baby elephant heads, lupine, monkey flower, and Sierra wallflower. You may see a lone whitebark pine, a conifer that in maturity can range from a 50-foot-high tree down to a knee-high bush. The bark of young lodgepole and whitebark pines looks similar; however, the former tree has two needles per bunch while the latter has five.

Your steep trail begins to level off near the top of the ridge, and on this stretch the flower "collector" may add spreading phlox, red mountain heather, buckwheat, and coyote mint to the day's journal. Atop the ridge, the well-earned view includes, clockwise from north, Gaylor Peak, Tioga Peak, Mt. Dana, Mt. Gibbs, the canyon of the Dana Fork, Kuna Peak, Mammoth Peak, Lyell Canyon, and the peaks of the Cathedral Range. From the vantage point you can see where red metamorphic rocks to the northeast are in contact with gray granites to the southwest. This division extends north to our locale.

As you move west on the ridgetop, the rocks underfoot become quite purplish, a hue shared by the flowers of penstemon and lupine that obtain their mineral requirements from these rocks. Now the trail descends steeply past clumps of whitebark pine to Middle Gaylor Lake, and skirts the lake's north shore. Across the lake, the peaks of the Cathedral Range seem to be sinking into the lake, for their summits barely poke above the water. Taking the trail up the inlet stream, we begin a short, gradual ascent to Upper Gaylor Lake. Surveying the Gaylor Lakes basin, we can see that campsites are so few and wood so scarce that only a few summers of camping, were it allowed, would finish off the environment here.

Upper Gaylor Lake, Gaylor Peak, and Middle Gaylor Lake, from near Great Sierra Mine

From the upper lake we can see a rock cabin, which bespeaks the activities of a mining company that sought to tap the silver veins that run somewhere under Tioga Hill, directly north of the lake. Should you go to the cabin, you can admire the skill of the dryrock mason who built this long-lasting house near the Sierra crest. Farther up the hill are other works—including one dangerous hole—left by the miners, in various states of return to nature. There are several other cabins in this area, and they are all that are left of the envisioned "city" of Dana, the site of the (not so) Great Sierra Mine.

Atop Tioga Hill, which is just beyond the cabins, you have all the earlier views plus a view down into Lee Vining Canyon.

From the saddle just between Tioga Hill and Gaylor Peak and across the crest lands to the north and south of Tioga Hill, there are myriad glacial striations that indicate the direction that a glacier originating from the Granite Lakes cirque flowed. Near Gaylor Peak the glacier flowed 80°, toward Tioga Lake, and progressively north of Tioga Hill it flowed 70°, not north or south. (Progressively south in the drainage, the glacial lobe flowed southeast.) This indicates that ice from this cirque flowed eastward, meeting ice from Mt. Dana that flowed westward. In the vicinity of Tioga Pass the ice may have split, flowing partly north and partly south, or perhaps it joined a branch of the Tuolumne River glacier that flowed north across the pass.

A scant mile northeast of and below Tioga Hill is another "city," Bennettville, sprang up near the mouth of a tunnel being dug to exploit the silver lodes. Its founder projected a population of 50,000! The white and lavender columbines and other living things around the summit may owe their lives to the absence of these hordes.

[S] **SIDE TRIP TO GRANITE LAKES:** From this general area, make your way west cross-country across a ridge and down to the easily found Granite Lakes, liquid gems backed by steep granite heights. (If you haven't hiked up to the cabins or Tioga Hill, then the best way to reach lower Granite Lake is from Upper Gaylor Lake, and you head directly west over a low ridge and down to it, a total distance of about 0.4 mile.) Like the upper lake with its near-shore island, lower Granite Lake is truly alpine and therefore too cold for comfortable swimming even during midsummer, as are the Gaylor Lakes. From lower Granite Lake you can follow its outlet stream as it curves from south to southwest about 1 mile down to Lower Gaylor Lake. In this meadowy upland you are likely to see many marmots and Belding ground squirrels. At this lake you may also see a few California gulls on the spit. Spotted sandpipers, identified by their bobbing walk, are also common summer visitors to High Sierra lakes. After a pleasant rest, make an easy, generally open, cross-country climb northeast 1 mile back to Middle Gaylor Lake, then follow the trail back to Tioga Pass. **END OF SIDE TRIP.**

CHAPTER 13

Trips of the Tuolumne Meadows Area South and East of the Tioga Road

Introduction to this Area

Except for Little Yosemite Valley, an outlier of Yosemite Valley, no other area in the park receives such intensive backpacker use. Consequently, it is highly recommended that you get a wilderness permit long before you start your overnight hike. The extreme popularity of this area is due, in part, to its supreme scenery, which is dominated by the Cathedral Range and the Sierra Crest. Its popularity is also due to its accessibility, for, in a few hours' hiking time, you can easily reach crest passes and subalpine lakes. How can one forget the alpenglow on the metamorphic Sierra Crest? The form of twin-towered Cathedral Peak? The expansive panorama from Mt. Dana? The beauty of an alpine wildflower garden? The enormous granite wall below Clouds Rest? These and many other sights continue to lure backpackers and dayhikers to this area year after year.

Half Dome's high point and Tenaya Canyon

Supplies and Services

Absolutely everything you'll need for a Yosemite outdoor experience can be purchased in the western foothills town of Sonora. This includes full backpacking and mountaineering gear, available at the Sierra Nevada Adventure Company. This town also has several large grocery stores, numerous dining places, and two hospitals.

Groveland, about 24 miles west of the park's Big Oak Flat Entrance Station, is the last town you'll pass on Hwy. 120; however, several resorts, gas stations, and campgrounds are found closer to the park. Gas, meals, and lodging are found at Evergreen Lodge, on Evergreen Road just 0.6 mile before it ends at the Hetch Hetchy Road in Camp Mather (for San Francisco residents).

Once inside the park, you can find virtually anything you'll need—other than fuel—down in Yosemite Valley, but this is crowded and out of your way. Should you need last-minute food or fuel, you can get them at Crane Flat. Fewer supplies are at White Wolf Lodge, the center for trips 18 to 21, though it offers breakfast and dinner.

Wilderness Permits

If you want to reserve a permit, rather than get one in person, see the "Wilderness Permits" section in Chapter 6. In person, if you are driving east up Hwy. 120, get a permit at the Big Oak Flat Information Station, which is immediately past the park's entrance station. Note that from about early April through late October, you can get a permit at the Hetch Hetchy Entrance Station (by the Mather Ranger Station). You cannot get a permit in the White Wolf area. If you are driving up Hwy. 140 or Hwy. 41, get your permit at the Visitor Center in Yosemite Valley, and if you are driving west down Hwy. 120, stop in Tuolumne Meadows.

If you are hiking Trip 49 or Trip 51 in reverse, you need to contact the Wilderness Permit Office in Bishop. For information, call 760-873-2485; to obtain a permit, call 760-873-2483. In person, you can obtain a permit at the Mammoth Ranger Station and Visitor Center, situated just before the bustling town/city of Mammoth Lakes.

Campgrounds

Ideally, you'll want to camp in Tuolumne Meadows Campground, situated at the east end of Tuolumne Meadows. About half of the number of its sites are reserved, while the remainder are on a first-come, first-served basis. Sometimes, it is full, it opens late, or it closes early, and then you may have to use Tioga Road campgrounds lying to the west of Tuolumne Meadows. Starting west up that road from Crane Flat, you have the following options: After driving east 3.75 miles up the Tioga Road from Crane Flat, branch right immediately before Gin Flat and follow the old Big Oak Flat Road for 3 winding miles to Tamarack Flat Campground. The next campground east is White Wolf Campground, on a short road branching east 14.5 miles up the Tioga Road from Crane Flat. Just 0.3 mile past the White Wolf Road junction is a junction with the old Tioga Road, on your right. Follow it 4.75 miles to the Yosemite Creek Campground. Finally, there is Porcupine Flat Campground, on the north side of the Tioga Road, 9.2 miles past the White Wolf Road junction. All of these campgrounds can be full, and, if you hope to stay at any of them, look for a site in midmorning, when most campers leave.

Alternatively, you can camp east of Tuolumne Meadows, north of and below Tioga Pass. Just beyond the pass on descending Hwy. 120, you'll see Tioga Lake Campground, and not much below it, at a junction with the Saddlebag Lake Road, are Sawmill Walk-in and Junction campgrounds, barely along this road. Just north below the junction is Ellery Lake Campground. All these campgrounds are small and often are full, so you may have to stay at one of several more campgrounds along the lower part of Hwy. 120 (beyond the end of the steep descent).

TRIP 40

Tenaya Lake to Upper Tenaya Canyon Cascade

E ⟋ DH, BP

DISTANCE: 4 miles out and back

ELEVATIONS: 7700´/8170´
+150´/-620´/±1540´

SEASON: Mid-July to mid-October

USE: Light

MAP: *Tenaya Lake*

TRAIL LOG:

2.0   Bottom of the cascade

INTRODUCTION: Back in 1977, Bob Fry led a Yosemite Association dayhike along this route. Ostensibly, we were to look at sub-alpine wildflowers, but in reality our group of amateur botanists ended up sightseeing and frolicking in the water. Probably some had gone before us, certainly many had gone after, given that the cross-country route had become a conspicuous trail. Therefore, I have included it in this book. Although it has an easy rating, this cross-country route can be potentially dangerous, especially in times of high water. Even when the route is dry, if you are not adept at walking on slick, if dry, water-polished slopes, you should not attempt this route.

DIRECTIONS TO THE TRAILHEAD: On the Tioga Road at the Tenaya Lake Trailhead parking area, at a highway bend near the lake's southwest shore, located 30.5 miles northeast of Crane Flat and 8.5 miles southwest of the Tuolumne Meadows Campground. Trail begins in map section E4.

DESCRIPTION: From the trailhead parking area, take a trail that heads east, and you soon cross the usually flowing outlet of Tenaya Lake. If you have to ford it, especially if it's up to your knees, the cascade on the creek near the end of our cross-country route will be impressive. If you can walk across stepping stones, it may be mundane. If the creek is barely flowing, the cascade will be disappointing, but the three potholes below it and the pool at the bottom of descent can be great for afternoon swimming and sunbathing.

Just beyond this crossing, you reach a trail junction. The left trail goes northeast to start a loop around the lake, and then it continues another 7 miles to the Cathedral Lakes Trail in Tuolumne Meadows. Consult the introduction to Chapter 12 (page 180) for a brief description of a myth about the origin of the lake's protruding tree stumps that you'll see along this trail. You veer right on a trail that heads south for a quarter mile along Tenaya Creek. From where it veers left away from the creek, you'll see a use path continuing down the creek, which is the start of our 1.5-mile cross-country route down to the upper part of Tenaya Canyon.

Except in times of very high water, you can follow this creekside trail for about a half mile to where it becomes vague and essentially dies out. If high water forces you up, return to the creek as soon as is practical. The trail parallels the creek first about 0.2 mile southwest, then about 0.3 mile south, passing occasional, tempting pools before coming alongside a conspicuous knoll rising from the west side of the creek. In this vicinity, the creek angles briefly southeast and we follow it about 100-plus yards to where it again turns south. At this bend, a tributary creek from the Sunrise Lakes joins Tenaya Creek.

If you continue ahead for 0.3 mile, you will traverse along the base of a low knoll on the east side of the creek and reach the top of the Tenaya Creek cascade, perhaps still with a warning sign about the danger ahead. Whereas mountaineers can negotiate the descent along the cascade, with slopes up to 35- or 40-degrees steep, this can be risky, especially since the slopes are polished and slippery. Therefore, take a safer route. Go a mere 200 or so yards south downstream from the creek junction to the north end of a ridge ascending to the top of the low, east-side knoll, then head a similar distance southeast to a conspicuous saddle just east of the knoll. From it, you descend about a quarter mile south across slabs that average in angle about 20 to 30 degrees down beside the cascade. A steepness of 20 to 30 degrees is not bad, and you can switchback down the slabs to lessen the grade. However, if you are not careful, you can find yourself on steeper slopes. Additionally, the glacier-polished slabs can be slippery even when dry, so take care. The slabs are open, and so we have an inspiring view down Tenaya Canyon.

The bottom of the cascade ends in a large pothole, which is safe for entry when the water is slowly flowing. Tenaya Creek then descends slabs, and, along it as well as just above the base of the slabs, you'll find two more large potholes. At the base, about 1.5 miles from the start of the cross-country route, is a rather large pool suitable for swimming, and, as at all three potholes, there are slabs for sunbathing.

You could continue 1.5 miles ahead through upper Tenaya Canyon to the brink of even more impressive Pywiack Cascade, but you'll have some bushwhacking to do, the worst of it at the beginning, where a rockfall has strewn debris across the uppermost part of the canyon's floor. Only qualified mountaineers with ropes for rappelling should attempt to follow the creek down to the floor of Yosemite Valley, and then only in times of very low water, such as in September. The route truly is life threatening (although extremely rewarding), and some have died attempting to either descend or ascend Tenaya Canyon proper. See "Side Trip up Lower Tenaya Canyon" at the end of Trip 58 (page 281) for the end of this inspiring route.

Upper Tenaya Canyon Cascade below Tenaya Lake

TRIP 41

Tenaya Lake to Sunrise High Sierra Camp via Sunrise Lakes

(M) ↗ DH, BP

DISTANCE: 11.6 miles out and back

ELEVATIONS: 8140′/9780′
+1890′/-710′/±5200′

SEASON: Mid-July to mid-October

USE: Heavy

MAP: *Tenaya Lake*

TRAIL LOG:

2.9   Forested saddle
3.4   Lower Sunrise Lake
4.1   Upper Sunrise Lake
5.8   Sunrise High Sierra Camp

INTRODUCTION: Considerable climbing at fairly high elevations normally makes this hike a moderate one, but its distance is so short that it's an easy backpack trip. Some hikers go only as far as Upper Sunrise Lake, an 8-mile round trip that is a good, moderate dayhike. However, if you camp near Sunrise High Sierra Camp, you are rewarded with a beautiful sunrise—the reason the camp is situated where it is.

DIRECTIONS TO THE TRAILHEAD: On the Tioga Road at the Tenaya Lake Trailhead parking area, at a highway bend near the lake's southwest shore, located 30.5 miles northeast of Crane Flat and 8.5 miles southwest of the Tuolumne Meadows Campground. Trail begins in map section E4.

DESCRIPTION: From the trailhead parking area, take a trail that heads east, and you soon cross the usually flowing outlet of Tenaya Lake. Just beyond this crossing, you reach a trail junction. The left trail goes northeast to start a loop around the lake, and then it continues another 7 miles to the Cathedral Lakes Trail in Tuolumne Meadows. Consult the introduction to Chapter 12 (page 180) for a brief description of a myth about the origin of the lake's protruding tree stumps that you'll see along this trail.

You veer right on a trail that heads south for a quarter mile along Tenaya Creek and then leaves it. Over the next half mile, it ascends southeast in sparse forest over a little rise and drops to a ford of Mildred Lake's outlet, which, like the other streams between Tenaya Lake and the Sunrise Trail junction, can dry up in late season. Beyond the Mildred Lake stream, the trail undulates and winds generally south, passing several pocket meadows browsed by mule deer. The trail then begins to climb in earnest, through a thinning cover of lodgepole pine and occasional red fir, western white pine, and mountain hemlock. As your trail rises above Tenaya Canyon, you pass several vantage points, from which you can look back upon its polished granite walls, though you never see Tenaya Lake. To the east, the canyon is bounded by Tenaya Peak; the cliffs of Mt. Hoffman and Tuolumne Peak are in the northwest.

Now on switchbacks, one sees the Tioga Road across the canyon and can even hear vehicles, but these annoyances are infinitesimal compared to the pleasures of polished granite expanses all around. These switchbacks are mercifully shaded, and where they become steepest, requiring a great output of energy, they give back the beauty of the finest flower displays on this trail, including lupine, penstemon, paintbrush, larkspur, buttercup, and sunflowers such as aster and senecio. Finally, the switchbacks end and the trail levels as it arrives at a junction on a shallow, forested saddle, from which point Trip 42 goes straight ahead.

Here, you turn left, contour east, cross a low gap, and descend north to Lower

Matthes Crest, from Sunrise High Sierra Camp

Sunrise Lake, above whose east shore you'll see excellent examples of exfoliating granite slabs. The large, talus slope beneath them testifies to the slabs' instability. Climbing from this lake and its small campsites, we reach a crest in several minutes; from it, one could descend cross-country an equally short distance north to more isolated, island-dotted Middle Sunrise Lake. The trail, however, veers east and gains a very noticeable 150 feet in elevation as it climbs to Upper Sunrise Lake, the largest and most popular lake of the trio. Campsites are plentiful along its north shore, away from the trail.

Leaving this lake, the trail climbs south up a gully, crosses it, and then soon climbs up a second gully to the east side of a broad gap, from which you see the Clark Range head on, piercing the southern sky. From the gap, which is sparsely clothed with mountain hemlocks, whitebark pines, and western white pines, you descend south into denser cover, veer east, and then veer north to make a steep descent to a backpackers' camp, complete with bearproof food-storage boxes. By walking briefly north from it, you'll reach Sunrise High Sierra Camp. An overnight stay at either camp gives you an inspiring sunrise over Matthes Crest and the Cathedral Range.

TRIP 42

Tenaya Lake to Clouds Rest, Half Dome, and Happy Isles

S / DH, BP

DISTANCE: 21.3 miles point to point

ELEVATIONS: 8140'/9926'
+2480'/-710'/±6380'

SEASON: Early July to early October

USE: Moderate

MAPS: *Tenaya Lake,*
Yosemite Falls, Half Dome

TRAIL LOG:

2.9	Forested saddle
5.2	Clouds Rest Trail
6.8	Horse trail
7.0	Clouds Rest
7.5	Horse trail
10.4	John Muir Trail
10.9	Half Dome Trail
13.0	Half Dome
15.1	John Muir Trail
16.4	Little Yosemite Valley
17.5	Junction northeast of Nevada Fall
21.3	Happy Isles

INTRODUCTION: Although Clouds Rest is higher than Half Dome, it is easier and safer to climb, and it provides far better views of the park than does popular, often overcrowded Half Dome. Except for its last 300 yards, the Clouds Rest Trail lacks the terrifying, potentially lethal drop-offs found along Half Dome's shoulder and back side, thereby making it a good trail for acrophobic photographers. If you're an avid photographer, you'll want to start this trek at the crack of dawn in order to reach this summit before shadows become poor for photography. All hikers should strive to reach this summit by noon or thereabouts, for lightning storms are a real possibility in the mid- to late afternoon.

Most hikers will go only as far as the Clouds Rest summit and then return, and the elevations listed are for this hike. However, a few will make the exhilarating route to the summits of Yosemite Valley's two loftiest, most scenic viewpoints—Clouds Rest and Half Dome. For this select few, I've described this as an alternate route. Attaining the two summits and then descending to Happy Isles requires more than 13,500 feet of climbing—more than double the total ascent to and descent from Clouds Rest. Good judgment is required for this hike, for both summit routes have potentially fatal drop-offs. Strong hikers can make this hike in one day, but many will want to take two. If you do, then plan to make a dry camp in the Clouds Rest environs or down along Sunrise Creek, so that you will reach the start of the Half Dome climb early on, avoiding both the hordes of people who start it later and the potential for an afternoon lightning storm.

DIRECTIONS TO THE TRAILHEAD: On the Tioga Road at the Tenaya Lake Trailhead parking area, at a highway bend near the lake's southwest shore, located 30.5 miles northeast of Crane Flat and 8.5 miles southwest of the Tuolumne Meadows Campground. Trail begins in map section E4.

DESCRIPTION: From the trailhead parking area, take a trail that heads east, and you soon cross the usually flowing outlet of Tenaya Lake. Just beyond this crossing, you reach a trail junction. The left trail goes northeast to start a loop around the lake, and then it continues another 7 miles to the Cathedral Lakes Trail in Tuolumne Meadows. Consult the introduction to Chapter 12 (page 180) for a brief description of a myth about the origin of the lake's protruding tree stumps that you'll see along this trail.

You veer right on a trail that heads south for a quarter mile along Tenaya

Creek and then leaves it. Over the next half mile, it ascends southeast in sparse forest over a little rise and drops to a ford of Mildred Lake's outlet, which, like the other streams between Tenaya Lake and the Sunrise Trail junction, can dry up in late season. Beyond the Mildred Lake stream, the trail undulates and winds generally south, passing several pocket meadows browsed by mule deer. The trail then begins to climb in earnest, through a thinning cover of lodgepole pine and occasional red fir, western white pine, and mountain hemlock. As your trail rises above Tenaya Canyon, you pass several vantage points from which you can look back upon its polished granite walls, though you never see Tenaya Lake. To the east, the canyon is bounded by Tenaya Peak; in the northwest are the cliffs of Mt. Hoffman and Tuolumne Peak.

Now on switchbacks, you can see the Tioga Road across the canyon and can even hear vehicles, but these annoyances are infinitesimal compared to the pleasures of polished granite expanses all around. These switchbacks are mercifully shaded, and, where they become steepest, requiring a great output of energy, they give back the beauty of the finest flower displays on this trail, including lupine, penstemon, paintbrush, larkspur, buttercup, and sunflowers such as aster and senecio. Finally, the switchbacks end and the trail levels as it arrives at a junction on a shallow, forested saddle, where Trip 41 branches left.

Now with all the hard climbing behind you, descend south along the Forsyth Trail. This switchbacks down to a shady, sometimes damp flat, and then it climbs up to a block-strewn ridge that sprouts dense clumps of chinquapin and aspen. Beyond it, the trail descends briefly to a tree-fringed pond—adequate for nearby camping—and then wanders south for a half mile before veering west to cross three creeklets, which will be your last reliable sources of water. After you cross the first creeklet, follow the trail briefly downstream, then veer left to cross the second creeklet before climbing up to the third. Beyond it, the trail rapidly

eases its gradient and soon reaches the Clouds Rest Trail junction.

The Forsyth Trail—not worth taking—forks left, but you keep right and, for about a mile, ascend the Clouds Rest Trail west to a forested, gravelly crest. From there, you follow the Clouds Rest Trail down to a shallow saddle. The final ascent begins here. After a moderate ascent of a quarter mile, you emerge from the forest cover to get your first excellent views of Tenaya Canyon and the country west and north of it. After another quarter mile along the crest, you come to a junction with a horse trail. If you're riding a horse from Tenaya Lake to Yosemite Valley via the Clouds Rest Trail—the most scenic of the possible routes to the Valley—you'll want to take this trail after first walking to the summit. The Clouds Rest foot trail essentially dies out here, so scramble a few feet up to the narrow and potentially dangerous crest. You might wish there was a hand railing in spots. Acrophobics and klutzes should not continue, but they can get some spectacular views of Tenaya Canyon, Half Dome, and Yosemite Valley that are nearly identical to those seen from the summit. Spreading below is the expansive 4500-foot face of Clouds Rest—the largest granite face in the park.

Those who follow the now steeper, narrow, almost trailless crest 300 yards to the summit are further rewarded with views of the Clark Range and the Merced River Canyon. Growing on the rocky summit are a few knee-high Jeffrey pines and whitebark pines plus assorted bushes and wildflowers.

Most hikers will return the way they came, but those intent on bagging Half Dome start south, negotiating short switchbacks down through a dense growth of chinquapin bushes. Then descend longer switchbacks past western white pines and a few Jeffrey pines to a junction with the Clouds Rest horse trail, which starts east. Red firs join the pines as you descend southwest from the junction, and chinquapins compete with pinemat manzanita, snow bush, and even sagebrush. The trail descends past the back sides of the two Clouds Rest "pinnacles," both broken with an abundance of horizontal fractures. Just beyond these, you reach a spur ridge with several bedrock knobs that are similarly fractured.

Most geologists interpret these fractures as the result of pressure release. These granitic rocks, which are a part of the 86-million-year-old Half Dome granodiorite pluton, solidified several miles beneath the earth's surface at pressures a few thousand times the atmospheric pressure they are exposed to today. Hence, the granitic rock tends to expand, cracking in the process, and eventually it unloads slabs.

From the low knobs and their adjacent western junipers, an initially steep descent yields to a more moderate one as you pass beneath the overhanging south wall of the southern Clouds Rest pinnacle. Your west-descending trail almost touches the rim of Tenaya Canyon before it begins about a dozen switchbacks, which drop into a vegetation zone that now includes huckleberry oaks and white firs. On this descent, you pass a trickling spring, flowing near Labrador tea, a water-loving bush that is easily identified by the turpentine smell of its crushed leaves. Don't be misled by its name; its leaves will not produce a suitable tea. Instead, they produce convulsions and paralysis. Another set of switchbacks drops you into sufficient forest cover to obstruct your recently plentiful views of towering Half Dome.

⑤ SIDE TRIP TO THE QUARTER DOMES: It is about here, at the end of a 400-yard-long switchback west—easily the longest—that adventurous hikers can start a cross-country traverse west for 0.3 mile to the Quarter Domes, the upper one providing an exceptional view of the face of Clouds Rest. You can then make a somewhat brushy cross-country descent southwest to the broad saddle midway between these domes and Half Dome. This alternate route saves you some 500 feet of climbing you will

have to do to approach that saddle via trail, and it also cuts 1 mile off the total length of your hike. **END OF SIDE TRIP.**

On the Clouds Rest Trail, your moderate-to-steep descent soon leaves red firs behind, and, through a forest of white firs and Jeffrey pines, you drop eventually to a junction with the John Muir Trail (Trip 44). Here, close to a tributary of Sunrise Creek, you'll find campsites. Just east on the John Muir Trail, between this tributary and Sunrise Creek, is a larger campsite. There are no more flat, desirable, near-water sites between here and the summit of Half Dome, about 2.6 miles farther. Be sure to bring sufficient water to last to your first reliable source, down in Little Yosemite Valley, a full 6 miles from your campsite.

From the campsite junction, we descend a half mile west along the John Muir Trail to a junction with the Half Dome Trail. If you don't want to climb to its summit, stick to the John Muir Trail and save yourself about 2.2 miles and about 1900 feet of ascent (and descent). Our trip, however, goes to the summit. Rather than carry your backpack all the way to the summit, hide it in some bushes and carry only a daypack up this strenuous section.

After about 0.6 mile, the Half Dome Trail bends west just before reaching a saddle, which is worth the minor effort for a viewful rest stop. In the next half mile, the trail first climbs through a forest of red firs and Jeffrey pines instead of white firs and incense-cedars. Half Dome's northeast face comes into view before the trail tops a crest. Here, you get a fine view of Clouds Rest and its satellites, the Quarter Domes, these accessible by a somewhat brushy cross-country ascent from the previously mentioned saddle. Between them and us, previous glaciers spilled into Tenaya Canyon. The shoulder of Half Dome, west of and above you, never was glaciated. You now have a 0.3-mile traverse, which reveals more views, including Tenaya Canyon, Mt. Watkins, Mt. Hoffmann, and much of the upper Merced River basin. This traverse ends all too soon at the base of Half Dome's intimidating shoulder.

Almost two dozen very short switchbacks guide us up the view-blessed ridge of the dome's shoulder. For too long, the real danger on this steep section was loose gravel, which could prove fatal if you fell off the trail—or were pushed off it due to heavy traffic—at one or more exposed spots. But in 2005, it was extensively reworked to make it safer. Topping the shoulder, you are confronted with the dome's even more intimidating pair of cables, which definitely cause some hikers to retreat. (Usually the cables are put up around mid-May and removed in early October.) The ascent starts out gently enough, but it, too, quickly becomes steeper, almost to a 45-degree angle. On this stretch, first-timers often slow to a snail's pace, clenching both cables with sweaty hands. Looking down, you can see that you don't want to fall. In recent years, hikers have used gloves for the cables and then left them for others. Perhaps fresh gloves may be better than sweaty hands, but old, well-used gloves seem just as slippery. Remember that even when thunderstorms are miles away, static electricity can build up here. Out of a seemingly fairweather sky, a charge can bolt down the cable, throwing your arms off it—or worse. If your hair starts standing on end, beat a hasty retreat!

The rarefied air certainly hinders your progress as you ascend, but, eventually, an easing gradient gives new incentive, and soon you are scrambling up to the broad summit of Half Dome, an area about the size of 17 football fields. With caution, most hikers proceed to the dome's high point (8842 feet), located at the north end, from where they can view the dome's overhanging northwest point. Stout-hearted souls peer over the lip of this point for an adrenaline-charged view down the dome's 2000-foot northwest face, perhaps seeing climbers ascending it. In the past, a few folks liked to camp overnight to view the sunrise, but in 1993 camping was banned.

From the broad summit of this monolith, which originated in the late days of the dinosaurs, you have a 360-degree panorama. You can look down Yosemite Valley to the bald brow of El Capitan and up Tenaya Canyon past Clouds Rest to Cathedral Peak, the Sierra Crest, and Mt. Hoffmann. Mt. Starr King—a dome that rises only 250 feet above you—dominates the Illilouette Creek basin to the south, while the Clark Range cuts the sky to the southeast. Looking due east across Moraine Dome's summit, you'll see Mt. Florence, whose broad form hides the park's highest peak, Mt. Lyell, behind it.

After your exploration of the dome's expansive summit, descend back to the John Muir Trail. The forested, switchbacking descent south is well graded, and after 1.3 miles, you arrive at a trail junction in Little Yosemite Valley.

A **ALTERNATE TRIP TO BACKPACKERS CAMP:** If you need water, continue straight ahead 0.2 mile past a spur trail northeast over to a rangers' camp, then past outhouses, and finally past a large backpackers camp with bearproof storage boxes to reach the Merced Lake Trail. From here, a short trail ahead goes to the Merced River. You could then take the Merced Lake Trail west a short half mile to the preferred route, which is 0.1 mile shorter. **END OF ALTERNATE TRIP.**

The preferred route goes a long half mile southwest to the alternate route, then, in another long half mile, your trail, the John Muir Trail, first briefly parallels the Merced River (get water here), climbs to a low notch, and then descends through brushy huckleberry oaks to a junction northeast of Nevada Fall, where we meet the top of the Mist Trail, with outhouses just above it.

A **ALTERNATE TRIP TO VERNAL FALL BRIDGE:** The trip's 21.3 miles is based on a descent along the John Muir Trail, but if you descend the Mist Trail, your hike will be 1.1 miles less, or only 20.2 miles. There are two caveats. First, if your knees hurt from all the thousands of feet of descent you have already done, take the JMT, which is better graded. Second, from the brink of Vernal Fall down to the end of the Mist Trail, the trail can be slippery and dangerous, particularly in the downhill direction. If you are exhausted and have sore knees, a mishap is even more likely, and so, normally, I would not recommend it. But if you are the type hell-bent for punishment—and if you hike this far, you will have gotten your fair share of it—why not some more?

The 1.6-mile Mist Trail begins with a 0.3-mile, 400-foot drop via short, steep switchbacks. Near their bottom, you see roaring Nevada Fall off to the left. The long half mile ahead is better graded, with occasional switchbacks, and you arrive at a bridge over the Silver Apron, which plunges into chilly Emerald Pool. Ahead, the trail goes about 100 yards west to a junction, from which a connecting trail switchbacks 0.4 mile southwest up to Clark Point, on the John Muir Trail.

The Mist Trail winds briefly down to a railing by the brink of Vernal Fall, passing outhouses along the way. When gusts of wind blow spray from the falls toward the last half mile of the well-named Mist Trail, you will get soaked, so be prepared. You begin by first following the railing south down steep steps to an alcove, then descending 300-plus steps, some of them treacherously wet and lacking a railing, down to easier hiking just before a junction with the John Muir Trail. **END OF ALTERNATE TRIP.**

From the junction with the top of the Mist Trail, the John Muir Trail traverses southwest toward nearby Nevada Fall.

S **SIDE TRIP TO NEVADA FALL VIEWPOINT:** Just a few yards before the Nevada Fall bridge, you can strike northwest to find a short spur trail that drops to a viewpoint beside the fall's brink. This viewpoint's railing is seen from the fall's bridge, thereby giving you an idea where the trail ends. A

bit of this short trail is exposed, so watch your step. **END OF SIDE TRIP.**

From the Nevada Fall bridge, we strike southwest and shortly end a gentle ascent at a junction, just beyond a seeping spring, with the Glacier Point-Panorama Trail. Onward, we have a high traverse that provides an ever-changing panorama of dome-like Liberty Cap and broad-topped Mt. Broderick—both overridden by glaciers and both standing as testaments to the ineffectiveness of glacial erosion. As you progress west, Half Dome becomes prominent, its hulking mass vying for your attention. Eventually, you descend to Clark Point, 1.1 miles from the last junction, where you meet a scenic connecting trail that switchbacks down to the Mist Trail. Backpackers, packers, and those wishing to keep dry continue down the John Muir Trail, which curves south into a gully, switchbacks down to the base of spreading Panorama Cliff, then switchbacks down a talus slope. Largely shaded by canyon live oaks and Douglas firs, it reaches a junction with a horse trail (no hikers allowed) that descends to the Valley's stables. Continue a brief minute more to a junction with the Mist Trail, 1.2 miles below Clark Point. Turn left here, and quickly reach the Vernal Fall bridge, from which you hike your last mile down to the shuttle-bus stop at Happy Isles.

Brink of Nevada Fall

TRIP 43

Tuolumne Meadows to Lower Cathedral Lake via John Muir Trail

Ⓜ ↗ DH, BP

DISTANCE: 7.6 miles out and back

ELEVATIONS: 8570'/9570'
+1070'/-350'/±2840'

SEASON: Early July to mid-October

USE: Heavy

MAP: *Tenaya Lake*

TRAIL LOG:

3.1 Lower Cathedral Lake Trail
3.8 Lower Cathedral Lake

INTRODUCTION: Justifiably popular Lower Cathedral Lake receives so much backpacker use that those who can visit this scenic lake in only one day—an easy task—should do so. Another option is to visit Medlicott and Mariuolumne domes, worthy goals in themselves. Since free shuttle buses operate between Tuolumne Meadows and Tenaya Lake, strong dayhikers have another option: After visiting Lower Cathedral Lake, follow the John Muir Trail to Sunrise High Sierra Camp (Trip 44), then head out and down to Tenaya Lake (Trip 41 in reverse), for a grand total of about 15 miles. Then take the shuttle bus back to your trailhead.

DIRECTIONS TO THE TRAILHEAD: In Tuolumne Meadows, 1.5 miles west on the Tioga Road from the Tuolumne Meadows Campground entrance, or about 0.75 mile east on the Tioga Road from the Pothole Dome parking area. On some summer weekends, vehicles are parked along quite a lengthy stretch of the Tioga Road, which,

of course, adds to your hiking distance. Trail begins in map section E4.

DESCRIPTION: From a trailhead beside Budd Creek, walk southwest 120 yards to a junction with the Tuolumne Meadows-Tenaya Lake Trail.

A **ALTERNATE TRIP TO YOSEMITE VALLEY:** Starting from the east side of Tuolumne Meadows Campground, this trail traverses west to our junction, then continues for a generally viewless 8.1 miles down to the trailhead near the southwest shore of Tenaya Lake. By continuing on Trip 30, you can descend to Mirror Lake, a hike that is the shortest route from Tuolumne Meadows to Yosemite Valley—about 19.75 miles. **END OF ALTERNATE TRIP.**

Now on the John Muir Trail, which has come west to this junction, we climb moderately up a stretch that can at times be objectionably dusty due to humus mixing with the abundance of glacial deposits. Lodgepoles dominate your 0.75-mile ascent to the crest of a lateral moraine, from which the trail briefly descends west before turning southwest.

S **SIDE TRIP TO FAIRVIEW DOME:** From this spot, you can hike cross-country a half mile northwest to the lower slopes of Fairview Dome, which can provide quite a view of the Tuolumne Meadows environs. During glacial periods, the Tuolumne Meadows glacier was so thick that it buried this dome under as much as 700 feet of glacier ice, which then overflowed the river basin to descend into Yosemite Valley via Tenaya Canyon. Non-climbers should not attempt to climb to its summit. **END OF SIDE TRIP.**

Follow the John Muir Trail southwest a half mile to a creeklet, which you cross, and then ascend short, moderate-to-steep switchbacks beneath the shady cover of lodgepole pines and mountain hemlocks. After 300 feet of climbing, your trail's gradient eases, and you traverse along the base of largely unseen Cathedral Peak, a mass of granodiorite towering 1400 feet above you that is the realm of the mountain climber. Your traverse leaves the Tuolumne River drainage for that of the Merced River, and soon, after a brief descent, you come to a junction with the Lower Cathedral Lake Trail.

This spur trail descends 0.6 mile to the bedrock east shore of Lower Cathedral Lake. A rust-stained waterline on the meadow side of the bedrock marks the high-water level, when the meadow floods in early season. Bear-frequented campsites abound on both the north and south shores; the northern ones are roomier. Campfires are not allowed. Due to high angler use, fishing for brook trout is likely to be poor. Because of the relative shallowness of this fairly large lake, swimming in it is tolerable despite its 9300-plus-foot altitude. From the lake's outlet, you can look across to Polly Dome, standing high above Pywiack Dome. Also seen are Mt. Hoffman and a bit of Tenaya Lake, nestled between Tenaya Peak and Polly Dome.

S SIDE TRIP TO MEDLICOTT AND MARI-UOLUMNE DOMES: By hiking cross-country 0.75 mile north from your lake's outlet, you can follow the rim of Tenaya Canyon to a seldom seen lakelet near the summit of Medlicott Dome. Seen from this lakelet, the dome in no way resembles a dome, but Mariuolumne Dome, a half mile north of it, bears a striking resemblance to Lembert Dome (Trip 38). Mariuolumne Dome gets its name from the nearby drainage divide, which separates Mariposa County from Tuolumne County. Both domes are worth visiting for their views, especially those from Mariuolumne. Its actual summit block takes a bit of climbing that is not too exposed; still, if you feel intimidated, don't climb it! To reach the two domes with a minimal effort, leave the John Muir Trail where it tops out at the Tuolumne-Merced drainage divide. END OF SIDE TRIP.

Cathedral Peak from Lower Cathedral Lake

TRIP 44

Tuolumne Meadows to Happy Isles via John Muir Trail

Ⓜ / DH, BP

DISTANCE: 21.7 miles point to point

ELEVATIONS: 4020′/9940′
+2470′/-7020′/±9490′

SEASON: Early July to mid-October

USE: Moderate

MAPS: *Tenaya Lake, Merced Peak, Half Dome*

TRAIL LOG:

3.1	Lower Cathedral Lake Trail
4.0	Upper Cathedral Lake
4.3	Cathedral Pass
7.0	Echo Creek Trail
7.8	Sunrise High Sierra Camp
9.5	Southeast-trending ridge
12.7	Forsyth Trail
12.8	High Trail
15.0	Clouds Rest Trail
15.5	Half Dome Trail
16.8	Little Yosemite Valley
17.9	Mist Trail
18.1	Nevada Fall
18.3	Glacier Point-Panorama Trail
19.4	Clark Point
20.6	Mist Trail
20.7	Vernal Fall bridge
21.7	Happy Isles

INTRODUCTION: This section of the John Muir Trail is perhaps the most popular route from Tuolumne Meadow to Yosemite Valley. For those who have done the first 190 miles of this famous trail, which originates at the summit of Mt. Whitney, these final scenic miles—most of them downhill—make a perfect ending. At 21.7 miles long, it is usually backpacked, but strong hikers can do this in about seven or eight hours. This is not particularly strenuous since there is only about 2000 feet of total ascent, of which more than half is done in the first 5 miles, when you are fresh.

You can make a longer variation of this route by following the Echo Creek Trail down to the Merced Lake Trail, then up to the backpackers campground near the Merced Lake High Sierra Camp. After spending the night at the lake, take the Merced Lake Trail down a very dramatic stretch of the Merced River canyon to a reunion with the John Muir Trail in Little Yosemite Valley. This route is about 10.5 miles longer than the one adhering to the John Muir Trail, but it is surprisingly easy, adding only about 1000 feet of additional elevation change, and most of that is elevation loss.

DIRECTIONS TO THE TRAILHEAD: In Tuolumne Meadows, 1.5 miles west on the Tioga Road from the Tuolumne Meadows Campground entrance, or about 0.75 mile east on the Tioga Road from the Pothole Dome parking area. On some summer weekends, vehicles are parked along quite a lengthy stretch of the Tioga Road, which, of course, adds to your hiking distance. Trail begins in map section E4.

DESCRIPTION: From a trailhead beside Budd Creek, walk southwest 120 yards to a junction with the Tuolumne Meadows-Tenaya Lake Trail, which continues west then southwest for a generally viewless 8.1 miles down to the trailhead near the southwest shore of Tenaya Lake. Now on the John Muir Trail, which has come west to this junction, we climb moderately up a stretch that can at times be objectionably dusty due to humus mixing with the abundance of glacial deposits. Lodgepoles dominate your 0.75-mile ascent to the crest of a lateral moraine, from which the trail briefly descends west before turning southwest.

The JMT traverses southwest a half mile to a creeklet, which you cross, and then ascend short, moderate-to-steep switchbacks beneath the shady cover of lodgepole pines and mountain hemlocks. After 300 feet of climbing, your trail's gradient eases and you traverse along the base of largely unseen Cathedral Peak, a mass of granodiorite towering 1400 feet above you that is the realm of the mountain climber. Your traverse leaves the Tuolumne River drainage for that of the Merced River, and soon, after a brief descent, you come to a junction with the Lower Cathedral Lake Trail. Visiting this lake adds about 1.5 miles to your hike's length.

From this junction, make an easy, mile-long climb to the southeast corner of very shallow Upper Cathedral Lake. Although camping is discouraged here, you may enjoy a rest on the south-shore peninsula, which offers a fine view of two-towered Cathedral Peak. The JMT then climbs a quarter mile to broad Cathedral Pass, snowbound but obvious in early summer, where the excellent views include Tresidder Peak, Cathedral Peak, Echo Peaks, and Matterhorn Peak far to the north.

Beyond the pass is a long, beautiful swale, the flowery headwaters of Echo Creek. The JMT traverses up the east flank of Tresidder Peak on a gentle climb to the actual high point of this trail, 9940 feet, at a marvelous viewpoint overlooking most of southern part of the park. The inspiring panorama here includes the peaks around Vogelsang High Sierra Camp in the southeast, the whole Clark Range in the south, and, farther away, the peaks on the park's border. Your high trail now descends slightly over the next half mile to pass below steep-walled Columbia Finger, then switchbacks quickly down to the head of the upper lobe of Long Meadow. Here, it levels off and leads down to a gradually sloping valley dotted with lodgepole pines to the head of the second, lower lobe of l-o-n-g Long Meadow. You soon reach a junction with the Echo Creek Trail; some hikers may wish to take this trail over to Merced Lake, but all should take the JMT south a half mile before bending west a quarter mile to pass below Sunrise High Sierra Camp,

perched on a granite bench just above the trail. South of the camp are some backpacker campsites, from which you can take in the next morning's glorious sunrise. Here you have bearproof food-storage boxes.

 ALTERNATE ROUTE TO MERCED LAKE: The next morning, backtrack 0.8 mile up the meadow to the Echo Creek Trail, on which you will immediately ford Long Meadow's creek on boulders. This trail, which takes us 7.2 miles to the Merced Lake Trail, quickly switchbacks up to the top of a forested ridge, about 200 feet above the meadow. It then descends through dense hemlock-and-lodgepole forest to a tributary of Echo Creek. Cross this, descend along it for 0.3 mile, recross it, and then momentarily reach the west bank of Echo Creek's Cathedral Fork, about 1.5 miles beyond Long Meadow.

From our trail beside the Cathedral Fork, we have fine views of the creek's water gliding down a series of granite slabs, and then the trail veers away from the creek and descends gently above it for more than a mile. Even in late season, these shaded slopes are watered by numerous rills that are bordered by still-blooming flowers. On this downgrade, the trail crosses the Long Meadow creek, which has found an escape from that meadow through a gap between two small domes high above our trail. The route then levels out in a mile-long flat section of this valley, where the wet ground yields wildflowers all summer but also many mosquitoes in the early season. Beyond this flat "park," the trail descends open slopes, and eventually you can see across the valley the steep course of Echo Creek plunging down to its rendezvous with its western Cathedral Fork. By the Cathedral Fork, your trail levels off and passes good campsites immediately before you take a bridge over Echo Creek.

Beyond the bridge, your trail leads down the forested valley and easily fords a tributary stream, staying well above the main creek. This pleasant, shaded descent soon becomes more open and steep, and it encounters fibrous-barked juniper trees and butterscotch-scented Jeffrey pines as it drops to another bridge 1.3 miles from the first one. Beyond it, the trail rises slightly, and the creek drops precipitously, so that you are soon far above it. Then the sandy tread swings west and diagonals down a brushy slope. Across it, the views are excellent of Echo Valley, which is a wide place in the great Merced River canyon below. On this slope, you arrive at a junction with the High Trail, which goes 3 miles west to a junction with the John Muir Trail. Leaving the dense growth of huckleberry oak, chinquapin, greenleaf manzanita, and snow bush behind, start southeast and drop 450 feet over 0.7 mile to the Merced Lake Trail junction in Echo Valley.

There is adequate camping here, but our goal is only 2.3 miles ahead. We go east, immediately bridging Echo Creek, pass through a burned-but-boggy area, then climb east, past the Merced River's largely unseen but enjoyable pools, to Merced Lake's west shore. Don't camp here, but, rather, continue past the north shore to Merced Lake High Sierra Camp and the adjacent campground, which you reach just before the camp.

On your third day, you hike about 14 miles to the floor of Yosemite Valley, which isn't that hard because it is mostly downhill and you've gotten sufficient exercise and acclimation to handle it. First, retrace your steps to Echo Valley, and then continue west on the Merced Lake Trail 7 miles to Little Yosemite Valley. This begins with a stroll 0.8 mile south and then west through spacious Echo Valley to reach a bridge south across the Merced River just above the brink of its cascades. Because dozens of previous glaciers were impotent at transforming the canyon from V to U in cross profile, we can't follow the river and must stay high for most of the 1.9 miles to a bridge north across the river.

This high traverse to a bench does have some benefits. First, from the bench, you can study the features of a broad, hulking granitic mass opposite you whose south face is bounded by an immense arch. A "hairline" crack along its east side indicates that a major rockfall is imminent, geologically speaking. Second, along your traverse, where you reach a highly polished bedrock surface, you can glance west and see Clouds Rest—a long ridge—standing on the horizon. And finally, not much farther, you reach a glade with a spring-fed profuse garden, bordered by aspens. In midsummer, this garden supports a colorful array of various wildflowers. Now we negotiate a series of more than a dozen switchbacks that lead us down 400 feet to the river, which we follow for 0.3 mile to the bridge north across the river. The bridge is here because the canyon floor has widened a bit.

Now we enter a second V gorge. Although the scenery may overpower you,

A fine view of Clouds Rest and its satellites, the Quarter Domes

past glaciers, which completely buried Bunnell Point, more than 1600 feet above you, were powerless to effectively erode this part of the canyon. They overtopped the point by several hundred feet, yet their massive thicknesses, exerting more than 100 tons per square foot on the lower slopes, failed to transform this canyon from a V to a U shape. Our trail becomes hemmed in as we traverse the north base of Bunnell Point on our left and pass an unnamed but imposing cliff on our right.

Beyond the squeeze, we switchback down past Bunnell Cascade, which, with the magnificent canyon scenery, can easily distract you from the real danger of this exposed section of trail. We've now entered Lost Valley, which, like Echo Valley and other U-shaped valleys, already was broad-floored well before glaciers set foot in it. In Lost Valley, no fires are allowed. In it, we head toward a glacier-smoothed dome, unofficially called the Sugar Loaf, and round its base, hemmed in by another short section of a V gorge. Just beyond it and 2.25 miles past the last bridge, we arrive at the east end of Little Yosemite Valley, graced by the presence of a beautiful pool—the receptacle of a Merced River cascade.

Now you embark on a shady traverse through the broad, flat valley. The valley's floor largely has been buried by glacial sediments, which, like beach sand, makes the trail more of a slog than a stroll, even though the trail is level. Progressing west through Little Yosemite Valley, we stay closer to the base of glacier-polished Moraine Dome than to the Merced River. After 2 miles, we arrive at a junction with the John Muir Trail, and the backpackers camp here tends to be a "Grand Central Station." **END OF ALTERNATE ROUTE.**

From about 9300 feet, just below the Sunrise High Sierra Camp, the John Muir Trail continues through the south arm of Long Meadow, then soon starts to climb up the east slopes of Sunrise Mountain. At about 9700 feet, you top a broad, south-east-trending ridge, and then, paralleling the headwaters of Sunrise Creek, descend steeply by switchbacks down a rocky canyon. At the foot of this descent, you cross a trickling creek, then climb a low moraine to another creek. In a short half mile, top the linear crest of a giant lateral moraine.

This moraine is the largest of a series of ridgelike glacial deposits in this area, and the gigantic granite boulders along its sides testify to the transporting power of the glacier that once overflowed Little Yosemite Valley. At its maximum, it had a surface higher than this Tioga-age moraine. Lower down, additional morainal crests appear on both sides of the trail, and you see Half Dome through the trees before your route reaches a junction with the Forsyth Trail. The steep hike up it to the Clouds Rest Trail is not worth taking. Look for fair campsites along Sunrise Creek about 150 yards north of this junction. Here, we turn south and, in a moment, reach the High Trail, coming in on the left. Turn right and descend southwest; your path is bounded first on the north by the south buttress of the Clouds Rest eminence, and then on the south by the northeast end of a ridge, Moraine Dome.

S **SIDE TRIP TO MORAINE DOME:** For admirable views and interesting geology, I strongly recommend you ascend south some 200 feet in elevation to attain the broad ridge-crest, then walk southwest along it to the obvious summit of Moraine Dome. This is named for a lateral moraine that descends southwest from just below the dome's summit. This moraine, hanging on the south side of Moraine Dome about 1750 feet above the floor of Little Yosemite Valley, does not represent the approximate thickness of the last glacier, geological experts to the contrary. It and earlier glaciers topped it by hundreds of feet. Atop Moraine Dome you'll see—besides an utterly fantastic panorama—two geologically interesting features. One is an 8-foot-high dike of resistant aplite, which stands above the rest of the dome's surface because it weathers more slowly. Nearby, just downslope, is a large erratic boulder that, unlike the rock of Moraine Dome, is composed of Cathedral Peak granodiorite, easily identified by its large feldspar crystals. Ongoing exfoliation of adjacent bedrock, aided by a lengthy root from a nearby Jeffrey pine, has left the erratic perched precariously atop a 3-foot-high pedestal. **END OF SIDE TRIP.**

Meanwhile, along the John Muir Trail a mile from the last junction, you ford Sunrise Creek in a red fir forest, then, in 0.75 mile, see a good campsite on a large, shady creekside flat. You then curve northeast to quickly cross the creek's tributary, which has two west-bank campsites. Immediately past these is the Clouds Rest Trail (Trip 42), and a half mile west from this junction, you meet the Half Dome Trail (Trip 68—about 4 miles round trip—an incredible hike that shouldn't be missed). From this junction, your shady path switchbacks down through a changing forest cover that includes some stately incense-cedars, with their burnt-orange, fibrous bark. At the foot of this descent, we reach a trail junction on the floor of Little Yosemite Valley. Due to the area's popularity, one or more seasonal rangers are stationed here. Just 0.1 mile ahead, past the backpackers camp and its bearproof food-storage boxes, you meet the Merced Lake Trail, which is the end of this trip's alternate route.

From here onward, you will meet dozens, if not hundreds, of hikers as you descend about 4.8 miles to Happy Isles in eastern Yosemite Valley. From here, you follow the Merced River a short half mile west to a junction, from which a shortcut route from the previously mentioned trail junction on the floor of Little Yosemite Valley comes a long half mile to join our route. Combined, the John Muir Trail first briefly parallels the Merced River, climbs to a low notch, and then descends through brushy huckleberry oaks to a junction with the top of the Mist Trail, with outhouses just above it. This trail descends 1.6 miles to a junc-

tion with the John Muir Trail, while that trail takes 2.7 miles to reach the junction. However, I don't recommend it because it is quite steep, and, in places, is wet and/or exposed. From the junction with the top of the Mist Trail, the John Muir Trail traverses southwest toward nearby Nevada Fall.

⑤ **SIDE TRIP TO NEVADA FALL VIEWPOINT:** Just a few yards before the Nevada Fall bridge, you can strike northwest to find a short spur trail that drops to a viewpoint beside the fall's brink. This viewpoint's railing is seen from the fall's bridge, thereby giving you an idea where the trail ends. A bit of this short trail is exposed, so watch your step. **END OF SIDE TRIP.**

From the Nevada Fall bridge, we strike southwest and shortly end a gentle ascent at a junction, just beyond a seeping spring, with the Glacier Point-Panorama Trail. Onward, we have a high traverse that provides an ever-changing panorama of domelike Liberty Cap and broad-topped Mt. Broderick—both overridden by glaciers and both standing as testaments to the ineffectiveness of glacial erosion. As you progress west, Half Dome becomes promi- nent, its hulking mass vying for your attention. Eventually, you descend to Clark Point, 1.1 miles from the last junction, where you meet a scenic connecting trail that switchbacks down to the Mist Trail. Backpackers, packers, and those wishing to keep dry continue down the John Muir Trail, which curves south into a gully, switchbacks down to the base of spreading Panorama Cliff, then switchbacks down a talus slope. Largely shaded by canyon live oaks and Douglas firs, it reaches a junction with a horse trail (no hikers allowed) that descends to the valley's stables. Continue a brief minute more to a junction with the Mist Trail, 1.2 miles below Clark Point, turn left, and quickly reach the Vernal Fall bridge, from which you hike your last mile down to the shuttle-bus stop at Happy Isles.

TRIP 45

Tuolumne Meadows to Budd Lake

Ⓜ ↗ DH

DISTANCE: 5.4 miles out and back

ELEVATIONS: 8570´/9980´
+1460´/-50´/±3020´

SEASON: Mid-July to early October

USE: Light

MAP: *Tenaya Lake*

TRAIL LOG:

2.7   Budd Lake

INTRODUCTION: Mountaineers take the unmaintained, de facto trail to Budd Lake, for it provides the fastest access to climbing routes on Cathedral Peak, Echo Peaks, the Cockscomb, and Unicorn Peak—all encircling the lake—and on Matthes Crest,

south of the Cockscomb. I would not describe this route were it not for significant geological features around chilly Budd Lake that are worth investigation.

DIRECTIONS TO THE TRAILHEAD: In Tuolumne Meadows, 1.5 miles west on the Tioga Road from the Tuolumne Meadows Campground entrance, or about 0.75 mile east on the Tioga Road from the Pothole Dome parking area. On some summer weekends, vehicles are parked along quite a lengthy stretch of the Tioga Road, which, of course, adds to your hiking distance. Trail begins in map section E4.

DESCRIPTION: The unsigned trail up to Budd Creek can be hard to find. From the trailhead, walk 120 yards southwest to a junction with the John Muir Trail, then start southwest up it toward the Cathedral Lakes. After a long quarter mile, a use trail starts south from a point where the John Muir Trail curves northwest—the only place it does so on the lower part of its ascent. The use trail quickly becomes more obvious and its first mile is easy to follow. However, it then levels off and forks. One branch makes a brief, gentle descent, but you should stay on the right branch, which

A young moraine arcs across Budd Lake, with Cathedral Peak in the background.

first climbs up to a granitic bench and then heads south along its brink. In about 0.3 mile, this branch rejoins the lower one; then the path can become vague just before crossing Budd Creek. Once on the east bank of Budd Creek, you may see a third branch, one that had split from the lower one. From the crossing, a single tread climbs a short mile up Budd Creek, crossing it again just before reaching Budd Lake.

Along your ascent of this trail, you'll note that Unicorn Peak, to the east, has three summits, not one, as you might assume from the name. At Budd Lake, camping is not allowed. Budd Lake is perhaps unique in Yosemite in that it contains two geologically recent moraines. The older moraine, perhaps formed only a few hundred years ago, rests along the north shore of 10,050-foot-high Budd Lake. The younger one, perhaps almost as old, arcs across the lake's south end.

 While you're admiring Cathedral Peak, the Echo Peaks, and the adjacent Cockscomb basin, you might take a close look at the granodiorite that composes them. Dated about 85 million years old, this Cathedral Peak pluton's mineral and chemical composition varies from place to place, but it generally becomes richer in feldspar and quartz toward the center. Despite the variation of its rocks, this pluton is easy to identify in Yosemite, for it contains large, blocky, protruding crystals of potassium feldspar. Climbers new to the Tuolumne Meadows area quickly discover that these make good holds.

TRIP 46

Tuolumne Meadows to Elizabeth Lake and Beyond

Ⓜ ↗ DH, BP

DISTANCE:	5 miles out and back
ELEVATIONS:	8690′/9510′ +820′/-40′/±1720′
SEASON:	Early July to early October
USE:	Heavy
MAP:	*Vogelsang Peak* (also *Tenaya Lake* for beyond Elizabeth Lake)

TRAIL LOG:

2.5   Elizabeth Lake

INTRODUCTION: Due to its accessibility, Elizabeth Lake ranks with Dog Lake (Trip 38) in popularity. Dog Lake is certainly better for swimming, while Elizabeth Lake is preferred for scenery. An optional trip, especially for backpackers, is a hike to fairly isolated Nelson Lake, which can be reached by a de facto trail from Elizabeth Lake.

DIRECTIONS TO THE TRAILHEAD: Near the horse camp loop of the Tuolumne Meadows Campground. Walk through the campground and find the trailhead just past campsite B49. Trail begins in map sections F3-F4.

DESCRIPTION: The signed Elizabeth Lake Trail in the campground goes about 100 yards up to a crossing of a trail that heads east to Lyell Canyon and west to Tenaya Lake. You then continue straight ahead for a steady southward ascent. Along this lodgepole-pine-shaded climb, the trail crosses several runoff streams that dry up by late summer. Before then, expect lots of mosquitoes. More than a mile out and with some considerable exertion, since we are now over 9000 feet, we veer near Unicorn Creek. If the music of this dashing, gurgling, cold-water stream doesn't make the climbing easier, the lesser gradient will. After rising 800 feet from its start, the trail levels off, and lodgepoles now are both stunted and spaced farther apart. You emerge at the foot of a long meadow, and, partway through it, take a short spur trail southwest to Elizabeth Lake. Unfortunately, at times, there have been a number of

Elizabeth Lake and Unicorn Peak

use paths, and the turf traversed by them has suffered. The problem is compounded by the difficulty of finding an adequate crossing of Unicorn Creek, and folks, especially in the high-water, early summer season, often go up and down the east bank looking for a narrow spot to jump across. A reworked trail with a footbridge would greatly reduce the human imprint on this fragile land.

Few places in Yosemite give so much for so little effort as this lovely subalpine lake, situated at 9508 feet. Backdropped by Unicorn Peak, the lake faces the snow-topped peaks of the Sierra Crest north of Tuolumne Meadows. From the east and north sides of the lake, the views across the 👁 waters to Unicorn Peak are classic. The glacier-carved lake basin is, indeed, one of the most beautiful in the Tuolumne Meadows area. Should you wish to camp in this vicinity, something I discourage due to heavy use, check out the forested bench rising above the lake's northwest corner.

⑤ **SIDE TRIP TO NELSON LAKE:** For more isolated camping, consider Nelson Lake, a 🏕 relatively modest 5.9 miles from the trailhead. From the Elizabeth Lake's spur trail junction, 2.4 miles into this hike, a very conspicuous and well-used unofficial trail heads south across meadow lands and, in 1 mile, climbs south to the southern of two shallow notches in the Cathedral Range. Over the next mile, it first descends steeply well below the spectacular Cockscomb crest, and then it eases its gradient. Over the next mile, you traverse southward, staying close to the east bank of upper Echo Creek before veering a half mile east, crossing two minor ridges, the second one damming 9605-foot Nelson Lake. From Nelson Lake and its population of brook trout, these backpackers can either head about 1 mile up-canyon to alpine 10,050-foot Reymann Lake or can head cross-country down Echo Creek for 4 miles to the creek's confluence with its Cathedral Fork (see Trip 44's alternate route). **END OF SIDE TRIP.**

TRIP 47

Tuolumne Meadows-Merced Lake Semiloop

Ⓜ ☊ BPx

DISTANCE: 32.8 miles semiloop

ELEVATIONS: 7220'/10,670'
+5950'/-5950'/±11,900'

SEASON: Mid-July to early October

USE: Heavy

MAPS: *Tioga Pass, Vogelsang Peak, Tenaya Lake, Merced Peak*

TRAIL LOG:

1.7	Rafferty Creek Trail
6.9	Tuolumne Pass
7.7	Vogelsang High Sierra Camp
9.2	Vogelsang Pass
10.7	Bernice Lake Trail
13.6	High Trail
14.6	Fletcher Creek Trail
15.8	Merced Lake Ranger Station
16.7	Merced Lake High Sierra Camp
18.8	Start up Fletcher Creek Trail
20.4	Babcock Lake Trail
22.6	Scissors junction
25.9	Tuolumne Pass
32.8	Tuolumne Meadows

INTRODUCTION: Although this hike can be made in three days, four are recommended because it is too scenic to hurry through. At this leisurely pace, you have time for most, if not all, of the side trips. That said, I realize that most hikers go only to Vogelsang High Sierra Camp or relatively nearby lakes. The total ascent and descent to the camp is about 4000 feet—that is, about a third of this suggested trip. Total distance to and from the camp as well as to one of its nearby lakes, such as Boothe, Upper Fletcher, Townsley, or Vogelsang, is about

half of this suggested trip. If you are an overnight backpacker and want to reduce stress rather than exacerbate it, the Vogelsang environs may be the right prescription.

DIRECTIONS TO THE TRAILHEAD: Drive to the large parking lot just beyond the start of the Tuolumne Meadows Lodge spur road. This road is reached by driving 0.6 mile northeast from the Tuolumne Meadows Campground entrance. During most of the summer, this large lot, immediately west of the spur road, has a small booth that dispenses wilderness permits. Trail begins in map section F3.

DESCRIPTION: Start on the John Muir Trail, which runs beside the Dana Fork of the Tuolumne River just yards south of the Tuolumne Meadows Lodge road. On the trail, you hike 0.3 mile up the Dana Fork to a junction with a spur trail that goes to the west end of the lodge's parking lot. Just before this junction is an underwater granite arch in the Dana Fork. From this junction, you bridge the Dana Fork and, after a brief walk upstream, reach a junction with a trail to the Gaylor Lakes. Unless you are riding a horse, you'll want to reach these lakes from Tioga Pass, via a much shorter route (Trip 39).

Veering right, the John Muir Trail leads over a slight rise and descends to the Lyell Fork, where there are two bridges. The meadows above these bridges are among the most delightful in all the Sierra. They are wonderful places to spend the last hour before dinner, something you might consider for your hike out to the Tuolumne Meadows Trailhead. Mt. Dana and Mt. Gibbs glow on the eastern horizon, catching the late sun, while trout dart along the wide Lyell Fork.

About 70 yards past the bridges, we meet a trail that comes about 0.75 mile up the river from the east end of the Tuolumne Meadows Campground. Turn left (east) onto it, and skirt around a long, lovely section of the meadow. Traveling through a dense forest cover of lodgepole pine, our route reaches a junction on the west bank of Rafferty Creek, from where the John Muir Trail (Trip 49) continues east, crossing the creek's two major branches.

Our route, the Rafferty Creek Trail, turns right and immediately begins a climb whose grade is moderate as often as it is steep. Fairly well-shaded by lodgepole pines, the climb eases well under a mile. Then, as the ascent decreases to a gentle grade, we pass through high, boulder-strewn meadows that offer good views eastward to reddish-brown Mt. Dana and Mt. Gibbs, and gray-white Mammoth Peak. Soon, the trail dips close to Rafferty Creek, and, after 2 miles of near-creek hiking, the gently climbing trail passes near the edge of a large meadow and continues its long, gentle ascent through a sparse forest of lodgepole pines.

In the next mile, you cross several seasonal creeks, and, about 3.5 miles up the Rafferty Creek Trail, reach an even larger meadow. Through this, you ascend easily up-canyon, having backward views north to the Sierra Crest between Tioga Pass and Mt. Conness and views ahead to cliff-bound, dark-banded Fletcher Peak and Vogelsang Peak to the right of it. After about 1.5 miles, you reach Tuolumne Pass, a major gap in the Cathedral Range. At the pass, some lodgepole pines and a few whitebark pines diminish the force of winds that often sweep through it. Taking the signed trail to Vogelsang from the junction here, you follow a path across a moderately steep slope, below which Boothe Lake and its surrounding meadows—part of your return route—lie serene in the west.

Finally, the trail makes a short climb, and tents of Vogelsang High Sierra Camp spread out before us at the foot of Fletcher Peak's rock glacier.

 This rock glacier likely has a complex origin. I believe that during the Little Ice Age, a large snowfield built up at the base of Fletcher Peak, and large granite blocks, falling from the peak's very fractured face, slid down the snowfield to its base. The accumulated blocks thus formed a crescent-shaped ring. Later, when conditions

warmed and the snowfields melted back, additional blocks fell, and these came to rest behind the crescent-shaped "dam" of earlier blocks, gradually filling in the void once occupied by the Little Ice Age snowfield.

At Vogelsang High Sierra Camp, a few snacks may be bought, or dinner or breakfast, if you have a reservation. Dispersed camping is not allowed. Rather, use a designated camping area just to the northeast at Upper Fletcher Lake. Backpackers, like camp visitors, must use the bearproof food-storage boxes. If you camp in this area, you might also take the time to explore Townsley and Hanging Basket lakes, above Upper Fletcher Lake.

Taking the Vogelsang Pass Trail from the camp, you descend slightly to ford Fletcher Creek on boulders and then begin a 600-foot ascent to the pass. The panting hiker is rewarded with increasingly good views. Fletcher Peak, with its dozens of good climbing routes, rises grandly on the left, far north is Mt. Conness, and Clouds Rest and then Half Dome come into view in the west-southwest. The trail skirts above the west shore of Vogelsang Lake as we look down on the turfy margins and the large rock island of this treeline lake. Nearer the pass, views to the north are occluded somewhat, but expansive new views appear in the south: From left to right are Parsons Peak, Simmons Peak, Mt. Maclure, the tip of Mt. Lyell behind Maclure, Mt. Florence, and, in the south, the entire Clark Range, from Triple Divide Peak on the left to Mt. Clark on the right.

From Vogelsang Pass, which has clumps of windswept whitebark pines, the trail rises briefly northeast before it switchbacks steeply down into sparse lodgepole forest. Many small streams provide moisture for thousands of lupines, with their light blue, pea-family flowers. The outlet stream from bleak Gallison Lake becomes clear as the trail begins to level off, and then you reach a flat meadow, through which the stream slowly meanders. There is a fine campsite beside this meadow, though wood fires are illegal here. After proceeding down a rutted, grassy trail for several hundred yards, you cross the Gallison outlet, top a low ridge, and make a brief, steep, rocky descent that swoops down to the meadowed valley of multibraided Lewis Creek. In this little valley, in quick succession, we boulder hop the Gallison outlet and then cross Lewis Creek on a log. In a few minutes, we reach the Bernice Lake Trail.

S **SIDE TRIP TO BERNICE LAKE:** This trail makes a steep half-mile climb to the lake. At that lake, among dwarf bilberry, red mountain heather, and stunted lodgepole and whitebark pines, you can find small, marginal campsites. Perhaps the lake's best use is as a treeline base camp for those who want to explore the snowfields and alpine lakes between here and Simmons Peak. The lake is also well located for enjoying the sight of alpenglow on the Sierra Crest. **END OF SIDE TRIP.**

In a short half mile from the Bernice Lake Trail junction, you cross a little stream, then descend to another equally small one as you wind a quarter mile through dense hemlock forest to a good campsite beside Florence Creek. This yearround creek cascades spectacularly down to the camping area over steep granite sheets, and the euphony of the water makes a fine sleeping potion if you should choose to camp here.

Leaving the densely shaded hemlock forest floor, the trail descends a series of lodgepole-dotted granite slabs, and Lewis Creek makes pleasant music in a string of chutes not far away on the right. Then, where the creek's channel narrows, the traveler will find on the left a lesson in exfoliation: granite layers peeling like an onion. One is more used to seeing this kind of peeling on Yosemite's domes, but this fine example is located on a canyon slope. As the bed of Lewis Creek becomes steeper to deliver the stream's water to the Merced River far below, the trail also becomes steeper, and your descent to middle altitudes reaches the zone of red firs and western white pines. After dipping beside the creek, the trail climbs away from it to a junction with the High Trail (Trip 75), which climbs south up to the east rim of the Merced River canyon. From here, the Lewis Creek Trail, now out of earshot of the creek, switchbacks down moderately, sometimes steeply, under a sparse cover of fir, juniper, and pine for 1 mile to a junction with the Fletcher Creek Trail. We'll be returning on this trail.

First, however, we'll hike to Merced Lake, which is visible on part of our descent toward it. Because cascading Lewis Creek is entrenched in a small gorge, our switchbacking trail keeps a short distance away from it, reaching a small flat with large Jeffrey pines before passing a small point with an excellent lake view. Half Dome stands on the distant down-canyon skyline. Open switchbacks lined with brush give way to ones with junipers and Jeffrey pines, and then, near the valley floor, to ones with white firs. Among lodgepoles on the valley floor, we come to a junction that is just 40 yards north of the Merced Lake Ranger Station. You could hike 2.25 miles up-canyon to Washburn Lake (Trip 75), which is more scenic than Merced Lake, but our Trip 47 takes us to the Merced Lake High Sierra Camp. A level, viewless mile walk west gets you to this camp and its adjacent riverside backpackers' campground. Here you will find bearproof boxes in which to store your food. Merced Lake, which is quite photogenic in late evening or in early morning, lies a quarter mile west of the High Sierra Camp. Some hikers prefer to continue from here down to Happy Isles (Trip 69), about 14 miles farther and a total distance of about 31 miles from your trailhead.

After your stay, return to the Lewis Creek Trail and ascend it to the Fletcher Creek Trail junction. Here, you turn left onto this path and descend on short switchbacks to a bridge over Lewis Creek. Just 50 yards past it is a good campsite, and then the trail enters more open slopes as it climbs moderately on a cobbled path bordered with proliferating bushes of snow bush and huckleberry oak. Just past a tributary a half mile from Lewis Creek, you have fine views of Fletcher Creek cascading down from the notch at the base of the granite dome before it leaps off a ledge in free fall. The few solitary pine trees on this otherwise blank dome testify to nature's extraordinary persistence.

At the notch, your trail levels off and reaches the Babcock Lake Trail.

 **SIDE TRIP TO BABCOCK LAKE:** This optional half-mile lateral trail arcs west to nearby Fletcher Creek, then northwest up to a low ridge. From it, the trail goes southwest, crosses a second low ridge, then reaches the lake's northeast end. Among fair lodgepole-shaded campsites by the southeast shore, the trail dies out short of the lake's tiny island. Better campsites are on the opposite shore. Suitable diving slabs are along both shores of this fairly warm lake. **END OF SIDE TRIP.**

From the Babcock Lake Trail junction, the sandy Fletcher Creek Trail ascends steadily through a moderate forest cover, staying just east of Fletcher Creek. After 0.75 mile, this route breaks out into the open and begins to rise more steeply via rocky switchbacks. From these, one can see nearby in the north the outlet stream of Emeric Lake—though not the lake itself, which is behind a dome just to the right of the outlet's notch.

A ALTERNATE TRIP TO EMERIC LAKE: If you wish to camp at Emeric Lake—and it's a fine place—leave the trail here for a short-cut route to it. First cross Fletcher Creek at a safe spot (do not attempt this in high water), and then climb along the outlet creek's west side and camp above the lake's northwest shore. The next morning, circle the head of the lake and find a trail at the base of the low granite ridge at the northeast corner of the lake. Follow this trail a half mile northeast to a scissors junction in Fletcher Creek valley. **END OF ALTERNATE TRIP.**

Cascading Fletcher Creek backdropped by an impressive dome

If you choose not to camp at Emeric Lake, continue up the trail into a long meadow guarded in the west by a highly polished knoll and presided over in the east by huge Vogelsang Peak. When you come to the scissors junction, take the left-hand fork up the valley and follow this rocky-dusty trail through the forest fringe of the long meadow that straddles Fletcher Creek. This trail climbs farther from the meadow and passes northwest of a bald prominence that sits in the center of the upper valley of Fletcher and Emeric creeks, separating the two. You might look for isolated camping sites in this vicinity, particularly above the far bank of Emeric Creek. Camping is not allowed at Boothe Lake. After topping a minor summit, your trail descends slightly and then winds on almost level ground past several lovely ponds that are interconnected in early season. Next is a lakelet, 100 yards in diameter, which would offer good swimming in some years. Just beyond it, the trail traverses northeast to a little swale with another possible swimming pond before reaching an overlook above Boothe Lake. Your trail then contours along meadowy slopes just east of and above the lake, passing a junction with a rutted use trail down to the lake. About a quarter mile farther, you pass another trail descending to this lake. Just ahead is Tuolumne Pass, and the junction with the trail to Vogelsang, from which we retrace our steps 7 miles north back to Tuolumne Meadows.

TRIP **48**

Tuolumne Meadows-Vogelsang-Lyell Canyon Semiloop

Ⓜ � BP

DISTANCE: 20.3 miles semiloop

ELEVATIONS: 8660'/10,600'
+2640'/-2640'/±5280'

SEASON: Mid-July to early October

USE: Heavy

MAPS: *Tioga Pass, Vogelsang Peak*

TRAIL LOG:

1.7	Rafferty Creek Trail
6.9	Tuolumne Pass
7.7	Vogelsang High Sierra Camp
11.3	Ireland Lake Trail
14.2	Floor of Lyell Canyon
18.6	Rafferty Creek Trail
20.3	Trailhead

INTRODUCTION: This is a popular weekend hike because you can reach the Vogelsang area in only a morning's walk, which gives you a whole afternoon to explore its half-dozen nearby lakes or more distant Emeric Lake. The second day's walk is mostly open, giving the hiker many interesting, diverse views. If you are a strong hiker, consider dayhiking this route, which has only about half of the elevation gain and loss, as does the popular dayhike to the summit of Half Dome (Trip 80).

DIRECTIONS TO THE TRAILHEAD: Drive to the large parking lot just beyond the start of the Tuolumne Meadows Lodge spur road. This road is reached by driving 0.6 mile northeast from the Tuolumne Meadows Campground entrance. During most of the summer, this large lot, immediately west of the spur road, has a small booth that dispenses wilderness permits. Trail begins in map section F3.

DESCRIPTION: Start on the John Muir Trail, which runs beside the Dana Fork of the Tuolumne River just yards south of the Tuolumne Meadows Lodge Road. On the trail, you hike 0.3 mile up the Dana Fork to a junction with a spur trail that goes to the west end of the lodge's parking lot. From this junction, you bridge the Dana Fork and, after a brief walk upstream, you reach a junction with a trail to the Gaylor Lakes.

Veering right, the John Muir Trail leads over a slight rise and descends to the Lyell Fork, where there are two bridges. About 70 yards past the bridges, we meet a trail that comes about 0.75 mile up the river from the east end of the Tuolumne Meadows Campground. Turn left (east) onto it, and skirt around a long, lovely section of the meadow. Going through a dense forest cover of lodgepole pine, our route reaches a junction on the west bank of Rafferty Creek, from where the John Muir Trail (Trip 49) continues east, crossing the creek's two major branches.

Our route, the Rafferty Creek Trail, turns right and immediately begins a climb south, where the grade is moderate as often as it is steep. Fairly well shaded by lodgepole pines, the climb eases well under a mile. Then, as the ascent decreases to a gentle grade, we pass through high, boulder-strewn meadows that offer good views eastward to reddish-brown Mt. Dana and Mt. Gibbs, and gray-white Mammoth Peak. Soon, the trail dips close to Rafferty Creek, and, after 2 miles of near-creek hiking, the gently climbing trail passes near the edge of a large meadow and continues its long, gentle ascent through a sparse forest of lodgepole pines.

In the next mile, you cross several seasonal creeks, and, about 3.5 miles up the Rafferty Creek Trail, you reach an even larger meadow. Through this, you ascend easily up-canyon, having backward views north to the Sierra Crest between Tioga

Pass and Mt. Conness and views ahead to cliff-bound, dark-banded Fletcher Peak and Vogelsang Peak to the right of it. After about 1.5 miles, you reach Tuolumne Pass, a major gap in the Cathedral Range. From here, you can hike southwest to nearby Boothe Lake or 3.7 miles to Emeric Lake, or you can follow this Trip 48 on a traverse south 0.8 mile to Vogelsang High Sierra Camp.

Here, a few snacks may be bought, or dinner or breakfast, if you have a reservation. Dispersed camping is not allowed. Rather, use a designated camping area just to the northeast at Upper Fletcher Lake. Backpackers, like camp visitors, must use the bearproof food-storage boxes. If you camp in this area you might also take the time to explore Townsley and Hanging Basket lakes, above Upper Fletcher Lake.

A **ALTERNATE TRIP TO IRELAND LAKE:** A good exercise in fairly easy cross-country hiking is to go to Ireland Lake from Upper Fletcher Lake. First, follow its inlet creek up to Townsley Lake, then climb northeast from it to a large, broad plateau. Strike east across this, and then climb up to the low part of a long ridge north of Peak 11500, a high point on the Cathedral Range. From the long ridge, the descent southeast to Ireland Lake is obvious. **END OF ALTERNATE TRIP.**

The trail, however, leaves Upper Fletcher Lake, climbs a half mile steadily up to an indeterminable drainage divide, eases its gradient, and passes through a flat-floored gully whose walls contain large, blocky feldspar crystals so typical of Cathedral Peak granodiorite. Beyond the gully, a far-ranging view opens, and, on a large flat below us, lies spreading, shallow, windswept Evelyn Lake, to whose outlet we now descend. The momentary ascent to the lake is worth it for the geologically inclined. In the process of solifluction, rising subsurface ice has lifted blocks on both sides of this unique lake's outlet to form a low, natural dam, slightly raising the lake's level.

[A] **ALTERNATE TRIP TO TUOLUMNE MEADOWS:** Hikers who would like to try a slightly adventurous, shorter alternative to the Lyell Canyon Trail as a route back to Tuolumne Meadows can descend the outlet creek along the west slope of its canyon. You pass through a beautiful, large, secluded meadow and walk beside delightful stretches of creek. Eventually, on the west side of the stream, you see a cliff that gradually diminishes in height. When the height has diminished to about 10 feet, find a place to scramble up the cliff and then walk a few hundred feet west to find the Rafferty Creek Trail. **END OF ALTERNATE TRIP.**

Leaving desolate Evelyn Lake and its population of Belding ground squirrels, we take the trail east, and then climb through an open forest of stunted whitebark pines before dropping to a smaller, unnamed lake. Though higher than Evelyn Lake, it has some whitebark pines nearby, providing protection from the wind for those who camp here. About a half-mile climb northeast from this shallow lake takes you up to a low point on a long, north-south crest, situated just above 2 miles in elevation. You have now left the Cathedral Peak pluton (a large, granitic body) behind and tread upon another pluton—one that lacks the conspicuous feldspar crystals. Descending from this viewful crest and its brushy whitebark pines, follow a 0.6-mile trail segment that contorts down slab after bedrock slab, bringing you to a junction with the 1.5-mile-long Ireland Lake Trail.

[S] **SIDE TRIP TO IRELAND LAKE:** Lying beneath both granitic and metamorphic peaks, this large alpine lake is unsuited for camping unless you've brought along a tent to protect you from the wind, which can become quite strong in the afternoon and into the evening. Also, the lake is not a good locality when thunderstorms are threatening. However, for those who like truly alpine environments, 10,735-foot Ireland Lake may be desirable, since it can offer dramatic lighting, as the sun's early morning rays strike high peaks and ridges to the north and northeast. The lands around the lake are both rocky and quite fragile, so practice environmentally sound camping. **END OF SIDE TRIP.**

Starting east from the trail junction, we soon descend gently south for half mile, then angle northeast to make a long, 2-mile descent that usually stays within earshot of Ireland Creek. We begin this descent first along its tributary creek, and we are in a dense forest of lodgepole and whitebark pines, but the latter give way before we reach the flat floor of Lyell Canyon, more than 1500 feet above the trail junction. On the floor of Lyell Canyon, the trail ends at a junction with the John Muir Trail. Look for many near-trail campsites in this part of the canyon.

The walk back to Tuolumne Meadows through this nearly level canyon is very easy—good therapy for the shocked knees you may have incurred on the descent you've just completed. We head north, down-canyon, and, from the more open parts of the trail, one has excellent views of the Kuna Crest as it slopes up to the southeast. The river itself has delighted generations of mountain photographers. In the meadows of Lyell Canyon, you can see Ragged Peak and its crest, to the northwest. The silent walker may come upon grazing deer in the meadows and an occasional marmot that has ventured from the rocky outcrops. Fields of wildflowers color the grasslands from early to late season, but the best time of the year for seeing this color is usually July.

After about 3 miles, the trail, which has become increasingly northwest oriented, begins to curve west where it climbs between two resistant granite outcrops. The trail traverses alternating wet-meadow and forest sections, with clouds of mosquitoes before August. Just before the Rafferty Creek Trail, 4.4 miles from the previous junction, you cross two branches of Rafferty Creek. The second ford may be difficult in early season. From the junction, retrace your steps 1.7 miles back to your trailhead.

TRIP **49**

Tuolumne Meadows to Silver Lake via John Muir Trail

Ⓜ ⟋ BP

DISTANCE: 25.9 miles point to point

ELEVATIONS: 7240'/11,060'
+3420'/-4850'/±8270'

SEASON: Mid-July to early October

USE: Heavy

MAPS: *Tioga Pass, Vogelsang Peak, Koip Peak, Mt. Ritter*

TRAIL LOG:

1.7 Rafferty Creek Trail
6.1 Trail to Vogelsang High Sierra Camp
9.0 Lyell Base Camp
13.0 Donohue Pass
15.4 Lower Marie Lake Trail
16.4 Rush Creek Trail
18.9 Trail to Weber and Sullivan lakes
20.4 Trail to Agnew Pass
21.1 Alger Lakes Trail
23.6 Agnew Lake dam
25.9 Silver Lake Trailhead

INTRODUCTION: This section of the John Muir Trail is described in its easiest direction—southbound—to the park's border. Then the description goes out to the first trailhead, although most hikers go no farther than upper Lyell Canyon. If you plan to hike Yosemite's entire section of the John Muir Trail, you'll want to start from Silver Lake, which is easier than starting from Yosemite Valley. You could start at Agnew Meadows or Reds Meadow, but the road to them is restricted and, being deeply buried by winter snow, is one of the last roads to open in the Yosemite region. Doing the whole walk from Silver Lake to Yosemite

Valley, you cover 51 miles. Following this hike's description in reverse, you can get to eastern Tuolumne Meadows, and then you walk west past the base of Lembert Dome to the iron-stained Soda Springs. From there, walk south across the western meadows, cross the Tioga Road, then, in a few minutes, traverse west to the start of Trip 51, which guides you to Yosemite Valley.

DIRECTIONS TO THE TRAILHEAD: Drive to the large parking lot just beyond the start of the Tuolumne Meadows Lodge spur road. This road is reached by driving 0.6 mile northeast from the Tuolumne Meadows Campground entrance. During most of the summer, this large lot, immediately west of the spur road, has a small booth that dispenses wilderness permits. Trail begins in map section F3.

If you are starting at Silver Lake, go 60 yards west on the spur road that is opposite the entrance to the Silver Lake Campground. This entrance is on the June Lake Loop Toad (State Route 158). From Hwy. 395, northbound drivers reach this spot by driving on the loop road (past June Lake) for 8.5 miles, while southbound drivers reach it by driving (past Grant Lake) for 7.1 miles.

DESCRIPTION: Start on the John Muir Trail, which runs beside the Dana Fork of the Tuolumne River just yards south of the Tuolumne Meadows Lodge Road. On the trail, you hike 0.3 mile up the Dana Fork to a junction with a spur trail that goes to the west end of the lodge's parking lot. From this junction, you bridge the Dana Fork and, after a brief walk upstream, you reach a junction with a trail to the Gaylor Lakes.

Veering right, the John Muir Trail leads over a slight rise and descends to the Lyell Fork, where there are two bridges. About 70 yards past the bridges, we meet a trail that comes about 0.75 mile up the river from the east end of the Tuolumne Meadows Campground, turn left (east) onto it, and skirt around a long, lovely section of the meadow. Going through a dense forest cover of lodgepole pine, our route reaches a junction on the west bank of Rafferty Creek, from where the Rafferty Creek Trail (Trip 48) climbs south.

Here, you head left and cross two branches of Rafferty Creek. The first ford may be difficult in early season. East of the creek, the trail traverses alternating wet-meadow and forest sections—with clouds of mosquitoes before August—then veers southward, climbing between two resistant granite outcrops. The silent walker may come upon grazing deer in the meadows and an occasional marmot that has ventured from the rocky outcrops. Fields of wildflowers color the grasslands from early to late season, but the best time of the year for seeing this color is usually July. From the more open parts of the trail, you have excellent views of the Kuna Crest as it slopes up to the southeast. The river itself has delighted generations of mountain photographers. In the meadows of Lyell Canyon, you can see Ragged Peak and its crest, to the northwest. About 4.4 miles past the last junction, your nearly level route passes a southwest-climbing trail to Vogelsang High Sierra Camp (Trip 48). Look for many near-trail campsites in this part of the canyon.

Beyond, the John Muir Trail fords multibranched Ireland Creek, passes below Potter Point, and ascends gently for 3 miles to the fair campsites at Lyell Base Camp, just beyond cascading Kuna Creek. This camp, surrounded on three sides by steep canyon walls, marks the end of the mead-owed sections of Lyell Canyon and is the traditional first-night stopping place for those touring the Muir Trail south from Tuolumne Meadows.

From Lyell Base Camp, the lodgepole-shaded trail ascends the steep southern terminal wall of Lyell Canyon, leaving an understory of sagebrush behind before reaching a granite bench. On it, you pass a few campsites just before the Maclure Creek-Lyell Fork confluence. Then the route crosses a bridge to the east side and switchbacks up to some popular campsites among clumps of whitebark pines just

before recrossing the fork at the north edge of a subalpine meadow. The rocky under-footing beyond the crossing takes you up past the foot of superb alpine meadows, from which views of the glaciers on the north faces of Mt. Maclure and Mt. Lyell are superlative. Hikers who wish to obtain a more intimate view or to ascend to these ice fields via the lake-dotted basin at their feet should take the ducked route that leaves our trail where we turn east and recross the infant Lyell Fork at the north end of a boulder-dotted pond.

From this ford, the John Muir Trail winds steeply up rocky going and eventually veers southeast up a long, straight fracture to Donohue Pass (11,056′) at the crest of the Sierra and on the park's border. Just before and just after the pass—not at it—one has great views of the Sierra Crest, the Cathedral Range to the northwest, and the Ritter Range to the southeast. At the broad pass, we enter Ansel Adams Wilderness. On a sometimes obscure trail, we descend northeast away from a prominent peak and go past blocks and over slabs before turning east for a seasonally wet slog across the tundra-and-stone floor of an alpine basin. West of this basin is a conspicuous saddle, which northwest-bound, early-season hikers too often mistake for Donohue Pass. When the JMT is largely snowbound, these hikers will have to remember to hike south-west up toward the prominent peak until the real Donohue Pass becomes obvious.

Beyond the alpine basin, whitebark pines rapidly increase in size and numbers as we drop farther. Generally heading southeast, the JMT winds excessively in an oft-futile attempt to avoid the boulders and bogs of the near-treeline environment. Three miles from Donohue Pass, you arrive at the Marie Lakes' outlet creek, which can be crossed at a jump-across spot slightly downstream. Immediately beyond the creek, down at about 10,050 feet elevation, we meet the Lower Marie Lake Trail, which climbs southwest.

[S] **SIDE TRIP TO LOWER MARIE LAKE:** About 0.8 mile farther along the JMT is the Rush Creek Forks area, popular with backpackers since it is sheltered. For those wanting a taste of solitude, Lower Marie Lake is a possibility. However, be aware that since it is alpine and just below the Sierran crest, campsites will be exposed to possible high winds, as well as to potential lightning strikes when thunderstorms are passing through. The 1.5-mile trail generally is moderately graded as it climbs about 800 feet to the lake, doing quite a bit of switch-backing and winding as it ascends first up slopes, and then up a ridge to a point just east of Lower Marie Lake's outlet. At about 0.6 mile long, the lake is one of our area's larger ones, although it is dwarfed by popular Thousand Island Lake, along the JMT about 3 miles to the east. If you've been to it, you might find 10,856-foot Lower Marie Lake similar, for it has a similar shape, a crenulated lakeshore, and many islands. **END OF SIDE TRIP.**

From the trail junction, we parallel the Marie Lakes' outlet creek 0.3 mile downstream to a low ridge. On it, you get your last good views of—east to west—Banner Peak, Mt. Ritter, and Mt. Davis, and then you descend via short, steep switchbacks to a junction with the Rush Creek Trail. This junction is in the Rush Creek Forks area, where campsites must be at least 100 feet from any creek or trail. Although you have left Yosemite, you have not left its black bears, for they have spilled beyond the park's boundaries in search of humans' food. If you camp here, expect to have these nighttime prowlers.

Among lodgepoles, you leave the John Muir Trail to follow the Rush Creek trail 9.5 miles down to Silver Lake. Immediately, you ford two of the creek's many forks, and then descend 0.6 mile to a small campsite on the west shore of Waugh Lake. Your trail hugs this lake, then, in about 10 minutes, you pass your second lodgepole-shaded, lakeshore campsite. After an easy mile hike beyond it, some of the distance being

past sagebrush, you leave the lake, switch-back down below the base of its dam and immediately meet a south-climbing trail to Weber and Sullivan lakes.

Paralleling Rush Creek, we continue down-canyon—now on a lodgepole-lined, closed service road of the Southern California Edison Company—and, in a few minutes, we reach a large campsite. Another campsite is passed just where the road leaves Rush Creek to climb through a 30-foot-high, glacier-polished granite gap. Beyond it, you hike down toward Rush Creek, curve northeast and, in a quarter mile, reach a short spur trail that goes south to a large creekside campsite. On the road, you quickly meet a junction with a trail to Agnew Pass. At this junction, turn left, then climb north past a pond and a closer, larger one, Billy Lake. In a quarter mile, top a low notch in a ridge that is composed of metavolcanic rocks. A short, steep descent east follows, and then a gentle one north. The road quickly descends to the west shore of Gem Lake, but, before it does so, you leave it to take a trail that traverses north a quarter mile to Crest Creek. Here, among an abundance of small-lodgepole-shaded campsites, you meet the Alger Lakes Trail.

[A] **ALTERNATE TRIP BACK TO YOUR TRAIL-HEAD:** By following Trip 51 in reverse, you can take this extremely scenic trail back into Yosemite National Park. From the Mono Trail's trailhead, you descend the Tioga Road 2.6 miles west to the Gaylor Lakes Trail, turn south onto it, and immediately cross the Tuolumne River's Dana Fork, which you parallel, usually at a distance, for 2 miles down to a junction with the John Muir Trail. This is just upstream from a bridge over the Dana Fork, and you retrace your steps 0.3 mile to your trailhead parking lot. This high-altitude loop is 41.5 miles long and is for those who want to escape the crowds at the expense of some strenuous climbing. **END OF ALTERNATE TRIP.**

In late season, we can rock hop Crest Creek, but, normally, you must cross it on a log. Aspens—brilliant in early fall—join ranks with lodgepoles in shading a creek-side campsite. Farther east, aspens give way to sagebrush, junipers, Jeffrey pines, and even an occasional whitebark pine. Your trail generally stays above Gem Lake's steep shoreline, then climbs to one ridge before descending and climbing to a second one—this one above the lake's dam. This ridge and the bedrock north and south of it are composed mostly of Paleozoic-age sediments that have been metamorphosed, usually to hornfels. These ancient rocks are roughly 100 times older than the dark andesite flows we see above Gem Lake's forested south slopes. These thick, horizontal flows originated in conjunction with faulting, which began about 3 million years ago, and which caused lands east of the Sierra Crest to subside.

We leave Gem Lake behind and, for a spell, Ansel Adams Wilderness, as we descend to the Agnew Lake dam. On this descent, mountain mahogany dominates the dry, south-facing slopes, in contrast to the forested, north-facing ones just below Agnew Pass. In the dam's vicinity grow giant blazing stars, whose oversized yellow flowers will be blooming for late-season hikers.

Beyond the dam, switchbacks lead you north down alongside a tramway, which you cross twice, and then descend slopes toward Silver Lake. At first, these slopes have mountain mahogany, juniper, and even pinyon pine, but then, not far beyond a small waterfall, they are gradually replaced with waist-high vegetation.

Draining west into Silver Lake is Reversed Creek, which has an interesting history. Glaciers originating near the Sierra Crest descended to the large canyon we're in, then split into two lobes, each going on one side of Reversed Peak. Each glacial lobe built up a considerable terminal moraine at its snout, and when these lobes finally retreated, a lake formed behind each moraine. The waters backing up behind the June Lake moraine were not able to breach it; rather, they overflowed southwest into Gull Lake and beyond. Today, these waters continue to flow in that direction—directly opposite that of the glacier's flow—as Reversed Creek. It is also reversed in the sense that it flows toward the range's crest rather than away from it.

Near Silver Lake's west corner, our trail almost touches the June Lake Loop Road, and then, in just over 0.3 mile, it arcs behind Silver Lake Resort and fords several branches of Alger Creek. It finally traverses behind Silver Lake Trailer Court to quickly end at the Silver Lake Trailhead parking area amid sagebrush, mule ears, rabbitbrush, and bitterbrush.

Mt. Lyell above Lyell Canyon, south of Evelyn Lake Trail

TRIP 50

Dana Meadows to Mono Pass

Ⓜ ↗ DH

DISTANCE: 8 miles out and back

ELEVATIONS: 9590′/10,610′
+1160′/-240′/±2800′

SEASON: Mid-July to mid-October

USE: Moderate

MAPS: *Tioga Pass, Mount Dana, Koip Peak*

TRAIL LOG:

2.2 Spillway Lake Trail
3.5 Parker Pass Trail
4.0 Mono Pass

INTRODUCTION: This dayhike to a historic pass on the Sierra Crest is great for alpine scenery, for the views improve constantly and culminate at the pass, where you can gaze down the great gash of Bloody Canyon to the vast, high desert east of the Sierra.

DIRECTIONS TO THE TRAILHEAD: Mono Pass Trailhead, which is 5.6 miles east of the Tuolumne Meadows Campground, and 1.4 miles south of Tioga Pass. Trail begins in map section F3.

DESCRIPTION: Starting under a dense canopy of lodgepole pines, you leave the trailhead, initially descending on a trail that once was a short part of a historic route across this region of the Sierra. In a meadow a quarter mile from the trailhead, lodgepoles, as elsewhere, ceaselessly attempt to invade this meadow, but wet years raise the water table and this may directly or indirectly kill them. These needles of these young trees are also suscepti-

ble to brown-felt fungus and to icy winter winds. About a half mile from the trailhead, you cross Dana Meadows creek and Dana Fork just above their confluence. Beyond these two crossings, your trail climbs to the crest of a low moraine, crosses two more, and then, near Parker Pass Creek, comes to the ruins of a pioneer log cabin. Sagebrush intermingles with lodgepoles as you pass creekside meadows that may have deer browsing in them. About halfway to Mono Pass, you come to a junction with the Spillway Lake Trail.

Ⓢ **SIDE TRIP TO SPILLWAY LAKE:** This trail climbs 1.9 miles gently up along Parker Pass Creek to shallow, meadow-bordered Spillway Lake (camping prohibited). This and other lakes of the Mono Pass-Tioga Pass area have California gulls as frequent visitors; these birds nest on islands in large, alkaline Mono Lake (Trip 52). From Spillway Lake, you could hike cross-country east up to alpine Parker Pass, then head back on a trail to the Mono Pass area. **END OF SIDE TRIP.**

Our trail up to the Spillway Lake Trail junction has been easy, but now it climbs nearly 700 feet, passing the ruins of a second pioneer cabin, on the right, just a quarter mile before the Parker Pass Trail junction. From that junction, near a large whitebark pine, Trip 51 describes that trail all the way to Gem Lake. After a quarter mile of nearly level hiking, our trail passes a lakelet situated between two ponds.

From the east shore of the lakelet, a trail starts south toward five old cabins but dies out. However, the cabins just south above you are easily reached. These cabins,  constructed from local whitebark pines, once housed workers on the nearby Golden Crown and Ella Bloss gold mines, both long defunct. If you visit these cabins, you'll get a good view north at Mt. Gibbs' south shoulder. Note the difference between its lower slopes and steeper higher ones. Whitebark pines are able to grow on the lower slopes, but not on the unstable upper ones. You'll also note that the upper

ORIGINS OF THE MONO TRAIL

Our hike has followed only a small portion of the Mono Trail, which is an old Indian trail that started near Cascade Creek, high above westernmost Yosemite Valley. This trail started like today's eastbound El Capitan Trail, but continued northeast along Bluejay Creek to Yosemite Creek, then up to Porcupine Flat, where it took a route similar to that of the later Old Tioga Road.

It was not discovered by Americans until 1852, when Army Lieutenant Tredwell Moore pursued Yosemite's Chief Teneiya band through Tuolumne Meadows and over Mono Pass. He failed to catch them.

From Mono Pass, the Mono Trail continued down Bloody Canyon, which may have been named for the reddish-color bedrock of metamorphosed sediments, but more likely was named for the treachery of this canyon. In 1864, William Brewer and Charles Hoffmann—two younger members of Josiah Whitney's State Geological Survey— descended Bloody Canyon. Brewer later said of it:

> You would all pronounce it utterly inaccessible to horses, yet pack trains come down, but the bones of several horses or mules and the stench of another told that all had not passed safely. The trail comes down 3000 feet in less than 4 miles, over rocks and loose stones, in narrow canyons and along precipices. It was a bold man who first took a horse up there. The horses were so cut by sharp rocks that they named it "Bloody Canyon," and it has held the name—and it is appropriate—part of the way the rocks are literally sprinkled with blood from the animals.

Today, this trail is still a steep descent over rocks and loose stones, but it is considerably safer. Upper Sardine Lake, only 0.75 mile away by this trail, is worth the effort of the 220-foot drop to it, but beyond it, a big drop to cold, deep Lower Sardine Lake makes for an exhausting return hike.

slopes have patterned ground, which indicates slope movement. In Yosemite's alpine areas, mass movement takes place only on slopes of metamorphic rocks, not those of granite, because ice wedging breaks metamorphic bedrock into many small, unstable rocks, whereas it heaps granite into large, relatively immobile blocks.

Just east of the cabins' spur trail, you encounter Summit Lake, straddling often breezy 10,600-foot Mono Pass. The lake appears to lie immediately east of the pass—the park's boundary—but careful scouting among the lake's west-end willows will reveal that the lake does indeed have a west-flowing outlet, as well as a more obvious east-flowing one. Nesting beneath the willows are white-crowned sparrows, which are usually seen with Brewer's blackbirds. The blackbirds nest at lower elevations during the spring but usually migrate up to these heights by the time the Mono Trail is snow free.

Mono Pass and the shoulder of Mt. Gibbs

TRIP 51

Dana Meadows to Silver Lake via Parker Pass

Ⓜ / BP

DISTANCE: 20 miles point to point

ELEVATIONS: 7240′/12,270′
+3440′/-5890′/±9330′

SEASON: Mid-July to early October

USE: Moderate

MAPS: *Tioga Pass, Mount Dana, Koip Peak*

TRAIL LOG:

3.5	Parker Pass Trail
5.2	Parker Pass
8.4	Koip Peak Pass
11.1	Alger Lakes
13.1	Gem Pass
15.2	Rush Creek Trail
17.7	Agnew Lake dam
20.0	Silver Lake Trailhead

INTRODUCTION: Knowledgeable backpackers prefer this route to the popular, nearby section of the John Muir Trail (Trip 49). Being mostly along metamorphic terrain, this route is certainly more colorful, and, if you stay high—at or above treeline—you'll notice a wild aspect about it. At these elevations, dark glasses and sunscreen are a must. This route is no place to be caught in a lightning storm or a snowstorm, so only weather-wise backpackers should attempt it. However, the 5.25 miles to Parker Pass makes a fine high-altitude dayhike for those in good shape. Those in excellent shape can dayhike the entire 20-mile route, which is a lot more down than up. This definitely is not a hike for those with bad knees.

DIRECTIONS TO THE TRAILHEAD: Mono Pass Trailhead, which is 5.6 miles east of the Tuolumne Meadows Campground, and 1.4 miles south of Tioga Pass. Trail begins in map section F3.

If you are starting at Silver Lake, go 60 yards west on the spur road that is opposite the entrance to the Silver Lake Campground. This entrance is on the June Lake Loop Road (State Route 158). From Hwy. 395, northbound drivers reach this spot by driving on the loop road (past June Lake) for 8.5 miles, while southbound drivers reach it by driving (past Grant Lake) for 7.1 miles.

DESCRIPTION: Follow Trip 59 3.5 miles up to the Parker Pass Trail junction just a half mile short of broad, deep Mono Pass. From a large whitebark pine near the junction, strike south-southwest 300 yards across a meadow, following ducks that guide you to a resumption of obvious tread. Continuing in the same direction, climb to the crest of a broad moraine that here and there has rusty exposures of Triassic-period metavolcanics (metamorphosed volcanic rocks). On this ascent, you pass many whitebark pines that are reduced to shrub height, and so get largely unobstructed views that include shallow Spillway Lake, lying at the base of the Kuna Crest. Note how the granitic upper slopes of this crest differ not only in color but in shape and texture from the lower metamorphic slopes.

Up at treeline, we see the deep cleft of Parker Pass more than a mile before we attain it. Stunted whitebarks and yellow-blossomed bush cinquefoils yield to mats of alpine willow—a favorite summer haunt of white-crowned sparrows. These bushes yield to sedges and, finally, at the broad, signed pass, to coarse gravel. A low, broad moraine south of you hides barren Parker Pass Lake, and it also provides a suitable habitat for marmots. Briefly, during midsummer, a marmot's sole food source may be Sierra wallflowers and Brewer's lupines. The first species can turn the moraine's slopes bright yellow and mask the presence of the equally prevalent lupine. Other plant species appear both before and after these two, and all provide the marmot with a diverse selection, which it readily consumes before going into hibernation in October. Our climb toward the pass is low gradient and uneventful, and it would be rated easy were it not for the high elevation. In due course, we reach 11,110-foot Parker Pass, where a well-deserved break is in store. Or, you may climb upward.

S **SIDE TRIP TO MT. LEWIS:** Starting from Parker Pass, you can wander first north about 0.75 mile up to an 11,800-foot crest that offers superlative views down Bloody Canyon and beyond to the Mono Craters and Mono Lake. If you are a peakbagger, follow the crest another 0.75 mile southeast up to the top of windswept 12,296-foot Mt. Lewis. However, don't attempt this technically easy but thin-air climb if the weather looks threatening. **END OF SIDE TRIP.**

At Parker Pass, backpackers enter Ansel Adams Wilderness and leave all vestiges of the granitic Yosemite landscape behind. Descending on Paleozoic-era metasediments, they first cross an outlet creek from two nearby ponds, recross it at a third, and then traverse southeast toward a series of ominous-looking switchbacks that climb the northwest slope of Parker Peak. About 0.75 mile beyond the pass, you cross a seasonally churning tributary that gets its vigor from a permanent snowfield lodged high on the slopes between Kuna and Koip peaks. Just past this tributary, the deep canyon cleft between Mt. Lewis and Parker Peak begins to open, and through it we see the Mono Craters (these days the Mono Domes) and the distant White Mountains.

A half mile closer to trail's end, you reach an alpine tarn, from which point you can gaze straight down the enormous Parker Creek cleft. Parker Lake is almost hidden, but larger Grant Lake, with its giant lateral moraines, is easily seen; This stupendous view may divert one's interest from the seemingly ordinary tarn.

This pond is, however, very un-Sierran, for near its outlet, the shallow, rocky bottom is patterned with a network of polygon stone rings. Repeated freezing and melting of ice over hundreds of years have separated the coarse rocks from the finer particles. If you step in the middle of one of these polygons—usually a hexagon—you'll sink into clay. This phenomenon is not seen at many High Sierra ponds because they typically exist in granitic terrain. This pond, however, is in metamorphic terrain, and at high elevations like here, metamorphic rock is shattered by ice wedging, which breaks it into many small, unstable blocks.

Beyond this tarn, we are confronted with a quarter-mile net vertical climb to Koip Peak Pass. First, we climb to our second snowfield-fed Parker Creek tributary. Panting up to the first of many switchbacks, take a breather, scan the ever-improving panorama, and now see most of large, alkaline Mono Lake and the summits of Mt. Gibbs and Mt. Conness, the latter rising above Parker Pass. During July, you may see the unmistakable sky pilot, a blue-petaled polemonium that thrives in the bleakest alpine environments. Around Yosemite, you'll rarely find it growing below 11,000 feet. Sharing this harsh habitat are members of the Draba genus, which has a dozen hard-to-key species that exist above treeline in the Sierra Nevada. You'll note that its yellow flowers are virtually identical to those of the Sierra wallflower, often seen west of Parker Pass, for both are mustards.

Finally, switchbacks yield to a gradually easing ascent southwest to shallow Koip Peak Pass, which at 12,270 feet is one of the Sierra's highest trail passes. Before early August, snowfields may cover parts of the trail to the pass, and they could present a problem, since you have 600 feet of steep, potentially fatal slopes below you.

Leaving the pass, you exchange views of Mt. Conness, Mt. Gibbs, Mt. Dana, and Mt. Lewis for ones of the Alger Lakes, the June Lake ski area, volcanic Mammoth Mountain, distant Lake Crowley, and the distant central Sierra Nevada crest. While topographic constraints made a string of short switchbacks necessary for your ascent, they are lacking for your descent, which is a pleasant, occasionally switchbacking drop deep into the Alger Lakes basin. As the trail's gradient eases, you cross Alger Creek, and then, with a low, fresh-looking moraine on your right, parallel the creek for 0.75 mile before crossing a multicrested moraine and descending past cairns for a quarter mile to a point between the two fairly large Alger Lakes. Only 50 yards and a 2-foot drop separate the two treeline lakes, and on the bedrock landmass that separates them, you can set up camp  among its windblown whitebark pines. These will be the first partly sheltered sites you'll encounter on this hike, for no camping is allowed in Yosemite's Dana Fork drainage and all possible sites this side of Parker Pass are above treeline. Immediately

beyond Lower Alger Lake's outlet you'll also find a trailside campsite.

From the outlet, we climb up our moraine's low crest, glancing back across the open terrain at the dramatic setting of this glaciated, somber-toned rock basin, which has metasediments composing the northeast canyon wall and metavolcanics composing the southwest one. Now 6 miles from Parker Pass and 4 miles from Gem Lake, you follow the generally open moraine's crest south past a nearby lakelet, then descend steeply about 300 feet to a second one, along whose fragile shore one should not camp. Along this morainal route, you'll probably note a flat-topped mass standing immediately east of Gem Pass. Your route ends near its base.

Your second lakelet has large rocks, and these form small islands that testify to the instability of a nearby cliff. Just 250 yards beyond this tarn, you enter your first stand of lodgepoles. Among its protective confines is a campsite, on the left, which is certainly the place you'll want to stay if you have to wait out a lightning storm. In only a minute's walk toward Gem Lake, you'll come to a shallow pond—the camp's closest water source. Beyond this pond, you climb for a half mile to forested Gem Pass, while Alger Creek, hundreds of feet below you, drops out of sight to your final goal, Silver Lake. Shortly before Gem Pass, the trail forks. The left branch descends, only to climb again, but it may be the better of the two in early season, when the snow is piled deep. From 10,500-foot Gem Pass, we have our first views of the famous Ritter Range, dominated by Mt. Ritter and Banner Peak. Now under a continual canopy of protective forest, we descend first through whitebark pines and then lodgepoles, cross Crest Creek after 0.75 mile, and switchback down alongside it, reaching well-used campsites above Gem Lake after a 2-mile, 1400-foot drop. Among these campsites, you'll meet the Rush Creek Trail, on which those on Trip 49 have descended east to our junction.

A marmot surveys its domain in an alpine fell-field near Parker Pass.

In late season, we can rock hop Crest Creek, but, normally, you must cross it on a log. Aspens—brilliant in early fall—join ranks with lodgepoles in shading a creekside campsite. Farther east, aspens give way to sagebrush, junipers, Jeffrey pines, and even to an occasional whitebark pine. Your Rush Creek Trail generally stays above Gem Lake's steep shoreline, and then it climbs to one ridge before descending and climbing to a second one above the lake's dam. This ridge and the bedrock north and south of it are composed mostly of Paleozoic-age sediments that have been metamorphosed, usually to hornfels. These ancient rocks are roughly 100 times older than the dark andesite flows we see above Gem Lake's forested south slopes. These thick, horizontal flows originated in conjunction with faulting, which began about 3 million years ago, and which caused lands east of the Sierra Crest to subside.

We leave Gem Lake behind and, for a spell, Ansel Adams Wilderness, as we descend to the Agnew Lake dam. On this descent, mountain mahogany dominates the dry, south-facing slopes, in contrast to the forested, north-facing ones just below Agnew Pass. In the dam's vicinity grow giant blazing stars, whose oversized yellow flowers will be blooming for late-season hikers.

Beyond the dam, switchbacks lead you north down alongside a tramway, which you cross twice, and then descend slopes toward Silver Lake. At first, these slopes have mountain mahogany, juniper, and even pinyon pine. But not far beyond a small waterfall, they are gradually replaced with waist-high vegetation.

Near Silver Lake's west corner, our trail almost touches the June Lake Loop Road, then in just over 0.3 mile, it arcs behind Silver Lake Resort and fords several branches of Alger Creek. It finally traverses behind Silver Lake Trailer Court to quickly end at the Silver Lake Trailhead parking area amid sagebrush, mule ears, rabbitbrush, and bitterbrush.

TRIP **52**

Mt. Dana and/or Dana Plateau

S ↗ DH

DISTANCE: 5.8 miles out and back

ELEVATIONS: 9940'/13,157' +3260'/-40'/±6600'

SEASON: Early July to mid-October

USE: Heavy

MAPS: *Tioga Pass, Mount Dana*

TRAIL LOG:

2.9 Mt. Dana's summit

INTRODUCTION: Dark glasses and good health are both necessary for this climb to the second highest summit in Yosemite. Only Mt. Lyell exceeds it—by about 60 feet—but the Lyell summit requires mountaineering skills. Because Dana vies with Mt. Hoffman as Yosemite's most accessible peak, it is very popular, and on weekends you may find dozens of people ascending it. Its summit views are among the Sierra's best, but turn back if the weather looks threatening.

DIRECTIONS TO THE TRAILHEAD: On Hwy. 120 at Tioga Pass—the park's east entrance. Trail begins in map section F3.

DESCRIPTION: The trail up Mt. Dana, like the one up Mt. Hoffmann (Trip 24), is one of use and not an officially maintained trail.

Dana's trail, however, is not random, but rather was established by Dr. Carl Sharsmith, Yosemite's eminent botanist, who, most likely in the 1930s, chose a route that would minimize damage to this area's fragile subalpine and alpine environments. Ironically, because he led botany trips every summer for decades, word of this peak spread, and before the close of the century, the alpine flora near the top of the mountain had been greatly reduced due to human traffic. The upper part of the route needs a well-constructed trail instead of the present tangle of use paths that impact the flora.

From Tioga Pass, the footpath starts due east, then meanders southeast between two tarns that are among two dozen ponds that developed when the last major glacier retreated.

Cirque glaciers originating on the Kuna Crest, about 6 miles south of us, coalesced to form a trunk glacier that mainly descended the Dana Fork to unite with the Lyell Fork glacier and create the Tuolumne glacier. Strengthened by dozens of feeder glaciers, this mammoth glacier, like the previous one, was able to descend tens of miles down-canyon, to an estimated 2 or 3 miles beyond the Tuolumne River's confluence with Cherry Creek, down at about 2000 feet elevation (see Trip 13). About 20,000 years ago, at the height of the Tioga glaciation, the Dana Fork branch was at least 1000 feet thick where it overflowed north across Tioga Pass to join the Lee Vining glacier. This originated in the nearby Hall Natural Area, and together they descended to spall icebergs into Lake Russell, a high-water predecessor of Mono Lake.

About 200 yards beyond the second pond, your path starts a moderate ascent; 0.3 mile later, it becomes a steep one and generally stays that way for almost 1500 feet of elevation gain. About midway up this steep stretch, you can rest in an alp—a miniature alpine pasture (see sidebar below). In this vicinity, at the top of a bowl, you are ascending before reaching gentler slopes.

The end of the steep section is well above treeline, and the obvious path ends

GLACIAL HISTORY

Near the alpine pasture above the second pond, take note of the small bedrock outcrop that was both polished and striated. USGS geologist Clyde Wahrhaftig had proposed that the Lee Vining Creek glacier massively overflowed south through Tioga Pass and into the Dana Fork drainage. If it had, the striations here should be oriented north-south. Instead, they are oriented west-southwest, that is, directly downslope.

There is another lesson here (besides the importance of doing serious fieldwork): For a glacier to impart polish, it had to be at least several hundred feet thick. The west-southwest descending glacier did not originate spontaneously at the top of the bowl, but must have flowed downslope from the higher, gentler slopes.

For the most part, these slopes are felsenmeer, a sea of rocks so fractured and broken that very little bedrock exists. One would not think to look for glacier polish up here, given the small likelihood of finding any bedrock. (Actually, some years ago, while on the Dana Plateau, to north of and below Mt. Dana, I speculated that the plateau had been covered with thin ice, based on the conspicuous lateral moraine on its southeast side, above Glacier Canyon. I had concluded that the moraine looked like a late-Tioga diachronous moraine, given the field relations.)

With this polish-and-striation evidence, it now appears that the gentle upland surfaces one sees above canyons and cirques also might have had glaciers, as in the case at Mt. Dana. (In the Alps and Himalayas, glaciers do occur on gentle upland surfaces.) Therefore, there was more ice volume in at least some of the High Sierra's glaciated drainages. One cannot assume that glaciers originated at cirques; they may have originated on gentle upland surfaces above the cirques. Being non-erosive, they did not change the land's morphology.

about 1.1 miles from and still 1400 feet below the summit. Several use paths, one more prominent than the others, head up the rubbly, ancient slopes to the windblown summit. Most people climb east to a shallow saddle, at about 12,150 feet in elevation, and immediately east of a crest high point, then hike southeast up the ridge to the top. Early in the hike, the views west are great, but the panorama continually expands with elevation, saturating the optic nerves with overpowering vistas. When you hike southeast up the ridge, your views take on another dimension, adding to your elation. However, take this ridge ascent slowly, for the atmosphere is thin, and in your euphoria you can easily overexert yourself. Being above the 12,000-foot elevation, July hikers may see the sky pilot blooming with its dense head of blue flowers.

At Mt. Dana's summit, at about 13,157 feet, your exhausting efforts are rewarded by a stupendous 360-degree panorama. The Sierra's east escarpment can be viewed as far as the Wheeler Crest, about 40 miles to the southeast. East of it extends a long north-south mountain chain, the White Mountains, which were a part of the Sierra Nevada until downfaulting created a proto Owens Valley, perhaps about 80 million years ago. Renewed faulting began much more recently, about 3 million to 4 million years ago, and for decades geologists have assumed—very incorrectly, as the abundant field evidence demonstrates—that Owens Valley began to form around then.

At the north end of the White Mountains stand the pale, isolated twin summits of Montgomery and Boundary peaks, both over 13,000 feet high. Gambling is legal on

MONO LAKE'S WATER

This lake's longevity was threatened by humans—water-hungry Los Angeles residents in particular, who have diverted inflowing creeks, thereby causing the lake to drop some 40 feet in historic times. This drop increased the lake's alkalinity almost to a pH of 10, which causes its water to feel like clothes-detergent water.

In addition, when the lake reached a low during the summer of 1977, a land bridge emerged, linking 1000-year-old Negit Island to the Black Point shoreline. This island, a major nesting ground for thousands of California gulls and other birds, thus became accessible to predators. With diminishing nesting sites and increasing alkalinity, the populations of gulls and other migrant birds have unfortunately decreased.

Fortunately, in a landmark 1994 decision, the State Water Resources Control Board mandated that diversions from the lake be reduced until it reaches a healthy water level of about 6392 feet, about 15 feet higher than its lower elevations in the 1970s and '80s. Additionally, streams gone dry due to diversions now have flowing water to support both trout and riparian vegetation.

During glacial times, Mono Lake was much larger than it is today. At its maximum size, Lake Russell—glacial Mono Lake—was about 345 square miles in area and up to 950 feet deep, versus about 86 square miles and 186 feet deep in historic time before Los Angeles started diverting water away from it. In the 1980s, the lake had shrunk to about 60 square miles and 150 feet deep. The volume of the lake at these three times respectively was about 120, 4, and 2 million acre feet.

Instead of being an alkaline desert lake, Lake Russell was a freshwater lake that at its maximum had icebergs, which were spalled from the snouts of the Lundy Creek, Lee Vining Creek, Walker Creek, and Rush Creek glaciers. In all of the lower 48 states, only two other large lakes are known to have had glaciers encroach upon them: Lake Tahoe and Lake Bonneville, now existing in dwarfed form as Utah's not-so-Great Salt Lake.

the Boundary Peak summit, for it is a quarter mile in from the Nevada border.

Below these twin summits rises Crater Mountain, the highest of Mono Domes' (formerly "Mono Craters") many volcanic summits, and, like most of them, less than 10,000 years old. The youthfulness of Mono Domes strongly contrasts with the ancient age of giant, orbicular Mono Lake, directly north of them. Lakes are generally short-lived features, but this one may be more than a million years old. Sediments beneath the lake are up to almost 4000 feet thick.

Below our summit is deep Glacier Canyon, which holds only the few-hundred-year-old Dana "glacier," which is more of a snowfield than a flowing glacier. Being only a two-hour hike up-canyon from Tioga Lake, this "glacier" is frequented by mountaineers who practice their ice-climbing skills up it. Another feature worth visiting (described, along with Glacier Canyon, at the end of this trip) is the broad, gently sloping, lightly glaciated Dana Plateau, with its rare, ankle-high snow willows. Like Peak 12568, which is 1.5 miles

southeast of our summit, this is a relict of an old, unglaciated or lightly glaciated landscape.

For that matter, Mt. Dana and Mt. Gibbs are left over from that landscape, as are many of this area's gentle-sloped peaks. By scanning the horizon, you can see a number of them and then you can mentally reconstruct the ancient eastern-Yosemite landscape. A nearly universal belief (unfortunately one I promulgated in previous editions and in other Sierra books), is that this gentle landscape existed until glaciers, starting in earnest some 2 million years ago, deeply eroded existing drainages. Not so. The gentle landscape is very ancient, having originated some 80 million years ago, and glaciers, despite their enormity, performed only minor deepening and widening of canyons.

Continuing your counterclockwise scan west, you see deep-blue Saddlebag Lake and, above it, the serrated Shepherd Crest. Next comes pointed North Peak, with its south-facing ancient surface, and then a true "Matterhorn," Mt. Conness. Beyond a sea of dark-green lodgepoles lies Tuolumne

Dana Plateau and Mono Lake, view northeast

Meadows and its sentinel, Lembert Dome, whose bald summit is barely visible. On the skyline above them stand Tuolumne Peak and Mt. Hoffmann, while south of these stand the craggy summits of the Cathedral Range. Examining it counterclockwise, you can identify blocky Cathedral Peak, north-pointing Unicorn Peak, clustered Echo Peaks, and the adjacent Cockscomb, plus the finlike Matthes Crest, extending south from it. A bit farther are sedate Johnson Peak, more profound Rafferty Peak, and broad Tuolumne Pass, through which former Tuolumne glaciers overflowed into the Merced drainage.

To the south-southwest, stands the park's highest peak, 13,114-foot Mt. Lyell, which also harbors the park's largest glacier, today cleft in two by a northwest-dropping ridge. When members of the Whitney Survey first climbed our summit in 1863, they saw a Lyell glacier twice the size at our new millennium, and it partly buried the ridge as well as extended north beyond it. With continued global warming, it and the several other remaining Sierran cirque glaciers will diminish to snowfields. Flanking Lyell is Mt. Maclure and its glacier to the west, and pointed Rodgers Peak to the southeast. Mt. Ritter and Banner Peak barely poke their summits above the temporarily stagnant Kuna Peak-Koip Peak glacier to the south. Finally, Parker Peak and Mt. Wood stand above closer Mt. Gibbs, while Mt. Lewis, of intermediate distance, projects just east of them. Once a part of a low continental borderland, all the red or dark metamorphic summits (including Mt. Dana's) are made of rocks with an extremely long history.

A **ALTERNATE TRIP TO GLACIER CANYON AND DANA PLATEAU:** To reach Glacier Canyon and/or the Dana Plateau, you have two logical starting points. The first is to start east from Tioga Pass along the Mt. Dana Trail. Just before it starts to climb, you branch north, traversing about 1 mile north-northeast to the creek emanating from the mouth of Glacier Canyon, at about 10,400 feet elevation. On this traverse, you have two choices: Drop below the extensive willows or traverse above them. The second starting point is vague; you park along the highway about 0.5 to 0.75 mile north below Tioga Pass, and then drop to near the inlet of Tioga Lake. Then you make a diagonal ascent up to Glacier Canyon's creek, which empties into the lake along its southeast shore.

With both routes, you head up the creek to the mouth of Glacier Canyon. Mountaineers and geologists will continue up the canyon to three small lakes and then much larger Dana Lake, all of them in a bleak setting above treeline. The lower edge of Dana Glacier is about 400 to 500 feet higher than the lake. Hikers only go about 0.3 mile up-canyon to where they will see, on their left, the obvious route to the Dana Plateau: a bouldery gully with a low notch on the skyline. A creek descends this gully, but most of its flow is below the boulders. After you gain about 400 feet elevation, you emerge onto the lower part of the plateau and follow the creek east.

After about 1 mile of relatively easy hiking eastward, you should reach a point on the brink of the Dana Plateau called "Cape Royal" by Professor Sharsmith. This projecting point is at about 11,680 feet elevation, and if you are at the right spot, you will know it. All of the eastern escarpment of the Dana Plateau is a very steep dropoff, but from base of the dropoff at the point, a conspicuous ridge drops northeast. A false Cape Royal lies about a half mile to the north-northwest, at about 11,440 feet elevation, as does another about a half mile to the west-northwest of it, at about 11,570 feet elevation; the two are between a north-slope snowfield.

From all three, you have a marvelous view of Mono Lake. True, you don't see the Sierran escarpment and the Owens Valley, but this hike requires just over half the effort of the one to Mt. Dana's summit. And if you like botanizing, you'll find more species along this ascent. **END OF ALTERNATE TRIP**

CHAPTER 14

Trips in Yosemite Valley and up from its Floor

Introduction to this Area

Rightly called "The Incomparable Valley," Yosemite Valley is a magnet that attracts visitors from all over the world. As John Muir noted long ago, the Sierra Nevada has several "Yosemites," though none matches Yosemite Valley in grandeur. Hetch Hetchy, to the north, is the foremost example of such a Yosemite. Though some of these "Yosemites" rival or exceed Yosemite Valley in the depth of their canyons and the steepness of their walls, none has the prize-winning combination of its wide, spacious floor, its world-famous waterfalls, and its unforgettable monoliths—El Capitan and Half Dome.

This hiking section is actually composed of two groups. Trips 53 through 58 are relatively flat, easy trails that acquaint you with the views and natural history seen along the Valley's floor. In contrast, trips 59 through 61 are strenuous, climbing quite steeply from the floor. Trips 59 and 60 guide you up to the Valley's north rim, first to the brink of Yosemite Falls, and then west to Eagle Peak and east to Yosemite Point and North Dome.

Yosemite Valley and Half Dome, looking east from Eagle Peak summit

Trip 61 guides you up to Stanford, Crocker, and Dewey points, along the western part of the valley's south rim.

Supplies and Services

Yosemite Village is a small-scale urban center—and, like one, it is all too crowded. Parking space is at a premium, so I recommend that you reach it by taking a free shuttle bus or by walking or bicycling. Located at the Village are the visitor center and museum, plus a general store, eating establishments, medical clinic, post office, and other services. The only service you'll find lacking at the Village is lodging, which is available, along with meals, at Yosemite Lodge to the west, the Ahwahnee Hotel to the east, and Curry Village to the southeast. West of Curry Village is its Housekeeping Camp, which currently has a laundromat next to its showers. Showers are also available at Curry Village proper and at Yosemite Lodge. These two operations each have a swimming pool, a bike-rental shop, and a post office. The prestigious Ahwahnee Hotel formerly had tennis courts and a nine-hole golf course, but now it offers only (besides elegant ambiance) a guest-only swimming pool. At Glacier Point, high above the Valley's southeast end, you can buy snacks, film, and a few other items. The same is true at the foot of the Glacier Point cliff—Happy Isles.

Wilderness Permits

Most of the hikes in this section are day-hikes. For multiday hikes, get your permit at the Wilderness Center, located in Yosemite Village. If you want to reserve a permit in advance, which I recommend you do for trips 59 through 61 (although I prefer dayhiking them), see the "Wilderness Permits" section in Chapter 6.

Campgrounds

Back in the early days, when visitation was light by today's standards, there were up to 14 campgrounds in the Valley. Today, there are only three regular campgrounds—North, Upper, and Lower Pines—plus two smaller, walk-in campgrounds—Camp 4 and Backpackers. The former is heavily dominated by rock climbers, and the latter is for backpackers who have a wilderness permit and need a place to stay the night before they start their hike. For most visitors, camping in the Valley will remain an unfulfilled dream.

TRIP 53

Valley Floor, Bridalveil Fall Loop

E ○ DH

DISTANCE: 6.9 miles loop

ELEVATIONS: 3880′/4000′
+550′/-550′/±1100′

SEASON: Early April to
late November

USE: Moderate (packed around
Bridalveil Fall)

MAP: *El Capitan*

TRAIL LOG:

0.2	Bridalveil Fall viewpoint
2.2	Cathedral Picnic Area entrance
2.7	Eastern edge of El Capitan Meadow
3.3	Climbers' trail
5.0	Valley View
5.2	Pohono Bridge
6.9	Bridalveil Fall parking lot

INTRODUCTION: This is the first of six Yosemite Valley floor hikes in this book, which are arranged from west to east. Because the Valley contains so much history, natural history, and spectacular scenery, the hike descriptions are long even though the hikes are relatively short. On this first loop hike, you'll see Bridalveil Fall, the Cathedral Rocks, and El Capitan—all at close range. Bridalveil Fall is extremely popular, and most people hiking from the fall's parking lot make no more effort than the brief walk up to and down from the fall's viewpoint. Once you leave the fall's vicinity, you'll have most of this route just to yourself.

DIRECTIONS TO THE TRAILHEAD: Bridalveil Fall parking lot, 120 yards before the descending Wawona Road reaches a junction on the floor of Yosemite Valley. Trail begins in map section C5.

DESCRIPTION: You could start this loop from any of several pullouts along the Valley's roads, but we're starting from the Bridalveil Fall parking lot, since it has the most parking space. From the lot's east end, you hike just two minutes on a paved trail to a junction, veer right and parallel a Bridalveil Creek tributary as you climb an equally short trail up to its end at the Bridalveil Fall viewpoint. During May and June, when Bridalveil Fall is at its best, your viewpoint will be drenched in spray, making the last part of the trail very slippery and making photography from this vantage point nearly impossible.

Early settlers named this fall for its filmy, veil-like aspect, which it has in summer after its flow has greatly diminished. However, their predecessors, the Miwok Indians, named it Pohono, the "fall of the puffing winds," for, at low volume, its water is pushed around by gusts of wind.

Of Yosemite's other falls, only Vernal Fall leaps free over a dead-vertical cliff, but its flow—the Merced River—is too strong to be greatly affected by the wind. The other major falls drop over cliffs that are less than vertical, and hence the falls partly glide down them. Bridalveil's cliff owes its verticality to vertical joints, along which the cliff's granite flakes off. The cliff and waterfall are very old, having changed little in the last 30 million years. Glaciers did very little to steepen or backwaste this cliff. For some 50 million years before then, under warm, wet climates Yosemite Valley widened principally through weathering and through rockfalls; glaciers played only a minor role in widening it. Along most of our easy hike, we'll be treading across sediments, some deposited since the glaciers left. Locally, they are as much as 1000 feet deep—2000 feet deep in the eastern part of the Valley—however, the bulk of this material likely is decomposed, subsurface bedrock that long ago had weathered in place.

After descending back to the trail junction and turning right, you leave behind most of the tourists, who return to their vehicles, and you quickly encounter several branches of Bridalveil Creek, each churning along a course that cuts through old rockfall debris. From a junction with a short trail to the Valley's eastbound Southside Drive, you continue ahead on our broad trail—the old Wawona Road, until 1933—and almost to the present road, then quickly veer right to climb up to the crest of Bridalveil Moraine. From it, you get a good view of the loose west wall of Lower Cathedral Rock and also the overhanging west wall of Leaning Tower.

Just past the moraine's crest, we enter a gully lined with big-leafed maples, and here we have an excellent head-on view of mammoth El Capitan. Then, only yards away from the base of the forbidding north wall of Lower Cathedral Rock, we can stretch our necks and look up at its large ledge, which is covered with canyon live oaks, that almost cuts the face in two. While violet-green swallows perform aerial acrobatics high overhead, we continue east through a conifer forest, soon crossing a narrow, open talus field.

At its base stands a second moraine, similar to Bridalveil, and, like all the Valley's moraines, it is recessional—that is, it was left where a glacier temporarily halted its retreat. Many geologists believed that the diminutive, essentially unseen El Capitan Meadow moraine, left by the Tioga-age glacier about 16,000 years ago, dammed the Merced River to create mammoth (though mythical) Lake Yosemite. After the last glaciation and ones before it, the Valley often may have been quite swampy due to temporary dams created behind recessional moraines or dams created by periodic rockfalls that originated on Lower Cathedral Rock's loose north wall, above us.

Indeed, the first visitors found the Valley too swampy and mosquito-ridden, so, in 1879, the large rockfall blocks clogging the nearby Merced River channel were blasted apart. This deepened the channel some 4.5 feet and thereby lowered the Valley's water table. The river, rather than meandering widely and changeably across the Valley, became entrenched, and ponderosa pines and incense-cedars invaded at the expense of wet-meadow vegetation and black oaks. The blasting was also expected to reduce all flooding, but major floods occurred about every 15 to 20 years. Two exceptionally large ones, which covered about two thirds of the Valley's floor, occurred in 1955 and 1997.

Walking among white firs, incense-cedars, ponderosa pines, Douglas firs, and black oaks, you continue on a generally view-impaired route to a brief climb almost to the base of overwhelming Middle Cathedral Rock. Here you'll find it worth your effort to scramble 50 yards up to the actual base. From it, you'll see most of El Capitan plus Middle and Lower Brother, North Dome, Sentinel Rock, and Taft Point. But greater than this panorama is a sense of communion with nature one gets just by touching the base of this rock's overpowering, 2000-foot-high, monolithic face. It can be a humbling experience.

Beyond the massive northeast face and its two pinnacles, you gradually descend to a level area, from which you could walk northwest a bit to a turnout on the eastbound road. From that turnout, you can plainly see the two Cathedral Spires. These spires, and the 500-foot buttress they stand on, resemble a two-towered Gothic cathedral—hence the name. Despite their apparent inaccessibility, both were first climbed way back in 1934, during the early days of Yosemite Valley rock climbing. Until the 1960s, both were popular climbs, but since rockfall altered the original ascent routes, they are somewhat dangerous and undesirable.

After about a 0.3-mile traverse across a forested flat, you arrive at a signed trail. Veer left, northwest, on it, and descend to a point on the eastbound road only 20 yards west of the Cathedral Picnic Area entrance.

S **SIDE TRIP TO CATHEDRAL PICNIC AREA:** The few people who head north to the picnic area will be rewarded with one of two classic views. The one of El Capitan still exists, but the other of the Three Brothers is disappearing as pines continue to grow skyward, obstructing their view. See the next trip for an elaboration of what you see. This excursion adds 0.3 mile to the length of the main route. **END OF SIDE TRIP.**

The main route continues northwest almost to a bend in the Merced River and then briefly west to the El Capitan Bridge, which lies just before busy Northside Drive. Here, by the eastern edge of El Capitan Meadow, the hiker gets a noteworthy view of the Cathedral Rocks, and one can see why the Miwok Indians visualized the lower monolith as a giant acorn. After Yosemite became a national park in 1890, El Capitan Meadow became the Valley's first free public campground, and Bridalveil Meadow soon became the second, though its use was mostly by US Army troops sent to patrol the park. Three other campgrounds—all in meadows—were soon operating, in contrast to the forested ones we have today. Back then, horse pasturage was a prime concern—hence the need for meadow sites. In 1906, however, all five were closed, because sanitation—or lack thereof—had become a problem.

Across the meadow are some trees that in spring 1979 were subjected to prescribed burning. Such intentional burning began in 1971, when the Park Service decided that fires were necessary in order to return Yosemite Valley's vegetation to its former character—a more open, mixed stand of oaks and conifers. The many years of fire suppression had seen the growth of a dense, view-obstructing conifer forest.

By building a parking strip along Northside Drive's meadowy stretch, the Park Service eliminated the parking jams that used to result in the '60s and early '70s, when visitors parked their cars in the road as they searched for climbers—just specks—ascending one or more of the

major routes up El Capitan. Today, one can park and leisurely set up a telescope without impairing traffic. During midsummer, sensible climbers stay off El Capitan's multiday routes, for then the rock's temperature often exceeds 100°F, requiring many gallons of extra water (and perhaps an ample supply of six-packs).

From the El Capitan Bridge, you walk north either along Northside Drive or its

Climbers on the "Nose" route of El Capitan

adjacent riverbank trail to a sharp bend. By continuing east about 250 yards, you can reach the site of Devils Elbow Picnic Area, closed in 1993 due to riverbank erosion from heavy use. However, above a second river bend, there is access to the sandy beach and its nearby mid-river boulder, which originated from a rockfall high on El Capitan's massive face. At the aforementioned sharp bend, which has parking for a dozen or so vehicles, you'll see a small meadow just north through the trees. By walking a few paces to it, you get a grand view of the towering east face of El Capitan. From the parking area, you start west along an old, former road and, in about 50 yards, you will see a trail branching right. This is a climbers' trail that provides access to El Capitan's east-face climbing routes. Our old road takes about 0.3 mile to cross a prehistoric, gigantic rockfall that emanated from El Capitan. At its west edge, we arrive at a small hollow, from whose north end a climbers' trail heads up to the nose of El Capitan. Southward, this trail curves increasingly southeast to end at the Valley's Northside Drive. If you're lucky, you might see a climbing team heading up it with some 100 to 200 pounds of gear.

⑤ **SIDE TRIP TO BASE OF EL CAPITAN:** For visitors who are new to Yosemite Valley, the size of El Capitan, like the Cathedral Rocks and other Valley landmarks, is too large to really comprehend, and many visitors who first try to estimate its size swear it is only 1000 or so feet high. If you take the climbers' trail up the left (southwest-facing) side of El Cap's "Nose," which you'll reach in about a quarter mile, you'll probably see rock climbers, who, hundreds of feet up the monolith's 3000-foot-high walls, are reduced to antlike stature.

The 3000-foot route from the foot up the Nose takes only several hours for world-class climbers. The first to ascend it without direct-aid slings was Lynn Hill. Rock climbing is a sport where women are on par with men.

The climbers' trail continues about another quarter mile up along the base to the left of the Nose, providing access to several dozen relatively short routes that go nowhere near the top. If you've ever wondered how it is possible to climb "unclimbable" cliffs, walk up the trail and observe climbers for yourself.

The trailside vegetation of whiteleaf manzanita and canyon live oaks, growing on talus deposits, is ideal for California ground squirrels and other animals, who, in turn, make suitable prey for rattlesnakes. You probably won't see these snakes, but they nevertheless are here, as are loose boulders, so please be safe. **END OF SIDE TRIP.**

Beyond the small hollow, your road rolls gently west and then southwest to a trail split. Ahead, the Valley's loop trail will cross two or more branches of Ribbon Creek, and, in times of high water, you will have a wet, but relatively safe, ford of at least one of them. (In pioneer days Ribbon Creek was known as Virgin Tears Creek— a name in harmony with Bridalveil Creek, across the Valley floor). If you don't want wet feet (typically in May and June), then, from the split, continue southwest along the old road to nearby Northside Drive at the west end of El Capitan Meadow. The drive's north side has no shoulder, so walk 0.2 mile west along its south shoulder— unnerving when vehicles whiz past you— and come to the bottom end of the old Big Oak Flat Road, on your right. Just 30 yards before this road, you'll pass the north end of the El Capitan recessional moraine, on your left.

From the trail split, the loop trail, which is 0.1 mile longer, continues west, crossing the tributaries of Ribbon Creek, and, after a quarter mile, it arrives at the old Big Oak Flat Road. You can either wind down along it to Northside Drive or take a sometimes amorphous path beside it to the same destination. Just before reaching Northside Drive, the Valley's little-used loop trail starts west, paralleling the drive.

S **SIDE TRIP TO RIBBON FALL:** For the adventurous and safety-minded cross-country hiker, an ascent to the base of Ribbon Fall is extremely rewarding. This is quite strenuous, following Ribbon Creek about 0.75 mile up at least 1400 feet to the slowly backwasting alcove, into which plunges the Valley's highest waterfall (about 1612 feet versus about 1430 feet for Upper Yosemite Fall). On both your ascent and descent, be wary of loose boulders and possible (although unlikely) encounters with rattlesnakes. The nearly vertical walls of the alcove are quite intimidating, and you may get the feeling that they are about to close in on you or at least spall rockfall, which is possible though very unlikely. **END OF SIDE TRIP.**

After walking about five minutes west on it, we cross a low recessional moraine, and then drop almost to the paved road's edge. Here, a turnout provides an unobstructed view of Bridalveil Fall. From this turnout, you might note that the Merced River's south-bank, water-laid deposits contrast with the angular north-bank rockfall deposits. We are now at the foot of deposits derived from an unstable band of highly fractured cliffs called the Rockslides. Continual rockfalls from the Rockslides eventually led to the closing of the old Big Oak Flat Road and the construction of its replacement with today's tunneled road in June 1940. Under the pleasant shade of ponderosa pines and incense-cedars, we continue west, passing some cabin-size rockfall blocks immediately before skirting the north end of the Bridalveil Meadow recessional moraine. There is no terminal moraine, since the last glacier ended lower down, in the Merced Gorge, which was too narrow to have one form and survive. Soon, we enter a swampy area with cattails, and at its west end, we cross trickling Black Spring. Here, pioneers got an oak-and-conifer-framed view of Bridalveil Fall and the Cathedral Rocks, but due to the park's old fire-suppression policy, incense-cedars and other conifers invaded the area,

totally obstructing the view. Past the spring, the trail more or less parallels the westbound road, shortly arriving above the back side of the Valley View scenic turnout.

S **SIDE TRIP TO VALLEY VIEW:** The Valley View scenic turnout on Northside Drive is perfectly obvious and about 100 yards away. Should you descend to it, you'll first reach an outhouse before reaching the drive. The view from the riverside turnout is one of the Valley's most famous, and it is a shame that the one-way road system prevents visitors from seeing this awe-inspiring view until they are ready to leave the Valley. Here, we see El Capitan, Bridalveil Fall, and the Cathedral Rocks magnificently standing high above the stately conifers that line Bridalveil Meadow. Barely rising above the trees are the distant landmarks of Clouds Rest, Half Dome, and Sentinel Rock. As elsewhere in the Valley, you'll see a sign showing how high the floodwater was at 11 PM on January 2, 1997, the largest flood in memory. The water here was sufficiently deep to flood the entire meadow lands you see. For a brief spell, Yosemite Valley had its Lake Yosemite, and you could have rafted across the inundated floodplain, from near the base of Half Dome west through forests and across meadows to the west edge of El Capitan Meadow. **END OF SIDE TRIP.**

From the Valley View area, we reach our trail's westernmost point at the Pohono Bridge, which is the current ending point of the north-Valley, one-way traffic. From a stream-gauging station across the bridge, our feet tread a riverside path past roadside Fern Spring, then past trailside Moss Spring. (Since the trail is below the road, you won't see Fern Spring, but where you cross its outlet creek, you can climb several paces up to the road and then cross it to the spring.) Pacific dogwoods add springtime beauty to this forest as sunlight filters down to light up their translucent leaves and their large, petal-like, creamy-white bracts. Douglas firs locally dominate the forest as we hike through it, and then our trail ends about 40 yards before the west edge of Bridalveil Meadow proper. The meadow is a gently sloping alluvial fan that contains enough ground water originating from south-side slopes to generally prevent trees from invading it.

From its edge, we see a panorama from Ribbon Fall clockwise past El Capitan, the Cathedral Rocks, and the Leaning Tower up to often-ignored points in the Valley's south rim. Avid map readers will identify Dewey, Crocker, Stanford, and Old Inspiration points, all of which are located along the Pohono Trail (Trip 61). Now you walk northeast along the road's side, staying above seasonally boggy Bridalveil Meadow. By the meadow's east edge, the trail resumes, and it goes north to a bend, where you cross the Bridalveil Meadow moraine.

From here, one can walk 40 yards north to a large rock by the Merced River's bank and see a plaque dedicated to Dr. Lafayette Bunnell, who was in the first-known party of white men—the "Mariposa Battalion"— to set foot in Yosemite Valley. Camping in the meadow on March 27, 1851, they held an evening campfire, at which Bunnell suggested the name "Yosem-i-ty," which he had incorrectly inferred was the name of the Indian tribe that inhabited the Valley.

From the moraine, you parallel the Merced River southeast almost to the eastbound road, which you can take 0.2 mile east back to the Wawona Road, then go briefly up it to the Bridalveil Fall parking lot. If you do this in springtime and early summer, you will avoid the possibility of getting your feet wet in the nearby fords of multibranched Bridalveil Creek. After the last ford, the trail parallels the creek's northern branch east about 300 yards to long turnouts on both sides of the eastbound road. Where the Valley's loop trail ends at the road, you cross it to find a trail starting south-southeast, going about 150 yards to meet the trail you originally started on. On it, retrace your steps 0.3 mile to the Bridalveil Fall parking lot.

TRIP 54

Valley Floor, Yosemite Lodge Loop

E ↻ **DH**

DISTANCE: 6.4 miles loop

ELEVATIONS: 3950'/4050'
+300'/-300'/±600'

SEASON: Early April to
late November

USE: Moderate (packed around
Yosemite Lodge and trails
below Lower Yosemite Fall)

MAPS: *Half Dome, El Capitan*

TRAIL LOG:

0.7	Leidig Meadow
2.2	El Capitan Picnic Area site
2.8	Devils Elbow
3.2	El Capitan Bridge
3.7	Cathedral Picnic Area
5.6	Four Mile Trail
5.9	Swinging Bridge Picnic Area
6.4	Lower Yosemite Fall complex

INTRODUCTION: Most of this loop is relatively quiet and lightly traveled. On it, you'll get inspirational views of some of the Valley's prominent landmarks, plus you will have strolls along the Merced River.

DIRECTIONS TO THE TRAILHEAD: Lower Yosemite Fall complex, which is immediately west of the Yosemite Creek bridge and immediately north of the entrance to the Yosemite Lodge grounds. Be aware that there is no parking here, since the former falls parking lot has been replaced with a picnic area and Yosemite Lodge's parking lots are for its visitors, not for hikers. Therefore, the best option is to walk to the west side of the Lower Yosemite Fall complex or to take a shuttle bus to it. You'll want to get off at shuttle-bus stop 6, which is 0.2 mile east of the entrance to Yosemite Lodge. The shortest way to the west side of the Lower Yosemite Fall complex is to take the trail that parallels Northside Drive west. The above mileages are from the west side of the complex; if you start from stop 6, add 0.2 mile to the mileages. Trail begins in map section D5.

DESCRIPTION: Starting from the west side of the Lower Yosemite Fall complex is a trail paralleling the Valley's Northside Drive west. On this trail, you almost touch the main road, then curve right to the base of Swan Slab, which is a low cliff that attracts many rock climbers.

Before 1956, when the new lodge opened, the main buildings of Yosemite Lodge were located here, while south of them, hundreds of tent cabins lay scattered around the forest floor. During the 1960s, the new lodge was shifting its orientation away from tent cabins to fairly luxurious motel units. Some people cried "profiteering," but, in fact, the vacationing public had changed: America had come to expect less spartan accommodations. Perhaps we can define an "old timer" as one who longs for the lodge's primitive, woodsy tent cabins.

A little less than a half mile from the falls' complex, we intersect the Yosemite Falls Trail (Trip 59), and then traverse just above Camp 4 (Sunnyside) Campground. Back in the '60s Camp 4 was specifically designated for dogs and climbers—the two being nearly indistinguishable in the eyes of many. Climbers, as evidenced by the many brightly colored climbing ropes seen around the camp, still make up most, if not all, of the camp's patronage.

Our Valley loop trail curves south along the west edge of Camp 4, and you'll see two trails branching right. The loop trail is the one you want; the one just past it diagonals quickly over to Northside Drive. The loop trail starts across what some Native Americans consider sacred land, the site of a former habitation, and it is possible that, in the future, the loop trail will be rerouted southward past it along the edge of Northside Drive. About a half mile from the campground, the loop trail once entered a flat, gravel turnout. This, however, is closed, having been littered with debris from a March 1987 rockfall.

If you look above the turnout, you'll see a huge, water-streaked wall, whose black streaks of moss mark the paths of the most persistent—though still ephemeral—streams of water. This wall has the Valley's best examples of glacier polish—in the form of small patches high on the wall and also near the base of Rixon's Pinnacle. Not a real pinnacle, this giant slab is recognized by canyon live oaks growing on its summit as well as by one prominent specimen growing on a ledge halfway up it. Note also the large, curving band of granite—a dike—cutting across the face of the wall. The wall's rock, solidifying beneath the earth's surface about 90 million years ago, was fractured and injected with this dike material. You get more views of these features after you cross the paved, one-way road, Northside Drive, and on a trail you parallel it southwest. In about a minute, you may see a trail, branching southeast along Leidig Meadow.

5 **SIDE TRIP TO LEIDIG MEADOW:** This unofficial path goes across the west edge of grassy Leidig Meadow to a sandy beach beside the Merced River, and then parallels it about a half mile upstream to a long, sturdy bridge that spans this river. From the west edge of the meadow, you can see a sandy beach on the opposite bank of the Merced River. This is only lightly visited by users of Sentinel Beach Picnic Area, reached from the Valley's eastbound, one-way road. In Leidig Meadow, you get one of the Valley's best views of North Dome, Royal Arches, Washington Column, Clouds Rest, and Half Dome. Partly obscuring Half Dome is a large, descending ridge on whose dry slopes the Four Mile Trail (Trip 66) zigzags down from Glacier Point.

Leidig Meadow—the original Camp 4 site—is named for George F. Leidig, an early resident who ran a hotel (popular because of his wife's cooking!) near the base of Sentinel Rock. As late as 1924, dairy cattle grazed in this and other Valley meadows. Looking west from this meadow, you get a clear view of the Three Brothers, named for three sons of Chief Teneiya taken prisoner here in May 1851 by the Mariposa Battalion. The vertical east face of the Middle Brother was the origin of the March 1987 rockfall and later rockfalls that left most of the rocky debris you are about to cross. Shrubs and young trees are invading the debris slopes—talus—but a future rockfall could eradicate them. **END OF SIDE TRIP.**

Ahead, the main trail is now confined to a narrow strip of vegetation between the busy, paved road above us and the quiet river at our feet. Soon, we leave the river's side and parallel the road at a short distance, hiking through a forest of ponderosa pine, incense-cedar, and black oak. After a mile of pleasant walking along the trail, part of it with fair views, we arrive at the El Capitan Picnic Area site, closed due to riverbank erosion from overuse (now no river access). This site is likely to go undetected, but from its east side, a trail (formerly a road) heads north-northeast about 200 yards to Northside Drive and the exit of the new picnic area. In 0.3 mile, we enter a meadow and have good views of many of the Valley's prominent features, particularly looming El Capitan, the angular Three Brothers, and the domed Cathedral Rocks. In the past, our path split in the meadow, the two branches then rejoining in about 0.1 mile at the roadside site of the Devils Elbow Picnic Area, also closed due to overuse. However, there still is access to its sandy beach and a nearby mid-river rockfall boulder that is perfect for diving. Should you wish to drive to this beach, park about 200 yards beyond it, at a conspicuous parking area where Northside Drive angles from west to south.

From the Devils Elbow environs, your trail quickly curves south, hugging both road and river for a quarter mile to the El Capitan Bridge—one of the Valley's most scenic spots (see Trip 53), where, again, there is river access. At the north side of the bridge's east end, the trail resumes, heads east to a bank opposite the south end of the Devils Elbow beach, then angles southeast to eastbound Southside Drive. Just 20 yards east lies the entrance to the Cathedral Picnic Area, which, at 0.3 mile round trip, is worth visiting.

S **SIDE TRIP TO CATHEDRAL PICNIC AREA:** On its road, walk north down to the riverbank for two famous and instructive views from the willow-lined Merced River. Look northeast and, through the growing pines, note the amazing similarity among the Three Brothers. They present a classic case of joint-controlled topography. Each is bounded on the east and south by nearly vertical joint planes and on the west by an oblique-angle joint plane. These three planes govern the shape of each brother, and when a rockfall does occur, the rock breaks off parallel to one of these planes, thus maintaining the triangular shape. Now look northwest and see the massive south face of El Capitan and, on the east part of it, identify the dark-gray "North America map," which is a band of diorite that intruded and then solidified within the slightly older El Capitan granite.

About five dozen extremely difficult climbing routes have been pushed up El Capitan. Perhaps the most famous route is the "Nose," which goes from the monolith's foot up its brow, and the most infamous one is the "Wall of the Early Morning Light," which ascends the blank wall just right of it. The former, first climbed continuously in 6.5 days in 1960, was scaled in a grueling 17-hour ascent in the mid-1970s. Later, faster ascents were done, and now to do it in one day is nothing special for first-rate climbers. The latter route, first climbed in 1970, took 26.5 days—an unheard of time—and the ascent upset many climbers, angered park officials, and received national press coverage. **END OF SIDE TRIP.**

On your main trail, cross the road, and walk 250 yards southeast to a junction with the valley's south-side trail. On it, we start east and immediately cross a creek bed that is densely lined with ponderosa pines. These pines probably sprouted after the usually dry creek became a swollen torrent during a flood and, like other creeks, created fresh soil exposures that became ripe for seed germination. Looking upstream you see overhanging Taft Point, then get other views of it as you progress east. After a half mile of shady, south-side walking, you come to a huge, trailside slab, on whose flat summit you'll find about 20 mortar holes used by the Indians to grind acorns to flour. Not a glacier-transported rock, this 1000-ton slab broke off a steep wall of this side canyon above us. After perhaps sliding down a layer of ice and snow, this slab came to rest at this spot centuries ago. As you continue on, Douglas firs and white firs mingle with the more dominant ponderosa pines, incense-cedars, and black oaks. Gray squirrels scamper about, and, in earlier days, they vied with Indians for acorns. However, they also benefited the Indians, for they buried many acorns and forgot about some, and these sprouted to produce the Indians' most cherished food source, the black oak.

Scattered views are obtained over the next mile from the big slab, and near its end, you cross Sentinel Creek—barely a trickle by the first day of summer. After summer solstice, you're lucky if multistage Sentinel Fall, seen high above the creek, is a even a gossamer mist. Voluminous only in flood stage, this fall is best seen in the warming days of late May, when runoff is about maximum and when winter's dormant seeds have awakened to dot the forest floor with a multitude of wildflowers. Sentinel Creek descends to Southside Drive, and just west of it is the entrance road to two picnic areas. Early on, the road splits, the right branch continuing north to the Sentinel Beach Picnic Area, the left branch soon bending west to head over to the Yellow Pine Picnic Area. Back around the 1970s, the latter was isolated Muir Tree Campground, and it is missed by us old-timers. After crossing Sentinel Creek, you come to an old spur road—the end of the Four Mile Trail from Glacier Point (Trip 66). In this vicinity, Leidig's Hotel, the westernmost of several pioneer hotels, once stood. Beyond here, your trail soon draws close to the Valley's eastbound road, and where you see a large roadside parking area, about a quarter mile beyond the old spur road, leave the trail, cross the busy road, and enter the Swinging Bridge Picnic Area.

Descending through the picnic area, you reach a long, sturdy bridge that replaces an earlier suspension bridge across the Merced River. From it, you have good views of Yosemite Falls, Royal Arches, Washington Column, North Dome, Clouds Rest, Sentinel Rock, the Cathedral Rocks, and the Three Brothers. From its far end, we take a broad, paved bike path north up-river and then beyond to a bend in the road on the grounds of Yosemite Lodge. The bike path next winds northeast, then heads

GALEN CLARK

Black's Hotel once stood in this area, together with Clark's cabin. Galen Clark was one of the Valley's first tourists, being one of about 30 visitors to see it in the summer of 1855. Later, discovering he had a serious respiratory condition, he returned to the mountains, perhaps to die, but Yosemite's environment acted like an elixir, restoring his health. He first established a small lodge at Wawona, and then he became Yosemite's first guardian. Later, he saw it made into a national park, and, in 1910—during the Hetch Hetchy controversy—he died at a ripe old age of 96.

north, finally crossing the Valley's North-side Drive on the east side of the entrance to the lodge's grounds, opposite the west side of the Lower Yosemite Fall complex, your starting point.

[A] **ALTERNATE TRIP TO TRAILHEAD:** If you started from shuttle-bus stop 6, the shortest way back to it—saving you 0.2 mile—is not through the grounds of Yosemite Lodge. Rather, from the Swinging Bridge Picnic Area, you take the bike path 0.6 mile east alongside Southside Drive, then branch left at the chapel and take another bike path 0.3 mile north, bridging the Merced River, over to stop 6. Most of this route is through meadow lands, so you'll have plenty of views. Furthermore, along a lengthy South-side Drive parking strip, a short trail north provides access to the Merced River. The only downside of this alternate trip is all the vehicle traffic. **END OF ALTERNATE TRIP.**

TRIP **55**

Valley Floor, Yosemite Falls Loop

E ↺ DH

DISTANCE:	1.1 miles loop
ELEVATIONS:	3960′/4040′ +160′/-160′/±320′
SEASON:	Early March to late November
USE:	Packed
MAP:	Half Dome

TRAIL LOG:

0.5	Lower Yosemite Fall
0.7	Junction
0.9	Second junction
1.1	Stop 6

INTRODUCTION: The brief walk to a bridge view of Lower Yosemite Fall may be the most popular hike in the park, rivaled only by briefer walks to a view of Bridalveil Fall and to the brink of Glacier Point. In our Trip 55, the vast majority of hikers only go to the bridge view of Lower Yosemite Fall and return the way they came, whereas I describe a slightly longer route, a 1.1-mile loop.

DIRECTIONS TO THE TRAILHEAD: Take the shuttle bus to stop 6. If you are driving, you might chance to find parking on both sides of Northside Drive just east of stop 6. Trail begins in map section D5.

DESCRIPTION: From Memorial Day to the Labor Day weekend, perhaps more than a thousand visitors daily make a short pil-grimage north to the base of Lower Yosemite Fall, many (if not most) arriving by tour buses and from out of state. And why not? Yosemite National Park is one of the most famous UNESCO World Heritage Sites, Yosemite Valley is its star attraction, and Lower Yosemite Fall is its most accessible fall. Therefore, the short route to it, and a slightly longer return route will be described first.

This loop trip, along mostly paved paths, begins along Northside Drive at from shuttle-bus stop 6, which is just east of the Lower Yosemite Fall complex. The shorter way to it is to take a paved path that parallels Northside Drive 0.2 mile west. The recommended slightly longer, quieter way is to start from the west side of the bus stop and take a path 70 yards north to a junction. You'll be finishing your loop on the path heading right, northeast. You head left, west, for 170 yards, bridging two branches of Yosemite Creek on your way to a building with restrooms and, immediately west of it, a drinking fountain and tables. In front of the building is a display that introduces you to this area. More displays lie ahead along our loop.

You are at the southeast edge of the Lower Yosemite Fall complex, and now you arc 80 yards northwest to the start of an arrow-straight path north. Folks from Yosemite Lodge and its tour-bus entourages join us here. Ahead, our broad path aims directly toward Lower Yosemite Fall and Upper Yosemite Fall behind it, this Kodak moment courtesy of many trees felled long ago. It seems that virtually all visitors attempt to take a photo of the falls and their family/friends, trying not to include all the others attempting the same task.

Ahead, the 0.3-mile path north to the lower fall is obvious. Your photogenic path soon reaches a loop with displays, including one that erroneously states that hanging valleys such as the one at the brink of Upper Yosemite Fall are due to glacial erosion. Not even François Matthes, who was the principal proponent of the Valley's erroneous glacial interpretations, made such a statement. On the path north from the loop, you quickly encounter rocks on your left, many the size of cabins and several the size of houses. These broke loose from the

cliffs above, and more rockfalls are likely in future years. Kids (and kid-like adults) often can be seen scrambling around, atop, and even under these giant boulders, but for this activity, caution is required. In one locale, there is Spider Cave, beneath some giant boulders. The cave derives its name not from spiders (I saw none), but from the multiple paths (legs) leading to the totally dark center (body).

Soon, the paved path begins to climb and curve gently, then moderately (the only part tough in a wheelchair), and, after several minutes, you arrive a wide bridge with a seasonally impressive view of Lower Yosemite Fall. In late spring and early summer, visitors are treated to the thunderous roar of the fall, a sound that reverberates in the alcove cut in this rock. During this time, the visitor is further treated to the fall's spray as well. But by mid-July, Yosemite Falls are somewhat diminished, and by late August the lower fall, like its upper counterpart, is usually reduced to a mist, and even this can be gone by the Labor Day weekend. So, most of the park's summer visitors are treated to a less than stellar water display. This was recognized early on.

In an article published more than a century ago, the July 16, 1892, issue of *Harper's Weekly* said, in brief part: "Yosemite Falls is one of the most famous features of the Yosemite scenery; but at a time when tourists find it most convenient to visit the Valley, there is no waterfall." It's been suggested to build dams above the brinks of Yosemite, Bridalveil, and both Vernal and Nevada falls so that their reservoirs could produce dramatic flow for each fall throughout the summer. And, one could add, the dams could generate electricity in the process. But dams and reservoirs are not built in national parks—unless you happen to be the City of San Francisco, whose hydroelectric project inundated the floor and lower slopes of the park's Hetch Hetchy Valley.

Dry or not, Lower Yosemite Fall should not be examined at close range, for even if boulder-choked Yosemite Creek is bone dry, its rocks are water polished to an ice-like finish. You may see climbers ascending the nearly vertical walls surrounding the fall, and being roped, they are in a safer environment than you are if you clamber around on the creek's rocks.

The wide bridge is occasionally swept away. It has been dislodged by winter's intense, flood-causing storms, which periodically occur, but it has also been dislodged by unseasonably warm springtime weather that causes rapid snowmelt. This, in turn, causes the huge snow cone at the base of the upper fall to swell with water and rapidly descend, avalanche-style, carrying the winter's rockfall debris with it as it plunges over the lower fall and slams into the bridge.

Before leaving the bridge, note how the lower fall has indirectly cut its alcove. Stream action has barely cut into the granitic bedrock since glaciers last left the Valley, but in winter, the fall's spray freezes in the surrounding rocks, expands, and pries loose lower slabs that in turn remove support from upper ones—hence the blocky nature of Yosemite Creek's bed in this area.

From the bridge, most folks return the way they came, but keeping to the clockwise loop, we take the paved path briefly northeast toward a cliff, then, on a short, counterclockwise loop, first southeast then northeast, traverse around slopes. In this vicinity, you may hear or see climbers on one of about a dozen difficult routes up the cliff just north of you. While some routes are short, others ascend to a long, linear ledge known as Sunnyside Bench, about 400 feet above you. After a couple of minutes walking eastward, you reach a junction, 0.2 mile beyond the bridge. If you're making the following, longer loop, described next, you'll head westward to this junction. Here, you turn right, take a gently winding, forested path south and slightly down between two branches of Yosemite Creek for another 0.2 mile to a second junction.

S **SIDE TRIP TO FALL VIEW:** Should you want another view of the falls, then turn right and walk 100 yards southwest to a dead-end above a branch of Yosemite Creek, where you'll find a James Hutchings bench and a John Muir plaque. In this vicinity, a sawmill once stood. It was located here because fast-flowing Yosemite Creek provided the water power necessary to turn the sawmill's large blade. John Muir built this sawmill for James Hutchings "to cut lumber for cottages...from the fallen pines which had been blown down in a violent wind-storm [winter of 1867-68] a year or two before my arrival." When not off on his treks, Muir sometimes worked at this mill, for at it he could enjoy "the piney fragrance of the fresh-sawn boards and be in constant view of the grandest of all the falls." His love of wilderness had grown so great that he preferred to spend the night perched on a ledge above the Valley floor, lulled to sleep by a splashing lullaby from nearby Lower Yosemite Fall. **END OF SIDE TRIP.**

Nearly through with our loop, we keep left and wind 150 yards south to the north edge of an informative exhibit area, complete with benches and a fine view of Upper Yosemite Fall. Continuing south through this area will get you to Northside Drive at a spot about 100 yards east of the start of our loop. This is your first way back to shuttle-bus stop 6. My preferred way—when Yosemite Creek is flowing briskly—is to branch right at the north edge of the area and take a path that parallels a creek branch west to a junction, from which you retrace your first steps 70 yards south to the west side of the bus stop.

TRIP 56

Valley Floor, Cooks and Ahwahnee Meadows Loop

E 🔄 DH

DISTANCE: 3.1 miles loop

ELEVATIONS: 3960'/4160'
+370'/-370'/±740'

SEASON: Early March to late November

USE: Moderate

MAP: *Half Dome*

TRAIL LOG:

0.3	Sentinel Bridge
1.0	LeConte Memorial Lodge
1.8	Church Bowl
2.7	Junction
3.1	Stop 6

INTRODUCTION: A loop route much less traveled than the previous one, this offers you photogenic views of dramatic landmarks of the east part of Yosemite Valley, which include Sentinel Rock, Yosemite Falls, Royal Arches, Washington Column, North Dome, Half Dome, and Glacier Point. Between the two meadows, you twice bridge the Merced River and pass innumerable boulders that testify to the primary cause of the Valley's widening: rockfall over tens of millions of years.

DIRECTIONS TO THE TRAILHEAD: Take the shuttle bus to stop 6. If you are driving, you might chance to find parking on both sides of Northside Drive, just east of stop 6. Trail begins in map section D5.

DESCRIPTION: As in the shorter, previous loop trip, you begin from stop 6, but head south, crossing Northside Drive and continuing south on a paved bike path that parallels an adjacent spur road on your right. Near its end, a water well was drilled in the early 1970s, and it went 1000 feet down before hitting either a large boulder or bedrock. Yosemite Valley is, in reality, a 4000-foot-deep canyon, for, on average, its bedrock floor is buried under 1000 feet of sediments and decomposed bedrock. Beneath the grounds of the Ahwahnee Hotel, 1 mile east of us, these reach 2000 feet in thickness.

After walking a minute or two south, you angle southeast to enter beautiful Cooks Meadow, with views of some prominent Valley features. Starting clockwise to the north, we see Upper Yosemite Fall and Lost Arrow to its left; Royal Arches and Washington Column to the northeast, with North Dome rising above both; Half Dome to the east; curving Glacier Point Apron and Glacier Point above it to the southeast; and Sentinel Rock to the south. Just within Cooks Meadow, we encounter a split. The preferred route is a footpath branching left, east, from the bike path. However, in times

---

THE INDIAN WARS OF 1851

Ironically, the Yosemite chapel stands close to the site of the Valley's first murder, which occurred in May 1851 during the so-called "Indian Wars." Two braves tied to a tree were allowed to free themselves so they could be shot down. The villainous soldier who planned this foul deed succeeded in killing only one of the Indians, but, unfortunately, it was Chief Teneiya's favorite son, and this certainly increased the old chief's mistrust of the intentions of the Mariposa Battalion. However, in all fairness, it must be stated that the battalion behaved with remarkable restraint when rounding up the chief's band, especially considering that some of its volunteers had suffered personal losses at the hands of the Indians.

of high water, it can be flooded and you'll have to take the bike path, which is about 200 yards longer. This heads to an obvious bridge raised high over the Merced River (so it won't be swept away in times of major flooding), then the path quickly ends at Southside Drive opposite the Yosemite chapel. To regain the primary route, take the bike path northeast over to a nearby road junction.

If you take the footpath east through Cooks Meadow, you soon end at a parking area just north of a 1994-vintage Sentinel Bridge, built immediately upstream from

the site of its predecessor. As elsewhere in the Valley, you'll see a sign showing how high the floodwater was at 11 PM on January 2, 1997, the largest flood in memory. The water here was sufficiently deep to flood the entire meadow lands you see. For a brief spell, Yosemite Valley had its Lake Yosemite, and you could have rafted across the inundated floodplain, from near the base of Half Dome west through forests and across meadows to the west edge of El Capitan Meadow. Head over to Sentinel Bridge, where, particularly during August, when Upper Yosemite Fall is only a vestige

JAMES HUTCHINGS AND THE VALLEY

By strategically locating their hotel in the area between this bridge and the chapel, Buck Beardsley and G. Hite in 1859 provided guests with the best of all possible views. Business, however, was poor, and, in 1864, James Hutchings—one of the Valley's first tourists—bought the hotel. Hutchings earlier had begun to attract tourists to the Valley by exposing this great California wonder to them in his magazine, *Hutchings' Illustrated California Magazine*, a monthly that existed from 1856 to 1860. As he closed his magazine, he replaced it with a book called *Scenes of Wonder and Curiosity in California*, a popular guide that had a long section on Yosemite. Hutchings also encouraged the development of the Valley area, both through words and investments, and there gradually arose what is now referred to as the "Old Village," which contained, among 21 structures, the National Park Headquarters. Today, the Yosemite chapel is the only significant structure remaining. Originally built between Black's and Leidig's hotels in 1879, it was later moved a half mile northeast up the road to its present site, and it stands as the Valley's oldest building.

A final point about Hutchings is that because he resided in the Valley for quite a few years, he became aware of almost all of the past geologic processes that created it. Nevertheless, because he was not a geologist, he was totally ignored by the geological establishment, which, due to a fatally flawed view on how mountain landscapes form, never did correctly determine how the Valley originated.

For over a century, visitors to the Valley have been treated to geological myths. An example of this may be at Sentinel Bridge, where you may see two explanations of the origin of Half Dome. The first is an Indian legend, the second is a White Man legend, presented as geologic fact. Past glaciers barely eroded the lower slopes of Half Dome, just as they barely eroded the curving Glacier Point Apron below Glacier Point. Half Dome's unglaciated northwest face, which you see, is somewhat unstable and has active rockfall, so, over millions of years, it has retreated. In contrast, its unseen back side is very stable, despite repeated glaciation, and it has hardly changed at all over millions of years. As you'll see if you take either Trip 56 or Trip 57, there are plenty of rockfall boulders along the northwest base, and these have accumulated over the last 15,000 years. If you take Trip 68 up to Half Dome, and look down at the southeast base from its shoulder, you'll see little or no debris.

of its springtime self, rafters with life vests slowly float down the river, adding a human element to the famous tree-framed view of stately Half Dome.

From the south end of Sentinel Bridge you can take the bike path eastward. Alternatively, you can walk east on a riverbank trail, sometimes below the road and sometimes beside it. When you arrive at the bustling Housekeeping Camp, cross the road to the bike path and soon come to a granite structure, the LeConte Memorial Lodge.

A student of the world-(in)famous Louis Agassiz, Joseph LeConte was invited to become the first professor of geology at Berkeley's then infant University of California. During the summer of 1870, he visited Yosemite Valley, met John Muir, and was profoundly impressed with both. As a pioneering geologist, he would later trek through much of the High Sierra, much as the Whitney Survey had done in Civil War days. However, like Muir, LeConte was not interested in topographic mapping and potential mining sites, but rather in the beauty and origin of this "range of light." Appropriately, LeConte died in one of his most loved sites, Yosemite Valley, in 1901. During 1902-03, the commemorative lodge was built, erected near the youthful Camp Curry (today's Curry Village). The camp, however, prospered and expanded, so, in 1919, the lodge was dismantled and then rebuilt, stone by stone, at its present location. This site was selected by Yosemite's foremost photographer, Ansel Adams, who chose it for its clear view up the Valley. As you can see, tall incense-cedars and ponderosa pines obstruct the view today. This lodge was once the terminal point of the John Muir Trail (trips 44 and 49), but today it ends at Happy Isles.

Leaving the LeConte Memorial, its trailside Indian mortar holes, and its large boulders chalked white by climbers, we cross the road and follow a short path north along the east side of the Housekeeping Camp, reaching a sturdy bridge to the site of flooded, closed Lower Riverside

Campground. Heading toward Yosemite Falls, we turn our backs on views of Glacier Point, the sweeping Glacier Point Apron, and Grizzly Peak as we follow a path downstream alongside alders and willows. On this short stretch, large blocks were laid along the bank to prevent the river from meandering into either camp. All told, the river was once lined with about 14,500 feet of riprap revetment. Ponderosa pines, incense-cedars, and black oaks provide shade until a small stretch of Ahwahnee Meadow, just before the Valley's central road, which we cross. Now we head north on a narrow, paved path along the west edge of Ahwahnee Meadow and have unobstructed views of North Dome, Royal Arches, Washington Column, and Half Dome. Below these towering landmarks stands one of America's grandest hotels, the Ahwahnee. Opened to the public in 1927, this magnificent granite-and-timber architectural treasure replaced Kenneyville, which, like the Old Village and Camp Curry, was a site of active tourism. Before that, there had been the nearby Harris Camp Grounds, established in 1878, in which, for a fee, you could camp. However, with the establishment of Yosemite National Park in 1890, free public campgrounds were opened, and this privately run camp folded.

After a scenic quarter mile, you cross the road east to the Ahwahnee Hotel by the west end of the Church Bowl.

Before continuing, first note that the Valley crossing you've just completed contains a sufficient diversity of plant species to allow selective feeding by all seven of the Valley's common summertime warblers. In the shady, moist confines immediately behind the LeConte Memorial, you might find MacGillivray's warblers foraging among the thimbleberries and bracken ferns. Just north, in the ponderosa pines and incense-cedars, you might stretch your neck and see yellow-rumped and hermit warblers. The larger, more common yellow-rumped warbler hunts for insects in the outer foliage of the trees' lower and middle

North Dome, Royal Arches, Washington Column, and Half Dome reflected in the Merced River

branches, while the misnamed hermit warbler hunts among the upper branches. Along the Merced River, you might observe yellow and Wilson's warblers, the former searching among the alders and cottonwoods, the latter searching lower down among the willows and adjacent shrubs. Along the northbound traverse of the edge of Ahwahnee Meadow, the Nashville warbler would be expected in the black oaks overhead, and, upon climbing into the canyon live oaks above the Church Bowl, you'd expect to see the black-throated gray warbler. Thus, you may see seven different warblers all hunting insects in Yosemite Valley. Yet none is in direct competition with any other, for each has found its own niche. Competition is mainly among individuals of the same species.

Rising from the east edge of the Church Bowl are some cliffs that are popular with rock climbers, and for some they put on quite a show. Ascending from the Church Bowl up past the unseen medical clinic, you quickly reach Indian Canyon Creek. This canyon was a principal Valley exit used by Indians heading up to the north rim, and early pioneers built a trail of sorts up it, then west to a Yosemite Falls overlook. In early season, you may note one of the Valley's lesser-known falls, Lehamite Falls, which plunges down a branch of Indian Canyon. "Lehamite" is actually the name Chief Teneiya's people gave to Indian Canyon.

Beyond the canyon's creek and its huge rockfall boulders, you climb northwest to avoid a mosaic of park buildings and residences of the "New Village," then contour west beneath sky-piercing Arrowhead Spire and the highly fractured Castle Cliffs. Approaching a spur trail down to the nearby government stables, you'll reach a very obvious talus slope, from which you'll spy Lost Arrow—a giant pinnacle high on the wall of Upper Yosemite Fall. Climbers who have ascended cliffs to Sunnyside Bench and don't want to rappel their climbing route walk east along the bench to this talus slope and then descend it. Sometimes even nature hikes are lead up this talus slope, but not west along the bench, which has some treacherous spots where a slip could be fatal. Heading west for a quarter mile, your trail first passes above the park's family-residence tract and its associated elementary school, and then comes to the junction just east of Lower Yosemite Fall. Here, as with others on the short Yosemite Falls loop, you follow the second half of that loop's description southward 0.4 mile back to shuttle-bus stop 6.

TRIP **57**

Valley Floor, Curry Village Loop

E ◯ DH

DISTANCE:	2.1 miles loop
ELEVATIONS:	3970′/4030′ +120′/-120′/±240′
SEASON:	Early April to late November
USE:	Moderate (locally packed)
MAP:	*Half Dome*

TRAIL LOG:

0.8	Happy Isles shuttle-bus stop
1.3	Medial Moraine
1.7	Clarks Bridge
2.1	Trailhead

INTRODUCTION: More like a stroll, this is one of the easiest hikes described in this guide. It is recommended for those who enjoy a leisurely pace and want to take the time to commune with the squirrels, birds, and wildflowers and to reflect on the Valley's natural and human history.

DIRECTIONS TO THE TRAILHEAD: Curry Village parking lot, in eastern Yosemite Valley. Trail begins in map section D5.

DESCRIPTION: From the Curry Village lot's southeast corner, start on a paved path east, at first paralleling the south edge of a paved road. The trail soon diverges away, and about a quarter mile into your hike, your path crosses a short spur road to a trailhead parking lot for wilderness-permit holders only (e.g. Trip 79).

This lot was a former garbage dump, which attracted bears, which were fed by rangers until 1941—the start of the bear problem. As backpackers became far more

BEFORE CURRY VILLAGE

Back in the 1860s, long before any car entered Yosemite Valley, the Curry Village parking lot was an apple orchard, and rows of these fruit trees are still seen in the area today. This orchard stands at the south end of Stoneman Meadow, whose grasses were nightly trampled by summer spectators watching the Firefall being pushed off Glacier Point—until the show was ended in January 1968. That meadow got its name from Governor George Stoneman, who was the state's chief executive when a large, state-financed hotel, the Stoneman House, was completed in 1887. Part of a political scandal, this pretentious but shoddy hotel began to fall apart almost as soon as it was finished, and, fortunately, it burned to the ground in 1896, thus ridding the Valley of one of its true eyesores. Today, Camp Curry's west-end shuttle-bus stop occupies the approximate site of that hotel. Three years after the fire, Camp Curry made a very modest start, and, as a company, it eventually outgrew all its competitors to become the park's largest concessionaire.

numerous in the 1960s, "delinquent" Yosemite bears that were trucked out of the Valley pursued them into new territory and eventually over much of the High Sierra. From this lot, you can also hike up to the base of broad, curving Glacier Point Apron, a good place to view climbers. "Sticky soled" shoes, developed in the 1980s, allowed climbers to waltz up new routes that would have been unthinkable in the '70s. Hence, new routes proliferated, and now more than 100 exist.

You could take the paved, roadside path to Happy Isles, but a quieter one begins from the east edge of the trailhead parking lot. Less than 100 yards past the parking lot's spur road, you'll see a trail branching right, which you take briefly to a junction with the trail from the parking lot. This we take as it rolls southeast, staying about 100 to 150 yards from the unseen shuttle-bus road. In 0.3 mile, you head east on planks across a boggy area, known as the Fen. Although mosquitoes may be bothersome in late spring and early summer, the bog then produces its best wildflowers. At a huge, lone boulder by the bog's east side, your trail heads 70 yards east to a paved, north-south road. On it, you can walk 80 yards north to the Happy Isles shuttle-bus stop, passing a restroom and its east-side drinking fountain just before it.

⑤ **SIDE TRIP TO HAPPY ISLES:** Rather than heading north, you can head south to the Nature Center, either 120 yards on the road, or better yet, on a paved riverside trail you'll find just east of the road. Beyond the Nature Center, the riverside trail quickly ends at a display of the July 10, 1996, rockfall, which originated high on a cliff southeast of and below Glacier Point. Before ending, the trail spawns another one, which bridges the lower Happy Isle, then continues to bridge the upper Happy Isle, ending near its upper end. In days past, these islands in the stream were heavily visited because one could bridge them over to the start of the John Muir Trail. However, once the bridge was removed, foot traffic fell precipitously. Consequently, you're likely to find the actual Happy Isles rather solitary, which is a plus. **END OF SIDE TRIP.**

From the Happy Isles shuttle-bus stop, we walk 100 yards east, first crossing the road's Happy Isles Bridge, then reaching a bend. South, trips 67 to 69 follow a broad path to the start of the John Muir Trail and beyond.

If you were to head south 0.1 mile along this path, you'd see that the USGS had a stream-gauging station on the Merced River. Records show that late in the summer, just before autumn rains, the river's discharge can fall to less than 5 cubic feet per second, while during a rampaging flood it can rise to a staggering 10,000 cubic feet per second! Most of the river's sediment is transported during times of high water, and since the Merced River's volume is considerably greater than that of Tenaya and Yosemite creeks, it brings a disproportionately large amount of sediment into the Valley. Overall, the historic rate of sediment is quite insignificant—according to my detailed calculations, about 2500 tons per year for the Merced River and 330 tons for all the Valley's remaining creeks. An undying myth is that a large Lake Yosemite, averaging about 200 feet in depth, occupied a basin covering most of the Valley floor, after the last glaciers left the Valley about 16,000 years ago. However, at best, the incoming sediments could have filled in only about 13 feet. Wind-blown silt plus rockfalls and mudflows could have added as much as 7 more feet. At best, Lake Yosemites that formed after each major glaciation were shallow; more likely, most were Yosemite Swamps.

Departing north from the Happy Isles bridge, you have a choice of three pleasant routes: the Merced's west-bank trail, its east-bank trail, and the shuttle-bus road's east-side trail. To reach the east-side trail, just walk briefly east from the bridge and you'll find it. On this trail, you pass some cabin-size, moss-and-lichen-covered rockfall blocks, and then, just as the trail climbs to cross the "Medial Moraine," you can walk a few paces west to reach the shuttle-bus road where the Merced River bends from north to northwest. Both riverbank trails are relaxing strolls along the azalea-lined river, but the east-bank trail may be more interesting since it traverses along the base of the west-trending moraine.

François Matthes, who produced a monumental report on Yosemite glaciation in 1930, concluded that this was a recessional end moraine that was probably left at the lower end of a glacier extending down Tenaya Canyon. Eliot Blackwelder, his contemporary, disagreed, saying it was a medial moraine—that is, one left between two glaciers, which, in this case, would be glaciers from Tenaya and from the upper Merced Canyon. However, a medial moraine exists only while the two joining glaciers exist, and when they melt away, the moraine is destroyed as its material is strewn about the area. After examining all the glacial evidence here and much in other Sierran canyons, I concluded that this west-trending ridge is a recessional moraine left by the retreating Merced Canyon glacier. There is more than one line of evidence for this, but the most convincing one is the kinds of boulders you see in the road cut through the moraine. The Tenaya Canyon glacier carried mostly boulders composed of Cathedral Peak granodiorite, which have unmistakable, large, blocky, feldspar crystals. In contrast, the Merced Canyon glacier carried relatively few of these boulders. Because very few of these exist in the road cut (you may not see any), the glacier that left the moraine must have been from the Merced Canyon.

Skirting the south base of this moraine, we take the east-bank trail northwest almost to the Valley stables and its adjacent shuttle-bus stop. Here, at the moraine's end, turn left and immediately cross Clarks Bridge, named for Galen Clark, the park's first guardian. From its west side, west-bank-trail hikers now join us for a brief walk past the entrances to the Upper and Lower Pines campgrounds. Beyond them, we presently come to a T, cross the road, and, on a trail, parallel the road northwest. Momentarily, you'll see a small campground reservation office at the nearby northeast corner of the Curry Village parking lot, and a trail branching left briefly over to it. By walking due south from this office of lost hopes, you'll soon arrive at your arbitrary trailhead in the lot's southeast corner.

TRIP **58**

Valley Stables to Mirror Lake

E ↻ DH

DISTANCE: 3.8 miles loop

ELEVATIONS: 3970´/4170´
+250´/-250´/±500´

SEASON: Early April to
late November

USE: Packed

MAP: *Half Dome*

TRAIL LOG:

0.8	Tenaya Creek Bridge
1.5	Path's end at Mirror Lake
2.2	Indian Caves area
2.9	Sugarpine Bridge
3.8	Clarks Bridge bus stop

INTRODUCTION: First cars and then shuttle buses once went to Mirror Lake and Indian Caves, but now the paved road is used by cyclists. Most hikers also use it, though paths offer quieter routes to these sites. Be forewarned that Mirror Lake is just a broad stretch of Tenaya Creek, not a true lake. In time of high water, typically in May and June, it is quite impressive and reflective, but in July the flow diminishes and the width of the "lake" greatly decreases, exposing widening stream banks. By late summer, the creek can entirely dry up. Also included under this trip is a side trip up the lower part of Tenaya Canyon.

DIRECTIONS TO THE TRAILHEAD: Walk or take the shuttle bus through the Pines campgrounds to a shuttle-bus stop just across Clarks Bridge, by the entrance to a parking lot for patrons of the Yosemite stables. Trail begins in map section D5.

DESCRIPTION: The shortest route to Mirror Lake is to take the road east from the shut-tle-bus stop to a junction, then the bike path north to the lake. This shaves 0.3 mile from the above mileages. The described route takes a longer, quieter way.

The low ridge you see just behind the shuttle-bus stop is the Valley's "Medial Moraine," a glacial deposit whose origin is mentioned near the end of Trip 57. A trail goes east along each side of the moraine, but the south-side trail is more scenic since it also goes along the Merced River. It is also quieter, for there aren't any trailside bicyclists. Take this riverside trail, walking east along the base of the smooth moraine to a junction and veer left up to the adjacent shuttle-bus road, which cuts through the moraine.

We follow the road through the moraine to a nearby road split with an adjacent shuttle-bus stop and nearby outhouse. The bus route goes counterclockwise west, while a paved bike path, the former Mirror Lake Road, goes north. Just north of this junction, you'll see a trail on your right, which you take about 40 yards east to a main trail. On it, we meander north, skirting an area of giant rockfall boulders that testify to the instability of Half Dome's west flank. Beyond them, we come to a trail intersection beside Tenaya Bridge. West, the trail parallels Tenaya Creek to the back side of the Yosemite stables.

S **SIDE TRIP TO MIRROR LAKE:** East, the trail heads about 0.8 mile to Mirror Lake and then about 1.3 miles beyond it to a bridge across Tenaya Creek. In the past, this trail has been signed for Mirror Lake and unwitting hikers have taken it instead of the paved bike path up to the lake. When you reach the lake, you may be surprised that it doesn't look like one—and it's not. Because of this, many hikers continue up-canyon to the bridge in search of Mirror Lake. On my last hike along this trail, most of the hikers I met above the "lake" were unaware they had passed it. This trail certainly needs a "Mirror Lake" sign at the lake to alert hikers to their arrival (and disappointment).

Before the big flood in early January 1997, you could take a bridge over Tenaya Creek immediately below a pond that lay immediately below Mirror Lake, but it got washed out and was never replaced. After the high-volume discharge diminishes, usually by late July, you can safely wade across Mirror Lake (a.k.a. Tenaya Creek) to get to the other bank and to the bike path up to it. **END OF SIDE TRIP.**

Standing on the Tenaya Bridge, you can get a good idea of the status of Mirror Lake. If Tenaya Creek is a raging torrent descending toward you, Mirror Lake will be worth the visit, but if there is only slow water or no water at all, you're likely to be disappointed.

From the north side of the bridge, a trail climbs briefly north to the Indian Caves area, which we'll visit later. First, we take the paved bike path northeast up to a junction with a bike path west to the caves, then we start east and momentarily spy a broad footpath branching left. You can choose either route northeast, both reuniting about 0.4 mile later near a shallow pond. If you don't mind all the hikers and cyclists, the bike path is more desirable since it is better graded and it ascends beside the engaging creek. When you reach the shallow pond, you may be disappointed; formerly, it was deeper and, until the mid-1990s, was a popular summertime swimming hole. But it is paralleling the evolution of adjacent Mirror Lake, reverting to just a broad stretch of Tenaya Creek. From the north side of the former swimming hole and just beyond an outhouse, a nature trail loops over to the southwest edge of former Mirror Lake, while the main trail continues briefly north to the lake's northwest edge. From this path's end, a former parking area, there is a horse trail that you can take southwest to Indian Caves or northeast up lower Tenaya Canyon.

In this vicinity, you'll see that Mirror Lake exists no more. The lake used to dry up by late September, and, at that time in past years, the Park Service would excavate the lake, sometimes removing thousands of tons of sand and gravel. This material was later spread on snow-covered winter roads to make them more drivable. It was an efficient system. Environmentalists, however, thought otherwise, so the procedure was stopped, and after 1971, Mirror Lake began to silt up. There will be many disheartened tourists to Mirror Lake, but perhaps as was with the Firefall (see the start of Trip 57), the public was led to expect the unnatural to be natural. Mirror Lake was not a deep, reflective gem when it was discovered; rather, it was a shallow, rockfall-dammed pond. However, with the addition of a manmade dam about 1890, the lake assumed its reflective qualities, which were then maintained from 1914 to 1971 by yearly excavation.

Today, visitors must console themselves with, at best, a broad stretch of Tenaya

Mirror Lake and Mt. Watkins

Creek in times of high runoff, and, at worst, a dry, gravel creek bed in late summer and early fall. To get the mirrored reflection of Mt. Watkins, take this hike in times of high water and take the broad path to its end, from which a conspicuously narrower hiker/equestrian path continues ahead (see the side trip at the end of this trip's description). For a few years, the Park Service expected the diminishing Mirror Lake to evolve into a meadow, and so called it Mirror Meadow, but this transition has not occurred, and is not likely to occur in the foreseeable future. If it were not signed Mirror Lake, no one would take it for a lake, and visitors mistakenly would hike up-canyon looking for a real lake.

Another nearby feature, remembered perhaps only by historians, is also gone: Iron Spring. Located by Tenaya Creek just 500 yards down the bike path from Mirror Lake's former satellite pond, the spring was the focal point of Camp 10, whose popularity exceeded available resources.

To resume your hike, look for the horse trail that starts at the end of the broad path. (It can be smelly, so perhaps most will simply descend the creekside bike path.) Starting south on the horse trail, you see, high above, North Dome and Half Dome. Next, your trail passes myriad oversize boulders that originated from the vertical east wall of Washington Column. Soon, your trail switchbacks briefly down to near the paved bike path, then goes 100 yards west to enter the Indian Caves area. In the past, this area was a favorite, with its several caves located among dozens of house-size boulders. However, apparently, there were too many climbing accidents and too much liability for the park, so, in the early 1990s, the area officially ceased to exist. If you bring children here, use the utmost caution. In this area, inspect a large, low slab that lies along the horse trail's north side. On its flat top are mortar holes made by the Yosemite Indians, who used them to pulverize acorns.

Continuing west, you have a choice: Either stay on the trail or take the paved bike path, just south of the caves. The two diverge, and, on this stretch, you pass under the forbidding south face of Washington Column. You may think you hear faint voices coming from high up on it. You actually might, for there are several popular crack systems on it that rock climbers ascend to the top. Where the trail and the bike path come together, you can look up a deep cleft—eroded along a vertical fracture—that separates Washington Column from that giant lithic rainbow, Royal Arches. After 150 yards of westward traverse, the two parallel paths cross a very low (and easily missed) deposit, mapped as a moraine. Actually, it is an old rockfall deposit similar to one immediately west of an upcoming campground.

Note that all the rocks are entirely covered with crustose lichens, a growth process that takes centuries. On the basis of their age, together with age estimates of the tall surrounding ponderosa pines and incense-cedars, one can see that a major rockfall has not occurred here for hundreds of years. Perhaps the source of the last major rockfall was the greatly thinned skyline arch, which is just a fraction of its former self. The large skyline arch just west of Royal Arches proper could fall any day, but then it might stand for millennia.

Where the horse trail and bike path come together, we approach the northeast corner of old Camp 9, which then became the Group Camp, and, finally, the new millennium's Backpackers Walk-In Campground. If you're going to start a backpack trip out of Yosemite Valley, or you've just descended into it, you can spend the night (one night only) here. By cutting south through the campground, one can save 0.3 mile. However, by continuing west for a few minutes along the bike path (the trail goes to the Ahwahnee Hotel), we reach the Sugarpine Bridge, named for a huge sugar pine growing by the northeast corner of the bridge. Like a royal arch, this stately, old-growth giant with a dead crown could fall any day. From the bridge, you take a trail first southeast up the Merced River, then briefly northeast up Tenaya Creek. Where you meet the southbound shortcut trail through the campground, you take it and immediately bridge Tenaya Creek, and then walk southeast past the back side of North Pines Campground and along the stables' road to the Clarks Bridge bus stop.

Under the old system of campground nomenclature, Upper, North, and Lower Pines campgrounds used to be, respectively, Camps 11, 12, and 14. Camp 13 never existed, for superstitious reasons. The camps' names were changed when they were modified to a fixed-site system. This system limited the number of vehicles per campground and greatly reduced the number of campers, who previously used to pack the camps until they overflowed. This dramatic campsite reduction resulted in a significant reduction in Valley sewage sent down to the Bridalveil Moraine sewage plant. In May 1976, this plant was replaced by a new sewage plant opened in El Portal, thus removing one more undesirable, man-made feature from the Valley.

The campgrounds may seem about as perfect as one could realistically desire—for the lucky minority who can get a site. However, there has developed relatively recently a crucial underlying problem: root rot. In prehistoric times, the Valley's vegetation was in part dynamically governed by periodic fires. After fire-suppression policies were introduced, the Valley's oak woodlands were invaded by conifers, resulting in the campground cover you see today. The conifer concentration, lacking periodic burns, invited attack by a root-rot fungus, *Fomes annosus*. The aging conifers are bound to fall, but the fungal invasion hastens their doom, and some people worry about the risk of camping in these forest groves. The lesson to be learned: Man's changes in Nature, even when well-intentioned, often lead to unwanted or unforeseen results.

S **SIDE TRIP UP LOWER TENAYA CANYON:** In addition to visiting "Mirror Lake," you get ever-changing views of Half Dome and other features of deep Tenaya Canyon by continuing 1.1 miles to the start of the Snow Creek Trail and then 0.3 mile beyond it to the main bridge over the principal branch of Tenaya Creek. Those who want to be physically challenged can ascend the Snow Creek Trail up to a vista point a full half mile above the canyon's floor. Finally, competent cross-country travelers can make a short diversion to the top of Tenaya Creek falls.

From the northwest arm of the former lake, you take a horse trail up-canyon. About 100 yards beyond it, you will come to a 1990s rockfall at the base of a cliff, which has conspicuous polish on it, imparted by a glacier before it retreated up-canyon about 15,000 years ago. In contrast to this glacier, the upper Merced Canyon glacier, which flowed through Little Yosemite Valley, lingered at the east end of Yosemite Valley for perhaps a few hundred years before it retreated up its canyon.

Your trail leads up-canyon under a shady forest cover, and soon you approach Tenaya Creek—a good picnic spot. Beyond it, your trail rolls northeast toward the south spur of Mt. Watkins, which is occasionally seen through the forest canopy. About 1.1 miles beyond Mirror Lake, you come to a junction with the Snow Creek Trail, which switchbacks more than 100 times in its 2600-foot climb out of Tenaya Canyon and into its hanging tributary of Snow Creek. Perhaps as many folks hike up this arduous trail as descend it. Averaging more than 20% gradient for 2.25 miles, you had better be in shape should you attempt it. The route up it is described in the last part of Trip 30, which includes a short diversion to what I call Snow Creek Point. Views on this trail generally improve with elevation, but you only have to do the first ten short switchbacks—about a 0.2-mile hike—to emerge above the forest and have a rewarding view. From it, you'll see, just up-canyon, the resistant bedrock cliff over which Tenaya Creek falls plunges.

Many believe that hanging tributary canyons like Snow Creek's became hanging because trunk glaciers eroded their canyons far deeper than tributary glaciers did theirs. However, a hike up treacherous Tenaya Canyon would show that in its steepest parts, where glaciers flowed fastest and should have eroded most, the canyon retains its preglacial V-shaped cross section. So, in this vicinity, where the floor is flat and glaciers flowed more slowly, erosion would have been less, and hence the U-shaped cross section is preglacial. And indeed, unglaciated, U-shaped Sierran canyons—both trunk and hanging tributary—do exist.

From the trail junction, our loop trail continues up-canyon, going a couple hundred yards to a bridge over a branch of Tenaya Creek, then a similar distance to a larger bridge over Tenaya Creek proper. Ahead, the loop trail is not worth taking, for it is largely viewless and it won't take you back to the bike path at Mirror Lake. Rather, it will continue beyond the easily missed lake down to Tenaya Bridge. Therefore, unless you want a viewless workout (the trail has its ups and downs), return the way you came back to your trailhead at Clarks Bridge. But first, for safety-minded and competent cross-country hikers, a brief visit to Tenaya Creek falls might be worth the effort.

From the bridge, a conspicuous use trail heads about 0.3 mile up along the south bank to the creek's falls, whose brim is a worthy goal. This use trail first goes up-canyon to a talus slope, from which you can continue ahead to the base of the falls, or else ascend the talus and traverse along a sloping and potentially dangerous (especially when wet) bedrock bench to the nearby falls.

This vicinity is near the end of a cross-country descent through Tenaya Canyon from Tenaya Lake. This strenuous descent is best done in late summer, when Tenaya Creek is barely flowing, since, in the lower parts, it is faster to hop thousands of the creek's boulders than to push through creekside vegetation. If you don't know the correct route (of several possibilities), you will need a rappel rope for the drop-offs. Even if you do know the correct route, in some spots, you may still wish you had a rope for safety. While for me it was my most exhilarating hike in the park, it also was the most dangerous—more so, in my opinion, than is a roped ascent of El Capitan. Why? Because these days, if you need a rescue off that monolith, you can radio for one, whereas in Tenaya Canyon you have no one to save you but the members of your own party. **END OF SIDE TRIP.**

TRIP **59**

Upper Yosemite Fall and Eagle Peak

S ╱ DH

DISTANCE: 7 miles out and back

ELEVATIONS: 3970′/6710′
+3000′/-410′/±6820′

SEASON: Late May to early November

USE: Heavy

MAPS: *Half Dome, Yosemite Falls*

TRAIL LOG:

1.2	Columbia Rock
1.6	Cryptic junction
1.7	Gate
3.2	Junction
3.5	Upper Yosemite Fall

INTRODUCTION: Most park visitors walk to the base of Lower Yosemite Fall. This popular trail gets you to the other end—the brink of Upper Yosemite Fall. For some, the hike is quite strenuous, and many ascend only to Columbia Rock, which is a worthy goal in itself. Like other early trails of Yosemite Valley, the Yosemite Falls Trail was privately built and then was operated as a toll trail. From 1873 to 1877, John Conway labored intermittently to produce a route to the Upper Fall's brink—a route to replace the defunct Indian path that once climbed Indian Canyon. After reaching the fall's brink, he extended the trail up to airy Eagle Peak.

Strategically located Eagle Peak, highest of the Three Brothers, provides commanding views both up and down Yosemite Valley. The hike to it also provides exciting views, and it is included here as a side trip. Taking this trip will increase your round-trip distance from 7 to 12.8 miles and your total elevation gain and descent by about 3000 feet, to 9000 feet.

DIRECTIONS TO THE TRAILHEAD: Park in the trailhead parking lot, which is the western of two lots immediately east of the climbers' Camp 4 Walk-In Campground, on the north side of Northside Drive, just past the Yosemite Lodge complex. The eastern lot is for campers, but climbers monopolize both. Consequently, you may have to park in the westernmost part of the Yosemite Lodge parking lot. Better yet, take a shuttle bus to this spot. Trail begins in map section D5.

DESCRIPTION: From beside Northside Drive, you begin on a north-heading trail that separates Camp 4 Walk-In Campground from its adjacent parking lot. In about 200 yards, reach the north-side Valley floor trail (Trip 54). By walking west on it about 25 yards, you reach the start of the Yosemite Falls Trail. We leave conifers behind as we start up nearly four dozen switchbacks. Characteristic of old trails, each switchback leg is short. Under the shade of canyon live oaks, which dominate talus slopes such as the one we're on, our so far viewless ascent finally reaches a usually dry wash that provides us with framed views of Leidig Meadow and the Valley's central features.

With more than one fourth of the elevation gain below you, you pass more oaks and an occasional bay tree as you now switchback east to a panoramic viewpoint Columbia Rock, which, at 5031 feet elevation, is just over 1000 feet above the Valley floor. At its safety railing, you can study the Valley's geometry, from Half Dome and the Quarter Domes west to the Cathedral Spires. Several steep, gravelly switchbacks climb after the viewpoint, the trail traverses northeast, drops slightly, passes an enormous Douglas fir, and then drops some more before it bends north for a sudden dramatic view of Upper Yosemite Fall. Here, at a minor low spot in the trail, is a cryptic junction.

S **SIDE TRIP TO OH MY GOSH ROCK:** On your right is the start of a 50-yard-long trail that descends to a railing, from which you're likely to say, "Oh my gosh," or something similar. From this small viewpoint, with room for about a half dozen hikers, if that, you look almost directly down on Lower Yosemite Fall and can trace Yosemite Creek up past its cascades to Upper Yosemite Fall. There is no other trail spot in the Valley where you can see the entire falls' sequence. Be forewarned, however, that the trail is somewhat exposed, and a careless step could result in a fatal slip over the brink of a cliff. **END OF SIDE TRIP.**

Next, the main trail quickly switchbacks to take you down to an adjacent gate, which is closed in times of potential danger, such as when covered with snow or when rockfall may be imminent. For example, in clear weather in November 1980, a 4000-ton slab, probably weakened by the May 1980 Mammoth Lakes earthquakes, fell from the site where you see a conspicuous scar on the cliffs west of and above the trail, killing three hikers. Smaller rockfalls have occurred, and, over tens of millions of years, countless rockfalls, more than glaciers, widened the Valley.

Your climb up a long, steep trough ends among white firs and Jeffery pines, about 135 switchbacks above the Valley floor. Here, in a gully beside a seasonal creeklet, you come to a junction, and your trail turns right while the trail to Eagle Peak continues ahead. Your trail makes a brief climb east out of the gully and reaches a broad crest and a trail heading south to Upper Yosemite Fall. If you are backpacking to this vicinity, continue east just a bit farther to a conspicuous use trail that goes 200-plus yards north to a large camping area near the west bank of Yosemite Creek. You can find relatively isolated campsites by going either west or north of this area.

Those bound for the fall keep to the crest as you follow a trail south almost to the Valley's rim; then, at a juniper, you veer east and descend more steps to a fenced-in viewpoint. If you're acrophobic, you should not attempt the last part of this descent, even though it has a hand railing, for it is possible, though unlikely, that you could slip on loose gravel or smooth bedrock and tumble over the brink. Beside the lip of Upper Yosemite Fall, you see and hear it plunge all the way down its 1430-foot drop to the rocks below. Just beyond the fall is a large roof—one that indicates the size of a slab that broke loose from this cliff in the not too distant past. On the skyline beyond the roof stands the pride of the Clark Range, finlike Mt. Clark.

Let's go back in time about 20,000 years, to the height of the last glaciation. How far did the tributary glacier descending south through Yosemite Creek's valley advance? Conventional geologic wisdom puts its terminus at about 6700 feet elevation, 0.3 mile above the fall's brink. However, if it and the preceding glacier both had stopped there, we would see a conspicuous terminal-moraine complex. But not a trace of a moraine is to be found. Rather, the two past glaciers advanced to the brink and were about 600 feet thick where each calved massive icefalls over the cliff onto the Valley's trunk glacier, more than 1000 feet below. Why didn't geologists reach this conclusion? Well, all believe that glaciers deeply erode, and, beginning just south of the imaginary terminus, there are shallow solution pockets on our low ridge. In reality, Sierran glaciers need to be more than 600 feet thick to plane away the solution pockets here and elsewhere.

After returning up the crest, you take a trail east briefly down to a bridge over Yosemite Creek and obtain water. However, be careful! Occasionally, people, wading in the creek's icy water, slip on the glass-smooth creek bottom and are swiftly carried over the fall's brink. From the creek's bridge, you could continue eastward 0.75 mile up a trail to Yosemite Point, a highly scenic goal.

⑤ **SIDE TRIP TO EAGLE PEAK:** Return to the junction in the gully west of the fall, from which most people descend 3.2 miles back down to the Valley floor. Bound for Eagle Peak, about 2.9 miles distant and about 1160 feet above your junction, you now commence a shady trek 0.6 mile north, climbing out of the gully, descending into a second, and climbing out of a third to a minor-divide junction. These gullies, plus the one north of the junction, are all in line and they probably owe their existence to relatively easy erosion along a straight, major fracture in the granitic bedrock. Leaving the Yosemite Creek environs, whose trail is described in the southbound direction in Trip 28, you momentarily cross Eagle Peak Creek and then climb more than 300 feet, at first steeply, before leveling off in a bouldery area—part of a terminal moraine which was left by a glacier that descended from the west slopes of Mt. Hoffmann. Now you turn south, generally leaving Jeffrey pines and white firs for lodgepole pines and red firs as you climb to Eagle Peak Meadows, whose north edge is blocked by another moraine. It is this moraine that diverts Eagle Peak Creek northeast, and it also dams up the meadow's ground water, thereby keeping conifers out of it.

Beyond the sometimes boggy meadow, we cross the headwaters of Eagle Peak Creek and, in a few minutes, reach a hillside junction, 1.7 miles from the last junction. From it, an old trail climbs and drops along a 1.8-mile course to the El Capitan spur trail. To reach the summit of that monolith, it is easier to start from Tamarack Flat Campground (Trip 27). From the junction, we branch left for a moderate 0.6-mile ascent to the diminutive summit of Eagle Peak. Like El Capitan, this summit has a register. From the weather-pitted, brushy summit, you have far-ranging views that extend all the way to the Sierra Crest along the park's east boundary. Below, central Yosemite Valley spreads out like a map, and, if you've brought along a detailed map of this Valley, you should be able to identify most of its major landmarks plus dozens of minor features.

At 3800 feet above the Valley floor, it's easy to appreciate the Valley's magnitude. About 2 million years ago, when glaciers may have first entered the Valley on a regular basis (some may have entered occasionally considerably earlier), it already was deep and quite wide, typical of some tropical granitic canyons. The Valley, you see, more than anything else, is the result of weathering and erosion under a warm, wet climate that lasted for about 50 million years, until about 33 million years ago. In tropical lands, subsurface chemical weathering is very intense, disintegrating highly jointed bedrock as much as 2000 feet below the surface. Coincidentally, the thickest "sediments" in the Valley are about 2000 feet, and below your summit, in Leidig Meadow, are about 1000 feet. These have been called glacial deposits because early geologists were unaware of

Looking southeast from Eagle Peak summit, you'll view Sentinel Rock, Sentinel Dome, and the cliff below Glacier Point.

subsurface chemical weathering. Glaciers certainly have left some deposits, perhaps up to 200 to 400 feet, so, ironically, the Valley has lost some of its depth because of this infilling. Glaciers, which performed very little erosion, were mammoth, but the largest never overtopped the Valley's rim, even at Royal Arches and Washington Column. The last glacier, where it passed below your summit, was about 1400 feet thick.

After your stay atop Eagle Peak, return directly to your trailhead, a distance of 6.1 miles. **END OF SIDE TRIP.**

TRIP **60**

Upper Yosemite Fall and North Dome

S ⁄ DH

DISTANCE:	17 miles out and back
ELEVATIONS:	3970′/7580′ +4650′/-1090′/±11,480′
SEASON:	Early July to mid-October
USE:	Heavy to Yosemite Falls; moderate beyond it
MAPS:	*Half Dome, Yosemite Falls*

TRAIL LOG:

3.5	Upper Yosemite Fall viewpoint
3.9	Yosemite Creek bridge
4.6	Yosemite Point
6.2	Indian Canyon Creek
6.6	Lehamite Creek Trail
8.0	Spur trail
8.5	North Dome

INTRODUCTION: The easiest route to North Dome is along Trip 29, which starts from the Tioga Road and reaches the dome with about half the distance and half the elevation change encountered in this trip, which has a round-trip elevation gain of more than 5700 feet. This is comparable to the ascent of Half Dome (Trip 68), which hundreds accomplish on good summer-weather days. The reason to take this longer trip is to combine the eminent views from North Dome with those from the brink of Upper Yosemite Fall and from Yosemite Point. If you're exhausted when you reach Yosemite Point, turn back. From late summer into October, Yosemite Creek can dry up, and if it does so, there may be no water along the entire route. If Upper Yosemite Fall has dried up, don't take this hike. Some folks backpack this route and then continue onward to descend along the Snow Creek Trail to the Valley's floor at Clarks Bridge, a total of 19.2 miles. Personally, I feel there is simply too much elevation gain and loss to do while laden down with a backpack and still have an enjoyable experience. Nevertheless, I've seen backpacking parties doing this route, and so I've written it up as an alternate trip.

DIRECTIONS TO THE TRAILHEAD: Park in the trailhead parking lot, which is the western of two lots immediately east of the climbers' Camp 4 Walk-In Campground, on the north side of Northside Drive, just past the Yosemite Lodge complex. The eastern lot is for campers, but climbers monopolize both. Consequently, you may have to park in the westernmost part of the Yosemite Lodge parking lot. Better yet, take a shuttle bus to this spot. Trail begins in map section D5.

DESCRIPTION: From beside Northside Drive, you begin on a north-heading trail that separates Camp 4 Walk-In Campground from its adjacent parking lot. In about 200 yards, reach the north-side Valley floor trail (Trip 54). By walking west on it about 25 yards, you reach the start of the Yosemite Falls Trail. We leave conifers behind as we start up nearly four dozen switchbacks. Characteristic of old trails, each switchback leg is short. Under the shade of canyon live oaks, which dominate talus slopes such as the one we're on, our so far viewless ascent finally reaches a usually dry wash that provides us with framed views of Leidig Meadow and the Valley's central features.

With more than one fourth of the elevation gain below you, you pass more oaks and an occasional bay tree as you now switchback east to a panoramic viewpoint Columbia Rock, which, at 5031 feet elevation, is just over 1000 feet above the Valley floor. At its safety railing, you can study the Valley's geometry from Half Dome and the Quarter Domes west to the Cathedral Spires. Several steep, gravelly switchbacks climb from the viewpoint, and then the trail

traverses northeast, drops slightly, passes an enormous Douglas fir, and then drops some more before it bends north for a sudden dramatic view of Upper Yosemite Fall. Here, at a minor low spot in the trail, is a cryptic junction.

S **SIDE TRIP TO OH MY GOSH ROCK:** On your right is the start of a 50-yard-long trail that descends to a railing, from which you look almost directly down on Lower Yosemite Fall and can trace Yosemite Creek up past its cascades to Upper Yosemite Fall. Be forewarned, however, that the trail is somewhat exposed, and a careless step could result in a fatal slip over the brink of a cliff. **END OF SIDE TRIP.**

Next, the main trail quickly switchbacks to take you down to an adjacent gate, which is closed in times of potential danger, such as when covered with snow or when rockfall may be imminent.

Your climb up a long, steep trough ends among white firs and Jeffery pines, about 135 switchbacks above the Valley floor. Here, in a gully beside a seasonal creeklet, you come to a junction, and your trail turns right while the trail to Eagle Peak continues ahead. Your trail makes a brief climb east out of the gully and reaches a broad crest and a trail heading south to Upper Yosemite Fall. If you are backpacking to this vicinity, continue east just a bit farther to a conspicuous use trail that goes 200-plus yards north to a large camping area near the west bank of Yosemite Creek. You can find relatively isolated campsites by going either west or north of this area.

Those bound for the fall keep to the crest as you follow a trail south almost to the Valley's rim; at a juniper, you veer east and descend more steps to a fenced-in viewpoint. If you're acrophobic, you should not attempt the last part of this descent, even though it has a hand railing, for it is possible, though unlikely, that you could slip on loose gravel or smooth bedrock and tumble over the brink. Beside the lip of Upper Yosemite Fall, you see and hear it plunge all the way down its 1430-foot drop to the rocks below. Just beyond the fall is a large roof—one that indicates the size of a slab that broke loose from this cliff in the not too distant past. On the skyline beyond the roof stands the pride of the Clark Range, finlike Mt. Clark.

After returning up the crest, you take a trail east briefly down to a bridge over Yosemite Creek and obtain water. However, be careful! Occasionally, people, wading in the creek's icy water, slip on the glass-smooth creek bottom and are swiftly carried over the fall's brink. From the creek's bridge, your climb to Yosemite Point first goes north, then east up short switchbacks on brushy slopes, and finally south to the rim of Yosemite Valley. Here at Yosemite Point, the view is even more spectacular than the one from the Yosemite Fall viewpoint. The dramatic panorama extends from Clouds Rest south past Half Dome and Glacier Point, then west to the Cathedral Rocks. Near you, a massive shaft of rock, Lost Arrow, rises almost to the Valley's rim. A better view of Lost Arrow would certainly be desirable, but to obtain it you have to get dangerously close to this spire.

Leaving Yosemite Point, you start up a crest and, in a few minutes, pass a quartz vein, the source of crystals you may have noticed on the slope just before you reached the point. About 120 yards farther, you encounter pitted boulders, which are not glacial erratics but merely local boulders that have been weathering more or less in place for hundreds of thousands of years, if not a million. Just higher on the crest, you pass a low, pitted knob of very weathered bedrock, and then climb moderately for 300 feet before crossing a forest-clad crest.

With no more major climbing between here and North Dome, we start a welcome, shady, gentle descent north. White firs and Jeffrey pines dominate the terrain, but by a trailside knoll, you'll see at least one mature sugar pine, recognizable by large cones growing at the tips of the tree's long branches. At about 7300 feet elevation,

these trees are close to the upper extent of their elevation range. Beyond the knoll, we dip into a shallow bowl, pass three more trailside knolls, and make a 0.3-mile descent through a red-fir-shaded gully. Indian Canyon Creek heralds the end of our descent and provides a well-deserved drink. After late July, this may be your last source for water, so be sure to stock up. Lehamite Creek, ahead, can dry up in early August, and Royal Arch Creek can dry in early July.

An Indian trail once descended Indian Canyon, hence the name. Early tourists used it to gain access to the north rim and then traverse west to Upper Yosemite Fall, but the trail fell into disrepair in the 1870s, particularly with the construction of the current trail to the fall, built by John Conway from 1873 to 1877. The Indian trail is long gone, but a cross-country descent down Indian Canyon is feasible. This route has minor but time-consuming obstacles in it, as well as some potentially dangerous spots if you do not know what you are doing, and so this canyon is definitely not a shortcut to the Valley floor. Beyond a low ridge east of the Indian Canyon Creek ford, you encounter the Lehamite Creek Trail and its namesake creek a minute's walk past it. The trail climbs 1.6 miles northeast up to a saddle, and then, reversing the start of Trip 29, it continues 1.8 miles northeast to the Tioga Road. No one would take such a route except in an emergency, since it bypasses this trip's major goal, North Dome.

Beyond generally flowing Lehamite Creek, which gives rise a half mile down to Lehamite Falls, you climb over a slightly higher ridge, then drop to seasonal Royal Arch Creek, shaded by white firs, Jeffrey pines, and sugar pines. These give way to brush, particularly huckleberry oak, as you climb to lower Indian Ridge. Ascending it, you quickly encounter a junction, from which Trip 29 has descended south. From the junction, a spur trail drops south a half mile to the summit of North Dome.

From the North Dome summit area, you can probably see more of Yosemite

Valley and its adjacent uplands than can be seen from any other summit except Half Dome. (The views from about 200 yards south of and below the summit area are even better.) The enormous 4000-foot face of Clouds Rest dominates the canyon's east side, and, to the south and west of it, stands mighty Half Dome, perhaps Yosemite's best-remembered feature. Continuing our clockwise scan, we next recognize Mt. Starr King, a steep-sided dome above Little Yosemite Valley. West of this unseen valley is joint-controlled Panorama Cliff, which bears the scar of a large rockfall near Panorama Point, close to Illilouette Fall. Extremely popular Glacier Point stands west of the fall's gorge, and, above and right of the point, Sentinel Dome bulges up into the sky. Looking down Yosemite Valley, we see Sentinel Rock, with its near-vertical north face, which is due to the unloading of slabs along the rock's near-vertical joint planes. Opposite the rock stand the Three Brothers, also shaped by joint planes, and beyond them protrudes the brow of El Capitan opposite the Cathedral Rocks.

A **ALTERNATE TRIP TO YOSEMITE VALLEY:** From the summit of North Dome, backtrack along its spur trail to the junction, then ascend a northbound trail climbing 1.2 miles up Indian Ridge to a second junction just beyond, only yards beyond a red fir saddle.

> **SIDE TRIP TO INDIAN ROCK:** Veering left is a trail signed for Indian Rock. The trail actually climbs very steeply a quarter mile up brushy slopes to a delicate arch, not a rock. About 1.5 feet thick at the thinnest part of its span, this 20-foot arch came into existence when the highly fractured rock beneath it broke away. **END OF SIDE TRIP.**

Continuing the alternate trip to Yosemite Valley, you make an initial drop and then traverse to a junction at a second red fir saddle, 1.1 miles past the first. To reach the Valley, start east. This shady trail, 2.8 miles long, descends to cascades along Porcupine Creek and then, in the realm of white firs, descends south to a junction near a bridge across Snow Creek. The acres

Indian Ridge arch

of lands just east of the creek are nearly level and there is abundant space for camping.

SIDE TRIP TO SNOW CREEK POINT: The 2.6-mile trail ahead to the floor of Tenaya Canyon has the greatest gradient of any trail into (and out of) Yosemite Valley, just over 20%. When wet, it can be treacherous. Before commencing this descent, you first might want to make brief diversion 0.2 mile southeast over to what I call Snow Creek Point for a good rest. Leave your trail about 250 yards from the junction near the bridge. You cross a broad area out to a minor but obvious high point, 6700 feet elevation. From it, you have a view directly across to Half Dome as well as up-canyon to Clouds Rest, partly blocked by the dome-like mass of Mt. Watkins. **END OF SIDE TRIP.**

Along the alternate trip to Mirror Lake, you make a spectacular descent to the floor of Tenaya Canyon, then walk southwest 1.1 miles to Mirror Lake. Since you're bound to be tired, end your hike by taking the shortest route—the 1.2-mile paved bike path—down to the shuttle-bus stop just east of Clarks Bridge. **END OF ALTERNATE TRIP.**

TRIP **61**

Wawona Tunnel to Stanford, Crocker, and Dewey Points

Ⓜ **↗** DH

DISTANCE:	11 miles out and back
ELEVATIONS:	4410′/7380′
	+3380′/-470′/±7700′
SEASON:	Mid-June to mid-November
USE:	Light
MAP:	*El Capitan*

TRAIL LOG:

0.6	Old Wawona Road
1.2	Inspiration Point
2.9	Artist Creek
3.3	Old Inspiration Point
3.7	Meadow Brook
4.2	Stanford Point
4.8	Crocker Point
5.5	Dewey Point

INTRODUCTION: Five viewpoints are visited: Inspiration, Old Inspiration, Stanford, Crocker, and Dewey. The first two, however, are somewhat blocked by vegetation. By hiking only to Stanford Point, you cut about 2.5 miles and 900 feet of climbing from your hike. The creeks found along this route typically dry up by early summer, so make sure you bring enough water.

DIRECTIONS TO THE TRAILHEAD: Discovery View, at the east end of Wawona Tunnel, on the Wawona Road 1.5 miles west of the Bridalveil Fall parking lot entrance. Trail begins in map section C5.

DESCRIPTION: Your signed trail starts at the west end of the south-side parking lot and makes a switchbacking, generally viewless

500-foot ascent for 0.6 mile up to an intersection of the old Wawona Road.

Constructed in 1875, this old stage route got a lot of use before it was closed with the opening of the newer Wawona Road in 1933. Today, the old road provides a quiet descent 1.6 miles down to the newer road, meeting it just 0.3 mile above the entrance to the Bridalveil Fall parking lot.

Beyond the intersection, your oak-and-conifer-shaded route continues all the way up another 500-foot ascent, keeping you relatively cool but also hiding most of the scenery. At Inspiration Point, we meet a bend in old Wawona Road, a point where early travelers got their first commanding view of El Capitan, Bridalveil Fall, and the Cathedral Rocks. Today, incense-cedars, black oaks, and ponderosa pines obstruct the view.

⑤ SIDE TRIP TO IMPENDING ROCKFALL: To visit the site of a colossal rockfall in the making, take the unmaintained old road 1.2 miles west, gaining 400 feet in the process. The site should be obvious because, at it, you will see on your right, immediately below you, a gap in the bedrock, about 50 feet deep, where a huge slab of bedrock has separated from the adjacent bedrock. If you climb up from the road, you will find additional gaps separating more slabs that have broken free. **END OF SIDE TRIP.**

With most of the climb still ahead, from Inspiration Point, you pace yourself while winding up 1200 vertical feet of the Pohono Trail to arrive at springtime-active Artist Creek. Sugar pines and white firs now replace the lower conifer species, though Douglas firs make sporadic appearances all the way to Stanford Point. From the creek, at an elevation with cool rather than warm afternoon temperatures, we make a steep, 300-foot climb 0.4 mile up to trailside 6920-foot Old Inspiration Point, whose view is in part blocked by a large sugar pine.

Red firs now add shade to the forest canopy as we briefly ascend before dropping to a welcome spring and nearby Meadow Brook. If any water remains along this trail through midsummer, it will be found here. Beyond the creek and its large grove of alders, head north and soon descend to your first significant viewpoint, at the end of a short spur trail—6620-foot Stanford Point. From it, you see the gaping chasm of western Yosemite Valley and identify its prominent landmarks: Leaning Tower, Bridalveil Fall, the Cathedral Rocks, El Capitan, and, seasonally, Ribbon Fall. This stunning panorama should motivate you to climb 0.6 mile farther to reach Crocker Point after more than 400 feet of elevation gain. Reached by a short spur trail, 7100-foot Crocker Point, at the brink of an overhanging cliff, provides a heart-pounding view similar to the last one,

Precipitous Crocker Point

through better. Now most of the Valley's famed landmarks stand boldly before us and we look over all the Cathedral Rocks to see the Three Brothers. To the left of Clouds Rest are twin-towered Cathedral Peak and broad-topped Mt. Hoffmann, with distant Mt. Conness between them, marking the Sierra Crest along the park's northeast boundary.

After the Crocker Point revelation, can you expect anything better? You'll have to judge for yourself after continuing 0.7 mile to 7385-foot Dewey Point.

Just east of this point, François Matthes of the US Geological Survey mapped ancient glacial deposits up to 7000 feet elevation, indicating glaciers deep enough to bury the Cathedral Rocks. In reality, none of his evidence exists, and neither did his glaciers.

Now closer to the Cathedral Rocks, your perspective is different, and you look straight down the massive face of Leaning Tower. Also intriguing is the back side of Middle Cathedral Rock, whose iron-rich, rust-stained surface stands out among the rest of the Valley's gray, somber colors. Finally, you see the Cathedral Spires head on so they appear as one. After scanning the Valley and the horizon, leave the point and descend the way you came.

Trips from the Glacier Point Road and Happy Isles

Introduction to this Area

As in the previous chapter, this one is actually composed of two groups: trails starting from the end or near the end of the Glacier Point Road, high above the east end of Yosemite Valley, and trails starting from Happy Isles, situated in the southeast end of the Valley. At first, these two groups may seem incongruous, but there is logic to their combination. Many people hike down from Glacier Point via Nevada and Vernal falls, while a lot more hike up Happy Isles to Vernal and Nevada falls. (Actually, I've put the descent from Glacier Point in the next chapter as Trip 74, since the route to Nevada Fall also serves as a first phase of hiking trips up the Merced River canyon.)

Glacier Point is arguably the best viewpoint in the entire park, if not in the entire Sierra, although I am sure many Sierran hikers have their favorites. (On my list, the views from Mt. Dana and Half Dome compete for first place; Mt. Whitney, the highest peak in the Sierra, is not one of them.) Whereas you can drive almost to Glacier Point (which is a brief walk), and you can drive to Washburn Point (nearly equally spectacular), you'll have to make short hikes (an hour or two round trip) to acrophobic Taft Point (Trip 63) or to

Mt. Watkins, Tenaya Canyon, and Clouds Rest seen from Half Dome's summit

broad-topped Sentinel Dome (Trip 64), both with "Kodak moments."

Trips 67 to 69 start from Happy Isles, and the hiker use is incredibly heavy on the first mile, up to the Vernal Fall bridge, but still is very heavy up to the brink of Nevada Fall. Beyond it, hundreds of people on a summer day continue to Little Yosemite Valley (the most popular backcountry site in the park), and most continue up Trip 68 toward Half Dome, with perhaps half of them daring to ascend its cables to the summit. In contrast, Trip 69 to Merced Lake is merely heavy.

Supplies and Services

For trips 62 to 66 along the Glacier Point Road, the only supplies are at a store at Glacier Point. This caters to tourists, offering postcards, picture books, souvenirs, and snack food. For trips 67 to 69, beginning from Happy Isles, the same items are available there. Should you need serious food or hiking gear, you'll need to try Yosemite Valley's Curry Village or the large store in Yosemite Village. If you are approaching Glacier Point Road from the south, you can get some last-minute items at a store beside the Wawona Hotel, but again, it caters more to tourists than to hikers. Also, there is an adjacent gas station. Be aware that there are no gas stations north along the Wawona Road, along the Glacier Point Road, or in Yosemite Valley.

Wilderness Permits

If you want to reserve a permit, see the "Wilderness Permits" section in Chapter 6. You can get permits in person either in Yosemite Valley or in Wawona. For the former, go to the Wilderness Center, located in Yosemite Village. For the latter, go to the Wawona District Office, which is at the end of a short road that branches right from the Chilnualna Road immediately past the Pioneer Yosemite History Center.

Campgrounds

Bridalveil Creek Campground is the only campground along the Glacier Point Road. Its entrance lies about 7.7 miles up this road, and campsites are on a first-come, first-served basis. If you plan to stay at it, look for a site, usually in mid-morning, when most campers leave. Your other choices are the Wawona Campground, about 1 mile north of the Wawona Hotel, and the Yosemite Valley campgrounds. Don't expect to get into any of these unless you have made reservations (see pages 4 and 5).

TRIP 62

Glacier Point Road to Dewey Point

Ⓜ ⟋ DH

DISTANCE: 8.2 miles out and back

ELEVATIONS: 6770´/7340´
+740´/-490´/±2460´

SEASON: Late June to mid-October

USE: Moderate

MAPS: *Half Dome, El Capitan*

TRAIL LOG:

0.8 McGurk Meadow
2.0 Pohono Trail
4.1 Dewey Point

INTRODUCTION: This is the easier of two routes to scenic Dewey Point, and it requires less than half the climbing effort of the previous hike, but then it doesn't visit Stanford and Crocker points.

DIRECTIONS TO THE TRAILHEAD: From a signed junction along the Wawona Road, drive 7.4 miles up the Glacier Point Road to the signed trailhead, on your left, which is a quarter mile before the Bridalveil Creek Campground spur road. Trail begins in map sections C5-D5.

DESCRIPTION: Most hikers will start from the Glacier Point Road. The lodgepole-shaded trail gently descends almost to the north tip of largely hidden Peregoy Meadow before topping a low divide. Next, it drops moderately and reaches the south edge of sedge-filled McGurk Meadow, in which we cross its creek. At times, the meadow may have an abundance of wildflowers such as shooting star, paintbrush, cinquefoil, and corn lily. Looking east from the meadow, note the low, unglaciated sum-

mits of the Ostrander Rocks, whose west slopes, at least one past geologist claimed, supported a small glacier that joined a Bridalveil Creek glacier. Actually, there is no evidence whatsoever of glaciation in the Bridalveil Creek drainage north of the Glacier Point Road.

Ⓐ **ALTERNATE TRIP TO DEWEY POINT:** If you are camping at Bridalveil Creek Campground, you have the option of starting from its entrance. Take a closed road that departs southwest away from the camp's Loop A. On it, you cross, in a quarter mile, a creek that drains Westfall Meadows, and then you immediately meet a trail. South, this undesirable trail passes through these meadows, then makes a brush-choked descent to an old logging area—a 1920s "battleground" between environmentalists and the Yosemite Lumber Company. The environmentalists won, but the scars remain. Next, take the trail north, which climbs gently over weathered terrain to the Glacier Point Road. This alternate start adds 0.9 mile to your hike to Dewey Point. **END OF ALTERNATE TRIP**

At Peregoy Meadow's north end, you first re-enter a lodgepole forest, soon crest a shallow, viewless saddle, and then descend at a reasonable gradient to a low-crest trail fork. The fork right quickly joins the Pohono Trail and drops to Bridalveil Creek. You could camp in this vicinity, obtaining water from this perennial creek. We fork left, quickly join that trail, and start west on it. Nearing a broad, low divide, we traverse a dry, gravelly slope dotted with streptanthus, pussy paws, and mat lupine.

The forest cover now becomes dominated by firs—both red and white—and, on the damp, shady floor beneath them, you may find wintergreen, snow plant, and spotted coralroot, the last two living off soil fungi. We cross Bridalveil Creek tributaries, then a smaller third one, before we start up a fourth that drains a curving gully. On the gully's upper slopes, Jeffrey pine, huckleberry oak, and greenleaf manzanita

El Capitan and Cathedral Rocks from Dewey Point

replace the fir cover. In a few minutes, we reach highly scenic 7385-foot Dewey Point, at the end of a short spur trail. Closer to the Cathedral Rocks than the viewpoints ahead, you look straight down the massive face that supports Leaning Tower. Also intriguing is the back side of Middle Cathedral Rock, with an iron-rich, rust-stained surface. Finally, you see the Cathedral Spires head-on, so they appear as one.

A ALTERNATE TRIP TO DISCOVERY VIEW: If you can get someone to meet you at the Wawona Tunnel, then descend to it along this highly scenic portion of the Pohono Trail, which passes Crocker and Stanford points. The remaining 5.5 miles are almost entirely downhill, and we descend 0.7 mile to Crocker Point, on the brink of an overhanging cliff, which provides a heart-pounding view similar to the last one. In addition to the Valley's famed landmarks, we can look over and beyond all the Cathedral Rocks to see the Three Brothers. To the left of Clouds Rest are twin-towered Cathe-

dral Peak and broad-topped Mt. Hoffmann, with distant Mt. Conness between them, marking the Sierra Crest along the park's northeast boundary.

TRAIL LOG: ALTERNATE TRIP

0.6	Old Wawona Road
1.2	Inspiration Point
2.9	Artist Creek
3.3	Old Inspiration Point
3.7	Meadow Brook
4.2	Stanford Point
4.8	Crocker Point
5.5	Dewey Point

A 0.6-mile descent takes us down to Stanford Point, at the end of a short spur trail. Its views are similar to those from Crocker Point, although not as spectacular. From that point, we climb 250 feet south and soon reach a welcome spring and nearby Meadow Brook, a half mile beyond the point. If any water remains along this trail through midsummer, it will be found here.

Among red firs, we make an undulating traverse for 0.4 mile to Old Inspiration Point, whose view is partly blocked. The actual point, identified on the map, is on the projecting spur below and northwest of us, and before construction of the old Wawona Road, a stock trail offered access to it. Our trailside point is at about 6900 feet elevation, and over the next 3.3 miles to trail's end at Discovery View, we'll drop a knee-knocking 2500 feet elevation. This begins with a steep 300-foot descent to close by Artist Creek.

Our longest drop is the next one, in which we lose 1200 feet elevation as we descend to Inspiration Point. Along this descent, we encounter sporadic Douglas firs among white firs and sugar pines. Down at the point, incense-cedars, oaks, and pines obstruct the view. Just to the west, we see a bend in the old Wawona Road, a point where early-stage travelers got their first commanding view of El Capitan, Bridalveil Fall, and the Cathedral Rocks.

Over the next stretch, we make a 500-foot descent mostly via short switchbacks, having oaks and conifers shade us but also hiding most of the scenery. After 0.6 mile, we make an intersection of the old Wawona Road. Built in 1875, this old stage route got a lot of use before it was closed with the opening of the newer Wawona Road in 1933. Today, it provides a quiet descent 1.6 miles down to the newer road, meeting it just 0.3 mile above the entrance to the Bridalveil Fall parking lot. Ahead, we complete the Pohono Trail with a similar, largely viewless, 500-foot descent mostly via short switchbacks for 0.6 mile to trail's end at the south-side parking lot of tourist-populated Discovery View, at the east end of the Wawona Tunnel. **END OF ALTERNATE TRIP.**

TRIP **63**

Glacier Point Road to Fissures at Taft Point

E   /   DH

DISTANCE: 2.6 miles out and back

ELEVATIONS: 7490´/7730´
+100´/-320´/±840´

SEASON: Late June to mid-October

USE: Moderate

MAP: *Half Dome*

TRAIL LOG:

0.7   Pohono Trail
1.2   The Fissures
1.3   Taft Point

INTRODUCTION: The views from Taft Point rival those from Glacier Point. However, since Taft Point is reached by trail, it is less visited than mobbed Glacier Point. Generally lacking protective railings, Taft Point and the Fissures are potentially dangerous, so don't bring along children unless you can *really* keep them under strict control.

DIRECTIONS TO THE TRAILHEAD: From a signed junction along the Wawona Road, drive 13.2 miles up to the Glacier Point Road to a scenic turnout, on your left, which is 2.3 miles before the Glacier Point parking-lot entrance. Trail begins in map section D5.

DESCRIPTION: From the road-cut parking area, you descend about 50 yards to a trail, turn left, and start southwest on it.

After about 150 yards of easy descent, you pass a trailside outcrop that is almost entirely composed of glistening whitish-gray quartz. It also has small amounts of pink potassium feldspar. Lacking the surrounding bedrock's dark minerals, which are more prone to weathering, this outcrop is eroding more slowly than the adjacent landscape, so it protrudes.

In a minute, we come to seasonal Sentinel Creek, whose limited drainage area keeps Sentinel Fall downstream from being one of Yosemite Valley's prime attractions. After boulder hopping the creek, follow an undulating trail west past pines, firs, and brush to a crest junction with the Pohono Trail (Trip 65). Just north of it are some large boulders. Not left by glaciers, these have weathered in place and will continue to become "taller" as the surrounding bedrock is stripped away.

From the junction, we descend to a seeping creeklet that drains through a small field of corn lilies. In this and two other nearby damp areas, you may also find bracken fern, lupine, paintbrush, bluebells (lungwort), mountain monkey flower, arrow-leaved senecio, Richardson's geranium, green gentian (monument plant), and alpine lily. The last two, like corn lily, can grow to head height. Descending toward the Fissures, you cross drier slopes that are generally covered with brush. Here, you may find two wildflowers belonging to the same wildflower tribe: the single-stemmed senecio and the soft arnica. The first has alternate leaves; the second, opposite. Two other yellow wildflowers seen are the sulfur flower, a buckwheat, and the Sierra wallflower, a mustard.

Soon you arrive at the Fissures—five vertical, parallel fractures that cut through overhanging Profile Cliff, beneath your feet. Because the Fissures area is unglaciated, it is well weathered, and a careless step could result in an easy slip on the loose gravel—dangerous in this area.

Beyond the Fissures, walk briefly up to a small railing at the brink of a conspicuous point and get an acrophobia-inducing view of overhanging Profile Cliff, beneath you. For the best views of Yosemite Valley and the High Sierra, walk west to exposed Taft Point. From it, you see the Cathedral Spires and Rocks, El Capitan, the Three Brothers, Yosemite Falls, and Sentinel Rock. Broad

Mt. Hoffmann stands on the skyline just east of Indian Canyon, and east of this peak stands distant Mr. Conness, on the Sierra Crest.

Taft Point was named to commemorate President William Howard Taft's October 1909 visit to Yosemite Valley. On it, he met John Muir, who hoped to convince the president to prevent construction of a dam in Hetch Hetchy. The president, tiring of Muir's arguments, jokingly suggested that Yosemite Valley also be dammed. Muir, not seeing the humor, was offended. To his credit, Taft did oppose the dam, but it was built later. From Taft Point, the Pohono Trail is described westward in Trip 65.

One of the five Fissures

TRIP 64

Glacier Point Road to Sentinel Dome

E ⟋ DH

DISTANCE: 2.4 miles out and back

ELEVATIONS: 7690'/8122'
+460'/-70'/±1060'

SEASON: Late June to mid-October

USE: Heavy

MAP: *Half Dome*

TRAIL LOG:

1.2 Sentinel Dome

INTRODUCTION: Sentinel Dome rivals Half Dome as the most-climbed dome in the park. Tuolumne Meadows' Lembert and Pothole domes almost rival them, but neither is a true dome; each is a roche moutonnée—an asymmetrical, glacier-smoothed ridge. Indeed, most of the Sierra's domes, glaciated or unglaciated, are asymmetrical ridges.

DIRECTIONS TO THE TRAILHEAD: From a signed junction along the Wawona Road, drive 13.2 miles up to the Glacier Point Road to a scenic turnout, on your left, which is 2.3 miles before the Glacier Point parking-lot entrance. Trail begins in map section D5.

DESCRIPTION: From the road-cut parking area, you descend about 50 yards to a trail, turn right, and make a curving, generally ascending traverse 0.75 mile north almost to the south base of Sentinel Dome. Here, we meet and briefly hike north on a road, which has several large boulders along it.

These boulders, and ones between this dome and Glacier Point, are widely thought to have been left by ancient glaciers. They were not; the boulders are locally derived. No glacier ever filled Yosemite Valley to its rim, not even to the tops of Royal Arches and Washington Column. On the road, we soon arrive at the dome's north end, where we meet a path ascending from Glacier Point. We now climb southwest up quite safe, unexposed bedrock slopes to the summit.

At an elevation of 8122 feet, Sentinel Dome is the second-highest viewpoint 👁 above Yosemite Valley. Only Half Dome—a strenuous hike—is higher. Seen from the summit, El Capitan, Yosemite Falls, and Half Dome stand out as the three most prominent Valley landmarks. West of Half Dome are two bald features, North and Basket domes. On the skyline above North Dome stands blocky Mt. Hoffmann, the park's geographic center, while to the east, above Mt. Starr King (an unglaciated, true dome), stands the rugged crest of the Clark Range. In years past, almost everyone who climbed Sentinel Dome expected to photograph its windswept, solitary Jeffrey pine, made famous by Ansel Adams. That tree, unfortunately, finally succumbed to vandalism in 1984.

Liberty Cap and Nevada Fall

TRIP 65

Glacier Point to Taft, Dewey, Crocker, and Stanford Points

M / DH, BP

DISTANCE: 13.5 miles point to point

ELEVATIONS: 4410'/7760'
+2180'/-4980'/±7160'

SEASON: Mid-July to mid-October

USE: Light

MAPS: *Half Dome, El Capitan*

TRAIL LOG:

0.9	Junction in a gully
1.7	Sentinel Creek
2.6	Broad-saddle junction
3.3	Taft Point
5.6	Bridalveil Creek
5.9	McGurk Meadow Trail
8.0	Dewey Point
8.7	Crocker Point
9.3	Stanford Point
9.8	Meadow Brook
10.2	Old Inspiration Point
10.6	Artist Creek
12.3	Inspiration Point
12.0	Old Wawona Road
13.5	Discovery View

INTRODUCTION: This hike, along the Pohono Trail, takes you past several excellent viewpoints, each showing a different part of Yosemite Valley in a unique perspective. After early June, carry enough water (usually one quart) to last you until the midpoint, Bridalveil Creek, which is the hike's only permanent source of water. Although this trip is recommended as a dayhike, you can backpack and spend the night near Bridalveil Creek.

DIRECTIONS TO THE TRAILHEAD: From a signed junction along the Wawona Road,

drive 15.5 miles up the Glacier Point Road to its end. If possible, take a park bus up to crowded Glacier Point, since, at times, the parking lot can be full. Trail begins in map section D5.

DESCRIPTION: On the low crest just east of the entrance to the Glacier Point parking lot, start south up a signed trail that quickly forks. Trip 74 branches left, but you branch right and under white fir cover momentarily cross the Glacier Point Road. Beyond it, you immediately branch right again since the path ahead climbs to a ranger's residence. Your still-climbing trail curves west up to a switchback, then south to a road. Cross the road and then continue up the relentless grade to a north-descending crest, which you cross before climbing briefly south to a junction in a gully. Our route, the Pohono Trail, goes west to the brink of Sentinel Fall, which is usually dry by midsummer.

[A] **ALTERNATE TRIP TO SENTINEL DOME:** The alternate route, which starts north before climbing south, goes to scenic summit of Sentinel Dome. Should you take this dome route, you can return to the Pohono Trail or you can take a more level route that adds 0.6 mile to your total distance. The 2.4-mile alternate route first climbs 0.4 mile up to the Sentinel Dome's north end, and we now climb southwest up quite safe, unexposed bedrock slopes to the summit. At an elevation of 8122 feet, Sentinel Dome is the second-highest viewpoint above Yosemite Valley. Only Half Dome—a strenuous hike—is higher. Seen from the summit, El Capitan, Yosemite Falls, and Half Dome stand out as the three most prominent Valley landmarks. West of Half Dome are two bald features, North and Basket domes. On the skyline above North Dome stands blocky Mt. Hoffmann, the park's geographic center, while to the east, above Mt. Starr King (an unglaciated, true dome), stands the rugged crest of the Clark Range.

Retrace your steps down to the dome's north end and then follow a trail 1 mile south to a trailhead on Glacier Point Road.

From here, you walk about 150 yards of easy descent. We pass a trailside outcrop that is almost entirely composed of glistening whitish-gray quartz. It also has small amounts of pink potassium feldspar. In a minute, we come to seasonal Sentinel Creek, whose limited drainage area keeps Sentinel Fall downstream from being one of Yosemite Valley's prime attractions. After boulder hopping the creek, we follow an undulating trail a half mile west to a broad-saddle junction with the Pohono Trail. **END OF ALTERNATE TRIP.**

Our route, the Pohono Trail, leaves the gully, traverses southwest across a lower face of Sentinel Dome, then drops to a gravelly gully with north-side boulders. The gravel and boulders here, like all the ones between Glacier Point and Sentinel Dome, are locally derived, not lingering deposits left by an ancient glacier. Your route stays gravelly on a short, sometimes steep descent to seasonal Sentinel Creek. Here, you can follow its bank 90 yards out to a point to get a good Valley view. Before mid-June, hikers will see upper Sentinel Fall splashing down a chute immediately west of the point.

Beyond the seasonal creek, climb past lodgepole pines and white firs, and then, before a broad-saddle junction, past Jeffrey pines and red firs. At the junction, the alternate route joins ours, and we now descend a half-mile trail segment to the Fissures and Taft Point. Be careful when exploring this scenic though precipitous area.

From the westernmost fissure, the Pohono Trail descends south, then contours west to a low ridge. By following the ridge about 250 yards out to its end, you'll reach an unnamed point that gives you a view down upon the Cathedral Rocks, lined up in a row. Descending from the low ridge, the shady Pohono Trail drops 700 feet to a bridge over Bridalveil Creek. Level ground is limited, so if you plan to camp, you can get water here, and perhaps camp in isolated spots on lands north and west of two nearby trail junctions. From the creek,

which is our hike's approximate midpoint, we climb shortly west to these two junctions with a lateral trail. This one climbs 2 miles south to the Glacier Point Road, then a short mile beyond it to Bridalveil Creek Campground.

On the Pohono Trail, we continue about 1 mile west to a broad, low divide with potential for making a dry camp. Now about 1.5 miles from Dewey Point, we first traverse a dry, gravelly slope, which becomes dominated by firs. On the damp, shady floor beneath them, you may find white-veined wintergreen, snow plant, and spotted coralroot, all deriving nutrients to varying degrees from soil fungi. Two Bridalveil Creek tributaries are crossed, then a smaller third one before we start up a fourth that drains a curving gully. On its upper slopes, Jeffrey pine, huckleberry oak, and greenleaf manzanita replace firs. In a few minutes, we reach prized 7385-foot Dewey Point, at the end of a short spur trail. Closer to the Cathedral Rocks than the viewpoints ahead, you look straight down the massive face that supports Leaning Tower. Also intriguing is the back side of Middle Cathedral Rock, with an iron-rich, rust-stained surface. Finally, you see the Cathedral Spires head on, so they appear as one.

The remaining 5.5 miles are almost entirely downhill, and we descend 0.7 mile to Crocker Point, on the brink of an overhanging cliff, which provides a heart-pounding view similar to the last one. In addition to the Valley's famed landmarks, we can look over and beyond all the Cathedral Rocks to see the Three Brothers. To the left of Clouds Rest are twin-towered Cathedral Peak and broad-topped Mt. Hoffmann, with distant Mt. Conness between them, marking the Sierra Crest along the park's northeast boundary.

A 0.6-mile descent takes us down to Stanford Point, at the end of a short spur trail. Its views are similar to those from Crocker Point, although not as spectacular. From that point, we climb 250 feet south, and we soon reach a welcome spring and nearby Meadow Brook, a half mile beyond the point. If any water remains along this trail through midsummer, it will be found here.

Among red firs, we make an undulating traverse for 0.4 mile to Old Inspiration Point, whose view is partly blocked. The actual point, identified on the map, is on the projecting spur below and northwest of us, and before construction of the old Wawona Road, a stock trail offered access to it. Our trailside point is at about 6900 feet elevation, and over the next 3.3 miles to trail's end at Discovery View, we'll drop a knee-knocking 2500 feet elevation. This begins with a steep 300-foot descent to close by Artist Creek.

Our longest drop is the next one, in which we lose 1200 feet elevation as we descend to Inspiration Point. Along this descent, we encounter sporadic Douglas firs among white firs and sugar pines. Down at the point, incense-cedars, oaks, and pines obstruct the view. Just to the west, we see a bend in the old Wawona Road, a point where early stage travelers got their first commanding view of El Capitan, Bridalveil Fall, and the Cathedral Rocks.

Over the next stretch, we make a 500-foot descent mostly via short switchbacks, having oaks and conifers shade us but also hiding most of the scenery. After 0.6 mile, we make an intersection of the old Wawona Road. Built in 1875, this old stage route got a lot of use before it was closed with the opening of the newer Wawona Road in 1933. Today, it provides a quiet descent 1.6 miles down to the newer road, meeting it just 0.3 mile above the entrance to the Bridalveil Fall parking lot. Ahead, we complete the Pohono Trail with a similar, largely viewless, 500-foot descent mostly via short switchbacks for 0.6 mile to trail's end at the south-side parking lot of tourist populated Discovery View, at the east end of the Wawona Tunnel.

TRIP 66

Glacier Point to Yosemite Valley via Four Mile Trail

E / DH

DISTANCE: 4.6 miles point to point

ELEVATIONS: 3980′/7200′
+20′/-3240′/±3260′

SEASON: Mid-June to mid-October

USE: Heavy

MAP: *Half Dome*

TRAIL LOG:
4.6   Southside Drive

INTRODUCTION: This trail provides a very scenic descent to Yosemite Valley—while acquainting you with the Valley's main features. This knee-knocking descent also gives you a feel for the Valley's 3000-foot depth. This hike is rated "easy" because not much energy is expended, but if you do a lot of braking on the dozens of switchbacks, you may consider it "moderate."

DIRECTIONS TO THE TRAILHEAD: From a signed junction along the Wawona Road, drive 15.5 miles up the Glacier Point Road to its end. If possible, take a park bus up to crowded Glacier Point, since, at times, the parking lot can be full. Trail begins in map section D5.

DESCRIPTION: Before building the Yosemite Falls Trail (Trip 59), John Conway first worked on this trail, completing it in 1872. Originally about 4 miles long, it was rebuilt and lengthened in 1929, but the trail's name stuck. Our trail starts west from the north side of a concessionaire's shop, which, along with other minor structures, replaced the grand Glacier Point Hotel. This three-story hotel, together with the adjacent historic Mountain House—built in 1878—burned to the ground in August 1969.

Descending west from the concessionaire's shop, you enter a shady bowl whose white firs and sugar pines usually harbor snow patches well into June. You then contour northwest, eventually emerge from forest shade, and, looking east, see unglaciated Glacier Point's two overhanging rocks capping a vertical wall.

One of Yosemite's popular geologic myths is that it at least once lay under as much 700 feet of glacier ice. In reality, the glaciers in this vicinity only buried the lower half of Yosemite Valley.

Soon, you curve west, veer in and out of a cool gully, then reach a descending ridge. On it, you generally exchange views of Royal Arches, Washington Column, and North Dome for those of Yosemite Falls, the Three Brothers, El Capitan, and, foremost, Sentinel Rock, which provides a good gauge to mark our downward progress.

Switchbacks begin, and where gravel lies on hard tread, it's easy to take a minor spill if you're not careful. Chinquapin, greenleaf manzanita, and huckleberry oak are shrubs that dominate the first dozen switchback legs, thereby giving us unobstructed panoramas, though making the hike a hot one for anyone ascending from the Valley floor on a summer afternoon. However, as you duck east into a gully, shady conifers appear, though they somewhat censor your views.

If you had been on this trail on some early morning through the 1970s until June 1990, when hang gliders were banned, you could have seen pilots land in meadows below you, taking sky trails from Glacier Point to the Valley floor.

About midway down the series of switchbacks, canyon live oaks begin to compete with white firs and Douglas firs, and your view is obstructed even more. After descending two thirds of the vertical distance to the Valley floor, the switchbacks temporarily end. A long, steady descent now ensues, mostly past canyon live oaks, whose curved-upward trunks are their response to creeping talus. These talus deposits were erroneously mapped by USGS topographer-turned-geomorphologist François Matthes as glacial deposits. Black oaks and incense-cedars also appear, and, after a quarter mile, you cross a creeklet that usually flows until early July. Down it, you have an excellent view of Leidig Meadow. Your steady descent again enters oak cover and you skirt below the base of imposing but largely hidden Sentinel Rock. At last, a final group of switchbacks guide you down to a former parking loop, closed about 1975, and you proceed briefly north, intersecting the Valley floor's southside trail, Trip 54, just before your end point, Southside Drive.

Sentinel Rock

TRIP 67

Happy Isles to Vernal Fall Bridge, Vernal Fall, and Nevada Fall

S **Ω** DH

DISTANCE: 6.5 miles semiloop

ELEVATIONS: 4020'/6000'
+2100'/-2100'/±4200'

SEASON: Early June to early November

USE: Packed

MAP: *Half Dome*

TRAIL LOG:

1.0	Vernal Fall bridge
1.1	John Muir Trail
1.6	Brink of Vernal Fall
1.7	Junction
1.8	Silver Apron bridge
2.7	John Muir Trail
2.9	Nevada Fall
3.1	Glacier Point-Panorama Trail
4.2	Clark Point
5.4	Mist Trail
5.5	Vernal Fall bridge
6.5	Happy Isles

INTRODUCTION: Popular, paved paths go to near the bases of Yosemite and Bridalveil falls, and a paved one also goes to the Vernal Fall bridge. Although the trail to the bridge is a mere 1 mile from the Happy Isles shuttle-bus stop, it is steep and intimidating for out-of-shape flatlanders. The total elevation gain and loss on this 2-mile, round-trip hike is about 900 feet, and perhaps a thousand or more hikers make this ascent on any sunny summer day. Fewer do it off season, which can last from early April through late November.

In contrast, "only" a few hundred go on to the brink of Nevada Fall. Mile for mile, this very popular hike may be the most scenic one in the park. The first part of this loop goes up the famous (or infamous) Mist Trail—a steep, strenuous trail that sprays you with Vernal Fall's mist, which cools you on hot afternoons but makes the mostly bedrock route slippery and dangerous. Take raingear or, if it is a warm day, strip down to swimwear, since you can dry out on slabs above the fall. For best photos, start after 10 AM

DIRECTIONS TO THE TRAILHEAD: Happy Isles shuttle-bus stop in eastern Yosemite Valley. Trail begins in map section D5.

DESCRIPTION: From the shuttle-bus stop, you walk briefly east across an adjacent bridge and head south, soon reaching the start of the famous John Muir Trail, which heads about 210 miles southward to the summit of Mt. Whitney. Bay trees, Douglas firs, and canyon live oaks dominate the forest canopy as we start up it, and, after a few minutes, we reach a small spring-fed cistern with questionably pure water. Beyond it, the climb south steepens, and, before bending east, you get a glance back at Upper Yosemite Fall, partly blocked by the Glacier Point Apron. This smooth, curving apron contrasts with the generally angular nature of Yosemite's topography.

Note the canyon wall south of the apron, which has a series of oblique-angle cliffs—all of them remarkably similar in orientation since they've fractured along the same series of joint planes. At the canyon's end, Illilouette Fall plunges 370 feet over a vertical, joint-controlled cliff. Just east of the fall is a large, light-colored scar that marks the site of a major rockfall that broke loose during the winter of 1968–69.

Climbing east, you head up a canyon whose floor, in times past, was buried by as much as 1800 feet of glacier ice. Hiking beneath the unstable, highly fractured south wall of Sierra Point, you cross a talus slope—an accumulation of rockfall boulders. The May 1980 Mammoth Lakes

Liberty Cap above Vernal Fall

earthquakes perhaps set up three rockfalls here, which finally occurred in conjunction with heavy rains in late spring 1986. More may occur. Entering forest shade once more, you ascend a steep stretch of trail before making a quick drop to the Vernal Fall bridge. From it, you see Vernal Fall, a broad curtain of water plunging 320 feet over a vertical cliff before cascading toward us. Looming above the fall are two glacier-resistant masses, Mt. Broderick (left) and Liberty Cap (right). Just beyond the bridge are restrooms and an emergency telephone (for emergencies such as heart attacks or slips on dangerous rocks).

About 200 yards beyond the bridge, you come to the start of your loop. Here, the Mist Trail continues upriver while the John Muir Trail starts a switchbacking ascent to the right. This is the route taken by those with horses or other pack stock. We'll go up the Mist Trail and down the John Muir Trail. You can, of course, go up or down either, but by starting the loop up the Mist Trail, you stand less chance of an accident. Hikers are more apt to slip or to twist an ankle descending than ascending, and the Mist Trail route to Nevada Fall has ample opportunities for mishaps.

Dressed for the upcoming mist, which can really soak you in May or June, start up the Mist Trail and soon, rounding a bend, receive your first spray. If you're climbing this trail on a sunny day, you may see one, if not two, rainbows come alive in the fall's spray. The spray increases as you advance toward the fall, but you get a brief respite behind a large boulder. Beyond it, complete your 300-plus steps, most of them wet, which guide you up through a verdant, spray-drenched garden. The last few dozen steps are under the shelter of trees; then, reaching an alcove beneath an ominous overhang, you scurry left up a last set of stairs. These, protected by a railing, guide you to the top of a vertical cliff. Pausing here, you can study your route, the nearby fall, and the river gorge. The railing ends near the brink of Vernal Fall, but, unfortunately, people venture beyond it, and some-

times people are swept over the fall. In the past, some sunbathers would wade to the far side of Emerald Pool, which lies just above the brink, but due to the danger of its treacherous current, wading and swimming are forbidden.

Plunging into the upper end of chilly Emerald Pool is churning Silver Apron, and a bridge spanning its narrow gorge is our immediate goal. At times, the trail has been vague in this area, due to use paths, but the correct route leaves the river near the pool's far (east) end, and you'll find outhouses here. After a brief climb south, the trail angles east to a nearby junction. From it, a view-packed trail climbs almost a half mile to Clark Point, where it meets the John Muir Trail. We, however, stay low and curve left over to the Silver Apron bridge. Beyond it, we have a short, moderate climb up to a broad bench, which was once the site of La Casa Nevada. Opened in 1870, it was managed by Albert Snow until 1891, when a fire burned the main structure to the ground.

Spurred onward by the sight and sound of plummeting Nevada Fall, you climb eastward, and soon commence a series of more than two dozen compact switchbacks. As you ascend them, Nevada Fall slips out of view, but you can see towering Liberty Cap. The climb ends at the top of a joint-controlled gully, where, on brushy slopes, we once again meet the John Muir Trail, with outhouses just up it. From this junction, we head southwest toward nearby Nevada Fall.

Along this stretch, you may notice boulders—rich in large, blocky feldspar crystals—that contrast strongly with the local bedrock. These boulders are erratics—that is, rocks left by retreating glaciers that were left here perhaps as recently as 15,000 years ago. Near the Merced River are patches of bedrock that have been polished, striated, and gouged by the last glacier.

S SIDE TRIP TO NEVADA FALL VIEWPOINT: Just a few yards before the Nevada Fall bridge, you can strike northwest to find a short spur trail that drops to a viewpoint beside the fall's brink. This viewpoint's railing is seen from the fall's bridge, thereby giving you an idea where the trail ends. Don't stray along the cliff's edge and, as advised earlier, respect the river—people have been swept over this fall, too. Standing near the tumultuous brink of the Merced River, you can look across its canyon—minimally eroded by glaciers—to unglaciated Glacier Point. Vernal Fall, which lies just beyond Emerald Pool, plunges over a vertical wall that is perpendicular to the steep one Nevada Fall plunges over. This part of the canyon contains major fracture planes, or joint planes, which account for the canyon's angular landscape. **END OF SIDE TRIP.**

From the Nevada Fall bridge, we strike southwest, immediately passing more glacier polish and erratic boulders, and shortly end a gentle ascent at a junction, just beyond a seeping spring, with the Glacier Point-Panorama Trail. Those descending from Glacier Point (Trip 74) join us here for a descent to Happy Isles along the John Muir Trail. This starts with a high traverse that provides an ever-changing panorama of domelike Liberty Cap and broad-topped Mt. Broderick—both overridden by glaciers and both standing as testaments to the ineffectiveness of glacial erosion. As you progress west, Half Dome becomes prominent, its hulking mass vying for your attention. Eventually, you descend to Clark Point, where you meet a scenic connecting trail that switchbacks down to Emerald Pool. If you enjoyed the Mist Trail, you can visit it again by first descending this lateral, but remember to be careful while descending the Mist Trail.

Backpackers, packers, and those wishing to keep dry continue down the John Muir Trail, which curves south into a gully, switchbacks down to the base of spreading Panorama Cliff, then switchbacks down a talus slope. Largely shaded by canyon live oaks and Douglas firs, it reaches a junction with a horse trail (no hikers allowed) that descends to the Valley's stables. Continue a brief minute more to a junction with the Mist Trail, turn left, and quickly reach the Vernal Fall bridge, from which you retrace your steps down to Happy Isles.

TRIP 68

Happy Isles to Little Yosemite Valley and Half Dome

S ⟳ DH, BP

DISTANCE: 15.5 miles semiloop

ELEVATIONS: 4020′/8842′
+5400′/-5400′/±10,800′

SEASON: Mid-June to early October

USE: Packed

MAP: *Half Dome*

TRAIL LOG:

1.0	Vernal Fall bridge
1.1	John Muir Trail
1.6	Brink of Vernal Fall
1.7	Junction
1.8	Silver Apron bridge
2.7	Junction northeast of Nevada Fall
3.3	Trail fork
3.8	Junction north of backpackers camp
5.1	Leave the John Muir Trail
7.2	Summit of Half Dome
11.7	Junction northeast of Nevada Fall
11.9	Nevada Fall
12.1	Glacier Point-Panorama Trail
13.2	Clark Point
14.4	Mist Trail
14.5	Vernal Fall bridge
15.5	Happy Isles

INTRODUCTION: Many a backpacker has spent his or her first night in the "wilderness" of Little Yosemite Valley. Indeed, more backpackers camp in it than in any other Yosemite backcountry area. Perhaps, too, more bears visit it than any other backcountry area. During the summer, rangers

stationed near the backpackers camp patrol this area. If you hike only this far, your entire semiloop route up the Mist Trail and down the John Muir Trail will be just 8.7 miles long, and the total ups and downs will be a mere 4800 feet. If you ascend and descend only along the Mist Trail, your round-trip distance is 7.4 miles; if you head entirely along the John Muir Trail, it is 9.6 miles.

For many camped in Little Yosemite Valley, the ultimate goal is the summit of Half Dome. On a good summer day, hundreds of hikers attempt this summit, but many turn back, either from exhaustion or from fear. If I, as a first-time visitor, were allowed to make only one dayhike in the park, I would unquestionably choose this hike—the one that introduced me to Yosemite and fired my desire to "climb every mountain."

However, Half Dome is certainly not for acrophobics, klutzes, those who are out of shape, or those who have bad knees. The hike up Half Dome's shoulder and its cables is exposed and potentially life threatening. Far too many "innocents abroad" attempt to make this climb, even in threatening thunderstorms. Do not attempt to climb the dome's shoulder and its cables if weather is threatening, for the exposed rock becomes very slippery and a lightning strike is possible. Occasionally, people die on this route; more fall and are injured. Do not take it likely. Although I've seen kids on the cables as young as 8, I discourage anyone under the age of 12. Call me a cautious parent. Half Dome's hiking season is limited to when its cables are in place, which depends a lot on the amount of snowfall and on the presence or absence of stormy weather. Cables may be placed as early as early May or as late as late June, and they may be removed any time in October. Therefore, if you're hiking before July or after September, be sure to inquire if the cables are up.

The preferred route between the Vernal Fall bridge and Nevada Fall ascends the Mist Trail and descends the John Muir Trail, for a total of 15.5 miles, exposing you to the maximum amount of scenery. If you ascend and descend only along the Mist Trail, your round-trip distance is 14.4 miles; if you head entirely along the John Muir Trail, it is 16.6 miles.

DIRECTIONS TO THE TRAILHEAD: Happy Isles shuttle-bus stop in eastern Yosemite Valley. Trail begins in map section D5.

DESCRIPTION: From the shuttle-bus stop, you walk briefly east across an adjacent bridge and head south, soon reaching the start of the famous John Muir Trail, which heads about 210 miles southward to the summit of Mt. Whitney. Bay trees, Douglas firs, and canyon live oaks dominate the forest canopy as we start up it, and, after a few minutes, we reach a small, spring-fed cistern with questionably pure water. Beyond it, the climb south steepens, and before bending east, you get a glance back at Upper Yosemite Fall, partly blocked by the Glacier Point Apron. This smooth, curving apron contrasts with the generally angular nature of Yosemite's topography.

Climbing east, you head up a canyon whose floor, in times past, was buried by as much as 1800 feet of glacier ice. Hiking beneath the unstable, highly fractured south wall of Sierra Point, you cross a talus slope—an accumulation of rockfall boulders. The May 1980 Mammoth Lakes earthquakes perhaps set up three rockfalls here, which finally occurred in conjunction with heavy rains in late spring 1986. More may occur. Entering forest shade once more, you ascend a steep stretch of trail before making a quick drop to the Vernal Fall bridge. From it, you see Vernal Fall, a broad curtain of water plunging 320 feet over a vertical cliff before cascading toward us. Looming above the fall are two glacier-resistant masses, Mt. Broderick (left) and Liberty Cap (right). Just beyond the bridge are restrooms and an emergency telephone.

About 200 yards beyond the bridge, you come to the start of your loop. Here, the Mist Trail continues upriver, while the John Muir Trail starts a switchbacking

ascent to the right. This is the route taken by those with horses or other pack stock. We'll go up the Mist Trail and down the John Muir Trail. You can, of course, go up or down either, but by starting the loop up the Mist Trail, you stand less chance of an accident. Hikers are more apt to slip or to twist an ankle descending than ascending, and the Mist Trail route to Nevada Fall has ample opportunities for mishaps.

Dressed for the upcoming mist, which can really soak you in May or June, start up the Mist Trail and soon, rounding a bend, receive your first spray. If you're climbing this trail on a sunny day, you may see one or two rainbows come alive in the fall's spray. The spray increases as you advance toward the fall, but you get a brief respite behind a large boulder. Beyond it, complete your 300-plus steps, most of them wet, which guide you up through a verdant, spray-drenched garden. The last few dozen steps are under the shelter of trees; then, reaching an alcove beneath an ominous overhang, you scurry left up a last set of stairs. These, protected by a railing, guide you to the top of a vertical cliff. Pausing here, you can study your route, the nearby fall, and the river gorge. The railing ends near the brink of Vernal Fall, but, unfortunately, people venture beyond it, and sometimes people are swept over the fall. In the past, some sunbathers would wade to the far side of Emerald Pool, which lies just above the brink, but due to the danger of its treacherous current, wading and swimming are forbidden.

Plunging into the upper end of chilly Emerald Pool is churning Silver Apron, and a bridge spanning its narrow gorge is our immediate goal. At times, the trail has been vague in this area, due to use paths, but the correct route leaves the river near the pool's far (east) end, and you'll find outhouses here. After a brief climb south, the trail angles east to a nearby junction. From it, a view-packed trail climbs almost a half mile to Clark Point, where it meets the John Muir Trail. We, however, stay low and curve left over to the Silver Apron bridge.

Beyond it, we have a short, moderate climb up to a broad bench that was once the site of La Casa Nevada. Opened in 1870, it was managed by Albert Snow until 1891, when a fire burned the main structure to the ground.

Spurred onward by the sight and sound of plummeting Nevada Fall, you climb eastward and soon commence a series of more than two dozen compact switchbacks. As you ascend them, Nevada Fall slips out of view, but you can see towering Liberty Cap. The climb ends at the top of a joint-controlled gully, where, on brushy slopes, we arrive at a junction northeast of Nevada Fall. Here, we once again meet the John Muir Trail, with outhouses just up it.

From this junction, you climb up a gully that is generally overgrown with scrubby huckleberry oaks. From its top, you quickly descend into forest cover and reach a fairly large swimming hole on the Merced River. Though chilly, it is far enough above the river's rapids to provide a short, refreshing dip. A longer stay would make you numb. Beneath lodgepole and Jeffrey pines, white firs, and incense-cedars, we continue northeast along the river's azalea-lined bank, and then quickly encounter a trail fork.

A **ALTERNATE TRIP TO LITTLE YOSEMITE VALLEY:** If you are backpacking first to Little Yosemite Valley, you should take the right fork, which parallels the Merced River upstream to the Valley's large backpackers camp with bearproof storage boxes. Just beyond it are outhouses and a spur trail northeast over to a rangers' camp. Just ahead of that is a junction with the left-fork route. **END OF ALTERNATE TRIP.**

Those bound for Half Dome generally take the left fork after first obtaining enough water from the Merced River, which is your last reliable source. This trail is 0.1 mile shorter than the right-fork route, but it climbs and then descends the low east ridge of Liberty Cap, negating its advantage over the level right-fork route, and it reaches a junction north of backpackers camp.

S **SIDE TRIPS TO LIBERTY CAP AND BEYOND:** Some nearby landmarks—all off trail—make interesting side trips: Liberty Cap, Mt. Broderick, Lost Lake, and the Diving Board. After starting on the "shortcut" trail, you can head west up the low east ridge of Liberty Cap and, if you're careful, quite safely reach its summit without climbing shoes or a rope. Mt. Broderick is another matter. You have to know how to use a map and how to climb. Some hikers may also want to bring a rope. Its summit, however, provides better views than does Liberty Cap's, particularly of Nevada Fall.

Both of these "domes" are merely high points on the down-canyon end of ridges, and, as such, are typical of tropical landforms. If glaciated, they are called roches moutonnées. Their asymmetry has very little to do with glaciation, for the amount of planing down their back sides and plucking away their steep down-canyon faces has been absolutely minimal. (Evidence for this is found early along Trip 5. You can see similar unglaciated roches moutonnées in the Dome Lands of the southern Sierra.)

Don't get lost looking for Lost Lake, a swamp at the east base of Mt. Broderick. Trapped between moraines left by a glacier receding up-canyon perhaps only 15,000 years ago, this "lake" has been slowly filling with sediments dominated by wind-blown silt and pollen. Lost Lake will appeal to the naturalist but probably not to anyone else. Beyond Lost Lake, one can climb to the steep-faced Diving Board, which, in my opinion, offers the best of all possible views of Half Dome's giant, intimidating northwest face. Good mountaineering sense and cross-country ability are prerequisites for this brushy ascent. From the low saddle just west of Lost Lake, descend sufficiently west down a gully before starting your climb. Small cliffs await those starting too soon. Be sure to study your route so you can find it when you descend. For a day-hike or overnight visit to the bench holding Starr King Lake, south of and high above the Merced River, consult Trip 74. For any of these side trips, you might consider first checking in with a ranger stationed in Little Yosemite Valley, then checking back when you have safely returned. **END OF SIDE TRIPS.**

From the junction north of backpackers camp, you've not yet expended half the energy required to reach Half Dome's summit. After 1.3 miles of forested ascent, you leave the John Muir Trail (Trip 44 in the downhill direction from Tuolumne Meadows), and you continue up the Half Dome Trail. After about 0.7 mile, the trail bends west just before reaching a saddle, which is worth the minor effort for a viewful rest stop. In the next half mile, the trail first climbs through a forest of red firs and Jeffrey pines instead of white firs and incense-cedars. Half Dome's northeast face comes into view before the trail tops a crest. Here, you get a fine view of Clouds Rest and its satellites, the Quarter Domes, which are accessible by a somewhat brushy cross-country ascent from the previously mentioned saddle. Between them and us, previous glaciers spilled into Tenaya Canyon. The shoulder of Half Dome, west of and above you, never was glaciated. You now have a 0.3-mile traverse, which reveals more views, including Tenaya Canyon, Mt. Watkins, Mt. Hoffmann, and much of the upper Merced River basin. This traverse ends all too soon at the base of Half Dome's intimidating shoulder.

Almost two dozen very short switchbacks guide us up the view-blessed ridge of the dome's shoulder. For too long, the real danger on this steep section was loose gravel, which could prove fatal if you fell off the trail—or were pushed off it due to heavy traffic—at one or more exposed spots. But in 2005, it was extensively reworked to make it safer. Topping the shoulder, you are confronted with the dome's even more intimidating pair of cables, which definitely cause some hikers to retreat. (Usually, the cables are put up around mid-May and removed in early October.)

The ascent starts out gently enough, but it too quickly steepens, almost to a 45-degree angle. On this stretch, first-timers often slow to a snail's pace, clenching both cables with sweaty hands. Looking down, you can see that you don't want to fall. In recent years, hikers have used gloves for the cables and then left them for others. Fresh gloves may be better than sweaty hands, but old, well-used gloves seem just as slippery. Remember that even when thunderstorms are miles away, static electricity can build up here. Out of a seemingly fair-weather sky, a charge can bolt down the cable, throwing your arms off it—or worse. If your hair starts standing on end, beat a hasty retreat!

The rarefied air certainly hinders your progress as you ascend, but, eventually, an easing gradient gives new incentive, and soon you are scrambling up to the broad summit of Half Dome, an area about the size of 17 football fields. With caution, most hikers proceed to the dome's high point (8842 feet), located at the north end, where you can view the dome's overhanging northwest point. Stout-hearted souls peer over the lip of this point for an adrenaline-charged view down the dome's 2000-foot northwest face, perhaps seeing climbers ascending it. In the past, a few folks liked to camp overnight to view the sunrise, but in 1993, camping became banned, ostensibly to protect the small population of Mt. Lyell salamanders (accumulating human feces may have been the real reason). Sharing the summit are golden-mantled ground squirrels. One of these squirrels, begging for food, may have followed you up the cables, staying close enough to you to avoid becoming the prey of a sharp-eyed hawk.

From the broad summit of this monolith, which originated in the late days of the dinosaurs, you have a 360-degree panorama. You can look down Yosemite Valley to the bald brow of El Capitan and up Tenaya Canyon past Clouds Rest to Cathedral Peak, the Sierra Crest, and Mt. Hoffmann. Mt. Starr King—a dome that rises only 250 feet above you—dominates the Illilouette Creek basin to the south, while the Clark Range cuts the sky to the southeast. Looking due

The cabled trail up Half Dome

east across Moraine Dome's summit, one sees Mt. Florence, whose broad form hides the park's highest peak, Mt. Lyell, behind it.

To return, backtrack 4.5 miles to the junction northeast of Nevada Fall, at the top of the Mist Trail. From here, the John Muir Trail traverses southwest toward nearby Nevada Fall.

S SIDE TRIP TO NEVADA FALL VIEWPOINT: Just a few yards before the Nevada Fall bridge, you can strike northwest to find a short spur trail that drops to a viewpoint beside the fall's brink. This viewpoint's rail-

ing is seen from the fall's bridge, thereby giving you an idea where the trail ends. A bit of this short trail is exposed, so watch your step. **END OF SIDE TRIP.**

From the Nevada Fall bridge, we strike southwest and shortly end a gentle ascent at a junction, just beyond a seeping spring, with the Glacier Point-Panorama Trail. Onward, we have a high traverse that provides an ever-changing panorama of dome-like Liberty Cap and broad-topped Mt. Broderick—both overridden by glaciers and both standing as testaments to the ineffectiveness of glacial erosion. As you progress west, Half Dome becomes prominent, its hulking mass vying for your attention. Eventually, you descend to Clark Point, 1.1 miles from the last junction, where you meet a scenic connecting trail that switchbacks down to the Mist Trail. Backpackers, packers, and those wishing to keep dry continue down the John Muir Trail, which curves south into a gully, switchbacks down to the base of spreading Panorama Cliff, and then switchbacks down a talus slope. Largely shaded by canyon live oaks and Douglas firs, it reaches a junction with a horse trail (no hikers allowed) that descends to the Valley's stables. Continue a brief minute more to a junction with the Mist Trail, 1.2 miles below Clark Point, turn left, and quickly reach the Vernal Fall bridge, from which you hike your last mile down to the shuttle-bus stop at Happy Isles.

TRIP **69**

Happy Isles to Merced Lake

Ⓜ / BP

DISTANCE: 28.4 miles out and back

ELEVATIONS: 4020′/7220′
+4480′/-4480′/±8960′

SEASON: Early July to mid-October

USE: Heavy

MAPS: *Half Dome, Merced Peak*

TRAIL LOG:

1.0	Vernal Fall bridge
3.6	Nevada Fall
3.8	Top of Mist Trail
4.9	Little Yosemite Valley
11.9	Echo Valley junction
14.2	Merced Lake High Sierra Camp

INTRODUCTION: Best done in three days with overnight stops at Little Yosemite Valley and Merced Lake, this hike is often done in two by energetic weekend hikers. Its route, up a fantastic river canyon, is one of the Sierra's best. Located at an elevation of about 7200 feet, relatively large Merced Lake is about 2000-plus feet lower than the popular ones reached from Tuolumne Meadows' trailheads. As such, it is snow free sooner, and may be relatively mosquito free by late July, when the higher populations are still profuse elsewhere.

DIRECTIONS TO THE TRAILHEAD: Just east of the day-use parking lot in Curry Village, drive 0.2 mile southeast on the shuttle-bus road to a short spur road branching right to a backpackers' parking lot. Trail begins in map section D5.

DESCRIPTION: This trip's mileage is based on starting from the Happy Isles bus stop and ascending the John Muir Trail. If you start from the trailhead parking lot just east of Curry Village, you'll have to walk a bit farther. You can take the paved, roadside path a half mile east to the bus stop, but a quieter route begins from the southeast edge of the trailhead parking lot. This rolls southeast, staying about 100 to 150 yards from the unseen shuttle-bus road. In 0.4 mile, it intersects a southbound stock trail that links the Valley stables to the John Muir Trail. Beyond this intersection, you head east on planks across a boggy area, and although mosquitoes may be bothersome in late spring and early summer, the bog produces its best wildflowers during that time. At a huge, lone boulder by the bog's east side, your trail angles southeast toward the hub of the Happy Isles area, and you head briefly north to its bus stop, 0.6 mile from the trailhead parking lot. Note that if you ascend and descend the Mist Trail instead of taking the John Muir Trail, you'll save 1.1 mile each way, reducing the distance to the Merced Lake High Sierra Camp to 13.1 miles.

From the Happy Isles shuttle-bus stop, you walk briefly east across an adjacent bridge and head south, soon reaching the start of the famous John Muir Trail, which heads about 210 miles southward to the summit of Mt. Whitney. Bay trees, Douglas firs, and canyon live oaks dominate the forest canopy as we start up it, and, after a few minutes, we reach a small, spring-fed cistern with questionably pure water. Beyond it, the climb south steepens, and before bending east, you get a glance back at Upper Yosemite Fall, partly blocked by the Glacier Point Apron. This smooth, curving apron contrasts with the generally angular nature of Yosemite's topography.

Entering forest shade once more, you ascend a steep stretch of trail before making a quick drop to the Vernal Fall bridge. From it, you see Vernal Fall, a broad curtain of water plunging 320 feet over a vertical cliff before cascading toward us. Looming above the fall are two glacier-resistant masses, Mt. Broderick (left) and Liberty Cap (right). Just beyond

the bridge are restrooms and an emergency telephone.

Now you hike 0.1 mile up to the start of the Mist Trail. The 1.1-mile shorter Mist Trail, to the brink of Vernal Fall, past Emerald Pool and across the Silver Apron, certainly is worth taking, but the steep stretch up to the top of Vernal Fall can be wet and slippery and potentially dangerous with a heavy backpack. Play it safe and take the John Muir Trail 2.7 miles up to the top of the Mist Trail.

This stretch has equal rewards. One is that the first 1.2 miles to Clark Point is along shady, moderately graded switchbacks, which are near ideal for the ascent. Beyond the point, you have less climbing to do, and most of it is with views across the canyon to Half Dome, Mt. Broderick, and Liberty Cap, the last above Nevada Fall. After 1.1 miles, you reach the Glacier Point-Panorama Trail, then descend 0.2 mile to the bridge over Nevada Fall. Just a few yards beyond the bridge, you can strike northwest to find a short spur trail that drops to a viewpoint beside the fall's brink. This viewpoint's railing is seen from the fall's bridge, thereby giving you an idea where the trail ends. Finally, about 0.2 mile later, you reach the top of the Mist Trail.

From the junction and its adjacent outhouses, we begin our 1-mile route to Little Yosemite Valley, first by ascending a brushy, rocky gully, then quickly descending and reaching both forest shade and the Merced River. Beneath pines, firs, and incense-cedars, we continue northeast along the river's azalea-lined bank, then quickly reach a trail fork. We keep to the main, riverside trail and go a short half mile to another junction, in the hub of Little Yosemite Valley, where the John Muir Trail branches north. Just up it is a large camping area with bearproof storage boxes, then outhouses, and, beyond them, a spur trail northeast over to a rangers' camp. Some hikers on their way to Merced Lake spend their first night here, which is about halfway up, measured by total elevation gain and loss.

You leave the northbound John Muir Trail to embark on a shady 2-mile stroll, following the Merced Lake Trail through the broad, flat valley. The valley's floor has been largely buried by glacial sediments, which, like beach sand, make you work, even though the trail is level. Progressing east through Little Yosemite Valley, we stay closer to the base of glacier-polished Moraine Dome than to the Merced River, and along this stretch, you can branch off to riverside campsites that are far more peaceful than those near the John Muir Trail junction, which tends to be a "Grand Central Station." The valley's east end is graced by the presence of a beautiful pool—the receptacle of a Merced River cascade. Leaving the camps of the picturesque area, we climb past the cascade and glance back to see the east face of exfoliating Moraine Dome.

Your brief cascade climb heads toward the 1900-foot Bunnell Point cliff, which is exfoliating at a prodigious rate. Rounding the base of a glacier-smoothed dome, unofficially called the Sugar Loaf, you enter Lost Valley, about 1 mile beyond the east end of Little Yosemite Valley, in which no fires are allowed. At Lost Valley's east end, switchback up past Bunnell Cascade, which has magnificent canyon scenery that can easily distract you from the real danger of this exposed section of trail.

Although the scenery may overpower you, past glaciers, which completely buried Bunnell Point, were powerless to effectively erode this part of the canyon. They overtopped the point by several hundred feet, yet their massive thicknesses, exerting more than 100 tons per square foot on the lower slopes, failed to transform this canyon from a V to a U shape.

Just beyond the V gorge, the canyon floor widens a bit, and, in this area, we bridge the Merced River. Our up-canyon walk soon reaches a series of more than a dozen switchbacks that carry us up 400 feet above the river—a bypass route necessitated by another V gorge. Our climb reaches its zenith amid a spring-fed profuse garden, bordered by aspens, which, in midsummer, supports a colorful array of various wildflowers. Alpine lily, monk's hood, and arrow-leaved senecio grow chest high, as if to divert our attention from the many smaller, though equally beautiful, wildflower species.

Beyond this glade, you soon come out onto a highly polished bedrock surface. Here, you can glance west and see Clouds Rest—a long ridge—standing on the horizon. Now you descend back into tree cover,

Cascading Merced River, from the switchbacks east of Bunnell Point

and, among the white boles of aspens, brush through a forest carpet of bracken ferns and cross several creeklets before emerging on a bedrock bench above the river's inner gorge. From the bench, you can study the features of a broad, hulking granitic mass opposite you whose south face is bounded by an immense arch. A hairline crack along its east side indicates that a major rockfall is imminent. Traversing the bench, you soon come to a bend in the river; at it, bridge the Merced just above the brink of its cascades. Strolling east, you soon reach the west end of spacious Echo Valley, and proceed to a junction at its north edge. From this Echo Valley junction near an Echo Creek campsite, there is the start of an alternate, less dramatic, high route you could take on your return back to the backpackers camp in Little Yosemite Valley. The overall distance is 7.7 miles, versus 7 miles along the Merced Lake Trail.

A **ALTERNATE TRIP ALONG HIGH TRAIL:** When your up-canyon Merced Lake Trail was completed in 1931, the old High Trail to Merced Lake fell into disuse, for it is almost a mile longer and climbs 750 feet more. It also has less water, fewer campsites, and fewer views. On the plus side, it does provide access to the rewarding summit of Moraine Dome (see Trip 44).

To return on this trail, you begin by first climbing about 450 feet over a distance of 0.8 mile, and passing a moraine about midway to a junction with the Echo Creek Trail (also Trip 44). On a 2.9-mile ramble to the John Muir Trail, the High Trail first branches west for a shorter climb to a broad granitic surface. Across bedrock, it winds briefly down to a stagnant lakelet. Beyond it, you get an incredible view—one that justifies the effort—of the glacier-smoothed slabs and walls that bound the Merced River canyon. Leaving the broad surface, the High Trail makes a brushy ascent to an ephemeral creek, crosses it, and, on gentle bedrock slopes, goes through a bouldery moraine. This feature, which you can trace west, is only one of many lateral moraines left high on the river canyon's north wall by the last glacier as it melted back up-canyon. The tremendous views soon disappear. You then begin a mile of exhilarating walking through a forest of Jeffrey pines, lodgepoles, and white firs, which shade patch after patch of vivid-green bracken ferns. Still in forest, you climb slightly, cutting across the crests of two lateral moraines just before a junction with the John Muir Trail. About 150 yards north up this trail, beyond yet another moraine crest, you'll find the south end of the Forsyth Trail, and a two-minute walk along it will get you to a good Sunrise Creek campsite.

From this vicinity, this alternate return route from the High Trail junction coincides with the John Muir Trail. On it, you descend 2.2 miles to a junction with the Clouds Rest Trail, with nearby camping near Sunrise Creek just before this trail. On the JMT, you descend just a half mile west to a junction with the Half Dome Trail. Should you want to reach Half Dome's summit, you'll make a strenuous, often waterless, 2-mile hike up to it. (See Trip 68 for details.) Onward, you drop 1.3 miles to a trail junction on the floor of Little Yosemite Valley. Just 0.1 mile ahead, past the backpackers camp and its bearproof food-storage boxes, you meet the Merced Lake trail. **END OF ALTERNATE TRIP.**

In Echo Valley and with Merced Lake as our first goal, we immediately bridge Echo Creek, strike southeast through burned-but-boggy Echo Valley, and climb east past the Merced River's largely unseen pools to Merced Lake's west shore. Don't camp here, but, rather, continue for 0.8 mile past the north shore to the Merced Lake High Sierra Camp and the adjacent riverside campground, about 9.25 miles beyond the John Muir Trail junction in Little Yosemite Valley. Be sure to use the bearproof food-storage boxes. As a large lake at a moderate elevation, 80-foot-deep Merced Lake supports three species of trout: brook, brown, and rainbow.

CHAPTER 16

Trips South and East of the Glacier Point Road

Introduction to this Area

This chapter is one of contrasts, ranging from 3250 feet at the bottom of the Alder Creek Trail, outside the park, up to 11,150 feet at Red Peak Pass. All of the park's plant communities are found within this altitudinal range. Along trips 70 and 71, few hikers will be met, but at Ostrander and Royal Arch lakes, trips 72 and 73/77, respectively, camping space may be at a premium. This chapter is unique in that it has a network of trails through a grove of giant sequoias (Trip 78); no such trail system exists at the park's two other groves (trips 16 and 17). Although thousands of people visit this chapter's Mariposa Grove each week during summer, the vast majority ride trams. The few who explore the grove on foot are richly rewarded.

Little Yosemite Valley, Cascade Cliffs, and Bunnell Point, from the Starr King bench

Supplies and Services

Wawona is the "urban" center for this area, with a large, historic hotel, a store, a gas station, and other amenities. In addition to a golf course, the hotel has a pool, but the natural pools on the South Fork Merced River are more enjoyable and get more use. Some of these are located just up from the river's covered bridge, as well as in spots upriver, while some are located beside and downriver from stretched-out Wawona Campground.

Just north of the river, the Chilnualna Road branches east from the Wawona Road—the main road—and it takes you past the History Center and its stables (with rides available) to North Wawona, a private in-park settlement with additional food and home rentals at The Redwoods in Yosemite (see Chapter 1's "Accommodations"). North of the Wawona area, you'll reach the start of the Glacier Point Road at a signed junction. At this road's end at Glacier Point, you can buy snacks, film, and various tourist-oriented items.

Food, lodging, gas, and most supplies are also available in Fish Camp, a small Hwy. 41 settlement just 2 miles south of the park's south entrance station. Oakhurst, a sprawling town about 13.5 miles south of this settlement, has virtually everything.

Wilderness Permits

If you want to reserve a permit, see the "Wilderness Permits" section in Chapter 6. However, only Ostrander Lake (Trip 72) is likely to reach its quota of backpackers, and then only on summer weekends. Therefore, most backpackers will probably get their permits in person at the Wawona District Office. This is at the end of a short road that branches right from the Chilnualna Road immediately past the Pioneer Yosemite History Center.

Campgrounds

This small area has only one option: Wawona Campground, about 1 mile north of the Wawona Hotel. Unfortunately, it is often full, and you may have to stay outside the park. An alternative to Wawona Campground is the small Summerdale Campground, about a half mile north of the settlement of Fish Camp, but it, too, is often full. If that's the case, you'll have to stay at more isolated Sierra National Forest campgrounds, such as those found along Forest Service Road 6S07, which starts east from the south end of Fish Camp. These are Big Sandy Campground (barely above the south edge of the park's topographic map), Little Sandy Campground, and Fresno Dome Campground.

TRIP 70

Bishop Creek via Alder Creek Trail

Ⓜ ↗ DH

DISTANCE: 6.4 miles out and back

ELEVATIONS: 3920'/4950'
+240'/-1270'/±3020'

SEASON: Mid-April to
mid-November

USE: Light

MAP: *Wawona*

TRAIL LOG:

3.2   Bishop Creek

INTRODUCTION: Your descent to Bishop Creek can be one of the Sierra's most pleasant springtime hikes, but by early summer, the creeks run dry and temperatures soar. Most of this trail's length is across rolling topography carpeted with one of my favorite plants, mountain misery; nowhere else in the park will you see such a spread of this low, aromatic shrub. Despite its sticky nature, it is a favorite food of deer. Another bush to look for is the large whiteleaf manzanita, easily recognized by its smooth, red bark and its gray-green leaves. The quiet forest shading these bushes is a classic ponderosa pine forest, though incense-cedars and black oaks prevail here and there, and, occasionally, a multitrunked foothill (gray) pine will be seen. In late May or early June, you're likely to see many wildflowers blooming, including Indian pink, mountain dogbane, soap plant, milkweed, miner's lettuce, small larkspur, and cinquefoil. Birds-foot, wood, and bracken ferns add spice to the carpeted forest floor, and at Bishop Creek, alders, azaleas, and creek dogwoods provide an interesting contrast. Most of these herbs, shrubs, and trees were used by the local Indians either for food, drink, or medicine, or for basketry, bows, or shelter.

DIRECTIONS TO THE TRAILHEAD: On the Wawona Road, 3.9 miles north of the Wawona Campground entrance and 280 yards west of the Alder Creek crossing; also 7.4 miles south of the Glacier Point Road junction. Trail begins in map section C6.

DESCRIPTION: From the road's bend near a cut through weathered granite, your trail drops below the Wawona Road and parallels it northwest. The trail quickly widens along an abandoned road, which it momentarily leaves. After about a half mile of traversing, it begins a long drop to the South Fork Merced River. About 1.2 miles from your trailhead, you leave the park, and, in the Sierra National Forest, descend 0.8 mile to a springtime creek. A short quarter mile beyond it, we climb to a low ridge, on which you'll find about a half dozen Indian mortar holes, perhaps covered with black oak leaves, just a few yards west of the trail. From the ridge, you have a steady descent that winds in and out of gullies as it drops about 550 feet to the banks of Bishop Creek. From there, you could continue down to the South Fork Merced River—a total drop of almost 800 feet along a dry, steep 1.4-mile course. However, the steepness, heat, and springtime ticks make the descent not worth it for many people.

TRIP 71

Bridalveil Creek Campground-Wawona Loop

Ⓜ ♫ BP

DISTANCE: 30.2 miles semiloop

ELEVATIONS: 4000'/7750'
              +5520'/-5520'/±11,040'

SEASON: Early July to mid-October

USE: Light

MAPS: *Half Dome,*
           Mariposa Grove, Wawona

TRAIL LOG:

1.6	Junction on a ridge
2.3	Second junction
4.9	Junction near a broad saddle
6.3	Junction just below Turner Meadows
9.2	Junction just above Chilnualna Creek
13.2	Trailhead
14.5	Alder Creek Trail
17.6	Mile-high junction
21.7	Alder Creek junction
23.4	Deer Camp
25.3	Junction near a broad saddle
30.2	Trailhead

INTRODUCTION: Sparkling lakes, deep canyons, and alpine crests are not found along this hike—but then, neither are the backpacking crowds. This is a hike for those who love quiet trails. Although most of it is forested, you will pass through areas that have been burned in lightning-caused forest fires. The trees are regenerating, and until they cast sufficient shade, shrubs and wildflowers will grow in greater abundance.

DIRECTIONS TO THE TRAILHEAD: Branch from the Wawona Road and drive 7.6 miles up the Glacier Point Road to the Bridalveil Creek Campground Road. Turn right and drive a half mile to the campground's entrance. Park at the campground's far end. Trail begins in map section D5.

DESCRIPTION: From the campground's far end, our trail, paralleling Bridalveil Creek, heads southeast and climbs only about 200 feet in the first 3.3 miles—an excellent way to start a backpack hike. Although white firs and red firs are present, they are greatly overwhelmed by a superabundance of lodgepole pines along this creekside stretch. After halfway along this easy stretch, we come to a junction on a ridge above nearby Bridalveil Creek. From here, a trail quickly descends to cross the creek before ending, in 1.7 miles, at the Glacier Point Road (Trip 72's trailhead).

A 1987 fire—one of several in the drainage—caused moderate damage to the forest here. The trail keeps above the creek for a short distance, then it curves over to a moderate-size camp along the creek's tributary. Like others we'll meet, this one can have lots of mosquitoes before late July. A two-minute walk upstream from the camp ends at the tributary's ford; on the east bank, we meet our second junction, 0.7 mile past the first. A sometimes obscure trail to the left climbs a short mile east to the Ostrander Lake Trail (Trip 72).

Turning right, we climb gently south for a mile to the tributary's upper basin. In it, your climb becomes first moderate and then steep as you struggle briefly up to a nearby crest that separates the virtually unglaciated Alder Creek drainage from the Bridalveil Creek drainage, which was glaciated only at its highest elevations. Jeffrey pines yield to red firs as you traverse slopes over to a junction near a broad saddle. The trail you'll return on climbs east to here from Deer Camp, down to the west. Starting southeast, you quickly cross the broad saddle and enter the Chilnualna Creek drainage, which also was glaciated only at its highest elevations.

S SIDE TRIP TO OFF-TRAIL CAMPING: In this vicinity, you have the opportunity for off-trail camping. Rather than start southeast down the trail, contour a quarter mile, first southwest, then west, to a second broad saddle. Peering through trees from its west edge, you should see a lakelet about 250 yards away and 100 feet below you. Its presence is evidence that the uppermost part of the Alder Creek drainage was glaciated. Originating on the north slopes of summit 8024, past glaciers here were about 1 mile long and descended to about 6700 feet elevation. These may be the lowest glaciers originating in the park. **END OF SIDE TRIP.**

From the broad saddle, you now begin a rolling, gentle 1.3-mile southeast descent that goes through several small meadows, all with abundant corn lilies. Your trail touches the east edge of long Turner Meadows, about 6 miles from your trailhead, and here you can make a fair camp. Just beyond Turner Meadows is a junction, and you veer right, hop Turner Meadows creek. Your old trail climbs unnecessarily 300 feet up to a ridge (originally, horses did the climbing, not hikers, so ups and downs were not an issue). On this moderate, shady ascent, one has a fine crest view of glaciated-but-subdued Buena Vista Peak, to the east. After topping out at 7750 feet—the route's highest point—you then start a 3800-foot drop to the Wawona area. On it, western white pines quickly yield to their cousins, sugar pines, while, farther down, red firs yield to the closely related white firs. A shrubby black oak appears at about 7540 feet elevation, near the top of its altitudinal range. Perhaps only on Smith Peak (Trip 15) can you find a specimen a couple of hundred feet higher. This oak is just past a secondary crest; from it, we plunge down to a creeklet, and then make an equally long drop to its larger counterpart. From its verdant banks, one has an easy half-mile descent to a junction just above Chilnualna Creek. Here, near the confluence of this creek and its southbound tributary, you can

find a suitable spot to spend your first night, 9.2 miles from your trailhead. You may want to first view Chilnualna Fall, just downstream, but be extremely careful if you do, for the rock can be treacherously slippery.

The next day, you descend the Chilnualna Creek Trail, 4 scenic miles to its end. Quickly, we have views extending over the forested Wawona area, soon followed by a switchback to get around a small gorge with a 60-foot cascade that is quite impressive in early season. Not far below, our trail comes to within a few yards of the brink of Chilnualna Fall proper. Now we diverge from the fall, traversing 0.6 mile west and having glances back, seeing the entire length of the fall, which churns for hundreds of feet down a deep, confining chute. Next, we have a moderately graded trail that, with more than a dozen switchbacks of various lengths, that take us 1000 feet lower and back to near Chilnualna Creek.

We descend along it a quarter mile and then descend west another quarter mile. Next, we descend south and have a few open spots to survey the Wawona area to the south, Wawona Point to the southeast, and Wawona Dome to the east. A forest of ponderosa pines and incense-cedars yields as we cross a manzanita-clothed ridge, and, not far below it, we come to a junction. We've been on a broad horse trail, which goes briefly west to a trailhead, but if you're not on horseback, take the hikers' trail. This heads east briefly to Chilnualna Creek, then descends steeply—and potentially dangerously—alongside it, passing its 25-foot fall just before reaching a road at our trailhead. Then, gradually descending west, walk 1.3 miles along a road that goes through the private in-holding of North Wawona, which has supplies, food, and lodging.

Your next trail, the Alder Creek Trail, begins about 0.3 mile beyond the settlement's school, and this trailhead is about 300 yards before the Wawona District Office, which dispenses information and wilderness permits.

S SIDE TRIP TO HISTORY CENTER AND SOUTH FORK MERCED RIVER: Before resuming your loop hike, you might consider a side trip to the Pioneer Yosemite History Center, which you enter just west of a junction with the district office's spur road. By walking 200 to 300 yards upstream from the center's covered bridge, you'll discover some small pools in the South Fork Merced River that, in summer afternoons, are among the warmest "swimming holes" in the park. END OF SIDE TRIP.

The Alder Creek Trail begins about 100 yards east of a west-heading service road. At your low elevation, temperatures often soar into the 80s by early afternoon, and water may be absent until Alder Creek, about 6 miles ahead. After a brief, initial, open climb north, your trail turns west to make an ascending traverse for 0.4 mile across small gullies. Then, at the end of a 2.7-mile, mostly viewless ascent, you reach a mile-high junction, from which a steep trail descends 0.7 mile to the heavily traveled Wawona Road.

LOGGING IN YOSEMITE

Along the last mile or so of this section, you may see railroad ties, which are the few tangible relics of a dark period in the park's history. From the early days of World War I through the 1920s, the Yosemite Lumber Company laid railroad tracks in and around western park lands to log some of the Sierra's finest stands of sugar pines. Ironically, some of this timber—more than 6 million board feet—was cut to use in the construction of Hetch Hetchy's O'Shaughnessy Dam, completed in 1923. More than a half billion board feet were cut before 1930, when John D. Rockefeller, Jr. and the US government split the cost of buying up the logging company's interests.

Starting east, we begin a 2.8-mile rolling traverse in and out of gullies and around or over low ridges to a view of 100-foot-high Alder Creek fall below.

Beyond the fall, our abandoned railroad route approaches lushly lined Alder Creek, parallels it north gently upstream for 1.25 miles, then crosses it to reach a nearby junction. Here, or elsewhere along Alder Creek, you can make your second night's camp.

S SIDE TRIP TO WAWONA ROAD: From the junction the trail climbs north 1.3 miles to an old logging road, which westbound goes about 1 mile to a junction with a spur road south, then 5 miles to the Wawona Road, ending about 50 yards south of the Yosemite West road junction. Limited parking is at the start of this trail, which makes an easy, nearly level hike worth taking before or after summer, when higher trails are under snow. Eastbound, you could follow the old logging road a half mile to a trail's resumption, which climbs a little more than 3 miles to the Bridalveil Creek Campground entrance. However, thick brush—the result of logging—makes this shorter route undesirable. END OF SIDE TRIP.

The recommended route angles to the right at the Alder Creek junction, immediately refords the broad creek, and then climbs east for 1.75 miles, paralleling a murmuring tributary. This white-fir-shaded stretch ends at Deer Camp, a roadend flat along the fringe of the former logging area. You can camp here, but it lacks aesthetics. Beyond it, your trail continues east and, typical of old trails, it winds and switchbacks all too steeply up most of a 1100-foot ascent. Midway up it, views expand, providing an overview of the Alder Creek basin. After about 1.25 miles of climbing, we top a crest, then momentarily descend to a usually flowing creeklet. Should you want to camp in this vicinity, do so at the nearby crest top if mosquitoes are abundant. Leaving the creeklet, we climb around a meadow—rich in sedges, willows, and corn lilies—and then make a final short push southeast up to the junction near a broad saddle, mentioned early in the trip. From it, retrace your first day's steps 4.9 miles back to the trailhead.

TRIP **72**

Glacier Point Road to Ostrander Lake

E ↗ DH, BP

DISTANCE: 12.8 miles out and back

ELEVATIONS: 7010'/8520'
+1720'/-210'/±3860'

SEASON: Early July to mid-October

USE: Heavy

MAP: *Half Dome*

TRAIL LOG:

1.4	First junction
3.0	Second junction
6.4	Ostrander Lake

INTRODUCTION: Ostrander Lake, as the closest lake to the Glacier Point Road, is the objective of many summertime weekend backpackers. It is also popular in winter and spring with cross-country skiers. You might consider dayhiking to it, since, with a daypack, it is only a two- to three-hour hike, and dayhiking lessens human impact on the lake's environment.

At the end of this trip is a 19.8-mile alternate trip, an even 7 miles longer than the round trip to Ostrander Lake. As a loop trip, it can be walked in either direction. It is described counterclockwise because the 2.25-mile cross-country stretch is easier to hike and follow in that direction. Its total loss and gain is about 6800 feet.

DIRECTIONS TO THE TRAILHEAD: From a signed junction with the Wawona Road, drive 8.9 miles up the Glacier Point Road to a turnoff on your right. This parking area is 1.3 miles past the Bridalveil Creek Campground spur road. Trail begins in map section D5.

DESCRIPTION: The first half of our hike is easy—a gentle ascent through a forest that is interspersed with an assortment of meadows. Start along a former jeep road and soon encounter the first of several areas of lodgepole forest badly burned in a 1987 fire. Farther up, on Horizon Ridge, you'll see a forest burned in a 1994 fire. Just 0.3 mile from the trailhead, we cross a sluggish creek, then amble an easy mile to a ridge junction. From it, a short lateral drops to Bridalveil Creek—possibly a difficult June crossing—then climbs equally briefly to the Bridalveil Creek trail (Trip 71).

From the junction, our route contours southeast past unseen Lost Bear Meadow, and, after a mile, makes a short ascent east up along a trickling creek to its crossing. Just beyond the ford, our route curves west to a nearby junction with a second lateral to the Bridalveil Creek Trail. Though we are now about halfway to Ostrander Lake, we've climbed very little, and, from this junction, we face 1500 feet of vertical gain, mostly through burned forests. Nevertheless, some trees survived, and they indicate the former (and future) forest type.

The steepening road climbs east through a mixed forest, then climbs more gently south across an open slab that provides the first views of the Bridalveil Creek basin. You then curve southeast into a Jeffrey pine stand, before climbing east through a white fir forest. These firs are largely supplanted by red firs by the time you top a saddle that bisects Horizon Ridge. Climbing southeast up that ridge, your road passes through a generally open stretch decked with lupines, sulfur flowers, and, surprisingly, sagebrush. About 400 feet above your first saddle, the road switchbacks at a second one, then curves up to a third. From it, the road makes a momentary descent southeast before bending to start a short, final ascent south into unburned forest surrounding Ostrander Lake. Near this bend, we get far-ranging views across the Illilouette Creek basin. We can see the tops of Royal Arches and Washington Column and, above and east of

Ostrander Hut, built atop a moraine

them, North, Basket, and Half domes. Behind Half Dome stands the park's geographic center, broad-topped Mt. Hoffmann. Reigning over the Illilouette Creek basin is Mt. Starr King and its entourage of lesser domes. To the east and northeast, the jagged crest of the Clark Range cuts the sky.

Beyond the short, final ascent south, we drop, in several minutes, to Ostrander Hut, on the north shore of Ostrander Lake. When it is snowbound, cross-country skiers can stay in it, if they've first obtained reservations from the Valley's Wilderness Center (see page 258, in Chapter 6). The hut is on a rocky glacial moraine left by a glacier that retreated perhaps 16,000 years ago. Behind it, lying in a bedrock basin, is 25-acre, trout-populated Ostrander Lake. Here, camping is good along the west shore.

[A] ALTERNATE TRIP TO HART LAKES AND MONO MEADOW: To begin your cross-country route to the Hart Lakes, start from the northeast shore of 8505-foot Ostrander

Lake and go southeast on a diagonal up-slope. If you're on course, you should approach the north shore of a pond after about a quarter mile of hiking. After reaching this checkpoint, you now strike east for an easier quarter-mile ascent to the north shore of a shallow lakelet—not a desirable camping area. Beyond the lakelet's east end, you soon curve northeast and climb 200 vertical feet up to a ridge, which you ascend southeast for about 200 yards. Then you make a 0.3-mile traverse, topping out at about 8950 feet and having distant views across the Illilouette Creek basin, to a view of the Hart Lakes. A brush-choked gully descends southeast to the larger Hart Lake, situated at about 8720 feet elevation. Even if you stay just north of the gully, chinquapin bushes still cause some problems down to this larger lake. Rimmed with lodgepoles, Labrador tea, and red heather, it harbors mosquitoes through late July, but should have pleasant camping after that. A tent helps before then. In the early morning, you may find the lake's placid surface occasionally broken by leaping rainbow trout.

Leave the larger Hart Lake at its northeast corner and go northeast about 250 yards to the east side of a low summit, then begin a moderate descent north toward soon-sighted Edson Lake, down at 8145 feet elevation. Midway between the Hart Lakes and this lake, you'll reach open granite slabs, across which you can head diagonally northeast to a moraine, and reach the Buena Vista Trail at roughly 8400 feet elevation. An efficient cross-country route from Ostrander Lake to this trail is about 2.25 miles.

As you begin to descend the Buena Vista Trail on the crest of a lateral moraine, you can see Edson Lake off to the northwest and about 200 feet below you. Should you wish to visit this shallow lake and camp at it, take the path of least resistance to it. After about 1.3 miles of hiking down this trail, you cross diminutive Edson Lake creek at roughly 1 mile below the lake. The trail now descends northeast for about 1.5

miles, and then it slowly curves to a northeast bearing. Over this 9.75-mile stretch, the trail is relatively close to Buena Vista Creek, and, while camping is poor along its west bank, it is good—and isolated—above the east bank. Fallen trees may provide access across the bouldery creek to these sites. Ahead, you have an easy descent northwest on the Buena Vista Trail, across gentle slopes and flats for about 3.4 miles to an intersection of the Mono Meadow Trail. East, this goes 300 yards east past campsites to ford broad Illilouette Creek, and then it climbs to a broad bench with more campsites.

We, however, go west 40 yards to a second junction, from which the Buena Vista Trail heads northwest, down-canyon, bound for the Glacier Point-Panorama Trail, which climbs to Glacier Point. Now we have a 3-mile, two-stage, rolling ascent to the Mono Meadow Trailhead. The first stage is a 600-foot ascent for 1 mile to a broad ridge, with views of North, Basket, and Half domes; Clouds Rest; and Mt. Starr King. You then head on a 200-foot descent from it for a half mile down to the western tributary of Illilouette Creek. You ford it at the brink of some rapids; in early season, this ford could be a dangerous one.

The second stage makes an initial ascent, then, in a 0.7-mile course, traverses west to lodgepole-fringed Mono Meadow. Until mid-July, you may face 200 yards of muddy freshets and meadow bogs before you reach the narrow meadow's east edge. During this period, desperate hikers try to circumvent the mire, and several paths may spring up to confuse you. The real trail crosses the meadow on a 300-degree bearing, and it becomes obvious once you're within the forest's edge. We complete the second stage with a 0.75-mile climb, the first half gentle, the second half moderate. Then, from the Mono Meadow Trailhead, we walk an easy 1.2 miles west down the Glacier Point Road to the Ostrander Lake Trailhead. **END OF ALTERNATE TRIP.**

TRIP 73

Mono Meadow to Buena Vista and Royal Arch Lakes

Ⓜ ↻ BPx

DISTANCE: 30.4 miles loop

ELEVATIONS: 6350'/9340'
+5240'/-5240'/±10,480'

SEASON: Early July to early October

USE: Moderate

MAPS: *Half Dome, Merced Peak, Mariposa Grove*

TRAIL LOG:

3.0	Buena Vista Trail
9.9	Trail leaves the crest
12.2	Crest junction
12.6	Buena Vista Lake
13.3	Buena Vista Pass
15.3	Royal Arch Lake
16.0	East-climbing trail
16.8	Johnson Lake
17.8	Crescent Lake
19.1	Grouse Lake
21.2	Hillside junction
21.9	Chilnualna Creek
22.8	Junction before Turner Meadows
24.2	Trail descending to Deer Camp
27.8	Ostrander Lake Trail
29.2	Glacier Point Road
30.4	Mono Meadow Trailhead

INTRODUCTION: The subalpine lakes nestled around Buena Vista Peak can be reached from North Wawona—Trip 77— or from three trailheads along the Glacier Point Road. This hike starts from one of these trailheads and visits five of the peak's lakes. Although this route is slightly longer than Trip 77, it requires 20% less climbing effort. Also see Trip 79 for a little-used

route to these lakes. While it can be done at a moderate pace in three days, I recommend a more relaxed pace in four or more days, so that you can savor the lakes you meet along this relatively easy route.

DIRECTIONS TO THE TRAILHEAD: From a signed junction on the Wawona Road, drive 10.1 miles up Glacier Point Road to a forested saddle with a parking area on your right. Trail begins in map section D5.

DESCRIPTION: At the trailhead, in a stand of red firs, ancient Bridalveil and Illilouette drainage glaciers once joined, just barely overtopping today's forested pass—according to François Matthes, who in 1930 produced a classic US Geological Survey "Professional Paper 160" on Yosemite Valley and environs. Interestingly, none of the ancient glacial deposits he mapped in these drainages existed, except in his imagination. Nevertheless, some still appear on the park's 1989 geologic map.

Looking for nonexistent glacial deposits, we start our trail with a steady, moderate descent north, followed by an easing gradient east to lodgepole-fringed Mono Meadow. Until mid-July, you may face 200 yards of muddy freshets and meadow bogs before you reach the narrow meadow's east edge. During this period, desperate hikers try to circumvent the mire, and several paths may spring up to confuse you. The real trail crosses the meadow on a 120-degree bearing, and it becomes obvious once you're within the forest's edge.

Beyond the meadow, your Mono Meadow Trail crosses a low divide, then makes a generally viewless, easy descent to a major tributary of Illilouette Creek. Here, 1.5 miles from your trailhead, is your first possible campsite. You ford the tributary at the brink of some rapids; in early season, this ford could be a dangerous one. From the tributary, you gain 200 feet on a short ascent to a crest, and, on your descent east from it, you're rewarded with views of North, Basket, and Half domes; Clouds Rest; and Mt. Starr King. After a descent through a fir forest, you emerge on an open slope with a thin veneer of grus, or granitic gravel. On the slope, you descend straight toward Mt. Starr King, the highest of the Illilouette Creek domes, and immediately after the view disappears, you reach a junction with the Buena Vista Trail, which links Glacier Point with the Buena Vista Peak area.

You turn right and go just 40 yards up-canyon to a second junction, where the Mono Meadow Trail goes 300 yards east past campsites to ford broad Illilouette Creek. From it, the trail climbs a slope veneered with glacial outwash—stream deposits from the last glaciers that existed up-canyon—then it crosses a bedrock bench with a veneer of grus. In "Professional Paper 160," Matthes said this grus was sediments of an ancient, glacial lake. Actually, this gravel, as elsewhere in glaciated and unglaciated granitic lands, is nothing more than weathered granitic bedrock. Real lake sediments are mud, not gravel.

Of more interest to the hiker is that this spacious bedrock bench is suitable for camping. Trip 75, descending Illilouette Creek from Merced Pass, traverses through this camping area, then follows the Buena Vista Trail northwest toward Glacier Point. From the junction before the creek crossing, our route heads southeast up the Buena Vista Trail. Over much of the route up toward Buena Vista Peak, the vegetation has been burned by several large, natural fires. Usually, a burn is quite unsightly for a year or two, but wildflowers often abound in one, and, after several years, brush and young trees soften the visual effect. In 1.25 miles, we come to a creeklet with a fair camp on its west bank. The trail's gradient gradually eases, then you cross a broad divide and, in a quarter mile, angle sharply left to descend along the edge of a sloping meadow. Beyond it are aspens that hide a step-across creek. Just a few minutes' walk east of it, you cross a slightly larger creek, then make a gentle ascent southeast across sandy soils to steep slopes above Buena Vista Creek. Camping is poor along the

west bank, but good—and isolated—above the east bank. Fallen trees may provide access across the bouldery creek to these sites.

Soon, our trail leaves Buena Vista Creek, curves southwest, and climbs moderately in that direction for 1.5 miles to a ford, between two meadows, of diminutive Edson Lake creek. From a poor campsite, the trail ascends along a moraine crest, then, in 1 mile, leaves it to angle southeast up to a higher crest. Where your trail makes this sudden angle left, you can leave it and contour 0.3 mile west over to a campsite at shallow Edson Lake. Our trail follows the higher moraine crest southwest for more than 300 yards, finally leaves the burned area, and then makes a quarter-mile, view-blessed descent to Hart Lakes creek. From where the trail leaves the crest at about 8400 feet elevation, you can continue cross-country southwest up it (alternate route at end of Trip 72), soon diagonal up slabs, and then climb south up to the Hart Lakes.

From brush-lined Hart Lakes creek, we make a short contour over to Buena Vista Creek, with a small campsite on its east bank. After a half mile of moderate ascent, you cross a creek that bends northeast, and then you continue south up a slightly shorter ascent to a recrossing of that creek. Immediately beyond, you cross its western tributary, then follow this stream south briefly up to two ponds, from which you switchback up a cirque wall with ice-shattered blocks to a crest junction. Trip 77, ascending from North Wawona, now joins our route for a loop around the lakes of Buena Vista Peak. The first lake we encounter, about 0.3 mile southeast from the junction, is rather bleak Buena Vista Lake, which has rainbow and brook trout. Nestled on a broad bench at the base of the cool north slope of Buena Vista Peak, this lake is the highest and coldest one we'll see. It does, however, have at least two good, if somewhat exposed, camps. In threatening weather, camp lower down. Starting at the lake's outlet, take short switchbacks up to a

nearby, broad, viewless Buena Vista Pass, which, at 9340 feet, is our trip's highest elevation.

S **SIDE TRIP TO BUENA VISTA PEAK:** From here, one can climb 0.75 mile southwest up a gentle ridge, gaining only about 270 feet elevation to reach the summit of Buena Vista Peak, from which you have an unrestricted panorama of the park's southern area. **END OF SIDE TRIP.**

From the pass, we descend 2 easy, winding trail miles to a favorite lake on this loop, Royal Arch Lake, which lies below a broad, granitic arch. This lake, like Buena Vista Lake, has rainbow and brook trout. Just past the outlet is an excellent, popular campsite.

S **SIDE TRIP TO MINNOW LAKE:** For more solitude, head cross-country 0.75 mile west up a ridge and then down it to less attractive Minnow Lake, which has brook trout. **END OF SIDE TRIP.**

Leaving Royal Arch Lake, we parallel its outlet creek for a half mile, then angle south across slabs to a junction with an east-climbing trail. Here, we meet the route of Trip 79, which starts northwest from Chiquito Pass, crosses the South Fork Merced River and climbs to Buck Camp, a ranger station about 1.5 miles from our junction.

Turning right, we descend west toward Johnson Lake, reaching good campsites along its northwest shore in just 0.75 mile—with hordes of mosquitoes in early season. You don't see large Crescent Lake, but on meeting its inlet creek, about 0.3 mile beyond a meadowy divide, you can walk 150 yards downstream, passing a fair camp before reaching the lake's shallow, trout-filled waters. You might visit or camp near the lake's south end, for, from its outlet, you can peer into the 2800-foot-deep South Fork Merced River canyon.

Former small ice caps that developed around Buena Vista Peak in part spilled south across the Johnson and Crescent lakes basins, descending toward the South Fork Merced River trunk glacier.

Beyond Crescent Lake's inlet creek, our trail quickly turns north, passes a small creekside meadow, and then climbs more than 150 feet to a second broad divide. From it, we descend into the headwaters of a Chilnualna Creek tributary. Your moderate-to-steep gradient ends when you approach easily missed Grouse Lake. Look for a trail that descends about 100 yards to a fair campsite on the north shore of this shallow, reedy lakelet.

Lodgepoles and red firs monopolize the slopes along your 2-mile descent from this lake down to a hillside junction. From it, hikers completing Trip 77 head west

Royal Arch Lake

down-canyon to their trailhead. Hikers on the second day of that hike join us for a short northwest stretch, first up over a nearby divide, then down more than 400 feet to Chilnualna Creek. Just above its north bank is a good, medium-size campsite, and just beyond that is another trail junction. From it, Trip 77 trekkers climb east. Should you want to visit the Chilnualna Lakes, take this 5.3-mile trail up past them to the crest junction, then backtrack 13.1 miles to your trailhead. This route is 10 miles longer than the following route, including its 1.2-mile walk along the Glacier Point Road back to the trailhead.

Spurning the longer option, we head northwest from Chilnualna Creek. During midsummer, our gently ascending traverse is brightened by the orange sunbursts of alpine lilies, growing chest high along the wetter parts of our trail. We encounter a junction before Turner Meadows, from which Trip 71 departs southwest down to the Wawona area.

You now backtrack along the first part of that hike, first ascending past and through a series of "Turner Meadows," then topping a forest pass to quickly meet a trail descending to Deer Camp. You, however, keep right, traverse to a crest, and descend to a tributary of Bridalveil Creek. But before reaching Bridalveil Creek, you meet a junction, turn left, and then cross the tributary creek. Along it, you momentarily pass a moderate-size campsite and then, in a half mile, reach another junction. The main trail continues 1.6 miles northwest to Bridalveil Creek Campground, but we veer right. Over the next 0.3-mile trail segment, we first drop to nearby Bridalveil Creek, ford it, and then make an equally short climb up to the Ostrander Lake Trail—a former jeep road. In 1.4 miles, this northbound route ends at the Glacier Point Road, beside which we walk 1.2 miles east to our Mono Meadow Trailhead.

TRIP **74**

Glacier Point to Yosemite Valley via Nevada and Vernal Falls

Ⓜ **╱** **DH**

DISTANCE: 9.2 miles point to point

ELEVATIONS: 4020′/7250′
+1020′/-4210′/±5230′

SEASON: Late June to mid-October

USE: Heavy

MAP: Half Dome

TRAIL LOG:

1.6	Buena Vista Trail
2.4	Wide bridge
4.4	Mono Meadow Trail
5.4	John Muir Trail
5.8	Nevada Fall and back
6.9	Clark Point
8.1	Mist Trail
8.2	Vernal Fall bridge
9.2	Happy Isles

INTRODUCTION: This is the most scenic of all trails descending to the floor of Yosemite Valley. Either take a bus up to Glacier Point or have someone drop you there and meet you down at Curry Village.

DIRECTIONS TO THE TRAILHEAD: From a signed junction along the Wawona Road, drive 15.5 miles up the Glacier Point Road to its end. If possible, take a park bus up to crowded Glacier Point, since the parking lot may be full. Trail begins in map section D5.

DESCRIPTION: Just east of the entrance to the Glacier Point parking lot, this trip starts south up a signed trail that quickly forks. The Pohono Trail, Trip 65, veers right, but

GLACIER POINT PLAY

From the early 1870s until January 1968, a large pile of embers was pushed off Glacier Point at evening darkness to create the renowned Firefall—a glowing "waterfall." Quite a spectacle. Then, from the early 1970s until June 1990, people in the chilly early morning hours would take running leaps from this vicinity out into space. This hang gliding was also quite a spectacle. However, one reason for establishing the park was to protect its natural lands, and you can see a spectacular part of them by making the short pilgrimage out to nearby Glacier Point before starting Trip 74.

ing in the creek could carry you swiftly downstream and over the fall.

Your trail soon passes just above the brink of Illilouette Fall, and gravels here are remnants of a thick accumulation that choked the creek when the uppermost part of the last glacier formed a low ice-dam across its mouth. The trail then starts a major climb along the slopes just above Panorama Cliff. It first climbs briefly along its rim, then it switchbacks away, soon returning near Panorama Point. The former viewpoint was in part undermined by a monstrous rockfall that broke loose during the winter of 1968–69. The rest of the viewpoint could break loose at any time. About 0.3 mile past this vicinity is a superlative panorama extending from Upper Yosemite Fall east past Royal Arches, Washington Column, and North Dome to Half Dome. Our forested, moderate

we veer left, on the Glacier Point-Panorama Trail, climbing a bit more before starting a moderate descent. A switchback leg helps ease the grade, and then we descend, often with views. A 1987, natural fire blackened most of the forest from near the trailhead to just beyond the upcoming Buena Vista Trail junction, but most trees survived. In open areas, black oaks are thriving, and shrubs have regenerated with a vengeance. Between charred trunks are occasional great views of Half Dome, Mt. Broderick, Liberty Cap, Nevada Fall, and Mt. Starr King. After 1.6 miles and an 800-foot drop, our Glacier Point-Panorama Trail meets the Buena Vista Trail. Over 2.2 miles, this first heads up-canyon to Illilouette Creek, and then it leads up along it to intersect the Mono Meadow Trail (Trip 73).

Our trail branches left and switchbacks down to a spur trail that goes a few yards to a railing. Here, atop an overhanging cliff, you have an unobstructed view of 370-foot Illilouette Fall, which splashes down over a low point on the rim of massive Panorama Cliff. Behind it, Half Dome rises boldly while, above Illilouette Creek, Mt. Starr King rises even higher. In a quarter mile, your trail descends to a wide bridge, wisely placed upstream. Still, wad-

Glacier Point Apron and Yosemite Falls cliffs, from atop Panorama Cliff

climb ends after 200 more feet of elevation gain, and then we descend gently to the rim for some more views, contour east, and have even more, these dominated by Half Dome, Mt. Broderick, Liberty Cap, Clouds Rest, and Nevada Fall. Your contour ends at a junction with the Mono Meadow Trail, which climbs southwest over a low ridge before descending to Illilouette Creek.

A fresh, Tioga-age lateral moraine descends northwest across the junction. François Matthes, in his classic 1930 paper, mapped many ancient lateral moraines above this one, but no one has been able to find any of them; just ascend any of the slopes to see for yourself.

S **SIDE TRIP TO STARR KING LAKE:** Worth an ascent from this junction is a visit to the Starr King Lake environs, to the southeast and about 1300 feet above you. The cross-country route 1.5 miles up to the west edge of the bench holding the lake is strenuous but straightforward, and it is not exposed. From any of three low summits along the north edge of the bench, one has stellar views of Mt. Starr King, Half Dome, Moraine Dome, and the features of Little Yosemite Valley that lie below them. Starr King Lake, although of ample dimensions, is so shallow that you can wade entirely across it. Sometimes it dries up in late summer, so if you want to camp here but find it dry, head a quarter mile southeast from the lake to a gully with a spring-fed creek. **END OF SIDE TRIP.**

Beyond the trail junction, we make a mile-long, switchbacking, generally viewless descent to a trail split, each branch descending a few yards to the John Muir Trail. You'll descend along it, but first walk over to the nearby brink of roaring Nevada Fall and back, a round-trip distance of about 0.4 mile.

S **SIDE TRIP TO NEVADA FALL VIEWPOINT:** Just a few yards beyond the Nevada Fall bridge, you can strike northwest to find a short spur trail that drops to a viewpoint beside the fall's brink. This viewpoint's rail-

ing is seen from the fall's bridge, thereby giving you an idea where the trail ends. Don't stray along the cliff's edge, and respect the river—people have been swept over this fall, too. **END OF SIDE TRIP.**

A **ALTERNATE TRIP TO HAPPY ISLES:** Rather than descend the John Muir Trail to Happy Isles, you could descend the Mist Trail, a shorter route, which begins a few hundred yards northeast of Nevada Fall. Because it is 1.1 miles shorter, it is also steeper, and harder on the knees, and it is potentially dangerous for those who try to descend it too rapidly. This wet route down the aptly named Mist Trail is described in the opposite direction in the first part of Trip 78. **END OF ALTERNATE TRIP.**

The recommended route is to take the John Muir Trail down to Happy Isles. This is described in the last part of Trip 78. In brief, from the junction with the Glacier Point-Panorama Trail, which we have descended, we start along the John Muir Trail, having grand views of Nevada Fall, Liberty Cap, Mt. Broderick, and Half Dome before we reach Clark Point. Ahead, the John Muir Trail is largely viewless, and on its well-graded switchbacks, we descend to the bottom of the Mist Trail and walk but a minute to the Vernal Fall bridge. From here, you hike your last mile down to the shuttle-bus stop at Happy Isles, where you can take a shuttle bus over to Curry Village.

TRIP 75

Glacier Point to Merced, Washburn, and Ottoway Lakes

S ⟳ **BPx**

DISTANCE: 51.1 miles loop

ELEVATIONS: 5920'/11,150'
+9020'/-9020'/±18,040'

SEASON: Early July to late September

USE: Moderate to Merced Lake, light beyond it

MAPS: *Half Dome, Merced Peak, Mount Lyell*

TRAIL LOG:

1.6	Buena Vista Trail
2.4	Wide bridge
4.4	Mono Meadow Trail
5.4	John Muir Trail
5.6	Nevada Fall
5.8	Mist Trail
6.9	Little Yosemite Valley
13.9	Echo Valley junction
16.2	Merced Lake High Sierra Camp
17.1	Merced Lake Ranger Station
19.5	Washburn Lake
26.4	Upper Triple Peak Fork
30.2	Turns southwest to climb
33.0	Red Peak Pass
34.7	Lower Ottoway Lake
37.7	Illilouette Creek Trail
44.3	Clark Fork
45.5	Junction
47.3	Buena Vista Trail
49.5	Glacier Point-Panorama Trail
51.1	Glacier Point Trailhead

INTRODUCTION: The park's trails exceed 11,000 feet in only three places: Donohue Pass (11,056', Trip 49), Parker Pass (11,100', Trip 51), and Red Peak Pass (11,150', trips 75 and 82). This trip reaches the highest—Red Peak Pass—by ascending the spectacular Merced River canyon. The length of this route gives you an appreciation for the magnitude of its past glaciers, several having extended as far down-canyon as the Merced Gorge beyond Yosemite Valley. From Red Peak Pass, which cleaves the multihued Clark Range, the route follows the shallow Illilouette Creek canyon—a very relaxing stretch—back to the trailhead.

There also is an alternate trip, which begins near the headwaters of the Merced River and follows the appropriately named High Trail north back to the Merced Lake Ranger Station. This 14.7-mile trip on the High Trail offers cross-country access to lakes and park-border peaks from Isberg Peak north to Mt. Lyell. Backtracking to your trailhead from the ranger station, you'll log 58.2 miles without any cross-country side trips, and you will gain and lose about 21,800 feet in elevation.

DIRECTIONS TO THE TRAILHEAD: From a signed junction along the Wawona Road, drive 15.5 miles up the Glacier Point Road to its end. If possible, take a park bus up to crowded Glacier Point, since the parking lot may be full. Trail begins in map section D5.

DESCRIPTION: Just east of the entrance to the Glacier Point parking lot, our trail starts south up a signed trail that quickly forks. The Pohono Trail, Trip 65, veers right, but we veer left, on the Glacier Point-Panorama Trail, climbing a bit more before starting a moderate descent. A switchback leg helps ease the grade, and then we descend, often with views. A 1987 natural fire blackened most of the forest from near the trailhead to just beyond the upcoming Buena Vista Trail junction, but most trees survived. In open areas, black oaks are thriving, and shrubs have regenerated with a vengeance. Between charred trunks are occasional great views of Half Dome, Mt. Broderick, Liberty Cap, Nevada Fall, and Mt. Starr King. After 1.6 miles and an

800-foot drop, our Glacier Point-Panorama Trail meets the Buena Vista Trail. Over 2.2 miles, this first heads up-canyon to Illilouette Creek, and then it leads up along it to intersect the Mono Meadow Trail (Trip 73).

Our trail branches left and switchbacks down to a spur trail that goes a few yards to a railing. Here, atop an overhanging cliff, you have an unobstructed view of 370-foot Illilouette Fall, which splashes down over a low point on the rim of massive Panorama Cliff. Behind it, Half Dome rises boldly while above Illilouette Creek Mt. Starr King rises even higher. In a quarter mile, your trail descends to a wide bridge, wisely placed upstream. Still, wading in the creek could carry you swiftly downstream and over the fall.

Your trail soon passes just above the brink of Illilouette Fall, and gravels here are remnants of a thick accumulation that choked the creek when the uppermost part of the last glacier formed a low ice-dam across its mouth. The trail then starts a major climb along the slopes just above Panorama Cliff. It first climbs briefly along its rim, and then it switchbacks away, soon returning near Panorama Point. The former viewpoint was in part undermined by a monstrous rockfall that broke loose during the winter of 1968–69. The rest of the viewpoint could break loose at any time. About 0.3 mile past this vicinity is a superlative panorama extending from Upper Yosemite Fall east past Royal Arches, Washington Column, and North Dome to Half Dome. Our forested, moderate climb ends after 200 more feet of elevation gain, and then we descend gently to the rim for some more views, contour east, and have even more, these dominated by Half Dome, Mt. Broderick, Liberty Cap, Clouds Rest, and Nevada Fall. Your contour ends at a junction with the Mono Meadow Trail, which climbs southwest over a low ridge before descending to Illilouette Creek.

Beyond the trail junction, we make a mile-long, switchbacking, generally viewless descent to a trail split, each branch descending a few yards to the John Muir Trail. You descend along it to the nearby brink of roaring Nevada Fall, its brink just beyond a bridge across the Merced River.

Royal Arches, Washington Column, and North Dome, from Panorama Cliff

⑤ SIDE TRIP TO NEVADA FALL VIEWPOINT: Just a few yards beyond the Nevada Fall bridge, you can strike northwest to find a short spur trail that drops to a viewpoint beside the fall's brink. This viewpoint's railing is seen from the fall's bridge, thereby giving you an idea where the trail ends. Don't stray along the cliff's edge and, respect the river—people have been swept over this fall, too. **END OF SIDE TRIP.**

Not far beyond the bridge, you reach the upper end of the Mist Trail. From this junction and its adjacent outhouses, we begin our 1-mile route to Little Yosemite Valley, first by ascending a brushy, rocky gully, and then by quickly descending and reaching both forest shade and the Merced River. Beneath pines, firs, and incense-cedars, we continue northeast along the river's azalea-lined bank, and then we quickly reach a trail fork. We keep to the main, riverside trail and go a short half mile to another junction, in the hub of Little Yosemite Valley, where the John Muir Trail branches north. Just up it is a large camping area with bearproof storage boxes, then outhouses, and, beyond them, a spur trail northeast over to a rangers' camp. You'll probably want to spend your first night here, or in the east end of the valley.

You leave the northbound John Muir Trail to embark on a shady 2-mile stroll, following the Merced Lake Trail through the broad, flat valley. The valley's floor has been largely buried by glacial sediments, which, like beach sand, make you work, even though the trail is level. Progressing east through Little Yosemite Valley, we stay closer to the base of glacier-polished Moraine Dome than to the Merced River, and, along this stretch, you can branch off to riverside campsites that are far more peaceful than those near the John Muir Trail junction, which tends to be a "Grand Central Station." The valley's east end is graced by the presence of a beautiful pool—the receptacle of a Merced River cascade. Leaving the camps of the picturesque area, we climb past the cascade and glance back to see the east face of exfoliating Moraine Dome.

Your brief cascade climb heads toward the 1900-foot-high Bunnell Point cliff, which is exfoliating at a prodigious rate. Rounding the base of a glacier-smoothed dome, unofficially called the Sugar Loaf, you enter Lost Valley, about 1 mile beyond the east end of Little Yosemite Valley, in which no fires are allowed. At the valley's east end, switchback up past Bunnell Cascade, which, with the magnificent canyon scenery, can easily distract you from the real danger of this exposed section of trail.

Just beyond the glaciated V gorge, the canyon floor widens a bit, and, in this area, we bridge the Merced River. Our up-canyon walk soon reaches a series of more than a dozen switchbacks that carry us up 400 feet above the river—a bypass route necessitated by another glaciated V gorge. Our climb reaches its zenith amid a spring-fed profuse garden, bordered by aspens, which, in midsummer, supports a colorful array of various wildflowers. Alpine lily, monk's hood, and arrow-leaved senecio grow chest high, as if to divert our attention from the many smaller, though equally beautiful, wildflower species.

Beyond this glade, you soon come out onto a highly polished bedrock surface. Here, you can glance west and see Clouds Rest—a long ridge—standing on the horizon. Now you descend back into tree cover, and, among the white boles of aspens, brush through a forest carpet of bracken ferns and cross several creeklets before emerging on a bedrock bench above the river's inner gorge. From the bench, you can study the features of a broad, hulking granitic mass opposite you whose south face is bounded by an immense arch. A hairline crack along its east side indicates that a major rockfall is imminent. Traversing the bench, you soon come to a bend in the river, where you bridge the Merced just above the brink of its cascades. Strolling east, you soon reach the west end of spacious Echo Valley and proceed to its north edge and the Echo Valley junction, near an Echo Creek campsite.

With Merced Lake as our goal, we immediately bridge Echo Creek, strike southeast through burned but boggy Echo Valley, and climb east past the Merced River's largely unseen pools to Merced Lake's west shore. Merced Lake—80 feet deep, large, and at a moderate elevation—supports three species of trout: brook, brown, and rainbow. Don't camp by the outlet, but, rather, continue for 0.8 mile past the north shore to the Merced Lake High Sierra Camp and the adjacent riverside campground. Be sure to use the bearproof food-storage boxes. Spend your second night here or about 3.3 miles farther, at Washburn Lake, our next significant goal.

From campsites near the east shore of Merced Lake, you climb around a low trans-canyon rib, down which the Merced River shoots to a churning pool. Beyond the rib, you have a level, 0.75-mile stroll past lodgepoles and aspens to a junction beside the Merced Lake Ranger Station. Descending to it is the Lewis Creek Trail, named for the multibranched creek we bridged just before this junction. An alternate trip, described just ahead, is a 23.9-mile loop from this junction; it ends along the last part of the Lewis Creek Trail. Don't hike this loop in the reverse direction; though it involves the same amount of climbing, the climbing comes in larger steps. The described route has a much more gradual ascent.

Starting southeast from the junction, we skirt along the edge of a broad, flat canyon floor, which, like the next 7.5 miles, is dominated by lodgepoles. The half-mile width of the canyon floor leads you to expect its sediments to extend more than 200 feet down to bedrock. One would expect to see a deep "Merced Lake" here, but not even a pond exists. At best, a swampy lake may have existed after the last glaciers retreated up-canyon, which may have disgorged prodigious sediments in

their voluminous outwash to fill it in by about 15,000 years ago.

About 0.75 mile south from the junction, we rejoin the Merced River at a point where a bedrock dam cuts across it, forming pools both above and below it. Just upstream is another bedrock dam, and then we see a large, smooth slab on the canyon's southwest wall, which, like other similar sites, in the past has borne avalanches. As your trail's gradient changes from level to a gentle ascent, junipers, Jeffrey pines, and white firs become prominent. Mule ears, found in abundance on volcanic soils, merely dot the slopes here, and at a large tributary, aspens radiate their own charm. Immediately beyond this tributary, the Merced River cascades through a small gorge, and beside it you'll find ochre-stained slabs—the artwork of soda springs. Climbing onward, note a progression toward dryness as expressed in a sequence from bracken fern to chinquapin to huckleberry oak and ultimately to sagebrush. Next, a river cascade is a treat, followed by a long, tempting pool, which lies just below a rocky moraine. You then pass an even larger pool, beside a trail blasted in bedrock, immediately before reaching bedrock-dammed Washburn Lake, at 7605 feet.

In Washburn Lake's cold waters—at least 86 feet deep—brook and rainbow trout await the skillful angler. The lake's north shore has been a popular camping area; nonetheless, most of the lake's campsites are along the lake's south end. Here, incoming sediments are slowly filling in the lake—a process that should be accomplished in about a half-million years. However, long before then, perhaps in the next few thousand years, a glacier will advance down-canyon and eradicate the lake sediments left after the last one retreated.

By the lake's inlet, notice the plant succession south from the shore. Sterile, newly deposited sand covers the shore, but a few feet back, sedges take hold. Farther back, willows start to shade them out and these, in turn, are shaded out by lodgepoles and aspens. Until late July, mosquitoes can plague campers here; before then, use the rocky, north-end campsites.

Beyond the lake, whose basin was buried under as much as 3000 feet of ice in past glaciations, we hike up-canyon, soon noting a cleft in our canyon's west wall—the result of erosion along a large, straight fracture. Momentarily, the trail approaches the Merced River, where you may see a good campsite 150 yards below a very photogenic fall. Continuing southeast, you leave most backpackers for an excursion into the upper reaches of the Merced River. In a half mile, your trail bends east, and beyond a tumultuous cascade, it gradually levels off, curves south, and passes a packer campsite about 40 yards before bridging the Merced River near its confluence with the Lyell Fork.

More cascades are passed as you make an effort south up the Merced Peak Fork canyon, whose east wall has one exposure of very massive dikes. Beyond this view, we soon bridge the fork beside another packer camp, then switchback eastward across open slopes. Along this ascent, you see the two summits of Mt. Florence, above the Lyell Fork canyon to the north-northeast, and the two summits of Merced Peak, above a cross-country route to the south-southwest. Once in the Triple Peak Fork canyon, about 4 miles beyond Washburn Lake, the trail first climbs for a half mile. It then makes a very gentle 2.25-mile climb across glaciated slabs and through a thinning lodgepole forest to a junction by the upper Triple Peak Fork. This is a scenic area for camping.

A **ALTERNATE TRIP BACK TO MERCED LAKE RANGER STATION:** This is the start of a 14.7-mile hike back to the junction by the Merced Lake Ranger Station. Only those wanting alpine solitude or alpine ascents will want to take this route. To begin it, look for a log to cross the wide tributary of Triple Peak Fork; then, back on the trail, head southeast to a quick ford of the fork. From the ford, your trail makes a gentle ascent south, paralleling the unseen fork for 0.8 mile to the start of a switchbacking climb northeast.

SIDE TRIP TO TURNER LAKE: Here is the place to leave the trail for an easy half-mile, cross-country jaunt up to seldom-visited Turner Lake, at 9531 feet. All the others we'll approach lie above the 9600-foot contour. **END OF SIDE TRIP.**

The 550-foot climb northeast is generally a viewless one, due to the lodgepoles and hemlocks, though you may get an occasional view north of the Mt. Florence ridge and of the Matthes Crest, in the distance west of it. Your climb ends 1.7 miles above your start at a junction on a small flat below the west spur of unseen Isberg Peak.

SIDE TRIP TO UNNAMED LAKE: For a campsite, you may want to follow that route for 0.3 mile, and then traverse a quarter mile east to a fairly large, unnamed lake, whose northwest shore is bordered with protective lodgepole pines. **END OF SIDE TRIP.**

Our hike, however, begins north along the High Trail, quickly reaching a step-across creek.

SIDE TRIP TO A SECOND UNNAMED LAKE: If followed upstream for an easy 0.75 mile, you would reach a treeline lake at 10,217 feet. **END OF SIDE TRIP.**

Blazes north mark your trail's route, which descends to a shallow, glaciated trough, then climbs up to three ephemeral creeklets.

SIDE TRIP TO A THIRD UNNAMED LAKE: From these, you could hike 0.3 mile cross-country up to a small subalpine lake. **END OF SIDE TRIP.**

Your ascent yields to a contour, then to a descent to a trickling creeklet, from which you climb to a low nearby saddle and then descend once again to another creeklet. A lake lies on a bench about a quarter mile east of it, but the climb to it is quite steep. In about a half mile, your high-altitude traverse, shaded by lodgepoles and hemlocks, crosses Foerster Creek, 2.5 miles along the High Trail. About 0.75 mile farther, you ascend to the second of two gently descending ridges, from which you can leave the trail for a quarter-mile contour east to a lovely little lake.

SIDE TRIP TO A FOURTH UNNAMED LAKE: This cross-country route begins about 30 yards before the trail makes a short, steep descent into a gully. Rather than camp on the fragile shoreline vegetation—which one should never do—camp just west of the lake. **END OF SIDE TRIP.**

Beyond the gully, our trail undulates to a forested, bouldery crest, which is our route's high point, at 10,050 feet. From this crest, you can look back and see the twin summits of rusty, metavolcanic Isberg Peak and the pointed summit of gray, granitic Post Peak. You can also identify slightly rusty Triple Divide Peak. West of it stands dark-gray, metamorphic Merced Peak, then the varicolored peaks of the Clark Range. In the distant northwest rise Clouds Rest and Mt. Hoffmann, and east of them stands the park's highest massif—the Mt. Lyell complex.

Leaving the crest, you descend for 1 mile into the deep, glaciated Lyell Fork canyon via dozens of short switchbacks—one with an excellent viewpoint—and then eventually reach the seasonally powerful Lyell Fork, 2.7 miles beyond Foerster Creek, and bordered by mountain hemlocks. This is the northernmost locality in which you'll want to set up your third night's camp. No camping space is found at the ford, so either follow the tumbling stream a couple of hundred yards downstream or go about 0.3 to 0.6 mile upstream. If you want to head upstream, leave the trail about 200 yards beyond the Lyell Fork, where it starts a traverse northwest.

The trail here might be hard to follow for a short distance, so watch for ducks and blazes. Soon starting a westward climb, you pass four large junipers, which add contrast to your typically pine-hemlock landscape. Beyond a conspicuous notch, you get a revealing panorama of the Clark Range and the expansive bench below it, which borders the rim of the deep Merced River gorge.

This "gorge within a canyon" topography has previously been interpreted as the result of two distinct major uplifts in the Sierra Nevada. However, the canyon below us lies parallel to the Sierra Crest, and therefore its river's gradient would not have been increased by any uplift. We now know that these inner gorges are tens of millions of years old. Despite having massive glaciers flow down them, they have been only slightly modified. (See the end of Trip 11 for evidence of virtually no erosion in the last 10 million years in the Tuolumne River canyon, where glaciers were as much as 4000 feet thick.)

After the view, we re-enter forest and cross a small Mt. Florence creek at the base of its splashing waterfall. From it, you climb past joint-controlled slabs, ascending almost 500 feet over a mile's course to a bouldery summit. Along the ascent to this forested summit, you come to a viewpoint that provides the trail's best panorama of the upper Merced River canyon, from Peak 11210 (about 1 mile east of us) south to Triple Divide Peak and then north along the entire Clark Range. The trail, which has climbed unnecessarily, now descends a half mile to a second Mt. Florence tributary, with camping potential, then climbs an equal distance to a slope below unseen Cony Crags, which you saw from points south of the Lyell Fork.

With no more major climbing to come until after Nevada Fall, you can enjoy the trail's course, which ducks down into a shallow but glaciated side canyon with a creekside campsite. Beyond the side canyon, the trail switchbacks more than 30 times on a mile-long descent to a junction in Lewis Creek canyon, 5.6 miles beyond the Lyell Fork.

From here, the Lewis Creek Trail, now out of earshot of the creek, switchbacks down moderately, sometimes steeply, under a sparse cover of fir, juniper, and pine for 1 mile to a junction with the Fletcher Creek Trail.

Because cascading Lewis Creek is entrenched in a small gorge, our switchbacking trail keeps a short distance away from it, reaching a small flat with large Jeffrey pines before passing a small point with an excellent Merced Lake view. Half Dome stands on the distant down-canyon skyline. Open switchbacks lined with brush give way to ones with junipers and Jeffrey pines, and then, near the Valley floor, to ones with white firs. Among lodgepoles on the Valley floor, we come to a junction that is just 40 yards north of the Merced Lake Ranger Station, and finish our loop. **END OF ALTERNATE TRIP.**

From the junction by the upper Triple Peak Fork, our trail angles west, begins a moderate ascent, and, in a few minutes, climbs steeply up a short, straight gully. Above it, the trail climbs moderately for about a 250-foot elevation gain, and then it rolls southwest across granitic benches. These, like the gully, are angular, and they were formed as a result of weathering and erosion along the many joints, or fractures, in the granitic landscape.

With more than half of your multiday hike behind you, you soon begin a switchbacking course northwest up to a granitic crest that divides the Triple Peak Fork from the Merced Peak Fork. Although the crest does support lodgepoles, mountain hemlocks, and whitebark pines, the forest cover is thin enough to permit views of many of the peaks that rim the upper Merced River basin. From the crest, you have a moderate though reasonably short descent to the two-branched Merced Peak Fork. You could camp in this vicinity or else hike cross-country 0.7 mile gently downstream to a shallow lake.

The trail to a second crest—one that separates the Merced Peak and Red Peak forks—has interesting nearby features and pleasant, tree-filtered views to divert your attention from the effort of the climb. We reach the second crest at a broad saddle (about 9900 feet) that conveniently holds a scenic lakelet, which makes a good place for an extended stop. Having a fair number of conifers, its surrounding slopes provide your last wind-shielded campsites this side of Red Peak Pass. Rather than climb toward that pass, the trail first makes an unnecessary descent north from the lakelet, then turns southwest to climb.

⑤ SIDE TRIP TO RED DEVIL LAKE: Here, at the start of the climb, you could descend cross-country northwest to Red Devil Lake, down at 9744 feet. About a half mile away, its lengthy, intricately winding shoreline provides the best near-treeline campsites. **END OF SIDE TRIP.**

Our trail, which, until now, has been across granitic terrain, enters a metamorphic one as it climbs to a broad bench. On it, you pass two sizable, windswept ponds, neither one having desirable camping. In midsummer, lowly wildflowers abound on this bench, attracting many pollinating insects that, in turn, may end up as food for resident yellow-legged frogs or altitude-transcending Brewer's blackbirds.

Leaving the bench, you climb northwest past the last holdout of whitebark pines, then switchback southwest up a bleak alpine ridge. On it, you have unobstructed views of the greater part of the upper Merced River basin. Tufts of sedge cluster around almost every available crack, and occasional wildflowers catch your eye as you struggle in a thin atmosphere up past tiny tarns toward a ragged, notched crest. Your trail, which soon becomes a series of short, steep switchbacks, heads for Red Peak Pass, which may be dangerously snowbound well into summer. And even when the switchbacks are not under snow, their rocky nature can easily turn your ankle if you take a careless step.

Along your ascent to Red Peak Pass, you might notice a small glacial moraine—a remnant of the Little Ice Age—lying at the edge of the Red Peak cirque. It may look like a collection of boulders that slid down Red Peak, but its large blocks are gray, not red, as they would be if they came from that peak. Rusty talus boulders, derived from the peak, do rest atop the moraine, whose gray blocks came from the south.

At 11,150-foot Red Peak Pass, you have views as far as Matterhorn Peak, along the park's north rim. Closer, Mt. Lyell crowns the upper Merced River basin and is flanked on the northwest by Mt. Maclure and on the southeast by Rodgers Peak. Twin-peaked Mt. Florence breaks the horizon west of this trio, while, east of all of them, the dark, sawtooth Ritter Range pokes above the park's eastern crest boundary. Below the peaks lies a broad upland surface that is cleft by the 2000-foot-deep Merced River canyon. Turning south, you have a tunneled, almost lifeless view of dark-gray Merced Peak, its western outliers, and rockbound Upper Ottoway Lake.

From Red Peak Pass, your descent to Lower Ottoway Lake—the ideal place to spend your third night—is a two-stage descent, each with more than two dozen switchbacks. The initial descent may appear to be lifeless—only cold granitic rocks and gravel—but closer inspection reveals the presence of alpine sedges and wildflowers. These are present in sufficient quantity to permit pikas to thrive up to the very pass itself. A high, nasal voice often gives away the presence of these diminutive, short-eared members of the rabbit family. They are preyed on by the short-tailed weasel, a small, voracious predator that dons a white coat in the winter.

Our first descent stage ends just above a pond and adjacent Upper Ottoway Lake. Neither of these cold, shimmering jewels has suitable camping, but you can make an interesting side trip over to them and then east up into the deep cirque that once held Muir's glacier. Today, only its moraines

exist, which show the size of the once-living snowfield.

Our second stage begins with a moderate descent west, followed by the usual short switchbacks. On this descent, many wildflowers are seen, including paintbrush, penstemon, monkey flower, baby elephant heads, columbine, phlox, leptodactylon, cinquefoil, yarrow, senecio, aster, and daisy. Sagebrush, heather, and dwarf whitebark pines appear before you reach the eastern arm of Lower Ottoway Lake. A slab above its northeast shore makes a good sunbathing area after a quick dip in its cold waters. Anglers can dangle lines for a tasty rainbow trout meal. You'll find the best camps under lodgepole and whitebark pines above the lake's northwest shore. The lake makes an ideal base camp for exploring the Merced Peak environs.

Back on the trail, you leave the lake just north of its outlet, and then parallel Ottoway Creek west. After 0.8 mile, you will, hopefully, find a log to cross it. Then you ramble southwest up and down a glaciated landscape for 1.8 miles, crossing Illilouette Creek before reaching a junction with the Illilouette Creek Trail. From it, you can start south up along the east bank of a creek, cross it after a minute's walk, and reach very good campsites along the west shore of Upper Merced Pass Lake. As elsewhere, bears may visit this lake.

Trip 82 descends north from nearby Merced Pass to our trail junction and then it climbs northeast up to Red Peak Pass. Our hike, however, descends northwest along the Illilouette Creek Trail, passing unseen Lower Merced Pass Lake in about 0.3 mile. To avoid mosquitoes at this relatively warm, shallow lake with a water-choked spongy shore, camp on the granitic ridge west of the lake. Below this nearby lake, your trail crosses several creeklets and, in places, may be hard to follow, so look for blazes on lodgepoles. About 1.8 miles below the last trail junction, you cross to the east bank of Illilouette Creek, which you then parallel for 3.8 miles. You can find several places to camp along the

JOHN MUIR AND SIERRAN GLACIERS

By late summer 1977, after two dry years, the Merced Peak snowfield had completely disappeared. When John Muir first saw it in the autumn of 1871, it was an active snow-field—that is, a small glacier. Muir was not the first to see a Sierran glacier, but he was the first to recognize one. On July 2, 1863, William Brewer and Charles Hoffmann—both members of Josiah D. Whitney's Geological Survey of California—climbed the Lyell Glacier and almost reached the summit of Mt. Lyell. However, several feet of fresh snow covered the glacier, and perhaps because of that, they saw no crevasses. In his journal, Brewer wrote:

> A great glacier once formed far back in the mountains and passed down the valley
> [Lyell Canyon], polishing and grooving the rocks for more than a thousand feet up on
> each side, rounding the granite hills into domes. It must have been as grand as any that
> are now in Switzerland. But the climate has changed, and it has entirely passed away.
> There is now no glacier in this state—the climate conditions do not exist under which
> any could be formed.

In *The Mountains of California*, John Muir disagrees. Muir was familiar with the charac-teristics of a glacier, as is revealed in the following passage of his 1871 discovery of the Merced Peak glacier:

> I observed a series of small terminal moraines ranged along the south wall of the
> amphitheater, corresponding in size and form with the shadows cast by the highest por-
> tions. The meaning of this correspondence between moraines and shadows was after-
> ward made plain. Tracing the stream back to the last of its chain of lakelets [the one
> above Upper Ottoway Lake], I noticed a deposit of fine gray mud worn from a grind-
> stone, and I at once suspected its glacial origin, for the stream that was carrying it came
> gurgling out of the base of a raw moraine that seemed in the process of formation. Not
> a plant or weather stain was visible on its rough, unsettled surface. It is from 60 to over
> 100 feet high and plunges forward at an angle of 38 degrees. Cautiously picking my
> way, I gained the top of the moraine and was delighted to see a small but well-charac-
> terized glacier swooping down from the gloomy precipices of Black Mountain [Merced
> Peak] in a finely graduated curve to the moraine on which I stood. The compact ice
> appeared on all the lower portions of the glacier, though gray with dirt and stones
> embedded in it. Farther up, the ice disappeared beneath coarse, granulated snow. The
> surface of the glacier was further characterized by dirt bands and the outcropping
> edges of the blue veins, showing the laminated structure of the ice. The uppermost cre-
> vasse, or "bergschrund," where the névé was attached to the mountain, was from 12 to
> 14 feet wide, and was bridged in a few places by the remains of snow avalanches.
> Creeping along the edge of the schrund, holding on with benumbed fingers, I discovered
> clear sections where the bedded structure was beautifully revealed. The surface snow,
> though sprinkled with stones shot down from the cliffs, was in some places almost pure,
> gradually becoming crystalline and changing to whitish porous ice of different shades of
> color, and this, again, changing at a depth of 20 or 30 feet to blue ice, some of the rib-
> bon-like bands of which were nearly pure, and blended with the paler bands in the most
> gradual and delicate manner imaginable. . .
>
> After this discovery, I made excursions over all the High Sierra, pushing my explo-
> rations summer after summer, and discovered that what at first sight in the distance

(continued on page 341)

(John Muir and Sierran Glaciers, continued)

looked like extensive snowfields, were in great part glaciers, busily at work completing the sculpture of the summit-peaks so grandly blocked out by their giant predecessors.

On August 21 [1872], I set a series of stakes in the Maclure Glacier, near Mt. Lyell, and found its rate of motion to be little more than an inch a day in the middle, showing a great contrast to the Muir Glacier in Alaska, which, near the front, flows at a rate of from 5 to 10 feet in 24 hours.

Thus, Muir can be credited with the first discovery of Sierran glaciers.

creek's east bank, or, if you cross to the west bank, even better ones.

Where the canyon's late-Pleistocene moraines force Illilouette Creek west over toward Buena Vista Creek, you continue northwest, cross the crests of five low moraines, and drop to the Clark Fork, which has several good campsites above its south bank. These sites, about 6.8 miles from your trailhead, are good choices for your fourth night on the trail.

From the camps, look for a log to cross the Clark Fork, and engage in an easy 1.25-mile traverse through a pleasant Jeffrey pine/white fir forest to a junction. Before reaching it, however, you pass some nearby boulders—one the size of a house—that fell from a dome north of here hundreds of years ago. Near these boulders and beyond, you'll see some evidence of 1970s and later forest fires that scar much of the landscape in the Illilouette Creek basin.

[A] **ALTERNATE TRIP TO TRAILHEAD:** From the junction, you can reach your trailhead at Glacier Point by two ways. Keeping right, you can make a high traverse to the Glacier Point-Panorama Trail, then reverse the first part of your first day's hike. This alternate route adds about 600 feet of climbing and a little more than 2 miles to your total hiking effort, but is worth it to those who enjoyed the spectacular Panorama Cliff traverse. **END OF ALTERNATE TRIP.**

Our hike's regular route branches left at the junction, immediately crosses a spring-fed creeklet, then starts down formerly burned slopes. Our moderate ridge descent

ends on a gravelly, open slope above Illilouette Creek. From here, the Mono Meadow Trail climbs north 2.3 miles back up to the trail we had earlier branched away from, while a use trail heads briefly ahead (west) toward some good, near-creek campsites. Your route turns south, descends the glacial outwash sediments to adjacent Illilouette Creek, and, on its sandy, fly-infested north bank, you find more camps, where a tent comes in handy. After a usually wet creek crossing, you reach this busy area's most popular camps, above the creek's south bank.

Beyond them, we hike a minute to a junction with the Buena Vista Trail (Trip 73), and a few yards farther, we reach a junction with the westbound Mono Meadow Trail (also Trip 73). The westbound trail climbs 3 miles up to the Glacier Point Road. Our route, the northbound Buena Vista Trail, descends along Illilouette Creek, climbs up to the Glacier Point-Panorama Trail, and then ascends it to our Glacier Point Trailhead. Because camping is prohibited within 4 trail miles of Glacier Point, you can't camp along this entire stretch. However, several places make fine rest stops.

TRIP **76**

North Wawona to Chilnualna Falls

Ⓢ ↗ DH

DISTANCE: 8.2 miles out and back

ELEVATIONS: 4200´/6410´
+2260´/-50´/±4620´

SEASON: Early May to late November

USE: Moderate

MAPS: *Wawona, Mariposa Grove*

TRAIL LOG:
4.1   Chilnualna Fall area

INTRODUCTION: Not all Yosemite waterfalls are found in Yosemite Valley; several are located along Chilnualna Creek. As in the Valley, the severely hanging canyon of Chilnualna Creek above the highest fall did not originate in response to glaciers deeply eroding the South Fork Merced River canyon. Rather, it slowly originated as the river eroded downward for some 50 million years under warm, wet climates, which existed until 33 million years ago.

DIRECTIONS TO THE TRAILHEAD: At the east end of the Chilnualna Road. The Chilnualna Road starts in the Wawona area immediately north of the bridge across the South Fork Merced River. On it, you drive past the Pioneer Yosemite History Center and a nearby fork right to the park's district office. In 0.1 mile, another road forks left, and, just beyond it, on the right, is a small parking area for the Alder Creek Trail, located a half mile along your main road. This northbound trail begins roughly 100 yards east of the road forking left. You then drive east 1.2 miles farther, to a short road branching down to a large parking area.

This road is located only 100 yards before the pavement on Chilnualna Road ends. Ahead, a dirt road descends to bridge Chilnualna Creek, while a paved road curves northwest. From the parking area, a trail climbs about 100 yards north-northeast to the actual trailhead. If you have stock, you will have to head about 250 yards up the paved road curving northwest to a road climbing north. Ascend this 0.2 mile to its second switchback, where a horse trail climbs about 280 yards east to the end of the foot trail. Trail begins in map section C6.

DESCRIPTION: The hikers' trail starts as a gently ascending dirt road, quickly giving way to a footpath that heads up Chilnualna Creek almost to its 25-foot-high fall.

Ⓢ **SIDE TRIP TO SWIMMING HOLE:** When the creek's flow is slow, hikers with some climbing skill can follow the creek several hundred yards up to a fairly large swimming hole, at the base of another fall. **END OF SIDE TRIP.**

Most stick to the trail, which becomes steep and potentially dangerous, especially when wet. Soon, it reaches the horse trail, and on that you climb to cross a manzanita-clothed ridge before entering a forest of ponderosa pines and incense-cedars. A few open spots allow one to survey the Wawona area to the south, Wawona Point to the southeast, and Wawona Dome to the east. Then, climbing east, you reach Chilnualna Creek in a quarter mile, and hike up along it another quarter mile. If you need water, get it before the trail leaves the creek. In mid- and late summer, the ascent can be hot and dry.

On a moderately graded trail, you now climb more than a dozen switchbacks of various lengths up into a cooler forest before making a fairly open traverse southeast toward the main Chilnualna Fall. Here, you see the entire length of the fall, which churns for hundreds of feet down a deep, confining chute. Your trail comes to within a few yards of the fall's brink, but due to loose gravel and lack of a protective railing, you should not venture any closer to it.

Not far above Chilnualna Fall proper is an upper fall, a 60-foot cascade that is quite impressive in early season. To get around this fall and its small gorge, your trail switchbacks north, then curves south above the lip of the gorge. Views extending over the forested Wawona area are left behind as you reach a trail junction. Just below this junction and also below the main trail east of it are several good campsites. From the junction, Trip 77 follows the trail, climbing generally northeast up Chilnualna Creek, while Trip 71 follows the trail that descends south to here from Turner Meadows.

While cautiously investigating the Chilnaulna Fall area, you might look for a small natural bridge below and just downstream from the trail junction. The stream was deeply undercutting a granite slab while, at the same time, its boulders were drilling a pothole through the slab. Eventually, the slab was drilled completely through, and the creekside rim of the pothole stands today as a small bridge.

TRIP **77**

North Wawona to Royal Arch, Buena Vista, and Chilnualna Lakes

Ⓜ **𝒫** BPx

DISTANCE: 28.3 miles semiloop

ELEVATIONS: 4200′/9340′
+6570′/-6579′/±13,140′

SEASON: Early July to late September

USE: Moderate

MAPS: *Wawona, Mariposa Grove*

TRAIL LOG:

4.1	Chilnaulna Fall area
4.6	Chilnualna Creek
6.6	Junction
7.3	Another junction
10.5	Southern Chilnualna Lake
12.7	Buena Vista Trail
13.1	Buena Vista Lake
15.8	Royal Arch Lake
16.5	East-climbing trail
17.3	Johnson Lake
18.3	Crescent Lake
19.6	Grouse Lake
21.7	Junction
24.2	Chilnaulna Fall area
28.3	Trailhead

INTRODUCTION: Glaciers originating on the slopes of Buena Vista Peak descended north, south, and west, and then retreated to leave about a dozen small-to-medium lakes. This hike visits seven of these, plus dashing Chilnualna Fall—one of the park's highest falls outside Yosemite Valley.

DIRECTIONS TO THE TRAILHEAD: At the east end of the Chilnualna Road. The Chilnualna Road starts in the Wawona area immediately north of the bridge across the

South Fork Merced River. On it, you drive past the Pioneer Yosemite History Center and a nearby fork right to the park's district office. In 0.1 mile, another road forks left, and, just beyond it, on the right, is a small parking area for the Alder Creek Trail, located a half mile along your main road. This northbound trail begins roughly 100 yards east of the road forking left. You then drive east 1.2 miles farther, to a short road branching down to a large parking area. This road is located only 100 yards before the pavement on Chilnualna Road ends. Ahead, a dirt road descends to bridge Chilnualna Creek, while a paved road curves northwest. From the parking area, a trail climbs about 100 yards north-north-east to the actual trailhead. If you have stock, you will have to head about 250 yards up the paved road curving northwest to a road climbing north. Ascend this 0.2 mile to its second switchback, where a horse trail climbs about 280 yards east to the end of the foot trail. Trail begins in map section C6.

DESCRIPTION: The hikers' trail starts as a gently ascending dirt road, quickly giving way to a footpath that heads up Chilnualna Creek, almost to its 25-foot fall. Ahead, the trail becomes steep and potentially dangerous, especially when wet. Soon, it reaches the horse trail, on which you climb to cross a manzanita-clothed ridge before entering a forest of ponderosa pines and incense-cedars. A few open spots allow you to survey the Wawona area to the south, Wawona Point to the southeast, and Wawona Dome to the east. Then, climbing east, you reach Chilnualna Creek in a quarter mile, and hike up along it another quarter mile. If you need water, get it before the trail leaves the creek. In mid- and late summer, the ascent can be hot and dry.

On a moderately graded trail, you now climb more than a dozen switchbacks of various lengths up into a cooler forest before making a fairly open traverse southeast toward the main Chilnualna Fall. Here, you see the entire length of the fall,

which churns for hundreds of feet down a deep, confining chute. Your trail comes to within a few yards of the fall's brink, but due to loose gravel and lack of a protective railing, you should not venture any closer to it.

Not far above Chilnualna Fall proper is an upper fall, a 60-foot cascade that is quite impressive in early season. To get around this fall and its small gorge, your trail switchbacks north, and then curves south above the lip of the gorge. Views extending over the forested Wawona area are left behind as you reach a trail junction in the Chilnualna Fall area. Just below this junction, and also below the main trail east of it, are several good campsites. While cautiously investigating Chilnualna Creek, you might look for a small natural bridge below and just downstream from the trail junction. The stream was deeply undercutting a granite slab while, at the same time, its boulders were drilling a pothole through the slab. Eventually, the slab was drilled completely through, and the creekside rim of the pothole stands today as a small bridge. Alternatively, you could camp about a half mile farther by taking the trail that makes a short, steep ascent northeast, then traverses southeast to Chilnualna Creek, with campsites along both its banks.

After crossing to its southeast bank, you head upstream, then veer away from the creek to make a short, moderate ascent to a low gap. Past it, you enter a damp meadow (an early-season mosquito haven) then climb for a mile, paralleling the usually unseen creek at a distance before intersecting its tributary, Grouse Lake creek. Generally a jump-across creek, it can be a 20-foot-wide, slippery-slab ford in June. Now just above 7000 feet, you feel the effects of a higher elevation as well as see them—as expressed in the predominance of stately red firs and occasional lodgepole pines. Before reaching a junction after a 0.7-mile ascent, note your first trailside western white pines.

At the junction, we join Trip 73 for a 0.7-mile stretch northwest, first up over a nearby divide, then down more than 400 feet to Chilnualna Creek. Just above its north bank is a good, medium-size campsite, and just beyond that is another junction. Here, we turn right while Trip 73 continues ahead, bound for Turner Meadows and the Glacier Point Road.

Eastbound, make a moderate 0.3-mile ascent, followed by a gentler one that goes an even mile along the lodgepole-shaded bank of Chilnualna Creek. After a 0.2-mile walk along this gentler stretch, you'll find an acceptable campsite. At the end of the stretch, you cross the seasonal creek that drains the middle and northern Chilnualna Lakes. With 1.9 miles left to our first lake, we first go a few yards along the larger creek that drains the southern and eastern Chilnualna Lakes, then leave it to cross a nearby bouldery ridge that is a recessional moraine left by a Tioga-age glacier about 15,000 years ago. At its maximum, about 20,000 years ago, this glacier calved icy blocks over the brink of Chilnualna Fall, as did some earlier glaciers. Young glacial evidence in the form of moraines, erratics, and polish is often seen along this shady climb to the waist-deep southern Chilnualna Lake, which has a fair west-shore campsite. Because it is so shallow, this is one of this route's warmest lakes for cooling off in.

[S] **SIDE TRIP TO A CHILNUALNA LAKE:** Perhaps the best of the Chilnualna Lakes is also one of the least visited: the lake at the base of Buena Vista Peak's western shoulder, about a half mile east-southeast of our trailside lake. A second goal is a more-frequented lake, which lies in the middle of this cluster of lakes. This one is easier to reach, and you do so by starting from the far end of our trailside, southern lake. Leaving it, you head 0.2 mile up its inlet creek to a small pond, then walk due north over a low ridge to the middle lake. From it, one can easily regain the trail by continuing north—no need to drop along its outlet creek. **END OF SIDE TRIP.**

Leaving the trailside lake, climb over a low, bouldery morainal ridge, skirt a small meadow, and cross the middle lake's ephemeral creek. Past it, you curve over to the northern lake's outlet creek, parallel it upward, and then, just a quarter mile before the lake, cross over to the north bank. Upon reaching the shallow, narrow lake, you find a good campsite among red firs and western white pines. If weather is threatening, camp here rather than climbing east to the exposed pass.

At that 9020-foot-high pass, about a 0.7-mile, winding ascent from the northern lake, we meet the Buena Vista Trail. Here, we join most of the second half of Trip 73, as it goes past Buena Vista, Royal Arch, Johnson, Crescent, and Grouse lakes. You may want to visit all of them, and you should plan to spend at least a day in this scenic glacier-lake area. The first lake we encounter, about 0.4 mile southeast from the junction, is rather bleak Buena Vista Lake, which has rainbow and brook trout. Nestled on a broad bench at the base of the cool north slope of Buena Vista Peak, this lake is the highest and coldest one we'll see. It does, however, have at least two good, if somewhat exposed, camps. In threatening weather, camp lower down. Starting at the lake's outlet, take short switchbacks up to a nearby, broad, viewless Buena Vista Pass, which at 9340 feet is our trip's highest elevation.

[S] **SIDE TRIP TO BUENA VISTA PEAK:** From here, one can climb 0.7 mile southwest up a gentle ridge, gaining only about 270 feet elevation to reach the summit of Buena Vista Peak, from which you have an unrestricted panorama of the park's southern area. **END OF SIDE TRIP.**

From the pass, we descend 2 easy, winding trail miles to a favorite lake on this loop, Royal Arch Lake, which lies below a broad, granitic arch. This lake, like Buena Vista Lake, has rainbow and brook trout. Just past the outlet is an excellent, popular campsite.

[S] **SIDE TRIP TO MINNOW LAKE:** For more solitude, head cross-country 0.4 mile west up to a ridge and then 0.2 mile down from it to less attractive Minnow Lake, which has brook trout. **END OF SIDE TRIP.**

Leaving Royal Arch Lake, we parallel its outlet creek for a half mile, then angle south briefly across slabs to a junction with an east-climbing trail. Here, we meet the route of Trip 79, which starts northwest from Chiquito Pass, crosses the South Fork Merced River, and climbs to Buck Camp, a ranger station about 1.5 miles from our junction.

Turning right, we descend west toward Johnson Lake. In just 0.8 mile, we good campsites along its northwest shore—where there are hordes of mosquitoes in early season. You don't see large Crescent Lake, but on meeting its inlet creek, about 0.3 mile beyond a meadowy divide, you can walk 150 yards downstream, passing a fair camp before reaching the lake's shallow, trout-filled waters. You might visit or camp near the lake's south end, for, from its outlet, you can peer down into the 2800-foot-deep South Fork Merced River canyon.

Former small ice caps that developed around Buena Vista Peak in part spilled south across the Johnson and Crescent lakes' basins, descending toward the South Fork Merced River trunk glacier.

Beyond Crescent Lake's inlet creek, our trail quickly turns north, passes a small creekside meadow, and then climbs more than 150 feet to a second broad divide. From it, we descend into the headwaters of a Chilnualna Creek tributary. Your moderate-to-steep gradient ends when you approach easily missed Grouse Lake. Look for a trail that descends about 100 yards to a fair campsite on the north shore of this shallow, reedy lakelet.

You complete your lake-blessed loop by descending a little more than 2 miles west of Grouse Lake to a junction, from which you began your loop. Now you retrace your steps, first down to the junction in the Chilnaulna Fall area, and then down the major descent to the trailhead.

Glaciated bedrock slopes above Johnson Lake

TRIP 78

Mariposa Grove of Big Trees

M 🔁 DH

DISTANCE: 6.2 miles semiloop
(other routes possible)

ELEVATIONS: 5620'/6810'
+1530'/-1530'/±3060'

SEASON: Late May to
early November

USE: Packed

MAP: *Mariposa Grove*

TRAIL LOG:

0.6 Grizzly Giant
1.7 Mariposa Grove Museum
2.0 Telescope Tree
2.5 Galen Clark Tree
3.0 Wawona Point
3.5 Crest saddle
5.1 Broad-crest junction
6.2 Parking lot

INTRODUCTION: Near the southwest end of the parking lot is an information kiosk where visitors can get information about the Mariposa Grove while waiting to take the tram. The tram ride gives you an instructive, guided tour of the grove's salient features and, at its stops, you can step off, explore the immediate area, and then get on the next tram. However, by hiking you get a more intimate experience with the giant sequoia, or Wawona, as the Indians called them.

Though almost all Mariposa Grove visitors drive to it, one can also walk to it, starting from the Wawona Hotel. From it, a trail climbs about 2000 feet over about 5 miles to the outer loop of the Mariposa Grove. This trail is written up as an alternate trip.

DIRECTIONS TO THE TRAILHEAD: From the park's south entrance station, drive east 2.1 miles up to road's end at the Big Trees parking lot. Be forewarned that by midmorning, it can be full, since the grove is very popular, receiving up to 2 million visitors a year. During summer and early fall, take the free shuttle bus that leaves from the Wawona Store, just northwest of the Wawona Hotel. Trail begins in map section D6.

The alternate trip begins from a road immediately before it crosses the high point of a west-dropping ridge. If you are staying at the Wawona Hotel, just walk east upslope to this nearby road. This road descends east-northeast to a junction that is located about 160 yards east of an RV dump station, which is east of the Wawona Store's parking area.

DESCRIPTION: Two trails, a northern and a southern one, leave from the eastern, upper end of the parking lot. The northern one is the Outer Loop Trail, which makes a switchbacking climb 0.6 mile north to a junction with a trail east, then a winding traverse 0.6 mile northwest to a junction with a trail down to Wawona.

A **ALTERNATE TRIP FROM WAWONA:** This trail is initially part of the Two Hour Ride Trail, begins eastward as a dusty horse trail locally adorned with excrement, urine, and flies. You quickly pass an old, abandoned canal, climb to a crest, and, in a short mile, reach a crest fork. To the left, a broad horse path descends to a summer camp. From it, the broad horse path climbs southeast back up to a junction with our trail. This junction is reached after a second short, dusty mile, most of it right along the forested crest. Views of large Wawona Meadow are generally poor or nonexistent. From the saddle where the broad horse path rejoins our trail, we turn south to briefly descend to within 40 yards of noisy, paved Wawona Road, where there is parking for several vehicles. Starting from here cuts 1.9 miles, each way, from the total distance.

Here, we leave the Two Hour Ride Trail, which crosses the Wawona Road to loop back to the Wawona area. Now on a much less-used, generally horse-free route, we climb east up a steepening ridge before veering south up to a usually flowing creek, 1.7 miles beyond the horse trail. Our trail maintains its moderate gradient as it next climbs south above the headwalls of two eroding, enlarging bowls. Then, in a half mile, it begins to switchback up to a broad-crest junction with a ridge trail, about 5 miles from your trailhead. **END OF ALTERNATE TRIP.**

Our route from the eastern, upper end of the Mariposa Grove's parking lot is the southern trail, which actually starts at the

---

THE GIANT SEQUOIA

One point worth elaborating is how difficult it is for a sequoia to successfully replace itself. For a seed to become a tree, first there must be a fire, which removes humus to expose mineral soil. For the seedling to survive, there must be adequate soil moisture. In the last 15 million years, summers generally have been too dry, and, almost invariably, seedlings died before fall rains arrived. Before then, summers were wetter, especially before 33 million years ago. Today, a seedling is likely to survive only if first there has been a ground fire, and then if there has been a heavy snow-pack, so that the soil will stay moist through the summer. Fortunately, a sequoia can live to more than 2000 years in age, producing more than a half billion seeds in this time, and only one seed is required to replace the parent. The oldest known sequoia—the Muir snag, in the Kings River's Converse Basin Grove—is estimated to have lived for about 3500 years. Sequoias survive today because they have "all the time in the world" to wait for proper regenerative conditions.

---

kiosk and runs along the edge of the parking lot. On this nature trail, you momentarily parallel the tram road east before crossing a creeklet and the road. The signs along this trail not only identify the notable sequoias, but also educate you on their natural history, including such items as bark, cones, fire, reproduction, and associated plants and animals.

At the tram-road crossing lies the Fallen Monarch, largely intact, including its roots. Note that they grew in shallow soil, because bedrock lies only a couple of feet down. Unfortunately, occasional severe winds can topple a tree before it reaches old age. From the south side of the road, your nature trail climbs a quarter mile east before crossing the road. At this spot stand the Bachelor and the Three Graces.

In a similar distance, your trail reaches the Grizzly Giant. Like the Leaning Tower of Pisa, this still-growing giant seems ready to fall any second, and one wonders how such a top-heavy, shallow-rooted specimen could have survived as long as it has. Though it's the largest tree in the park—and probably the oldest, at almost 3000 years—there are at least 25 specimens elsewhere larger than it. It has a trunk volume of about 34,000 cubic feet, compared to about 52,500 cubic feet for the largest, the General Sherman, in Sequoia National Park's Giant Forest Grove. The Grizzly Giant has enough timber to build about 20 homes, but, fortunately, sequoia wood is very brittle, shattering when a tree falls—a feature that saved it from being logged into oblivion.

Heading north from the east end of the enclosure circling the Grizzly Giant, we reach, in 50 yards, the California Tree, also enclosed, but with a path through it. It once had a deep burn, which was cut away in 1895 so that tourists could ride a stage through it. Beyond this tree, a trail traverses a half mile west to the Outer Loop Trail. We, however, take an ascending trail that parallels the tram road north for 250 yards before crossing it. Our trail then climbs to a nearby switchback, where a lightly used trail winds southeast down to an old road. We start north and quickly reach a lackluster trail that traverses northwest to the tram road, where another trail, equally lackluster, descends southwest to the Outer Loop Trail. Additionally, a switchbacking one climbs northeastward to a loop in the upper part of the tram road.

Our trail gains 400 feet elevation climbing to the same spot, starting north and then going briefly east before switchbacking to wind northwest to the upper end of the switchbacking trail; the junction is about 15 yards from the tram road. Here, too, is the Upper Loop Trail, which parallels the tram road counterclockwise as both circle the upper grove. (Although our area is called the Mariposa Grove, it is really two groves, a lower one, which includes the Grizzly Giant and trees below it, and an upper one, which mostly is encircled by the Upper Loop Trail.)

This guide's suggested route from the junction is to start on a trail a few paces away that descends north about 90 yards to a junction with an east-west trail (along the most direct way to the Mariposa Grove Museum from the alternate trip). This winds about 250 yards eastward, skirting below restrooms and then passing a west-heading nature trail before reaching the museum, with an adjacent water fountain. In the museum, you will find information and displays on the giant sequoia, its related plants and animals, and the area's history. From just east of it, you could take a trail 0.3 mile east up to the tram road, beside which you'd spy the lower end of the Fallen Wawona (Tunnel) Tree, which toppled during the late winter or spring of 1969. This 2200-year-old giant, like many others, had a fire-scarred base, and it was enlarged in 1881 for first stagecoaches and much later automobiles to pass through it. An old timer is one who remembers waiting in a long line while each car drove through, stopping to have a passenger get out and photograph the momentous event. Today, the tree is not much to look at.

The suggested route continues from the museum, momentarily east along the tram road, to a bend. Here is the amazing Telescope Tree, which has been hollowed out by fire. Inside it, you can look straight up to the heavens. Despite its great internal loss, this tree is still very much alive, for its vital fluids—as in all trees—are conducted in the sapwood, immediately beneath the thick bark. The heartwood is just dead sapwood whose function is support.

From the back side of the tree, you take a trail that climbs 50 yards to the Upper Loop Trail, mentioned earlier. On it, you hike 0.3 mile counterclockwise to pass just above the Fallen Wawona Tree, then continue about 250 yards to a crest saddle. Just

The Mariposa Grove Museum, situated in a Brobdingnagian forest

40 yards east of it is the Galen Clark Tree, a fine specimen named for the man who first publicized this grove and later became its first guardian. From the saddle, a road branches from the tram-road loop, and, on it, you make an easy climb half mile to Wawona Point. No sequoias grow along this route, probably because of insufficient ground water. From the point, you see the large, partly manmade meadow at Wawona, to the northwest, and the long, curving cliff of Wawona Dome, breaking a sea of green, to the north.

After returning a half mile to the crest saddle, descend west along the Outer Loop Trail, which takes you down almost 3 essentially viewless, sequoia-less miles to the parking lot. The descending trail winds westward about 0.7 mile to a junction. From here, a connecting trail goes about 270 yards southeast down to the tram road and the adjacent west end of the nature trail. Onward, the Outer Loop Trail descends about 200 yards to a second connecting trail, descending about 150 yards southeast to cross the grove's tram road. We continue 0.8 mile southwest on the Outer Loop Trail, down to the broad-crest junction, where one could follow the alternate trip in reverse 5 miles down to Wawona. Instead, we start south on the Outer Loop Trail, which soon begins a winding, rolling traverse a half mile southwest over to a junction with a northeast-climbing trail. Walk 0.1 mile farther to another junction, where the eastbound trail from it leads to the California Tree and the Grizzly Giant. Unless you want to make another visit to them (and add about a half mile to your hike), continue southward a half mile down to the parking lot.

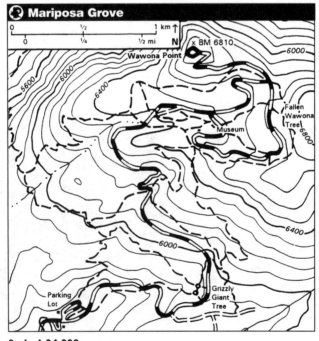

Scale 1:24,000

CHAPTER 17

Trips of Yosemite's Southeastern Lands

Introduction to this Area

This section explores the back ways into southeastern Yosemite. As roads in the Sierra National Forest were steadily upgraded—particularly Forest Route 7 (old Road 5S07)—more and more hikers discovered, and returned to, this scenic area. The Chain Lakes and the lakes of the southwest part of Ansel Adams Wilderness already rival many of the park's better-known lakes in popularity. Much of the landscape is lodgepole pine forest, but around Fernandez, Post Peak, and Isberg passes, the vegetation shifts to subalpine. Truly alpine Red Peak Pass, at 11,150 feet, is the highest trail point in the entire park. Two of this section's natural attractions are not found anywhere else in the other sections: a broad, scenic subalpine plateau and an unbelievable mottled-granite landscape—both seen along Trip 82 and the optional extension of Trip 83.

The largest Staniford Lake

Supplies and Services

Oakhurst, at the crossroads of highways 41 and 49, has just about everything you'll need for a backcountry hike. Closer to the trailheads is a settlement at the south end of Forest Route 7 (Beasore Road), just above the north shore of Bass Lake. Here, in Pines Village, are cafés and restaurants, a market, a gas station, and tourist-oriented business-es. After driving 13.5 miles north up Forest Route 7, you'll reach Jones Store, with a few but very pertinent food items. Also sell-ing food, plus other assorted items, is the Minarets Pack Station, located on Road 5S88 (see the third trailhead description in Trip 81). This large pack station, located near Miller Meadow, serves the western part of Ansel Adams Wilderness and the southeastern part of Yosemite National Park.

Wilderness Permits

Get one at the Forest Service office (559-658-7588) in the Yosemite-Sierra Visitors Center, located in downtown Oakhurst. For trips 81 through 83, you can get one at the Clover Meadow Ranger Station, locat-ed close to their trailheads. (When the sta-tion is not staffed, you may find permits outside to complete.) Permits are also avail-able at the Mariposa-Minarets Ranger Dis-trict Office (559-877-2218), located in the tiny settlement of North Fork, but, for most people, this is out of the way.

Campgrounds

If you are driving up late at night, you might want to stop at Chilkoot Camp-ground, 4 miles up Forest Route 7. Other-wise, use Upper Chiquito Campground for trips 79 and 80. You branch left from For-est Route 7 about 1 mile beyond a junction with Road 5S04, opposite Globe Rock. For trips 81 through 83, use Bowler Group Camp, if you are in a group, or else use Clover Meadow Campground. Both are mentioned in Trip 81's trailhead informa-

tion. For Trip 83, you can also use Granite Creek Campground, mentioned in its trail-head information. You can also use a de facto camping area on an old road near the trailhead. This is described under Trip 83's directions to the trailhead.

Globe Rock

TRIP 79

Royal Arch Lake via Chiquito Pass

Ⓜ / BP

DISTANCE: 19.4 miles out and back

ELEVATIONS: 7240′/8900′ +3040′/-1590′/±9260′

SEASON: Early July to late September

USE: Light

MAPS: *Sing Peak, Mariposa Grove*

TRAIL LOG:

2.9	Chiquito Pass
4.1	Gravelly Ford
6.0	Connector trail
6.6	Junction atop a second ridge
7.5	Buck Camp Ranger Station
8.5	Route's high point
9.0	Buena Vista Peak loop trail
9.7	Royal Arch Lake

INTRODUCTION: The shortest way to Royal Arch Lake is along this route from Chiquito Pass—only 7.6 miles from the alternate trailhead. Perhaps because the hiker has to first drive about an hour along dirt roads, this route is spurned in favor of routes from North Wawona (Trip 77) or from the Glacier Point Road (Trip 73). Each approach to Royal Arch Lake and other lakes around Buena Vista Peak has its own merits. Finally, this trip includes a side trip to lightly visited Givens Lake, which is about 9 to 9.5 miles from the trailhead, depending upon which route you use to reach it. If you like solitude, this lake may be for you.

DIRECTIONS TO THE TRAILHEAD: From the Hwy. 49 junction in Oakhurst, drive north on Hwy. 41 for 3.5 miles up to a junction with Road 222. Follow this east 3.5 miles to a fork, veer left and continue east 2.4

miles on Malum Ridge Road 274 to a junction with north-climbing Forest Route 7, or Beasore Road. (South, Beasore Road descends briefly to Pines Village, just above the north shore of Bass Lake.) Paved Forest Route 7 climbs north 4 miles to Chilkoot Campground, then it climbs to an intersection at Cold Springs Summit, 7.4 miles beyond the campground. Road 6S10 (an alternate, 0.2-mile-longer route to Cold Springs Summit) heads west from this intersection, winding 5.5 miles over to a junction near Kelty Meadow, mentioned in the next paragraph. From the summit, Forest Route 7 winds 8.6 miles, going past Beasore Meadows, Jones Store, Muglers Meadows, and Long Meadow before coming to a junction with Road 5S04, opposite Globe Rock, 20 miles from the start of Forest Route 7. Turn left and drive up the road 2.4 miles to a signed trailhead atop a small, flat ridge area. Trail mileages for trips 79 and 80 are based from this trailhead. From it, a trail climbs 2.9 miles to Chiquito Pass.

A lesser-known route gets you to a trail that drops to Chiquito Pass in only 0.8 mile—which will save you 2.1 miles each way. This higher, later-opening alternate route is a mile shorter to drive than the one just described, but because it is on narrower roads, it takes a little more time to drive. Starting from the Hwy. 49 junction in Oakhurst, you drive north on Hwy. 41 for 3.5 miles up to Road 222, then continue 0.6 mile past it to a right turn onto Forest Route 10 (Sky Ranch Road). After climbing 11.4 miles from Hwy. 41, this meets a junction near Kelty Meadow, mentioned above, where one can veer right toward Cold Springs Summit. You, however, veer left, driving 1.7 miles north to a junction with Road 6S07, on the left, which descends 8.2 miles west to Hwy. 41 at the southern fringe of the town of Fish Camp. This rocky road has one potentially bad creek ford and is not recommended for automobiles.

Your road curves right and immediately passes the Fresno Dome Campground entrance. Just 1.5 miles past your junction with Road 6S07, a road branches left toward the Star Lakes area. Beyond this junction, you could get lost. At most junctions, your road is the wider, obvious one. (Because new logging spurs may be built, this guide will mention only the important junctions.) Your road divides after 3.1 miles past the Star Lakes junction, and you curve left and wind 0.9 mile up to another junction. Here, you keep right, on the level road, rather than climb left, and drive 4.5 miles to a major junction. If you're on the correct road, you should cross two saddles, pass Lost Lake (on your right), and pass a trail to Grizzly Lake (on your left). A rockslide area along this 4.5-mile stretch sometimes releases boulders that temporarily block the road—the only real gamble with this route.

From the major junction with a wide road branching left, your wide Sky Ranch Road traverses 2.7 miles, veers right around a descending ridge, and, in a half mile, reaches a spur road branching left. Follow this road 0.4 mile to a turnaround at its end, 26.7 miles from Hwy. 41. From here, a short trail descends northeast to Chiquito Pass, while a branch from it descends east toward the southwest shore of Chiquito Lake. In early season, you may not be able to drive this road all the way. The Sky Ranch Road goes 0.4 mile to an unofficial camping area, with tables and a spring, then 0.6 mile to a turnaround. Trail begins in map section E6.

DESCRIPTION: On a flat area atop a granitic ridge, our Chiquito Lake Trail traverses northwest away from curving Road 5S04. Jeffrey pines largely dominate the broken forest cover, and cattle are often grazing beneath them. These may be with us on and off until we leave Sierra National Forest at Chiquito Pass. About 0.3 mile from our trailhead, we cross a short-lived creeklet, then climb moderately an equal distance to a junction with a long-abandoned trail. Progressing northwest from it, you have an easy traverse that takes you past another creeklet and over to the bank of Chiquito

Creek. Now your climbing begins in earnest as you gain about 500 feet over a short, mile-long ascent up a large, dusty lateral moraine. Hikers descending this occasionally steep Chiquito Lake Trail sometimes take shortcuts, resulting in confusing paths, but these always quickly rejoin the main trail, should you be led astray. Fortunately, your moderate ascent is usually shaded by red firs and by western white, Jeffrey, and lodgepole pines.

The climb is essentially over when the moraine gives way to a small bedrock knoll. After traversing for a few minutes beyond it, you drop to ford seasonally wide Chiquito Creek. Once across it, you crest the top of a low moraine and arrive at a spacious campsite—one of several—along the south shore of disappointing Chiquito Lake. Were Chiquito Lake not dammed, it would be little more than a waist-deep swamp. Even with the dam, it is little better, its tainted waters attracting both cows and mosquitoes. Should you, for some reason, decide to camp beneath lodgepoles by this sedge-lined lake, bring a tent and treat the water.

Just beyond, at the lake's southwest corner, we take a path 250 yards west to a junction with the alternate route mentioned in the trailhead description. Those taking it join us for a 0.3-mile walk north over to Chiquito Pass, where we leave the grazing cows and their muddy shoreline environment behind.

Note that Chiquito Pass, at just over 8000 feet, sits atop a long, multicrested moraine. A Tioga-age glacier that once spilled over Chiquito Pass and down the upper Chiquito Creek drainage left this moraine as it retreated from this vicinity about 16,000 years ago. Except for its ridgecrests and mountaintops, the entire South Fork Merced River basin, north of us, lay under a sea of ice during these and earlier glacial times. Your 500-foot ascent was up an eastern lateral moraine left during the Tioga glaciation, which was cold and wet enough to create a glacierette on the north slopes of Quartz Mountain, near the alternate trailhead.

Just within the fence—and Yosemite National Park—at Chiquito Pass, the trail splits. Trip 80 goes right, northeast, along the moraine, while we go left and descend northwest away from this bouldery, multi-crested feature. Our descent into a red fir/lodgepole pine forest momentarily abates at wide Spotted Lakes creek, which, in early season, you cross on large boulders. Leaving its banks of alders, willows, and wildflowers, you continue on a lesser gradient, your trail curving west to cross the South Fork Merced River at Gravelly Ford. A medium-size camp exists on each bank, and to get from one to the other, you'll probably have to wade, unless a large log is handy.

After leaving the gravelly banks, climb up a low, dry, sagebrush-clothed slope, then curve down to the west end of rightly named Swamp Lake. Beyond it is a wet meadow, which, like the lakelet, sires hordes of mosquitoes that last well into August. This is unfortunate, for in July and early August, it also has one of the better assemblages of tall, water-loving wildflowers. Leaving the wet flat for better-drained, less-mosquitoed slopes, we climb northwest 1 mile up a gradually steepening trail. The gradient becomes an exhausting one just before you top a gravelly, boulder-strewn moraine ridge. From it, you plummet down to diminutive Givens Creek, only to climb again. After an easy 0.3 mile of climbing, you meet a little-used though perfectly good connector trail that goes 3.5 miles east to a junction with the Chain Lakes-Moraine Meadows Trail. About 2.8 miles east along this trail, you'd find a short spur trail that descends a few hundred yards to a cold, bubbly, rust-stained soda spring similar to the ones in Tuolumne Meadows.

Starting west, we go but 60 yards before a sometimes faint trail branches right. Staying out of sight, it parallels our conspicuous trail a quarter mile before it climbs northwest an equal distance to a main trail. Bound for Royal Arch Lake, we

climb 0.6 mile west to the aforementioned main trail, first crossing a glacier-polished ridge before meeting the junction atop a second ridge.

[S] SIDE TRIP TO GIVENS LAKE: Starting on the previously mentioned northeast-bound main trail, you can make a 2- to 2.5-mile ascent to Givens Lake. First, you climb 0.3 mile northeast to a slightly higher ridge that has a junction with the upper end of the faint trail, this just after a shallow saddle by an exfoliating cliff. About 250 yards later, you reach a wide gap, and on it, your trail passes through a tiny, seasonal pond that lies due west of a minor summit. Now you make a short descent to Givens Creek, which you parallel briefly east to its crossing. In early season, you may have to use large boulders just upstream.

Now you have a choice of two routes. The shorter one is cross-country, and it ascends more or less north along Givens Lake's outlet creek, which has descended to your ford. If you are efficient, you can reach the lake, about 600 feet higher, with about 0.7 mile of hiking. The longer route is to keep to the trail. This switchbacks eastward, climbing 1 mile up about 650 feet to a shallow saddle on a south-trending ridge. Here, you'll see a faint, ducked path—your route—climbing northwest up a broad ridge. The route can be sketchy at times, but, basically, you meander in a west-northwest direction for 0.6 mile, crossing three prominent lateral moraines before ending at the northeast shore of Givens Lake. You'll find the best campsite near the blunt peninsula at the lake's south end.

What makes the lake's lateral moraines prominent is not their height (which isn't great), but rather the way they stand out so sharply above the bedrock bench they lie upon. The innermost moraine curves around Givens Lake, enclosing its bedrock basin as what appears to be an amazingly leakproof earthfill dam. Actually, youthful moraines such as this one are very leaky; the lake is dammed by a very low bedrock ridge buried beneath the moraine. All three of these moraines were left as the Tioga-age glacier, which once covered the South Fork basin and extended almost to Wawona until about 20,000 years ago; it retreated to oblivion by about 15,000 years ago. **END OF SIDE TRIP.**

From the junction atop a second ridge, we descend southwest through a red-fir-dominated forest interspersed with sunlit, grassy openings. Lodgepoles and Jeffrey pines increase in number westward, and then you climb northwest to the meadowy environment of Buck Creek. Just west of it and south of the main trail stands Buck Camp Ranger Station—the summer "headquarters" for patrols through the South Fork Merced River basin.

A mile-long slog, first along and through wet, sloping meadows, confronts you beyond Buck Camp. You end this moderate-to-steep, 720-foot climb northwest in a fairly deep ridge cleft, the route's high point, at about 8900 feet, where views are blocked by red firs and western white pines. An equally steep trail segment, descending almost a half mile west, ends at the Buena Vista Peak loop trail. Here, we turn right and make an easy ascent 0.7 mile up to an excellent campsite at the southwest corner of beautifully backdropped Royal Arch Lake. As in trips 73 and 77, you could make a circuit of the Buena Vista Peak Lakes. The last part of Trip 73 describes this loop from Buena Vista Lake south past Royal Arch, Johnson, Crescent, and Grouse lakes, while the last part of Trip 77 describes the rest of this loop past the Chilnualna Lakes.

TRIP 80

Chain Lakes via Chiquito Pass

M ✎ **BP**

DISTANCE:	16.4 miles out and back
ELEVATIONS:	7240′/9300′ +2360′/-300′/±5320′
SEASON:	Early July to late September
USE:	Moderate
MAP:	*Sing Peak*

TRAIL LOG:

2.9	Chiquito Pass
4.8	Moraine-dammed meadow
6.3	Junction
6.7	Lower Chain Lake
7.3	Middle Chain Lake
8.2	Upper Chain Lake

INTRODUCTION: Reached in three hours from the standard trailhead and only two from the alternate one, these lakes receive considerable backpacking pressure. Only the long road to each trailhead prevents them from being overrun. The charm of Middle Chain Lake draws the crowds while the shore of Upper Chain Lake provides a base camp for peakbagging mountaineers.

This trip also offers other side trips in the upper South Fork Merced River basin, allowing one to visit Moraine Meadow and Givens Lake, and, for mountaineers, to bag Merced and Triple Divide peaks.

DIRECTIONS TO THE TRAILHEAD: From the Hwy. 49 junction in Oakhurst, drive north on Hwy. 41 for 3.5 miles up to a junction with Road 222. Follow this east 3.5 miles to a fork, veer left, and continue east 2.4 miles on Malum Ridge Road 274 to a junction with north-climbing Forest Route 7, or Beasore Road. (South, Beasore Road descends briefly to Pines Village, just above the north shore of Bass Lake.) Paved Forest Route 7 climbs north 4 miles to Chilkoot Campground, then it climbs to an intersection at Cold Springs Summit, 7.4 miles beyond the campground. Road 6S10 (an alternate, 0.2-mile-longer route to Cold Springs Summit) heads west from this intersection, winding 5.5 miles over to a junction near Kelty Meadow, mentioned in the next paragraph. From the summit, Forest Route 7 winds 8.6 miles, going past Beasore Meadows, Jones Store, Muglers Meadows, and Long Meadow before coming to a junction with Road 5S04, opposite Globe Rock, 20 miles from the start of Forest Route 7. Turn left and drive up the road 2.4 miles to a signed trailhead atop a small, flat ridge area. Trail mileages for trips 79 and 80 are based from this trailhead. From it, a trail climbs 2.9 miles to Chiquito Pass. Trail begins in map section E6.

A lesser-known route gets you to a trail that drops to Chiquito Pass in only 0.8 mile—which will save you 2.1 miles each way. This higher, later-opening alternate route, described under Trip 79's trailhead directions, is a mile shorter to drive than the one just described but, because it is on narrower roads, it takes a little more time to drive.

DESCRIPTION: On a flat area atop a granitic ridge, our Chiquito Lake Trail traverses northwest away from curving Road 5S04. Jeffrey pines largely dominate the broken forest cover, and cattle are often grazing beneath them. These may be with us on and off until we leave Sierra National Forest at Chiquito Pass. About 0.3 mile from our trailhead, we cross a short-lived creeklet, then climb moderately an equal distance to a junction with a long-abandoned trail. Progressing northwest from it, you have an easy traverse that takes you past another creeklet and over to the bank of Chiquito Creek. Now your climbing begins in earnest, as you gain about 500 feet over a short, mile-long ascent up a large, dusty lateral moraine. Hikers descending this occasionally steep Chiquito Lake Trail

sometimes take shortcuts, resulting in confusing paths, but these always quickly rejoin the main trail, should you be led astray. Fortunately, your moderate ascent is usually shaded by red firs and by western white, Jeffrey, and lodgepole pines.

The climb is essentially over when the moraine gives way to a small bedrock knoll. After traversing for a few minutes beyond it, you drop to ford seasonally wide Chiquito Creek. Once across it, you crest the top of a low moraine and arrive at a spacious campsite—one of several—along the south shore of disappointing Chiquito Lake. Were Chiquito Lake not dammed, it would be little more than a waist-deep swamp. Even with the dam, it is little better, its tainted waters attracting both cows and mosquitoes. Should you, for some reason, decide to camp beneath lodgepoles by this sedge-lined lake, bring a tent and treat the water.

Just beyond, at the lake's southwest corner, we take a path 250 yards west to a junction with a trail descending east from a trailhead at the end of a spur road, which branches left just 1 mile before the end of Sky Ranch Road. (This shorter, alternate route is mentioned in Trip 79's "Directions to the Trailhead," on page 353.) Those taking it join us for a 0.3-mile walk north over to Chiquito Pass, where we leave the grazing cows and their muddy shoreline environment behind.

Just within the fence—and Yosemite National Park—at Chiquito Pass, the trail splits. Trip 79 goes left, west, but we go right, northeast. We soon pass by a stagnant pond trapped between the crests of two bouldery, brushy moraines. The one on our left stays with us for a full half mile before we cross it and make a slight descent to a flat-floored forest. In early summer, several creeks and creeklets are flowing, and, during those times, the traverse can be a muddy one that hikers hurry along to evade a marauding horde of mosquitoes so typical of this shady, damp environment. The last creek crossing is the widest, and beyond it, you have a mile-long ascent up to a small, moraine-dammed meadow, at about 8400 feet elevation.

[S] **SIDE TRIP TO SPOTTED LAKES:** From the meadow, one could contour east cross-country over to a creek draining Spotted Lakes. However, these lakes are best reached by starting from the end of a jeep road that traverses the southwest slopes of Red Top. From this road, which ends 4.4 miles beyond the Chiquito Pass Trailhead, you have only a 1.5-mile, cross-country hike to these trout-inhabited lakes. Furthermore, from the end of an east branch of this jeep road, you can reach the summit of Red Top in less than a mile's ridgecrest hike. This rusty peak, composed largely of ancient, metamorphic rocks, contrasts with our granitic trailside landscape. **END OF SIDE TRIP**

From the moraine-dammed meadow, we climb a short half mile up to a low point on a glacier-polished ridge, cross it, and make a rolling, short, mile-long traverse northeast to a junction on the north bank of boulder-choked Chain Lakes creek.

[S] **SIDE TRIPS IN THE UPPER SOUTH FORK MERCED RIVER DRAINAGE:** Although the upper South Fork Merced River drainage contained sizable glaciers, they excavated few basins, and so cirques are mostly lake free, and where lakes exist, they are small. Hence, trails—and people—are few. From the junction, you can begin a loop route back to Chiquito Pass by first taking a trail descends Chain Lakes creek a half mile to another junction. West, a trail descends 0.7 mile to a spur trail, which descends a few hundred yards south to a cold, bubbly, rust-stained soda spring that is similar to the ones in Tuolumne Meadows. You may find this feature interesting and may want to camp nearby, between the spur trail and the South Fork, just west of it. Ahead, this connector trail is not worth taking. It climbs and drops 2.7 viewless miles west across ground moraines and bedrock slabs, terminating at a trail bound for the Buck Camp Ranger Station and beyond, along Trip 79.

That trail also provides a shorter way to Givens Lake.

From the junction east of and above the spur trail to the soda spring, one can meander north on a winding, rolling path, first passing a couple of stagnant ponds. From bedrock benches and slabs, you see forested Moraine Mountain, a broad mass to the northwest. Nearing the South Fork Merced River, note that the landscape becomes gentler—almost flat—and the lodgepoles, being ideally suited to it, completely exclude red firs and western white pines from the forest's cover. Above the south bank of the South Fork, you'll find a medium-size camp that is good by late July, after mosquitoes diminish. Once you ford the South Fork, you'll find a similar camp, used by equestrians, 90 yards downstream. From the bank, you head north through one of the Moraine Meadows, which is more of a forest than a meadow, and, in 200 yards, you come to an east-west trail, about 1.9 miles from your last junction.

East, you could climb 3.4 miles to Fernandez Pass, and then descend into the lake-blessed lands just outside of the park, but Trip 81 provides much easier access to these lakes. Alternatively, mountaineers and recluses could head east just 1 mile to a trail ford of the upper South Fork. Leave the trail here and head upstream to explore the alpine headwaters of the South Fork or climb either Merced Peak and/or Triple Divide Peak.

West, the trail traverses 1.5 miles west to a junction with a trail that climbs 1.7 miles to viewless Merced Pass. The loop route goes another 1.5 miles, this time southwest, climbing more than 300 feet to a forested, boulder-strewn pass midway along this stretch. From the pass, you could make an easy cross-country ascent north to Moraine Mountain, but why bother, since trees prevent summit views. Beyond the midway point, you descend past a wet meadow, rich in corn lilies, then continue down across slopes down to a lower saddle. Here, you'll see a faint, ducked path—your route—climbing northwest up a broad ridge, ending in 0.6 mile by the northeast shore of Givens Lake, another goal for recluses.

Ahead, you'll finish your loop by first descending the main trail about 650 feet to Givens Creek, then continuing west upstream, then southwest through a wide gap with a tiny, seasonal pond. Continue 250 yards to a faint trail just before a shallow saddle by an exfoliating cliff. This trail descends a half mile to the Chiquito Pass-Buck Camp Trail, but if it looks hard to follow, continue 0.3 mile ahead to this same trail and take it 0.6 mile west to the faint trail, which is 60 yards east of a connector trail, mentioned earlier. From this junction, you have a 1.9-mile route down to the South Fork, first descending to Givens Creek, then climbing a low, broad ridge before descending to a meadow and Swamp Lake—mosquito heaven—just west of Gravelly Ford. Here, you cross the South Fork and make an easy ascent of 1.2 miles to Chiquito Pass. **END OF SIDE TRIPS.**

The vast majority of hikers will not explore the upper South Fork drainage, but rather will head to the Chain Lakes. Therefore, we turn right, upstream, and hike east on a moderate-to-steep trail up to shallow Lower Chain Lake, at about 8950 feet elevation. This fairly warm lake is too shallow for swimming, but it is heavily fished. Its trout may periodically die, though it can be repopulated from the middle lake's trout. Camps here are inferior to those by the deeper middle lake.

From the outlet of the moraine-rimmed lower lake, your trail climbs over a low ridge and drops to a de facto north-shore foot trail at the lake's far end. Next, you make a short, fairly steep ascent up along a creek to picturesque, island-dotted Middle Chain Lake. The warm bedrock islands are easily reached, particularly from the excellent oversized camp along the lake's southwest shore. To reach that camp, cross the lake's two outlet creeks and then follow a primitive path along the west shore. Twenty feet deep, this is a classic subalpine lake,

rimmed with lodgepole pines, western white pines, and mountain hemlocks and understoried with Labrador tea, red heather, western blueberry, and dwarf bilberry. The last two plants, both huckleberries, produce edible berries in late summer, after the crowds have left, and then the birds, bears, and golden-mantled ground squirrels have a feast.

Beyond the middle lake, the trail is less traveled. It climbs steeply to the bouldery crest of a moraine, winds over to a stagnant pond, and drops south to a photogenic lakelet. Near this lakelet, the trail may divide and reunite, and then it briefly climbs to deep Upper Chain Lake. Cold, windswept, and rock-rimmed, it offers marginal camping, but it is a good staging area for experienced mountaineers planning to climb slopes up to Gale Peak and the park's southeast boundary crest. Anglers may have a better chance up here than down at heavily fished Middle Chain Lake.

TRIP 81

Vandeberg-Lillian Lakes Loop

E 🏃 DH, BP

DISTANCE: 12.3 miles semiloop

ELEVATIONS: 7530′/9020′
+2650′/-2650′/±5300′

SEASON: Early July to late September

USE: Heavy

MAP: *Timber Knob*

TRAIL LOG:

0.4	Junction
1.7	Near-crest junction
1.9	Crest junction
4.3	Junction above Madera Creek
4.7	Trail to Lady Lake
5.4	Trail to Chittenden Lake
5.6	Trailside pond
6.2	Lillian Lake
7.4	Fernandez Trail
9.0	Junction
9.3	Madera Creek
10.4	Lillian Loop Trail
12.3	Trailhead

INTRODUCTION: If you are in shape, you could hike this entire circuit in one day without overexerting yourself. However, it is so scenic that three days are recommended—sufficient time to visit Lady, Chittenden, Staniford, and Rainbow lakes. Visiting all four of these desirable lakes lengthens your route to about 21 miles, adds about 2400 feet of ascent and descent, and changes its classification to a moderate three-day hike.

DIRECTIONS TO THE TRAILHEAD: From the Hwy. 49 junction in Oakhurst, drive north on Hwy. 41 for 3.5 miles up to a junction with Road 222. Follow this east 3.5 miles to a fork, veer left, and continue east 2.4 miles on Malum Ridge Road 274

to a junction with north-climbing Forest Route 7, or Beasore Road. (South, Beasore Road descends briefly to Pines Village, just above the north shore of Bass Lake.) Paved Forest Route 7 climbs north 4 miles to Chilkoot Campground, then it climbs to an intersection at Cold Springs Summit, 7.4 miles beyond the campground. Road 6S10 (an alternate, 0.2-mile-longer route to Cold Springs Summit) heads west from this intersection, winding 5.5 miles over to a junction near Kelty Meadow, mentioned in the next paragraph. From the summit, Forest Route 7 winds 8.6 miles, going past Beasore Meadows, Jones Store, Muglers Meadows, and Long Meadow before coming to a junction with Road 5S04, opposite Globe Rock, 20 miles from the start of Forest Route 7.

Continue along your road, an obvious route, 7.5 miles to a junction with Road 5S86. This junction is 0.4 mile past the Bowler Group Camp entrance and 100 yards before Forest Route 7 crosses Ethelfreda Creek. Your first of three trailheads lies at a road's end parking area above Norris Creek, 1.9 miles up this road. Be aware that there may be a rough creek bed crossing about a half mile before the parking area. This trailhead provides the shortest mileage for any hike along the Lillian Loop Trail. It is also the start of a trail to Norris Lake and the Jackass Lakes, the latter being worthy goals. F6.

The second trailhead—the one from which this trip's trail mileages are based—is at the end of Road 5S05. This forks left only 100 yards after Forest Route 7 crosses Ethelfreda Creek. Take Road 5S05 2.3 miles to the trailhead and its large turnaround/parking area. Former logging operations have added spurs to this road, but you should have no problem finding the trailhead. By starting at it, you hike 0.6 mile farther in each direction than you would from the first trailhead. F6.

The third trailhead is in the Clover Meadow area. On Forest Route 7, drive east from the Road 5S05 fork, passing Road 5S88, which branches south 0.4 mile to Minarets Pack Station and then, in 250 yards, reaches a junction. Here, 30 miles from the start of Forest Route 7, you meet the end of Forest Route 81, a.k.a. Minarets Road, ascending 52 paved miles north from community of North Fork. (From that town, this route starts east as Road 225 and is signed as the Mammoth Pool Road. Also, between North Fork and its eastern, adjacent neighbor, South Fork, Malum Ridge Road 274 heads north 9 miles to the start of Forest Route 7. You can make a relatively scenic 91-mile loop by taking roads 7, 81, 225, and 274, allowing four-plus hours to do so, since you can't travel too fast and there are many spots worth stopping and investigating.)

From the junction where Forest Route 7 ends and 81 begins, drive northeast 1.8 miles on Road 5S30 to a junction at the Clover Meadow Ranger Station. Turn left here, get your permit (if you haven't gotten one in advance), then continue past the station about 0.3 mile to the Clover Meadow Campground entrance. Midway along your road, the Fernandez Trail starts from its south (left) side. You can also locate this trail at the far end of the campground. This trail climbs 1.4 miles west to the north side of the parking area at the second major trailhead. Trail begins in map section F6.

DESCRIPTION: From the second trailhead at the end of Road 5S05, you start west up the Fernandez Trail, passing through a typical mid-elevation Sierran forest: white fir, Jeffrey pine, lodgepole pine, and scrubby huckleberry oak. After 0.3 mile of gentle ascent across morainal slopes, you reach the lower end of a small meadow and meet a junction at its west side. From it, a trail meanders almost a mile to the vicinity of the first trailhead before climbing up to Norris Lake and the Jackass Lakes. Beyond the junction, your trail's gradient becomes a moderate one, and red firs quickly begin to replace white firs. The forest temporarily yields to brush—huckleberry oak, chinquapin, greenleaf manzanita, and snow bush—as we struggle up short, steep

switchbacks below a small, exfoliating "dome." Now entering Ansel Adams Wilderness, we have a steady, half-mile pull up to a near-crest junction with a steep, mile-long trail from the first trailhead. If you come up this short, exhausting route, remember this junction, for if it is not properly signed, it can be easy to miss as you later descend the Fernandez Trail. We continue a moderate ascent up the Fernandez Trail for only a few more minutes, and then reach a crest junction. This lakeless route bypasses the best part of our trip, but it will save you 2.4 miles in your ascent to Fernandez Creek. You would take it only if you are in a hurry to get beyond our basin.

Heading west toward peaks and lakes, we veer left and start up the Lillian Loop Trail. This trail's first 2 miles are generally easy. Conifers shade your way first past a waist-deep pond, on your right, then past two often wet, moraine-dammed meadows—both mosquito havens. Then the trail climbs to a bedrock notch in a granitic crest. On the crest, you arc around a stagnant pond, then make a short descent to a junction above Madera Creek. If you plan to camp at very popular Vandeberg Lake, at 8650 feet, you could leave the trail here and descend southwest to find some campsites along its east shore.

From the junction, the right branch—for horses—descends north to Madera Creek, then circles counterclockwise 0.3 mile to rejoin the left branch above the lake's west shore. We take the left branch, curving above good-to-excellent campsites along the lake's north shore. From them, steep, granitic Peak 9852, on Madera Peak's northeast ridge, is reflected in the lake's placid early-morning waters. Where the two branches of the loop trail reunite, you start a 250-yard climb up bedrock to the edge of a lodgepole flat that has a junction with a trail to Lady Lake.

⑤ **SIDE TRIP TO LADY LAKE:** Here, a spur trail takes off south and climbs gently to moderately a half mile up to a large campsite on the north shore of granite-rimmed

8908-foot Lady Lake. On the east-shore moraine that juts into the lake, you'll find an even better campsite, though not quite as large. This lake's irregular form, speckled with several boulder islands, makes it a particularly attractive lake to camp at or to visit, especially since it is backdropped by hulking, metamorphic Madera Peak. Like all the lakes you might visit along this hike, Lady Lake has trout. Because it is shallow, it is a good lake for swimming from late July through mid-August. **END OF SIDE TRIP.**

Beyond the Lady Lake Trail junction, your Lillian Loop Trail crosses the lodgepole flat, then climbs a couple of hundred feet up fairly open granitic slabs. On them, you can stop and appreciate the skyline panorama from the Minarets south to the Mt. Goddard area in Kings Canyon National Park. During past glaciations, virtually all of this panorama, except for high crests and mountain peaks, was under ice. Descending northwest from a ridge on a moderate-to-steep gradient, you reach, in 0.2 mile, an easily missed junction—if it is not well-signed—with a trail to Chittenden Lake.

[S] **SIDE TRIP TO CHITTENDEN LAKE:** Here, close to a Staniford Lakes creek, one can start a mile-long climb up to cliffbound 9182-foot Chittenden Lake. (If you miss this junction, then you probably wouldn't be able to follow the obscure trail to that lake anyway.) Where this trail curves from northwest to southwest at the lower end of a small, wet meadow, you could follow an equally obscure trail 0.2 mile northwest up to extremely shallow Shirley Lake, which is not worth most hikers' efforts. The last slabby trail section to Chittenden Lake is so steep that equestrians rarely visit it. Chittenden may be the most beautiful of all the lakes in this part of Ansel Adams Wilderness, though Lady and Rainbow lakes offer competition. Although Chittenden's water usually does not rise above the low 60s, the lake's three bedrock islands will certainly tempt some swimmers. If there are more than two backpackers in your group, don't plan to camp at this fairly deep lake, for flat space is really at a premium. **END OF SIDE TRIP.**

On the Lillian Loop Trail, you go north only about 200 yards past the Chittenden Lake Trail junction before you see one of the Staniford Lakes. A waist-deep, grass-lined lakelet, this water body, like Shirley Lake, is best avoided. After a similar distance, you'll come to a trailside pond atop a broad granitic crest.

[S] **SIDE TRIP TO LARGEST STANIFORD LAKE:** In this vicinity, you can leave the trail, and, on your third optional excursion, descend southeast briefly cross-country on low-angle slabs to the largest of the Staniford Lakes, lying at 8708 feet. This is certainly the best lake to swim in, and if any sizable lake along this route will warm up to the low 70s in early August, it will be this one. The great bulk of the lake is less than 5 feet deep, its only deep spot being at a diving area along the west shore. Among the slabs, you can find camp spots. **END OF SIDE TRIP.**

More ponds are seen along the northbound Lillian Loop Trail before it dips into a usually dry gully. It then heads diagonally up a ridge with many glacier-polished slabs. You soon cross the ridge, then quickly descend to Lillian Lake's outlet creek. A short walk upstream ends at the lake's low dam and an adjacent, lodgepole-shaded area that once comprised the largest campsite in this part of the wilderness. Since camping is prohibited within 400 feet of the northeast shore, be inventive and try elsewhere. As the largest and deepest lake you'll see along this hike, Lillian Lake is also the coldest—not good for swimming. However, its large population of trout does attract anglers.

With our basic hike now half over, we leave the lake's outlet and descend a mile east past lodgepoles, hemlocks, western white pines, and red firs down to a two-branched creek with easy fords. The Lillian Loop Trail ends in 0.3 mile, after a short, stiff climb over a gravelly knoll. Here, at a junction on a fairly open slope, we rejoin the Fernandez Trail. Trip 82 describes this trail from this point upward.

[S] **SIDE TRIP TO RAINBOW LAKE:** Your fourth optional side trip ascends this trail 1 mile northwest up to a junction, from which the Rainbow Lake Trail first wanders 0.9 mile southwest up a ridge that is just north of Lillian Lake. On the ridge, the trail may become vague on bedrock slabs where it bends from southwest to northwest, and unsuspecting hikers may continue southwest down toward Lillian Lake, 400 feet below, before realizing their error. If you are good at cross-country hiking, you can start from the northeast shore of Lillian Lake and hike up this "erroneous" route, and, just beyond its ridge's crest, locate the trail, saving about 2 miles of hiking. From the ridge, the Rainbow Lake Trail then rollercoasters northwest 0.7 mile to the prized lake, where camping is prohibited within a quarter mile of the lakeshore. One can cross this multilobed lake by swimming from island to island. **END OF SIDE TRIP.**

From the Lillian Loop-Fernandez trails junction, we descend 0.3 mile east on the Fernandez Trail to a linear gully, follow it a bit, and then drift over to the crest of a moraine, about a half mile from the previous junction. From here, a now abandoned, former route of the Fernandez Trail once ascended this ridge for about 0.7 mile northwest to the Twin Lakes, then a similar distance and bearing up to a minor saddle now crossed by the current route. Your route, which has been eastward, now turns southeast and follows the crest to its end, where you soon engage a few short switchbacks near some junipers, and get a good view of much of your basin's landscape.

Below the switchbacks, the Fernandez Trail descends a half mile to a junction. If you were to follow the trail north 70 yards to a crest saddle, you would see that it forks into the Post Creek Trail (left) and the Timber Creek Trail (right). The Post Creek Trail ends after a 1.9-mile climb to a packer camp on the West Fork of Granite Creek. Just below this spot is the creek's confluence with Post Creek. A faint trail—essentially cross-country—more or less parallels

Rainbow Lake

this creek northward 1.5 miles to the Post Peak Pass Trail (Trip 82). The Timber Creek Trail climbs about 5.8 miles up to the Joe Crane Lake Trail (Trip 83).

From the junction, the Fernandez Trail descends briefly past lodgepoles and junipers to a gravelly flat along the north bank of Madera Creek. This spacious flat is well suited for camping, and, from it, you can inspect the dark plug of olivine basalt, above you, which was once part of the throat of a cinder cone. Glaciers removed the cinders but were too feeble to erode the lava. On the flat, you may see an old trail heading east, the former Walton Trail, which crossed Madera Creek about 250 yards below the Fernandez Trail ford, which once provided an alternate route to our trailhead. With that goal in mind, cross the creek and gain about 500 feet on the Fernandez Trail. Our ridge ascent after a brief contour southeast to a wilderness-boundary junction with the start of the Lillian Loop Trail. From it, retrace your steps to your trailhead.

TRIP 82

Fernandez-Red Peak-Post Peak Passes Loop

S **◯** BPx

DISTANCE: 48 miles loop

ELEVATIONS: 7530′/11,150′
+10,250′/-10,250′/±20,500′

SEASON: Early July to late September

USE: Moderate

MAPS: *Timber Knob, Sing Peak, Merced Peak, Mount Lyell*

TRAIL LOG:

0.4	Junction
1.7	Near-crest junction
1.9	Crest junction
4.3	Junction above Madera Creek
4.7	Trail to Lady Lake
5.4	Trail to Chittenden Lake
5.6	Trailside pond
6.2	Lillian Lake
7.4	Fernandez Trail
8.4	Meadowside junction
9.7	Fernandez Creek
10.8	Rutherford Lake Trail
12.4	Fernandez Pass
13.0	Breeze Lake Trail
15.8	Moraine Meadows
17.3	Junction
19.0	Merced Pass
19.8	Junction
22.4	Lower Ottoway Lake
24.5	Red Peak Pass
31.1	Triple Peak Fork
32.8	Junction
34.2	Meadowy junction
35.3	Post Peak Pass
35.8	Porphyry Lake
37.9	Post Creek
39.5	Slab Lakes Trail
39.8	Fernandez Trail
42.1	Lillian Loop Trail

44.7   Junction
45.0   Madera Creek
46.1   Lillian Loop Trail
48.0   Trailhead

INTRODUCTION: Along this double-loop hike, you cross four major divides and sample lakes in the Granite Creek, South Fork Merced River, Illilouette Creek, and Merced River basins. On one divide, you cross Red Peak Pass, which, at 11,150 feet, is the highest pass in Yosemite National Park.

DIRECTIONS TO THE TRAILHEAD: From the Hwy. 49 junction in Oakhurst, drive north on Hwy. 41 for 3.5 miles up to a junction with Road 222. Follow this east 3.5 miles to a fork, veer left, and continue east 2.4 miles on Malum Ridge Road 274 to a junction with north-climbing Forest Route 7, or Beasore Road. (South, Beasore Road descends briefly to Pines Village, just above the north shore of Bass Lake.) Paved Forest Route 7 climbs north 4 miles to Chilkoot Campground, then it climbs to an intersection at Cold Springs Summit, 7.4 miles beyond the campground. Road 6S10 (an alternate, 0.2-mile-longer route to Cold Springs Summit) heads west from this intersection, winding 5.5 miles over to a junction near Kelty Meadow, mentioned in the next paragraph. From the summit, Forest Route 7 winds 8.6 miles, going past Beasore Meadows, Jones Store, Muglers Meadows, and Long Meadow before coming to a junction with Road 5S04, opposite Globe Rock, 20 miles from the start of Forest Route 7.

Continue along your road, an obvious route, 7.5 miles to a junction with Road 5S86. This junction is 0.4 mile past the Bowler Group Camp entrance and 100 yards before Forest Route 7 crosses Ethelfreda Creek. Your first of three trailheads lies at a road's end parking area above Norris Creek, 1.9 miles up this road. Be aware that there may be a rough creek bed crossing about a half mile before the parking area. This trailhead provides the shortest mileage for any hike along the Lillian Loop

Trail. It is also the start of a trail to Norris Lake and the Jackass Lakes, the latter being worthy goals. F6.

The second trailhead—the one from which this trip's trail mileages are based—is at the end of Road 5S05. This forks left only 100 yards after Forest Route 7 crosses Ethelfreda Creek. Take Road 5S05 for 2.3 miles to the trailhead and its large turnaround/parking area. Former logging operations have added spurs to this road, but you should have no problem finding the trailhead. By starting at it, you hike 0.6 mile farther in each direction than you would from the first trailhead. F6.

The third trailhead is in the Clover Meadow area. On Forest Route 7, drive east from the Road 5S05 fork, passing Road 5S88, which branches south 0.4 mile to Minarets Pack Station. In 250 yards, reach a junction. Here, 30 miles from the start of Forest Route 7, you meet the end of Forest Route 81, aka Minarets Road, ascending 52 paved miles north from community of North Fork. (From that town, this route starts east as Road 225 and is signed as the Mammoth Pool Road. Also, between North Fork and its eastern, adjacent neighbor, South Fork, Malum Ridge Road 274 heads north 9 miles to the start of Forest Route 7. You can make a relatively scenic 91-mile loop by taking roads 7, 81, 225, and 274, allowing four-plus hours to do so, since you can't travel too fast and there are many spots worth stopping and investigating.)

From the junction where Forest Route 7 ends and 81 begins, drive northeast 1.8 miles on Road 5S30 to a junction at the Clover Meadow Ranger Station. Turn left here, get your permit (if you haven't gotten one in advance), and then continue past the station about 0.3 mile to the Clover Meadow Campground entrance. Midway along your road, the Fernandez Trail starts from its south (left) side. You can also locate this trail at the far end of the campground. This trail climbs 1.4 miles west to the north side of the parking area at the second major trailhead. Trail begins in map section F6.

DESCRIPTION: From the second trailhead at the end of Road 5S05, you start west up the Fernandez Trail, passing through a typical mid-elevation Sierran forest: white fir, Jeffrey pine, lodgepole pine, and scrubby huckleberry oak. After 0.3 mile of gentle ascent across morainal slopes, you reach the lower end of a small meadow and meet a junction at its west side. From it, a trail meanders almost a mile to the vicinity of the first trailhead before climbing up to Norris Lake and the Jackass Lakes. Beyond the junction, your trail's gradient becomes a moderate one, and red firs quickly begin to replace white firs. The forest temporarily yields to brush—huckleberry oak, chinquapin, greenleaf manzanita, and snow bush—as we struggle up short, steep switchbacks below a small, exfoliating "dome." Now entering Ansel Adams Wilderness, we have a steady, half-mile pull up to a near-crest junction with a steep, mile-long trail from the first trailhead. If you come up this short, exhausting route, remember this junction, for, if it is not properly signed, it can be easy to miss as you later descend the Fernandez Trail. We continue a moderate ascent up the Fernandez Trail for only a few more minutes, then reach a crest junction.

[A] **ALTERNATE TRIP ON FERNANDEZ TRAIL:** If you are in a hurry, you can keep right, staying on the Fernandez Trail. This lakeless route will save you 2.4 miles in your ascent to Fernandez Creek. **END OF ALTERNATE TRIP.**

Heading west toward peaks and lakes, we veer left and start up the Lillian Loop Trail. This trail's first 2 miles are generally easy. Conifers shade your way first past a waist-deep pond, on your right, then later past two often wet, moraine-dammed meadows—both mosquito havens. Then the trail climbs to a bedrock notch in a granitic crest. On the crest, you arc around a stagnant pond, then make a short descent to a junction above Madera Creek. If you plan to camp at very popular Vandeberg Lake, at 8650 feet, you could leave the trail

here and descend southwest to find some campsites along its east shore.

From the junction, the right branch—for horses—descends north to Madera Creek, then circles counterclockwise 0.3 mile to rejoin the left branch above the lake's west shore. We take the left branch, curving above good-to-excellent campsites along the lake's north shore. From them, steep, granitic Peak 9852, on Madera Peak's northeast ridge, is reflected in the lake's placid early morning waters. Where the two trail branches of the loop trail reunite, you start a 250-yard climb up bedrock to the edge of a lodgepole flat that has a junction with a trail to Lady Lake.

[S] **SIDE TRIP TO LADY LAKE:** Here, a spur trail takes off south and climbs gently to moderately a half mile up to a large campsite on the north shore of granite-rimmed, 8908-foot Lady Lake. On the east-shore moraine that juts into the lake, you'll find an even better campsite, though not quite as large. This lake's irregular form, speckled with several boulder islands, makes it a particularly attractive lake to camp at or to visit, especially since it is backdropped by hulking, metamorphic Madera Peak. Like all the lakes you might visit along this hike, Lady Lake has trout. Because it is shallow, it is a good lake for swimming from late July through mid-August. **END OF SIDE TRIP.**

Beyond the Lady Lake Trail junction, your Lillian Loop Trail crosses the lodgepole flat, then climbs a couple of hundred feet up fairly open granitic slabs. On them, you can stop and appreciate the skyline panorama from the Minarets south to the Mt. Goddard area in Kings Canyon National Park. During past glaciations, virtually all of this panorama, except for high crests and mountain peaks, was under ice. Descending northwest from a ridge on a moderate-to-steep gradient, you reach, in 0.2 mile, an easily missed junction—if it is not well-signed—with a trail to Chittenden Lake.

$\boxed{S}$ **SIDE TRIP TO CHITTENDEN LAKE:** Here, close to a Staniford Lakes creek, one can start a mile-long climb up to cliffbound 9182-foot Chittenden Lake. (If you miss this junction, then you probably wouldn't be able to follow the obscure trail to that lake anyway.) Where this trail curves from northwest to southwest at the lower end of a small, wet meadow, you could follow an equally obscure trail 0.2 mile northwest up to extremely shallow Shirley Lake, which is not worth most hikers' efforts. The last slabby trail section to Chittenden Lake is so steep that equestrians rarely visit it. Chittenden may be the most beautiful of all the lakes in this part of Ansel Adams Wilderness, though Lady and Rainbow lakes offer competition. Although Chittenden's water usually does not rise above the low 60s, the lake's three bedrock islands will certainly tempt some swimmers. If there are more than two backpackers in your group, don't plan to camp at this fairly deep lake, for flat space is really at a premium. **END OF SIDE TRIP.**

On the Lillian Loop Trail, you go north only about 200 yards past the Chittenden Lake Trail junction before you see one of the Staniford Lakes. A waist-deep, grass-lined lakelet, this water body, like Shirley Lake, is best avoided. After a similar distance, you'll come to a trailside pond atop a broad granitic crest. On your first hiking day, plan to spend your first night either at the largest Staniford Lake or 0.6 mile farther at Lillian Lake.

$\boxed{S}$ **SIDE TRIP TO LARGEST STANIFORD LAKE:** In this vicinity, you can leave the trail, and, on your third optional excursion, descend southeast briefly cross-country on low-angle slabs to the largest of the Staniford Lakes, lying at 8708 feet. This is certainly the best lake to swim in, and if any sizable lake along this route will warm up to the low 70s in early August, it will be this one. The great bulk of the lake is less than 5 feet deep, its only deep spot being at a diving area along the west shore. Among the slabs, you can find camp spots. **END OF SIDE TRIP.**

Relaxing in largest Staniford Lake

More ponds are seen along the northbound Lillian Loop Trail before it dips into a usually dry gully. It then heads diagonally up along a ridge with many glacier-polished slabs. You soon cross the ridge, then quickly descend to Lillian Lake's outlet creek. A short walk upstream ends at the lake's low dam and an adjacent, lodgepole-shaded area that once comprised the largest campsite in this part of the wilderness. Since camping is prohibited within 400 feet of the northeast shore, be inventive and try elsewhere. As the largest and deepest lake you'll see along this hike, Lillian Lake is also the coldest—not good for swimming. However, its large population of trout does attract anglers.

With our basic hike now half over, we leave the lake's outlet and descend a mile east past lodgepoles, hemlocks, western white pines, and red firs down to a two-branched creek with easy fords. The Lillian Loop Trail ends in 0.3 mile, after a short, stiff climb over a gravelly knoll. Here, at a junction on a fairly open slope, we rejoin the Fernandez Trail.

From this point, we make a mile-long, winding climb northwest up granite slabs through an open forest to a meadowside junction immediately below a low gap. From here, a trail, described in Trip 81, climbs 1.6 miles up to rewarding Rainbow Lake. We, however, keep to the Fernandez Trail, climbing a half mile north to a broad crest, then traversing 0.8 mile northwest to a junction beside Fernandez Creek. Early on this traverse, you recognize the park boundary's two named summits, broad Triple Divide Peak and narrow Post Peak. At the junction, above the south bank of Fernandez Creek, a trail branches right, eventually climbing to Post Peak Pass, and we'll descend this trail to our junction.

Keeping to the Fernandez Trail, you immediately pass a good campsite, on your left, jump across Fernandez Creek, and, above its north bank, meet a connecting trail that briefly descends northeast to a meadow and the Post Peak Pass Trail. More campsites are found near this mead-

ow. Our Fernandez Trail climbs west and, after a half mile, it switchbacks high above Fernandez Creek to offer down-canyon views. These disappear as you curve right into a bowl and meet the Rutherford Lake Trail.

S SIDE TRIP TO RUTHERFORD LAKE: This short trail gains about 200 feet in elevation to climb 0.3 mile to 9730-foot Rutherford Lake. If you make this side trip, you'll find the best camps along the east shore, about 200 yards beyond the south-end dam. Another dam is at the lake's northeast bay. END OF SIDE TRIP.

Beyond the Rutherford Lake Trail, you face a two-stage ascent to Fernandez Pass. Short switchbacks elevate you 200 feet to a broad, shallow gap, from which you descend into a large, granitic bowl. After crossing its subalpine meadow, you begin your second stage—far more taxing—which climbs by more than two dozen switchbacks 450 feet almost up to an unnamed crest saddle. From the saddle, which is well dressed with whitebark pines and mountain hemlocks, the view west is surprisingly unimpressive. However, from our trail, the view east is quite impressive, ranging over much of the Granite Creek basin and extending to the Ritter Range and the central Sierra Nevada crest. From the saddle, you traverse south 0.3 mile across generally open slopes, heading toward a fin on the boundary ridge just yards before dropping to 10,175-foot Fernandez Pass.

This is named for Sergeant Joseph Fernandez, who, with Lieutenant Harry Benson and others, explored, mapped, and patrolled the Yosemite backcountry in the 1890s. They also planted trout, starting a practice that continued without serious question until the 1970s, when biologists began to study the ecological effect of fish in the high country.

At the pass, decked with ragged hemlocks, lodgepoles, and whitebark pines, your views are far more restrictive than from the previous saddle. You may note an old trail that drops northeast down a gully to the granitic bowl. Though still used by many hikers, this trail was abandoned decades ago because of its steepness and the long-lasting snowfield that lingered in much of the gully. Unlike our overly engineered ascent to the pass, our descent is steep, dropping about 650 feet along an old trail to a junction with the Breeze Lake Trail. Along this descent, you see Breeze Lake, where you might spend your second night.

S SIDE TRIP TO BREEZE LAKE: From the junction, follow a winding path 0.4 mile toward this lake. Midway to it, the path may become vague along the west shore of a pond, but continue upward, soon entering a straight, joint-controlled gully that takes you to deep, rockbound Breeze Lake. Because it is larger than average and also lies in a cirque below the slopes of towering Gale Peak, the lake often lives up to its name. A few small campsites can be found along the lake's north and west shores. END OF SIDE TRIP.

From the Breeze Lake Trail, head northwest down the main trail. Midway to a couple of marshy ponds and an adjacent chest-deep lake, about a half mile past the trail junction, you pass some giant mountain hemlocks and mature lodgepoles—among the best to be seen in the park. During the afternoon, the lake can provide a refreshing swim, and its shore makes a good spot for a trail break. From here, your descent along morainal ground quickly steepens, then you cross the lake's creek for an easing descent to the wildflowered banks of the South Fork Merced River. Once on its north bank—sometimes reached by a ford—you walk a viewless mile along a rolling trail to a junction in Moraine Meadows. By walking south 200 yards through the lodgepole-invaded meadow, you can reach the South Fork, which has a medium-size camp above its south bank and a similar one 90 yards downstream on its north bank.

Continuing west on our trail, we pass through a bedrock gap after a half mile, then soon swing northwest down into a small though impressive gully with straight, vertical walls. About 0.3 mile farther, we cross a small creek, then, in a like distance, climb southwest to a meadowy junction, passing a crescentic pond midway.

Bound for Merced Pass, we turn right and contour north a half mile to the wild-flowered creek we crossed earlier, crossing it twice more. A short, steep climb ensues, bringing you up to a small meadow, at whose head you cross the now trickling creek. With the pass now more or less in sight, you climb easily over to your final creek crossing—hardly worth noting—then make a final, short push up to 9295-foot Merced Pass. Lodgepoles and western white pines totally preclude any view, so, after catching your breath, descend 0.8 mile to a creek that drains Upper Merced Pass Lake. Just before this creek, you can traverse east across slabs to the nearby lake, which is blessed with very good campsites.

Above the northeast bank of the lake's outlet creek, we come to a junction, from which Trip 75 descends northwest down Illilouette Creek canyon. Now you ramble northeast up a glaciated landscape for 1.8 miles to Ottoway Creek, cross it, perhaps on a log, and then parallel the creek east 0.8 mile up to the outlet of Lower Ottoway Lake. Spend your third night here. You'll find the best camps under lodgepole and whitebark pines above the lake's northwest shore. Also, a slab above its northeast shore makes a good sunbathing area after a quick dip in its cold waters. Anglers can dangle lines for a tasty rainbow trout meal. Finally, the lake makes an ideal base camp for exploring the Merced Peak environs.

On day four, you climb 1.7 miles to Red Peak Pass in two stages, each with more than two dozen switchbacks. The first is up to a spot just above a pond and adjacent Upper Ottoway Lake. Up here in alpine lands, neither of these cold, shimmering jewels has suitable camping, but you can make an interesting side trip over to them and then east up into the deep cirque that once held Merced Peak's Little Ice Age glacier. Today, only its moraines exist, which show the size of the once-living snowfield.

After resting, begin the second stage, switchbacking to view-blessed, 11,150-foot-high Red Peak Pass. From it, you have views as far as Matterhorn Peak, along the park's north rim. Closer, Mt. Lyell crowns the upper Merced River basin and is flanked on the northwest by Mt. Maclure and on the southeast by Rodgers Peak. Twin-peaked Mt. Florence breaks the horizon west of this trio, while east of all of them, the dark, sawtooth Ritter Range pokes above the park's eastern crest boundary. Below the peaks lies a broad upland surface that is cleft by the 2000-foot-deep Merced River canyon. Turning south, you have a tunneled, almost lifeless view of dark-gray Merced Peak, its western outliers, and rockbound Upper Ottoway Lake. By late summer 1977, after two dry years, the Merced Peak snowfield had completely disappeared. When John Muir first saw it in the autumn of 1871, it was an active snowfield—that is, a small glacier. Muir was not the first to see a Sierran glacier, but he was the first to recognize one. On July 2, 1863, William Brewer and Charles Hoffmann—both members of Josiah D. Whitney's Geological Survey of California—climbed the Lyell Glacier and almost reached the summit of Mt. Lyell. However, several feet of fresh snow covered the glacier, and, perhaps because of that, they saw no crevasses, and so thought it a snowfield.

From alpine Red Peak Pass, you begin a generally descending, 6.6-mile trek to a trail junction beside a tributary of the Triple Peak Fork of the Merced River. Your trail, a series of short, steep switchbacks, may be dangerously snowbound well into summer. But even when the switchbacks are not under snow, their rocky nature can easily turn your ankle if you take a careless step. As you level out lower down, you might notice a small glacial moraine—a remnant of the Little Ice Age—lying at the edge of the cirque.

Now you switchback northeast down a bleak alpine ridge. On it, you have unobstructed views of the greater part of the upper Merced River basin. You momentarily end your descend on a bench, where you marginally enter the subalpine realm, which here has scattered clusters of whitebark pines. On this bench are ponds and lakelets, but all are too exposed for desirable camping. Leaving the bench, the trail heads east down toward a nearby, scenic lakelet, but rather than going to it, the trail unnecessarily descends north below it, only to climb up to its northeast shore. Here, among a fair number of conifers, are your highest wind-shielded campsites this side of Red Peak Pass.

From near the lakelet, the trail crosses a crest at a broad saddle, then it takes a tightly winding course southeast, dropping only 300 feet in a mile-long course to the two-branched Merced Peak Fork, with camping potential among sheltering trees. Onward, we climb to a second broad crest, reached in 0.7 mile with only 200 feet of ascent. Although the crest does support lodgepoles, mountain hemlocks, and whitebark pines, the forest cover is thin enough to permit views of many of the peaks that rim the upper Merced River basin. Leaving this crest, which divides the Triple Peak Fork from the Merced Peak Fork, you face almost 2 miles of descent, initially curving southeast for a spell, and then, from a shallow-cirque floor, descending 1.5 miles northeast from bench to granitic bench to a junction just before the Triple Peak Fork. Ideally, here you spend your fourth night somewhere in this vicinity.

Look for a log to cross the wide tributary of Triple Peak Fork; then, back on the trail, head southeast to a quick ford of the fork. From the ford, your trail makes a gentle ascent south, paralleling the unseen fork for 0.8 mile to the start of a switchbacking climb northeast.

S SIDE TRIP TO TURNER LAKE: Here is the place to leave the trail for an easy half-mile cross-country jaunt up to seldom-visited Turner Lake, at 9531 feet. All the others we'll approach lie above the 9600-foot contour. END OF SIDE TRIP.

The 550-foot climb northeast is generally a viewless one, due to the lodgepoles and hemlocks, though you may get an occasional view north of the Mt. Florence ridge and of the Matthes Crest, in the distance west of it. Your climb ends 1.7 miles above your start at a junction on a small flat below the west spur of unseen Isberg Peak. You head south, and, in 0.3 mile, you enter a broad, open expanse—an awesome landscape of a sort not seen anywhere else along Yosemite's trails.

S SIDE TRIP TO LAKE: From the northwest edge of this expanse, you could traverse 0.2 mile east to a fairly large, windswept lake with a sandy beach along its north shore. Protective lodgepole pines shelter a campsite near it. END OF SIDE TRIP.

On your open trail, you see a pond lying immediately west of the unseen lake, then soon enter a grove of struggling lodgepoles growing on rocky ground. Venturing beyond this grove is unwise in threatening weather, for you won't find any protective cover until you cross Post Peak Pass and descend below Porphyry Lake.

From the grove, our trail gradually curves left, and, looking back, we have a startling view: We seem to be at land's end, with the world dropping off beyond our broad, alpine surface. Starting to climb, one can scan an entire stretch of crest from Isberg Peak clockwise to Triple Divide Peak. After a moderate ascent for a 200-foot gain, we arrive at a meadowy junction. The trail left, the Isberg Trail, makes a traversing ascent 0.6 mile north to Isberg Pass, from which it descends 12.5 miles in a mostly southern direction to a trailhead on Road 5S30, about 0.3 mile above Granite Creek (Trip 83).

From the junction, you climb 0.3 mile up to an unnamed saddle—at 10,620 feet— on the boundary crest. You now have a view of the Ritter Range, one of Upper Ward Lake, below you, and much of the enormous San Joaquin River basin. Staying at or near the crest, you traverse south for a half mile, getting high from the spectacular views as well as from the rarefied air. At last, you climb almost to the top of Post Peak's northern satellite, then drop to desolate, 10,770-foot Post Peak Pass. Despite its height, its orientation prevents one from having the far-ranging views found along the crest traverse.

Our trail descends from Post Peak Pass via short, very steep switchbacks that force us to constantly brake. Be careful on this descent, for there are many loose boulders and this is no place for an injury. After dropping more than 550 feet, you skirt across bedrock benches above the east shore of tiny Porphyry Lake, which is a suitable place to rest your aching knees. Camp space, however, is nonexistent.

The "beach balls" (see sidebar on page 372) stay with us for at least 0.3 mile south of Porphyry Lake, and we leave them only after our moderately descending Post Peak Pass Trail crosses a gully and takes on a gentler gradient. Now the trail makes a traverse south through wet meadows before entering a lodgepole forest. In it, you soon start down the snout of a giant lateral moraine, briefly angle east, then descend 0.7 mile southwest to Post Creek. Crossing to the west bank of Post Creek, you'll find an adequate campsite. It would be rated "good" were it not for the seasonal abundance of mosquitoes. A tent is highly desirable here before August. Still, this may be a choice for your last night in the wilderness, or at a site just ahead.

The route climbs southwest from the Post Creek camp, cutting through a low divide after a quarter mile, then descending toward a reedy lake. On the short descent to it, you'll see some more exposures of intruded quartz diorite. Your trail skirts along the southeast shore of the small lake,

BEACH BALLS IN THE BACKCOUNTRY?

This area looks like it came down with a very bad case of measles. And not just the lakeshore. The "outbreak" spreads across hundreds of acres, dotting the landscape with countless thousands of dark, tightly packed, beach-ball-size spheres. Nowhere else in the Sierra will you find such a landscape. One explanation for this phenomenon is that the "beach balls" are quartz-diorite inclusions in a matrix of rock known as the "granite porphyry of Post Peak." The lighter-colored granite porphyry, which has quartz and feldspar crystals in a fine-grained groundmass, intruded a mass of quartz diorite about 98 million to 100 million years ago. The intrusive process broke the quartz diorite into thousands of angular blocks, and the molten granite, before it solidified, began to melt the blocks, the way water melts ice cubes floating in it. Because the molten-granite pluton intruded the solid quartz-diorite pluton at a relatively shallow depth, the granite cooled faster than usual. Had the intrusion taken place at the usual, greater depth, the quartz diorite might have been greatly or completely melted, and a typical granitic landscape would have developed.

though, at its outlet, a second trail briefly descends the north bank, only to climb back up the south bank. Take this trail when the first is flooded. From the lake's southwest end, you can continue a few yards in that direction and make camp—away from most of the mosquitoes—on a low divide. Leaving this gap, the trail drops southwest a quarter mile, crossing a creek bed immediately before a junction with the Slab Lakes Trail.

[S] **SIDE TRIP TO TRIPLE DIVIDE PEAK:** This primitive trail, which is essentially cross-country along its last 0.8 mile, climbs 2.3 miles to the two treeline lakes. They can serve as a staging area for a strenuous but safe ascent for competent mountaineers up Triple Divide Peak. **END OF SIDE TRIP.**

Just 50 yards west of the trail junction, you cross the main Slab Lakes creek—one of three parallel washes—then momentarily enter a small meadow. Camps can be found among lodgepoles near the confluence of Slab Lakes creek and Fernandez Creek, as well as up Fernandez Creek. At the meadow's southwest end, we meet Fernandez Creek, with a trail ascending each bank. Cross the creek and climb 250 yards up to a junction with the Fernandez Trail. Now you backtrack 2.3 miles down this trail, passing a junction with the Rainbow Lake Trail, then continuing for another mile down to a junction with upper end of the Lillian Loop Trail.

From the Lillian Loop-Fernandez trails junction, we descend 0.3 mile east on the Fernandez Trail to a linear gully, follow it a bit, then drift over to the crest of a moraine, about a half mile from the previous junction. From here, a now abandoned, former route of the Fernandez Trail once ascended this ridge for about 0.7 mile northwest to the Twin Lakes, then a similar distance and bearing up to a minor saddle now crossed by the current route. Your route, which has been eastward, now turns southeast and follows the crest to its end, where you soon engage a few short switchbacks near some junipers, and here get a good view of much of your basin's landscape.

Below the switchbacks, the Fernandez Trail descends a half mile to a junction. If you were to follow the trail north 70 yards to a crest saddle, you would see that it forks into the Post Creek Trail (left) and the Timber Creek Trail (right). The Post Creek Trail ends after a 1.9-mile climb to a packer camp on the West Fork of Granite Creek. Just below this spot is the creek's confluence with Post Creek. A faint trail—essentially cross-country—more or less parallels this creek northward 1.5 miles to the Post Peak Pass Trail, which you were just on. The Timber Creek Trail climbs about 5.8 miles up to the Joe Crane Lake Trail (Trip 83).

From the junction, the Fernandez Trail descends briefly past lodgepoles and junipers to a gravelly flat along the north bank of Madera Creek. This spacious flat is well suited for camping, and, from it, you can inspect the dark plug of olivine basalt, above you, which was once part of the throat of a cinder cone. Glaciers removed the cinders but were too feeble to erode the lava. On the flat, you may see an old trail heading east, the former Walton Trail, which crossed Madera Creek about 250 yards below the Fernandez Trail ford, which once provided an alternate route to our trailhead. With that goal in mind, cross the creek and gain about 500 feet on the Fernandez Trail, our ridge ascent ending after a brief contour southeast to a wilderness-boundary junction with the start of the Lillian Loop Trail. From it, retrace your steps 1.9 miles to your trailhead.

TRIP 83

Cora and Joe Crane Lakes via Isberg Trail

Ⓜ ✓ DH, BP

DISTANCE: 18 miles out and back
ELEVATIONS: 6980'/9630'
+2980'/-330'/±6620'
SEASON: Early July to late September
USE: Moderate
MAP: *Timber Knob*

TRAIL LOG:

2.4	Ansel Adams Wilderness
2.8	Stevenson Trail
4.3	Middle Cora Lake
5.0	Chetwood Trail
7.4	Joe Crane Lake Trail
8.2	Timber Creek Trail
9.0	Joe Crane Lake

INTRODUCTION: Granite Creek Campground, by your trailhead, was designed with equestrians in mind. Because your trailhead is one of the most remote in the Sierra Nevada—a 1.5-hour drive from the nearest settlement, Bass Lake—there are relatively few hikers. Beyond Cora Lakes, a favorite with packers, you'll have most of the glaciated, subalpine scenery to yourself. If your time is limited to one or two days, Middle Cora Lake is a worthy goal in itself. It is 8.6 miles round trip, has about half of the elevation gain (and loss) as the route to Joe Crane Lake, and it makes a good dayhike. Finally, those looking for multiday alpine adventures can head up the Isberg Trail to explore Yosemite's southeastern backcountry.

DIRECTIONS TO THE TRAILHEAD: As in the description of the route to Trip 81's third trailhead, drive 30 miles northeast up Forest

Route 7 to a junction with Road 5S30, located just 0.2 mile east of a spur road south to the Minarets Pack Station. (Ahead to the south, the main paved route is Forest Route 81, an alternate road to this junction, and is mentioned under the Trip 81 trailhead information.) Drive 1.8 miles northeast on Road 5S30 to the Clover Meadow Ranger Station, and get your permit there if you haven't gotten one in advance. Then continue a half mile to a road branching right, an alternate trailhead.

This alternate goes about 1 mile north to diffuse Granite Creek Campground, which is frequented by equestrians. Start your route from its northern creekside sites. There, a jeep road heads east across south-flowing Granite Creek, which is a wet ford most of the hiking season. (A bridge formerly existed about 300 yards downstream, but it was washed out.) From the east bank, the road goes briefly east to an old east-bank road, and, here, the flat used to be the old trailhead parking area. From this road intersection, the old trail from it climbs a little over 0.3 mile to diagonal across a newer road, up which you walk about 40 yards to the newer trailhead.

To reach the newer trailhead and its parking area, stay on Road 5S30, driving a winding mile past the Granite Creek Campground road to a bridge across West Fork Granite Creek. Now you parallel the creek 0.8 mile east to where the creek turns south. At this point, the old road branches southeast before turning south, and, along about a 0.2 mile stretch, to the old trailhead parking area, where you can find several de facto camping spots, sans toilets, which is preferred by hikers. The newer version of Road 5S30 keeps left and climbs 0.3 mile to the signed trailhead. Trailhead parking lies just 100 yards up the road, about 2.6 miles from the Clover Meadow Ranger Station. Ahead, the road ends in 2.7 miles at the Mammoth Trail. This trail is beyond the scope of this book, but besides being favored by equestrians, it is favored by long-distance runners who jog to Devils

Postpile National Monument (or beyond) and then jog back—quite a workout.

DESCRIPTION: Our Isberg Trail starts northward easily up past lodgepoles, and, in a quarter mile, we approach bouldery East Fork Granite Creek, on our right. The creek's large boulders, like our flat's gravels, were left by a retreating glacier. During past glaciations, almost the entire Granite Creek basin (both forks) lay under ice. Only the metavolcanic summit of Timber Knob, high above Cora Lakes, rose above the sea of ice, which extended continuously to Mt. Goddard, in northern Kings Canyon National Park, about 42 miles southeast of us.

After paralleling the East Fork for 0.3 mile, you begin to climb through a lodgepole pine and white fir forest, and our trail's gradient increases to moderate. With distance, our terrain evolves from a very shallow gully to a well-defined one, and a steep ascent guides up it to a forested divide separating a 7842-foot-high knoll from the south end of the Post Peak-Timber Knob crest. From the divide, which is about 700 feet above our trailhead and represents over half of the ascent to Middle Cora Lake, you make an ascending circle clockwise, the last part across open, bedrock slopes that afford views to the south and southeast, including pyramidal Squaw Dome, 6 miles to the south, and also broad, gentle Kaiser Ridge, on the far horizon behind it. Our ascent momentarily ends by a deep cleft known as the Niche. By the Niche, at a small flat beside East Fork Granite Creek, we enter Ansel Adams Wilderness.

The next 0.3 mile is up the creek's minor gorge past unseen Green Mountain, just to the east, and then we quickly reach a junction with the Stevenson Trail. This trail immediately crosses the East Fork—usually a ford if no log is handy—then it gives rise to other trails that radiate across the upper San Joaquin River basin. These routes are favorites with equestrians, including the route to Devils Postpile and Reds Meadow.

Still on the Isberg Trail, you curve left for a 0.3-mile stroll upstream to a second creek crossing. An often plentiful supply of mosquitoes tends to discourage camping by this bank. After making the typically wet ford of the East Fork, you go momentarily east to a bend north. Just east of the bend, you're likely to see a packer camp, which, being farther from the creek, tends to have fewer mosquitoes. From here, a former 0.2-mile lateral trail once continued east over to the Stevenson Trail.

Your Isberg Trail angles north from this lateral and soon makes a short, steep climb that fortunately yields to a gentle 0.8-mile ascent through a verdant, rich forest growing on deep, morainal soils. Your ascent ends just after you cross Cora Creek and arrive at the southeast corner of Middle Cora Lake. Camping is prohibited within 400 feet of its south and east shores, but good sites are along the north shore. The lake is shallow, making it warm and excellent for swimming, yet it is deep enough to support trout. You can also find small, isolated campsites along the broad, low, south-descending ridge that separates Middle Cora Lake from Upper Cora Lake, just west of the ridge. This smaller lake is attractive but is too shallow for decent swimming and certainly too shallow to support any trout. Incidentally, Lower Cora Lake, which is easily reached by following the south bank of the middle lake's outlet creek for a few minutes, is more of an oversize, overgrown pond that is not worth visiting.

Beyond Middle Cora Lake, you make a short, dusty climb to the top of a low volcanic ridge, which still exists despite some 2 million years of repeated glacier attacks on it. As everywhere else in the range, the evidence here testifies to the inefficacy of glacial erosion. From the ridge, an even shorter descent takes you to a junction with the eastbound Chetwood Trail.

[A] **ALTERNATE TRIP TO TRAILHEAD:** If you are hiking only to Middle Cora Lake but would like an alternate route back, you can take this easy trail 2.2 miles over to the Stevenson Trail, then go a half mile southwest down that trail to the East Fork and the Isberg Trail. The total distance of this semiloop hike is 10.8 miles. **END OF ALTERNATE TRIP.**

Although you now leave most equestrians and backpackers behind, you may meet cattle, which in some summers are still brought up to graze in this wilderness. Your 2.4-mile hike northwest to the Joe Crane Lake Trail is an amazingly easy one. At first your trail hugs the base of a volcanic plateau, keeping just above wet meadows. After 1.1 miles you pass Knoblock Meadow, once the site of Knoblock Cabin, which was located just past your first view of Isberg and Post peaks. You could camp by the meadow's end, by which you cross East Fork Granite Creek. However, better camping lies along its west bank. After a mile of fairly easy ascent, you cross Joe Crane Creek, and about mile beyond it reach the Joe Crane Lake trail.

[A] **ALTERNATE TRIP TO ISBERG PASS AND BEYOND:** For weekenders, Joe Crane Lake is a worthy goal. However, for serious backpackers looking for tens of miles of hiking and 10,000-plus feet of elevation change, several long routes are possible. They all

Post Peak above treeline, from Joe Crane Lake

begin by following the Isberg Trail to Isberg Pass and beyond.

Northbound on the trail, you make an easy up-canyon climb 0.6 mile to a ford of East Fork Granite Creek. Now a multistage climb to Isberg Pass begins. Up at around 9000 feet, short, steep switchbacks can tire hikers. The gradient abates after more than 300 feet of precious altitude gain, and after a relaxing 0.2-mile creekside ascent, you reach a junction with the McClure Lake Trail. This lake, at 9594 feet, is not worth the small effort to reach it because a dam on the lake's outlet offsets its aesthetic appeal. Furthermore, the tightly rimmed lake has no flat space for adequate camping.

Better camping is found at 9362-foot Sadler Lake, which the Isberg Trail reaches in less than 200 yards beyond the McClure Lake Trail junction. An even 9 miles from the trailhead, our trail curves to the lake's north shore, along which no camping is allowed within 400 feet of it. Try small sites, such as one near the inlet on the lake's west shore or ones on level spots on bedrock slopes just above the lake. These sites are the last good ones until Post Creek. Sadler Lake, though fairly large, is extremely shallow—barely chest deep.

From the north shore of Sadler Lake, the trail starts its second steep ascent, making feeble efforts to switchback up the slopes. As before, after 300 feet of ascent, the gradient eases and, at a sharp bend left, you may find a sign pointing toward alpine McGee Lake, about 10,100 feet in elevation, unseen on a broad bench a half mile to the northeast. Now you climb southwest, reaching a ridge that dams shallow, bedrock-lined lower Isberg Lake, at 9820 feet. On the short descent to the north shore of this lake, you'll probably note some giant erratics, looking as fresh as on the day a glacier dropped them. You could camp among lodgepoles north of the lake, but the sites are definitely inferior to those at Sadler Lake.

If you haven't done so already, don your dark glasses for the climb south up the lake's inlet creek, leave it, and pass a large mountain hemlock before reaching the McClure Lake vista, on a barren, granitic ridge. From it, you see the deep lake lying at the base of a forbidding cliff. A moderate climb, made difficult by thinning air, takes us 0.3 mile west up to truly alpine, 10,300-foot Upper Isberg Lake. The trail keeps its distance from the lake's shore in order to avoid its fragile alpine turf. It then does something remarkable: It zigzags more than two dozen times, climbing more than 300 feet northwest away from Isberg Pass. From the top of this climb, you have nearly a half-mile traverse over to 10,500-foot Isberg Pass, 12.5 miles from the trailhead.

Leaving Isberg Pass and its prostrate whitebark pines, we enter Yosemite National Park and actually climb a bit, going from ledge to ledge, before dropping a half mile on an irregular course to a junction. Near the junction, you can scan most of the upper Merced River basin, rimmed by a spectacular alpine crest. The Clark Range borders the basin to the west, the Cathedral Range to the north, and the park's boundary crest to the east. With map and compass, you can identify many peaks, including Mt. Hoffmann and Tuolumne Peak on the distant skyline about 18 miles northwest.

From this junction, you have several choices, of which two are worth the effort. The first would be to head north 1.4 miles to the High Trail and explore the lakes between Isberg Pass and Mt. Lyell and Mt. Florence (see the alternate trip in Hike 75, page 336). A second option would be to head north 1.4 miles to the High Trail, and then to descend 1.7 miles from it to the Triple Peak Fork, climb west toward Red Peak Pass (Hike 75), and explore the off-trail lakes below the Clark Range. (Large, alpine Edna Lake is seldom visited and is ideal for mountaineers). From either route are climbing opportunities for peakbaggers. Notable peaks along the former are Mt. Lyell, Maclure, and Florence; along the latter, Triple Divide, Merced, and Red peaks.

END OF ALTERNATE TRIP.

APPENDIX

Campgrounds and RV Parks

Yosemite National Park Campgrounds

HETCH HETCHY:
Hetch Hetchy Backpacker

BIG OAK FLAT ROAD, EASTWARD:
Hodgdon Meadow
Crane Flat

TIOGA ROAD, EASTWARD:
Tamarrack Flat
White Wolf
Yosemite Creek
Porcupine Flat
Tuolumne Meadows

YOSEMITE VALLEY:
North Pines
Upper Pines
Lower Pines
Sunnyside Walk-in (Camp 4)
Backpackers Walk-in

GLACIER POINT ROAD:
Bridalveil Creek

WAWONA:
Wawona

National Forest Campgrounds

For each chapter on hiking trips, campgrounds close to the trailheads are listed. However, these are often full, so you may have to stay in a campground that is a considerable way from your trailhead. Below is a list of campgrounds for each national forest, and these are listed in the order you will encounter them as you drive toward the park or its adjacent Forest Service lands. For the east-side (Hwy. 395) campgrounds in the Humboldt-Toiyabe and Inyo national forests, the campgrounds are listed from north to south. Campgrounds located miles away from routes to the trailheads are not listed. There is an (R) listed next to campgrounds that take reservations.

HWY. 41—SIERRA NATIONAL FOREST

WEST OF FISH CAMP:
Summit Campground

EAST OF FISH CAMP:
Big Sandy Campground
Little Sandy Campground
Fresno Dome Campground (R)

NORTH OF FISH CAMP:
Summerdale Campground

BASS LAKE:
Crane Valley Campground
Forks Campground
Lupine/Cedar Campground
Spring Cove Campground
Wishon Point Campground

**FOREST ROUTE 7
(NORTH FROM BASS LAKE):**
Chilkoot Campground (R)
Upper Chiquito Campground
Bowler Campground
Clover Meadow Campground
Granite Creek Campground

**FOREST ROUTE 81
(NORTH FROM NORTH FORK):**
Fish Creek Campground
Rock Creek Campground
Soda Springs Campground

**HWY. 108—STANISLAUS NATIONAL FOREST
(WEST OF SONORA PASS)**
Meadowview & Pinecrest
Cascade Creek
Mill Creek
Niagara Creek
Boulder Flat
Dardanelle
Pigeon Flat
Eureka Valley
Baker

**HWY. 108—HUMBOLDT-TOIYABE NATIONAL
FOREST (EAST OF SONORA PASS)**
Sonora Bridge
Leavitt Meadow

**HWY. 120—STANISLAUS NATIONAL FOREST
(WEST OF YOSEMITE NATIONAL PARK)**
The Pines
Lost Claim
Sweetwater

CHERRY ROAD:
Cherry Valley

EVERGREEN ROAD:
Dimond O

**HWY. 120—INYO NATIONAL FOREST
(EAST OF YOSEMITE NATIONAL PARK)**
Lower Lee Vining
Cattleguard
Boulder
Moraine
Aspen Grove
Big Bend
Ellery
Junction & Sawmill Walk-in

Tioga Lake
Saddlebag Lake

**HWY. 395—HUMBOLDT-TOIYABE NATIONAL
FOREST**

SOUTH OF HIGHWAYS 108/395 JUNCTION:
Obsidian

FS ROAD 017 WEST OF BRIDGEPORT:
Buckeye

**TWIN LAKES ROAD
SOUTH FROM BRIDGEPORT:**
Honeymoon Flat
Robinson Creek
Paha
Crags
Lower Twin Lakes

**GREEN CREEK ROAD 142
SOUTH OF BRIDGEPORT:**
Green Creek

**VIRGINIA LAKES ROAD 021
SOUTH FROM CONWAY SUMMIT:**
Trumbull Lake

HWY. 395—INYO NATIONAL FOREST

NORTH OF LEE VINING:
Lundy Canyon

JUNE LAKE LOOP:
Oh! Ridge
June Lake
Reversed Creek
Gull Lake
Silver Lake

OBSIDIAN DOME ROAD:
Hartley Springs

GLASS CREEK ROAD:
Glass Creek

DEADMAN CREEK ROAD:
Deadman

MAMMOTH LAKES:
Shady Rest
Pine Glen

DEVILS POSTPILE:
Agnew Meadows
Upper Soda Springs
Pumice Flat
Minaret Falls
Devils Postpile
Reds Meadow

Private Campgrounds and RV Parks Outside Yosemite National Park

The following is a list of private facilities for camping. Most of these are RV parks, which cater more to those with motorhomes, fifth wheels, and trailers than to those with tents, who are more likely to camp in one of the Forest Service campgrounds near the park. For each of the western Sierra highways below, the facilities are listed by their distance to the park, starting with those in the closest sites or towns. For east-side Hwy. 395, the facilities are listed from north to south.

HWY. 41—BASS LAKE

Bass Lake Recreational Resort:
559-642-3145

HWY. 41—OAKHURST

Elks Lodge: 559-683-2717
High Sierra RV & Mobile Park:
559-683-7662
Oakhurst RV Park: 559-642-4488

HWY. 120—EAST OF BUCK MEADOWS

Yosemite Lakes RV Park:
209-962-0121

HWY. 120—GROVELAND

Pine Mountain Lake Campground,
Groveland: 209-962-8615, -8625
Yosemite Pines RV Resort,
just east of Groveland:
877-962-7690

HWY. 140—MIDPINES

KOA Yosemite-Mariposa:
209-966-2201
Yosemite Trail Camp: 209-966-6444

HWY. 140—MARIPOSA

Mariposa Fairground,
south on Hwy. 49:
209-966-3686

HIGHWAY 395—BRIDGEPORT

Annett's Mono Village,
at Upper Twin Lake:
760-932-7071

HWY. 395—BETWEEN BRIDGEPORT AND LEE VINING

Lundy Lake Resort: 626-309-0415

HWY. 395—LEE VINING

Mono Vista RV Park, Lee Vining:
760-647-6401

HWY. 395—JUNE LAKE AND SILVER LAKE

June Lake RV & Lodge:
760-648-7967
Pine Cliff RV Resort: 760-648-7558
Silver Lake Resort & RV Park:
760-648-7525

Hotels, Lodges, Motels, and Resorts

I've tried to list all reputable facilities other than B&Bs, since B&Bs have a tendency to come and go. My apologies to the owners and managers of good facilities that I failed to mention in this edition. On the internet, you can access most of these. For additional facilities, you might start by visiting www.yosemite.com for accommodations and services outside the park. For each of the western Sierra highways below, the facilities are listed by their distance to the park, starting with those in the closest sites or towns. The east-side Hwy. 395 facilities are listed from north to south.

Yosemite National Park

Delaware North: 559-252-4848,
www.yosemitepark.com

YOSEMITE VALLEY

Ahwahnee Hotel
Camp Curry
Housekeeping Camp
Yosemite Lodge

WAWONA

Wawona Hotel

TIOGA ROAD

Tuolumne Meadows
 High Sierra Camp
White Wolf

PRIVATE LODGING

The Redwoods in Yosemite:
 559-375-6666,
 redwoodsinyosemite.com
Yosemite West: 559-642-2211,
 www.yosemitewest.com

Outside the Park

HWY. 41—FISH CAMP

Apple Tree Inn: 559-683-5111
Narrow Gauge Inn: 559-683-7720
Tenaya Lodge at Yosemite:
 559-683-6555

HWY. 41—BASS LAKE

Forks Resort: 559-642-3737
Pines Resort: 559-642-3121

HWY. 41—OAKHURST

America's Best Value Inn:
 800-658-2888
Best Western Yosemite Gateway Inn:
 800-545-5462
Comfort Inn-Oakhurst:
 800-321-5261
Days Inn: 800-DAYSINN
Oakhurst Lodge: 800-OKLODGE
Ramada Limited Yosemite:
 559-658-5500
Shilo Inn: 800-222-2244
Sierra Sky Ranch Resort:
 559-683-8040

HWY. 120—BUCK MEADOWS

Yosemite Westgate Lodge:
800-253-9673

HWY. 120—GROVELAND

Groveland Hotel:
209-962-4000, -7865
Pine Mountain Lake Realty
(vacation home rentals):
209-962-7156

HWY. 140—EL PORTAL

Cedar Lodge: 209-379-2612
Yosemite View Lodge: 209-379-2681

HWY. 140—MIDPINES

Bear Creek Cabins: 209-966-5253
KOA Yosemite-Mariposa:
209-966-2201
Muir Lodge Motel: 209-966-2468
Whispering Pines Motel:
209-966-5253
Yosemite Bug Lodge & Hostel:
209-966-6666

HWY. 140—MARIPOSA

Best Value Mariposa Lodge:
209-966-3607
Best Western Yosemite Way Station
Motel: 209-996-7545
Comfort Inn-Mariposa:
209-966-4344
E C Lodge Yosemite: 209-742-6800
Mariposa Lodge: 209-966-3607
Miners Inn: 209-742-7777
Mother Lode Lodge: 209-966-2521
Super 8 Motel: 209-966-4288

HWY. 395—BRIDGEPORT

Annett's Mono Village
(at Upper Twin Lake): 760-932-7071
Best Western Ruby Inn:
760-932-7241
Big Meadow Lodge: 760-932-9801
Bodie Motel: 760-932-7020
Bridgeport Inn: 760-932-7380
Redwood Motel: 760-932-7060
Silver Maple Inn: 760-932-7383
Walker River Lodge: 760-932-7021

HWY. 395—LEE VINING

Best Western Lake View Lodge:
760-647-6543
El Mono Motel: 760-647-6310
Heidelbert Inn: 760-648-7718
Lee Vining Motel: 760-647-6440
Murphey's Motel: 760-647-6316
Tioga Lodge
(west of Hwy. 395 near Tioga Pass):
760-647-6423

HWY. 395—JUNE LAKE & SILVER LAKE

Boulder Lodge: 760-648-7533
Double Eagle Resort: 760-648-7004
Fern Creek Lodge:
760-648-7722, -7741
Four Seasons: 760-648-7476
Gull Lake Lodge: 760-648-7516
The Haven: 800-648-7524
June Lake Motel & Cabins:
760-648-7547
June Lake Pines Cottages:
760-648-7522
June Lake Villager: 760-648-7712
Lake Front Cabins: 760-648-7527
Reverse Creek Lodge: 760-648-7535
Silver Pines Chalet: 760-648-2403
Whispering Pines Motel:
760-648-7762

HWY. 395—MAMMOTH LAKES

There are dozens of lodging opportunities in the small city of Mammoth Lakes. Online, you might start by visiting www.mammothweb.com.

Bibliography
and Suggested Reading

General

Browning, Peter. *Place Names of the Sierra Nevada*. Berkeley: Wilderness Press, 1991.

Browning, Peter. *Yosemite Place Names*. Lafayette, CA: Great West Books, 1992.

Medley, Steven P. *The Complete Guidebook to Yosemite National Park*. El Portal: Yosemite Association, 2002.

Muir, John. *The Mountains of California*. Berkeley: Ten Speed Press, 1977.

Muir, John, and Galen Rowell. *The Yosemite*. San Francisco: Sierra Club, 1989.

Robertson, David. *West of Eden: A History of the Art and Literature of Yosemite*. El Portal: Yosemite Association, 1984.

Backpacking and Mountaineering

Arce, Gary. *Defying Gravity: High Adventure on Yosemite's Walls*. Berkeley: Wilderness Press, 1996.

Beck, Steve. *Yosemite Trout Fishing Guide*. Portland, OR: Amato Publications, 1995.

Darvill, Fred, Jr. *Mountaineering Medicine*. Berkeley: Wilderness Press, 1998.

Graydon, Don, and Kurt Hanson, eds. *Mountaineering: The Freedom of the Hills*. Seattle: The Mountaineers, 1997.

Jordan, Ryan, ed. *Lightweight Backpacking and Camping: A Field Guide to Wilderness Hiking Equipment, Technique, and Style*. Bozeman: Beartooth Mountain Press, 2006.

King, Clarence. *Mountaineering in the Sierra Nevada*. Lincoln: University of Nebraska Press, 1997.

Rowell, Galen A., ed. *The Vertical World of Yosemite*. Berkeley: Wilderness Press, 1974.

Secor, R.J. *The High Sierra: Peaks, Passes, and Trails*. Seattle: The Mountaineers, 1992.

Winnett, Thomas, and Melanie Findling. *Backpacking Basics*. Berkeley: Wilderness Press, 1994.

Winnett, Thomas, and Kathy Morey. *Guide to the John Muir Trail*. Berkeley: Wilderness Press, 1998.

History

Brewer, William H. *Up and Down California in 1860-64*. Berkeley: University of California Press, 1974.

Bunnell, Lafayette H. *Discovery of the Yosemite in 1851*. El Portal: Yosemite Association, 1990.

Farquhar, Francis P. *History of the Sierra Nevada*. Berkeley: University of California Press, 1965.

Muir, John. *My First Summer in the Sierra*. San Francisco: Sierra Club, 1990.

Reid, Robert L. *A Treasury of the Sierra Nevada*. Berkeley: Wilderness Press, 1983.

Righter, Robert W. *The Battle Over Hetch Hetchy*. Oxford: Oxford University Press, 2005.

Russell, Carl P. *100 Years in Yosemite*. El Portal: Yosemite Association, 1992.

Sanborn, Margaret. 1989. *Yosemite: Its Discovery, its Wonders and its People*. El Portal: Yosemite Association, 1989.

Geology

Bateman, Paul C. *Plutonism in the Central Part of the Sierra Nevada Batholith, California*. US Geological Survey Professional Paper 1483, 1992.

Bateman, Paul C., and Clyde Wahrhaftig. "Geology of the Sierra Nevada." In *Geology of Northern California* (Edgar H. Bailey, ed.). California Division of Mines and Geology Bulletin 190, 1966. [Classic article on the Sierra Nevada, but now extremely dated.]

Graymer, Russell W., and David L. Jones. "Tectonic Implications of Radiolarian Cherts from the Placerville Belt, Sierra Nevada Foothills, California: Nevadan-age Continental Growth by Accretion of Multiple Terranes." *Geological Society of America Bulletin*, v. 106, 1994.

Gradstein, Felix, James Ogg, and Alan Smith. *A Geologic Time Scale 2004*. Cambridge: Cambridge University Press, 2004.

Greene, David C., Richard A. Schweickert, and Calvin H. Stevens. "Roberts Mountains Allochthon and the Western Margin of the Cordilleran Miogeocline in the Northern Ritter Range Pendant, Eastern Sierra Nevada, California." *Geological Society of America Bulletin*, v. 109, 1997.

Gutenberg, Beno, John P. Buwalda, and Robert P. Sharp. "Seismic Explorations on the Floor of Yosemite Valley, California." *Bulletin of the Geological Society of America, v. 67*, 1956.

Harwood, David S. *Stratigraphy of Paleozoic and Lower Mesozoic Rocks in the Northern Sierra Terrane, California*. US Geological Survey Bulletin 1957, 1991.

Howell, David G., ed. *Tectonostratigraphic Terranes of the Circum-Pacific Region*. Houston: Circum-Pacific Council for Energy and Mineral Resources.

Huber, N. King. *Amount and Timing of Late Cenozoic Uplift and Tilt of the Central Sierra Nevada, California—Evidence from the Upper San Joaquin River Basin*. US Geological Survey Professional Paper 1197, 1981. [Foremost paper on Sierran uplift; but hopelessly flawed.]

Huber, N. King. *The Geologic Story of Yosemite National Park*. US Geological Survey Bulletin 1595, 1987. [Good bedrock geology; poor uplift and glacial geology.]

Jones, David L. "Uplift of the Sierra Nevada: Fact or Fancy?" *Guide to the Geology of the Western Sierra Nevada: Sacramento to the Crystal Basin*. Northern California Geological Society, 1997.

Lahren, Mary M., and Richard A. Schweickert. "Sache Monument Pendant, Central Sierra Nevada, California: Eugeoclinal Metasedimentary Rocks Near the Axis of the Sierra Nevada Batholith." *Geological Society of America Bulletin*, v. 106, 1994.

Matthes, François E. *Geologic History of the Yosemite Valley*. US Geological Survey Professional Paper 160, 1930. [The widely acclaimed classic on Yosemite Valley, but in reality an artificial construct at odds with the geologic evidence.]

Matthes, François E. *The Incomparable Valley*. Berkeley: University of California Press, 1950. [Popular account of the above, and equally flawed.]

McNulty, Brendan A., Weixing Tong, and Othmar T. Tobisch. "Assembly of a Dike-fed Magma Chamber: The Jackass Lakes Pluton, Central Sierra Nevada, California." *Geological Society of America Bulletin*, v. 108, 1996.

Molnar, Peter. "The Rise of Mountain Ranges and the Evolution of Humans: A Causal Relation?" *Irish Journal of Earth Sciences*, v. 10, 1990. [A serious spoof of the widespread geomyth of recent uplift of the world's ranges.]

Oldow, John S., and others. "Phanerozoic Evolution of the North American Cordillera; United States and Canada." In *The Geology of North America; An Overview* (The Geology of North America, Volume A, Albert W. Bally and Allison R. Palmer, eds.). Boulder: Geological Society of America, 1989.

Ratajeski, Kent, Allen F. Glazner, and Brent V. Miller. "Geology and Geochemistry of Mafic to Felsic Plutonic Rocks in the Cretaceous Intrusive Suite of Yosemite Valley, California." *Geological Society of America Bulletin*, v. 112, 2001.

Ruddiman, W.F., and H.E. Wright, Jr. *North America and Adjacent Oceans During the Last Deglaciation* (The Geology of North America, Volume K-3). Boulder: Geological Society of America, 1987.

Saleeby, Jason B. "On Some Aspects of the Geology of the Sierra Nevada." Geological Society of America Special Paper 338, 1999. [Excellent synopsis of the evolution the Sierra Nevada batholith and its subsequent unroofing and uplift.]

Schaffer, Jeffrey P. *The Geomorphic Evolution of the Yosemite Valley and Sierra Nevada Landscapes: Solving the Riddles in the Rocks.* Berkeley: Wilderness Press, 1997. [The only comprehensive source on Sierran uplift and glaciation based solely on field evidence.]

Schaffer, Jeffrey P. (unpublished manuscript completed in 2005). *Seeing the Elephant: How Perceived Evidence in the Sierra Nevada Biased Global Geomorphology.*

Schweickert, Richard A., and Mary M. Lahren. "Triassic Caldera at Tioga Pass, Yosemite National Park, California: Structural Relationships and Significance." *Geological Society of America Bulletin*, v. 111, 1999.

Shelton, John S. *Geology Illustrated.* San Francisco: W.H. Freeman, 1966. [Perhaps the best geology text ever written; a true classic.]

Wahrhaftig, Clyde. "Stepped topography of the southern Sierra Nevada." Geological Society of America Bulletin, v. 76, 1965. [Another flawed classic, negated by its own evidence, but nevertheless awarded geomorphology's highest honor, the Kirk Bryan award.]

Wieczorek, Geralld F. *et al.* "Unusual July 10,1996, Rock Fall at Happy Isles, Yosemite National Park, California." Geological Society of America Bulletin, v. 112, 2000.

Geologic Maps

Alpha, Tau Rho, Clyde Wahrhaftig, and N. King Huber. *Oblique Map Showing Maximum Extent of 20,000-year-old (Tioga) Glaciers, Yosemite National Park, Central Nevada, California.* US Geological Survey Map I-1885, 1987. [Considerably underestimates the lengths and thicknesses of these glaciers.]

Bailey, Roy A. *Geologic Map of the Long Valley Caldera, Mono-Inyo Craters Volcanic Chain, and Vicinity, Eastern California.* US Geological Survey Map I-1933, 1989. [Some glacial deposits are misdated.]

Bateman, Paul C. *Pre-Tertiary Bedrock Geologic Map of the Mariposa 1° by 2° Quadrangle, Sierra Nevada, California; Nevada.* US Geological Survey Miscellaneous Investigations Series Map I-1960, 1992.

Bateman, Paul C., and others. *Geologic Map of the Tuolumne Meadows Quadrangle, Yosemite National Park, California.* US Geological Survey Map GQ-1570, 1983.

Bateman, Paul C., and Konrad B. Krauskopf. *Geologic Map of the El Portal Quadrangle, West-Central Sierra Nevada, California.* US Geological Survey Map MF-1998, 1987.

Calkins, Frank C., and others. *Bedrock Geologic Map of Yosemite Valley, Yosemite National Park, California.* US Geological Survey Map I-1639, 1985.

Chesterman, Charles W. *Geology of the Matterhorn Peak Quadrangle, Mono and Tuolumne Counties, California.* California Division of Mines and Geology Map Sheet 22, 1975.

Dodge, F.C.W., and L.C. Calk. *Geologic Map of the Lake Eleanor Quadrangle, Central Sierra Nevada, California.* US Geological Survey Map GQ-1639, 1987.

Huber, N. King. *Preliminary Geologic Map of the Pinecrest Quadrangle, Central Sierra Nevada, California*. US Geological Survey Map MF-1437, 1983.

Huber, N. King, and C. Dean Rinehart. *Geologic Map of the Devils Postpile Quadrangle, Sierra Nevada, California*. US Geological Survey Map GQ-437, 1965.

Huber, N. King, Paul C. Bateman, and Clyde Wahrhaftig. *Geologic Map of Yosemite National Park and Vicinity, California*. US Geological Survey Map I-1874, 1989. [Dates on metamorphic rocks are poor; glacial deposits are inaccurate.]

Kistler, Ronald W. *Geologic Map of the Mono Craters Quadrangle, Mono and Tuolumne Counties, California*. US Geological Survey Map GQ-462, 1966.

Kistler, Ronald W. *Geologic Map of the Hetch Hetchy Reservoir Quadrangle, Yosemite National Park, California*. US Geological Survey Map GQ-1112, 1973.

Peck, Dallas L. *Geologic Map of the Merced Peak Quadrangle, Central Sierra Nevada, California*. US Geological Survey Map GQ-1531, 1980.

Peck, Dallas L. *Geologic Map of the Yosemite Quadrangle, Central Sierra Nevada, California*. US Geological Survey Map I-2751, 2002.

Stewart, John H., John E. Carlson, and Dann C. Johannesen. *Geologic Map of the Walker Lake 1° by 2° Quadrangle, California and Nevada*. US Geological Survey Map MF-1382A, 1982.

Wagner, D.L., and others. *Geologic Map of the Sacramento Quadrangle, Scale 1:250,000*. California Division of Mines and Geology Regional Geologic Map Series, Map No. 1A, 1981.

Wahrhaftig, Clyde. *Geologic Map of the Tower Peak Quadrangle, Central Sierra Nevada, California*. US Geological Survey Map I-2697, 2000.

Biology

Sierra Nevada Ecosystem Project, Final Report to Congress (Vol. I: Assessment Summaries and Management Strategies. Vol. II: Assessments and Scientific Basis for Management Options. Vol. III: Assessments, Commissioned Reports, and Background Information.). Davis: University of California, Centers for Water and Wildland Resources, 1996.

Barbour, Michael, and others. *California's Changing Landscapes: Diversity and Conservation of California Vegetation*. Sacramento: California Native Plant Society, 1993.

Botti, Stephen J., and Walter Sydoriak. *An Illustrated Flora of Yosemite National Park*. El Portal: Yosemite Association, 2001.

Edelbrock, Jerry, and Scott Carpenter, eds. *Natural Areas and Yosemite: Prospects for the Future* (Yosemite Centennial Symposium Proceedings). El Portal: Yosemite Association, 1990.

Gaines, David. *Birds of Yosemite and the East Slope*. Lee Vining: Artemisia Press, 1992.

Gibbens, Robert P., and Harold F. Heady. *The Influence of Modern Man on the Vegetation of Yosemite Valley*. Berkeley: University of California Division of Agricultural Sciences Manual 36, 1964.

Grater, Russell K., and Tom A. Blaue. *Discovering Sierra Mammals*. El Portal: Yosemite Association, 1978.

Hartesveldt, Richard J., and others. *The Giant Sequoia of the Sierra Nevada*. Washington, D.C.: National Park Service, 1975.

Harvey, H. Thomas, Howard S. Shellhammer, and Ronald E. Stecker. *Giant Sequoia Ecology: Fire and Reproduction*. Washington, D.C.: National Park Service Scientific Monograph Series No. 12, 1980.

Heyl, George R., Stromquist, Arvid A., Swinney, C. Melvin, and Wiese, John H. *Geologic Map of the Sonora Quadrangle*. California Division of Mines and Geology Special Report 41, Plate 2, scale 1:24,000, 1955.

Hickman, James C., ed. *The Jepson Manual: Vascular Plants of California*. Berkeley: University of California Press, 1993.

Horn, Elizabeth L. *Sierra Nevada Wildflowers.* Missoula, MT: Mountain Press, 1998. [This contains over 220 photographs of common shrubs and wildflowers. It is a good introduction for those who prefer plant identification by photos rather than by keys.]

Jameson, E.W., Jr., and Hans J. Peeters. *California Mammals* (California Natural History Guide 52). Berkeley: University of California Press, 1988.

Klikoff, Lionel G. "Microenvironmental Influence on Vegetational Pattern Near Timberline in the Central Sierra Nevada." *Ecological Monographs,* v. 35, 1965.

Leopold, A. Starker, and others. *The Jawbone Deer Herd.* Sacramento: California Division of Fish and Game, Game Bulletin 4, 1951.

McGinnis, Samuel M. *Freshwater Fishes of California* (California Natural History Guide 49). Berkeley: University of California Press, 1984.

Niehaus, Theodore F., and Charles L. Ripper. *A Field Guide to Pacific States Wildflowers* (Peterson Field Guide 22). Boston: Houghton Mifflin, 1981.

Ornduff, Robert. *An Introduction to California Plant Life* (California Natural History Guide 35). Berkeley: University of California Press, 1974.

Peterson, Roger T. *A Field Guide to Western Birds.* Boston: Houghton Mifflin, 2001.

Petrides, George A., and Olivia Petrides. *A Field Guide to Western Trees* (Peterson Field Guide 44). Boston: Houghton Mifflin, 1998.

Sawyer, John O., and Todd Keeler-Wolf. *A Manual of California Vegetation.* Sacramento: California Native Plant Society, 1995.

Sibley, David Allen. (*National Audubon Society's*) *The Sibley Guide to Birds.* New York: Alfred A. Knopf, 2000. [The *new* bird authority.]

Stebbins, Robert C. *A Field Guide to Western Reptiles and Amphibians.* Boston: Houghton Mifflin, 1998.

Storer, Tracy I., Robert L. Usinger, and David Lukas. *Sierra Nevada Natural History.* Berkeley: University of California Press, 2004. [A classic, but erroneous, century-old glaciation and uplift geology.]

Watts, Tom. *Pacific Coast Tree Finder.* Berkeley: Nature Study Guild, 1973.

Weeden, Norman F. *A Sierra Nevada Flora.* Berkeley: Wilderness Press, 1996.

Willard, Dwight, 1994. *Giant Sequoia Groves of the Sierra Nevada: A Reference Guide,* 1994. [Self-published, excellent, but unfortunately out of print. A real collector's item.]

INDEX

The author (left) and his twin brother, Greg, at the Nevada Fall bridge

About the Author

Jeffrey P. Schaffer made his first backpack trip in a 1962 traverse of the Grand Canyon, at age 19. The following year, the climbing frenzy seized him, and in 1964 he began climbing in Yosemite National Park, where he has completed some 70 different roped ascents, including several first ascents, such as the very popular Pine Line at the base of El Capitan. In 1972, he began work on his first book for Wilderness Press, *The Pacific Crest Trail*. Since then, he has written and contributed to more than a dozen Wilderness Press guidebooks, including the *Hikers Guide to the High Sierra: Yosemite*, and he has mapped about 4000 miles of trail. Schaffer has logged more than 1000 miles on trails in Yosemite. Today, he teaches a variety of natural sciences courses at San Francisco Bay Area community colleges, does Sierran geomorphic research, lead-climbs both outdoors and in climbing gyms, and lives the good life with his wife in the Napa Valley.